Teaching Skills

to Children with Learning and Behavior Disorders

Teaching Skills

to Children with Learning and Behavior Disorders

Thomas M. Stephens

The Ohio State University

Charles E. Merrill Publishing Company
A Bell & Howell Company
Columbus   Toronto   London   Sydney

Published by
Charles E. Merrill Publishing Company
A Bell & Howell Company
Columbus, Ohio 43216

This book was set in Times Roman and Helvetica.
The Production Editor was Lynn Walcoff.
The cover was prepared by Will Chenoweth.

Library of Congress Catalog Card Number: 77-73775

ISBN: 0-675-08533-0

PHOTO CREDITS

p. 12: Faculty for Exceptional Children, The Ohio State University (top)
    Tim Williams (bottom)

p. 13: Faculty for Exceptional Children, The Ohio State University

p. 122: Bernstein Photos

p. 123: Bernstein Photos

p. 124 Bernstein Photos and Faculty for Exceptional Children, The Ohio State University (bottom)

pp.241–243: Bernstein Photos
pp. 360–361: Bernstein Photos

3 4 5 6 7 8 — 82 81 80 79 78

Printed in the United States of America

To My Evelyn

Acknowledgments

To paraphrase a common saying, God looks after fools, drunkards, and professors. At least this professor has been fortunate to have had many fine colleagues, students, and friends as well as a very tolerant and supportive wife. In addition, I had the benefit of a tolerant publisher, Tom Hutchinson, and an extremely capable secretary, JoAnn Van Schaik.

To each of the following and those many unnamed students, children, teachers, and friends with whom I have had the privilege of working for more than twenty years, I express my gratitude:

For their review of the entire first draft of this manuscript–
    Dr. John O. Cooper, The Ohio State University
    Dr. Cecil D. Mercer, University of Florida
    Dr. Sara Tarver, University of Virginia
    Dr. Jill E. McGovern, College of Charleston
For their reviews of chapter 12—
    Dr. A. Carol Hartman, The State University of New York at Binghamton
    Dr. Virginia Lucas, Wittenberg University
For his review of selected chapters—
    Larry Magliocca, The Ohio State University
For their contributions to chapter 3—
    Joseph Fisher, Director of Special Education, Illinois State Department of Education
    Thomas O. Iles, Assistant Director of Special Education, West Virginia State Department of Education
For their contributions and assistance—
    the staff of The Directive Teaching Instructional Management System Project, who are named in chapter 9.

T. M. S.

Contents

Preface

Concern for students with learning and behavior problems has increased rapidly in recent years. These children are at long last receiving the attention from school personnel that all students deserve. This attention is being reflected in financial and other human resources administered by state, federal, and local school officials. With increased attention, instructional technology, relevant theory, and better trained teachers, more students with problems can be helped in the public school environment.

The diagnostic prescriptive teaching movement has greatly changed special education practices; more changes, as a result of the emerging skill training stream of this movement, are still to come. In this text I attempt to present the possibilities for using a skill training orientation. I view academic and social learning problems as deficits which are essentially inherent in the social and/or educational systems. In addition, there are differences among humans which require the schools to provide alternative ways for students to be successful.

My rationale for placing the weight of responsibility on changing the educational environment is simply that differences among humans represent a scientific fact. Different experiences, rates of learning, interests, social preferences, and attitudes are to be expected.

Part I of this book contains information which forms the foundation for present and future educational practices in behalf of the learning disabled and behaviorally disordered.

Part II of this text represents a handbook to be used as a reference for teachers. Chapter 9 describes an instructional management system. It is designed to give readers an overall view of the integral parts of classroom instruction. Suggested tactics for classroom management are described in chapter 10. Included in that chapter is a teacher's handbook for organizing the classroom and/or using positive reinforcement. Ways to teach social behavior are described in chapter 11; also in the chapter is a procedure for developing a social skills curriculum. Chapter 12 provides suggestions for teaching basic academic skills. It also contains many sample teaching strategies from the DTIMS program. Chapter 13 contains suggestions and strategies for special teachers to be effective when working cooperatively with those people who are so very important in children's lives.

Part II of this text is an attempt to be of help to teachers who have one of the most challenging and crucial jobs in our society. While limitations of space do not permit this author to provide entire components of the DTIMS program, readers should feel free to write to him in requesting additional materials, sharing suggestions, and making recommendations. Address all comments and requests to:

Dr. Thomas M. Stephens
Professor and Chairman
Faculty for Exceptional Children
College of Education
The Ohio State University
Columbus, Ohio   43210

This book was written for use in courses directed at college students preparing to become teachers of the mildly handicapped. It is my hope that this text contains sufficient information and teaching suggestions for it to be helpful to special teachers and, through them, beneficial to their students.

T.M.S.

Teaching Skills

to Children with Learning and Behavior Disorders

part I

Information for Teaching Learning Disabled and Behaviorally Disordered Children

Educational Programming

This chapter provides an overview of educational considerations for learning and behaviorally disordered children (L&BD). The following points are discussed:

1. Special education's role is to serve students who cannot be successful in school without supportive or corrective instruction.

2. A common instructional program should be used for children with learning and behavioral problems.

3. Maladaptive responses may occur in academic learning, behaviors related to academic performance, social behaviors, and emotional behaviors.

4. A traditional view sees maladaptive behavior as being symptomatic of the true causes of performance problems, but a contemporary view treats performance problems directly.

5. Both biological and environmental factors may contribute to learning and behavioral problems.

6. Students with learning and behavioral disorders may be placed in regular classes, special classes, special schools, or resource rooms or provided tutoring services.

7. Supportive and ancillary services are provided by a variety of school personnel including instructional consultants, school psychologists, visiting teachers, and parent trainers.

8. Criteria for identifying students with learning and behavioral problems vary, making it difficult to establish the extent of these problems.

9. A functional approach begins with an assessment of students, followed by instruction based upon that assessment information. An evaluation of instruction is used to determine if performance meets criterion.

10. There are different uses for information concerning L&BD students. Some information may have educational value but may not be instructionally relevant.

Introduction

Throughout the history of special education three themes have appeared repeatedly: (1) concern for students with unique needs, (2) attempts to individualize instruction and, allied to the latter, (3) a continual improvement of instructional technology.

As a subsystem of general education, special education provides for those school-aged children who are inadequately served by regular elementary and secondary education situations. Thus, children with handicapping conditions — physical, mental, and emotional — are typically representative of the special education population. Intellectually gifted children are sometimes a part of this subsystem since they too are often inadequately provided for in regular school programs.

The term *handicapped* is often associated with physical anomalies. Consequently, crippled children and those suffering from other obvious impairments often comprise the public's view of handicapped children. Yet children possessing less apparent barriers to learning and adjustment are also handicapped — the mentally retarded, those whose cognitive abilities are significantly behind their chronological ages, the blind and visually handicapped, and the hearing handicapped.

Attempts to individualize instruction have become standard parts of special education programs, as reflected by corrective instruction occurring in special schools, full-time special classes, and services provided by itinerant and resource personnel. Accompanying the attempts to individualize instruction is the need to improve teaching technology (Skinner, 1968). Findings concerning a scientific basis for human behavior and learning (Gilbert, 1962; Skinner, 1953; Suppes, 1964; Zifferblatt, 1973) have helped to generate specific methods and teaching techniques which comprise the *teaching technology*.

As our society becomes more accepting of individual differences, special education services will be delivered to more handicapped children in regular school environments. Until recently, many of these children were assigned to restrictive settings such as special schools and institutions. And when, on occasion, these children were adequately provided for in regular schools, they were more often than not placed in special classes to be segregated from their normal peers. This is not to suggest that all handicapped children are better educated in regular instructional programs; however, special instruction for many handicapped children can be a part of regular educational programs.

Learning and Behavioral Disorders

One segment of the school population whose handicaps are not always apparent are termed *learning disabled,* while another group is sometimes referred to as *behaviorally disordered.* Together these students represent the handicapped population of concern in this text. The term *L&BD* is used in this text when both groups are combined.

Two separate bodies of literature have evolved in the areas of educating children who have learning problems and those who display behavior maladjustments. Specific diagnostic terms and categories have been created to lend scientific credence to each area. Among the terms used synonymously to describe children with learning disorders are learning disabled, Strauss syndrome, learning handicapped, slow learner, brain-injured, perceptually handicapped, minimal brain dysfunction, neurologically impaired, dyslexic, and aphasic. Labels for behaviorally disordered children are emotionally disturbed, behaviorally handicapped, autistic, emotionally maladjusted, delinquent, sociopathic, character disordered, emotionally immature, and emotionally inadequate.

In addition to a lack of agreement concerning diagnostic labels, definitions of learning disorders and behavioral problems are inconsistent. Hewett and Black (1973) noted that emotionally disturbed children have been described, defined, and classified from at least five points of view and, within each classification, several different definitions have emerged. Students handicapped by learning disorders have also been defined in many different ways. As Gearheart (1973) correctly stated, a definition of "learning disabilities" raises almost as many questions as it answers. One of the longer definitions is contained in the *First Annual Report of the National Advisory Committee on Handicapped Children* (1968). The committee, chaired by Samuel A. Kirk, excluded from its definition all learning problems which were due primarily to "visual, hearing, motor handicaps, mental retardation, emotional disturbance or to environmental disadvantage." Included in the definition were problems of listening, thinking, and talking and difficulties in the academic skill areas.

Generally, regardless of terminology used, children who are classified by any of the above labels may be viewed as having learning problems. From an instructional point of view, students who exhibit any of the behaviors implied by these labels need to learn different responses to their environments. Since their behaviors are considered to be maladaptive, both the learning disabled and behaviorally handicapped possess learning problems. In addition, children of average or better measured intelligence and who are free of physical and sensory handicaps may on occasions present learning problems. In such instances their difficulties tend to be the result of environmental conditions and biological factors. Yet instructional procedures need not differ as a function of the differences in diagnoses. Etiological factors typically form the bases for diagnosis, but such factors seldom have any instructional relevance.

Types of Maladaptive Behaviors

Regardless of the causative factors, if students display a deficit performance in behaviors that are required of all students they will have trouble learning. If normal behavior is used as the standard, all behaviors significantly below that standard may be considered deviant. But if one uses normal behavior as the criterion for acceptable performance, one must have a clear notion of what constitutes that performance. Many *typical* behaviors are expected of school-aged children, and these may be categorized into four groups: academic performance, behaviors which are related but not central to academic performance, social behavior, and emotional behavior. Figure 1.1 contains two examples of each category.

Students who display academic or social deficits engage in maladaptive behaviors. Although various maladaptive behaviors are found among children, some examples follow:

Academic Performance

Generally low academic achievement in relation to measured intelligence

Poor quality academic performance in specific skill areas

Poor quality performance and difficulty in at least one basic academic area

Difficulty in maintaining an acceptable level of academic performance, e.g., erratic academic performance

Lack of prerequisite responses for formal schooling, e.g., failure to obey simple directions, short attention span, or poor discrimination of likenesses and differences among objects and sounds

Failure to profit from typical teaching methods

Failure to generalize academic responses learned in one situation to other situations

Behaviors Related to Academic Performance

Negative reactions to academic tasks, e.g., violent reaction or no response at all

Difficulty in attending to relevant stimuli, e.g., response to details of events rather than to major themes

Trouble with sequencing events

Failure to integrate experiences into wholes

Difficulty in following directions

Poor control of motor responses

Social Behaviors

Physical aggression exceeds acceptable limits for setting

Over-emission of responses, e.g., behavior is disruptive, boisterous, hyperactive, and overly aggressive

Under-emission of responses, e.g., withdrawal from regular social interactions; overly quiet or shy behavior

Difficulty with peers, e.g., a child is a loner, has few friends, does not participate in group games; is not encouraged by peers to participate

Emotional Behaviors

Emission of inappropriate emotional responses

Display of unreasonable fears

Show of undue need for reassurance

The maladaptive behaviors which have been described in this section are commonly found among children who have been diagnosed as *learning disabled* and among those often considered to be *emotionally disturbed*. Since the behaviors are likely to be related to both diagnostic categories, for purposes of instruction the two groups are treated as one throughout this text.

1.0 Academic Performance
—achieves in skill areas at a rate closely approximating the average for his or her age and grade

—acquires concepts typically learned by students for his or her age and grade

2.0 Behaviors Related to Academic Performance
—follows directions for performing academic and social responsibilities

—attends to relevant stimuli in the school environment

3.0 Social Behaviors
—participates in play with peer group in acceptable fashion

—responds to requests in socially acceptable fashion

4.0 Emotional Behaviors
—displays expected emotions when experiencing events that typically evoke laughter, joy, sorrow, and pain

—shows preferences towards people and things including maintaining friendships and acquaintances

---

FIGURE 1.1 Examples of normal student behaviors

Traditional and Contemporary Views of Learning and Behavior Problems

Concern for locating the etiological bases for children's academic and emotional learning problems is a natural outgrowth of medical practitioners' interests and their contributions to special education. Since they must concern themselves with those biological factors causing physical anomalies, their view was transferred to problems of learning and behavior. It was a natural, but fallacious, notion to believe that an approach which had contributed significantly to health problems would also serve to correct other human performance difficulties. Figure 1.2 depicts a traditional view of learning problems which was a logical outcome of the medical influence in special education.

Step 1: A dysfunction is observed.

Step 2: Why does the child present learning problems?

Step 3: Speculation as to primary causes of problems (e.g., brain damage, genetic factors, family relationships).

Step 4: Speculation of secondary causes of learning problems (e.g., poor coordination, visual-perceptual problems, emotional problems).

Step 5: Treatment focus is on secondary causes (e.g., visual-motor training, personal and family counseling, medication).

FIGURE 1.2 A traditional view of learning problems

As seen in Figure 1.2, the traditional approach views behavior, which constitutes incorrect responses, as symptomatic of the *real causes* of maladaptive performances. Consequently, defective processes of learning are often treated, e.g., visual motor training, perceptual training, memory training, and so forth. In the traditional view, a more direct approach toward performance problems, such as academic or social skill instruction, is frequently viewed as supplemental to the more "basic treatment."

The contemporary approach deals more directly with the problems of functioning. From a behavioral perspective, steps for instructional treatment are:

1. a dysfunction is observed;
2. the behavior constituting the performance difficulty is analyzed and specified;
3. treatment is instituted consisting of those responses directly related to performance.

In the behavioral view, causes of dysfunction are the inappropriate responses themselves and treatment consists of developing the desired behavior. Instructional treatment of this sort does not mean that biological and other factors are ignored. Rather, when medical or other types of treatment are provided they are viewed as supplemental to the instruction since the major outcome is a change in behavior (performance).

Even though interest in the "causes" of learning and behavioral problems is natural and understandable, teachers should not find it necessary to search for them in order to effect changes in performance. Unfortunately, many people feel that one cannot correct a problem of human functioning without first locating its "basic cause," based on the mistaken belief that treatment can only follow diagnosis.

There are sound reasons for *special educators* to be aware of causes for learning and behavior problems. First, as professionals they should be knowledgeable about their area of specialty. Second, such knowledge makes them aware of the complex nature of learning and behavioral handicaps. And third, their research activities often must take into account the probable causes of handicapping conditions.

Many factors, both biological and environmental, interact to form the bases for most human conditions (Dobzhansky, 1962); rarely does a single event or factor represent the sole cause of adequate or defective performance. Instead, multiple factors usually contribute to the quality of any type of human functioning.

Even though most thoughtful teachers are aware of the multiplicity of causes contributing to problems of learning and behavior, many continue the quest to find out "why." Perhaps it is reasonable to seek such explanations. Yet, teachers' knowledge of those etiological factors contributing to students' disabilities will not facilitate their teaching or the students' learning for at least three reasons.

First, teachers' roles permit them to deal solely with student behavior. That is, while they may refer students to other specialists within or outside the confines of school, their expertise and professional roles mitigate against providing medical and social services (such as family intervention or assistance) to students.

Second, a large portion of behavior is a function of instructional treatment and social interactions. Thus, while biological factors may contribute to problems of adjustment in school, almost all performance problems can be improved through skillful teaching.

Third, in those instances where medical treatment is necessary to ameliorate physical problems, performance can rarely be improved without changes in responses by the learner. For example, when students are medicated so as to reduce their hyperactivity, this provides a prerequisite condition for learning to attend to relevant stimuli. However, in such instances students must still learn to identify those relevant stimuli as well as other responses that together are often referred to as *paying attention*.

Causes of Academic Learning Problems

Academic learning problems may be due to biological factors, environmental conditions, or a combination of both. Although there is often no single reason for academic learning problems, some conditions are found to predispose children to such difficulties. Predisposing factors tend to be related to biological conditions such as genetic factors, brain injury, glandular defects, and malnutrition.

Environmental conditions also serve to precipitate learning problems. These events are conditions such as gaps in learning experiences, inadequate teaching, lack of incentives for responding, and psychological trauma.

It is reasonable to assume that in many instances a combination of biological and environmental conditions contribute to learning difficulties. Regardless of causation, however, faulty learning is the result and, at that point, special instruction is needed.

Biological Conditions

Biological defects have been attributed to a wide variety of academic learning failures. In fact, the history of learning disorders is closely tied to questions concerning the effects of neurological abnormalities upon memory and other aspects of learning (Birch, 1964; Cruickshank et al., 1961; Goldstein, 1942; Strauss & Lehtinen, 1947). In addition to neurological factors, academic learning problems have been associated with prematurity and low weight at birth (Harper, Fisher, & Rider, 1959). As more premature newborns survive, an increase in the number of children with learning disorders can be expected.

Rourke (1975) and his associates have conducted extensive clinical research concerning the causes of learning disabilities among children. They concluded that some deficits found among those diagnosed as learning disabled are due to cerebral dysfunction. Their findings, they believe, warrant an explanation of learning disabilities as rooted in neuropsychological problems. It is of interest to note, however, that performance deficits of their subjects, such as poor attention, were successfully treated through the use of positive reinforcement.

Genetic factors are also believed to contribute in important ways to learning difficulties (Erlenmeyer-Kimling & Jervek, 1963). In some instances where certain familial learning disorders have been observed, there is a belief among some authorities that these are genetically linked from father to son (Lennenberg, 1967). In an early study, over 42% of 276 children studied had a family history of dyslexia. Within that group 88% of the families had other members with learning problems (Hallgren, 1950).

Environmental Conditions

Regardless of the effects of biological and inherited factors on learning difficulties, environmental conditions greatly influence the expression of students' innate potentials. Many children with persistent learning problems have normal medical histories with no positive signs of brain injury. When the measured intelligence of these same children is low-average or higher and accompanied by persistent difficulties in academic skills, it is reasonable to assume that their performance deficits are due to factors within their learning environments.[1]

School environmental factors are interactions between students' strengths and weaknesses and specific classroom situations. The latter group may include methods of instruction, teacher characteristics, and quality of teaching. In addition to classroom factors, student and familial value systems may also contribute to insufficient academic performance.

Causes of Social Behavior Problems

Human emotions as reflected in behavior are varied and complex. Because of this complexity, diverse factors have been attributed to maladaptive social and emotional behaviors. Combined biological and environmental factors are generally believed to cause serious emotional disorders.

Interestingly enough, the term *mental illness* suggests that the resultant behaviors are due to a biological condition (disease) rather than to environmental factors.

---

1. Both home and school represent learning environments. In fact, all settings in which children acquire experiences are environments where learning occurs.

Szasz (1960) has presented persuasive arguments to demonstrate that the concept of "mental illness" is fallacious. He views it as a metaphorical expression which should not be confused with a basis for treatment. Thus while problems in living may be alleviated through treatment, mental illness is not amenable to treatment. Szasz and other critics do not deny the genetic and constitutional determinants of behavior, but they do emphasize that the deviances are socially determined.

While biological factors may establish the extent to which social responses can be acquired, the maladaptive behavior is relative to social and cultural values. In social situations where a wide range of deviant behavior is acceptable, the percent of "emotionally disturbed" individuals will be lower than in groups where the behavioral parameters are more restrictive. However, emotional problems are known in all societies, but the degree and nature of the problems differ (Benedict & Jacks, 1954).

Biological Conditions

Physical health and genetic factors contribute to behavior disorders. Glandular dysfunctions and other physiological factors such as abnormal blood pressure cause irritability, depression, and other reactions which may result in maladaptive behavior. Similarly, genetic factors may predispose children to emotional disorders.

Although biological factors undoubtedly contribute to maladaptive behavior, medical treatment alone will not correct the behaviors. Learning correct responses must occur in conjunction with medical treatment. Thus, children who display adjustment problems or even more serious emotional difficulties need to *learn* coping skills and appropriate behaviors.

Environmental Conditions

Social and psychological conditions are major contributors to emotional and behavioral problems. Such problems are more prevalent among lower socioeconomic populations (Hollingshead & Redlich, 1958), suggesting that maladaptive behavior is related to or caused by poor economic conditions.

Situational factors can also contribute to behavior disorders. While some disorders may be of a temporary duration, such behaviors, if handled incorrectly, can develop responses which children will emit when confronted with similar stressful situations.

While genetic and biological factors do influence social behavior, the major contributors are rooted in environmental experiences. These may include events which serve as rewards for inappropriate behavior and lack of rewards for desirable behavior. A lack of exposure to appropriate social models can also result in undesirable social behavior.

As other socializing agencies provide less direct influence and, consequently, less impact in shaping children's attitudes and social behavior, schools are expected to provide more instruction. Thus, as families change from nuclear units with set guidelines to varying styles where social rules and controls are less definite, and often less effective, an increase in social adjustment problems is likely to occur. In addition, failure to receive instruction in acceptable social values and behaviors or failure to profit from such teaching will also contribute to maladaptive behavior.

Just as there are many ways in which environmental conditions may contribute to student adjustment problems, there are ways in which they can alleviate such problems. Anecdote 1.1 describes three situations in which adjustment problems were handled.

1. *At home*. When the visiting teacher, Jack Pangborn, visited Ann Smith's home, he gained insight into a number of her behavior problems. Ann, an excessively overweight ten-year-old, had few friends at school, and her school attendance was erratic. When she was in attendance, her teacher reported that Ann seemed apathetic and withdrawn. Her face was usually expressionless and she took little interest in anything and showed no initiative. At times, she burst into tears when asked to answer a question in class.

Ann was referred to the visiting teacher because of her frequent absences from school. Mr. P. found that Mrs. Smith used food as a way to soothe Ann's loneliness, for she had no playmates. An only child, Ann was encouraged to eat instead of seeking friends. Whenever she complained of physical ailments, which was frequent, she was encouraged to stay at home instead of attending school. Ann and her mother spent most of their time watching television and snacking. Since Mrs. Smith had few friends, Ann and she were often companions. Mr. P. established a friendly relationship with Mrs. Smith and, through a series of meetings, encouraged her to seek assistance from a community agency which provided counseling to adults. He also obtained counseling at school for Ann.

2. *In school*. The instructional specialist, Mary Super, provided a first grade teacher with assistance in changing a "school phobic" child's behavior. Tod, a six-year-old, often refused to attend school. When taken to school by his parents, he frequently left and returned home on his own.

Thelma Robinson worked with the parents so that they would reward Tod for going to school and not reward him for staying home. Previously, they permitted him to play at home when he feigned illness or refused to attend school. With Thelma's help, they now confined him to his bedroom (which he disliked) when he did not go to school and permitted him to play longer in the evenings on the days when he willingly went to school.

Ms. Super assisted the teacher to develop a system of rewarding events for Tod when he was in attendance. His teacher began with a frequent schedule of positive reinforcement when Tod entered the classroom. She gave Tod much personal attention upon his entering the classroom. She greeted him pleasantly; encouraged him to engage in free play with other classmates; permitted him to lead the class in opening activities; and had another child purchase the job of being Tod's aide.

Later, as he began to adjust to regular school attendance, the teacher was assisted in developing Tod's behavior toward less noncontingent rewards and more independent performance. Thus, he was gradually assigned more school tasks prior to selecting those events which he preferred. Every attempt was made throughout to make certain that his school experiences were pleasant.

Thelma taught Tod's parents how to reward him for school attendance and for willingly going to school. She also encouraged them to make after school experiences at home pleasant ones for Tod.

3. *On the playground*. Clement Elementary School had gained an earned reputation as a tough school with serious behavior problems because of the many fights which occurred on the playground. When Mrs. Rules became principal, she decided to do something to change the students' playground behavior. Generally, her approach consisted of two separate tactics. The first was to initiate social skills into the cirriculum, and second, a management system was implemented for the playground.

Social skills instruction consisted of a school-wide curriculum in which one unit of study included playground behaviors. The curriculum contained eight components, appropriate for the ages of each student group. Teachers were trained to implement the curricular ideas. Included in their training was the use of behavior rehearsing, role

Instructional situations vary and may involve teachers and students as well as parents, consultants, and other concerned individuals.

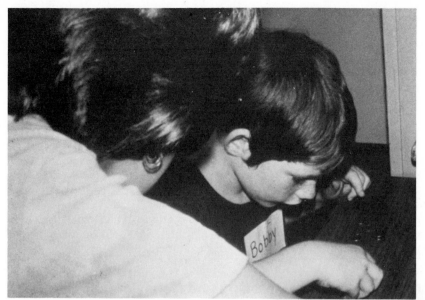

playing and conducting group discussions. All recommended lessons contained suggested functional assignments so that students were expected to apply those behaviors which they discussed and practiced in the classrooms.

The playground management system consisted of providing rewards for classes of students who engaged in proper play behavior. In order to use the playground, it was necessary for all students to wear armbands which designated their classrooms. Teachers and volunteers were then able to recognize readily those students who were frequent violators of playground rules as well as those who obeyed the rules. Playground supervisors made notes of those students who were violating playground rules. Those classrooms not represented by students on the playground supervisors' reports were recipients of rewarding events (such as special movies, popcorn parties, field trips, extra playground time, magazines, and other rewards).

The supervisors were also trained to use personal attention and other means of recognition to encourage students in appropriate play behavior. Frequent rule violators were assigned to special instruction on how to play properly.

Instructional Views of Learning and Behavioral Problems

Past

In the past two separate instructional approaches developed for teaching learning disabled children and those with behavioral problems (L&BD).[2] Learning handicapped children have been taught on the basis of presumed causative factors and stereotyped characteristics. Thus, those authorities who emphasized the neurological deficits believed to be common to this population often advocated sterile classroom environments as a way to reduce hyperactivity (Cruickshank et al., 1961) or figure/ground problems of perception (Strauss & Lehtinen, 1947), to cite a few examples.

Similarly, emotionally disturbed children were taught on the basis of assumptions surrounding the causes and effects of maladaptive behavior. A typical example of these faulty assumptions is the "emotional blocks" that presumably interfered with academic performance. If certain academic content was believed to arouse the emotions of a given student, it was not presented. Instances of emotional blocking typically required that the emotional block be removed prior to teaching.

Present

Placement and Special Services

Effective instruction for children with learning and behavioral problems requires organizational arrangements which facilitate the delivery of services. While organizational schemes are not highlighted here, it may be helpful for readers to keep in mind specific settings in which activities described in this text are likely to occur and to identify those types of services which will help make teaching more effective. The descriptions which follow are presented in order to begin the process of relating the content found in this text to school settings.

There are many possible educational placements for school-aged children with learning problems and behavioral disorders. These include *regular elementary* and *secondary classes* where selected students are placed for the entire time or for

---

2. Hereafter throughout this text L&BD will be used to denote *children with learning and behavioral disorders*.

portions of their days. When placed in such settings, these students may be considered *Target Students*; that is, special instruction and related services are provided to them in conjunction with or as supplementary to their placements.

Full-time special class placement at any level has been used traditionally for placing students who have extraordinary needs. Under this organizational plan, students spend all of their school day in a special class. While such classes often have been criticized for various social (Rist, 1970) and educational reasons (Christopolos & Renz, 1969), these classes have continued to represent the basic placement vehicle for a large percentage of such children who are receiving special instruction. However, there is evidence to support the belief that students placed in special classes and their parents tend to view such placements favorably (McKinnon, 1970). Some questions have also been raised regarding the evaluation of special class placement effects as well as the importance of those variables which have been studied (MacMillan, 1971).

Special schools have been used traditionally for placement purposes. While the trend is clearly away from special schools, these continue as educational arrangements for many severely disturbed and learning handicapped children (Berkowitz & Rothman, 1960). Among the advantages often cited in support of special schools are (1) the total environment within special schools is oriented toward that particular population; and (2) adjunct medical and psychological services are presumably well integrated into the educational programs.

Resource rooms are typically found in both elementary and secondary schools. This particular organizational scheme was borrowed from the education of visually handicapped children. As early as 1913, the Cleveland Public Schools developed a cooperative plan whereby partially sighted children engaged in activities requiring special materials and techniques in special classes but participated with normally sighted students in activities not requiring close visual work (Stephens, 1966).

Variations on this same plan have been adapted widely for children with learning and/or behavioral problems who are in need of special instruction of an individualized nature for portions of their school days. Instruction and opportunities for interacting with regular students are available to them through regular class placement for the balance of the time.

Typically, students are taught in resource rooms in small groups, although at times tutoring and counseling are provided on a one-to-one basis. In either instance, instruction is delivered by a special teacher with the anticipation that these students will gradually spend increasingly more time in regular classes with a corresponding reduction of time in the resource room.

Tutoring has long been a way to provide basic or supplementary instruction to handicapped children on a ratio of one teacher to one student. It has developed into a viable and important means of assisting learning disabled children in many schools. State departments of education often provide financial assistance to school districts in order to encourage its use.

Tutoring may provide supplementary or basic instruction to learning and behaviorally disordered children. When it supplements other instruction, the tutor teaches a student in addition to the instruction which is provided in either special or regular classes.

As basic instruction, tutoring is provided in residential or school settings where it is the sole means of schooling for the child. Often, this condition exists with severely handicapped students who, otherwise, cannot be maintained in group instructional settings.

Supportive and Ancillary Services

Psychological testing has been the cornerstone for most special education programs. In the United States instructional services for the mentally retarded, emotionally disturbed, and learning disabled have grown out of the testing movement (Wallin & Ferguson, 1967). More recently, assessment approaches have become a bridge between academic instruction and identification procedures using standardized tests for measuring intelligence, achievement, and personality. Usually assessment for instructional purposes tends to be keyed more specifically to teaching and has more immediate instructional value than standardized testing.

In addition to psychological services, ancillary personnel may consist of medical (nurses, psychiatrists, and physicians) and paramedical practitioners (physical and occupational therapists, audiologists, and dental hygienists). Counselors, school administrators, and instructional supervisors and consultants are usually involved in supportive roles. In residential settings, social workers and cottage parents tend to be key members of treatment teams.

Anecdote 1.2 describes how school programs can be organized to provide instruction to children with learning and behavioral problems. Settings and services of this type are used to facilitate the instructional approaches described throughout this text. While titles of the special education team may differ in other school programs, those functions which each member performs are necessary services regardless of the job titles.

ANECDOTE 1.2

Regular Elementary Class – Two Target Students

Ms. Lecture, a fourth-grade teacher at Main Street Elementary School (Newton School District) has two students who have been termed "target children" by the special education team among her 27 students. These two students are attending a regular class full time for the first time in two years. Matt, an eight-year-old has spent his entire first and second years of school in a special class for children with "adjustment problems." Toward the latter part of his third year in school, he began to be phased into the general instructional program by spending a portion of his school day in a regular third grade. For the remainder of the school day, Matt was in a special class. Doris, an early ten-year-old, was in Ms. L's class for the last six weeks during the previous school year. She had been in a special class for children with learning problems during most of her first year and all of the second year of schooling. She is now in a regular fourth grade with 26 other children but will continue to receive some special education services as well as special attention from her teacher, Ms. L.

Special Class – Elementary School

Mr. Sigmund teaches a special "adjustment class" at Main Street Elementary School. The eight children in his class have been diagnosed as having moderate to severe emotional problems. Because of the management and learning problems presented by these children, aged from eight to twelve years, a teacher's aide is assigned to work under Mr. S's direction.

As individual children demonstrate more typical (for their ages) social and academic functioning, they are scheduled into regular classes for small portions of the school day. The time out of Mr. S's class is gradually increased until they no longer attend the special class, although they may continue to receive special education services in various forms.

Consultation to regular teachers may be provided by special education personnel in order to assist the teachers in maintaining target children's social and academic adjustment. More direct instructional services may also be provided to the children through special tutoring.

Special Elementary School

Mrs. Rules is principal of the Clement Elementary School, a special public school for seriously disturbed elementary aged children. The average daily enrollment at Clement is 145 students between the ages of 8 and 14. In addition to evidencing problems of social adjustment (such as disruptive, violent behavior and withdrawn behavior), students also present moderate to severe academic learning problems. There are 14 classroom teachers at Clement, a physical education teacher and full-time art, music, and industrial arts teachers. A school psychologist, a visiting teacher, and a speech therapist are assigned half time to serve students and teachers at the school.

Resource Room – Middle School

Mr. Ambi Dextrous is a resource teacher at Harding Middle School where he is responsible for 18 students, ages 12-16, for portions of the school day. Students come for instruction in clusters of four or five, although individual students also enter his room for short intervals. All of the students present academic deficits in one or more subject areas. Twelve of the 18 display moderate to mild social adjustment problems. The remaining six students have such serious academic learning problems that they require daily assistance in order to maintain their academic skills. As these students improve they will spend less time with Mr. D. and more time in their regular classes. Hopefully, each will eventually receive instruction entirely in regular classes.

Resource Room – High School

Mrs. Rehab teaches senior high school students whose academic and social behaviors are inadequate. She typically teaches 12 students, aged 15 to 18. Approximately four or five students are in her room at any given time during the school day.

When they are not being taught by Mrs. R., four students are in selected academic classes. Three students are employed outside the school as a part of a work-study program each afternoon. And the remaining five students are scheduled for nonacademic subjects (art, shop, physical education, home economics, homeroom, and driver education) with other teachers but receive the remainder of their instruction from Mrs. R.

Tutoring Services – Elementary School

Mrs. Flack tutors 10 children each day. Each child comes to her for instruction for approximately 20 minutes. She usually teaches basic skills in language (listening, speaking, reading, writing, and spelling) and arithmetic. Although at times, it is necessary to teach social responses which she does through behavior rehearsing and discussion. Mrs. F's role includes meeting with each child's teacher regularly in order to determine where progress is occurring and which areas are in need of more emphasis.

Special Education Team

The Special Education Team serves all Newton Public schools: elementary, middle, high, and special schools. Each team is composed of an instructional consultant, a school psychologist, a visiting teacher, and a parent trainer. When the team serves a given school, the building principal becomes an ex officio member. Similarly, any teacher receiving its services is an ex officio team member while team services are provided to that class.

Team members and their roles are:

Tony Rodriquez, *school psychologist:* He observes, assesses and makes school placement recommendations for students referred for special services. Occasionally, he consults with classroom teachers, building principals, and other teachers regarding the instruction and management of selected children referred to the team. Tony also serves as team leader in six of the twelve schools served by his team.

An *instructional specialist*, Mary Super, typically provides consultation to teachers. While her main focus is on the child referred to the team, she also assists and advises teachers in management and instruction of all children in their classes.

Jack Pangborn, the team's *visiting teacher*, serves as a liaison person between schools and homes in particular for those children who are in need of special assistance. He also refers parents to other community agencies and specialists for additional services. Jack works as an advocate for children in the community, with the courts, and in the school. He shares the leadership of the team when it is working in the remaining six schools.

Thelma Robinson is the *parent trainer*. She conducts on-going parent education and training programs in small groups at schools. And she provides follow-up assistance to them in their homes. While Thelma provides information to parents concerning child growth and education, her primary function is to train parents in child management techniques.

The Extent of Learning and Behavioral Problems

Children of school age who display learning and behavioral problems appear to constitute a varying percentage of that population, depending upon the criteria used for identification. Since there is little agreement as to which deficits constitute learning and behavioral problems, prevalence estimates vary from school to school, state to state, and district to district. In states where diagnosis of emotional problems or learning disabilities must include biological factors, the prevalence of such disorders tends to be less than where instructional services are provided solely on the basis of performance criteria.

Percentages of behaviorally troubled children in classrooms vary due to differences in criteria but indicate a substantial occurrence of problems within different sample populations. Glavin (1967) reported that 12.9% of school-aged children in Tennessee could be termed emotionally disturbed. Stennett (1966) found 22% of children in a Minnesota school district to be moderately or seriously emotionally handicapped.

Mothers of 482 children, ages 6 to 13, were interviewed by Lapouse and Monk (1958). They found that 28% of the children had frequent nightmares, 48% were considered to be ill-tempered, and 43% had a high number of fears and worries. In another study (Werry & Quay, 1971), behavior ratings were obtained on over 1500 kindergarten, first-, and second-grade children. They found an average of 7.6 deviant behaviors for girls and 11.4 deviant behaviors for boys.

In one of the few reported longitudinal studies of L&BD children, Rubin and Balow (1971) found that over 41% of their sample population were placed in special classes (2.3%) or repeated one grade (11.6%) or were identified by teachers as displaying problems of attitude and behavior (28%); in addition, they found that 18% were referred for special services.

Since their study only followed the population through the third year of school, it can be assumed that even a higher number of the sample population might fall into the above categories later in their school lives.

Of course, those categories used in the Rubin and Balow study do not necessarily mean that learning and behavioral problems existed among all 41% of the subjects. All those identified by teachers as displaying attitudinal and behavioral problems probably would not qualify for special education services. Nor should all of the students referred for psychological and other services be considered to possess moderate to severe learning and behavioral problems. This study does show, however, the extent of requests for special education services among that particular population. It also suggests that considerably more than 10% of some populations may be considered to have learning and behavioral problems. Perhaps more importantly, it points out that teachers are faced with many children who present various degrees of learning problems and behavior difficulties.

In a longitudinal study of emotionally disturbed children, McCaffrey and Cummings (1967) found that most children identified as emotionally disturbed by their teachers during their second year of school were not so rated by teachers in the fifth year of school. If behaviors related to emotional disturbance are as transitory as suggested by this study, then the wide variance in estimated emotional disturbance among school-age populations may be attributed to the temporary nature of many emotional problems.

It is reasonable, however, to believe that problems of social adjustment and difficulties in academic learning represent serious handicaps for a substantial number of children. Teachers are faced with assisting these students in classrooms in almost all public elementary and secondary schools.

Interrelatedness of Learning and Behavioral Problems

From a behavioral perspective, the interrelatedness of learning and behavioral problems is based upon the notion that both academic and social behaviors are performances. In fact, academic learning problems or emotional problems are identifiable only when these are manifested in behavior.

Regardless of the type of response—academic, social, or emotional—it can be improved or changed through instruction. Children with problems in reading, for example, can be helped through an instructional approach. Similarly, emotionally disturbed children can be taught to respond in more normal ways. By attending to the behavioral aspects of students' adjustment and academic learning problems, teachers can deal directly with performance problems.

Academic Learning Problems

Academic learning problems exist only when students fail to perform. Often learning handicapped students demonstrate significant discrepancies between their functional intelligence, as reflected in IQ scores, and academic achievement test scores. Consequently, they are often referred to as *underachievers* because they perform academically at a level below which they seem capable of achieving.

Children with severe academic learning deficits have such pronounced problems when faced with academic tasks that they are readily identifiable by teachers and their peers. Unfortunately, they are sometimes mistakenly considered to be mentally retarded because of their significantly poor academic functioning.

However, unlike for those who are mentally retarded, the primary educational approach for learning disabled children should consist of corrective academic instruction. Since the typical learning handicapped child possesses sufficient mental ability to profit from the regular educational program, the major barrier is one of correcting academic deficits.

Behavioral Problems

Students who display maladaptive behavior problems clearly present performance difficulties. Such students often demonstrate any one of or combination of the following: bizarre behavior, weak control of impulses, and under- or over-emissions of responses.

Since emotional problems are reflected in behaviors, it is the response which must be changed if the behavior is to be modified. For many years, teachers and others who sought to help children with emotional problems attempted to deal with theoretical constructs which were believed to be contributing to behavioral disorders. As a result of such attempts, teaching practices were expected to be related to the *causes of maladaptive behavior* rather than to the behavior itself (Woody, 1969). Because of these expectations, questionable teaching practices have been applied to behaviorally disordered children.

Technical names can hinder instruction. When children are referred to as having strephosymbolia or dyslexia or dysphasia or any of the many other pseudoscientific terms that have become associated with the learning disabilities movement, instruction cannot (and should not) proceed until descriptions of the students' problems are obtained. For instructional purposes, it would be more facilitative if the meaning of technical terms were conveyed instead of the terms. For example, if an eight-year-old child is not reading and the reasons for his failure are not apparent and he possesses sufficient intelligence and has adequate vision, he should be described as having a reading problem. To label him "dyslexic" is to add an additional step to the instructional information which is needed to help him. Diagnostic labels convey little meaningful information to teachers and other practitioners since they do not indicate the type of instruction needed or even a precise definition of the problem (Adams, 1969).

An Instructional Approach

Until recently, children with academic learning problems and those displaying social learning difficulties were not viewed from an instructional point of view. Nor is there common agreement among special educators as to what constitutes an instructional point of view (Fink & Glass, 1973).

This text has an instructional focus. It deals with teaching students who present social and/or academic deficits. How teachers assess students, manipulate learning environments, manage classroom activities, and implement and evaluate instructional strategies are considered in this text.

An instructional point of view begins with descriptions of a student's performance in comparison with specific behaviors to be learned. Instructional plans are implemented to assist in achieving those behaviors. Lastly, student performance is evaluated to determine if the performance meets acceptable criteria. If it does, additional responses to be learned are identified. If performance is unacceptable, additional instruction, with possible changes in strategy, is used until criterion is met.

In Figure 1.3, an instructional approach is shown schematically using the Directive Teaching System as a model. Upon entry into an instructional experience (a unit of study, beginning of a school year, or any point where new skills or concepts are to be learned), students are assessed against the instructional objectives for that particular experience.

Those who demonstrate mastery of specific tasks may be provided with, or choose, a related enrichment experience or they can continue to be assessed until tasks are identified which they have not yet mastered but have the prerequisite skills to learn.

When tasks students are ready to learn[3] are identified, a directed teaching-learning experience occurs, usually in a form of a teaching strategy.

After students have had instruction, reassessment of their responses to the task takes place. If after several instructional sessions (about three) students fail to meet performance criteria, a different instructional approach is used. This teaching/assessing cycle continues until performance criteria are met.

One key to an instructional approach is to base teaching on specific tasks for which the student has the prerequisite skills and concepts to master. Another is for teachers to avoid responding to irrelevant information. Types of information irrelevant for instructional purposes include home conditions, parental information, test scores, and diagnostic information.

Generally, any information which cannot be directly translated into activities for improving students' learning are instructionally irrelevant. It should be noted that some information has educational relevance for administrative purposes but has no instructional value.

Home Conditions

A search for home factors that have influenced students' learning and behavioral deficits is commonplace in education. Undoubtedly such factors do contribute to academic and social performances, but teachers typically have no direct influence over the home conditions of their students. While knowledge of students' home life may help teachers understand their students, this information should not affect the instruction of those children. Such information is not necessary to teach students and is therefore irrelevant to the instructional process.

Information about Parents

A similar rationale relates to information concerning students' parents. Relationships students have with their parents may be of central concern to other professionals such as social workers, psychologists, and psychiatrists, but teachers have no useful purpose for such information.

Some authorities argue that teachers can develop empathy for children whose parents have some kind of problem, but this rationale implies that teachers should not be empathetic to all students. Those students whose home problems are unknown to their teachers are also in need of kindness and empathy.

Test Scores

Standardized test results have considerable educational and informational value. They may be used for curriculum planning when, for instance, test results suggest that groups of students are in need of remedial assistance or more vocationally oriented programs. Test results are also helpful in providing educational and vocational counseling when students are planning their career goals. They are useful for comparing the students' performances in a given school against national norms. This information is often used to provide the public with an understanding of how students rank in regard to other sample populations.

---

3. "Ready to learn" implies that the responses are within students' repertoires of responses; that is, the tasks are not beyond their present performance levels.

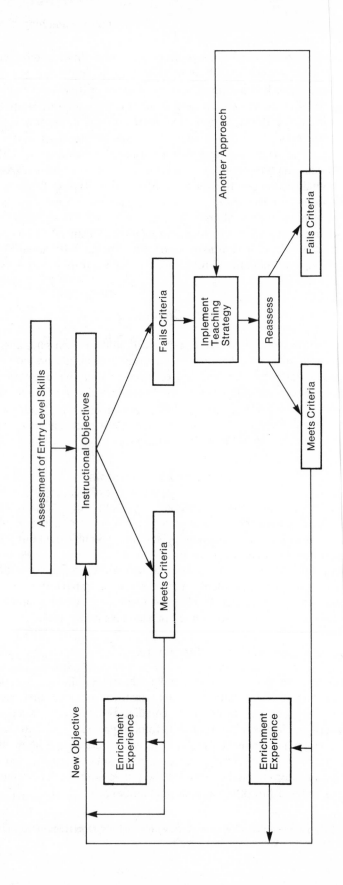

Instructionally, however, tests scores of individuals have practically no value. A reading grade score, for example, does not indicate which responses students have already mastered, which they are ready to learn, or which they have not yet learned. Part of the problem is the nonspecific nature of test scores. Another factor is the manner in which standardized tests are developed and the purposes for which they are made. These issues are discussed more fully in chapter 6.

Diagnostic Information

Diagnosis is made either on the basis of causation or on the basis of behaviors typical for a particular disorder. Diagnosis is directly related to classification and is used in medicine as a means of treating the causes of an illness rather than its symptoms. In special education, diagnosis precedes educational services. Thus, after a child is diagnosed as "brain-injured" he or she may be placed in a special class or provided with other special services such as tutoring or home instruction.

In this sense, diagnosis can have *educational* value since it provides a mechanism for identifying and placing those children who are in need of special help. But its *instructional* value is questionable. Even when a diagnosis is made on the basis of behavior, it has little or no instructional value since a teacher cannot instruct children on the basis of general behaviors such as "hyperactivity," "perseveration," and "perceptual problems." Teachers need task-specific and recent information concerning student performance. Ways to acquire current task-specific information are discussed in chapter 6.

If an instructional basis were widely accepted for considering L&BD children, the two categories of *emotional disturbance* and *learning disabilities* would not exist for school purposes. Rather, a single category based upon learning variables would be used. One proposed grouping is that of *learning and behaviorally handicapped* (Stephens, 1970). The behavior-oriented rationale for an instructional basis for a single label is:

> Classifications that are derived from etiological thinking seldom have educational relevance and do not suggest directions for teaching or for curriculum development. Terminology that is based on the biological conditions of children presents three implications. First, body deficits are assumed to cause inadequate behavior. Second, it suggests that by identifying physical disabilities teachers can change the behavioral responses of children. Third, it equates educational treatment with medical treatment.
>
> One must not negate the importance of etiological and biological considerations with respect to disabling conditions. Such factors may be of the utmost importance for those who engage in prevention of disabilities and certain forms of treatment, but we are concerned here with teaching children who are presented to schools after having acquired the biological factors which are presumed to cause learning and behavioral handicaps.
>
> Teachers instruct and manage children on the basis of overt manifestations. Therefore, they respond to the behavior of children not to diagnostic labels or medical conditions. Those who teach children labeled as having *minimal brain dysfunction*, for example, typically begin by assessing each child's academic skills in order to establish individual instructional levels. If a child is easily distracted, the teacher attempts to control environmental stimuli as a means of reducing the child's hyperactivity. Similarly, children who are labeled *emotionally disturbed* are managed by teachers in an attempt to accommodate the children's behavior to the learning environment. Teachers would continue to be faced with diverse learning rates and variable behavior among children even if it were possible to classify and group them along clear disability lines. (Stephens, 1970, pp. 2-3)

Summary

L&BD students are identified as those individuals who display mild to moderate academic learning and behavior adjustment problems. There is a sound rationale for considering such children for educational placement and instruction on the basis of their functioning rather than on presumed etiological factors. Contemporary views of learning and behavior problems deal directly with performance difficulties.

There are multiple causes for most academic learning and social behavior problems including biological and environmental conditions. However, teachers need not identify such causes since they should *focus* on students' current functioning.

Included in possible educational placement of L&BD students are regular classes, special classes, resource rooms, and special schools. Tutoring may also be provided for basic or supplemental instruction.

The prevalence of L&BD students among various school populations varies widely due to differences in identification criteria.

Characteristics of Children with Learning and Behavior Problems

Characteristics commonly associated with children who display learning difficulties and behavioral disorders are discussed in this chapter. Such characteristics include three levels of awareness termed observable, inferential, and hypothetical. While school-related characteristics for both groups of students are not identical, there are many behaviors common to both.

Children with learning problems present moderate to severe academic performance problems. They also display problems of motor control and attention.

Two models of instruction are associated with the learning disability movement: the ability training model and the skill training model.

Behaviorally disordered students tend to present a higher rate of deviant behavior than do the learning disabled, but school-related characteristics for both groups of students have many behaviors in common.

Introduction

It is necessary to identify students in need of assistance in a systematic way if they are to be served. Teachers, parents, and other school personnel should be sensitive to those signs which suggest children may need special instruction. In order to locate these children, it is necessary to know their characteristics.

Many authorities have characterized learning disabled and behaviorally disordered children. But prior to categorizing students in any particular way, samples of behavior should be obtained. Although a single act can result in labeling students, such as in the instance of delinquent behavior, clusters of behavior are usually needed. A cluster of characteristics results in the classification of *syndromes*. Characteristics common to a particular disorder form a syndrome. Depending upon one's theoretical orientation, syndromes may focus on observable characteristics or hypothetical constructs or a combination of both.

Syndromes have been useful in medical practice where a patient's outward signs provide clues to the practitioner as to the origin of an illness. The syndrome concept has been adopted by psychologists and special educators as a way to locate children in need of special assistance. Some believe that a knowledge of syndromes by teachers can serve to identify children who may be in need of assistance as described in anecdote 2.1.

Joey Devlin's first-grade teacher noticed during the first few months of school that he performed and behaved quite a bit differently than most of the children. His coordination and motor activities were poor in comparison to the others. In general, he was clumsy, often falling and tripping at play. When Ms. Henson, the teacher, discussed Joey's lack of coordination with his mother she stated that he had always been "accident prone." During his preschool years he had broken an arm, sprained a wrist, and often turned his ankles.

Ms. Henson also noticed that Joey had lapses of memory and sometimes would strike himself in the head in such a way as to punish himself for his forgetfulness. Academically, he demonstrated a diverse range of work in various subjects: his coloring and pencil work were of poor quality but his speaking vocabulary was above average. When printing, he frequently reversed numerals and letters.

As a result of her observations, Ms. Henson requested assistance from the Special Education Team. When the school psychologist, Tony Rodriquez, contacted her she was able to provide him with specific descriptions of Joey's difficulties.

By knowing which behaviors are deviant for a student's age and grade placement, teachers are better able to determine when additional assistance should be requested. For example, Joey's behavior provided Ms. Henson with sufficient information to indicate a need for consultant services.

Checklists have been developed for teachers' use. Schleichkorn (1972) identified 121 items teachers could use to recognize problems of learning.

Behaviors such as those in Figure 2.1 should be viewed only as tentative signs of the need for assistance. Particularly when seeking to identify preschool or kindergarten children who may have learning problems, it is essential to recognize that most academic learning problems have not yet developed. As Keogh and Becker (1973) have noted, children who have not yet been exposed to reading instruction cannot be considered to have reading problems.

FIGURE 2.1. A checklist for teachers (From Jacob Schleichkorn, The teacher and recognition of problems in children, *Journal of Learning Disabilities* 1972, *5*, 55-56. Reproduced with permission of the author and publisher.)

The classroom teacher is afforded an excellent and unique opportunity to note slight deviations in the behavior of children which may be precursors of greater problems. To assist the teacher in recognizing developing problems I have prepared a checklist, based on material submitted by a graduate class in special education at Hofstra University. The teacher can pull out this checklist and use it as a guide; where problems so-indicate, she should seek the assistance of appropriate specialists. The checklist follows:

Coordination and Motor Activities

1. Has difficulty in walking up stairs.
2. Cannot skip.
3. Holds a pencil or pen in a weak or clumsy grasp.
4. Has difficulty in using scissors.
5. Has jerky movements.
6. Trips often.
7. Bumps into objects.
8. Cannot tie knots, zip zippers, button buttons.
9. Turns head from side to side in a rhythmic pattern.

FIGURE 2.1—*Continued*

10. Demonstrates poor balance.
11. Touches other children all the time.
12. Startles easily.
13. Appears hyperactive.
14. Fatigues easily.
15. Can't manage two subjects.
16. Is clumsy in general.
17. Can't catch a ball.
18. Has sloppy eating habits.
19. Has difficulty in walking a straight line.
20. Cannot balance objects.
21. Cannot stay neat for any length of time.
22. Drools.
23. Displays weakness in an extremity.
24. Walks with feet turned inward.
25. Walks on toes.
26. Favors one extremity.
27. Drags a foot.
28. Shuffles feet.

Responses (aural)

1. Repeats what is told before he acts or responds
2. Asks the same question over and over.
3. Tends to forget what he heard.
4. Overreacts to normal situations with continuous talk.
5. Is unable to differentiate sounds and noises.
6. Cannot distinguish direction of sound.
7. Requests directions time and time again.
8. Attempts to read lips.
9. Speaks extremely softly.
10. Talks in loud voice all the time.
11. Cannot hear certain sounds.

Communication (verbal)

1. Has delayed speech
2. Has poor articulation.
3. Has infantile speech.
4. Is unable to read orally properly.
5. Stutters.
6. Has trouble with certain sounds such as *s* and *th*.
7. Mumbles.
8. Loses the endings of words.
9. Lisps.
10. Is unable to vocalize thought rapidly.
11. Uses dirty words to replace good vocabulary.
12. Feels the urge to make irrelevant remarks.
13. Cannot recall pertinent facts about self.
14. Refuses to speak.

Behavior

1. Has poor concept of time.
2. Stamps on the floor.
3. Hits head against the wall.
4. Hits his head with his hand.
5. Drums fingers on the table constantly.
6. Bites nails.
7. Twists hair.
8. Always looks downward.
9. Becomes frustrated easily.
10. Cannot tolerate changes in routine.
11. Is forgetful.
12. Has lack of emotional control.
13. Appears hostile.
14. Has tics.
15. Has lapse of memory.
16. Has difficulty with peer relationships.
17. Is gullible.
18. Appears disorganized in activities.
19. Is distractible.
20. Is impulsive.
21. Has catastrophic reaction to minor problems.
22. Is withdrawn.
23. Is unable to control behavior.
24. Is generally excluded by his peers.
25. Daydreams.
26. Suffers sudden removal from reality.
27. Is anxious.
28. Exhibits moods of unhappiness.
29. Cannot make social judgments.
30. Has bizarre fears.
31. Is short tempered.
32. Has frequent temper tantrums.
33. Maintains a blank expression.
34. Is overly meticulous.
35. Constantly rocks in chair.
36. Picks at paper and tears small pieces.
37. Is unable to concentrate on activity.

FIGURE 2.1—continued

38. Perseverates.
39. Is extremely shy when asked
    to talk.
40. Has *petit mal* seizures.

Conceptual Ability
1. Does not comprehend what is said.
2. Does not follow simple directions.
3. Constantly asks neighbors for help.
4. Cannot apply former experiences to
   new situations.
5. Demonstrates unequal work in
   various subjects.
6. Is two or more grades below
   vocal reading ability.

Perception
1. Is unable to focus on one item.
2. Squints.
3. Obvious constant copying errors
   (i-e)(f-l)(g-q)
4. Has crossed eyes.
5. Blinks.
6. Has poor judgment of
   distance.

7. Juxtaposition of letters.
8. Cannot spell words he can
   read.
9. Has special orientation
   problems.
10. Is disorganized.
11. Has short reading attention
    span.
12. Has difficulty in reading from
    the blackboard.
13. Makes extremely peculiar
    drawings.
14. Has difficulty differentiating
    subjects.
15. Cannot reason abstractly.
16. Has difficulty in returning eyes
    to left margin when reading or
    writing.
17. Has poor aim.
18. Is unable to classify objects.
19. Holds paper at an angle.
20. Is unable to copy.
21. Has faulty body image.
22. Confuses right from left and
    left from right.

Lists, similar to those in Figure 2.1, often are misleading and confusing. The language of many items is imprecise, making the reliability and validity so low as to make the list of questionable value. Often the terms are not descriptive, contributing to poor reliability of interobserver agreement. If two people using the list at the same time on the same sample population do not agree at least 80% of the time, its reliability should be considered inadequate (Cooper, 1974). Checklists often are related to specific theoretical orientations which, by implication, require users to accept those theories of causation.

Levels of Syndromes

Ysseldyke and Salvia (1974) detailed the importance of differentiating between two fundamentally different theoretical models of teaching, both of which have grown out of the diagnostic-prescriptive teaching movement. They termed these the *ability training model* and the *task analysis model*.

While the differences between these two models are discussed later in this chapter, it should be noted here that the ability training model is based upon more unproven assumptions than is the task analysis model. It is important to be careful when attributing a degree of significance to certain maladaptive responses.

Characteristics obtained from observations should be related to a level of awareness. Three levels of thinking generally form the bases for syndromes. These are observable, inferential, and hypothetical. At the observable level, behaviors are noted which in themselves are viewed as maladaptive. At the inferential level, inferences are made concerning problems based upon the observed behavior. The third level of thinking results in the formulation of hypotheses concerning the causes of observed maladaptive behaviors.

The same pupil may be described differently, as shown in Figure 2.2, depending upon the level of categorization used. Not only are different terms used to describe the maladaptive behavior, but also the relevancy of the descriptors vary. Child A's teacher, for example, will find brain injury irrelevant and distractibility too general.

Child	Level	Terminology
A	Observable	Short attention
	Inferential	Distractible
	Hypothetical	Brain injured
B	Observable	Reverses letters when printing
	Inferential	Perceptual-motor problem
	Hypothetical	Neurological deficit
C	Observable	Threatens teachers with physical harm
	Inferential	Is overly aggressive
	Hypothetical	Has difficulty with authority figures
D	Observable	Talks to imaginary people
	Inferential	Fantasizes
	Hypothetical	Is psychotic

FIGURE 2.2. Observational, inferential, and hypothetical levels of human behavior

Observable Level

Characteristics of behavior which are derived strictly from descriptions of student functioning are at an observable level. Since these characteristics are descriptive, they do not infer from the actual performance which factors may be contributing to the maladaptive responses. At the observable level there is no attempt made to speculate as to the basic cause(s) of the aberration. The task analysis model of instruction (Ysseldyke & Salvia, 1974) draws heavily from the observable level of thinking. Maladaptive responses are described and related to specific acts as seen in anecdote 2.2.

ANECDOTE 2.2

Ms. Henson conferred with Mr. Rodriquez, the school psychologist, concerning Joey's problems. He asked the teacher to begin recording the incidents when Joey falls at school. She was to note when (day and time) this occurred, what he was doing at the time, and where it happened.

Similarly, he requested that Ms. Henson keep specimens of his paper/pencil products, dating each.

At the observable level, the characteristics were to meet these criteria:
1. the behavior must be descriptive,
2. it must be related to specific acts, and
3. it must be reliable.

Descriptive Criterion

When describing behavior it is necessary to select precise words and whenever possible to obtain samples of written products. With the accessibility of electronic devices in schools, it is often possible to have samples of behavior as supplements to verbal descriptions.

When the *descriptive* criterion is applied to the list in Figure 2.1, it is apparent that all items do not meet this requirement. For example, "is gullible," item 17 under the category *behavior,* is not descriptive. Rather, it is a conclusion that must be derived from specific behaviors. Is the child gullible because he believes exaggerated statements made by peers? Or is he gullible because he sold his coat for five cents?

On the other hand, behaviors such as the following (shown in Figure 2.1) are descriptive:

> trips often
> can't catch a ball
> squints
> blinks
> has crossed eyes
> drags a foot
> hits head against the wall
> bites nails
> twists hair
> asks the same question over and over

Relation to a Specific Act

In addition to being descriptive, it is important that the observed characteristic is related to performance. When does he trip? While walking, running, or both? Does it matter which type of ball he is to catch? And who is present when he is required to catch it?

The descriptive criterion can be met if the act is specified and those conditions under which the behavior occurs are described. Thus, *has difficulty walking a straight line* adequately describes the act but fails to indicate the conditions. What is the length of the line?

Similarly, *blinks* fails to convey conditions of the behavior. Does blinking occur while reading, talking, or at anytime regardless of the tasks being performed?

Of course, the act itself must be descriptive. For example, *he shouts when playing* fails to describe the type of play. Is it a ball game on the playground or an educational game in the classroom?

Reliability Criterion

To satisfy the criterion of reliability, it is necessary for two or more observers to agree most of the time. Usually, an 80% level of agreement is considered adequate. This is a stiff criterion to apply to a list of observed characteristics. However, it is reasonable to expect a characteristic to be reliable given the importance of its purpose.

Reliability can be improved by describing those responses which constitute the act. For example, *has difficulty walking a straight line* can be made to describe precisely what will represent difficulty as well as the length of the line. The item might read as follows:

Given a straight line of twenty feet in length and asked to walk the line by placing one foot after the other on the line, falling one time or more and/or failing to place a foot on the line each time.

Inferential Level

Inferences are one step removed from descriptive observations. Although they should be derived logically from the actual behavior, inferences should also be determined carefully since the potential for error is great. It is a sound policy to infer only from several observations of the same characteristic since a cluster of behaviors is needed to form a generalizable inference. In Figure 2.2, for example, several observations of Child A indicated that attending for reasonable time intervals was not often achieved, resulting in the generalization that the student was distracted easily.

Inferential thinking tends to deal with general categories of behavior, e.g., visual-motor problems. It also uses a cluster of related behaviors, e.g., aggression. Correct inferences are logically related to observed behaviors. For example, a child may be said to fantasize (inference) because she has been observed talking to imaginary people and telling wild stories.

Groups of behaviors are generally thought of as comprising a syndrome. The Strauss Syndrome (Stevens & Birch, 1957), for example, is characterized by hyperactivity, distractibility, disinhibition, and perseveration. Unfortunately these characteristics are often not descriptive and lead to the problems of reliability and validity commonly associated with the ability training model (Ysseldyke & Salvia, 1974).

Typically, each characteristic is related to a particular type of behavior, such as incoordination being reflected in children's poor quality of printing and handwriting.

Behaviors within a cluster are expected, at least logically, to be related. Thus, the characteristic of incoordination might consist of problems of body balance, poor quality paper-pencil work, difficulty in catching and/or throwing, and frequent tripping or falling.

In one sense, related behaviors may be considered to be symptomatic of a given characteristic. Any one of the behaviors alone would not usually be sufficient to characterize a child. For example, poor handwriting skills without the presence of other deficits would not constitute incoordination.

Inferences are not valid unless they are related directly to observed performances. Children who lie, for example, are not necessarily fantasizing, but frequent exaggerations related to other imaginary events may constitute fantasy. The behaviors from which the inferences are derived must have a direct and logical relationship. For example, a low score on the *Illinois Test of Psycholinguistic Abilities (ITPA)* should not be used as evidence of a learning problem unless daily academic performance in the classroom supports this belief. Observed behavior (daily academic performance) is always more valid than predicted performance *(ITPA)*. The ability-training orientation has been criticized justifiably because of its heavy reliance upon instruments such as the *ITPA* (Ysseldyke & Salvia, 1974).

Even correctly derived inferences are, at best, one step removed from the actual behavior. Because of the remoteness of inferential thinking from responses, when instruction is based upon inference rather than description, the most obvious instructional need should be met, rather than attempting to treat on the basis of explanations for the maladaptive performance.

Hypothetical Level

Hypothesis testing is an acceptable and standard scientific practice. When it occurs based on observations, conditions are arranged so that specific factors are evaluated to determine if they contribute to causation. When hypotheses are not tested or testable but assumptions are made indicating that maladaptive behavior has particular causes, then they are being used in lieu of the actual behavior or to account for that behavior. Practices of this sort can be misleading and detrimental.

Some advocates of ability training, for example, often rely upon hypothetical constructs to provide explanations for maladaptive responses. They claim that instruction should be differentiated on the basis of aptitude scores. Yet research evidence in support of that position has not materialized (Quay, 1973; Ysseldyke, 1974). Problems can be minimized by carefully formulating and testing hypotheses as well as avoiding the tendency to treat hypothetical constructs as evidence of real behavior.

Obviously, hypothetical thinking is of a different order than observational or inferential thinking. Note that student D, in Figure 2.2, behaved in a bizarre way, as if he were conversing with unseen individuals. Thus, *fantasizing* is a reasonable inference. To label the behavior psychotic, however, implies that a thorough psychological examination and observations of behavior over long time intervals revealed serious emotional disorders.

Correct hypothetical thinking must be related logically to inferences concerning the observed behavior. It must be testable, and it must take into account other possible explanations for maladaptive behavior.

Combining Levels

Often the three levels of thinking for dealing with syndromes are combined as shown in Figure 2.1. While this is a common practice, it does tend to confuse the purposes for which a list of behavioral characteristics is to be used. For example, a list of descriptive behaviors is necessary if teachers are to identify students in need of assistance with a high degree of accuracy. When a list of characteristics used for purposes of identification contains nondescriptive words, the reliability will be poor. As a result, many children who are in need of assistance will be overlooked. Conversely, many will be identified who are not in need of help. In addition, great variability in using the list will occur since the meanings of terms will differ from teacher to teacher.

Since school practitioners have different role expectations, their use of information varies with their job functions. If expected outcomes for a school position are general, they then have the latitude to use inferential or even hypothetical information. Conversely, if their jobs demand specificity with performance outcomes, descriptive information will be most useful to them.

Teachers should be concerned primarily with descriptive information since their roles require them to improve school performance, although, at times, it may be useful for them to infer from observations in order to generalize across time, settings, tasks, and other conditions. By describing student behavior, teachers are able to prepare specific instructional treatments. Further, they can then evaluate the effects of their instruction against their initial descriptions of the behavior.

Those who want to assist teachers find it necessary to use descriptive information for the same reasons. Instructional consultants and other resource personnel will do well to emphasize behavior descriptions when working with teachers.

Curriculum planners and other leadership personnel may use inferences since they are often responsible for groups of students across time and tasks. Long-term planning requires a degree of generalization that is related naturally to inferential thinking.

Hypothesis testing is used by researchers in order to answer the question *why.* School psychologists and other diagnosticians who are engaged in diagnostic labeling sometimes find it impossible to test hypotheses. However, while hypothetical thinking may serve to facilitate educational activities in other ways, it has little if any instructional value for individual students. Diagnostic classification schemes should never be used in lieu of descriptive information for instructional personnel.

Difficulties in Describing Learning Disabled Children

Characteristics believed to be common to learning disabled children have been reported in the educational and psychological literature for many years (Strauss & Lehtinen, 1947; Clements, 1966; Meier, 1971; Kirk, 1971). Some of these characteristics have not been recorded at the observable level, however. There are clusters of syndromes combining inferential and hypothetical characteristics with observable ones. For example, a list of characteristics reported by Clements (1966) included:

Hyperactivity
Perceptual-motor impairment
Emotional lability
General orientation defects
Disorders of memory and thinking
Specific learning disabilities in academic skill areas
Disorders of speech and hearing
Equivocal neurological signs
Motor perseveration

Almost all of the above characteristics must be inferred or hypothesized from observable behavior. Because in many instances the responses lack standard observable criteria, attempts to measure these characteristics do not tend to possess reasonable interobserver reliability.

Perceptual-motor impairments, for example, must be inferred from daily observations or from medical or psychological examinations. Since *perception* itself is a cognitive process, the reliability with which this characteristic is measured tends to be low. Further, many tests which purport to measure perception have established very low reliability correlations, thus opening to question whether they even measure perception (Salvia & Clark, 1973). Damage to the neurological system, as implied by the term *perceptual-motor impairment,* is not directly observable by nonmedical personnel. Therefore, the *effects* of possible damage to the central nervous system are often referred to as the *disability.* This level of language is also confusing since, in fact, a disability is not directly observable and is, as Stevens (1962) has noted, inferred from a handicapping condition. But the term has been so loosely used in reference to children with learning problems that it has assumed the status of an observable event, rather than a possible condition which may be contributing to maladaptive learning.

Children with learning problems would be served better if educational terminology were standardized. And if similar terms used by related disciplines conveyed the same meanings when used in special education, interdisciplinary communications would be improved. Additionally, common terminology would improve the reliability, and consequently the validity, of identification procedures.

School personnel can improve communications among one another by focusing on performance aspects of problems, rather than on presumed causative factors which are often outside their areas of expertise. Since teachers deal only with behaviors on school-related tasks, their emphasis, in particular, should be on performance in school settings.

Since an emphasis on behavior requires school practitioners to *describe* performance, a likely result seems to be more useful terminology. Descriptive terms help teachers both to assess students more effectively and to provide the necessary instruction more often. In Figure 2.3, examples of descriptive terms are shown in comparison to those terms more often used when referring to characteristics of learning disabled students.

Nondescriptive	Descriptive
disability	academic learning problem slow learner handicapped learner
specific disability	reading problem expressive language problem listening problem
perceptual disability	poor visual discrimination poor auditory discrimination difficulty in visual tracking
perceptual/motor disability	traces objects poorly difficulty in copying designs has trouble catching a ball
dyslexic	reads poorly does not comprehend what is read does not read sentences

dissociation	responds to parts not to entire
	  figure, problem, etc.
	has trouble putting segments of
	  story, puzzle, etc. together
	does not relate one event to
	  another

FIGURE 2.3 Some descriptive terms in comparison to other terms

Characteristics of Learning Disabled Children Related to Academic Performance

Children with learning problems present perplexing teaching and management problems. Often they function at a low-average or higher level of intelligence on standardized measures. Yet they present moderate to severe academic learning problems, often showing significant deficits in one or more academic skill areas.

Sometimes, they display problems in controlling their motor responses and in attending to relevant stimuli.

A syndrome of behavior has been associated with these children. While all students possessing learning problems do not display each characteristic, many of these are observed in their functioning. Stereotypes are invariably superfluous, and syndromes which lead solely to labeling are particularly misleading. However, characteristics may be useful as aids for identifying students in need of special help. For that purpose, behaviors are discussed within the following problem areas: cognitive problems, body management problems, academic learning problems, attitudinal problems, and emotional adjustment problems.

Cognitive Problems

ANECDOTE 2.3

Harry Sweet at age five seems very frustrated in kindergarten and his teacher Ms. Chin is puzzled. Since coming to school in September, Harry has been continually troubled. Now after twelve weeks, when all the children are expected to be responsive to the classroom routines, Harry continues to have school adjustment problems.

He seemingly doesn't understand verbal directions, is unable to skip, does not play well in a group, has toilet accidents, cannot print letters from copy, does not sit still in the story circle, cannot button his clothing, mispronounces simple words, is clumsy, and is generally behind the other children in motor development.

Yet, Harry is likable and tries very hard to please. His teacher feels he *knows* more than he shows. Like many retarded children, she reasons, his is a case of uneven development, or *developmental lag;* that's what one of her textbooks termed it in the section on mentally retarded children.

In discussing Harry with the principal, it is decided that more information is needed before referring him to the program for the mentally retarded. A school psychologist, Tony Rodriquez, is called in to consult with Ms. Chin. After a brief discussion with the teacher and a period of observing Harry, Mr. Rodriquez is convinced that the child needs help but he is uncertain as to the type of instruction needed.

Following a conference with Harry's parents, arrangements are made, on a trial basis, for two weeks of daily tutoring services. At the end of that time, the tutor, the psychologist, and the teacher are to discuss Harry's performance. Mrs. Flack, the tutor, feels that Harry is not mentally retarded but rather has severe learning problems. Although she believes that if Harry were administered the Stanford-Binet he might test below an IQ of 80 because so many of the test items below age six require nonverbal, motor, and discrimination responses. It is agreed that Mrs. Flack will continue tutoring Harry daily for 20 minutes in addition to his kindergarten attendance.

Epilogue: In April of his kindergarten year, Harry was administered an individual test of intelligence. His full-scale IQ score on that test was 83. The following year he was placed in a primary special class for children with learning problems.

Difficulties in cognitive processes encompass more areas than low or uneven measured intelligence since children at any level of intelligence may have learning problems. For administrative and funding purposes, the minimum IQ for inclusion in programs for the learning disabled varies from state to state. Generally, those who have measured intelligence below low-average are not served through such programs. Thus, an IQ of about 80 represents the lower limit of this population.

   While pseudoretardation, as seen in anecdote 2.3, is not common, young children
with serious learning problems have been known to be diagnosed incorrectly as
being mentally retarded. In addition to the higher measured intelligence of learning
handicapped children, better reasoning ability generally differentiates these children
from those who are mentally retarded. They tend to demonstrate higher *levels* and
rates of learning than do the mentally retarded. When comparing children's learning
over a period of time, the retarded have lower and longer curves of learning,
representing slower acquisition and longer time required for mastering those tasks.
In Figure 2.4, two children's hypothetical rates of learning the same task are compared. The steeper and shorter curve for the learning handicapped child graphically
shows the faster rate of mastering school tasks such children generally display in
comparison to mentally retarded youngsters. However, children with severe learning and/or behavior problems at times display learning curves more typical of the
mentally retarded. Learning-rate differences should not alone be a basis for determining placement or instruction of any handicapped youngster. The best way to
determine what and how to teach any child is to try systematic instruction for a
given period of time, while carefully evaluating the child's performance, as described in anecdote 2.3.

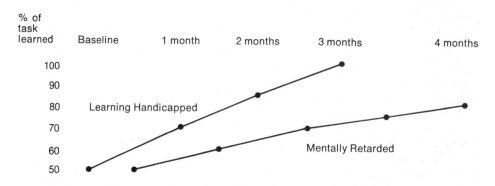

FIGURE 2.4.   Rate of learning the same task for a learning handicapped child and a
   mentally retarded child

   Uneven performance on tests of intelligence is another characteristic found
among children with learning problems. This is most noticeable when tests yielding
two or more IQ scores are administered. There may be, in such instances, a
15-point or more spread between the verbal and performance IQ scores (Clements
& Peters, 1962). In instances where there is a great IQ-score discrepancy between
the verbal and performance areas, performance IQs tend to be higher. In a study by
Ackerman, Peters, and Dykman (1971), 82 boys diagnosed as having specific learning disabilities were compared with a control group of 34 boys displaying adequate
academic performance using the *Wechsler Intelligence Scale for Children (WISC)*
as a measure. Verbal IQ scores were lower for the learning disabled population in
comparison to the control group. Their findings also point out problems which may
occur when criteria for special instruction require a minimum IQ of 90 since over
7% of the learning disabled subjects had full-scale IQ scores below 90 on the *WISC*.
   Deficit scores are commonly used as an identifying characteristic of children with
learning problems. Often this concept takes the form of a discrepancy between
achievement test scores and measured intelligence (Bateman, 1965). This notion,
however, has been falling into disrepute because of the lack of confidence in the

underlying assumptions upon which it rests. Salvia and Clark (1973) have warned against a rigid adherence to the use of deficit IQ scores as the sole criterion for identifying learning disabled children. They found that while deficits can be used as clues, alone this criterion may be misleading.

Among the assumptions made when using a discrepancy score for identifying learning disordered children are that:

1. intelligence is a stable characteristic,
2. measures of intelligence and achievement are valid for that population,
3. both measures are reliable, and
4. the discrepancy score's reliability is high.

When considering the above assumptions and other problems inherent in using discrepancy scores, it appears that this criterion for identifying children with learning handicaps has questionable predictive validity. As is the case with other hypothetical constructs, the value of deficit scores is not yet proven but continues to remain a characteristic which may have some use to clinicians and researchers as a sign of learning difficulties.

Difficulty in sequential ordering is believed to be a cognitive characteristic found among the learning handicapped population (Johnson & Myklebust, 1967). The ability to sequence events, words, experiences or other phenomena is considered important for school success. Some children with severe learning problems have trouble ordering events or thinking in a systematic fashion. This problem has been attributed to the lack of, and consequently a need for, structure. Epstein (1961) found that even among adults structured lists of nonsense syllables are recalled better than unstructured lists of similar type syllables.

Tendency to think in concrete terms is another characteristic. While thinking literally is common among young normal children and among the mentally retarded of any age, older students with learning problems often give only concrete explanations for events, word definitions, and other phenomena. For example, literal definitions may be provided for such sayings as:

Where there's smoke, there's fire.

Don't judge a book by its cover.

We don't know the worth of water until the well runs dry.

Big oaks from little acorns grow.

Don't throw diamonds before swine.

Man lives not by bread alone.

Difficulty in using symbols is common with primary-level learning disabled children. They may respond to letters and words by commenting on their shapes ("a T is a big I with a hat on").

Body Management Problems

School success, particularly in the early grades, demands motor control. Lack of body control is believed to contribute to poor visual/motor performance and inattention in learning situations. Clumsiness, untidiness, and unkempt appearance are body management problems often associated with learning disabled children. In addition, their failure to form letters and geometric designs properly and/or neatly when writing have frequently been noted (Strauss & Lehtinen, 1947; Johnson & Myklebust, 1967; Fernald, 1943; and Gillingham & Stillman, 1965).

Preschool- and primary-aged children are faced with many motor-related tasks in relation to the total number of tasks demanded of older students. As children acquire more language facility, body management demands decrease in importance, although motor and attending skills continue to be necessary for school success. Among motor-related tasks typically useful for school learning are:

SPEAKING	*OTHER*
tongue control	sitting
lip and mouth formations	walking
voice control	running
	standing
READING	throwing
	skipping
eye movements	dancing
head control	jumping
holding reading material	catching
	bending
WRITING	lifting
	pulling
holding writing instruments	shoving
control of writing instruments	

Meier (1971) reported a study where teachers checked behaviors commonly found among learning handicapped children. Using a checklist with 80 behavioral items, he found several requring body control frequently checked by the teachers.

Twenty-four of the items were categorized arbitrarily, by this writer, as primarily body management items. Of those 24, Meier reported that 6 were checked for at least 25% of the children ($N=284$), 3 for 50%, and 1 for approximately 66% of the pupils. These items are shown below:

Checked for 187 children: Easily distracted from school work (can't concentrate with even the slightest disturbances from other student's moving around or talking quietly).

Checked for 159 children: Repeats the same behavior over and over.

Checked for 147 children: Poor handwriting compared with peers' writing.

Checked for 140 children: Points at words while reading silently or aloud.

Checked for 131 children: Poor drawing of crossing, wavy lines compared with peers' drawings.

Checked for 121 children: Poor drawing of a man compared with peers' drawings.

Checked for 112 children: Avoids work requiring concentrated visual attention.

Checked for 102 children: Poor drawing of a diamond compared with peers' drawings.

Checked for 101 children: Tense or disturbed (bites lips, needs to go to the bathroom often, twists hair, high strung).

Checked for 96 children: Overactive (can't sit still in class, shakes or swings legs, fidgety).[1]

Related Characteristics

Many body management behaviors are interrelated, requiring coordinated physiological functions. Children who have difficulty performing intricate physical tasks necessary for academic achievement are often found to have problems in any one

---

1. Adapted from John H. Meier, Prevalence and characteristics of learning disabilities found in second grade children, *Journal of Learning Disabilities*, 1971, *4*, (1), 20-21. Reprinted with permission of the publisher and author.

or combination of five areas: visual-motor coordination, figure-ground perception, perceptual constancy, position in space, and spatial relationships. Otto, McMenemy, and Smith (1973) indicated that these critical visual-motor areas may be improved through remedial help. And while performance in these areas may be improved, recent studies indicate that improvement in such areas does not result in higher academic gains. In studies using control groups, no significant gains in reading were found when the gains made by the experimental subjects were compared with those made by the control groups (Jacobs et al., 1968; Elkind & Deblinger, 1968; Wiederholt & Hammill, 1971; Falik, 1969). While improvement may be possible in the five critical visual-motor areas, that improvement does not appear to be related to reading achievement. Accordingly, a more critical attitude toward visual-perceptual training programs by school personnel certainly seems indicated as suggested by anecdote 2.4.

ANECDOTE 2.4

Assistant Superintendent George Wilson requested services from Mary Super, Special Education Instructional Specialist. It seems that Dr. Wilson, who is in charge of all instruction in the school district, wants to prevent learning problems by instituting a visual-motor training program among all kindergarten and first-grade students. Such a program would, in his opinion, reduce the number of children requiring special instruction later in their school careers. It was, as Dr. Wilson explained it, sort of an immunization program.

Mary Super listened to Dr. Wilson explain how a certain commercial program could be purchased and, if Mary would train the teachers to use the material, it could be used as a part of the reading readiness program. Mary was aware of a recent review of some 60 studies regarding the relationship of visual perception to reading, arithmetic, and spelling measures. She knew that Larsen and Hammill (1975) had concluded that the relationship was not of such significance to be of instructional value. Yet she also believed that the reading readiness program could stand improving.

After Dr. Wilson was finished explaining what he wanted Mary to do she suggested that perhaps language skills could be incorporated into the training program. After obtaining his interest in the suggestion, Mary outlined the type of inservice program that would be presented. It follows:

1.0 Ways to develop children's speaking skills
2.0 How to develop listening skills
3.0 Reading pictures
4.0 Story telling
5.0 Sequencing pictures to develop stories
6.0 Discriminating big words from little words
7.0 Teaching basic sight words
8.0 Relating table games to reading instructions
9.0 Teaching reading through experience stories
10.0 How to encourage children to participate in group discussions

Dr. Wilson was led to see how visual-motor skills could be developed as a natural part of the above activities without purchasing the commercial materials and by helping teachers select a variety of instructional materials which related to the ten topics.

Academic Learning Problems

Problems often associated with learning handicapped children are those commonly considered to be in the academic learning area. These are represented by problems of attending, discriminating relevant stimuli, and basic skill difficulties.

Attending Difficulties

Attention to relevant stimuli is a prerequisite for successful school learning. Students must not only know to what their attention should be directed but also have the facility to attend after having identified the correct stimuli. Among the characteristics associated with attending problems are hyperactivity, distractibility, perseveration, and short attention span.

Hyperactivity has long been a noteworthy characteristic of learning handicapped students (Strauss & Lehtinen, 1947). In one study, designed to measure task-oriented and social behavior of learning disabled and normal children in the classroom, Bryan (1974) reported that learning disabled children spent significantly less time in attending behavior. She found that learning disabled children attended less than normal children in almost all subject areas.

Among the behaviors which mark children as hyperactive are: frequent head movements, squirming, tapping feet and/or hands, fidgeting, general and frequent body movements, and extreme talkativeness.

Perseveration is a type of hyperactivity. It is seen in motor responses where drawing or writing continues beyond what is required, or in talking where the same topic or word is repeated ad infinitum. Perseveration is characterized by responses which exceed what is required, is necessary, or is appropriate.

Distractibility impairs attention. Children who readily and frequently dart from one topic or stimulus to another are distractible. Often they have a tendency to focus on details rather than on central issues or items. Anecdote 2.5 describes such a child who, among other things, is easily distracted.

ANECDOTE 2.5

Ever since Cliff Hanger was a toddler his mother noticed that he had trouble "paying attention." At first she believed that he was just stubborn but as he got older it became obvious that there was something wrong. One day, when he was four years old, he was playing with a miniature truck, and a wheel fell off. Mrs. Hanger watched Cliff try to push the wheel on to the axle. At once he began to cry because he was not successful on his first attempt.

Cliff seemed to be in "high gear" all day, rarely slowing his pace. By evening he went to bed completely exhausted. Watching television with Cliff was no fun. After a few minutes, he was running about the room, making it impossible for others to relax.

He was a menace in the car, jumping from front to back as well as up and down. Auto trips frequently included spanking him for his "misbehavior."

By the time Cliff went to kindergarten, he had broken an arm and sprained both wrists. His hyperactivity continued in kindergarten where his teacher termed him a "wall climber" and where he frequently pushed and shoved classmates. His teacher reported that Cliff often had difficulty telling a story from pictures or relating events in the order in which they occurred. After six weeks in kindergarten, he was removed from school because of his "immaturity." It was recommended that he return to kindergarten next year.

Short attention spans are frequently found among children with learning problems. Often they seem to lose interest quickly or just flit from one activity to another. Their apparent inability to attend for reasonable time intervals is closely associated with their academic problems since perseverance is often one essential ingredient for school success.

Problems of Discrimination

A major portion of academic learning requires proficient discrimination skills because different student responses are necessary for different stimulus situations. Within each situation, students are also expected to reply correctly to finer task requirements. For example, the teacher may instruct primary-grade students in a small reading group to *Bring your workbooks to the reading circle*. At this point, they must select the proper workbook and not another subject-related workbook such as writing, spelling, or arithmetic.

Once seated in the circle, they are expected to discriminate further. Using both visual and auditory discrimination skills, students will need to follow the teacher's verbal instructions: *Looking at page 12 on the first line, place an X on the capital D*. Visually they must note the difference (discriminate) between the capital and lowercase letters. At higher grade levels, even more complex discriminations are required, such as those required in learning advanced mathematics or foreign languages.

The demands for learning academic tasks are further complicated because the accuracy of discrimination in one mode affects student performance in another mode. For example, written spelling accuracy is hindered or improved by the student's pronunciation of words, e.g., *probly-probably* or *hunderd-hundred*.

Some of the problems associated with sensory discrimination skills observed among learning disordered children at the primary grade levels are listed below.

Prereading and Prearithmetic
   confusing or not noting differences among environmental things and inhabitants
   confusing similar sounding words (e.g., *then* and *than*; *their* and *they're*; *beg* and *big*
   errors in articulating
   substitutes incorrect words or sounds
   is not fluent when speaking;
   presents confusing phraseology, e.g., "Shopping for toys I saw a horse with Mommy," for "When Mommy and I went shopping for toys, I saw a horse."
   confuses simple concepts, e.g., says *up* for *down*; *over* for *under*
   does not differentiate pictures of animals
   fails to differentiate colors, odors, and tastes
   does not note details in pictures
   has difficulty in repeating events
   does not respond to verbal requests
   fails to differentiate and/or match shapes, designs, and words
   fails to discriminate numerals and letters
   does not identify rhyming words when heard, e.g., tree-see or look-book
   does not match same amounts of different objects, e.g., 9 oranges with 9 cars; 3 dots with 3 books
   does not match similar coins, e.g., pennies with pennies, nickels with nickels

Reading and Arithmetic
   confuses verbal and/or written instruction
   does not differentiate visually differences in words, e.g., hen-her; went-want
   has trouble hearing the correct number of parts (syllables) in words
   has trouble rhyming words
   fails to write letters or words which are spoken, e.g., writes *t* for *th*; *pig* for *peg*

does not indicate the number of objects which were correctly counted, e.g., counts 9 animals but writes the numeral 6
has trouble determining the arithmetical process when the sign is shown, e.g., adds instead of subtracts
is confused when arithmetic problems are presented horizontally, e.g., $12 + 6 =$
confuses place value
has trouble reading a clock
confuses names of money items

Problems in Basic Skills

Mastery of basic academic skills is a prerequisite for school success. Reading, writing, and arithmetic make up the foundation of academic learning. From these skills, almost all future academic success develops.

Since a considerable number of school children exhibit basic skill deficits, federal and state compensatory education programs have tended to focus on improving reading instruction. However, less attention has been given to improving arithmetic performance.

Learning disabled children often have much more acute academic deficiencies than the typical candidate for remedial instruction. It is not just that their acquisition of basic skills is slow or of poor quality. Unlike those who are in need of remedial instruction alone, the other characteristics described previously, hyperactivity, perserveration, distractibility, short attention span, and discrimination problems, serve to confound basic skill learning.

Problems in basic skill areas are characterized generally by some form of language dysfunction. These problems may be observed in poor speaking, reading, written expression, or comprehension. After all, reading, arithmetic, and writing are language skills. Anecdote 2.6 describes an eight-year-old boy with moderate problems in basic academic areas.

ANECDOTE 2.6

Kevin Frank is beginning his second year in third grade. Now at the age of eight, he is one year "behind his grade level." Since kindergarten, Kevin has displayed academic learning problems. His kindergarten teacher recalls that Kevin had trouble pronouncing ordinary words such as airplane and pumpkin. By the end of that year in school, he still had trouble copying letters of the alphabet, coloring, and verbally communicating with others.

While he is not a disobedient child, Kevin often disturbs others and quickly becomes bored with learning activities. His academic learning problems became more pronounced in first and second grades, where he learned to read haltingly. With great effort, he did print and write legibly. Although, he often reversed letters and numerals when printing.

The accumulated effect of poor academic skills became too much for Kevin by the third grade. His spelling, reading, and arithmetic skills were the poorest in the class, although he occasionally demonstrated good reasoning ability. Kevin became confused when faced with problems different from the ordinary, such as missing addend problems or horizontal problems.

Spelling is particularly difficult for Kevin. Beyond the most simple words, he demonstrates no consistency in spelling words. He seems to have little facility for phonics which, of course, affects his independent reading and spelling skills.

Even at the kindergarten level early signs of learning problems in language deficiencies can be detected by observant teachers. Cowgill, Friedland, and Shapiro (1973) found that speech and language problems were among those traits which significantly differentiated learning disabled from normal children. They studied the feasibility of predicting learning problems from kindergarten teachers' anecdotal reports. Thirty-seven boys, already identified as learning disabled, were compared with their classmates. The learning disabled group was rated as having more immature traits, more traits suggesting short attention spans, being impulsive, having poor motor control, and having more speech and language problems.

Student Attitude

Teachers sometimes attribute students' failures to "poor attitude." Yet since student attitudes are learned, they may be shaped by teachers:

> *Attitude*, a learned predisposition to react consistently in a given manner (either positively or negatively) to certain persons, objects or concepts. Attitudes have cognitive, affective and behavioral components. (Wolman, 1973, p. 34)

As English and English (1958) noted, attitude is one of many terms that refers to an aspect of personality inferred to account for persistent and consistent behaviors toward related situations or objects. Since attitude is believed to be learned behavior, we should expect children with learning problems to display negative attitudes toward school-related activities. Generally, this does seem to be the case. For example, Begley (1973) found that low measured intelligence correlated highly with poor attitudes toward school along with other behavioral variables. It is, therefore, somewhat surprising to note that many young children with persisting academic learning problems continue to enjoy school work. When this condition is observed, their attitudes usually seem to be related to sensitive, hard-working teachers who differentiate instruction for these children and to understanding parents who are reasonable in their expectations.

Children with learning difficulties often do view academic tasks as unpleasant since many of their failure experiences take place at school. Sometimes their negative attitudes are directed toward specific academic subjects in which they have experienced particular difficulties. At other times, negative attitudes pervade all school-related activities.

Emotional Adjustment Problems

ANECDOTE 2.7

1. Seven-year-old Shirley often cried in school. It appeared, at first, that crying behavior occurred for no apparent reason. Closer observations by her teacher indicated that Shirley had so much trouble doing academic tasks that she cried out of frustration.

2. Eight-year-old Carl, while doing handwriting assignments, often would say *God damn* and tear up his paper.

3. When under pressure in school, twelve-year-old Art began to twist his hair, often pulling it from his scalp.

4. Mary Lou had toilet accidents in school. These occurred during arithmetic time, a subject in which she had great trouble.

5. Six-year-old Jeffrey bit his fingernails to the quick, often resulting in bleeding. He usually began nail biting in school when given independent seat work assignments to complete.

6. Mario, at age nine, was a frequent daydreamer in school. He often sat at his seat, staring into space. When asked to respond, he rarely gave relevant replies.

A wide range of emotional adjustment problems have been observed among learning handicapped children. Begley (1973) reported immaturity, excessive withdrawal, and excessive suffering among learning disabled, low IQ (80-89) children.

Children react to school problems in many different ways. But in almost all instances, some degree of emotional maladjustment should be expected among those having learning problems. The behaviors depicted in anecdote 2.7 are not unusual among children with learning disorders. Such problems can be expected to be prevalent in school situations where special provisions are not available to assist learning disordered students and where instruction is not differentiated in relation to prerequisite requirements.

Reactions from those within students' environments are believed to create adjustment problems as well. For example, Rhodes (1967) has suggested that emotional disturbance may be a function of the interactions between students' behaviors and the responses those behaviors provoke from others in their environments. From this viewpoint, maladaptive behaviors are considered to be disturbing to others rather than merely disturbed behavior.

Relevance of Characteristics

Characteristics of students in need of special assistance are relevant only in terms of those purposes for which students are to be identified. That is, characteristics useful for identifying students' needs must relate functionally to subsequent instructional treatment. This requirement is not always met, and there are instructional and diagnostic orientations which have not bridged the gap between identification and instruction.

Quay (1973) and Ysseldyke and Salvia (1974) have differentiated between theoretical models which have emerged from the diagnostic-prescriptive teaching movement. These models have been referred to as (1) the ability training model and (2) the task analysis model (Ysseldyke & Salvia, 1974). The models differ in several important respects and dictate to a great extent which student characteristics are relevant for instructional purposes. (Since a task analysis approach is sometimes advocated by those committed to the ability training viewpoint, the second model should more appropriately be referred to as the *skill training model*, a phrase which serves to describe and emphasize the inherent ingredient of this orientation.[2])

The Ability Training Approach

Advocates of the ability training approach emphasize remediating those underlying processes believed to be contributing to inadequate functioning. Major proponents and their findings are summarized in Figure 2.5.

Testing and ability training. Within the ability training model, the search is toward identifying abilities in which weaknesses are noted. Instruction then emphasizes strengthening the weaker ability areas. Most often the abilities of concern are related to perceptual-motor processes (Kephart, 1971; Barsch, 1967; Frostig, 1964; Getman, 1962).

---

2. Actually, Ysseldyke and Salvia (1974) combined categories originally presented by Quay (1973), though their use of the phrase *task analysis* was not a part of Quay's discourse. *Skill training model* was not used in either article but is used here by this writer.

Bateman, 1965: Emphasizes the use of a wide range of standardized tests to describe the process used by students for learning.

Cruickshank, 1961: Advocates a thorough diagnosis of learning disabled children. Instruction is based upon the disabling conditions, e.g., reducing unessential auditory and visual stimuli.

Delacato, 1966: Treatment is prescribed in order to improve the development of specific areas of the brain and neurological system.

Frostig, 1967: Views visual perception as essential for complex body functions. Instruction is prescribed on the basis of results derived from *The Developmental Test of Visual Perception*.

Johnson & Myklebust, 1967: Relates academic deficiencies to perceptual problems, difficulties in imagery, disorders in symbolic processes, and trouble in conceptualizing.

Kephart, 1960: Emphasizes the importance of sensorimotor development to learning performance.

Kirk, McCarthy, & Kirk, 1968: Bases instruction on results of the *Illinois Test of Psycholinguistic Abilities* which emphasizes visual-perceptual skills.

FIGURE 2.5:   Major advocates of ability training

Advocates rely heavily on testing aptitudes in order to locate the *causes* of poor performance. Many tests purporting to measure perceptual abilities are available. One widely used test within the ability training movement is the *Illinois Test of Psycholinguistic Abilities (ITPA)* (Kirk, McCarthy, & Kirk, 1968).

Twelve subtests comprise the *ITPA*, yielding subtest scores and a total language age. A diagnostic profile may also be obtained and used as a basis for remediation. The twelve subtests are: auditory reception, visual reception, auditory association, visual association, verbal expression, manual expression, grammatic closure, visual closure, auditory closure, sound blending, auditory sequential memory, and visual sequential memory. The auditory closure and sound blending tests are optional.

Carroll (1972) critically reviewed the *ITPA*, citing several weaknesses including (1) it is misnamed, (2) its norms do not include data on handicapped children, and (3) as a diagnostic instrument it is no better, and perhaps not as good, as other individual aptitude tests.

Because only about half of the subtests in the *ITPA* involve a language system, Carroll did not believe it met the requirements of a test of psycholinguistics. He noted that the authors purposely omitted handicapped children from the standardization population in order to have a reference group for comparing with handicapped children. This omission resulted, he stated, in unfair assessment of lower-class and handicapped children.

Regardless of the tests used, advocates of the ability training approach must accept at least three major assumptions:

1. that there are reliable and valid measures for testing aptitudes,
2. that the aptitude deficits can be corrected, and

3. that the performance deficits are related causally to the aptitude weaknesses.

Ysseldyke & Salvia (1974) have analyzed the assumptions upon which the ability training approach rests. They concluded that hypothetical constructs as measured by aptitude tests should be rejected as causative factors of children's difficulties. They presented both research evidence and logical arguments in support of their beliefs. In order to arrive at a point where reliable and valid aptitude measures are linked to effective instructional strategies, these authorities believe extensive research and experimentation are needed.

Relevant characteristics for ability training. Characteristics of students to be instructed within the ability training model include both observable responses and those which can only be identified through psychological testing. For example, low performance on various aptitude measures include such items as those measured by the *ITPA*.

The *Marianne Frostig Developmental Test of Visual Perception* (Frostig & Horne, 1964) serves as another source for assessing psychological characteristics. The characteristics evaluated are eye-motor coordination, figure-ground discrimination, constancy of shape, position in space, and spatial relationships. There are many other ability tests similar to the two mentioned. Basically, all presume to measure various abilities which are believed to be essential for successful academic learning.

In general, advocates of the ability training approach view students' poor performances as symptomatic of underlying and more basic problems. Delacato (1966), for example, views problems of laterality, cerebral dominance, and handedness as contributing to academic learning deficits.

The Skill Training Approach

Those who advocate a skill training approach emphasize identifying those precise responses which are in error and advocate teaching the correct response. Assumptions are not made as to the causes of the dysfunctionality and, in most instances, causality is deemed irrelevant for instructional treatment. Major advocates of this orientation are identified in Figure 2.6.

FIGURE 2.6   Major advocates of skill training

Bijou, 1973: Recommends an emphasis on behavioral analysis when teaching the mentally retarded.

Englemann, 1969: Emphasizes skill assessment and teaching of deficit skills and a system of reinforcement.

Haring & Phillips, 1972: Focuses on behavior analysis and various behavior modification tactics.

Lovitt, 1970: Demonstrates how self-management skills can be taught to L&BD students for improving their academic and social behaviors.

Mann, 1971: Advocates a more scientific approach to instruction, less emphasis on hypothetical constructs and more direct instruction.

Staats, 1963: Complex responses are shaped through direct behavioral interventions.

Stephens, 1970: Stresses direct instruction of response deficits in associations with behavior modification techniques.

The skill training approach emphasizes observations of performance and assessment through permanent products (Cooper, 1974) and criterion-referenced measures (Stephens, 1975). Once the defective performances are pinpointed, corrective instruction begins. While psychological testing may be used within this orientation, no attempt is made to relate the results to instruction. Rather, test results are typically used as gross screening devices generally for purposes of administrative planning.

Advocates of the skill training approach assume that:

1. direct skill instruction will correct faulty responses,
2. behavior changes and develops as the result of its consequences, and
3. students can be taught to generalize responses across conditions.

Relevant characteristics for skill training. Descriptive characteristics of students being instructed are needed in the skill training model. Their performances on curriculum tasks must be described. Since skill training instruction is based upon observed behavior, any response which is below a specified criterion may be considered a relevant instructional characteristic. A list of characteristics for skill instruction could include any task in which a given student is deficient. This list could include any academic and social skill which is a part of the school's curriculum.

Lower order academic and social skills are more likely to be relevant, however, for teaching students with learning and behavioral problems. The majority of children with such problems are believed to possess deficit responses in basic academic skills and in routine social behaviors.

One group of lower order skills is referred to as *visual motor*. These are often characterized by the following behaviors:

difficulties in coordinating visual movements with body movements
trouble differentiating figures from their backgrounds
problems in identifying forms of objects
confusion when faced with a page of printed or written material
poor performance in coloring prepared figures
focusing on details rather than wholes
difficulty in consistently recognizing items when their physical properties are different, e.g., differences in color or size
confusing spatial relationships, such as position of objects in relation to self or other fixed points
confusion of directions
problems in relating one object, sound, or event to another
difficulty in categorizing items or events in terms of primary features

It should be emphasized that, according to the skill training approach, visual-motor skills would be taught only in order to improve those specific responses. This differs from the ability training advocates who believe such skills comprise aptitudes which, when deficient, are *causing* academic learning problems.

Characteristics of Behaviorally Disordered Children

Maladaptive behavior in school is commonplace. Mild adjustment disorders are usually expected by classroom teachers: the bright ten-year-old who seemingly cannot settle down to do seatwork; the first grader who is seen toying with his genitals; the twelve-year-old who avoids participating in group play; the fourth-grade girl who must be reassured frequently by her teacher; the teenager who refuses to dress for gym class. Rarely would these types of behaviors alone be cause for concern since many are well within the normal range of behavior.

Signs of maladaptive behavior, however, become more obvious as the focus is shifted to pronounced disorders: the student who often daydreams; the seven-year-old who bites classmates; the adolescent who physically attacks teachers; the child who steals from classmates; and the child who acts as the classroom bully.

Behavioral disorders in school run the gamut from minor misbehaviors to severe psychological reactions of violence or withdrawal. The most severe disorders, e.g., autism, are rarely found in schools. The relatively small number of children, for example, suffering from childhood psychoses (Rimland, 1964) are typically institutionalized. But an increasing number of acting-out students are attending school in special day and residential settings.

Considered here is that population often referred to as emotionally disturbed, delinquent, or character disordered. Regardless of their diagnostic labels, they are found in sizable numbers in public elementary and secondary schools. Sometimes they are identified and placed in special classes or even special schools, but as Morse (1958) noted, the majority of moderately disturbed children continue to be found in regular classrooms.

Identifying Maladjusted Students

Various authorities have suggested behaviors which are characteristic of maladaptive adjustment. Some, such as Bower (1960, 1969), have attempted to validate items to be used for early identification of emotionally disturbed, school-aged students. Others have listed characteristics which are based solely on theory and experience (Hammer, 1970). Some lists, however, have been carefully validated (Quay, Morse, & Cutler, 1966).

At times behavioral characteristics have been developed into checklists for the purpose of differentiating emotionally disturbed from learning handicapped children. For example, Wagonseller (1973) studied three groups of students: those diagnosed as learning disabled, those diagnosed as emotionally disturbed, and those institutionalized as emotionally disturbed. Differences were found among the groups on various measures. Because of the differences in performance on achievement tests and behavior checklists, he concluded that a systematic approach to differential diagnosis could be developed, implying that different diagnostic findings should result in varying instructional treatment.

Assigning students for special instruction on the basis of diagnostic categories assumes all members of that group, such as the behavior disordered, have a significant number of characteristics in common to differentiate them from other students. Quay (1963) questioned this assumption, noting that within a group of emotionally disturbed children there are great differences in terms of educational needs. His suggestions encouraged identification practices to focus less on hypothetical characteristics, which typically form the basis for psychological measures, and more on direct observations of classroom behavior.

More recently, Quay (1973) examined those concepts concerned with educational exceptionality and how they lead toward various instructional approaches. These different notions have resulted in the different instructional approaches often used with students having similar educational handicaps. He maintains that, in some instances, the approaches are incompatible, leading to inadequate results. Quay suggested that special education should move toward more specific, short-term evaluation criteria.

Barr and McDowell (1972) investigated the extent of differences between observed deviant behaviors of emotionally disturbed children in special classes and learning disabled children in special classes. The frequency of three deviant behaviors for both groups was obtained. Eight emotionally disturbed and eight learning disabled children, matched for age, sex, IQ, and time in special program, were observed as to their out of seat behavior, negative physical contact, and vocalizations.

Significantly more deviant behavior was exhibited by the emotionally disturbed group on two dimensions. When examining each of the three deviant behaviors, they found that the emotionally disturbed children showed a high frequency of inappropriate vocalizations and negative physical contacts. While the emotionally disturbed group also had a higher frequency of out-of-seat behavior, differences between the groups were not, however, statistically significant.

Results of this study suggest that, when specific behaviors are used for observational purposes, the two handicapping groups may be differentiated by a comparison of the frequency of their behaviors. It would be premature, at this time, to generalize results from this study to the larger issue of differences in characteristics among these two groups. Sampling procedures, the manner in which students were selected, the small number of subjects, and the limited number of behaviors used as variables would suggest that much more study is needed prior to answering the question of whether or not there are significant differences between the behaviors of learning disabled and emotionally disturbed children.

More progress has been made in differentiating behaviorally disordered children from their normal peers. Nelson (1971) used an observational technique to investigate differences between children classified as conduct disturbed and normal on the basis of ratings given by their regular classroom teachers. Those rated as conduct disturbed engaged in significantly more deviant behavior and significantly less task-oriented behavior than subjects rated as normal on a 10-item rating scale.

Bullock and Brown (1972) identified four factors of behavior as reported by 112 teachers of emotionally disturbed children. The factors were *aggressive/acting out, withdrawn, tense/anxious, and irresponsible/inattentive.*

Aggressive/acting-out students were characterized as fighters, and as being threatening and generally socially aggressive. The withdrawn students were described as passive, shy, timid, self-conscious, and most apt to play alone. Tense/anxious children were not clearly described in the report, but the irresponsible/inattentive students were frequent rule violators.

The multivariate approach used by Bullock and Brown has been used by a number of other researchers. Hewitt and Jenkins (1946) analyzed case histories of problem children, listing behavior traits. They identified three primary behavioral syndromes which they termed "unsocialized aggressive behavior," the "socialized delinquent," and the "overinhibited child."

In another study, Peterson (1964) found that 58 descriptive behavior items were factored into two separate categories which he labeled as (1) conduct problem and

(2) personality problem. The first group consisted of aggressive behavior and the second of withdrawn behavior. Of course, Peterson's findings were influenced by the items in the checklist. Thus, behaviors which were not included on the list could not be identified by teachers. This may account for the difference between his findings and those reported by others.

Studies reviewed above suggest that it is possible to identify children who present behavior problems when compared with normal behavior. But it is not as yet always possible to differentiate those with behavior problems as to whether they are primarily learning disabled or conduct disordered.

Acting-out Behavior

ANECDOTE 2.8

Kurt, a twelve-year-old, was placed in a full-time special class for behaviorally disruptive students as a result of his misbehavior in a regular sixth-grade class. When Tony Rodriquez, the school psychologist, received a referral to evaluate Kurt, he began by talking to his sixth-grade teacher, Mr. Hall. He had anticipated his visit and had an anecdotal record of Kurt's misbehavior over a seven-day period. It follows.

Fri., Sept. 24

   Sat on top of bookcase to catch flies.

   Broke all pencils in room.

   Spread corn around room.

   Tore book apart at noon.

   Went on the fire escape.

Mon., Sept. 27

   Tore pen apart.

   Drank ink and smeared it all over.

   Dismissed from gym for failure to behave.

   Spit on floor of room.

   Exposed himself before girls and urinated on floor.

Tues., Sept. 28

   Put boys' gym equipment into toilets.

   Smashed girls' lunchpail in cafeteria.

   Swore openly in the classroom.

   Ran through cafeteria lines until he was made to sit on stool there.

   Took money from one of the girls.

   When girls went to gym, he went to restroom, kicked lunchpails, and tore geography books. Girls also said he was standing in front of frosted windows.

   Marked two new desks with crayolas.

   Ran on the highway three times.

   Chased neighbor's ducks.

   Turned the gas pumps on behind the school.

   Spit on cafeteria windows.

   Continually running and yelling in halls.

   Disturbing classes.

Wed., Sept. 29

   This morning he ate almost half an apple at his desk until I took it away from him. I had to get after him several times for talking aloud.

   I had missed candy several times from my desk drawer. More was missing today when I returned from lunch. Another boy in the class told me that when he came back to the room from lunch he saw Kurt taking candy from the drawer of my desk.

During the afternoon he was noisy, talked all the time, did not mind, threw his paint shirt up on top of the tall cupboard so he had an excuse to climb up after it, sharpened the paint brush handles while I was helping someone else. In general, he was just impossible!

Thur., Sept. 30

He was noisy, talking at the top of his voice even when I was trying to explain something to the whole group. He refuses to do most of the work even on his own ability level unless someone is working with him most of the time.

Fri., Oct. 1

Kurt bent a pair of school scissors which were supposed to be in my drawer. He had them without permission. He was unlocking the heater with them when he bent them. He crawled up on the window sill, up on top of the cupboard on the west side of the room, down into the sink and back to the floor. He said, "Just make me," when I told him to be quiet. I have to lock the door to keep him out of the room if he finishes his lunch before I do. He talked loudly or yelled many times today. I did not count them. He gets other boys to misbehave with him.

Mon., Oct. 2

Kurt yelled or talked loudly many times when he did not get my individual attention. When I told him to zip his zipper, he pulled it down farther and showed himself to other children. He came in after lunch with a grasshopper which I made him throw out the window. He got out of the door before I could stop him and brought the grasshopper back to the room. He put it in a girl's desk. Out the window again went the grasshopper. Kurt slipped out once more and got it, but out the window it went again. About a half hour later he said he was sorry and would not do those things again.

Mr. Rodriquez decided it would be advisable for him to observe Kurt and also to obtain additional descriptions of his behavior. The following are behaviors recorded by Mr. Rodriquez during two observation periods.

First Observation: Time — 90 minutes

Talked incessantly, very loud, in class.
Broke up several pencils for no apparent reason.
Punched the teacher when he was correcting him.
Climbed into the cupboard and shut the door on himself.
Climbed up on the window sill.
Climbed up on the window sill, across the cupboard, down into the sink, and back to the floor.

Second Observation: Time — 50 minutes

Said, "God damn you," when the teacher tried to correct him. Took scissors from the teacher's desk without permission. Stole candy from the teacher's desk.

Three days elapsed between the first observation, which was during reading instruction, and the second observation. In addition, Mr. Rodriquez discussed Kurt's behavior with the building principal.

The principal reported that Kurt was new to the school in September, having moved to the community from another state. His report card indicated he had been a C and D student last year and had satisfactorily completed fifth year work. He also said that during the first week of school Kurt had been reported by the school patrol for climbing onto the trunk of the mailman's car and taking a short ride unnoticed by the mailman.

Kurt had been referred to the office on other occasions during the first few months of the school year. He was referred by a teacher who had observed Kurt spit on another boy in the hallway.

The playground supervisor complained that he swears at her. Mr. M, physical education teacher, refuses to have Kurt in class because he will not do anything he is told or even sit down and be quiet while he is giving directions.

The bus driver has been in complaining that she cannot do anything with Kurt on the bus. As an example, one day Kurt was hanging from the waist up out the window while the bus was moving down the highway. He also has been using obscene language on the bus.

Finally, Mr. Rodriquez administered an individual test of intelligence and standardized achievement tests to Kurt with parental permission. He found him to have a measured IQ of 109. Reading achievement was at the beginning third grade level (3.1) and arithmetic at middle fifth grade.

It was recommended to the special education team that Kurt be placed in the special adjustment class at Main Street Elementary School.

Kurt (anecdote 2.8) is a behaviorally disordered child, displaying a high rate of acting-out behavior in and about school. In addition, he also has inadequate reading achievement. While the school system could provide his teacher with consultant assistance while modifying his disruptive behavior, the school psychologist's observations suggest that two factors make that a poor option.

First, his high rate of inappropriate behavior would require frequent behavioral tactics, perhaps too often to implement in a regular classroom with 29 other children. Second, the extent of Kurt's reading difficulties indicates that tutoring services would not provide sufficient remedial assistance. Placement considerations must take into account such important factors when assisting students.

Other examples of acting-out behavior can be found in viewing juvenile delinquents. While all adjudicated delinquents are not necessarily of the acting-out type, the large majority are (Stratton & Terry, 1968) since most are considered delinquent for violating norms and/or laws.

Schools, and consequently teachers, are confronted with an increasing number and percentage of students who are destined to be juvenile delinquents. Over one million juvenile delinquency cases, excluding traffic offenses, were estimated as being processed by all juvenile courts in the United States in 1971. These juveniles represented almost 3% of all children between ages 10 through 17 in the country (U.S. Department of HEW, 1972).

Acting-out behavior is characterized by acts which are of a serious type directed against property and/or others. These acts may consist of physical attacks on others or may be an infringement against other students' rights, such as interfering with their instruction. In addition to the seriousness of the acts, frequency of acting-out behavior should also be considered. In Kurt's case, his norm-violating behavior was emitted at a high rate. A high rate of emission contributes to the seriousness of a behavior problem.

Withdrawn Behavior

Shy, quiet, and conforming children can be overlooked in classrooms. Results of studies have been inconsistent as to the extent to which teachers are able to identify withdrawn children. However, some findings indicate that teachers are successful in locating such children (Bower, 1960), while others (Goldfarb, 1963) indicate that teachers continue to overlook withdrawn behavior.

Withdrawn behavior is characterized by low rates of response and underemission of behavior. Such a child is depicted in anecdote 2.9. Note that Michelle's lack of responses and her failure to initiate normal activities were major determiners for obtaining psychological assistance.

Nine-year-old Michelle was referred to the school psychologist by her fourth grade teacher. Mr. Wood, the teacher, had noticed since the beginning of the school year that Michelle was alone on the playground and rarely interacted with her peers in the classroom. He had also observed that Michelle almost never volunteered an answer or participated in class discussions.

Michelle seemed lethargic, doing just what was required and no more. Yet her academic work was average for the class and her IQ, as measured by a group test, was within the average range.

Mr. Rodriquez discussed Michelle's withdrawn behavior with the teacher. Mr. Wood expressed concern that Michelle had emotional problems since she always seemed so sad, never smiling or laughing as did the other children.

Michelle was observed in the classroom by the school psychologist. During those 30 minutes, Mr. Rodriquez recorded the following behavior:

During class discussion of current events, while most children were requesting permission to be heard, Michelle sat with her head lowered playing with a rubber band wrapped around a pencil. Only when the teacher directed a question to her did she respond. Her answer, while correct, was hardly audible.

Michelle was observed later, for about 10 minutes, on the playground. During that time, she stood on the edge of the playground, occasionally stopping to pick up a stone which she examined and discarded. At one point, a bigger child shoved Michelle and ran off. Michelle appeared to be on the verge of tears.

Tony Rodriquez briefly interviewed Michelle. He found her to be aloof and almost inaudible. The school psychologist concluded that Michelle needed some supportive counseling and assertive training. It was recommended that Michelle be seen for tutoring services and that she be provided counseling by the elementary counselor under Tony Rodriquez' supervision. Mary Super, the instructional specialist, agreed to provide consulting assistance to the teacher in order to help him elicit more responses from Michelle. Mr. Pangborn, visiting teacher, was asked to visit Michelle's home and to make a determination if the parents needed and could profit from assistance in helping her.

In anecdote 2.9 Michelle was not placed in a special class because those classes with available space consisted of many acting-out students. When withdrawn children are faced with aggressive peers, they often become more fearful and withdrawn. The first step in dealing with withdrawn behavior is to elicit responses. This objective is difficult to achieve in classrooms where hostile, acting-out behavior is common.

Children who emit low rates of behavior may not be extremely withdrawn and may not be in need of special assistance. There are quiet, socially competent students who are well adjusted. One important factor to consider is the effectiveness of the youngster's coping skills. Answers to questions such as the following may help to determine if a student possesses adequate coping skills:

Does he or she protect himself or herself from more aggressive peers?

Does he or she volunteer for tasks in which he or she has success?

Does he or she have some friends or playmates among the peer group?

Does he or she actively participate in play or other social activities with his or her peer group?

Does he or she initiate discussion, play, social interactions with others?

Does he or she accept challenging assignments in which he or she must compete against others?

Positive responses to the above six questions indicates that a student has some skills for dealing with the school environment. Although, even with a degree of competencies, some children may still be in need of special assistance.

At times withdrawn behavior is precipitated by emotional environmental factors, such as illness or death in the family. Concerns of parents, such as unemployment, may result in psychological withdrawal by children. In instances of this kind, children sometimes express their concerns. For example, ten-year-old Herman expressed great concern because his father, a realtor, had not sold a house in several months. Herman listened to his parents discuss their financial problems and had been told that gifts at Christmas would be curtailed because of his father's inability to sell property. Because Herman was not typically an overly quiet child, his teacher, a sensitive person, asked him what was bothering him. The teacher, in this instance, was able to provide some supportive counseling. Although, had Herman become more concerned and withdrawn, consultant services for the teacher and perhaps professional counseling for Herman would have been indicated.

Bizarre Behavior

Strange responses which may be neither too aggressive or too infrequent but are inappropriate represent what is meant here by bizarre behavior. Children on the extreme fringe of bizarre behavior have been labeled *autistic*. Such children are often indifferent to others as well as to the environment. They may use instructional materials in odd ways. Preferring solitary play, these children rigidly respond in the same way often reacting negatively to change or interference from others (Stott, 1971).

Traditionally, childhood psychosis (Werry, 1972) represents the most severe adjustment problem of children. Bizarre behaviors are typically classified under this diagnostic term, although many children who exhibit bizarre behavior would not be considered psychotic. Among those who are considered psychotic is the autistic child. First described by Kanner (1943), the autistic child demonstrates a lack of responsiveness to people beginning at birth, failure to use language for communicating, and a rigid need for sameness (Rimland, 1964).

Bizarre behavior may consist of aggressive or withdrawn responses or a mixture of the two. In essence, it is incongruous behavior. Children who frequently emit strange responses or behave in ways which are inappropriate for the conditions exhibit bizarre behavior. Anecdote 2.10 contains examples of such behavior.

ANECDOTE 2.10

Clem usually displays inappropriate affect, laughing when others cry and crying when laughter is expected.

Eight-year-old Celeste washes her hands dozens of times daily. Immediately after handling books, pencils, or door knobs she must wash her hands.

Kenneth enjoys punishing animals. One of his favorite pastimes is to pull wings from house flies and to set cats afire.

Sidney makes animal noises and other sounds throughout the school day in addition to exhibiting many other nervous habits.

Jane, at 10 years of age, weighs 125 pounds and eats constantly. She is an indiscriminate eater and frequently brings candy and other foods for snacks to school.

Sixteen-year-old Harold exhibits unusual fears. Animals, darkness, thunder, and heavy winds all provoke fear in him.

Martha is an obsessive liar. Often she lies about events and people for no apparent reason.

Phil bites teachers and peers when provoked. Now at age seven, he has inflicted severe wounds on two classmates and bitten his teacher's hand when she was trying to show him how to hold a pencil for cursive writing.

Behaviors of the sort described in anecdote 2.10 may be considered strange if they occur frequently and are unusual for the settings. Age and intelligence are factors to be considered when determining if behaviors are bizarre. For example, it is not unusual for four-year-olds to attempt to eat nonedible items, but it is strange for eight-year-olds of normal intelligence to do so. Similarly, mentally retarded individuals may behave in ways that, while expected of them, would be viewed as odd when emitted by the nonretarded.

Bizarre behavior may take many forms. It may be seen in terms of antisocial behavior, verbalizations, physical contortions, strange dress, odd mannerisms, unrealistic beliefs, and habit rooted in fantasy. Essentially, it is behavior which exceeds the bounds of reasonableness in view of the conditions under which it is emitted.

Relating Characteristics of Behaviorally Disordered Children to Instruction

Observed characteristics among students should be related to instruction. It seems reasonable to assume that those characteristics used for selecting students for special help are useful for determining the type of instruction they will receive. Attempts to make such relationships, however, have not been entirely successful.

Often attempts to relate diagnosis to school placement fail because diagnostic categories tend not to be descriptive. Weissman (1970), for example, discussed factors to consider when determining school placement for children with emotional and social problems. He related personality categories to instructional provisions. By using diagnostic categories for determining instructional needs, he was using theoretical constructs as a basis for prescribing instruction. He argued that the educational implications for children with neurotic disorders differ from those with deficits in social conduct. He reasoned that children with neurotic conflicts are more amenable to tutoring than are the undersocialized. Since he failed to describe those behaviors which constitute each group, it is difficult to determine how placement or instruction would be differentiated.

There have been some efforts to conceptualize more functional classification schemes. Quay (1973) cited the need for classification systems to have a direct relationship to instructional treatment. Our failure to achieve a closer relationship, he believes, has been due in part to different and conflicting conceptions of the nature and causes of educational exceptionality. Until criteria for successful treatment in special education are standardized, it will be difficult to evaluate the effects of various instructional approaches.

Readers should remember that there are no homogeneous groups of exceptional learners, requiring specific instructional procedures or materials. Rather, teachers should focus on the specific performances of each learner throughout the instructional process. All students have differences which require teachers to assess each regularly as a part of their instructional planning.

Establishing Identification Procedures

Establishing a close relationship between identifying and instructing handicapped students requires three procedures. First, it is necessary to detail the specific tasks in the school curriculum. Second, the curricular tasks should be stated as to observable behavior. Third, students not possessing those behaviors should be selected for corrective instruction.

Specifying Instructional Tasks

Those skills, concepts, and attitudes to be mastered in school at various age/grade levels can be identified. These may take the form of statements which are categorized into various groups such as the following seven categories for prereading skills. One sample task for each category is also shown.

1.0 Labeling
.1 child finds object from verbal label when presented with four objects.

2.0 Answering Questions
.8 child listens to a statement containing at least three facts and answers three questions about it.

3.0 Picture Decoding
.8 child anticipates events from pictures.

4.0 Following Sequence
.5 child views pictures in three-step sequences, listens to three-step sequences, listens to three-step incidents about them, and relates the steps in order while viewing the picture.

5.0 Repeating Verbal Symbols
.1 child repeats simple sentences

6.0 Discriminating Letters
.2 child matches letters of the alphabet.

All academic skill areas and social behaviors can be categorized with specific items, similar to those shown above.

Relating Tasks to Behavior

Criterion-referenced measures and behavior observations can be used to relate instructional tasks to performance. Criterion-referenced measures consist of sets of items, minimum levels of acceptable performance, and the task which each set of items represents. Students' performances are then compared against a fixed criterion. Figure 2.7 shows an example of a criterion-referenced measure.

FIGURE 2.7. A criterion-referenced measure

Task: Child demonstrates comprehension by underlining a picture described in a paragraph he has read.

Criterion: 18/20

Say: "Read this story and draw a line under the picture that goes with it."

1. Stop Jimmy.   2. Here we go, Sue.
   Stop for me.   Here we go for a ride.

3. Look at me Pepper.   4. Jimmy, here is Pepper.
   See me go for a ride.   Stop for Pepper.

5. I look for a toy.   6. I see a toy for Pepper.
   It is a toy for Sue.   Here is the toy.

7. Look, Sue.
   Look at my toy.
	8. Look here, Pepper.
	   See the toy for Jimmy and Sue.

9. Look for the train.
   See the little train go.
	10. Here is a little airplane.
	    See the airplane come down.

11. Look for the airplane.
    See the airplane go up.
	12. Here is a toy for Jimmy.
	    Look for the toy train.

13. Here is a toy for Pepper.
    Look for it.
	14. Here is a toy for Jimmy.
	    Look for a big toy.

15. Here is a big toy.
    It is a toy for Sue.
	16. Here is a toy.
	    It is a toy for Pepper.

17. Look at the train.
    See it go.
	18. Here is a little toy.
	    It is for Pepper.

19. Here is a big airplane.
    See it go up.
	20. Look at the toy airplane.
	    It is in the train.

By assessing students on criterion-referenced measures, teachers are able to determine exactly which responses the students have mastered, are in the process of learning, or have not yet begun to acquire.

Observational tactics are used in assessing the social behavior of children. Teachers may develop their own format for observing students or commercially available forms may be used. A teacher-devised observational form is shown in Figure 2.8.

Child _____ Age_____

Date_____ Place_____

Observer_____ Time of Day _____

Specify the observed behavior. Indicate under reactions: + for positive, − for negative, and o for neutral. Add notations if necessary.

1. Reactions to Instruction   Time_____

      Activities   *Reactions*

                        +   −   o

2. Reactions to Others   Time_____

      Names   *Reactions*

                        +   −   o

3. Reactions to Assignments   Time_____

      Assignments   *Reactions*

                        +   −   o

FIGURE 2.8. Observation form for in-class behavior

Students who demonstrate poor performance when assessed on academic measures and/or when observed as to social behavior should be eligible for special instruction. Aptitude tests, administered by qualified personnel, are sometimes necessary prior to special placement. Children who score low on tests of intelligence are usually placed in programs designed for mentally retarded students. In such instances, however, academic assessment and observation of social behavior will also prove valuable for instructional purposes.

Summary

Children with learning and behavior problems have been characterized differently depending upon various theoretical orientations. Generally, such children display a wide range of academic deficits and/or social adjustment problems. These behaviors may consist of problems in thinking, body management, attitude, and emotional adjustment and aggressiveness.

Two different orientations have been identified as approaches to teaching learning disabled students. Ability-training advocates focus on correcting learning processes, while skill-training proponents emphasize correcting deficient responses.

In order to relate behavioral characteristics to instruction, it is necessary to establish a close relationship between identifying and instructing students.

Educational Placement: Legal and Ethical Considerations

This chapter focuses upon educational provisions for L&BD students and those legal and ethical conditions necessary for special education programming. Three major areas are discussed: special education services, identification and placement of students, and due process and confidentiality of information.

School placement options are considered under special education services. These include activities of the special education team, regular classroom placement, consultation services, supplemental services (tutoring, resource rooms, and counseling), special classes, and special school placement. Six rules are presented to be followed when returning students to regular programs.

Procedures for identifying and placing students consist of locating students with problems, selecting and using screening instruments, and selecting students for testing.

The chapter closes with a discussion concerning due process and confidentiality of information. Legal factors and ethical considerations are related to procedural safeguards. Suggested policies and procedures are presented with respect to the confidentiality of students' records.

Introduction

Over the years various arrangements have been adopted in an attempt to accommodate the special needs of students. Such attempts have been aimed at individualizing instruction and have taken many different forms. Generally, however, each has been an attempt to improve education for handicapped children.

Related to individualized instruction are efforts to provide alternative ways to educate such children. The bases for alternative programming for handicapped learners are reflected in a statement made by The National Advisory Committee on Handicapped Children (1973). In their report, the committee noted that:

1. all handicapped children have a basic right to an education,
2. instruction must be designed to meet each child's needs,
3. our societal institutions must assume major responsibilities for educating all handicapped learners, and

4. instruction should occur within the context of general education and in association with nonhandicapped populations.

These four statements are ideal goals — objectives for which to aim. Great strides have been made toward achieving these goals by creating special educational services and establishing procedures for identifying children in need of such provisions.

Special Education Services

Educational provisions consist mainly of organizational arrangements and services designed for facilitating instruction. These are broader in scope than instructional services and tend to be managerial in character. A system for locating, identifying, and placing students with learning and behavioral problems into one or a series of educational services should be directly related to those organizational arrangements and instructional services.

School districts have followed various procedures for locating and placing students in special programs. One model is summarized in Figure 3-1 and described below.

Step 1:   Screen all students through scheduled testing and teacher/parent referral.

Step 2:   Parental approval for individual testing and/or observations.

Step 3:   Identified students are considered for special services.

Step 4:   Special assistance is provided.

Step 5:   Student's progress is followed.

FIGURE 3.1.   Steps for identifying and placing students

1. *Screening*

Someone (school personnel or parents) expresses concern about a student's school performance and/or behavior. Or standardized testing, physical examinations, or other mass surveys suggest that a student may need special assistance.

2. *Identifying*

Current observational data are gathered. These may be derived from checklists, teachers' reports, or parental information. With parental permission, psychological tests may be administered.

3. *Placement*

The special education team considers the pupil's needs in relation to test results and available services. With parental and possibly student involvement, the team determines which services are necessary in order to assist the pupil.

4. *Implementation*

The pupil is provided with special assistance. It may take the form of consultant assistance to the teacher, tutoring, counseling, or a change in educational placement. Special services are provided with parental consent.

5. *Follow-up*

A monitoring system is maintained to follow the pupil's progress and to determine when a change in special services is needed.

Program options and qualification of students are dictated by several conditions. A primary concern is one of funding requirements. Special education programs are generally funded partially or entirely by state or federal sources. Regulations, of course, accompany state and federal funds. These may be related to student characteristics (handicapping condition), socioeconomic factors (family income), and/or program requirements (maximum number of students to be served).

Other conditions which help determine types and numbers of educational provisions include availability of physical facilities and transportation services. Some program options require additional space, e.g., special classes, while others demand less room, e.g., tutoring.

Anecdote 1.2, page 16, described the various educational settings and services which may be available in any one school district for students with learning and behavioral problems. These are regular class placement with supplemental services provided to teachers and/or students, tutoring services, resource room instruction, full-time special class placement, and special school placement.

Deno (1970) presented a *cascade system* of special education services consisting of seven levels. She termed the first six levels "out-patient programs"; these included:

Level 1   Children in regular programs, handicapped but able to accommodate to regular classes with or without supportive services,

Level 2   Regular class placement with supplementary instructional services,

Level 3   Part-time special class placement,

Level 4   Full-time special class placement,

Level 5   Special stations, e.g., special schools, and

Level 6   Homebound instruction.

Level 7   represents what Deno termed as "in-patient programs." These are facilities controlled by health and/or welfare agencies such as hospitals and treatment centers.

Requirements for each placement should be specified. These may include IQ, age, and severity of problem, depending upon local board of education policies and state and federal requirements. The policies and requirements for receiving each service should be written and available to all school personnel and to the public.

School Placement Options

Special education placement and services for children with learning and behavioral problems require accurate information concerning individual children's educational needs, a thorough knowledge of available programs and services, and awareness of students' and parents' rights. Placement decisions are generally made as a part of the duties of a special education committee or team. A team approach contributes to decisions which are carefully considered and should serve to ensure due process for students.

Special Education Team

The special education team evaluates pertinent information and recommends, most often to the superintendent of schools, educational placement and services. Among the team's responsibilities is to make certain that prior to placing or removing students from special education programs, conferences are held with the parents.[1]

---

1. *Parents* in this discussion refers to the child's natural parents, legal parents, guardians, or their designated representatives.

During the conference, the advantages and disadvantages of change in school assignment should be discussed. Conferences with parents should be held at a mutually convenient time and place.

It is the team's responsibility to make available to parents all personnel who have had a part in the recommendations so that they can interview and discuss with each person the reasons for the recommendations and the anticipated results. Parents should have the opportunity to request and present reasonable supportive data (such as test results from other clinicians and medical reports) concerning the team's recommendations. If the parents wish other professional opinions and request assistance in locating such personnel, the team should recommend competent sources and take their results into consideration when making final recommendations. The team should also be responsible for informing parents about other educational assistance for their children beyond that provided by the school district.

While the team recommends placement and services, in most states the school superintendent has final responsibility for educational placement. Typically, superintendents designate a representative to assume the actual responsibility for this function, but parents are permitted to appeal any committee recommendations through an appeal procedure established by the school district. In anticipation of an appeal, the special education team must maintain records of their deliberations and parental conferences.

Parents may waive, of course, in writing the opportunity to participate in these due process procedures. By doing so they give, in effect, their consent to whatever placement and services are provided. No special education placement or service should be provided without written parental permission, or in the case of appeals, until all appeals have been completed.

The special education team may be composed of various personnel as described in anecdote 1.2. Teams may have different organizational structures. In some instances, team leadership does not rotate, as it does in anecdote 1.2. The leader may be an administrator designated by the superintendent or school board to serve that function.

In addition to considering placement and services for individual students, the team should be responsible for routine reviews of each student's progress. In large special education programs, reviews will be time-consuming and may result in team members having major time commitments for placement and reviews of student progress.

Reviews of student progress may be initiated by teacher and other school personnel, parents, or team members. It is necessary to review the progress of every student receiving special education services at least once every two years (*PARC* v. *Commonwealth of Pennsylvania*, 1972).

Regular Classroom Placement

Many children with learning and behavioral problems can remain in regular classes while receiving special assistance. In some cases, improvement in children with behavioral problems has occurred without special services. Glavin (1972), for example, found that 70% of the students identified as behavior disordered were not identified using the same screening process four years later, although no special assistance was provided. He concluded that, based on his findings, about two-thirds of all emotionally disturbed children will show spontaneous improvement.

However, as he noted, it is not possible to predict which children will improve or to know which conditions contribute to spontaneous recovery.

Similar studies conducted in Onondaga County, New York (1964), however, suggested that major reasons for spontaneous treatment were students' improved academic performances and school adjustments. When considering these findings, *spontaneous improvement* may be a misnomer since the treatment, in the form of schooling, did result in improvement. It is reasonable to assume that academic success improves emotional adjustment among school-aged children since schooling represents a significant portion of their lives. The acquisition of academic skills and the feeling of school success can go far to improve children's feelings about themselves and to change their teachers' and parents' attitudes toward them.

Some authorities, such as Lilly (1971), recommended that all children with mild to moderate learning and behavior problems be maintained in regular classes. He described a training based model for special education services in order to help regular classroom teachers to cope with mildly handicapped children including the emotionally disturbed and behaviorally disordered. He proposed that special educators shift from teaching mildly handicapped children to training regular classroom teachers to deal with such children.

Cartwright and Cartwright (1972) expanded on Lilly's recommendations and suggested a diagnostic teaching model to enable regular classroom teachers to develop needed competencies. They described the diagnostic teaching model as requiring the following teacher behaviors:

1. Identify characteristics of individual children that indicate the need for special teaching or management procedures.
2. Specify relevant educational objectives for individual children.
3. Select techniques for effective classroom management.
4. Choose and use specialized teaching strategies for reaching specific objectives for children with varying behavioral and learning characteristics.
5. Choose and use special materials in association with specific strategies.
6. Identify and use appropriate evaluation procedures.
7. Draw upon existing sources of information regarding specialized strategies and materials.
8. Consult with available resource persons for assistance.[2]

Children who are identified as having learning and behavioral problems may remain in regular programs for various reasons. Sometimes there are no special provisions available, and consequently students in need of special assistance must be maintained in regular classes. Often parents refuse to permit special placement, and school officials choose not to pursue a change in placement. And in some cases, it is believed that students will profit from remaining in regular programs when special assistance to them or the teacher is provided.

For children remaining in regular classes, special education services generally take any one, or combination, of these forms:

Consultation to teachers may be provided.
Services may be given to the parents.
Students may receive supplemental services.

2. From G. Phillip Cartwright and Carol A. Cartwright, Gilding the Lilly: Comments on the training based model, *Exceptional Children*, 1972, *39*, 231-234. Copyrighted by The Council for Exceptional Children 1972. Reproduced with permission.

Davis Jones was referred for psychological services by his third grade teacher Ms. James early in the school year. She had noticed that Davis read haltingly and his handwriting was almost illegible. More careful observations by Ms. James revealed that Davis played team games poorly because he had trouble following the rules. She further noted that he displayed immature speech, mispronouncing several common words.

Following psychological testing and conferences with the parents and teacher, the psychologist recommended to the special education team that Davis be continued in the regular program with consultation services to the teacher and parents. These services would consist of the following:

> Assistance to the teacher from an instructional specialist to train Ms. James in reading assessment and to provide materials and techniques for individualizing reading instruction.

> Assistance from the speech correctionist to aid Ms. James in helping Davis correct his poor articulation.

> Training of the parents by the parent trainer to reinforce correct articulation and to help Davis increase interest in reading for pleasure.

Consultation to teachers and parents.   In anecdote 3.1 consultation was provided to the teacher by two different specialists. Additional services were given to train the parents. But these types of services are not always feasible. A child's problems, for example, may be too severe for the regular teacher to correct. Or conditions in a classroom may be such that the teacher has neither the time or the competencies to give special instruction. Special education teams should be aware of the complexities teachers face when asked to provide prescribed instruction. For that reason, it is a sound policy to have teachers serve as members of teams. A teacher can bring to the team a realistic perspective of what can be expected of regular classroom teachers.

Teaching of the type described in anecdote 3.1 within a regular classroom is difficult. Teachers who are to carry out special instruction must willingly plan regularly for the special child, possess competencies to implement special strategies, and have access to understanding, supportive consultants and building principals.

As more children with learning and behavioral problems are served within regular classrooms, it is essential that consultation and follow-up services be provided to teachers and parents routinely and regularly. Sometimes busy consultants soon forget to maintain a regular schedule of services, particularly if teachers do not remind them of their need for assistance. And such placements should not be viewed as inexpensive ways to serve handicapped students. Proper consultation, follow-up, and supplemental instructional services are very likely to be financially more costly than special class placement.

Supplemental Assistance

Regardless of class placement, it is often necessary to provide special instructional and/or supportive services to handicapped children. Assistance may take the form of tutoring, small group instruction within a resource room, and counseling.

Tutoring.   Tutoring is typically considered to be one-to-one instruction for part of the school day. It is commonly provided to many children with learning and behavioral problems. Funds are available in many states for partial or total reimbursement of tutoring costs.

In states where reimbursement for costs of tutoring is provided, regulations usually specify student characteristics for eligibility, qualifications of tutors, and level of reimbursement to school districts. Requirements sometimes also include tutoring services in relation to local program provisions. In Ohio, for example, state-supported tutoring of L&BD children may be provided in lieu of special class placement, for assisting children who have been in special classes and for those who have been returned to regular classes, and for those who are not in need of special class placement but require assistance to remain in regular classes (Ohio Department of Education, 1973, pp. 55-57).

While tutoring of children with learning and behavioral problems is widely practiced, there is little research evidence reporting its effects. In one study using comparison groups (Stephens, Hartman, & Cooper, 1973), disadvantaged readers taught according to a skill-training model significantly exceeded an equivalent group who received standard reading instruction. First- and second-year students were tutored individually twice a day for ten minute intervals, once in the morning and once in the afternoon. Materials were programmed for the tutors and packaged so that each had assessment tasks and lesson plans for each task. The tutors were trained to provide frequent verbal reinforcement and to enter into short-term contingency contracts with each child. At the end of the school year, the tutored group exceeded significantly an equivalent group who only received standard reading instruction. In addition, the tutored group's reading achievement surpassed the average achievement of those children who, at the beginning of the year, were reading too well to qualify for special instruction (although this latter gain was not statistically significant).

In a follow-up study, Merriman located 60 pupils three years after having been tutored. Data on each participant were collected from records on test variables related to the project reported in 1973 (Stephens, Hartman, & Cooper). Included in the data were test results administered as a part of the school's regular testing program. Results indicated that the original gains in reading were sustained three years later. The study revealed that 8% of the students continued to need directive teaching. Other findings indicated that the probability of reading success is higher for students whose treatment began in first grade, rather than second grade, success is not necessarily the result of more than one year of tutoring, and the probability of success is not necessarily a product of continuous year to year treatment.

Tutors have some managerial responsibilities in many schools. These may consist of some or all of the following:

1. Beginning assessment of students, specific academic assessments, and specific social skills assessment.
2. Conferring with the classroom teacher to gather pertinent data on the child in the classroom setting.
3. Observing the child in classroom settings.
4. Making initial recommendations to the classroom teacher, principal, and supervisor, including:
   a. the number of hours a child should be tutored.
   b. initial goals and objectives to be accomplished by the tutor.
5. Making subsequent recommendations for adjustments in tutoring hours or situations, including the classroom situation.

6. Conferring with classroom teachers regularly concerning the children's progress.

7. Maintaining a record of objectives, methods, and materials employed, and progress of each student.

8. Maintaining contact with the building principal.

9. Completing final assessment and evaluation, and making recommendations for students' further instruction.

10. Reporting changes in the tutoring situation to classroom teachers, principals, and supervisors.

11. Conferring with parents on the progress of students in the tutoring setting.

12. Attending staffings of the placement committee concerning students in their program and students being considered by the committee for the tutoring program.

13. Attending staff meetings in the building assigned and those conducted for the district's special education staff.

In addition to these managerial responsibilities of tutors, their most important activity is that of instruction. While instruction takes many forms, a systematic tutoring program requires the use of teaching strategies or plans. A sample teaching strategy for tutoring is shown in anecdote 3.2.

ANECDOTE 3.2

During the tutoring session on October 10, Timmy's tutor implemented this teaching strategy.

Tasks:
1. To have student say a long *g* when shown the letter symbol with 100% accuracy.
2. To have student say aloud and point to the word *and* when presented along and with other words with 90% accuracy.
3. To have student read aloud sentences with known words and the new word *and* with 90% accuracy.

Strong modality: Auditory

Incentives: Listen to story on cassette at end of oral reading, and then tell story to teacher.

Use social praise in an operant manner as student gives correct responses. Teacher will say, "that's good" or "great."

Materials and Activities:

5 min. of presenting auditory stimulus by teacher saying a word and student point-name.

10 min. of concentration game with pairs of the following letters:

$$p \quad b \quad d \quad f \quad g \quad q$$

5 min. of presenting auditory stimulus by teacher saying a word and student pointing to the word. The following will be used:

A and are funny little are and
A can are go and jump funny

10 min. of making up sentences and reading aloud the sentences using known words and the new word *and*, e.g.,

Tim and Joe can go.
"Tim, go and jump."

"Joe, go and jump."
Wow! Can Tim go.

10 min.   of writing sentences by student — an indepentent activity

10 min.   of listening to cassette

5 min.   of review

Evaluation:

Tim said the letter *q* with 100% accuracy
Tim did not meet mastery on the word *and* when reading in context.
Tim attended to task and demonstrated appropriate reinforcement was used.

Tutors must be trained to assess children, to observe them, to instruct them, and to evaluate their achievement. While each of these tasks are discussed in detail later in this text, they are also presented extensively in earlier texts (Stephens, 1970, 1976).

The importance of designing sound teaching strategies cannot be overstressed. For tutors of children with learning and behavioral problems, the points listed below should be helpful.

1. There is a high correlation between good planning and student achievement.
2. The clearer teachers are about teaching strategies, the higher the probability for successful learning experiences.
3. Plan incentives as carefully as academic tasks are planned.
4. Emphasize small steps and small blocks of time for intensive instruction.
5. Begin with success; after difficult tasks use easy ones.
6. Provide opportunity to use the information being taught as soon as possible.
7. Overteach.
8. In teaching language arts, remember to include experiences in listening, speaking, reading, and writing.
9. Stick with the planned schedule. Consistency in schedules will provide a more comfortable learning environment.
10. Don't overlook evaluation. Record immediately, so the information will be as accurate as possible.
11. Keep tasks and materials meaningful to the student. A rural child may not identify with city-oriented programs or vice versa. Find the student's interest and use this interest to plan lessons.
12. Build a backlog of success experiences for each child. These may be used from time to time for review and as rewarding experiences.[3]

Cross-age tutoring.   Tutoring in regular education programs is common, and there is considerable literature describing and evaluating its effects (Cloward, 1967). Among those tutoring programs outside of special education, cross-age tutoring (Lippert & Lohman, 1965) has received much attention in recent years.

Cross-age tutoring occurs when older children tutor younger children in various subject areas. It is based upon beliefs that older children can provide models for younger students, that students can be trained to teach academic skills, and that older students also will profit from the tutoring relationships by being motivated to achieve in school.

Johnson and Bailey (1974) reported the results of a cross-age tutoring program. In their study, five fifth-grade students tutored five kindergarten children in beginning

3. The writer appreciates this contribution from Dr. Jerry Barnett and Dr. Virginia Lucas who, as doctoral students, developed a workshop for tutors from which these points were abstracted.

arithmetic skills for seven and a half weeks. A control group of kindergarten children was matched with the experimental group in arithmetic ability. Results demonstrated that the experimental group made far greater gains than the control group on posttesting.

An analysis of arithmetic skills was also conducted which revealed that these skills improved only when tutoring for that skill occurred. In this study, it should be noted that the fifth-grade students were trained as tutors in three half-hour sessions. The training included role playing and demonstrations.

Graubard and Rosenberg (1974) described a cross-age project in a junior high school. Seventh- and eighth-grade students were trained daily in two-hour sessions for six weeks. The students were taught to use behavior modification principles, to write behavioral objectives, and to use tutoring skills. Following training, students tutored fourth, fifth and sixth graders for six weeks, two hours daily. The tutoring was judged to be "extremely successful" (p. 121) and was continued a second year.

Apparently, cross-age tutoring has some potential for services to children with learning and behavioral problems. It should be noted, however, that successful cross-age tutoring seems to require:

> careful selection of tutors
> training of tutors in using reinforcement and other behavioral techniques
> regular meetings of tutors to monitor their activities and for maintaining their interest
> specific tutoring assignments, including scheduled times for tutoring

Resource Rooms

Part-time placement in rooms where special instruction occurs by trained personnel has been referred to as *resource rooms*. Although an extensive evaluation of resource rooms for L&BD children has not been reported, it is widely advocated and may be the most prevalent organizational scheme for L&BD students (Wiederholt, 1974).

Ferinden, Van Handel, and Kovalinsky (1971) described and reported results of a resource room instructional program for learning disabled children. Eleven students remained in regular classes while receiving supplemental instruction. Treatment emphasized instruction in perception, arithmetic, and reading skills. Using Strauss and Lehtinen's (1947) early definition of perception, *a mental process which precedes thinking and integrates sensations*, the authors' major goal was to correct the children's perceptual disturbances.

After eight months of treatment based on a pretest and posttest design, their results were:

> gains in reading achievement were not significant, although the average gain for the group was 8 months.
> arithmetic gains were 18 months, resulting in statistically significant improvement.
> gains in perceptual achievement were significant, as measured by the *Bender Gestalt Test*.

Although the students (ages 7 to 11 years) remained in their regular classes, they were assigned to meet with a special teacher in a resource room located in the same building. Instruction consisted of perceptual training in the areas of visual motor coordination, tactile discrimination, visual memory, auditory discrimination, distance judgment, spatial relation, kinesthetics, and figure-ground perception. In addition, reading and arithmetic instruction were emphasized.

Limitations of this study clearly relate to the lack of a control group and failure to control important variables, such as the differences in teaching competencies among the regular classroom teachers in which the 11 children were enrolled. Despite its limitations, this study is a valuable contribution in that the curriculum was extensively described. One wonders, however, if reading achievement would not have been greater had more instructional time been devoted to teaching these skills directly rather than emphasizing perceptual training.

Glavin, Quay, Annesley, and Werry (1971) reported results of the Temple Resource Room Project. Children in the experimental group were assigned to a resource room program during those periods of the day in which they were functioning least effectively in their regular classes. The program emphasized academic instruction using contingency contracting. They reported that the experimental group made significantly greater gains in reading vocabulary and arithmetic fundamentals than did a comparison group. Changes in social behavior also occurred, with the greatest improvement among the experimental group while they were in the resource room.

In the Glavin et al. study, 27 students with a mean age of 10 years constituted the experimental group. Thirty-four children, mean age 9 years, 4 months, made up the comparison group. The authors concluded that increases in attending behaviors and decreases in deviant behaviors in the resource rooms appeared immediately after placement. They also found that behaviors acquired in resource rooms were not generalized to regular classes unless mechanisms were developed between the teachers in both placements. For example, deviant social behaviors continued in the regular classes even though they were improved in resource rooms. Clearly, recently acquired academic and behavior skills developed in resource rooms tend not to be maintained in regular classrooms if left to chance.

Glavin (1974), in a follow-up to the study reported above, sought to determine if gains were maintained in regular classes following one- or two-year placement in regular classes. He found that generalization of social behavior never occurred in regular classes. That is, in the absence of specific procedures for maintaining the desirable hehavior which was taught and displayed in resource rooms, social behavior was not improved in regular classes even though that behavior was quickly changed in resource rooms. Glavin could not account for the lack of significant results in arithmetic attainment. While the experimental group's arithmetic performance had improved more significantly than the controls in the initial study, the difference between the two groups was not maintained in the follow-up study.

Based on Glavin's follow-up study it appears that the following strategies would have improved the chances of generalizing behavior and academic achievement to regular classes:

1. Gradually phase out placement in resource rooms by having the student attend fewer and fewer days for shorter and shorter intervals.

2. Train the regular classroom teachers so that they can reinforce the gains made by students while they were in resource rooms.

3. Develop procedures where resource room and regular teachers routinely discuss tactics for maintaining behavior of specific children.

4. Assist classroom teachers to individualize instruction so that academic gains can continue.

Counseling

Most school districts have full-time guidance counselors in secondary schools but they are found less frequently at the elementary school levels. Yet personal assistance by school counselors can be an important way to provide support and personal contact with L&BD children as described in anecdote 3.3.

ANECDOTE 3.3

Claude, a 12-year-old youngster, has been returned to the regular classroom after having spent two years in a special class for L&BD children. In order to be successful in the class, he is receiving daily tutoring in academic skills. He has also been assigned to the counselor at Main Elementary school for bi-weekly counseling.

Mr. Rogers, the counselor, meets with Claude on Tuesdays and Thursdays for 30 minutes. He and Claude have discussed the purposes of the counseling sessions and have agreed that he is someone that Claude can talk to about "how things are going in school." Mr. Rogers will also help Claude to have better self-control.

The special education team assigned Claude for counseling because he did not have a father at home and because he had demonstrated a quick and violent temper at school as well as at home. His mother appreciated the counseling for Claude. She reported after about six weeks that he had already used some self-regulating tactics in order to avoid trouble at home and in the neighborhood.

Counseling of L&BD children is not commonly practiced in most schools. But as guidance counselors are trained in specific behavioral tactics, they could become important ancillary personnel. Among the methods which have promise for counseling L&BD students are:

1. Teaching them to regulate their own behavior, such as resisting temptation, delaying gratification, and tolerating unpleasant stimuli.

2. Helping students to form positive relationships with other children through the use of role playing and behavior rehearsing.

3. Providing support to students by allowing them to discuss their concerns and problems without being evaluated adversely.

4. Teaching students how to study and to use resources for learning.

5. Helping them develop better relationships with teachers and other adults.

6. Training passive and inhibited students to be assertive. Assertive training (McFall & Lillesand, 1971) involves instruction and modeling behaviors.

Special Class Placement

In the early 1960s, Morse, Cutler, and Fink (1964) found special class placement to be the most common organizational plan for the behaviorally disordered, and it appears to continue to be most frequently used. According to Rogan and Luken (1968), 58% of all teachers of behavior disordered children were in self-contained special classes. Eighty-six percent of the states use special classes for learning disabled children, and of this group 41% use it as the only provision for such children (Chalfant, 1972).

McCarthy and McCarthy (1969) estimated that less than 1% of learning disabled children are placed in self-contained classrooms. Although their estimate may appear to differ with Chalfant's, theirs was based on numbers of students while his data base were numbers of states. Since many more children can be served in resource rooms and by itinerate tutors, it is likely that the McCarthys are correct Due to the differences in criteria and varying definitions of "learning disabilities" from state to state, no definite statement can be made as to the numbers of L&BD children who are in any one organizational arrangement.

It is understandable that frequent use of special classes has been made for L&BD children. Historically, special education started with self-contained classes and special schools when regular education failed to assist handicapped children. The relatively recent categories of handicaps, such as learning disabilities and behavior disorders, tended naturally to follow the established pattern. Within regular schools, special class placement continues to be used for those children who cannot be taught or managed for any part of the school day in regular classes.

Placement in special classes is misused when:

children are placed there because teachers are unwilling to adapt the instruction to their individual needs.

when teachers are incompetent and, therefore, cannot instruct or manage students,

when adequate supportive services are not provided to regular teachers so that L&BD children can be maintained in their classes.

Some research evidence on special classes for L&BD students has been accumulated. Vaac (1968) studied two groups of emotionally disturbed children, ten years of age. One group, consisting of 16 children, were in special classes. These were matched with 16 emotionally disturbed children who were identified but continued in regular classes. At the end of one year, he reported greater gains by children in special classes on all areas.

In a follow-up study a few years later, however, Vaac (1971) found no significant differences between the two groups. Due to school changes, the follow-up population consisted of 11 students from the special class group and 10 from regular classes. It should be noted that after two years in special classes, those in special classes were returned to regular class placement. He compared this group with those who had not experienced special class instruction. He concluded that special classes do not result in long-term changes for emotionally disturbed children over those who are not placed in special classes. His findings suggest that special class gains are lost once children leave the special program.

Among the implications of Vaac's studies is the importance of continuing special instruction after class placement is completed. Special instruction may consist of those supplemental activities discussed in the previous section.

Whelen (1966) studied emotionally disturbed children between the ages of 9 and 12. He studied the feelings of 15 emotionally disturbed boys in special classes, 10 similar children who were in regular classes awaiting treatment at a child guidance center, and 15 boys who were judged normal and well-adjusted. All subjects responded to an interview containing questions regarding school, family, and self. He found that emotionally disturbed special class and normal regular class boys attached more positive meanings to school, self, and family than did the emotionally disturbed boys in regular classes. The boys assigned to special classes viewed such placement as positive and valuable. Positive meanings were not revealed for emotionally disturbed children in regular classes.

Fink (1972) analyzed teacher-pupil interactions in 15 special classes for emotionally handicapped children. He developed an interactive analysis system, encompassing the variability and complexity of teacher and pupil behaviors. Its use in the 15 classes revealed wide differences in teacher-pupil behavior. He concluded that the almost equal division between task and nontask activities suggests the importance of nontypical patterns of behavior in the life of special classroom children and teachers.

Concerns regarding parents' and pupils' perceptions of special class placement were studied by McKinnon (1970). He considered 88 students (mean age 14 years) who had spent an average of 17 months in special classes for the emotionally disturbed and their parents. He concluded that generally parents felt their children were assisted with schoolwork and behavior problems. Students indicated an awareness of and appreciation for the assistance they received in managing their behavior and their improved academic achievement.

Although placement trends in special education are away from a heavy reliance on special classes this does not mean that special classes for L&BD children will soon be extinct. As Birch (1971) noted:

> There is and probably will continue to be a substantial need for many exceptional children to spend most of their school days with teachers specifically prepared to apply special education approaches. But there are other exceptional children for whom the regular personnel programs can be used with fully satisfactory results. (p. 77)

Special School Placement

Private and public special schools are available for children with learning and behavioral problems. The private schools tend to be residential types where the children live, receive special treatment, and attend school.

Special schools administered by public school districts are almost always day schools, where students attend school during the day but return to their homes after school. There are exceptions, of course. Some school districts administer school programs in residential facilities, such as in state mental health institutions or agencies for adjudicated delinquents or dependent and neglected children.

Special education teams may, in certain instances, recommend placement in a special school. Generally, factors which should be considered when recommending special school placement are:

1. *Severity of problem.* The student's learning and/or behavioral conditions are such that special care and/or instruction and treatment are needed to such a degree that public school services are insufficient.

2. *Protection.* The student's behavior is so extreme that he or she is dangerous to himself or herself or to others and therefore must be placed in a residential setting.

3. *Insufficient public school services.* The public school district lacks the special services needed and, with parental permission, provides the cost for instruction in a nearby day school.

4. *Family conditions.* Home and family problems are of such a magnitude that the student will be further disturbed by staying at home. In cooperation with juvenile court, the child is placed in a residential setting.

5. *Parental requests.* The parents request that their child be placed in a private setting where adequate treatment and instructional services are available. Although school authorities may not need to participate in decisions of this type, some states and/or school districts provide tuition or partially pay the costs for schooling.

ANECDOTE 3.4[4]

The Lafayette School is a private nonprofit day school for children with learning disabilities in Philadelphia, Pennsylvania. The school is approved by the Bureau of Special

---

4. This description is reproduced from The Lafayette School brochure with the permission of Dr. Jerry G. Miller, Director.

Education, Department of Education, Harrisburg, Pennsylvania, and is licensed by the State Board of Private Academic Schools, Commonwealth of Pennsylvania. It is non-sectarian and is open to children of all racial, religious, and national backgrounds.

Tuition: Instructional costs are paid by state government for those children approved for admission by the local school district and the State Department of Education. Students receive free bus transportation by the Philadelphia School District.

Student Population: Children with learning disabilities, ages 4 through 16, caused by minimal brain damage are served.

Educational Program: The Lafayette School is concerned with academic, social and physical learning. It has adopted an individualized learning program "Directive Teaching," originated by Thomas M. Stephens of The Ohio State University. By assessing and instructing each child at the place in his learning where he has the prerequisite skills to learn, performance and motivation are encouraged through earned rewards for gains he has made at his level of achievement.

The school is structured for individual learning in size, grouping, and staffing. Each classroom is staffed with a teacher and an aide.

Each individual child learns to work correctly and for certain goals.

Rewards are a part of the learning process. Objectives are set for a child to learn and reach goals systematically. Rewards are then slowly reduced and removed, and the individual continues to learn at his own pace. Thus, accurate and effective performance become rewards to the learner.

Each child is assessed as to his social and academic functioning in a highly specific way. Information is obtained concerning those events within his environment that serve as incentives to encourage his development.

Individual academic prescriptions are developed and generated by computer based specific objectives and criterion measures. Prescriptions are continually updated and revised. The computer is also used for grouping children according to skill level and teacher accountability.

Teachers are instructed to know each child well. Based upon assessment findings, they can set specific learning priorities for the child. In-service workshops are routinely provided for teachers to enable them to remain current in educational advances.

Most large school districts have special public schools for disruptive and disturbed students. Berkowitz and Rothman (1960) described the program for one such school in New York City. Public special schools are often criticized for being "blackboard jungles" and for ignoring the necessity for disruptive students to have contact with normal peers. As social problems escalate, it is inevitable that special schools will continue to be placement options for some disruptive students.

The Montgomery County, Maryland Public Schools have a special day school for students, grades 5–12, who "fail to achieve academically, to exercise proper judgment, to organize their thoughts and energies for constructive activities, or to behave in socially acceptable ways." Mark Twain School (Montgomery County Schools, 1975) operates for 12 months each year and enrolls students for a maximum of two years. Its major objective is to promote academic skills and social behaviors so students can return to regular classrooms.

Private residential schools also offer alternative placement for L&BD students. Devereux Schools are among the more noted residential settings. Owned and operated by The Devereux Foundation, a non-profit organization, there are Devereux campuses in Pennsylvania, California, Texas, Arizona, and Georgia. Students placed there tend to have moderate to severe learning and/or emotional problems. Placements are often made by parents or by the courts. In some instances, the costs are partially borne by school districts.

The Devereux Foundation was established in 1912 as a residential and day treatment center for emotionally disturbed and mentally retarded children. It operates as a rehabilitation center rather than as a custodial institution. A treatment team typically consists of two educators, a psychiatrist, a physician, a psychologist, and a social worker.

Residential facilities are believed to have the advantage of providing multidisciplinary services to the students. Under conditions where services are well coordinated this advantage can exist. But sometimes professional rivalries and other personnel problems result in disjointed and inefficient services. School personnel who have placement responsibilities should visit those residential facilities where they intend to recommend placement. They should also investigate the accreditation of the school programs to determine if instruction will be at least as good as it is in the school district.

Among the factors to consider when determining private residential placement for L&BD children are the following:

1. Does the facility have an accredited school program?

2. Are their students similar in age and severity of problems to that of the youngster being considered for placement?

3. Is the teacher-pupil ratio adequate to allow for individualized instruction?

4. Are there support services such as psychological, social, medical, and recreational?

5. Is the average stay reasonable or are large numbers of children placed there for prolonged periods?

6. Are provisions made to help the children return to day schools and to home?

7. Is adequate supervision provided in the living quarters?

8. Are the living quarters "homelike"?

9. Are the costs reasonable in relation to the services which are provided?

10. Is the school program considered to be important to the success of students, or is it merely an adjunct service of the treatment?

Procedures for Reintegrating Students

Placing students in special programs, or providing special services to children in regular classrooms, begins a process of following the students in order to modify their placements as needed. Students in special settings should be returned to regular programs as soon as they are able to make successful adjustments. Due process procedures are also operable by the special education team when students are evaluated and being considered for return to regular classes.

Research evidence is limited concerning the adjustment of L&BD children returned to regular classrooms. In addition to the Vaac (1974) and McKinnon (1969) studies discussed earlier, two others were reported.

Hayball and Dilling (1969) investigated the classroom adjustments of 57 students who had been returned to regular classes from different types of classes: an opportunity class for slow learners, a class for children with perceptual difficulties, those having multiple handicaps including behavioral problems, and those in special reading programs. Using a questionnaire distributed to the receiving regular classroom teachers, they found that personal and social adjustments were rated as similar for students from all four groups. Interviews with the students indicated that all groups gave favorable ratings concerning their feelings about regular classes. The slow learner group gave the highest number of positive responses.

Saunders (1971) studied the influence that the behavior of emotionally disturbed children had on their normal peers in fourth-, fifth-, and sixth-grade classes. After three months of study, he could find no evidence of a behavioral contagion in any of the classes. His findings suggest that, contrary to beliefs of many, emotionally disturbed students do not adversely influence normal peers' behaviors and attitudes. Of course, more study of this important concern is needed.

McKinnon (1969) studied 65 children who had been returned to regular classes for an average of three years. Previously they had been in special classes for the emotionally disturbed. He concluded that:

— academic gains were greater for those who had fewer academic learning problems initially, who were younger at the time of special placement, had higher measured intelligence, and came from higher socioeconomic families.

— behavior adjustment gains were greater for those who had more severe learning problems initially, were younger at the time of special placement, had the greatest lack of self-confidence at the end of special placement, and came from higher socioeconomic families.

In an unpublished study concerned with attitudes of educators toward integrating L&BD children from special classes to regular classes, Levin (1974) surveyed teacher educators, special classroom teachers, regular classroom teachers, and regular classroom teachers who had already received L&BD children from special classes. She found that the three groups significantly agreed as to the necessity to integrate L&BD children into regular classes, but there were differences among the three groups as to the effectiveness of special integration procedures. Levin's study points out the need for research evidence, rather than opinion, as a basis for determining which procedures to use when returning students to regular classes from special classes.

In view of the limited research findings available as to how best to proceed, some basic rules are stated here derived mainly from this writer's experience.

Rule One

Change in placement should be based on performance factors. While psychological testing may be required to satisfy state and local school district regulations, decisions for placement should be made on the basis of student's daily academic and social behaviors. School performance, on day-to-day tasks, is the best indicator of the chances of success in a new placement, as anecdote 3.5 depicts.

ANECDOTE 3.5

Eleven-year-old Colleen Howe had been in a self-contained special class for L&BD children for the past two and one half years. Psychological testing, at the time of placement, indicated that she had a measured intelligence in the low 90s and that she was deficient in reading by over three years. At the age of 8 years 7 months, she was reading at the prereading level. Because of her serious reading problem and hyperactive and destructive behavior, she had been placed in a special class with 11 other children. In addition, parent training was provided to her mother with follow-up sessions to help Mrs. Howe maintain the management skills she had acquired in training.

In December of the current school year, the special class teacher, Ms. Franklin, indicated to her consultant that Colleen was one of two students whom she believed could be returned to regular classes. She based this belief on her improved reading performance; she was now reading on a late fourth grade level. She knew this because she frequently read from fourth grade readers and because her library selections tended to be written at the fourth grade level. Further, Colleen was rarely a behavior problem now and had become a class leader.

After conferring with the building principal and a fifth-grade teacher, the consultant suggested to Ms. Franklin that she begin to send Colleen to that fifth-grade class with a note for the teacher. At times, she took a note to the playground when the fifth-grade class was at recess and was encouraged to participate in play with the others.

The consultant brought the request for Colleen's new placement to the special education team with her recommendation that she be gradually phased into a regular fifth-grade class. She also indicated that she and the building principal had met with Mrs. Howe and that she had readily agreed to the change, giving written consent.

At the team's request, Colleen was first assigned to a regular class during arithmetic instructional time since this was her strongest skill area. She also began taking physical education, music, and art instruction with the fifth grade.

Gradually, she spent most of her school day in the regular class except for a small portion of the time when she received supplemental tutoring in reading in the special class. By the end of the school year, Colleen was a regular fifth grader.

Rule Two

Students and their parents should be helped in adjusting to the change when special education services are reduced or modified. Some welcome the change, although later they may feel something is amiss as the child's school marks drop below average. Others resist the change, knowing that they will be leaving teachers who understand them. The insecurity faced by some children when leaving special classes, in particular, is a real but unstudied problem in special education.

Parents' concerns can be alleviated through careful and systematic contacts with them throughout their children's special education placement. They will have more confidence that the school personnel know their children and have a sound basis for recommending the change. Parents should be prepared for their children's change in daily performance; it may be more difficult to do as well in regular classes. They should also be prepared for their children's concerns. Suggestions should be made as to how they can help make the placement transition as nonanxiety ridden as possible.

Of course, students' concerns must be alleviated. Phasing them into a new situation, helping them to get to know their new teacher and classmates, assuring them that they can stop by and talk with their former special teacher, and above all, making certain they have the necessary academic and social skills to cope in the new class will serve to make the transition smoother.

Rule Three

Trial placements should be used only when essential. A setback can be a serious psychological blow to any student with learning and behavior problems. Trial placements imply that the child may not make the new adjustment and will be returned to a special class. Such placements may be harmful to students.

If a trial placement is necessary, then poor planning has occurred. The method described in anecdote 3.5 serves to eliminate the need for trial-and-error placements.

On occasions, the most carefully planned placement will not be successful. In such rare instances, students may need to be given another placement or more supplemental assistance. They will also need psychological support. Those performance factors which led to the failure should be identified and corrected.

Rule Four

Receiving and sending teachers should be involved in placement decisions, and they should share performance observations. Teachers are the key factors in successful reintegration. Their active involvement, prior to placement decisions, will contribute to smooth transitions for students. How to proceed, where the child should best be seated, when to phase him or her into the class, his or her personality characteristics, and his or her new peers' attitudes are ingredients that teachers can best discuss.

Sending teachers may want to participate in some seatwork plan initially to help the student gain success. Sharing with the receiving teacher the student's academic strengths and what he or she is now beginning to learn will facilitate the transition.

Feedback regarding the child's performance from the receiving teacher to the sending teacher can serve two purposes. First, it will encourage teachers to share ideas on how to help students, and, second, it will give the sending teacher a chance to evaluate the effects of the special program.

Rule Five

Fading approaches should be used when changing placements. Several references have already been made to "phasing in" students and this was a part of the process described in anecdote 3.5.

In a fading process, students are moved gradually from spending time in one setting to spending an increasing amount of time in the new placement. Clearly, fading requires careful planning and cooperation from teaching personnel. It may require modifying teaching schedules so that, for example, subject matter is taught at a different time than it is usually.

Fading procedures also include a systematic use of supportive services. As the sending teacher fades from the scene, other personnel provide services to help maintain the student in the new placement. Supportive services may include direct instruction to the student in the form of tutoring, resource room instruction, and services from speech therapists and counselors. Or services may be provided to the receiving teacher in the form of consultants or special materials or equipment. Services to the parents are also sometimes provided during transition periods.

Rule Six

Due process procedures should be followed when reintegrating students into regular classes. Parents should be involved in all placement decisions. Basically, the same procedures which are followed when special services are first considered should be followed when changes in special assignments are contemplated.

A sound policy to follow is to maintain routine contact with parents of all children receiving special education services. This contact may be accomplished by teachers, consultants, or other representatives of the special education team. By having continual contact, any change in placement can be considered a natural part of conversations with parents. And as progress reports are made to them, they will be ready for new services and placements.

Procedures for Identifying
and Placing Students

Students in need of special services must first be located, usually within the regular school program, prior to special placement. Procedures for locating L&BD students require specifying behavioral characteristics, screening target population, and selecting students for formal testing.

Locating Students with Problems

Detection of children who need special assistance should be a basic concern of all school personnel. Students who behave differently from others, those who have trouble learning, and those displaying attitudinal problems may need special help. All teachers who are concerned about their pupils and who attempt to individualize instruction should not hesitate to request help for such students.

Directly related to concern for students is a process for systematically screening all pupils in order to locate those in need of assistance. Procedures are needed which routinely alert personnel to pupils who need help. These procedures must involve classroom teachers since they have frequent opportunities to observe students.

Keogh and Becker (1973) presented guidelines for the early identification of children with learning problems. They recommended that techniques be emphasized which are short-term, educationally oriented, and based upon functional aspects of children's behavior in classroom settings.

Buktenica (1971) discussed identifying children early in order to prevent and remediate learning disorders. He argued that screening methods are needed to identify perceptual and cognitive factors at an early age. Buktenica concluded that group assessment procedures are needed for preventing learning problems, that assessment procedures must be consistent with instructional goals, and that learning characteristics of children should be matched with instructional methods.

While Buktenica's arguments were persuasive, he cited no research evidence in support of his thesis that learning disabilities could be prevented through an early intervention program which focused on nonverbal factors, such as perception and cognition. In fact, Jacobs, Wirthlin, and Miller (1968), in an evaluation of a visual-perceptual training program, concluded that first-grade children who are trained in Frostig's Visual Perception program have no advantage in reading achievement as compared to pupils who do not take the Frostig program.

A research-based screening program for reading problems among first graders was reported by Hartlage and Lucas (1973). They developed an approach to screening problems among beginning readers. The group screening procedure was initially administered to over one thousand beginning first graders. At the end of first grade, these same children's reading skills were tested. They found that their group screening test can be of more value in predicting the reading success of first-grade children. Of more significance, however, was their finding that teachers' ranking of beginning first graders correlated well (.83) with reading test scores at the end of the school year.

Ozer and Richardson (1974) described an approach whereby teachers observe children performing certain tasks. Their "neuro-developmental observation" is an examination process which includes assisting the child with difficult tasks and observing those tactics which facilitate his or her learning.

Wedell (1970) presented another approach to diagnosis. In response to what he termed "the inadequacy of the psychological assessment of children with learning difficulties," he proposed an ongoing process of hypothesis testing. It should be noted that Wedell's suggestions are based upon the unproven assumption that instruction should be related to the etiology of learning problems.

Many tests and testing techniques purport to identify adjustment problems and learning disorders among children. For example, Mecham, Jones, and Jex (1973) reported on the use of the *Utah Test of Language Development* for screening children with language disabilities. They developed percentile norms for kindergarten children and suggested an abbreviated form of that test for quick screening.

The *Bender Gestalt Test* (Bender, 1938) has frequently been used to diagnose brain injury and to predict reading problems in elementary school children. Koppitz (1970), however, has cautioned that while the Bender is an effective screening test for school beginners, it only identifies reading problems when these are related to visual-motor perception. Koppitz claims that the Bender Test does not identify reading problems when caused by "language disabilities or specific memory deficits."

Swanson and Jacobson (1970) tested the validity of the *Slosson Intelligence Test (SIT)* as a screening instrument for identifying children with learning problems. They correlated the *SIT* scores of 64 second graders, referred as having learning problems, with scores on the *Wechsler Intelligence Scale for Children (WISC)*. The *SIT* was found to be essentially a measure of verbal ability since it correlated high (.64) with the *WISC*'s verbal IQ but low (.10) with its performance IQ.

Bower's (1969) materials have been widely used to screen for emotionally disturbed children. But Salvia, Schultz, and Chapin (1974) point out that Bower's process requires a fixed number of children in each class to be identified as potentially disturbed regardless of their emotional status. At the end of the process, the teacher identifies those five children with the highest percentages of negative ratings. As the authors correctly note, this process is an arbitrary way to identify potentially disturbed children since a fixed percentage of each class must be negatively rated.

Many tests and standardized procedures are available to assist school personnel in screening and diagnosing children with learning problems and behavioral disorders. Interested readers are referred to Buros' *Seventh Mental Measurements Yearbook*, which is available in most reference libraries.

Specifying Student Characteristics

Students' behavioral characteristics should be described in written form for use by classroom teachers, so that they can identify those in need of further study. Another purpose for specifying those characteristics, which make students eligible for special education services, is for placement considerations. Since special placement and services are often limited, it is important to have a rational way to prioritize students. Thus, a written statement concerning eligibility can serve as a basis for waiting lists when special services are in short supply.

Funding sources usually dictate the nature of those students to be served. State departments of education, for example, often specify program standards for special education. State standards usually contain those student characteristics necessary for placement in that state's approved programs.

At the classroom screening level, an observation form may be developed drawing upon those characteristics. An analysis of Ohio's requirements would show children with L&BD problems being characterized as:

— possessing low average or higher IQ
— being below average academically
— having social behavior which deviates from the norm of regular class
— demonstrating a significant deficit in one or more basic academic skills (reading, math, language, spelling, writing). (Ohio Department of Education, 1973, pp. 24-29)

These items could serve as a basis for classroom teachers' use in Ohio. Checklists, observation forms, and other types of written reports could also be structured around the above items for classroom screening purposes.

Screening Procedures

Procedures are needed which provide for mass screening of all students in school. It is important to screen routinely at critical points in the school lives of children. Typically, these are considered to be during the first year in school, at the start of the middle elementary years (fourth year), and at the beginning of adolescence (seventh school year). In addition, emotional problems sometimes become acute among high school students. Bower (1975) indicated that screening should occur at points of transition between institutions, such as home and school.

Learning disorders are usually detected during the elementary school years, though special provisions for many children will continue to be needed through high school. In cases where students have deficits which interfere with learning in typical ways, but where they have learned to achieve well in school with special help, provisions may need to be extended through the college years.

Screening student populations usually involves these procedures:

1. Instructional provisions for which students will be identified are described.
2. Characteristics of students necessary for placement in special programs are specified.
3. Student populations to be screened are identified.
4. Screening instruments are selected or developed.
5. Student screening is conducted.
6. Students identified in screening are considered for individual testing.

Each of these six procedures involves several activities which are a part of the procedure. For example, number 1 may include developing new programs for students who are not presently being taught adequately. It might also involve locating physical space and qualified teaching personnel so that program expansion can occur.

Selecting and Using Screening Instruments

Mass screening is, at best, a gross means of locating students who may be in need of assistance. In addition to those limitations which are inherent in screening, there are other factors which contribute to its ineffectiveness. These are often associated with the nature of screening instruments as well as the difficulties of differentiating students who are progressing normally from those who have mild problems.

First, the screening instruments to be used and variables to be measured should be directly related to instructional treatment. That is, the curriculum and instruction should be reflected in the screening instruments. Since many standardized measures are purposely imprecise so that they will appeal to a wide market, most commercially available tests will not alone meet this first requirement.

Second, teacher observations and judgments should provide heavy weight to the screening process. Several reviews of studies (Balow, 1966; Glavin & Quay, 1969; Lambert, 1967; Lambert & Hartsough, 1968; Morse & Dyer, 1963; Morse, Finger, & Gilmore, 1968) support the effectiveness of teachers in identifying behavior problems of children. Their ability to identify such problems is further improved when assistance is obtained from others, such as psychologists and the peer group.

Lovitt (1967) described a direct behavioral assessment as the first step in teaching children with learning problems. Four procedures to be conducted by teachers consisted of (1) baseline assessment, (2) assessment of behavioral components, (3) assessment based on referral, and (4) generalization of assessment. In the first phase the teacher conducts a direct analysis of target behavior. The second procedure is the assessment of those behavioral components that maintain and modify behavior (stimulus or antecedent events). The third factor considers the referring adult by assessing the competencies of the parent and/or teacher. Lovitt's fourth step is meant to transfer assessment results into instructional procedures.

Emotionally handicapped children have been identified using a process involving teachers and the peer group. Schultz, Manton, and Salvia (1972) compared the results of the *Behavior Problem Checklist* (Quay & Peterson, 1967) with those obtained on the same rural population using Bower's (1969) *A Process for In-School Screening of Children with Emotional Handicaps, Elementary Level*. All children and teachers from third and fourth grades in two rural counties were screened using both instruments plus Schultz's (1967) *Fundamental Interpersonal Relations Orientation – Behavior, Adult form and Children's form*. Their findings indicated that teacher and peer selections were not biased by the absence of interpersonal compatibility. A statistically significant but low relationship was also found between Bower's process and Quay and Peterson's checklist. This finding suggests that the same children are not always identified by both instruments.

Two types of methods are commonly used by teachers for locating school-aged children with behavior problems. One is through the use of tests, and the other is by direct observation. Since, at the screening level, large numbers of children are involved, tests are often represented by checklists·which serve to structure teacher observation. These are differentiated from other observations made by teachers in that checklists often yield scores that are related to populations upon which the measures were standardized.

Teacher observations are essential when screening students. Since they have many opportunities to note behavior under various situations, their observations are indispensable for locating children in need of assistance. Observations may occur during different forms of instruction, small group as well as large, at play, while eating, and during social interactions. Rick (1976) argues that educational placement error is unavoidable when using testing procedures for individual placement of students. He described an observation approach in which teachers take frequent, direct measures of social and academic behaviors of target students. This single subject approach permits educational decisions to be based upon actual data of specific students rather than on predictive data derived from standardized testing.

Harth and Glavin (1971) reported their attempts to validate a screening technique using teacher judgment concerning emotional problems. They compared teacher ratings of students with their scores on the *California Test of Personality*. Their student population consisted of 786 children from grades five through eight in a small county school system. They concluded that:

1. teacher rating is a valid way for screening for emotionally disturbed children,
2. other measures may be needed in order to identify different types of emotionally disturbed children,
3. an academic achievement index should be used instead of the *California Test of Personality*, and
4. ratings should be supplemented by classroom observations.

Once teachers have located children who seemingly need more intensive study, they may initiate requests for such services as depicted in anecdote 3.6:

ANECDOTE 3.6

The Newton School District provides each primary grade teacher with a list of items to be used when observing children who appear to need special assistance. Teachers are reminded by the special education team each December that they may wish to observe closely children who appear to be in need of further study. The observation form is brief and covers these areas:

1. Student identification and personal data
   —name
   —date of birth
   —school placement
2. School progress
   —results of standardized tests
   —school achievement in relation to the group
   —record of school absences and tardiness
3. Social conduct
   —class behavior
   —behavior with peers
   —behavior with teacher
4. Parental reports
   —adjustment at home
   —interactions with playmates

An observation form used in gross screening encompasses areas such as those shown in anecdote 3.6. The actual items included in the form may vary depending upon the types of special services which are available. For example with the availability of psychological services, some schools use completion of a teacher's request for service form, as a referral source. Upon receipt of a completed form, contact is made with the teacher by a school psychologist. Figure 3.2 shows a form typically used by teachers when requesting assistance for an individual child.

FIGURE 3.2.   Request for individual study form

Name of Student _____

Home Address _____

Home Phone _____

Parents or Guardians _____

Date of Referral _____
                        Yr.   Month   Day

Date of Birth _____
                        Yr.   Month   Day

School _____

School Placement _____

Teacher(s) _____

Reason for Referral _____

Standardized Test Results

Test	Scores	Date

Briefly describe problem:

_____

_____

_____

Are the parents aware of the problem?

_____   _____
Teacher's Signature   Principal's Signature

Selecting Students for Testing

A screening procedure should identify students who need more careful consideration. As a result of screening, referrals for assistance are typically directed to
psychological service personnel. Of course, requests may be initiated by someone
other than a teacher. Within schools, counselors, nurses, and supervisors may refer
children through building principals. Parents, physicians, and mental health agencies are referral sources from outside the school.

Psychological services may provide a number of different ways to respond to
requests from teachers, depending upon referral information. In many instances,
psychological testing is a routine response. In others, teacher conferences and
observations of students may precede testing.

Psychological testing in schools is motivated by the need to obtain valid information in order to aid students. As Oakland (1937) has noted, school psychologists are
relied upon by special educators for classifying children in order to achieve educational placement goals. For that reason, school psychologists are often integral
members of the special education team.

Psychological Assessment

Psychological assessment includes more than testing. It is an overall study of the
student's school adjustment. A thorough psychological evaluation should include
the following but not necessarily in this order.

—Teacher interview
—Observation in school
—Reading student's school record
—Principal conference
—Parent conference
—Administering an individual test of intelligence
—Administering standardized academic achievement tests
—A written report including interpretation of test results and recommendations.

Often school psychologists will incorporate into their reports results of prior tests, relevant information contained in student files, and summaries of all conferences regarding the students.

Reasonable expectations for psychological evaluations are to gain an estimate of the seriousness of the problem, identify alternate educational planning, determine the prognosis for helping the student, and determine the student's eligibility for special education services.

Parent and Student Involvement

Parents and students are involved in locating children in need of special help in two ways. They may serve as referral sources, and they are included in those procedures for protecting the rights of students.

Parents may often be the first to suspect that their children have adjustment or learning problems. While anecdote 3.7 describes an unusually perceptive parent, it is also typical because parents have many opportunities to observe their preschoolers and consequently may detect early signs of learning problems.

ANECDOTE 3.7

Since the age of three years, Mrs. V suspected that something was different about Bryan. Although he was an only child, when he was three, his mother, a registered nurse, believed that he was much too active physically to be normal. The family physician in their small town tried to assure Mr. and Mrs. V that Bryan was simply "all boy" and would soon "outgrow" his hyperactivity.

Bryan was first seen at a county mental health facility when he was three and a half years old. His mother described his behavior as overly active; he was in constant motion all day. His evening meals with both parents present were impossible because Bryan could not or would not sit at the table for any reasonable amount of time. By bedtime, Bryan was physically exhausted as was his mother.

Although psychological testing could not be thorough due to Bryan's hyperactivity and age, the clinician estimated that he was of average intelligence. And because there were no known birth complications or accidents during infancy, treatment focused on Bryan's relationship with his parents.

Play therapy was provided for Bryan supplemented by parental counseling. Treatment and counseling, however, were terminated by the parents after only a few sessions. It seemed that Mr. and Mrs. V resented the implication that the father rejected Bryan and, because his birth was unplanned, he was therefore not wanted.

At the age of four years, eight months, Mrs. V brought Bryan to the Exceptional Children's Clinic at a major university requesting assistance.

Bryan's behavior was essentially as it had been earlier, except that his mother questioned his readiness for kindergarten. He was unable to maintain any attention while a story was read or told to him. His coloring and other paper-pencil activities were primitive, equivalent to a late two-year-old's. He displayed little ability to play with other children of his age. Often attempts to play resulted in Bryan's crying or the other children complaining about his physical contacts.

Mrs. V was trained to manage Bryan at home. Training sessions involved her bringing Bryan to the clinic where she and he were trained together. Through the systematic use of a kitchen timer, Bryan was taught to sit for increasingly longer periods of time at the dinner table without being disruptive. In addition, many other management tactics were taught to Mrs. V.

The parents were also referred to a competent pediatrician, one who was knowledgeable about learning disabled children. Medication was prescribed and for some time, approximately 18 months, Bryan took this drug.

While the school district in which Bryan resided had limited services for learning disordered children, he was provided with a sensitive kindergarten teacher. Initially, he attended kindergarten for only an hour. But by the end of the year he often was able to spend the entire morning there.

___

Many parents are not as persistent as was Bryan's mother, but they often can identify problems which their children display at home and in the neighborhood. Information regarding learning and behavioral problems of children should be disseminated through newspapers and other media and as a regular part of parent teacher group meetings. As parents become sensitized to observable characteristics which suggest maladaptive behavior and learning problems, more referrals for assistance will emanate from them.

Oberst (1973) described a community approach to learning disabilities. The program included a component for publicizing the problems of children who have learning disorders. A program of this type can encourage parents to be more aware of their childrens' learning problems and to seek assistance for them.

Parents of children with learning and behavioral problems are often in need of counseling in order to deal with their attitudes and concerns toward their handicapped child. Wetter (1972) found that mothers and fathers of learning disabled children demonstrated a greater disagreement between themselves when judging their child's overall adjustment than did parents of children who did not present learning disorders. Since there was a greater disagreement among the experimental group's opinion of the child's adjustment than among the control group, he concluded that parents' attitudes toward their learning disabled children are distinctive. It is also likely that disagreements between parents are generated by their children's handicapping conditions. Because of the likelihood of differences in attitude between mothers and fathers of learning disordered children, school services are needed for aiding these parents.

Parents sometimes hesitate to seek help from school personnel. Reasons for their hesitation are probably related to several factors. First, parents may feel that the school will evaluate them and their children unfairly if their problems and concerns are revealed to them. In this instance, the school is not viewed as a helping agency. Rather, it is seen as a place where parents and their children will be punished because of their limitations.

Second, parents may feel that the school will violate the confidentiality of the information. When parents have little confidence in the schools, they tend to suspect that the information will be misused or otherwise be used to ridicule them. Or if they have knowledge that teachers and other school personnel have discussed, on occasions, confidential information with unauthorized individuals, they will have good reason to believe that their confidentiality will be violated.

Third, parents may have no confidence in the school's capacity to be helpful. In this instance, they believe that school personnel are not competent to alleviate their children's problems or that the school system is incapable of dealing with atypical problems.

Students may help to identify those in need of services. While they may not serve as referral sources, peers have been effective in screening procedures. Bower (1969) includes the peer group in the process, which he and Lambert (1967) developed, for in-school screening of children with emotional handicaps.

Observant teachers can identify students who are in need of special assistance by noting interactions among the peer groups. Children who are frequently chosen last for competitive games, those who have few friends, those who are bullies, or are easily bullied, those who are often reported for copying the work of others, those who are often accused of stealing, lying, cheating, or other norm-violating conduct are excellent prospects for more careful study.

A system for placing students should include mechanisms for protecting children's legal rights. Dauterman and Ambrose (1974) discussed the legal aspects of special education placement. They advocated open parent-school discussions in order to meet the legal requirements of knowledge of consent. That is, in order for parents to give their consent for testing and placing children, they must have accurate information concerning the nature of the service. In addition, they should be informed concerning the possible implications special placement may have on the pupil's future educational alternatives, such as school placement following special assistance and the effects on school promotions.

Due Process and Confidentiality of Information

Special education services are provided to students after careful screening, assessment, and conferences with parents. Throughout the processes of identification, placement, and follow-up, it is essential that the students' and parents' rights be guarded. Following due process procedures is one way to protect their rights. Another safeguard must be provided by protecting the confidentiality of students' records.

Legal and Ethical Considerations

Placement practices in special education have come under scrutiny in recent years. Woody (1974) presented the legal aspects of mental retardation. Drawing heavily upon laws affecting the emotionally disturbed, he emphasized the importance of due process in protecting both the individual and society.

In at least two instances, courts have required that placement in classes for the handicapped be preceded by a formal due process hearing if parents oppose the placement. Some states have legislated similar requirements (Kirp, Kuriloff, & Buss, 1975).

While the legal issues are yet unclear, ethical considerations are easier to specify.

1. Parents should be contacted prior to formal assessment;
2. Parents should be provided with an accurate description of the problem;
3. Parents should be informed about placement procedures and advised as to the placement options;
4. Written parental permission should be obtained prior to psychological examinations;
5. Parents should be provided with accurate information concerning test results;
6. Parents should be advised as to placement recommendations; and
7. Written parental permission should be obtained prior to special placement.

It is important that school personnel monitor the progress of pupils in special programs. Ethically, if students are not profiting from special placement, parents should be notified and involved in determining if the placement should be changed.

Anecdote 3.8 describes the due process procedures followed by one school district in helping Billy, a nine-year-old, behaviorally disruptive child.

Billy is a nine-year-old fourth grader. His classroom behavior is described by Miss Kling, the teacher, as defiant, disruptive, and generally not in keeping with her expectations. He has physically attacked classmates on the playground, in the cafeteria, and in the classroom. Seemingly with little provocation, he loses his temper. He recently told his teacher to "go to hell" when she ordered him to quit annoying a female classmate.

Billy's school work has steadily deteriorated this year to the point where he is failing most subjects. His teacher has difficulty gaining his cooperation, and he appears to have trouble concentrating on school tasks.

In April, the building principal, Ms. Fort, referred Billy for psychological services. Her request had been preceded by two conferences with Billy's parents. At the first conference, Miss Kling and Ms. Fort discussed their concerns regarding his school adjustment problems. His parents expressed worry about the general deterioration of his behavior at home. And they could not identify any recent stresses in the home which might have precipitated his difficulties.

At the second conference, Billy's parents reported a further decline in his behavior and expressed concern that, as the eldest of three children, he might be setting a poor example for the others, ages six and eight. Ms. Fort described the various programs available within the school system for which Billy might be eligible. She further indicated that in order for Billy to be considered for any of these services, he must be examined and observed by a school psychologist. The parents consented to a request for psychological services, signing the necessary permission forms, a copy of which was given to them.

After Mr. Rodriquez, the school psychologist, examined and observed Billy in various settings at school, Ms. Fort called Billy's parents to invite them to a conference with him. Since Billy's father was unable to leave his job as a bookkeeper in a small business, his mother attended the conference alone.

Test results and observations were interpreted to the mother by Mr. Rodriquez. With her permission, Billy's case was referred to the special education team for review. The possible services for which Billy may be eligible were again described. At this point, Billy's mother requested that he not be placed in a special school. She was willing to have him placed elsewhere including a special class in a nearby school if necessary.

After reviewing Billy's case and the parents' wishes, the special education team made the following decisions:
1. that Billy be placed in a special class in a nearby elementary school beginning the following September,
2. that Mr. Rodriquez be assigned to monitor Billy's progress and make a report to the team by January of the next school year.
3. that Thelma Robinson, the parent trainer, invite Billy's parents to attend the parent training program scheduled to begin in two weeks.

It should be noted in anecdote 3.8 that Billy's parents were given information as to his problems and concerning those programs for which he might be eligible. Permission was sought and obtained for testing and placing Billy. Had his condition been serious enough to require special school placement, the parents would have been so informed and given a right to appeal the placement before a review panel. They could, if they desired, bring legal counsel with them. Also, if the parents refused to attend the training sessions and if Billy's behavior appeared to be due to parental negligence, school personnel could file child neglect charges against them.

Mechanisms for assuring students and their parents due process should not be used as excuses for school personnel to abrogate their responsibilities. In most states, placement provisions and services which are in the best interest of the pupil may be provided even over parental objections if due process procedures have been followed.

Federal Requirements[5]

Public Law 94-142 expands the provisions of Public Law 93-380, known as the *Education for All Handicapped Act.* Provisions in both acts include areas that must be incorporated into a state plan to be approved by the U.S. Office of Education, Bureau of Education for the Handicapped.

Each state's plan must cover at least seven areas: (1) full educational opportunities, (2) procedural safeguards, (3) placement of children in the least restrictive alternative, (4) nondiscriminatory testing, (5) conformance with the *Family Educational Rights and Privacy Act,* (6) the development of an educational plan for each handicapped student, and (7) the state must develop an advisory council to consider present programs, program revisions, funding and state legislation in behalf of the education of handicapped children.

Full educational opportunities means that every handicapped child regardless of place of residence and nature or severity of handicap will receive an appropriate educational program. Highest priorities must be given to children presently receiving no educational services, those receiving some education but no special education services, and handicapped children who are receiving inappropriate or inadequate special education services.

Provisions for *procedural safeguards* cover six areas: (1) parents of each handicapped child must be notified whenever individual evaluation, placement, or change in educational program is scheduled for the child; notification must be by certified mail or a visitation to the home and signed consent or other means that can be documented; (2) due process procedures will be initiated whenever the parent or school believes that agreement between the home and school cannot be reached; (3) hearings in a due process procedure must be initiated before an impartial hearing officer and testimony and examination of witnesses must be documented by a recorded and/or typed transcript; (4) decisions of hearing officers will be final with appropriate appeal procedures to the state superintendent and board of education with subsequent appeals to the courts; (5) parents may seek an independent evaluation of their child, costs to be borne by them; and (6) surrogate parents will be appointed to serve children who have no parents or legal guardians.

Programs must be designed and developed to ensure that each child is educated in the *least restrictive alternative.* This provision requires that handicapped children be placed in as close to a regular class setting as their performances permit. Whenever possible, special education services are to be conducted within regular classrooms.

Nondiscriminatory testing means that children will be evaluated with instruments that are normed to their culture and/or socioeconomic backgrounds. Testing must be conducted in the child's primary language.

When selecting students for testing or for informal assessment and observation, advanced written permission from the parents must be obtained. The letter requesting permission should:

---

5. Thomas O. Iles, Assistant Director of Special Education, West Virginia State Department of Education, provided substantial assistance to the author in writing this section.

1. state the reasons for requesting the evaluation;
2. name the person who initiated the request;
3. contain a statement indicating the right of the parents or students to refuse the evaluation;
4. indicate that the school can request a hearing in order to obtain approval to conduct the evaluation;
5. state that parents have the right to review all relevant records concerning their child;
6. indicate that the parents will be fully informed as to the results of the evaluation;
7. declare that their child's educational status will not be changed without the knowledge and written approval of the parent or, failing that, until the notice and due process procedures have been exhausted.

By following the above procedures, school personnel may safeguard the rights of students as well as involve parents in important educational decisions.

Confidentiality of Records

Programs for L&BD children require the maintenance of accurate and current records. Decisions regarding identification, placement, and referral to other agencies are based upon recorded information. All school districts should have written policies concerning record keeping which conform to legal and ethical practices in order to keep such information confidential.

Due process procedures include both maintaining the confidentiality of records and making *all* records of children available to their parents or guardians (Teitelbaum, 1973). Yet, as recently as 1970, only 46 school districts of 160 districts surveyed had a written policy defining the maintenance and release of student information (Barone, 1971). In the past, parents have been refused access to their children's records while at the same time officials have opened these same records to others both inside and outside the school (Goslin & Bordier, 1970).

Suggested Policies and Procedures

Policies and procedures for record keeping are applicable, of course, for all children in schools. While the discussion here relates only to L&BD children, it may be useful in developing policies and procedures for all school children.

Informed consent is a principle to be followed. This involves collecting only that information about which parents and students have been informed and to which the parents have consented. Parents and, when feasible, children should know which information will be collected and where it will be deposited.

Procedures should be established for verifying the accuracy of all information in records. These procedures should also include guidelines for periodically destroying that information which is no longer needed.

Parents should have full access to all information regarding their children. They should also have the right to challenge the accuracy of that information.

No agency or persons other than the parent or school personnel who deal directly with the student should have access to that pupil's file without written parental permission.

Written procedures should be established by school districts to ensure the confidentiality of student records. These procedures should ensure that:

1. all records be maintained in a central location,
2. any authorized personnel wishing to examine such records must do so on school property and that the records be signed in and out by that person.
3. copies of records only be made after authorized, written approval by the parents,
4. copies of records or information from records only be forwarded to other agencies upon written approval from the parents,
5. a system for destroying records be established. This system should include a schedule and methods by which records are to be destroyed.

Summary

Any consideration of educational provisions should be accompanied by legal and ethical practices which assure children and their parents that their rights will be protected. Educational arrangements for L&BD students include: regular class placement with special services, teacher consultations, tutoring, resource rooms, special classes, special day schools, and residential schools.

Screening and identifying students in need of help are two necessary procedures prior to placement. Following placement, instruction is implemented and monitoring of student progress is maintained.

Practices to ensure due process for students include early notification of parents regarding observation and testing, involvement of them in placement options, and providing them with all necessary information concerning their children's performance.

When returning students to regular programs, due process procedures should also be followed. In addition to making placement decisions on the basis of performance factors, students and parents should be helped to adjust to changes in placement, and phasing into new situations should be a common practice.

Record keeping should include a system of confidentiality and written policies and procedures for maintaining and discarding student files.

4

Instruction and Curriculum for L&BD Students

This chapter is concerned with instruction and how it relates to what should be taught to L&BD students. Among the points emphasized are:

1. L&BD students need to acquire the same academic and social skills and concepts as those required of regular students.
2. Authorities are not in agreement as to how best to teach L&BD students. Disagreements concerning methods are rooted in theories concerning causes of learning dysfunctions and appropriate treatments.
3. Teaching methods affect curriculum often in terms of content emphasis.
4. Questions concerning curriculum for L&BD students relate to those assumptions upon which instruction is based, the issue of performance deficits as opposed to attempting to correct underlying problems, treating deficits or focusing on performance, and the quest for special teaching methods.
5. Academic skills include two major groupings: motor performance and language facility.
6. Concepts, general classes of ideas, are a part of academic and social learning.
7. Thinking processes should also be taught. These include labeling, organizing, inferring, and generalizing.
8. Social skills and attitudes consist of school-related behaviors and those necessary for adjusting in other settings.

Introduction

Social expectations for L&BD students dictate the type of curriculum they need. Their educational goals are essentially the same as those for nonhandicapped children since all students are expected to live in an economically competitive society and to adjust within our social system. In addition to economic demands which are ultimately placed upon most adults, citizenship responsibilities have become increasingly important in our crowded, highly technological society.

Schools in a democracy are expected to perform several important functions. They are supposed to transmit the cultural heritage, help civilize the young, develop academic skills, shape social attitudes, foster ideas, and provide worthwhile environments for those too young to work. And as other institutions in our society such as the family and the church become less influential, schools may find it necessary to assume additional responsibilities, such as teaching social values and behaviors.

Although authorities generally agree that L&BD students need to acquire the same basic academic and social skills and concepts as do other students, there appear to be differences of opinion concerning (1) how to teach L&BD students and (2) what constitutes prerequisite competencies for acquiring advanced skills and concepts. Curriculum is the main focus in this chapter and, consequently, the second of these two issues is an integral part of the present discussion. However, teaching methodology influences and shapes content in at least four ways. First, methods help determine if the content will tend to be more general or specific. For example, those methods concerned with learning processes, such as perceptual approaches, tend to be less task-specific and more general. For example, in an ability training model teachers may focus on activities for improving memory by using exercises that contain digits and/or nonsense words. Or in instances where meaningful content is used, the content is not necessarily specific to the outcome (evaluation) measures. For example, students may be encouraged to walk a balance beam in order to improve their motor development, or, so as to improve their verbal expression, they may be asked to relate recent events. Since in these examples the performance outcomes are general, the activities (content) cannot be specific to the outcomes.

Second, methods may help generalize learning, or may interfere with transferring learning to other settings. Task-specific approaches, for example, which do not provide training in a variety of formats may tend to inhibit the use of skills in different circumstances. A typical way in which generalizing and transferring of learning can and cannot be aided is described in anecdote 4.1.

ANECDOTE 4.1

In seatwork assignments, Mary does well in converting fractions to decimals, e.g.:

$$\frac{64}{100} = .64$$

But when asked what percentage of the class is absent, she does not know how to answer the question.

In order to help Mary transfer this computational skill to practical applications, Ms. Howard, the teacher, did the following:

1. She taught Mary to consider which factors are necessary for calculating any percentages.
2. She assigned seatwork problems within the context of practical applications.
3. She had Mary develop practical application problems.
4. She assigned Mary the task of explaining when calculating percentages might be useful at home, such as when determining which percentage of the budget is used for food.

Third, the teaching method may tend to emphasize one content area to the exclusion or neglect of others. For example, Barsch (1965) believes that movement is the basis for learning and, consequently, tends to exclude language experiences from his Movigenic curriculum.

Fourth, a teaching method may be used for treatment per se rather than to facilitate content acquisition. For example, methods that are corrective, in the sense that they attempt to remediate etiological factors of long-standing duration (such as psychological problems), use content for treatment purposes rather than for acquisition. Stories may be used as bibliotherapy rather than for their own value or for acquisition of reading comprehension skills.

Teaching methods and curriculum are separate areas in instruction, although each influences the other. Methods represent the *how*. These are instructional approaches. Curriculum, however, is the *what* — the content to be taught. Since each affects the other, some gaps in academic and social learning may be a function of inadequate curriculum or inappropriate methodology rather than students' handicapping conditions.

Special Education Curricular Issues

Programs for learning disabled (LD) students have varied considerably as to content. Much of this variance can be attributed to differences in theory regarding causes of disabilities and to teaching methods arising from the various theories. Similarly, behaviorally disordered (BD) students have experienced wide differences among their school programs for essentially the same reasons. When the two handicapped groups are combined into an L&BD cluster, the basic issues in terms of curriculum are not compounded but remain basically the same. Questions surrounding curriculum for L&BD students include:

1. What are the assumptions upon which the instructional approaches and content are based?
2. Should the instructional focus be on immediate, short-term functioning, or should it emphasize those factors underlying the dysfunctionality?
3. Should performance problems be treated directly, or should current performance be viewed as a point of departure for instruction?
4. Are there distinct methods of instruction and different curricula for LD and BD students which justify separate programs?

What are the assumptions concerning the relationship between curriculum and subsequent instruction?

Numerous assumptions underly all instructional approaches. These may relate to rationales for emphasizing a given content area or for valuing one set of skills over others. In particular, assumptions abound when considering remedial or corrective instruction. Remedial teaching relies upon certain notions concerning students' deficit performances as well as attributing particular effects to selected teaching approaches. Because of the widespread, often unthinking acceptance of remedial instruction, there are few published criticisms of remedial approaches in special education.

Quay (1973), in one of the few critiques, discussed those assumptions, techniques, and evaluative criteria which have formed the basis for three types of remedial approaches to the same observable educational handicaps. He noted that, in some instances, approaches are incompatible. And he pointed out the great range of variability among the evaluative criteria when measuring the effects of remediation. Three types of strategies were identified.

Type 1 strategies involve activities which are expected to result in behavior change at some future time. He cited as examples the use of gross motor training to produce improved reading at a later time, or situations where psychotherapy provided at one point in time is expected to improve achievement in future years. In type 1 strategies, the exact ways in which change is expected to occur are never fully or rationally explained.

Type 2 approaches are also expected to result in future change in performance. The difference between the two approaches, however, is that type 2 activities are at least logically related to the expected terminal behavior. Examples provided by Quay in describing type 2 strategies include:

> teaching form discrimination in order to improve reading performance,
> teaching sound blending,
> attention training, and
> "... most all perceptual discrimination training programs . . ." (Quay, 1973).

Type 3 techniques involve direct instruction of either the terminal behavior or its close antecedents. While the instruction may be sequenced, each activity is a direct part of the terminal behavior. Quay described type 3 characteristics:

> each activity is an actual part of the terminal behavior,
> there is no attempt to correct deficiencies which are not directly related to the required performances, and
> the ameliorating of prior adverse experiences is not considered necessary.

In summarizing the three types, several points are important. *Type 1* strategies generally have weak empirical and theoretical links between specific activities and desired instructional outcomes. Consequently, there is little reason for continuing to practice Type 1 activities. *Type 2* approaches are worthy of consideration where the activity is clearly a precursor of the terminal behavior. But where the activity is only "test-related," with weak relationships to the outcome behavior, little consideration of this type should be given. *Type 3* activities should always be considered first as teaching approaches, only to be discarded when proven ineffective.

It is important to note that an activity varies as to type depending upon the desired terminal behaviors. Anecdote 4.2 attempts to clarify the differences among the three types.

ANECDOTE 4.2

Fred S. has been in a special class program for three years, having been diagnosed as "learning disabled with emotional problems" during his first year in school, at the age of six.

Type 1   Example

During his first year in special class, the teacher, Ms. Wink, had noted that Fred demonstrated poor gross motor skills, and she related this observation to his inability to read. Her consultant, being of the type 1 persuasion, reinforced Ms. Wink's belief that Fred's reading failure was due to "poor visual-motor skills." Ms. Wink was encouraged to use a new product which consisted of various sizes of bean bags accompanied by other apparatus. These materials enabled Fred to shoot the bags into the air and to practice catching the bags in the classroom. In addition to catching skills, Ms. Wink arranged various other activities which required Fred to use gross motor skills for much of the school day.

Type 2 Example

Mrs. Green was Fred's teacher during his second year in special class. Mrs. Green noted Fred's continued lack of reading progress and discovered, while reading Ms. Wink's report, that he had experienced an intensive gross motor training program. Both she and the new consultant agreed that a "prescriptive teaching approach" should be taken with Fred.

After administering a test of visual-perceptual performance, Mrs. Green set out to use the training material materials which accompanied the test as a part of Fred's reading program.

Type 3 Example

In March of his second year in special class, Fred demonstrated only a modest gain in beginning reading. His ability to draw forms and to catch bean bags had, however, improved somewhat more than his reading. Mrs. Green, concerned about Fred's poor progress in reading and his failure to participate in baseball at recess because of his poor performance in fielding and hitting, decided to take a more direct instructional approach. The course which she had just completed at the local university included several readings which described very direct instruction to performance problems. Here is a strategy Mrs. Green used to teach Fred a reading skill:

Skill: To use the letter sounds *a, i, n, p, t, m* in reading words

Materials: Letter cards *a, i, n, p, t, m*
A card for each word, with a captioned picture on reverse side.
Come in. (someone greeting a child at a door)
I see an ant. (an ant)
Look at the pin. (a pin)
See the pan. (a pan)
Sam takes a nap. (Sam napping)
The dog can nip the man. (Nip nipping a milkman)
This is a ball. Look at it. (a ball)
Sam can pat a cat. (Sam patting Tab)
See this tin can? (a tin can)

Procedure: (What Mrs. Green does)
1. Review letter sounds. Present each word as combined letter sounds.
2. When each word is taught, read the sentence on the card's reverse side, letting the child read the new word.
3. Build tin, pin from "in"; pan from "an"; turn nip and nap around to spell pin, pan. Build pat from "at."
4. Show 10 words, one at a time for child to read. Use pictures on reverse side as cues; cover initial consonant in tin, pin, pat, pan to help child if he hesitates.

Activity: (What Fred does)
1. Gives sound for each letter.
2. Reads the "new" word in each sentence as teacher reads sentences, pausing for him to supply the word.
3. Reads new words as they are built, or are made by "turning around" another word.
4. Reads words from flashcards, practicing with cues until cues are no longer needed.

Here is a teaching strategy used to teach Fred to catch a baseball:

Skill: To catch a baseball when thrown from 30 feet away

Materials: A fielder's glove
          A baseball
          A sixth-grade boy
          The playground

Procedure and Activity:
For 15 minutes daily, an older student will play catch with Fred. The student will be instructed how far to stand away from Fred and to begin by throwing "easy to catch" balls. Later a variety of fielding situations will be practiced.

As can be seen in anecdote 4.2, when considering the three types of approaches, activities may be relative to a particular type depending upon the expected outcomes. For example, bean bag catching would be a Type 3 activity if the terminal behavior were to catch bean bags or it might serve as a subtask to catching baseballs. But it is a Type 1 activity when its outcome is to improve reading performance by developing visual-motor skills.

Should the instructional focus be on the immediate short-term functioning?
Or should it emphasize those factors underlying the dysfunctionality?

Curricula tend to include activities such as perceptual training and various forms of psychotherapy when concerns center around underlying factors for poor performance or for maladaptive behavior. Perceptual training seemingly is viewed as essential for those children possessing academic deficits. Psychotherapy is often used when problems are considered to be rooted in attitudinal or emotional difficulties.

Perceptual Training

Perceptual problems have long been viewed as an integral part of many LD students' difficulties. Similarly, distorted interpretations of events and others' behaviors have often been associated with problems of behavioral disturbance. With the latter, maladaptive social behavior has sometimes been attributed to, or concomitant with, a distortion of reality, while LD students have been believed to have problems integrating sensory stimuli.

In particular, much attention has been given to developing visual-perceptual skills among LD populations. There are several approaches which emphasize perceptual development. Typically, these attempt to relate perception to visual-motor activities. Some of the advocates of training students in order to improve their visual-motor skills and one major publication of each are:

Barsch, R. H. *Achieving perceptual-motor efficiency.* Seattle: Special Child, 1967.
Delacato, C. H. *Neurological organization and reading.* Springfield, Illinois: Charles C. Thomas, 1966.
Frostig, M. *Movement education: Theory and practice.* Chicago: Follett, 1970.
Getman, G. *Pathway school program.* Boston: Teaching Resources, 1969.
Kephart, N. *The slow learner in the classroom* (2nd Ed.). Columbus: Charles E. Merrill, 1971.

There are, of course, differences among those advocating visual-motor training, ranging from those who view such training as a way to improve language-related performance to those who consider it as a means for improving visual-motor skills only. The first group assumes that visual-motor integration is a necessary condition for academic success. While in the second group, an assumption is made that these skills are improved through training. Both groups evidently believe that valid and reliable measures exist for determining students' visual-motor performances.

When reference is made to *visual perception,* measurement becomes even more complicated. Technically, perception is a cognitive process and is not observable, although its results may be measurable. Perception, as a function of the brain, involves integrating and interpreting stimuli as well as relating them to previous experiences. Unfortunately, *visual discrimination* is often used synonymously with *visual perception.* Discrimination is more easily measured, and its results are readily observed.

Some research evidence is available concerning the effects of training in visual perception. In an extensive discussion of the issue relating to training of visual perception, Hammill (1972) concluded that little correlation existed between measures of visual perception and tests of reading comprehension. He emphasized that current training programs purporting to train visual-perceptual skills have no positive effects on reading and little effect on visual perception. Less attention has been directed to other sensory areas. although auditory perceptual training has begun to emerge as a more commonly advocated practice than it was in the 1960s.

Empirical research[1] on the effects of perceptual training suggests that young children with learning disabilities sometimes make gains in visual perceptual skill development. But in such studies, when academic achievement measures are used, gains in visual-perceptual skills typically are not accompanied by gains in academic performance.

Falik (1969) studied the effects of perceptual-motor training on the beginning reading skills of normal kindergarten children. Those falling within the lower two-thirds of their group on a reading readiness test were randomly assigned to experimental or control groups. The groups were compared for readiness for reading at the end of the first year and reading achievement at the end of the second grade. No significant differences were found. It was suggested that training of perceptual-motor skills, for typical beginning readers, is of questionable value. Curriculum for perceptual-motor training followed that as advocated by Kephart (1960) including chalkboard training, sensory-motor training, training for ocular control, and form perception training. While the study contained only 42 children, its findings should caution general educators away from the notion that they will improve reading performance through a concerted visual-motor training approach.

Frostig's visual-perceptual program (Frostig & Horne, 1964) is often cited in association with teaching learning disabled students (Wallace & McLaughlin, 1975; Wallace & Kauffman, 1973; Hammill & Bartel, 1975; Gearheart, 1973; McCarthy & McCarthy, 1969). Yet only a limited number of empirical studies have been reported using the Frostig Visual-Perceptual Training Program. In a series of studies, Jacobs (1967, 1968) sought answers to these questions:

   1. Do children in pre-kindergarten, kindergarten, and grade one who take the Frostig program achieve better than controls on the *Frostig Visual-Perception Tests?* Is the benefit uniform among the grades tested?
   2. Do kindergarten "Frostig" children achieve higher on the *Metropolitan Reading*

---

1. In this context, *empirical research* refers to a research method using one or more comparison groups with control of appropriate variables.

Readiness Test at the end of their kindergarten year as compared to controls?

3. What is the predictive validity of the Frostig test as compared to the *Metropolitan Reading Readiness Test?*

4. Do Frostig trained children achieve better on reading tests as compared to controls?

5. Do children exposed to two years of the Frostig program achieve better on reading tests as compared to one year Frostig children and controls? That is, is there a cumulative effect due to Frostig involvement in reading achievement?

Results of his studies are provided in relation to each question.

1. The average difference between experimental subjects and controls revealed a significant difference in favor of the Frostig trained pupils. Jacobs (1968) concluded that the Frostig program does produce higher Frostig scores in comparison to controls with the largest gains occurring among first graders. He also found that pupils who take the Frostig program for two consecutive years achieve higher on the Frostig test compared to pupils who take the Frostig program for one year and who, in turn, achieve better than pupils who do not take the Frostig program in either grade.

2. Kindergarten pupils who take the Frostig program generally show higher Metropolitan Reading Readiness scores.

3. The Metropolitan tests seem to be better indicators of reading achievement than the Frostig tests.

4. There is little relationship between Frostig scores and reading achievement. It is apparent that high Frostig test performance is no guarantee of higher reading achievement.

5. The Frostig program does have a cumulative effect on Frostig test scores; the longer one is trained on the Frostig, the higher one's scores are on the Frostig test.

Jacobs concluded that pupils who take the Frostig program seem to have no particular advantage for future reading achievement. It appears that the Frostig program should be used if the terminal behavior is higher Frostig scores. But these higher scores do not contribute to higher reading achievement, according to Jacobs' studies.

Wiederholt and Hammill (1971) reported a study using the Frostig tests. They randomly assigned 170 inner-city kindergarten and first-grade pupils to experimental and control groups. They concluded that the use of the Frostig program as a supplement to readiness activities or as a means of facilitating the acquisition of reading and arithmetic skills is not warranted. They found that performance by non-perceptually handicapped pupils on the Frostig test was improved. But those in a perceptually handicapped group demonstrated no significant gains over the control group on the Frostig test.

Smith and Marx (1972) concluded that the Frostig test does not measure what it purports to measure, that it weakly correlates with IQ, and that it is unrelated to reading ability. Their findings raise serious questions concerning the test's validity. They used factor analysis to compare the test performances of 43 elementary school children who had been referred for educational assessment. All students were tested on the Frostig, *Wechsler Intelligence Scale for Children,* and a reading achievement measure. Their findings indicate that the Frostig measures a single general factor rather than discrete aspects of perception.

Black (1974) reported a study of the relationship between performance and visual-perceptual performance in LD children. With intelligence controlled, reading-test performance of the low perceivers was significantly higher than that of the high perceiver. No significant differences were found in spelling and arithmetic. The author concluded that the current practice of offering remedial instruction based upon the Frostig test is not supported by his results.

Other areas of perceptual training, in addition to visual-motor skills, are advocated by some authorities in the learning disabilities field. While each has curriculum implications, none is as prevalent as is visual-motor training. It appears that visual-motor perception is emphasized because an underlying assumption, for these approaches, is that visual-motor problems contribute to or cause academic learning problems. And unless these difficulties are corrected, students will continue to have trouble learning. To date, there is little evidence in support of this assumption.

Treating Underlying Problems of Behaviorally Disordered Students

Children labelled as behaviorally disordered (BD) are also typically exposed to special treatment presumably because their emotional problems are interfering with school performance and adjustment. But there is little evidence in support of that belief.

McNeil (1969) noted that two major theories have influenced the education of BD students. One is learning theory (by which he seemingly meant behavioral practices) and the other is what he referred to as "psychodynamic theory." He maintained that neither approach used instructional materials in other than ordinary ways. His statement is questionable, however, since both orientations use materials in ways that are germane to certain assumptions concerning the causes of emotional problems. The various forms of psychotherapy, for example, rely upon the notion that certain approaches and content will facilitate or interfere with emotional development.

In the following discussion, some forms of psychotherapy are considered. As may be noted, these practices differ depending upon assumptions concerning the nature of emotional problems and the needed corrective treatment. Behavioral approaches are discussed extensively in chapters 10 and 12.

Psychotherapy. In this discussion, *psychotherapy* refers to any approach dealing with the emotional states of students as a primary function of academic and social learning. When psychotherapy is provided in order to facilitate school learning, it is assumed that emotional problems are interfering with school learning. Such beliefs are widespread, particularly among teachers of disruptive and inhibited students. While psychotherapy may also be provided as an adjunct to schooling, the use of it for that purpose is not considered in this discussion, though it is discussed in chapter 11. Of concern here are those practices which assume that emotional problems must be resolved prior to expecting improved academic functioning and those situations where psychotherapy is an integral part of the instructional program.

Perhaps advocates of psychodynamic interventions in school learning are the major proponents of the need to resolve emotional conflicts in order to facilitate learning. Cheney and Morse (1973) categorized, what they termed, *milieu intervention* as intervention through reality interpretation, expressive therapeutic interventions, and interventions by facilitating the identification processes.

Reality interpretations have been advocated by Redl (1959) and Glasser (1965). Their themes are based upon the belief that outside conflicts result from individuals' interpretations and motivations. *Life Space Interviewing* (Redl, 1959) is based on the belief that an individual's life space may be filled with cues which are too suggestive. According to this view, teachers should try to arrange students' outer worlds in ways that facilitate coping with their environments.

Glasser (1965) starts with outside conflicts in his *Reality Interviewing* and relates these to the inner-motivations of students. He views school failure as a source of many conflicts (Glasser, 1969). School failure is due to a lack of "caring" by teachers. According to Glasser, teachers of BD children should value emotional change as more important than academic performance.

Expressive interventions are rooted in the belief that catharsis (expressing strong feelings) is therapeutic. Many school practices, for both normal and disturbed children, are based upon the cathartic assumption. Play therapy, verbal catharsis, music, art, and role playing have all been used as ways to express unacceptable feelings. These practices are related to psychodynamic theory which holds that externalizing feelings and conflicts results in socially productive behavior and cleanses the individual of guilt and other unhealthy feelings (Kessler, 1966).

Interventions for improving identification are based upon the belief that BD children need to identify with certain role models. "School-Mom" programs (Donahue & Nichtern, 1965), where children have opportunities to relate to warm, affectionate mothers, represent one practice derived from the identification notion. Another, filial therapy, (Andronico & Guerney, 1967) teaches parents how to conduct nondirective play therapy with their children.

In classrooms BD children are sometimes assigned to particular teachers because they are in need of certain types of male or female models. This type of therapy often encourages the use of school volunteers to function as tutors or teacher aides or to otherwise perform services.

Almost all of the teaching practices derived from psychotherapy involve special techniques. Each activity consumes part of the school day and in that sense it is a part of the curriculum.

Bibliotherapy (Schulthesis, 1973), psychodrama (Moreno, 1946), values clarification (Raths, Harmin, & Simon, 1966), and other methods for learning through imitation and/or suggestion often include the use of special materials in the form of stories, plays, and skits. Shaftel and Shaftel (1967) have proposed the use of role-playing as a method for improving values as a part of the teaching of social studies. They have suggested special themes and plays for that purpose.

Should performance deficits be treated as such? Or should current performance be viewed as a point of departure for instruction?

Concepts concerned with deficit functioning are common in special education. L&BD students are typically identified as needing special assistance on the basis of shortcomings in relation to what is typical or normal for their age/grade peers. At the observable or descriptive level, deficit performances can be detected as described in anecdote 4.3.

ANECDOTE 4.3

1. Academic deficits from test scores
   During the second month of Michael's sixth year in school, his class was administered the *Stanford Achievement Test,* Intermediate II, Complete Battery. His grade scores by subtests were as follows:

   Word Meaning   4.9

Paragraph Meaning	4.1
Spelling	3.0
Language	3.9
Arithmetic Computation	6.3
Arithmetic Concepts	5.2
Arithmetic Application	6.5
Social Studies	4.6
Science	4.3

Since Michael has consistently tested within the average range of intelligence on group IQ tests and his current grade placement is 6.2, it has been determined, based on the above test scores, that he has serious performance deficits in reading, spelling, language, social studies, and science areas. He is achieving as expected in arithmetic computation and is one year behind in arithmetic concepts.

2. Academic deficits from observations

Ms. Vulcain noted that eight-year-old Jill's oral expression was confusing. She tended to mispronounce common words and often misnamed common objects and things, such as referring to cows as horses and plants as trees. Ms. Vulcain further observed that Jill's speech was immature, being considerably inferior to that of other eight-year-olds.

From these observations, the teacher concluded that Jill had serious deficits in oral language and concept formation.

3. Social behavior deficit

Twelve-year-old Mildred refuses to speak in class. When called upon, she will not respond. Her teacher has discussed this problem with Mildred and indicated that she has a "terrible fear" of speaking in a group. The problem is of recent origin since her last year's teacher indicated that, while Mildred was always somewhat reserved, she did speak when called upon in class.

As a result of the above information, observations of in-class behavior, and interviewing of Mildred, the school psychologist has concluded that Mildred has developed fears which are related to physiological changes. In this sense, she has a personality deficit.

Some practices, however, identify deficit performances and attempt to relate these to hypothetical or inferential causes. Zach and Kaufman (1972) discussed an aspect of one such attempt. They found that many kindergarten children, from a group of 70, were able to discriminate designs well but performed poorly on the *Bender Visual Motor Gestalt Test*. Conversely, they found others who did well on the Bender but discriminated poorly. They concluded that it was a questionable practice to diagnose children as having perceptual problems on the basis of scores on the Bender. The practice of subjecting these same children to a training program in visual discrimination was criticized as well.

Some of the assumptions which practitioners accept when using the concept of deficit functioning are:

1. The measures used to determine performance are valid and reliable.

2. The standards or norms established as the expected performance are valid and reliable.

3. Teaching will rectify the deficits.

4. Correcting the deficits will improve students' performances.

In practice, these assumptions are not always met. For example, Zach and Kaufman's (1972) findings suggest that the Bender failed to meet those assumptions regarding validity and reliability of measures and norms. Depending on what is being taught, assumptions 3 and 4 are not easily met. For example, as indicated previously in this chapter, if in using the Frostig program one's purpose is to improve performance on the Frostig test, assumption 3 will probably be met. However, if the goal is to improve reading performance through the use of the Frostig Training Program, more often than not assumption 4 will not be met.

Teaching may begin with the assumption that L&BD students possess no social or academic performance deficits, and that their functioning is normal for them at that time. While this is not a commonly accepted concept regarding L&BD students, features of it have been advocated by both special and general educators.

Bloom (1968) formulated a rationale for mastery learning for all students. He began with these assumptions:

> Over 90% of students can master what is taught;
>
> It is essential to define what is meant by mastery and to identify methods and materials for students to achieve mastery;
>
> Because the United States is highly developed and demands a sophisticated level of performance among its citizenry, completion of secondary and advanced education can no longer be for only the few;
>
> If quality and rate of instruction are related to learner characteristics, the majority of students will achieve subject mastery.

Many special educators, however, would emphasize that Bloom is referring to nonhandicapped students, though some who advocate skill training tend to emphasize a nondeficit approach to teaching L&BD students. For example, in Directive Teaching (Stephens, 1976) L&BD students are taught those skills that have the prerequisite responses within their repertoires. When they achieve mastery, they proceed to higher order tasks.

A nondeficit approach to L&BD students is also predicated upon several assumptions. Among these are:

1. Given enough time and sound instruction, students will learn what is taught.

2. Social and academic skills can be sequenced in a hierarchy from simple to complex.

3. Defective processing and inadequate abilities do not prevent the acquisition of performance skills.

4. Technology is currently available for identifying where students are on a continuum of performance skills and for teaching the specific responses needed to master each skill.

5. Parents, teachers, and other interested parties are amenable to changing their beliefs concerning poor academic performance and undesirable behavior.

The first assumption does not mean that anyone can learn anything regardless of prerequisite skills and abilities. It does imply, however, that sound instruction includes a wise choice of tasks for teaching students. By matching students' responses to task requirements, learning will occur, given sufficient time and incentives.

Assumption 2 does not imply the existence of a natural hierarchy of skills. It does require, however, sequencing of tasks in such a way that prerequisite responses precede higher order skills. This notion of task analysis is relatively new to education and requires retraining of teachers and other school personnel.

Assumption 3 may be the most contested of the five. Deficit-oriented approaches assume that defective processing of stimuli and problems in other ability areas must be improved so that academic skills can be acquired. In this sense, those abilities are considered to be prerequisites for academic achievement.

Nondeficit approaches may accept the validity of measures of perception and other abilities while maintaining their unimportance for academic achievement. By beginning with the tasks to be mastered and analyzing those tasks as to each response to be acquired, nondeficit approaches teach those skills needed to perform any given task. It is around this assumption that advocates have disagreed, particularly with respect to teaching LD students.

Assumption 4 is evidently not considered to be an issue by many authorities as reflected by titles of their texts, e.g., Block, *Mastery Learning;* Lessinger, *Accountability in Education: Every Kid A Winner;* Mager, *Preparing Instructional Objectives;* Nagel and Richman, *Competency-Based Instruction: A Strategy To Eliminate Failure;* Popham and Baker, *Establishing Instructional Goals;* Stephens, *Implementing Behavioral Approaches in Elementary and Secondary Schools.*

Describing teaching technology, of course, provides no assurance that the technology is applicable or effective. An accumulation of research evidence using such techniques suggests that the necessary teaching technology is in fact available for developing a continuum of social and academic skills and for teaching those skills.

Assumption 5 may be the major barrier to a nondeficit approach to instruction. For decades, teachers and parents have been taught to believe that L&BD children possess deficits and that these must be corrected. Our culture seems to be imbued with the deficit notion: *find and correct the underlying causes.* This belief appears to be deeply rooted in contemporary American education. A nondeficit approach in special education requires major changes in understandings, attitudes, and practices of those adults who staff schools, their trainers, parents of students, as well as others who provide the financial and political support for special education.

Are there distinct methods of instruction and different curricula for LD and BD students which justify separate programs?

One thesis of this text is that, from an educational point of view, the instructional needs of mildly and moderately disturbed students are essentially the same as those who are termed *learning disabled.* Throughout the state of Ohio, this particular premise has been demonstrated. Programs in that state have been operational for serving students with moderate to severe learning problems (LD) and for those who are mildly to moderately behaviorally disturbed (BD). From all appearances, these programs appear to be effective, although, of course, the quality of programs varies widely from school to school.

It should be clearly noted that in this text the severely emotionally disturbed are excluded from the L&BD population. This very small population of school-aged children do require separate and special programs. They must often be provided total and continual care, including medical and other specialized treatment. For these reasons, instruction for such children often occurs in residential settings. However, mild to moderately handicapped students with learning and/or behavioral problems have been taught together while separated from normal students for portions of the school day.

Historically, separate school programs have been established for LD students and for BD students. Various beliefs have evolved in support of the necessity for distinguishing between the two groups. Rationales for separating LD students from BD students appear to include the following three factors:

1. *Etiological differences* — arguments along this line emphasize that the origins of the handicapping conditions are different and consequently instruction should be different.

2. *Differences in functioning* — children who have behavior problems do not necessarily have academic learning problems; similarly, learning disabled students do not always present behavioral problems. Consequently, instructional treatment should differ.

3. *Ancillary services* — the two groups require different kinds of supportive services. LD children are in need of adaptive physical educators, vision specialists, and remedial tutors. BD children often need psychological and social work services.

The above arguments fail to recognize the roles of teachers and schools as well as the fact that individualized instruction and services are needed regardless of the bases for grouping. As was noted in an earlier publication:

> Teachers instruct and manage children on the basis of overt manifestations. Therefore, they respond to the behavior of children, not to diagnostic labels or medical conditions. Those who teach children labelled as having *minimal brain dysfunction,* for example, typically begin by assessing each child's academic skills in order to establish individual instructional levels. If a child is easily distracted, the teacher attempts to control environmental stimuli as a means of reducing the child's hyperactivity. Similarly, children who are labelled *emotionally disturbed* are managed by teachers in an attempt to accommodate the children's behavior to the learning environment. Teachers would continue to be faced with diverse learning rates and variable behavior among children even if it were possible to classify and group them along clear disability lines. (Stephens, 1970, p. 3.)

Students who display extremely deviant behaviors should be identified and provided appropriate instruction and services. The differentiated treatment should not be based upon etiological factors but rather on functioning. Thus, those who display primitive emotions or autistic-like behavior should be treated in response to their low functioning. In this way, the range of academic and social skills to be taught is narrowed as individualized instruction is provided.

Since behaviorally disordered children are primarily characterized by social and emotional adjustment problems, a related issue is *how to change behavior.* When instruction is the primary means for changing behavior, an L&BD combination seems rational. When, however, problems are viewed as outside the purview of teaching, combining the two handicapping conditions seems irrational. Often such problems involve attitudes, social values, and social behavior.

Issues Regarding Teaching Social Values

Two fundamental issues are involved when considering the place of social values and behavior in the curriculum. The first is related to the efficacy of teaching such content. The second is concerned with the school's role in our society.

Effectiveness in teaching social behavior has been widely documented. It is known, for example, that information alone does not change behavior in any predictable ways. But when consequences are included for behaving in certain specified ways, then the behavior is far more predictable. Burgess, Clark, and Hendee (1971) demonstrated the effects of incentives for reducing littering. In their study, viewing an antilittering film resulted in no appreciable change in such behavior. But in one theater where a dime was used as an incentive, 94% of the litter was properly disposed of. And in another where theater tickets were used as rewards, 95% of litter was deposited in litter bags.

There are only a few published studies, however, that deal with the long-term effects of teaching social behavior using incentives. While this issue is an important consideration in another context, the major point here is that social behavior can be taught effectively using behavioral approaches.

Considerable controversy has always been associated with the school's role in our society. The issue, however, is philosophical rather than practical since social behavior and values are inevitably acquired through schooling. The question is whether or not these will be systematically taught or merely left to happenstance.

There is a logical need to teach social behaviors and values to L&BD students. Presumably such children are identified for special instruction due to maladaptive performance in either or both social and academic areas. Unless their performance is changed, they will continue to present difficulties. Consequently, programs that are to be responsive to L&BD children's needs must include instruction in social behavior.

Normal students appear, also, to need improved social behavior. The U.S. Senate subcommittee to investigate juvenile delinquency in the nation's elementary and secondary schools (1975) reported 70,000 serious physical assaults on teachers and hundreds of thousands of assaults on students. The committee found that extortion, drug, and prostitution rings are flourishing in suburban and urban schools. Of the 757 school districts surveyed, there were over 100 students murdered on school grounds during the 1973 calendar year.

Terkel (1972) interviewed typical working people. By their own accounts, many found their jobs and lives boring, and they described hostile feelings toward their jobs. Attitudes of this type, which appear to becoming more prevalent in our society, surely must have some implications for schools' curricula.

Academic Skills and Concepts

Most school curricula generally include, among other items, skills and concepts which are taught to students. Those skills and concepts relating to academic subject matter are discussed briefly in this section.

Academic Skills

Academic skills are complex responses to school tasks. In order for students to be successful in school, it is necessary for academic skills to be mastered so that they are performed with both ease and precision. Speaking, reading, writing, and the use of symbols are all language based. Some typical academic skills are adding two-place numerals, pronouncing words correctly, reading maps, spelling words, printing words, identifying the main idea in a paragraph, and writing one's name.

All academic skills are based upon prerequisite skills. These prerequisite skills must be within students' response repertoires if higher order skills are to be mastered. When students demonstrate difficulty performing a given skill, an analysis of their performance on prerequisite, lower order skills should be done, as Figure 4.1 indicates. The five steps in Figure 4.1 are applied in anecdote 4.4.

FIGURE 4.1. Steps for analyzing skill problems

Step 1:   Performance on a skill is inadequate.

Step 2:   Which responses are immediately below those required to use the skill?

Step 3:   Does student demonstrate those responses identified in step 2?

Step 4:   Teach those skills which were not demonstrated.

Step 5:   After student demonstrates mastery of the prerequisite skills, request that the original skill be demonstrated.

ANECDOTE 4.4

Task: Divide four-digit problems by two-digit problems

Problem: 43$\overline{)8815}$

Step 1:   *Student's performance is inadequate*

$$\begin{array}{r} 250 \\ 43\overline{)8815} \\ 86 \\ \hline 215 \\ 215 \\ \hline \end{array}$$

Step 2:   *Which responses are immediately below those required to use the skill?*
Knowing when to place a zero in the quotient.

Step 3:   *Does student demonstrate those responses identified in Step 2?*
After having the student do five different problems, it was found that three out of five times he incorrectly placed the zero.

Step 4:   *Teach those skills which were not demonstrated.*
Using problems where one digit is divided into three digits, the student is taught where to place zeros, e.g.,

2$\overline{)205}$

Then using problems where two digits are divided into four digits, the student is taught where to place zeros, e.g.

25$\overline{)2550}$

Step 5:   *After student demonstrates mastery of the prerequisite skills, request that the original skill be demonstrated.*
Five different problems, each requiring the use of a zero in its quotient are presented to the student. Each, also, consists of dividing four digits by two digits.

Motor Skills

Motor dexterity is well developed in normal six-year-olds entering first grade. Typical school beginners have already demonstrated the facility to use gross and fine motor skills. Many L&BD children have not mastered such skills by the time they enter school. This does not mean, however, that a heavy emphasis on motor training is warranted in the curriculum. It does suggest that motor skills, typically acquired at early ages, may need to be taught systematically as a part of the curriculum for L&BD students if those skills are essential for mastering school tasks.

Some of the motor skills which are immediate prerequisites to more advanced academic skills are control of eye movements, use of hands for grasping writing tools and proper manipulation of those tools, and good body balance and body posture.

There are several theories of learning involving motor development, some of which have curriculum suggestions and materials associated with them. In addition to Barsch's Movigenic theory (1965, 1967), other popular programs include Kephart's (1964), Getman's (1969), and Doman and Delacato's (Doman & Delacato, 1966).

This author questions the heavy emphasis placed upon motor training in the area of learning disabilities. The direct benefits to academic performance in any of the above motor training programs are questionable. Generally, it is a sound practice to teach motor skills as a part of a specific academic task, such as holding or using a pencil, rather than as a means for improving academic functioning in general.

Language Skills

Language facility is the basis for most academic learning. Skills requiring the use of language may be grouped into two major categories: speaking and prereading and decoding skills and concepts.

Speaking and prereading. Labeling, speaking, and writing are basic skill areas at the preschool and first-grade levels. Labeling consists of the use of language to differentiate various stimuli. Auditory and visual discrimination and language labeling are believed to be essential skills for reading and arithmetical reasoning.

Speaking is an essential means of communicating and the inability to use meaningful speech is a profound handicap for school-age children. L&BD children who have difficulties in verbal communication, when they do not use meaningful language or when they misuse basic words, are not uncommon. It is for this reason that speaking skills represent an important area of the curriculum for teachers of many L&BD children.

Writing is also an avenue of communicating. The use of writing symbols by students is a skill area which is routinely required in schools.

Decoding skills. Listening, reading, interpreting numbers and math symbols, and writing from dictation are all skills which require students to interpret or decode.

Schooling demands much listening. It serves as a way to learn new language labels as well as for obtaining information and directions for school tasks.

Reading is the primary mode for receiving information at advanced levels. It is perhaps the most essential skill for self-learning. Poor reading is one of the major performance problems of LD children. A heavy emphasis on reading skills, effectively taught, should be the hallmark of all programs for such children.

Another type of reading is that of interpreting numbers and math symbols. Correctly reading symbols is essential for mathematical reasoning. In addition, these skills have functional uses in daily living, e.g., telling time and making change.

Outlining and note-taking are important skills for taking dictation and when studying.

Concepts

Concepts are general classes of ideas that are related in some fashion. English and English (1958) define concepts as things one can think about as well as any object of awareness. Certainly, the formation of concepts represents the essence of schooling. Concepts are represented in school curricula, though teaching of concepts has not yet achieved the level of effectiveness as have skills.

Fortunately, most children acquire concepts through active interactions with their environments. L&BD students may need much more systematic instruction than their normal peers if they are to acquire many of the academically related concepts. Since the acquisition of many concepts comes through reading, children with reading problems have less chance to learn concepts through independent activities.

Some examples of academic concepts are value of numbers, place value, addition, subtraction, big, little, division, and the concept of government. Of course, there are thousands of concepts which students must learn if they are to be successful in school. A sampling of concepts and skills typically acquired through schooling are listed in Figure 4.2.

FIGURE 4.2.   Academically related skills and concepts

SPEAKING AND PREREADING
Labeling
  names common objects
  names body parts
  gives own name
  names real objects, e.g., apple
  names parts of objects, e.g., seeds
  names aspects of objects, e.g.,
    flavor
  names objects from pictures and
    models
  identifies words
  identifies letters and names
  names coins

Speaking
  responds to questions
  initiates conversations
  relates experiences
  tells stories from pictures
  uses appropriate greetings
  uses courtesy words

Writing
  uses pencil or crayon for drawing
  prints some letters and numbers
  prints own name
  prints some words

Number Concepts
  counts by rote to ten or more
  relates numbers to amounts
  selects a nickel as more than a
    penny
  selects a dime as more than a
    nickel

DECODING SKILLS AND
    CONCEPTS
Listening
  follows verbal directions and
    instructions
  relates listening experiences
  repeats verbal directions

Reading
  reads from left to right
  names all letters of alphabet
  matches lowercase letters with
    uppercase letters
  reads basic sight words
  uses word-attack skills to decode
    unfamiliar words
  reads sentences
  reads stories
  reads for information
  reads for pleasure
  follows written directions
  reads orally
  reads with inflection
  demonstrates meanings of
    punctuation symbols

Numbers and Math Symbols
  reads number symbols
  reads math symbols
  associates amounts with number
    symbols
  does simple addition
  does simple subtraction
  carries in addition
  borrows in subtraction
  does one-step problems
  does two-step problems

Writing from Dictation
  uses capitalizations correctly
  uses punctuation   correctly
  uses correct tense
  spells common words correctly
  forms letters and words legibly

ADVANCED SKILLS AND
    CONCEPTS
Reading
  uses reference skills
  reads maps, graphs, tables, and
    other illustrative devices
  uses study skills when reading
  reads newspapers, magazines,
    and other recreational matter
  scans and skims for selective
    reading
  draws inferences and conclusions
    from printed matter

Mathematics
  uses mathematical symbols
  adds, subtracts, multiplies, divides whole numbers
  adds, subtracts, multiplies, divides common fractions
  adds, subtracts, multiplies, divides decimal fractions
  changes decimals to percents
  changes common fractions to percents
  changes percents to decimals
  changes percents to common fractions
  determines interest
  reads and uses roman numerals
  describes and lists elements of number sets
  uses common measures, e.g., feet, yards, miles, pounds, tons
  reads time
  reads temperatures
  uses constant symbols
  uses variable symbols
  uses equations and inequations
  uses distributive property and its inverse
  factors polynomial expressions
  derives sets of quadratic equations by factoring
  transforms algebraic fractions
  performs fundamental operations with algebraic fractions
  uses ratios to compare quantities
  develops and uses proportions
  formulates direct and inverse variations
  uses tables of powers and roots
  extracts square roots of numbers
  derives solution sets for quadratic formulas
  derives and uses quadratic formulas
  uses trigonometric ratios to measure distances
  uses tables of trigonometric ratios
  solves problems using trigonometric ratios

Spoken Expressions
  participates in group discussions
  shares time in group discussions
  speaks to audiences
  modulates voice
  pronounces combinations of letters and words correctly
  differentiates between colloquial expressions and formal expressions
  uses terms and phrases correctly

  uses plural nouns correctly
  uses possessive case of nouns when modifying verbal nouns
  uses pronouns for definite antecedents
  uses verbs in agreement with subjects in number and person
  uses nouns and pronouns in proper case

Written Expressions
  uses period, question, and exclamation marks
  uses commas
  uses pair of commas to enclose phrases
  uses semicolon
  uses colon
  uses parentheses
  uses single dash
  uses pair of dashes
  uses quotation marks
  uses brackets
  uses three dots
  uses capital letters in spelling proper names and for beginning sentences
  uses abbreviation point
  uses decimal point
  uses comma in numbers
  uses hyphen for compound words
  uses apostrophe for writing contractions and plurals
  divides words into syllables
  pronounces words correctly
  identifies roots of words
  identifies prefixes
  identifies suffixes
  uses words with different meanings in various contexts
  forms plurals of nouns
  adds suffixes to words
  uses a dictionary as a tool in writing
  writes personal letters
  writes business letters
  addresses envelopes
  writes bank checks
  combines equal thoughts with conjunctions
  combines equal sentences to form compound sentences
  combines supporting thoughts with main thoughts
  uses prepositions and conjunctions correctly
  uses adverbs in reference to verbs
  uses adjectives in reference to nouns and pronouns
  engages in creative writing

Thinking Processes

Thinking involves a complex set of processes which require the use of several skills. Attempts have been made to teach some of the skills believed to facilitate thinking. Riegel, Taylor, and Danner (1973) trained LD children to classify and remember. Using a sequence of activities aimed at improving grouping and memory processes, they randomly assigned 28 children, who lacked the skills and maturity necessary for first-grade placement, to experimental and control groups. Their findings suggest that young children can be trained to organize information systematically.

It should be noted that the above study is merely one of many needed prior to determining if thinking processes can be developed through such training. Because of the necessity to deal with hypothetical models when considering thinking, it is important to identify behaviors considered to be the results of thinking. Four such behaviors are labeling, organizing, inferring, and generalizing.

Labeling. Labeling may be as simple process as associating words with objects, or as abstract as developing new symbols in order to communicate or develop a mathematical model. Labeling is perhaps the first step in the language process. Naming of objects, events, and people should begin long before first grade. A curriculum for preschool L&BD children should stress skills in language labeling within the context of relevant experiences. L&BD students often assign their own idiosyncratic labels to objects and experiences in attempting to communicate and to understand their environments. Correct names must be taught to these children.

Organizing. Information must be organized in some meaningful way by learners if they are to use it. Experienced learners (adults and successful students) probably use their own personal systems for organizing information automatically. Children with learning problems may be helped by a better understanding of the organization of information (Riegel, Taylor, & Danner, 1973).

Ausubel (1960) proposed the use of advanced organizers as a means of improving retention of verbal information. By providing brief outlines and key phrases in advance of reading or listening, it appears that those receiving the information tend to retain it for longer periods of time.

Inferring. Inferences are based upon facts or other judgments which have been established as proven. Inferring involves deducing or drawing conclusions from facts, observations, or other inferences which have been established as correct.

Students can be taught the steps to use in inferring from written passages, from their observations, and from statements made by others. They should also be trained to verify their inferences since procedures for inferring can lead to faulty conclusions.

Generalizing. Generalizations are conclusions based on judgments concerning a group or class of experiences. These are often formulated from inferences or a series of conclusions which seem to support a general belief. Anecdote 4.5 contains examples of generalizing.

Teachers of L&BD children should include training of thinking processes in association with and as a part of regular academic content. For example, skills of inferring and generalizing should be taught as a part of reading and in content areas such as social studies and science. Training students to use thinking skills in isolation is not advocated by this writer.

ANECDOTE 4.5[2]

1. Sammy Jones read the word *triangle* in a magazine. In context, he associated this word with this design:

   Later, in other contexts, Sammy saw these symbols referred to as triangles:

   Generalization: From these experiences, Sammy correctly generalized that "Three-sided geometric figures which formed three angles were classified as triangular." Later he learned that within this class of figures each type of triangle has a particular name.
2. Marsha Jones, Sammy's older sister, learned that "an adverb is a word that modifies a verb, an adjective, or another adverb," Examples of adverbs, presented by the text and the teacher, were words ending in *ly,* e.g., remarkably, rapidly, quietly.
   Generalization: Marsha correctly concluded that most adverbs end in *ly.* She generalized as follows: "Adverbs usually end in *ly* and modify either verbs, adverbs, or adjectives."
3. David Haney recalls from his study of American history that the Harding administration was noted for its scandals.
   Generalization: David incorrectly concluded that Harding and all members of his cabinet were scoundrels and engaged in schemes to bilk the taxpayers. David later found that this was a false generalization, that Warren G. Harding and all but one member of his cabinet were never accused of or considered to be involved in the scandals.
4. Marsha Jones typically forms the plurals of nouns by adding *s.*
   Generalization: Marsha has incorrectly concluded that all nouns form their plurals by adding *s* to the singular form.

Academic curricula for L&BD students currently consist of a hodgepodge of skills and concepts which are often based more upon hope than empirical evidence. Considering our current knowledge of what such children need to learn in school, academic skills and concepts should generally be the same as those taught to normal children. Teaching must be differentiated and individualized for L&BD children. Instructional approaches for individualizing instruction are discussed in part II of this text.

Social Skills and Attitudes

Although elementary and secondary schools in our society serve as basic socializing agencies, few conscious attempts are made to teach social skills and attitudes. Inkeles (1966) related the absence of necessary social competencies of many adults in our society to the neglect of social training in schools. As was indicated earlier in this chapter, there is considerable need for schools to deal with socialization in systematic ways.

Social skills typically involve adaptive behaviors. Hops and Cobb (1972) believe that social behaviors required for school success may be divided into personal interaction skills and task-related skills. They refer to personal interaction skills as

2. Reproduced from Thomas M. Stephens, *Implementing behavioral approaches in elementary and secondary schools.* Columbus, Ohio: Charles E. Merrill, 1975, p. 165.

behaviors such as helping, sharing, smiling, greeting, speaking positively to others, and controlling aggression. Task-related skills are behaviors such as attending, compliance to teachers' requests, following directions, punctuality and perseverance.

Attitudes, unlike skills, are not directly observable. Results of attitudes are manifested in student behaviors. Negative attitudes, for example, may be reflected by uncooperativeness, anger, physical violence, and withdrawal. Because so many different behaviors may be precipitated by a given attitude, it is customary to speculate as to the reasons for such behaviors. More recently, however, it has become evident that dealing with the behaviors, without reference to the attitudes, will result in changes in behavior, as described in anecdote 4.6.

ANECDOTE 4.6[3]

Positive school environments facilitate favorable attitudes toward learning. When students have good feelings toward teachers and schooling, they are typically more responsive to instruction. Many students come to school with negative attitudes and display behavior management problems. Values derived from home tell them that education is alien to their way of life, and that authority, represented by the school, is unfair and favors more affluent students. In short, the strange feelings associated with differences in values and environments tend to make some students feel uneasy.

Behavioral and learning problems are related, in part, to a conflict in value systems. Some students have learned that one must be aggressive, harsh, and ready to fight in order to survive. These same attitudes, when displayed in school, are greeted with punishment. The students become confused. They are punished at school for behavior that is acceptable at home. Thus, they may interpret a rejection of their behavior as a rejection of themselves. Consequently, such students may soon become alienated from school, reject what teachers value, and more importantly, reject what schooling can offer.

Teachers who gain rapport with students can change negative attitudes to positive ones. This is accomplished by being firm, fair, friendly, and understanding, by being sensitive to what students communicate, and by recognizing and reflecting the feelings of students.

When a student says, "No, I ain't goin to," should the teacher threaten him? Or should he or she respond by asking, "John, you don't want to do this assignment?" If his feelings are recognized at first, it is often possible to discuss the problem with him. But if the teacher reacts defensively, the student is likely to become even more uncooperative. Teachers who behave in a defensive manner typically argue with students, lecture them concerning their poor attitudes and misbehavior, nag them, use sarcasm with them, and ridicule them.

On the other hand, responses toward students which tend to indicate an understanding by teachers are verbalizing students' expressed feelings, informing students of the requirements for courses, units of study, and assignments, reminding students of the desirable consequences of their performance, and recognizing students' rights to profit or suffer from the consequences of their actions.

Bases for Teaching Social Behavior

As children grow and become socialized into their families and communities, they learn ways of behaving in different situations and with different people.

---

3. Adapted from Thomas M. Stephens, *Implementing behavioral approaches in elementary and secondary schools.* Columbus, Ohio: Charles E. Merrill, 1975, p. 93.

Often they learn by imitating the behavior of others who are models for them — parents, peers, teachers, and other people in their environments. As they attempt new behaviors, they receive positive or negative feedback which tells them which behaviors to continue and discontinue. Children who lack opportunity for learning correct behavior through imitation or who receive insufficient feedback may fail to learn important social behaviors. Others who are frequently exposed to models who provide inappropriate opportunities for imitation or those who receive rewards for undesirable behavior may also fail to learn necessary social skills and attitudes.

Consequently there are several sound reasons for teaching social behaviors in schools. First, desirable social behavior in school is strongly related to academic achievement. Second, appropriate social behavior contributes to better social adjustment. Third, L&BD children are often socially inadequate and the school's curriculum should reflect their need for social competencies.

Social Behavior and Academic Achievement

A positive relationship between desirable social behavior and academic achievement has been demonstrated repeatedly (Eichorn, 1965; Fieldhusen, Thurston, & Benning, 1967, 1970; Swift & Spivack, 1968; Atwell, Orpet, & Meyers, 1967; Lahaderne, 1968; Cobb, 1970). In a study of 200 third- and sixth-grade children, Fieldhusen, Thurston, and Benning (1967) found that those students exhibiting socially appropriate behavior performed significantly better academically than those displaying socially maladaptive behavior. In another longitudinal study, the same researchers (Fieldhusen, Thurston, & Benning, 1970) found that aggressive and disruptive students achieved significantly below that of appropriately behaving peers.

Swift and Spivack (1968) compared teacher ratings of classroom behavior with scores on academic achievement tests. They found that students who were rated high on classroom misbehavior obtained significantly lower test scores.

Teachers also recognize the influence of certain social skills on the academic performance of students. Milburn (1974) asked special and regular class teachers to rate 136 social skills. The teachers indicated the degree to which they felt a child should possess a specific social skill in order to succeed in their classrooms. These skills were arranged in four general categories: social initiative, on-task behavior, relationship rules, and basic socialization. The 265 teachers in her study expressed the highest agreement with the skills in the latter three categories. Generally, teachers tended to place the greatest importance upon skills involving order, rules, obedience, and responsibility in academic and interpersonal areas.

There have been efforts directed toward developing social curricula for L&BD students. Minuchin, Chamberlain, and Graubard (1967) reported an effort to teach learning skills to disturbed and delinquent students. They taught six boys, who were in a residential treatment center, skills involving ten different lessons. Role playing and games were used to teach listening skills, storytelling, taking turns in discussions, categorizing and classifying information, and asking relevant questions.

It seems logical that skills needed for achieving in school do include listening, categorizing and classifying information, and responding in relevant ways. There are, however, several unstudied issues concerning *how* students acquire such skills. Use of an ability training model, where the skills are taught unrelated to the content, may prove as ineffective as has isolated perceptual training on reading performance.

Use of a skill training model, where the behaviors are tied to specific content and settings, raises questions concerning the extent to which skills are generalized across conditions. Skill training can help students acquire the responses under a given set of conditions. It cannot assure that the behaviors will be emitted or even maintained under different conditions. Advocates of skill training should routinely remind practitioners that they must arrange conditions so as to elicit behaviors which are within students' repertoires.

Social Behavior and Social Adjustment

It seems axiomatic that appropriate social behavior positively influences interpersonal adjustment. Rhodes (1970) emphasized the influence that environment has on social adjustment. He stressed the need to intervene into the surroundings of disturbed children while simultaneously treating their adjustment difficulties. Since there is a continuous exchange between individuals and their surroundings, social adjustment cannot be divorced entirely from environment. This interaction results in certain behaviors which, when inappropriate to the conditions, are considered disturbed.

An ecological model, as described by Rhodes (1967), poses important curriculum implications since from this view both the environments in which maladaptive behaviors occur and the students are disturbed. Using this model, curriculum modifications would need to take into account such factors as students' performance levels, their goals, ways in which students can learn to shape schools' cultural and environmental conditions, and mechanisms for encouraging harmonious exchanges between and among school personnel and students. With these factors incorporated into schools' environments, the social adjustment of students would improve primarily because those conditions under which they behave would have been changed.

From a reinforcement point of view, improved social behavior will result in more positive reinforcement for students. Rewards gained from better social behavior encourage students to adjust to the demands of schools. Social adjustment, then, is the result of improved social behavior.

Many specific behaviors comprise social adjustment. In school, these may include behaviors related to academic performance, peer interaction, and interpersonal relations with teachers. Some of the behaviors which contribute to good social adjustment in these areas are listed below.

School Achievement

perseverance
following directions
recognizing academic limitations
asking relevant questions
using time wisely
listening
communicating clearly

Peer Interactions

sharing time and resources
being a sensitive listener

being fair
accepting leadership and participant roles
recognizing individual differences
being friendly
following game rules
being pleasant
greeting others

Relations with Teachers

recognizing teacher's authority
greeting teachers
accepting differences among teachers
reinforcing teachers for good performances
being pleasant
obtaining assistance from teachers

Social Competencies for L&BD Students

Many authorities have noted that L&BD students often lack necessary social skills.
Graubard (1969) demonstrated that a group of delinquent students can be trained to
learn. He reported the results of a study where eight adjudicated delinquent males
(ages 10 to 12) improved in reading and classroom behavior because rewards for all
students were made contingent on each student's behaving appropriately. Dupont
(1974) stated, "It is reasonable to think of most disturbed children as retarded in
social development . . . " (p. 355). Learning disabled students, the other population
of concern in this text, are also often socially inadequate. Such children have been
characterized as having poor self-concepts, being overly dependent, having peer
acceptance problems, and generally being viewed as different or strange by peers
and adults.

Children with pronounced learning problems sometimes have physical stigmata.
Misshapen heads and other odd physical appearances are not uncommon among
this group. These types of conditions tend to make the students feel inadequate
since they are often rejected by their more normal appearing peers.

Play and team sports are important parts of children's and youths' lives. Inadequate motor performance, distractibility, and other problems often associated
with LD students can affect their play. As a result, they are often chosen last to play
team games and viewed as the team's liability.

Language problems as reflected in speaking, reading, spelling, and writing difficulties contribute to social inadequacies. Our information-dependent society
often demands independent language skills at an early age. Difficulties in communicating may result in social incompetencies. Failures in receiving and/or understanding information create serious social adjustment problems.

Socially competent students are able to enjoy their lives and to develop their
personal skills in socially worthwhile ways. Many LD students, until their social
and academic skills are effective, live anxiety-filled days, often fearing that their
inadequacies will be apparent to others.

School-related Social Skills

Children spend a considerable amount of their time in school. Since a significant
measure of students' competencies is the extent to which they cope with the

school's environment, the curriculum should include the development of social skills that facilitate adjustment in school. Children engage in many activities requiring high levels of social functioning.

A social skills curriculum is contained in the Directive Teaching Instructional Management System (DTIMS).[4] It covers four categories of behavior: environmental, interpersonal, self-related, and task-related behaviors.

Environmentally Related Behaviors

Numerous behaviors may be related to the school's environment. In the DTIMS social skills curriculum, there are four general areas included which cover twelve skills. (See Figure 4.3.)

1.0 Care for Environment
 .1   to dispose of trash in the proper container
 .2   to drink properly from water fountain
 .3   to clean up after breaking or spilling something
 .4   to use classroom equipment and materials correctly
 .5   to use playground equipment safely

2.0 Dealing with Emergency
 .1   to follow rules for emergencies
 .2   to identify accidents or emergency situations which should be reported
 .3   to report accidents or other emergencies

3.0 Lunchroom
 .1   to use eating utensils properly
 .2   to handle and eat only one's own food
 .3   to dispose of unwanted food properly

4.0 Movement around Environment
 .1   to walk through the hall quietly at a reasonable pace
 .2   to enter classroom and take seat without disturbing objects and other people
 .3   to form and walk in a line
 .4   to follow safety rules in crossing streets

FIGURE 4.3. Environmentally related behaviors in the directive teaching social skills curriculum

As can be seen in Figure 4.3, each area lists several behaviors to be taught. In addition, concepts are taught which may be applicable across all four areas. For example, one concept is the recognition that public property belongs to all citizens. When it is misused, *our property* is damaged.

Interpersonal Behaviors

Certainly, how students interact with others in school determines the extent to which they can cope with that environment. There are numerous behaviors essential to good interpersonal skills; some are listed in Figure 4.4.

Ten areas are covered: accepting authority, coping with conflict, gaining attention, greeting others, helping others, making conversation, organized play, positive attitude toward others, informal play, and care of property. These represent routine, but important, interpersonal behaviors.

4. DTIMS was originated and conceptualized by the author. However, many former students should be credited with the development of the social skills. Gwendolyn Cartledge, A. Carol Hartman, Michael Kabler, George Levin, and JoAnn Milburn should receive special recognition for the content.

FIGURE 4.4. Interpersonal behaviors in the directive teaching social skills curriculum

1.0 Accepting Authority
 .1 to comply with requests of adults in positions of authority
 .2 to comply with requests of peers in positions of authority
 .3 to know and follow classroom rules
 .4 to follow classroom rules in the absence of the teacher
 .5 to question rules which may be unjust

2.0 Coping with Conflict
 .1 to respond to teasing or name calling by ignoring, changing the subject, or some other constructive means
 .2 to respond to physical assault by leaving the situation, calling for help, or some other constructive means
 .3 to walk away from peer when angry to avoid hitting
 .4 to refuse the request of another politely
 .5 to express anger with nonaggressive words rather than physical action or aggressive words
 .6 to handle constructively criticism or punishment perceived as undeserved

3.0 Gaining Attention
 .1 to gain teacher's attention in class by raising hand
 .2 to wait quietly for recognition before speaking out in class
 .3 to use *please* and *thank-you* when making requests of others
 .4 to approach teacher and ask appropriately for help, explanation, and instruction.
 .5 to gain attention from peers in appropriate ways
 .6 to ask a peer for help

4.0 Greeting Others
 .1 to look at others when greeting them
 .2 to state one's name when asked
 .3 to smile when encountering a friend or acquaintance
 .4 to greet adults and peers by name
 .5 to respond to an introduction by shaking hands and saying "how-do-you-do?"
 .6 to introduce oneself to another person
 .7 to introduce two people to each other

5.0 Helping Others
 .1 to help teacher when asked
 .2 to help peer when asked
 .3 to give directions to a peer
 .4 to offer help to teacher
 .5 to offer help to a classmate
 .6 to come to defense of peer in trouble
 .7 to express sympathy to peer about problems or difficulties

6.0 Making Conversation
 .1 to pay attention in a conversation to the person speaking
 .2 to talk to others in a tone of voice appropriate to the situation
 .3 to wait for pauses in a conversation before speaking
 .4 to make relevant remarks in a conversation with peers
 .5 to make relevant remarks in a conversation with adults
 .6 to ignore interruptions of others in a conversation
 .7 to initiate conversation with peers in an informal situation
 .8 to initiate conversation with adults in an informal situation

7.0 Organized Play
 .1 to follow rules when playing a game
 .2 to take turns when playing a game
 .3 to display effort in a competitive game
 .4 to accept defeat and congratulate the winner in a competitive game

8.0 Positive Attitude toward Others
 .1 to make positive statements about qualities and accomplishments of others
 .2 to compliment another person
 .3 to display tolerance for persons with characteristics different from one's own

9.0 Play Informally
 .1 to ask another student to play on the playground
 .2 to ask to be included in a playground activity in progress
 .3 to share toys and equipment in a play situation
 .4 to give in to reasonable wishes of the group in a play situation
 .5 to suggest an activity for the group on the playground

10.0 Care of Property
 .1 to distinguish one's own property from the property of others
 .2 to lend possessions to others when asked
 .3 to use and return others' property without damaging it
 .4 to ask permission to use another's property

Self-related Behaviors

Accepting consequences for one's actions, ethical behavior, expressing feelings, positive attitude toward self, responsible behavior, and self-care are included under self-related behaviors.

FIGURE 4.5. Self-related behaviors in the directive teaching
social skills curriculum

1.0 Accepting Consequences
 .1 to report to the teacher when spilling or breaking something
 .2 to apologize when injuring or infringing on another
 .3 to accept deserved consequences of wrong-doing

2.0 Ethical Behavior
 .1 to distinguish truth from untruth or fantasy in one's own statements
 .2 to answer truthfully when asked about possible wrong-doing
 .3 to identify consequences of behavior involving wrong-doing
 .4 to avoid doing something wrong when encouraged by a peer

3.0 Expressing Feelings
 .1 to describe one's own feelings or moods verbally
 .2 to recognize and label moods of others

4.0 Positive Attitude toward Self
 .1 to say "thank you" when complimented or praised
 .2 to be willing to have one's work displayed
 .3 to make positive statements when asked about oneself
 .4 to undertake a new task with a positive attitude

5.0 Responsible Behavior
 .1 to be regular in school attendance
 .2 to arrive at school on time
 .3 to hang up one's clothes in required place
 .4 to keep one's desk in order
 .5 to take care of one's own possessions
 .6 to carry messages for the teacher
 .7 to bring required materials to school

6.0 Self-care
 .1 to use toilet facilities properly
 .2 to put on clothing without assistance
 .3 to keep face and hands clean

These six areas, as shown in Figure 4.5, provide for teaching many behaviors relating to the self. All such behaviors cannot be taught in school. By teaching the various concepts which these behaviors represent, students will have opportunities to generalize behaviors and attitudes to other situations.

Task-related Behaviors

Tasks which relate directly to academic behaviors are shown in Figure 4.6. Behaviors in this section are divided into ten areas: asking and answering questions, attending behavior, classroom discussion, completing tasks, following directions, group activities, independent work, on-task behaviors, performing before others, and quality of work.

FIGURE 4.6. Task-related behaviors in the directive teaching social skills curriculum

1.0 Asking and Answering Questions
 .1 to answer or attempt to answer a question when called upon by teacher
 .2 to acknowledge not knowing the answer to a question
 .3 to volunteer an answer to teacher's question
 .4 to ask a question appropriate to the information needed

2.0 Attending Behavior
 .1 to look at the teacher when a lesson is being presented
 .2 to watch an audio-visual presentation quietly
 .3 to listen to a speaker in the class
 .4 to listen to assignment directions
 .5 to listen to answers to questions
 .6 to look at the chalkboard for assignment directions

3.0 Classroom Discussion
 .1 to use tone of voice in classroom discussions appropriate to the situation
 .2 to make relevant remarks in a classroom discussion
 .3 to participate in a classroom discussion
 .4 to bring things to class relevant to classroom discussions
 .5 to express opinion in classroom discussion even when contrary to opinions of others
 .6 to provide reasons for opinions expressed in group discussion

4.0 Completing Tasks
 .1 to complete assigned academic work
 .2 to complete assigned academic work within the required time
 .3 to continue working on a difficult task until it is completed
 .4 to complete and return homework assignments

5.0 Following Directions
 .1 to follow teacher's verbal directions
 .2 to follow simple directions
 .3 to follow written directions
 .4 to follow directions for taking a test

6.0 Group Activities
 .1 to share materials with others in a work situation
 .2 to work cooperatively on a task with a peer
 .3 to carry out plans or decisions formulated by the group
 .4 to accept ideas presented in a group situation different from one's own
 .5 to initiate and help carry out a group activity

7.0 Independent Work
 .1 to attempt to solve a problem with school work before asking for help
 .2 to find productive use of time while waiting for teacher assistance
 .3 to find acceptable ways of using free time when work is completed

8.0 On-Task Behaviors
 .1 to sit straight at desk when required by teacher
 .2 to do a seat-work assignment quietly
 .3 to work steadily for the required length of time
 .4 to ignore distractions while doing seatwork
 .5 to discuss academic material with peers when appropriate
 .6 to change from one activity to another when required by the teacher

9.0 Performing before Others
 .1 to participate in role playing
 .2 to read aloud in a small group
 .3 to read aloud before a large group
 .4 to make a report before a small group
 .5 to make a report before a large group

10.0 Quality of Work
 .1 to turn in neat papers
 .2 to accept correction of school work
 .3 to use teacher's corrections for improving work
 .4 to review work to correct errors

The DTIMS social skills curriculum is not intended to include every behavior students need to acquire while in school. It is, however, an attempt to assist teachers to consciously and systematically instruct students in social behavior. Most behaviors are acquired by children indirectly through various life experiences. Those students who have not mastered essential social behaviors should be taught them in school. Since L&BD students are often so labeled because they lack such behaviors, the curriculum should reflect this need. Procedures for teaching social behaviors are presented in chapter 11.

Summary

L&BD students should have educational goals similar to those for their normal peers. While the school curriculum should reflect the standard academic and social needs, teaching methods will vary depending upon several factors. Curricular issues in special education include the assumptions upon which instruction and content are based, immediate functioning vs. underlying causes, correcting performance deficits vs. teaching to current functioning, and the issue regarding the need for methods and curricula for learning disabled children which are distinct from those for the behaviorally disturbed.

Academic skills are complex responses to school tasks. These are developed from lower order or prerequisite skills. Motor and language skills are necessary for school achievement. Concepts are related general classes, and concept formation is an essential part of learning. Attempts have been made to improve thinking by teaching related skills such as organizing, labeling, inferring, and generalizing. Social skills and attitudes are, for the most part, learned indirectly. Because of the importance of these behaviors, school curricula should include social skills and concepts. These should be taught systematically to all students who have not yet demonstrated a mastery of them.

There are educational opportunities for all learning and behaviorally disordered students.

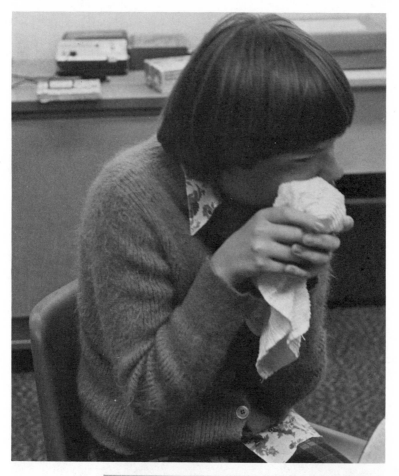

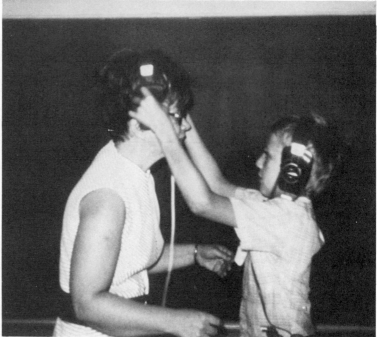

5

Student Variables for Learning

Introduction

Teaching methods, curriculum, and competencies of teachers are conditions in schools affecting student learning. L&BD students who are taught academic and social tasks effectively have a better chance of learning these behaviors than do those who are not taught systematically. In addition to those factors within school environments, there are other variables within students to be considered.

All students bring to school personal attributes which may facilitate or inhibit learning. In many instances, those barriers to learning contained within L&BD students can be overcome, or reduced, given proper assessment and treatment.[1] In this chapter, factors internal to L&BD students that tend to interfere with their learning are discussed. These consist of physical health and psychological problems. Health problems include illnesses and physical handicaps. Psychological conditions are problems of temperament, family-related problems, intellectual factors, inappropriate learning, and sensory-expressive difficulties.

Some conditions inherent to students are more amenable to change by school personnel than are others. But because some of these conditions cannot be corrected, or even changed, by teachers does not mean that they should be overlooked. Referring to other agencies, assisting parents by identifying possible problems, helping students adapt to certain conditions, and providing supportive services for students to aid them in accommodating to their problems are possible responses by school personnel to those conditions that extend beyond the school's control.

Psychological problems, however, often may be reduced or corrected through instruction. Teachers of L&BD students will always find it necessary to differentiate instruction on the bases of student performances since inappropriate responses may often be corrected through careful instruction.

---

1. *Treatment* includes instructional activities as well as medical and psychological services.

Physical Problems

Health problems and physical handicaps are found among some L&BD students, and these conditions may complicate learning and teaching. Those with physical problems will not necessarily present learning and behavioral disorders, but when they do, they often have special needs.

Health Problems

Carol B., an eight-year-old, had been in a special class for L&BD students for a year and a half. One day her teacher, Ms. Badger, had noticed that Carol seemed less interested in school, appeared tired, and complained of an upset stomach. During the following few days Carol's school work diminished in quality. Her mother sent a note to school with her on one of the days indicating that she did not feel well but didn't seem sick enough to stay home.

One day, shortly after the note was received at school, Ms. Badger noticed a yellow cast to Carol's eyes. She was immediately referred to the school nurse who, fearing hepatitis, contacted the family's physician. Carol's illness was diagnosed as infectious hepatitis. Because it was possible that others in the school were infected, the health department had a medical team examine all students and school personnel in the building and also provided to parents a description of the symptoms and signs of that illness.

Illnesses can create physical discomfort, reduced ability to attend, low energy levels, and general weakness. Obviously, physical conditions of this sort do affect school performance. Anecdote 5.1 describes how an illness can disrupt an entire school, creating a medical emergency. In this case, the teacher's attention to her students' bodily conditions enabled her to identify and refer a student for medical attention. While the actual treatment was provided by other specialists, the teacher's awareness probably helped to prevent the infection of others.

L&BD Students and Illnesses

L&BD students are probably no more likely to become ill than are any other group of children. Although this question has not been widely studied, it is reasonable to assume that illnesses are more a function of socioeconomic conditions and access to medical attention than to behavior and learning performances.

Students are subjected to a wide variety and range of illnesses, such as influenza and the various childhood illnesses, and most of these can adversely affect behavior and school performances. For this reason, teachers are expected to note changes in students' physical conditions and to know the correct procedures for medical referrals.

Policies concerning referrals for medical attention vary among, and sometimes within, school districts. In some schools, teachers are expected to initiate requests through building principals. In others, teachers may request services directly from the school nurse. Generally, school policies discourage teachers from referring parents directly to medical specialists. In situations where teachers are expected to make medical referrals, or when policies are nonexistent, teachers should avoid specifying a particular practitioner. Referral to "your family physician" is a more judicious suggestion.

A school nurse is an excellent source prior to making referrals for medical services. Nurses will often prefer to contact parents themselves after observing students' conditions. When parents request the name of a medical practitioner to contact, it is a sound policy for school personnel to provide them with several names in alphabetical order. Parents then may choose a physician to contact.

Regular contacts with parents also help teachers to be aware of student illnesses. Calling the home after two consecutive days of absences is a wise practice. Similarly, when there are frequent single days of absences, a contact with parents is advisable. As a result of being familiar with each other, teachers and parents will be able to more readily share concerns about a student's need for medical attention.

Side Effects of Drug Treatment

Pharmacotherapy, better known as drug treatment, is widely used in treating L&BD students, particularly those who are hyperactive. Stimulant drugs are often prescribed for hyperactive children. Tranquilizers have been used to prevent seizures and with behaviorally disturbed children who demonstrate abnormal electroencephalograms (Fish, 1975). The use of stimulants with hyperactive children has received much attention in special education, and Fish (1975) has emphasized, in regard to the use of this treatment, that:

— hyperactive children are a heterogeneous group and stimulants are not effective with all of them;
— stimulants may have limited effectiveness even when they are useful;
— medication should be preceded with a comprehensive psychological and medical examination;
— careful observation of the child during medication is essential;
— children with learning problems require other interventions in conjunction with medication.

Teachers should know when students are on drug treatment, and physicians should inform them of possible side effects. Since medical practitioners tend to communicate with parents rather than teachers, it may be necessary for teachers to obtain such information from the parents. Teachers' roles in this situation should be clear; it is one of noting changes in students' behaviors and school related performances and to relay the observational information to the parents. It is *not* one of recommending drug treatment, changes in dosages, or changes in medical personnel. Teachers should not, of course, deal directly with a student's physician without parental approval. Such contacts should only occur at the requests of parents or physicians and with parental approval.

Side effects from prescribed drugs can result in physical difficulties and a subsequent increase in school problems. Fish (1975) noted that stimulant drug treatment of hyperactive children often requires trial use of several drugs. While locating the right drug and dosage for a given child, many physical problems of a temporary nature can develop. Excess drug dosage can cause sleepiness, tiredness, tenseness, and difficulties in sleeping and eating. Freeman (1966), in an extensive review of studies of drug therapy on children, noted that many of the drugs commonly used can result in dysfunctions of the central nervous system and cause jaundice and liver damage.

Connors (1971) reviewed studies concerning the effects of stimulant drugs on hyperactive children's general behavior, motor organization, learning, physiological responses, and attention. He noted that several studies found that the students general behavior was improved with the use of stimulant drugs. Inattention and undirected motor responses were reduced under drug treatment. He also found that the quality of motor behavior was improved. Performance on laboratory learning tasks was better, in several cases, with the use of stimulant drugs. Connors concluded that attention is more likely to show improvement from stimulant drug treatment than other behaviors. He also indicated that tranquilizers, as compared to stimulants, tend to result in impairment of learning and thinking.

There continues to be controversy regarding the use of drug treatment for purposes of improving students' school performance. Critics point to the dangerous side effects and the lack of controlled studies of such problems as the effects of drugs over long periods of time. Proponents, however, cite the large number of children who have been successfully helped through such treatment. It is a controversy with ethical overtones when critics accuse parents and teachers of chaining children with drugs (Vonder Haar, 1975). Disagreements concerning drug therapy undoubtedly will continue for some time. School personnel can be of assistance by:

— encouraging and cooperating with researchers who seek to predict side effects of drug therapy;
— advising parents to seek competent medical advice prior to using drugs;
— attempting to manage hyperactive students through various nondrug approaches (see chapter 10 for a discussion of these approaches);
— observing and recording changes in behavior of students who are receiving drug therapy;
— cooperating with parents and medical personnel when they seek information concerning students' behaviors.

Physical Handicaps

Learning and behavioral disorders are not uncommon among physically handicapped children. Since physical handicaps may exacerbate academic and social learning problems, their impact on learning can be extensive.

Among the physical defects of children are amputations, asthma, cerebral palsy, congenital heart disease, convulsive disorders, cystic fibrosis, diabetes, muscular atrophy, muscular dystrophy, poliomyelitis, rheumatoid arthritis, and sickle cell anemia.

ANECDOTE 5.2

1 Eight-year-old Mary Jane was stricken with rheumatic fever two years earlier. As a result, she missed three months of school in the first grade and has a damaged heart. The early gaps in her skill and concept development were not corrected, and she accumulated additional learning problems in language arts and arithmetic. Her heart condition contributes to a low energy level which results in an apathetic interest in school. Her parents have tended to overprotect her; she is rarely permitted to play with other children and to participate in activities typical of eight-year-olds. Consequently, she tends to withdraw from peer activities in school and seeks attention frequently from the teacher.

2. Sam was born with a cleft lip. While surgery for his harelip was recommended during his infancy, his mother could not afford the costs. Being on welfare and husbandless, Sam's mother has difficulty paying the rent and feeding her four children. At the age of seven, Sam's speech is poor and seems to impair his total language development. He is hostile to classmates and has on occasion fought with them, claiming they have mimicked his speech.

3. Wilhelmina, a nine-year-old girl from a low-income family, has extremely irregular teeth which interfere with pronunciation and closing her mouth. Her reading and spelling performances are low. Additional problems are extreme shyness and reluctance to participate in social interactions.

4. Jeff has been nonambulatory since he lost the use of his legs in an auto accident when he was seven. Now, at the age of eleven, he is doing poorly in school subjects and is a frequent behavior problem. His teacher reports that he refuses to try, has temper tantrums, shouts obscene words, often argues, and is mean to fellow students.

Structural Defects and L&BD Students

A defect or weakness in the body structure may be obvious, e.g., loss of limbs. Others are less obvious, e.g., a heart condition, While these physical conditions do not necessarily contribute to learning problems or adjustment difficulties, they are factors that when present can affect learning.

As anecdote 5.2 shows, physical defects of a structural nature may involve body organs, limbs, and facial features, in addition to many other body deformities. Even though all such defects will not necessarily cause or contribute to learning and behavioral difficulties, some L&BD children have such handicaps. Teachers should focus on these students' performances but may also need to make adaptations in their instruction and schedules in order to accommodate their physical handicaps. Since students' poor physical conditions are additional considerations for teachers, ancillary services, frequent contacts with the parents, and medical consultations may be necessary.

Functional Defects and L&BD Students

Other handicapping conditions exist in which the trouble is more in using the body part than in a defect in its structure. Example four in anecdote 5.2 is an instance where a physical handicap of a functional nature is associated with an L&BD problem. Jeff's legs are presumably correctly formed, but he is unable to use them. Similar physical functioning problems occur with students who have cerebral palsy where damage to the brain may cause difficulty in using certain body parts even though they are structurally normal.

Difficulty in speech may also present functional problems. Since speaking involves many body parts (lips, tongue, teeth, lungs, and diaphragm), speech problems are common handicaps among school-aged children. Incorrect speech can contribute to problems in spelling and reading. In spelling, the speech-handicapped child may have trouble using phonetic analysis and his or her mispronunciation can contribute to incorrect spelling of words. Word attack skills and other auditory discrimination errors, often found among children with speech problems, can interfere with acquiring reading proficiency. Poor speech may also be one part of a total language problem as noted in anecdote 5.3.

ANECDOTE 5.3

Since starting school, Gerald has performed poorly in all areas of language. He mispronounces common words, often stutters, displays low reading performance, his handwriting and printing are of poor quality, and he spells few words correctly. His mother reported that he was delayed in speaking and did not begin to use intelligible language until age four. In kindergarten he was initially considered to be mentally retarded but the school psychologist recommended that he be reevaluated a year later in order to obtain more valid results.

Upon retesting at the age of seven, Gerald earned a full scale IQ of 94 on the *WISC.* The verbal IQ was 80, but the performance IQ was 108. Because of his poor achievement and classroom behavior, Gerald received a variety of specialized services. Speech therapy and academic tutoring were provided. His teacher was also given consultant services in order to manage him better within the classroom.

Students with hearing and visual limitations may also present learning and behavior problems. These sensory handicaps require modifications in methods and materials. When such children have problems learning after necessary modifications have occurred, special tutoring, systematic instruction, and extensive behavior management approaches will often be necessary.

Psychological Problems

Many children bring to learning situations psychological factors which contribute to learning and behavioral problems. Difficulties may range over problems of temperament, family centered problems, intellectual difficulties, poor training and learning, and problems in sensory-expressive areas.

Problems of Temperament

Temperament is thought of as one's predisposition to emotional reactions (Wolman, 1973; English & English, 1958; Thomas, Chess, & Birch, 1968; Cattell, 1950). And, regardless of origin, children's temperaments influence their academic and social functioning. Among those characteristics of temperament affecting L&BD students are impatience, anger, rigidity, and high or low activity levels.

Impatience

Patience is relative to one's age. Young children tend to be less patient than are older children, and generally, most children are inclined to be less patient than are adults. But patience among children varies widely (Kagan & Moss, 1962), and those who are impatient often have trouble in academic and social learning situations.

Impatient students tend not to persist in tasks for reasonable amounts of time. They may seem less understanding of others' limitations and overly demanding of them. L&BD students who are impatient are less inclined to complete assignments or to follow through. They may create nervousness among peers and teachers because of their tendencies to rush through activities.

Anger

Angry reactions are undoubtedly learned responses, although it appears that a biological predisposition may influence the frequency, nature, and quality of anger (Thomas, Chess, & Birch, 1968). Anecdote 5.4 describes how anger in one student was an early sign of behavioral problems.

ANECDOTE 5.4

At the age of 14, Kent S. and his mother (his father died when he was 10) faced a juvenile judge. Kent was there to be sentenced to a state facility for delinquent juveniles since his mother had, in the words of the judge, " . . . demonstrated an inability to control your son."

The final act which resulted in court sentencing was Kent's burning of a neighbor's cat. Several weeks before Kent has been before the same judge for taking a neighbor's car for an all day joy ride. In retaliation for filing charges against him, Kent had set that same neighbor's cat afire, killing the cat and seriously upsetting the neighbors' and their children.

Kent had a history of acts committed in anger. Between ages three and four, his mother recalled how Kent would burst into tears and become uncontrollable in response to her verbally correcting him. He would withhold bowel movements until he received his wishes.

In elementary school, teachers complained that he frequently lied about his misdeeds and had poor relationships with other children. While his measured intelligence was above average (IQ-112) throughout his school career, he consistently achieved at low levels on his daily work.

Later, when older, he would curse and shout at his mother when she corrected him or otherwise attempted to control him.

During his first year in junior high (eighth grade) Kent was often caught smoking in the boy's restroom. Once a female teacher reported him to the office for threatening her if she "opened her big mouth" about seeing him smoking in the hallway. With his explosive anger, Kent was increasingly involved in fights at school and in the neighborhood. Although he was not a strong boy, he was feared by many students because of his verbal threats and violent behavior.

Anger of the type depicted in anecdote 5.4 is not easily changed at school for several reasons. First, the responses have had many years of practice and positive reinforcement prior to school attendance. Second, the behavior is an integral part of the child's personality, occurring outside of school as well. Third, the factors precipitating the angry reactions were not always apparent. Fourth, his mother did not have the necessary respect to gain control of his behavior outside of school hours.

Although a behavior problem of this magnitude is not corrected easily, such behavior can be controlled within school as discussed in chapters 10 and 11. And such behavior may be changed through a concerted program between school and home as described in chapters 13 and 14.

Rigidity

Rigidity has frequently been termed a characteristic of behavior disorders. Fears, compulsions, and inhibitions are often associated with rigid, invariant behavior. An inflexible personality may be characterized as emitting a limited number of responses to a wide variety of stimuli or situations.

Some L&BD students tend to respond within a more restricted range of behavior than do normal children. Such children often begin schooling with rigid demands of others and, seemingly, an inability to change. Because school performance requires a divergent number of behaviors to a wide variety of academic and social situations, students with these characteristics often have trouble achieving well in school and may present serious social adjustment problems.

High and Low Activity Levels

Motor behavior seems to be an integral part of some children's temperament (Thomas, Chess, & Birch, 1968). This behavior includes the level of motor activity (high, average, low), its tempo, and its frequency. High activity levels among L&BD students are represented by behaviors such as frequent tapping of fingers and/or feet, unusual body movements, head rolling and jerking, poking and thrusting of arms or legs into the air, frequent running and jumping, and twisting and turning of limbs and body.

Low activity levels may be characterized by sitting or standing or lying still for long periods ot time, slow body and/or limb movements, rarely running or jumping, writing and/or printing unusually slowly and speaking too slowly.

Behaviors of this sort have been modified through classroom instruction. In some cases, teachers are only able to control the behavior and cannot significantly modify it. Instructional and behavioral approaches for modifying high and low motor activities are discussed in chapters 10 and 11.

High activity levels.   Children with high activity levels can endanger their own or others' safety. If, for example, a child often runs in the school building or at home, frequent bruises and other injuries may result. Running into others can also cause serious injuries.

Highly active students may present various management problems depending upon other attributes. For example, when distractibility is combined with high levels of activity, the behavior may be unpredictable. Intense, highly active children are known to unwittingly injure others by pushing them vigorously.

Children who learn to control their tendencies to be overly active can become effective students. Their high energy levels may be directed toward worthwhile school and physical tasks. If their coordination is good, they can develop into successful athletes and often will profit from the discipline which accompanies a sound physical education program. On the other hand, those who do not acquire body control and who are left to "use up their excess energies" without well-defined programs may present serious conduct problems and become poor students.

Low activity levels.   Students who are slow moving and content to remain in one place for excessively long periods of time may also have academic and social performance problems. Their slow responses are often irritating to other students and to teachers. They may delay in going to lunch or recess or in beginning new classroom activities. Also, because of their slowness, they often fail to complete time-bound tasks and may be penalized for late completion of other assignments.

Intellectual abilities of slow-responding students are sometimes understimulated by teachers and parents. In early grades, such children may be detained because of their slowness, particularly in classrooms where high premiums are placed upon quickness and promptness.

Older students who respond slowly are sometimes misjudged as uncooperative or "passive-aggressive" because they seemingly comply too slowly. When they are compared with other students or siblings who are faster responders, they tend to be rated lower. With the emphasis on speed and quickness in our culture, L&BD students who have low activity levels may be particularly handicapped since learning and behavior problems when combined with slow motor responses place unusually difficult burdens on these students.

There are, of course, instructional techniques for increasing motor responses: speed reading, using incentives, providing easier tasks, using mechanical devices, giving shorter assignments, and others, some of which are described in part II of this text. The use of such techniques with those students who respond slower because of constitutional factors will probably increase their levels of activity but may decrease the quality of their responses.

Family-related Problems

Families influence students in a multiplicity of ways. Some have inherent conditions which enhance students' strengths, while others contribute to their problems. Parents, much like students, are prisoners of their past and present circumstances. Most want their children to be worthwhile, happy people, but some are unable to contribute to that dream. Others may mistakenly believe that their actions are for their children's betterment when, in fact, they contribute to their detriment. Family problems of L&BD children do impact upon their schooling.

Teachers' knowledge of specific family problems need not be extensive, though a general understanding of family influences upon behavior and school achievement is basic. For years teachers have been prepared with the misconception that a more intimate knowledge of students leads to better learning and effective teaching. This notion is still widely proclaimed even though no research evidence is available to support such beliefs. Hoyt (1955) found no gains in academic achievement when teachers had an increased understanding of their students. Bush (1958), in reviewing research on the topic, concluded that there is no important advantage to pupils as a result of teachers' understanding of them. Thus, it seems that a basis for acquiring information about students' families should not be for purposes of "better understanding of their problems." In most instances it is not necessary to have extensive information about L&BD students' home lives, though there may be times in which assistance to families may need to be provided by other school personnel or other agencies. In situations of child abuse, monetary crises, and marital discord school personnel may be of assistance.

Child Abuse

Public Law 93-247 defines child abuse and neglect as maltreatment of a child under the age of 18 by a person who is responsible for the child's welfare with indications that the child's health or welfare is harmed or threatened. The incidence of child abuse and neglect in the United States has been estimated at between 60,000 and 500,000 cases annually, and it appears that child battering is the most common cause of death in children (Martin, 1974).

Children are easy targets for abusive adults, particularly in the home where they must rely upon adults for their basic living needs. Problems of child abuse cut across socioeconomic levels and all handicapping and normal conditions of children. After a comprehensive review of the problem, Soeffing (1975) reported that *no major research* had been reported which examined the relationship of handicapping conditions or causes of child abuse and neglect. However, some authors (Sandgrund, Gaines, & Green, 1974) have speculated that mentally retarded and neurologically handicapped children tend to elicit abuse from some parents.

Several studies (Gil, 1970; Martin, Beezley, Conway, & Kempe, 1974) have reported the handicapping characteristics of abused children populations. There is little reason at this time, however, to believe that L&BD children are abused more frequently than are other children. Every teacher, however, should be aware of the problem, be sensitive to possible signs, and know which procedures to follow. Some school districts provide inservice training of teachers so that they can recognize early signs of abuse and neglect; others have policies which specify procedures teachers should follow in reporting suspected cases (Soeffing, 1975).

Children may be abused physically through sexual assaults and beatings, lack of nourishment, and lack of proper supervision and care. They may also be abused in more subtle, psychological ways. While not easily detected, extensive damage to students may occur due to psychological abuse. Such abuse may occur as a result of verbal assaults, long periods of inattention, acts of cruelty, and invasions of childrens' privacies.

Most local communities and states vigorously prosecute adults who are found guilty of abusing children. Although most child abuse occurs at home, there are instances where teachers and other school personnel have abused children. The L&BD teacher's responsibility for notifying the proper authorities when child abuse is suspected is no less when the incidents occur at school as when the acts are believed to occur in homes.

ANECDOTE 5.5

Eight-year-old Maria appeared to be a quiet, somewhat shy child. To her special class teacher, Ms. Ross, she seemed frightened much of the time. Recently, she had noticed that Maria had bruises about her face and arms. These appeared mostly as black and blue marks, although, on a few occasions, her skin was broken, indicating that some bleeding had occurred.

Ms. Ross questioned Maria about her wounds after they became more common. On one occasion she had the school nurse examine and treat some of the cuts. When questioned, Maria refused to talk about how she received the bruises. Since the family did not have a telephone, it was necessary for Ms. Ross to write notes home calling to the parent's attention Maria's condition. She received no replies.

One day when Maria was particularly badly bruised she told the nurse, in reply to her questioning, that her father had come home drunk and beaten her mother, brother, and her. That day the visiting teacher filed a complaint with the county prosecutor's office and that office began an investigation of the home.

As described in anecdote 5.5, cases of child abuse generally result in criminal prosecution following these steps:

1. physical or behavior signs suggest that the child is injured;
2. the child and/or siblings are questioned;
3. attempts are made to notify the parents of the child's condition;
4. some evidence is obtained which suggests that the injuries were inflicted on the child;
5. legal authorities are notified of the suspected child abuse — these may be children's services boards, county welfare departments, or the police;
6. following investigation, charges may be filed against those adults believed to be inflicting the abuse.

In some communities and states, child abuse offices are available to investigate suspected cases. Regardless, however, there are laws to protect minors from such acts of cruelty, and, when necessary, school personnel should aid children through the use of such laws. All states require that school authorities report suspected cases of child abuse and stipulate fines and imprisonment for those failing to report.

Additional information concerning child abuse and neglect may be obtained from:

National Center for the Prevention and Treatment
   of Child Abuse and Neglect
1205 Oneida Street
Denver, Colorado   80220

National Committee for Prevention of Child Abuse
Suite 510
111 East Wacker Drive
Chicago, Illinois   60601

Parental Problems

There have been several studies in which pupil problems were found to be related to family and parental difficulties. Goldstein et al. (1970) studied family structures in relation to school performance among 94 L&BD boys. They found that family socioeconomic status and parental ambition for their children were related to school performance. Socioeconomic status was related positively to IQ, achievement scores, and grades in reading and arithmetic. Maternal and paternal ambitiousness were also related positively to school performance.

Peck and Stackhouse (1973) compared 15 families in which one child had reading problems with 15 families in which all children were normal readers. They found that families with reading problems took longer to reach decisions, spent less time discussing their reading, had more off-task comments, and had fewer exchanges of information during family decision-making tasks.

While the problems cited in the above studies are not solely related to parental difficulties, both studies reveal the complexities involved when relating family factors to schooling. Problems which L&BD students may possess as a result of parental related difficulties may include personal problems of one or both parents as well as marital problems.

Personal problems of parents.   Personal problems of parents may affect their children's learning and behavior. Children often worry about their parents' problems and, due to limited experiences with such problems, may believe that resolutions are not possible.

About one-tenth of the population of the United States will have, at some time, an emotional disorder serious enough to require hospitalization. And when such breakdowns occur among parents, their children may need special assistance as well. The assistance may take the form of providing accurate information concerning the meaning of emotional illness. When other students tease a youngster concerning his or her "crazy" parent, it may be useful for the teacher to discuss with the class the meaning and prevalence of emotional problems. Assistance to the family by a social work agency may also be helpful. Referrals to such agencies can be made by teachers through designated school personnel, such as visiting teachers or social workers.

Physical illness among parents may also affect students. In some instances parents must rely upon their school-aged children to assume major responsibilities at home due to parental illnesses. In others, where parents are hospitalized or have prolonged illnesses, young children can feel that the parents are neglecting them and they may express such feelings in angry reactions or other undesirable ways at school.

Marital problems.   Children are almost always involved when parents have marital difficulties. Separated or divorced parents may vie for their children's affection. Such situations are often confusing and difficult for children. Often because of marital problems, parents are overwhelmed with their personal concerns and are unable to assist their children with theirs.

L&BD students sometimes are not able to obtain the necessary support and assistance from their parents because of their marital problems. Similarly, teachers may find parents, in such situations, unresponsive to school requests in behalf of their children. While marital problems usually exceed the school's direct influence, teachers should be aware of the impact of such problems on schooling and, when feasible, refer children and parents to family agencies for counseling and assistance.

Sibling Problems

L&BD students may be confronted with problems that are rooted in relationships with their brothers and sisters. Such problems may take many different forms. When parents and teachers make an unfavorable comparison between a L&BD student and a less troubled sibling, or when an older sibling influences the L&BD student in undesirable directions, the student of concern here may be adversely affected.

Comparing siblings.   Historically teachers have compared students with their older siblings. Teachers may have several children from the same family in their classes over a period of years. While it is probably natural to make such comparisons, the thoughtlessness with which these comparisons may be made is often unfair.

> *Your sister was a good student. Why aren't you?*
> *Your brother Mark never acted that way!*
> *How come you aren't more like Jack? He was always so pleasant.*

Comments such as the above, when made by parents or teachers, may convey to the child that he or she is less good or in some way is inferior.

Teachers can influence parents and their students toward having a more realistic view when comparing siblings by stressing the individuality of all children. This can be done in class by instructing students about individual differences; these concepts can also be presented to parents in conferences. In such discussions, emphasis should be on the differences rather than on the values often placed on those differences. For example, L&BD students are often compared unfavorably with siblings during their preschool years. Since their attitudes and feelings of worthlessness may already be firmly established before entering special programs, their teachers should recognize feelings of inferiority as having instructional implications. Attitudes of inferiority are sometimes exhibited behaviorally in the form of self-deprecating verbal statements or daring feats and verbal excesses (overcompensation).

Simply telling children they are individuals and are worthy will not be of much value, but helping children to become effective and successful academically and socially will go far toward improving their feelings and attitudes. An emphasis on what children do of value as human beings will also help alleviate their feelings of inferiority. Teachers can help students to evaluate their own performances. Self-recording of specific responses and achievement on a regular basis will encourage them to be more objective in considering their progress.

Sibling influences.   Many children imitate older siblings' attitudes and behaviors. Often such imitation enhances the youngster's performances, particularly in cases where emulating an older sibling results in better social and academic behavior. But negative attitudes toward school, misbehaviors, and a dislike for learning may also be learned through imitating older brothers or sisters.

Of course, teachers rarely have opportunities to intervene when students are adversely influenced by their siblings. On occasion, some parents do recognize such problems and may discuss their concerns with teachers. Assistance for the sibling can then be recommended. Sometimes the behavior being emulated by a younger sibling is appropriate for older children. In these circumstances, parents and teachers may be able to obtain the cooperation of the older brother or sister so as to influence the student properly.

Financial Problems

Two types of family financial problems are reflected in schools. The first is characterized by temporary crises where the family, accustomed to a reasonable income, suddenly must adjust to a lesser amount. Low income as a way of life characterizes the second group. Behaviors and attitudes within the two groups are often very different.

Financial crises. Unemployment, reduced income, unexpected expenditures, and other financial problems produce serious difficulties for families. Their problems may be reflected in children's behavior and school achievement, as noted in anecdote 5.6.

ANECDOTE 5.6

Ten-year-old Manuel had always been a pleasant child even though he had academic learning difficulties. Because of his poor reading skills, he received tutoring each day as a part of the L&BD program. His regular classroom teacher noticed that Manuel was not as happy or pleasant as he had been just a few weeks before. She also noticed that he was much less talkative than usual.

In their weekly discussion concerning progress of each student being tutored she asked the tutor, Mr. Wolf, if he had noted any changes in Manuel. He had and indicated that Manuel's dad was laid off from his job.

Manuel was suddenly aware of unemployment compensation and food stamps. Since his father was now at home all day, Manuel's routine at home had changed and, along with the financial worry, had contributed to Manuel's concerns and fears.

It seems that Manuel had openly discussed his worries with Mr. Wolf during recent tutoring sessions. While he could not, of course, deal directly with Manuel's concerns, he was able to reassure him by letting him know that the family's current financial problems were of a temporary nature and not uncommon. He discussed his own experiences with unemployment and suggested ways that Manuel could help the family by being cooperative and understanding.

Problems of low income. Children from low income families live with financial problems continually. Welfare payments and food stamps are a way of life for them. Unlike Manuel's problem, their financial crises are not temporary. Because of the permanent nature of their family's financial conditions, their life-styles are often affected permanently.

Family income is highly correlated with school success. Because of the long-term effects of poverty, many children from such low socioeconomic homes are placed in programs for the mentally retarded early in their school lives. In some instances, such placements are precipitous, and more careful evaluations result in a need for instructional services commonly available for L&BD students. This issue is discussed in more detail in the following section.

Children of poverty often present problems in school that are qualitatively different from their middle-income peers. Often their values, in terms of behavior and school performance, are at variance with those of their teachers. Fighting and strong rhetoric are often their solutions to interpersonal problems; their eating habits and nutritional levels also tend to be poor.

Resultant effects on schooling for students from lower socioeconomic levels should be obvious. School lunch and breakfast programs should be made available to them. Teachers should be knowledgeable concerning the various social service programs available to children from low-income families. When necessary, children and parents who are not using such services fully should be identified and referred to the proper school and community offices.

Intellectual Problems

Intelligence has been a useful concept to special educators for many years. In fact, the measurement of intelligence gave scientific credence to identifying those children who were intellectually limited and in need of special instruction (Wallin & Ferguson, 1967). It is important to recognize that intelligence is only one aspect of human behavior, however, and in that sense it is crudely measured. Behaviors that are believed to be products of reasoning and that can be quantified are observed and related to fixed scales of previous measures. As a result, students' aptitudes, generally subsumed under the heading *intelligence,* are assigned scores on a previously determined scale.

Whether differences in intelligence are genetically determined or environmentally conditioned has been the subject of considerable controversy. Regardless of the bases for such differences, intellectual functioning is inherent to individuals in the sense that they bring to classrooms certain styles of thinking and levels of thinking power (IQ) which influence their learning.

Differences in Thinking Styles

Wide variations in styles of thinking are sometimes seen within the same student. The styles of thinking students bring to classrooms affect their learning in many ways.

First, thinking styles may conflict with or be incompatible with the manner in which curriculum content is presented. For example, a slow, methodical but power thinker (high IQ) may be penalized by teachers who expect and reward quickness. Students in such situations may be considered *underachievers* because their daily academic achievement is below their anticipated levels of achievement as determined by their IQ scores. Some learning situations require estimations rather than precise answers within limited time conditions. A compulsively methodical but slow thinker will tend to do poorly under such restrictions.

Second, students' thinking styles may be inconsistent and not in harmony with changing task demands. In these instances, students modify their rates and types of responses, but their changes are unrelated to what is required in a given learning situation. A problem of this type is described in anecdote 5.7.

ANECDOTE 5.7

Eleven-year-old Steve has been receiving special instruction in an L&BD program since he was seven. After having spent three years in a special class he is currently in a regular sixth grade and spending approximately two hours each day in a resource room. While Steve consistently scores in the average range (90-109) on IQ tests, his academic performance is erratic even within the same lesson on the same day. For example, he may at one moment give an extraordinary quick and correct answer to a reasoning problem in arithmetic and yet within a few minutes fail to comprehend why his response to an easier reasoning problem is incorrect.

Steve's great fluctuation in performance is not limited to math; he displays the same variability in reading comprehension and in other areas where reasoning is required. His earlier school records evidenced similar fluctuations in beginning academic skill learning as well.

During his first year in school this problem was viewed as symptomatic of *brain injury with emotional overlay.* Although the neurologist reported no clear signs of brain dysfunction he was placed on medication for awhile in hopes that it would result in a more consistent learning pattern. He performed no differently with medication and consequently it was no longer prescribed.

The emotional disturbance theory was then hypothesized and Steve was placed in a special class for L&BD children, thus satisfying the state's requirement for a *psychological or a medical diagnosis* for placement. Steve's teacher Miss Pantic, however, did not concern herself with the diagnosis and began to instruct him on the basis of where he seemed to be performing but that starting point was elusive since it changed so rapidly.

Considerable progress was made in the special class. After a few months of frustration Miss P. conferred with the consultant who observed Steve and then spent some time assessing him on task-specific items. She found that Steve's responses (and conduct) varied greatly. But a *base performance* on the skill continuum was found below which his responses were relatively consistent. Because of his age, this base performance level was quite low and seemed to Miss P. to be "too easy" for Steve. But, having confidence in her consultant's judgment, she proceeded to follow her recommendations and did find that Steve began to progress, ever so slowly, toward higher and higher levels where his performance was consistent.

Third, some students tend to focus on details to the exclusion of more general aspects of problems or tasks. Their ability to recall items within a paragraph, for example, may be quite good but they have trouble identifying the major theme or main idea of that paragraph. Problems of this sort may be noted in oral language as well when students participate in group discussions but fail to relate the various points to an overall principle or moral.

A fourth problem of thinking may be observed where students are unable to deal with specifics and are too general in their responses. Problems of this type are more noticeable among older students who have acquired language sophistication. They can, because of their language acquisition, discuss or write in generalities ("talk around problems") but have trouble coming to grips with the specifics of an issue.

L&BD students whose thinking styles interfere with learning conditions, should be provided with the needed individual assistance. Help should generally take the form of (a) personalizing assignments and/or (b) modifying their responses so as to be more flexible as the demands of tasks change. Both approaches are described in chapters 11 and 12.

Differences in Thinking Power

There are differences in performance on IQ tests which are related to learning. These differences are considered here as low measured intelligence, uneven intelligence, and specific intellectual deficiencies.

Low measured intelligence.   L&BD students, as discussed in this text, are distinguishable from other children with learning and behavior problems on the basis of measured intelligence. Their scores on aptitude tests are above the upper limits of those generally established for the mentally retarded. Since the IQ criterion for L&BD varies from state to state, as it does for the mentally retarded, there is no one IQ score that represents the minimum, although the absolute minimum appears to be around a score of 80.

When L&BD students with IQ scores in the 80s and 90s score below average on achievement tests, their performances may be incorrectly viewed as inadequate. Palkes and Stewart (1972) compared a group of hyperactive students with a matched group of normal students. They found that the mean full-scale, verbal and performance IQ scores on the *Wechsler Intelligence Scale for Children* were significantly lower for the hyperactive group. Their achievement test scores were consistent with their lower IQ scores.

Minde et al. (1971) found a similar result when they compared group IQ scores of hyperactive children with a normal (nonhyperactive) group. In their study, hyperactive students scored lower on group tests of intelligence and in academic subjects.

Uneven intelligence.   Qualitative differences in measured intelligence and thinking processes are sometimes associated with L&BD students. An IQ score is the sum of its parts, and students who score very high on some factors and low on others may receive average scores yet display problems of intelligence because of their uneven performances. Similarly, two students obtaining the same IQ scores may be functioning intellectually in very different ways.

Roth (1974) demonstrated how conventional test scores can hide qualitative differences in student responses. Using the *Peabody Picture Vocabulary Test* he tested a sample of black and white children at school and retested them at home. All testing sessions were tape recorded, and analysis of the transcripts showed that children from both racial groups demonstrated conceptual performances which were not measured by the Peabody. While Roth's sample was not drawn from an L&BD population, his study does show that tests of intelligence do not necessarily measure important differences in thinking.

Kirk and Kirk (1971) described the importance of using aptitude tests that yield scores showing discrepancies in growth and abilities within students. They argued for diagnostic tests that delineate abilities in such a way as to pinpoint strengths and weaknesses within an individual's overall performance. They based the *Illinois Test of Psycholinguistic Abilities* on the belief that learning disabled children have specific disorders in one or more areas of the communication process.

The extent to which disproportionate abilities affect learning among L&BD students has not been fully studied, but clinical evidence does suggest that the kind of performance described in anecdote 5.8 is frequently found among the L&BD population.

ANECDOTE 5.8

Twelve-year-old Myra has had serious problems achieving even moderately well in most language skills. Throughout her school career she has had difficulty in reading, spelling, and written language. Although her oral language is about average for her age, Myra's reading skills are at about a third grade level and her spelling is equally low. Yet her arithmetic computation and reasoning are at a seventh-grade level.

Myra's academic achievement is reflected in her aptitude test scores. She consistently scores on performance test items (nonlanguage) at around 110 IQ, but her verbal IQ scores are about 85.

A careful analysis of her achievement test responses shows that she has poor word attack skills in using syllabication and phonetics. Similarly, her aptitude subtest results show low performance on items which require reading and language, such as information and vocabulary.

Since Myra's teacher is more concerned about her achievement test results than her aptitudes, she developed a teaching plan based upon the former.

Specific intellectual deficiencies. Another form of uneven intellectual functioning is noted when students show consistent performance in all but one aptitude area. For example, problems of memory can result in poor academic performance because of the reliance on recall for success in schools. Students with memory difficulties may perform adequately on problem-solving tasks but do poorly in activities where informational items must be recalled. Beginning reading skills are affected by poor memory where there is a need for instant recognition of sight words. Similarly, spelling performance is also impaired by poor memory.

Where there is specific reasoning impairment, for example in mathematics, students may do well in all subject areas except math. Reasoning may be intact in subjects where word symbols are used but poor when using numbers or formulas in reasoning.

Other examples of specific problems are seen where tone deafness contributes to an inability to carry a tune or to play musical instruments or when a failure to see perspectives results in limited art skills. These types of aptitude defects tend to be more readily accepted by teachers and parents than similar problems in academic areas.

Inappropriate Learning

Previous learning experiences may serve to facilitate or inhibit new learning. Students with inadequate life experiences bring to school limitations which may have accumulated over many years. Their inadequacies may be attributed to many different factors. For example, poor training at home and/or poor teaching in school can contribute to insufficient and/or incorrect learning. Under these circumstances students may have acquired behavior standards that conflict with those required at school, or their limited language acquisition handicap their learning in school. Anecdote 5.9 depicts how home and school experiences contribute to academic and social learning problems.

ANECDOTE 5.9

1. Sammy, at age 14, is considered a school failure, a behavior problem, and an emotionally disturbed teenager by his teachers. Because he displays so many problems, he has repeatedly been recommended for special L&BD class placements. However, his parents, particularly his mother, refuse to approve special placement as recommended by the special education team. It seems that Sammy has a history of needing special help but his parents have consistently denied that he was in need of assistance.

2. Eight-year-old Norma has frequently been absent from school, averaging one day each week in the past two years. She and her mother enjoy spending week days together at home watching TV. Because of her frequent absences, Norma has gaps in

her academic skills. She has also developed a poor attitude toward school.

3. Harvey's middle-income family rarely reads books or magazines. Consequently, his home is devoid of reading materials and he has not acquired those values towards learning which are important for school success.

4. Margaret's second-grade teacher taught the entire class of 30 pupils reading from the same text and at the same time. Even though Margaret had difficulty acquiring reading skills as rapidly as most of the class, her teacher persisted in continuing to move her through the reading series without any individualized instruction. By the end of the year Margaret had acquired several poor reading habits, often miscalling words and misinterpreting passages.

5. Clem finds arithmetic processes confusing. His fourth-grade teacher, however, simply discards written arithmetic assignments and is unaware of Clem's inadequate understanding.

Items 1, 2 and 3 in anecdote 5.9 indicate how values and attitudes at home influence children's schooling. Similarly, items 4 and 5 show that teachers who fail to conduct instruction in dutiful ways can impair students' academic achievement. There are, of course, many other known examples of how previous learning hinders childrens' school success. Fortunately, parents who encourage children in their learning and teachers who conscientiously individualize instruction are more numerous than those who do not.

Reinforcement History

From a behavioral view, students' past learnings are the result of their reinforcement histories. Their conduct, interests, efforts, and attitudes are shaped and maintained by previous events which were satisfying or punishing to them.

Inappropriate, inadequate, and conflicting reinforcement in students' past and present environments affects their schooling. L&BD students who have extensive histories of these kinds of reinforcement often require extensive special instruction and services. In some cases it is necessary to retrain parents or other school personnel when the new behavior must be maintained across other classrooms or at home. This is not to suggest that teachers cannot change students' performances because of past reinforcement experiences. It does require, however, that teachers recognize that a systematic reinforcement approach may take longer to be effective with those who have lengthy histories of different reinforcement. Older students, in particular, may require extensive special treatment for this reason.

There is no question that rewards and punishment influence academic performance and social behavior. Those not familiar with studies in support of their effects often mistakenly view "behavior modification" as only effective in changing conduct disorders. They fail to recognize that academic performance is also a type of behavior.

Wadsworth (1971) demonstrated the effects of reinforcement approaches on school behavior and reading performance on third-grade learning disabled children. Fifteen boys, diagnosed as having visual-motor integration, auditory discrimination, and reading problems were taught under three conditions. With the boys serving as their own controls, clinical tutoring in reading, reinforcement techniques in a self-contained classroom, and reinforcement in a resource room were used as treatments. Reinforcement in both class settings resulted in significant reading gains and a reduction in misbehavior. Traditional tutoring in a private clinic, however, did not change reading behavior or conduct problems significantly.

Seven-year-old Rocko was referred to the special education team because of his severe conduct problems. During his first year in school Rocko was repeatedly sent to the principal's office for disruptive classroom behavior and fighting in the lunchroom and on the playground.

Two conditions seemed to maintain Rocko's maladaptive behavior. First, he was stronger than any of his classmates and a good fighter. Thus, he received recognition and gained status among his peer group because of his superior strength and fighting skills. Second, the school personnel believed that such behavior was symptomatic of emotional problems and responded to Rocko's misbehavior by counseling him and by providing him with special privileges. For example, when he was sent to the principal he was provided with an opportunity to discuss his problems with her. She also encouraged him to play with clay as a means of "expressing his hostility."

Receptive/Expressive Modalities

Two factors influencing learning are students' abilities to receive stimuli and to respond selectively to them. There is some question as to the basis for this ability, its nature, and instructional effects on it. Authorities, however, have speculated as to the receptive and expressive processes which are used in human learning. Some (Osgood, 1957; Chalfant & Scheffelin, 1969; Ensminger, 1970) have related these modalities to various theoretical models of learning. Others have assumed that teachers of children with learning and behavioral problems need to relate classroom instruction to those neurological deficits which are presumed to have caused or contributed to the students' handicaps.

Prescriptive teaching methods, both those rooted in the ability training model and those related to skill training, point toward an assessment of students' modes of learning in order to relate instruction to those modes (Stephens, 1970; Meyen, Vergeson, & Whelan, 1972). While an approach of this type seems logical, those few research studies which have been conducted have failed to support or deny its importance for learning (Hammill, 1972; Snyder & Pope, 1972; Waugh, 1973; Hartman, 1974). It seems reasonable, however, to recognize that sensory modes are important for academic and social learning. Sensory channels are our only means for receiving stimuli, and that reception influences our expressions.

Receptive Modalities

Humans have the capacity to receive stimuli through five senses. We can obtain visual, auditory, olfactory, gustatory, and haptic stimuli. While experiences acquired through all of these senses influence learning, the visual and auditory modes are heavily emphasized in schools, and there is some research evidence to suggest that reading instruction for L&BD students should be determined by their proficiencies in visual and auditory learning (deHirsch, Jansky, & Langford, 1966). Visual stimuli include printed and written symbols and thus make reading skills highly dependent upon discrimination and recall of these symbols.

Auditory discrimination and recall are essential for all language learning. Because of its importance, the acquisition of language is the most necessary skill for advanced academic achievement.

Olfaction has not been emphasized in academic learning, although there are commercially available materials for using the olfactory mode in reading (Rowland,

1971). In one study, Hartman (1974) used odors as paired stimuli with words with beginning readers. She found that olfactory cues did not result in significant gains in reading over other experimental subjects. Performance of the subjects in the olfactory group was superior, however, to that of controls.

Gustatory stimuli undoubtedly influence our food preferences but have almost no influence on formal learning.

Fernald (1943) and others have noted the importance for learning through touch discrimination, which is one aspect of haptics. The sense of touch through its broadest sense, *haptics,* encompasses all of the skin area.

Expressive Modes

Expressive behavior is observed in students by their activities. Their behavior may include moving, speaking, hearing, smelling, tasting, and touching. The quality of students' responses usually determine their academic success and their social behaviors suggest their emotional and social adaptability.

Expressive behavior also reveals students' abilities to discriminate across social and academic situations. Students who have difficulty in distinguishing among various academic stimuli are often considered to have learning problems. Similarly, those who fail to discriminate correctly within a social context, and consequently behave inappropriately, may be termed socially or emotionally disturbed.

Summary

This chapter considered those important variables that are inherently a part of attributes which students bring to teaching/learning situations. These are not necessarily conditions which cannot be changed. They are, however, factors over which school personnel have limited control. These factors include problems of health, including the effects of medication on behavior and physical handicaps.

Psychological factors are problems of temperament, family related problems, sibling problems, and financial difficulties. Intellectual problems include factors which are directly related to school success, such as differences in styles of thinking, intelligence, past learning, and differences in using receptive/expressive modes for learning.

Teacher Assessment of Students

Instruction of L&BD students should begin with an assessment of their performances on tasks that are to be taught. Selection and use of assessment materials are related to the type of instructional program and to teachers' understanding of the relationship of instruction to assessment.

Student assessment may be conducted with standardized tests and through nonstandardized approaches. Often both types of testing are used. Standardized approaches consist of aptitude, academic achievement, information processing, and personality tests. Such measures have limitations in terms of their usefulness and validity and reliability.

Nonstandardized approaches include teacher devised measures, direct observations, and criterion-referenced measures.

Introduction

Almost all teachers of L&BD students recognize the importance of individualizing instruction. While they might disagree as to what constitutes the procedures for individualizing, they certainly would view it as an essential ingredient of successful special programs. Gathering information concerning students' performances is the first step in any instructional program that is designed to provide individualized approaches. This step is referred to here as assessment.

Assessment has various meanings to different school practitioners. Because its meaning is not standardized, teachers who assess children prior to instruction may be engaging in widely diverse activities. Assessment may essentially be thought of as testing through the use of aptitude and standardized achievement measures. Or it may be used to convey the notion of a general appraisal of a student's past and present performance levels as well as delving into psychological, medical, and family backgrounds. Assessment is used by this author in a more restricted sense: *a survey of student functioning to determine those responses and skills that are adequate and those yet to be learned or mastered.*

Teachers and Assessment

Teachers are responsible for determining the academic learning and social behavior needs of L&BD students. In order to determine those specific needs, it is essential for teachers to conduct assessments of their students.

Depending upon one's expectations and orientation to instruction, one may attempt to obtain information about students from various diagnostic tests, inventories, and other sources. Those teachers who precede instruction with assessment are faced with several issues that determine for them the meaning of assessment, its nature, variables that will be assessed, and the uses to which assessment information will be put.

Three overriding issues are related to assessment of students by their teachers. These are what to assess, how to assess, and how to use assessment findings.

What to Assess

Questions as to which performances or behaviors to assess are related to teachers' approaches to instruction. Those who are inclined toward prescriptive teaching are faced with the differences between ability training and skill training.[1]

Ability training draws heavily from those tests based upon information processing, while skill training approaches rely upon measures that evaluate performances in terms of products. Differences in how the two models affect teachers' assessment of students are exemplified by the use of direct observational information, as seen in anecdote 6.1

ANECDOTE 6.1

1. Sandy Smith, an eight-year-old boy, is in a special class for learning disabled children. His teacher has noted that he sometimes reads *was* as *saw*, prints and writes poorly, at times reverses some numerals and letters when reproducing them, and appears to be clumsy when running and walking.

2. Twelve-year-old Gerald has trouble reading. His teacher observed that he has poor word attack skills, has trouble following verbal instruction, and appears not to be attentive during class discussions.

3. Sarah, at seven years of age, is very hyperactive. She has difficulty attending even for short periods of time in school or at home. She also uses pencils and crayons crudely and draws poor circles and squares. While most of her classmates are already reading, she knows very few sight words.

Sandy might be considered to have a visual-perceptual problem by teachers who are steeped in an ability training orientation. Those who are skill-training oriented, however, would approach each of Sandy's problems as skills to be corrected. Similarly, ability trainers would consider Gerald as having auditory-perceptual difficulties. Whereas, skill trainers would identify those responses Gerald was ready to learn and proceed to teach them to him. Since Sarah's problems are more general, ability trainers might proceed to use the *ITPA* or the Frostig tests to determine which ability areas were in need of remediation. Skill trainers would undoubtedly seek more specific measures of her performances prior to teaching her correct responses.

In ability training, abilities and processes are assessed. Ability trainers assume that responses on tests are related to terminal behaviors because they are sometimes shown to be correlated to such behaviors. Correlation is used in lieu of

---

1. Readers are referred to chapter 2 for an extended discussion concerning skill training and ability training.

causation by ability trainers. Conversely, skill trainers value what is assessed for its own worth since they do not need to relate poor performance to causation.

How to Assess

How to assess is related to Quay's (1973) three types of remedial techniques.[2] Ability trainers are clearly Type 2 oriented because they rely upon factors which are "... either empirically or at least logically related to the terminal behavior" (Quay, 1973, p. 167). Quay's caution in this regard is that the responses should not merely be test related but should be demonstrated to be precursors of the terminal behavior.

Proponents of ability training often cite the importance of teaching generalizable responses, those that consist of subsets. Similarly, critics of skill training note that it ignores processes and tends to inhibit generalizability of responses. In sum, advocates of ability training emphasize measuring students' abilities "... in such a way that remediation and training can follow" (Kirk, 1975, p. 45).

Skill trainers rely upon direct instruction, citing the failure of ability training (Ysseldyke, 1974). They respond to the criticism of neglecting generalizability by recommending that specific responses can be taught across various conditions in order to facilitate generalizing (Stephens, 1975).

Direct observation of responses is a common technique for skill trainers. They may count the number of times target students engage in certain maladaptive behaviors or the frequency of words that are misspelled or misread. When observation is used by ability trainers, it is either for confirming a diagnosis or as a preliminary means of suggesting the abilities to be examined.

ANECDOTE 6.2

Nine-year-old Geraldine reverses letters when printing (M,W,d,b,p,q). She confuses small words when reading (saw, was, at, it, he, she, for, ant, and). Her handwriting and printing are of poor quality. She also tends to be inattentive and somewhat hyperactive.

Ability Training Assessment

Ms. Hamm, Geraldine's resource room teacher, has related the above observations, which she made, to the scores on the Frostig and *ITPA*. Her observations seemed to confirm the test scores, low on visual-motor subtests on the *ITPA* and low on eye-motor coordination, position in space, and spatial relations subtests on the *Frostig Developmental Test of Visual Perception.*

Skill Training Assessment

Had Geraldine been assigned to Ms. Franklin's special class, and had she noted those same observations, her instructional program would have been different. Instruction would have been based upon those observations. In reading, small words would be emphasized with special practice assignments directed at those words not yet mastered. Correct formation of letters in printing would be systematically taught. Conditions would be arranged so that attending skills would be reinforced.

How to Use Assessment Results

Perhaps the most important question to ask prior to assessing students is *How will the assessment results be used?* Clearly, assessment information should be useful

2. Readers are referred to chapter 4 for a detailed discussion of Quay's three types.

for instructional purposes. And, of course, the teacher's orientation will determine the nature of instruction. For example, ability trainers use their findings to suggest training procedures for improving abilities, as noted in anecdote 6.3.

ANECDOTE 6.3

Ms. Hamm, following the suggested training procedures by Frostig (1975), has set up these activities in relation to the test findings:

Eye-Motor Coordination — eye movement training, arts and crafts, handwriting exercises, and manipulative exercises.

Position in Space — exercises to promote awareness of body position in space, physical education program, and learning directions.

Spatial Relations — using jig-saw puzzles and copying patterns.

Skill trainers do an analysis of those tasks which students have not yet mastered. Those subtasks which are established as comprising the desired skill are then systematically taught. For example, Ms. Franklin might have arranged the following instructional activities for Geraldine:

printing: Those letters in which reversals occurred would be taught by first having her trace each letter and then having her copy the letter from a model on the same paper. Later she would print the letter from dictation. Mastery of each step would be demonstrated prior to moving to the next step.

reading: Small words that she tended to confuse would be placed individually on cards. The teacher would say a sentence, flashing each card in lieu of saying the word, and Geraldine would be required to read the word, e.g., Teacher: We call a boy *he* and a girl _____. Geraldine: *she*.

Assessment results may also be used to suggest *how* to teach. For example, some students may respond well to repetition, or particular modalities may seemingly be effective presentation modes for selective students. As seen in Figure 6.1, sensory modes may be assessed in relation to academic performances.

The Use of Standardized and Clinical Tests[3]

Norm-referenced measures are tests in which performance of one individual is compared with that of others in the reference group upon which the test was standardized. Because of the way in which norm-referenced measures are constructed, they are often referred to as standardized tests. Clinical tests may or may not be normed, although they almost always have some type of a scoring system. These are often individually administered instruments requiring psychometric or psychological training, particularly for interpreting the results, and are referred to as clinical tests because of their frequent use in clinic settings. Projective tests and other personality measures are typically considered to be clinical instruments.

Tests are available for measuring aptitude and school achievement, for diagnosing specific learning problems, and for determining personal adjustment. Critical analyses of standardized, commercially available tests are available in Buros' *Mental Measurements Yearbooks* and *Reading Tests and Reviews*.[4]

---

3. Dr. Mary Boehnlein, Cleveland State University, provided information concerning specific tests for this section. Her contribution is appreciated.

4. See O. Buros, *The seventh mental measurements yearbook*. Highland Park, N.J.: Gryphon Press, 1972; O. Buros, *Reading tests and reviews*. Highland Park, N.J.: Gryphon Press, 1972.

Dates of Assessment

	Sense Skill	Stimulus	Criterion Score	Performance Score	Analysis Code	(○ at criterion; − below; + above) Comments
A U D I T O R Y	Discrimination	20 pairs of words — subject to indicate same or different	18	18	○	answered 18 or 20 correctly; failed sit-set; knit; net
	Immediate Recall	Story: "Katy"	3	3	○	answered 3 of 3 questions
	Delayed Recall	Same	3	3	○	
V I S U A L	Discrimination	220 Dolch Words	220	214	−	word recognition improves when detail is called to her attention
	Immediate Recall	word selection — 4 trials	2	3	+	recognized correct, circle, halo; missed suggestion
	Delayed Recall	word selection — 4 trials	3	4	+	recognized all 4 including suggestion
H A P T I C S	Discrimination	objects letters	8	9	+	geometric designs recognized letters T, P, O, Q, recognized
	Immediate Recall	Spelling words: correct, heaven, believe	3	1	−	recalled "correct"
	Delayed Recall	Same	1	0	−	failed all 3 words
O L F A C T O R Y	Discrimination	Chocolate candy, cinnamon, orange, onion, banana	3	3	○	missed cinnamon, banana; at criterion
	Immediate Recall					
	Delayed Recall	Same	3	3	○	at criterion

FIGURE 6.1. Sensory-expressive learning summary form. (From Thomas M. Stephens, *Directive teaching of children with learning and behavioral handicaps.* Columbus, Ohio: Charles E. Merrill, 1976, p. 133.)

Tests for specific purposes are also listed in some textbooks, such as the following:

Gearheart, Bill R., & Willenberg, Ernest P. *Application of pupil assessment information for the special education teacher* (2nd ed.). Denver: Love Publishing Co., 1974.

Harris, Albert J. *How to increase reading ability* (5th ed.). New York: David McKay Company, Inc., 1970.

Miller, Wilma. *Identifying and correcting reading difficulties in children.* New York: Center for Applied Research in Education, Inc., 1971.

Teachers of L&BD students who use normed measures for assessment purposes generally use either achievement tests and/or diagnostic prescriptive tests. In addition, personality measures and aptitude measures are sometimes used by such ancillary personnel as psychologists and counselors and are interpreted for teachers.

Aptitude Measures

Aptitude tests are used for predicting students' performances. They consist of items believed to correlate highly with scholastic performance. Many aptitude tests yield IQ scores and are often referred to as tests of intelligence. Some can only be individually administered, thus requiring trained psychometrists. Others may be used with groups.

Generally, individually administered intelligence tests are composed of a variety of problems requiring the ability to use ideas and symbols. Tests of intelligence measure abstract and scholastic abilities and are seldom good predictors of nonschool performances. A selected number of individually administered tests of intelligence are listed below:

Ammons Full-Range Picture Vocabulary Test. Preschool-Adult. A test of verbal intelligence. Answers are given by pointing to the correct picture. New York: The Psychological Corporation.

Cornell-Coxe Performance Ability Scale. Ages 6-15. An individual nonlanguage performance scale. Chicago: Stoelting.

Goodenough-Harris Drawing Test. Ages 3-12. Measures nonverbal intelligence through a standardized procedure of scoring human figure drawings. New York: Harcourt, Brace, and World, Inc.

Peabody Picture Vocabulary Test. Ages 2-18. A test of verbal intelligence. Circle Pines, Minnesota: American Guidance Services, Inc.

Stanford-Binet Intelligence Scale. Ages 2-16. Perhaps the most commonly used individual test of general intelligence. Boston: Houghton-Mifflin Co.

Vineland Social Maturity Scale. Preschool-Adult. An observation and interview scale for measuring self-care and social behavior. Circle Pines, Minnesota: American Guidance Services, Inc.

Wechsler Intelligence Scale for Children. Ages 5-15. Yields verbal, performance, and full-scale IQ scores. New York: The Psychological Corporation.

Group tests of intelligence are similar in content to individual intelligence scales. Both attempt to minimize routine school learning and present problems demanding reasoning and generalizing. Many group tests of intelligence require reading ability and have strict time limits. Both of these conditions may provide serious limitations to L&BD students and often result in depressed scores. The following is a list of selected group tests of intelligence. These are not necessarily the best group aptitude measures; they are presented here solely as samples from a wider selection of available tests.

California Tests of Mental Maturity. K-College. Available in short form and long form. Provides separate IQ scores for language, nonlanguage, and total scores. Monterey, California: California Test Bureau.

Culture Fair Intelligence Tests. Ages 4-Adult. General intelligence tests not requiring reading and considered free of educational and cultural influences. Champaign, Illinois: Institute for Personality and Aptitude Testing.

Henmon Nelson Tests of Mental Ability. Grades 3-12. A self-marking group intelligence test requiring reading. Boston: Houghton-Mifflin Company.

Kuhlmann-Anderson Measure of Academic Potential. K-12. Yields a general intelligence score. Content below fifth grade does not require reading. New York: The Psychological Corporation.

Lorge Thorndike Intelligence Tests. Grades 3-13. Provides verbal, nonverbal, and total scores. Boston: Houghton-Mifflin Company.

Otis Quick Scoring Mental Ability Tests. Grades 1-9. Tests below grade four require no reading. New York: Harcourt, Brace, and World, Inc.

SRA Primary Mental Abilities Test. Grades K-12. Provides separate IQ scores for verbal meaning, number facility, reasoning, perceptual speed, and spatial relations. Total IQ is also provided. Chicago: Science Research Associates.

Academic Achievement Measures

Standardized scholastic achievement measures are used routinely in schools in order to determine how much pupils know about subjects they are studying or will be studying. These tests are useful for surveying a group's standing in relation to that of the norm group and for curriculum development and change.

Attempts have also been made to use these tests for determining students' weaknesses and strengths. Some of the tests provide a form for conducting an item analysis of each student's performances. Because each subtest contains a limited number of items, however, an analytical approach is questionable. Some of the skills are often measured by only two or three items, giving teachers very little information for making instructional decisions.

Five tests of academic achievement are listed below as examples of this type of measure.

California Reading Tests. Lower primary, grades 1, 2; Primary, grades 3, lower 4; Elementary, grades 4-6; Junior High, grades 7-9; Advanced, grades 9 to college. Each test has two main parts, vocabulary and comprehension, with several subtests in each part. Two to four forms at each level. Monterey, California: California Test Bureau.

Iowa Tests of Basic Skills. Grades 3-8. Tests for all grades in one reusable booklet. Test V, vocabulary; Test R, reading comprehension; Test W, word-study skills. Boston: Houghton-Mifflin Company.

MacMillan Reader Placement Test. Individual test containing graded book samples and word lists. New York: The MacMillan Company.

Metropolitan Achievement Tests. Primary 1, Battery, end of grade 1, Word knowledge, word discrimination, reading, arithmetic. Primary II Battery, grade 2.0-3.5. Word knowledge, word discrimination, reading, spelling, arithmetic. Elementary Reading, grades 3, 4. Paragraph comprehension, vocabulary. Intermediate Reading, grades 5, 6. Advanced Reading, grades 7, 8. Paragraph comprehension, vocabulary. New York: Harcourt, Brace & World, Inc.

SRA Achievement Series: Reading. Grades 1, 2. Verbal-pictorial association, language perception, comprehension, vocabulary. Grades 2-4, grades 4-6, grades 6-9, comprehension and vocabulary. Grades 4-6, Word-study skills. Chicago: Science Research Associates.

Diagnostic Measures

Ensminger and Sullivan (1974) have indicated that the frequent use of diagnostic-prescriptive tests with learning disabled children " . . . has been to provide greater sophistication in diagnosing learning assets and deficits in children and in formulating educational programs to improve their school learning" (p. 53). Diagnostic achievement tests are designed to identify students' strengths and weaknesses in subject areas or in information processing. Selected diagnostic tests in reading and subject areas include:

Diagnostic Reading Tests. A series of survey and diagnostic tests from grade 1 to college.

Kindergarten-grade 4. Reading readiness; Survey section, Booklet I, grade 1; Booklet II, grade 2; Booklet III, grades 3, 4; Section IV, word attack, Part 1, Oral.

Lower Level, grades 4-6. Booklet I, comprehension and word attack; Booklet II, vocabulary and rate; Section IV, word attack, oral, for individual administration. Forms A, B, each booklet.

Higher Level, grades 7 to college. Includes a Survey Test of vocabulary, comprehension, and rate, with seven forms, A to H; and a Diagnostic Battery with eight separate booklets: vocabulary, silent comprehension, auditory comprehension, general rate, rate in social studies, rate in science, oral word attack (individual), and silent word attack; forms A, B, each part. Mountain Home, North Carolina: Committee on Diagnostic Reading Tests.

Durrell Analysis of Reading Difficulty. A battery of diagnostic tests for intensive analysis of reading difficulties. Includes a set of reading paragraphs, a cardboard tachistoscope, word lists, and a record blank. Provides tests of oral and silent reading, listening comprehension, word analysis, phonics, faulty pronunciation, writing, and spelling. New York: Harcourt, Brace & World, Inc.

Gates-McKillop Reading Diagnostic Tests. Battery of tests for individual diagnosis of retarded readers from nonreader up. Paragraphs for oral reading, word perception, flashed and untimed; phrase perception; syllabication, letter names and sounds, visual and auditory blending, spelling. New York: Teachers College Press, Columbia University.

Lincoln Diagnostic Spelling Tests. Intermediate, grades 5-8; grades 8-12. Designed to disclose causes or areas of difficulty; pronunciation, enunciation, and use of rules. Indianapolis: Bobbs-Merrill Company.

Roswell-Chall Diagnostic Reading Test. A short series of tests for analyzing phonic knowledge and skills. New York: Essay Press.

Silent Reading Diagnostic Tests. Grades 3 and up. Group test providing a detailed analysis of many word recognition and phonic skills, with eleven subtests. Chicago: Lyons and Carnahan, Inc.

Measures of Information Processing

Information processing theories have influenced the development of diagnostic tests designed to identify students' strengths and weaknesses in receiving and integrating stimuli. Such tests have been extraordinarily influential in programs for learning disabled children; in the diagnostic-prescriptive movement these measures are widely used in many areas of special education.

Some tests of information processing attempt to incorporate most of the sensory channels, such as the *Illinois Test of Psycholinguistic Abilities (ITPA),* while others deal with a single mode, e.g., *Assessment of Children's Language Comprehension,* which seeks to measure receptive language abilities. A sampling of such tests are:

Assessment of Children's Language Comprehension. Ages 2-6, determines difficulties in receptive language. Missoula, Montana: Psychological Test Specialists.

Bender Visual Motor Gestalt Test. A clinical test of ability to copy visual designs. New York: Psychological Test Corporation.

Benton Visual Retention Test, Revised. An individual test of ability to draw designs from memory. New York: Psychological Test Corporation.

Frostig, Marianne, Developmental Test of Visual Perception. Ages 4-9. Includes group tests of five aspects of visual perception. Chicago: Follett Educational Corporation.

Goldman-Fristoe-Woodcock Test of Auditory Discrimination. Ages 4 and above. Evaluates auditory discrimination under both quiet and background noise conditions. Prerecorded tape included. Circle Pines, Minnesota: American Guidance Services, Inc.

Illinois Test of Psycholinguistic Abilities. Ages 4-9. Nine individually administered subtests measuring abilities basic in communications. Urbana, Illinois: University of Illinois Press.

Memory for Designs Test. Ages 8 and above. Assists in screening for brain damage or perceptual motor problems. Missoula, Minnesota: Psychological Test Specialists.

Picture Story Language Test. Ages 7-17. Assess written language productivity, syntax, and development of abstract and concrete language. New York: Grune and Stratton, Inc.

Screening Tests for Identifying Children with Specific Language Disability. Levels for grades 1-2, 2-3, and 3-4. Intended for use in locating children who have or are likely to develop disabilities in reading, spelling, and handwriting. Visual copying, memory, and discrimination; three auditory group tests; one individual auditory test. Cambridge, Massachusetts: Educators Publishing Service.

START: Screening Test for the Assignment of Remedial Treatments. Ages 4-6. Group tests of visual memory, auditory memory, visual copying, visual discrimination. Skokie, Illinois: Priority Innovations, Inc.

Valett Developmental Survey of Basic Learning Abilities. Ages 2-7. A compendium of 233 tasks in seven areas: motor integration, tactile discrimination, auditory discrimination, visual motor coordination, visual discrimination, language development, conceptual development. Palo Alto, California: Consulting Psychologists Press.

Wepman Auditory Discrimination Test. Ages 5-9. Tests ability to distinguish whether two spoken words are the same or slightly different. Chicago: Language Research Associates.

Woodcock Reading Mastery Tests. Grades K-12. Yields six scores: letter identification, word identification, word attack, word comprehension, passage comprehension, and total reading. Provides options for use as a criterion-referenced test and as a normed test. Two parallel forms. Circle Pines, Minnesota: American Guidance Services, Inc.

Personality Measures

Personality has been evaluated in three ways: by rating scales, by questionnaires and inventories, and by what has been termed *projective* tests. It is technically incorrect to consider some of these devices as standardized tests since they often fail to meet acceptable criteria for validity and reliability. Further, teachers often find that personality measures do not provide useful instructional information. The following are listed here merely for informational purposes:

California Test of Personality. Primary, kindergarten to grade 3; Elementary, grades 4-8; Intermediate, grades 7-10; Secondary, grades 9 to college. An analytical group personality questionnaire providing scores on self-adjustment and social adjustment. Monterey, California: California Test Bureau.

Children's Apperception Test. Ages 4-10. An individually administered projective test of personality, to be used only by trained psychologists. New York: The Psychological Corporation.

Michigan Picture Test. An individual projective test for elementary school children. Chicago: Science Research Associates.

Rorschach Psychodiagnostics. Preschool to adult. A projective test of personality. New York: The Psychological Corporation.

Thematic Apperception Test. Ages 6 to adult. A projective test of personality. New York: The Psychological Corporation.

Of the five tests listed above, the *California Test of Personality* is the only paper-pencil instrument. The others are projective instruments and require special training for administering and for interpreting results.

Limitations of Standardized Tests for Assessment

Almost all public schools in the United States use standardized tests regularly. Similarly, clinical measures are often used by nonteaching school personnel such as counselors and psychologists. Both standardized tests and clinical instruments should be considered with respect to their possible limitations: their usefulness for instruction, their validity and reliability, and their ease of use. Each of these possible limitations are discussed below.

Usefulness for Instruction

Academic assessment measures can be evaluated as to their usefulness by comparing the results they yield with the desired outcomes of the instructional program. Thus, usefulness of assessment measures is based upon the types of information needed in order to teach L&BD students and to provide them with meaningful educational programs.

Usefulness can be determined by considering the target population's characteristics, how well the assessment measures are related to the instructional program, and the level of specificity of information yielded by assessment instruments.

Target Population Description

Mager (1972) considers target population description as " . . . a careful examination of the characteristics of those for whom instruction is intended" (p. 8). Of course, such descriptions can be at varying levels of specificity. For example, school placement may require gross information elements (aptitude scores, achievement grade scores, and evidence of certain types of personal adjustment).

At the instructional level, however, descriptions of students' performances should be related to their existing skills and compared with the desired skills. Information of this type must be more precise than that needed for school placement. In addition to precision, it must also be directly related to what is to be taught. All information useful for classroom instruction can be used for program assignment decisions, although such precise information is not essential for placement purposes.

Information which is provided through test scores is often of value only for purposes of program assignment because test scores do not provide sufficient precision for instruction Program assignment decisions involve a range of possible student services such as classroom instruction, tutoring, counseling, remedial instruction, special schools, and health services. Because of this range, diverse (but accurate) information is useful for making program assignment decisions.

Decisions made by instructional personnel are of an immediate nature (e.g., which skills does the child need in order to complete this unit?). While such personnel should be *involved* in placement decisions, the accountability for placement rests with administrative and supervisory personnel.

Relatedness to Instruction

Relevance is a major criterion of usefulness. If test results are not directly related to what is to be taught, it is not instructionally relevant for assessment purposes. The issue of curriculum (what is to be taught?) is tied to the question of relevance for assessment. Few standardized or clinical tests meet the requirement of relevance to curriculum. Only those measures that have been developed in conjunction with a curriculum, or those that provide remedial programs as a result of the tests (e.g., *ITPA*, Frostig), may meet this requirement.

Rarely are aptitude measures accompanied by related instructional programs. This is not surprising since aptitude measures are based upon the belief that they are predictive tests and would be invalidated if used for teaching purposes. Similarly, personality measures are generally not tied directly to instructional items because they are often not viewed as having instructional value. Rather, projective test results are used to assess an individual's personal adjustment.

Some textbooks provide achievement tests to accompany workbooks and other instructional materials. Many of these, however, are used to help determine which graded book students should be assigned (e.g., *MacMillan Reader Placement Test*). Such a determination does not meet the requirements of specificity or instructional relevance.

Some diagnostic measures, particularly those based upon information processing theory, do provide curriculum materials to be used following assessment. However, the effectiveness of such programs has not been consistently verified.

Jacobs (1967; 1968) demonstrated that the Frostig Program for the Development of Visual Perception (Frostig & Horne, 1964) results in higher scores on the Frostig test but not on reading scores for regular class students. Wiederholt & Hammill (1971) had similar findings. Non-perceptually handicapped pupils scored higher on the Developmental Test of Visual Perception following training but not higher on academic and readiness tests. Perceptually handicapped pupils, however, failed to score higher on the test after training on Frostig materials.

The *ITPA* has not fared well either as a basis for remedial instruction. Although Kirk & Kirk (1971) report studies of individual students who improved as a result of following their guidelines for remediation, Waugh (1975) has pointed out the fallacy of generalizing individual reports to groups of children. Following an extensive review of the *ITPA*, he concluded: "Remediation directed toward strengths and weaknesses in sensory or perceptual processing has not been effective" (p. 468).

However, Riegel, Taylor, and Danner (1973) found that young children (mean age 6½ years) scored higher on the Visual Association subtest of the *ITPA* following training in organizing information. The effects of this training on academic performance, however, were not studied.

Level of Specificity

Instruction demands a high degree of specificity. Consequently, those assessment measures that yield descriptive information, or are readily amenable to item analysis, are most likely to meet the criterion of specificity.

Certainly an item analysis can be conducted on any test. However, some are more easily analyzed because their formats encourage it. As noted previously, however, item analysis of standardized tests has limited value since there are so few items for each subtest. Figure 6.2 shows the number of items for each subtest for two popular achievement tests.

California Achievement Tests,
Complete Battery[1]

Subtest	Number of Items[2]
word form	25
word recognition	20
meaning of opposites	15
picture association	15
reading comprehension	15
arithmetic meaning	30
arithmetic problems	15
addition	25
subtraction	20
capitalization	20
punctuation	20
word usage	25
spelling	20

Stanford Achievement Test,
Complete Battery[3]

Subtest	Number of Items[4]
word meaning	48
paragraph meaning	64
spelling	56
language usage	38
punctuation	38
capitalization	36
dictionary skills	24
sentence sense	18
arithmetic computation	39
arithmetic concepts	32
arithmetic applications	39
social studies content	45
social studies skills	30
science	50

1. *California Achievement Tests*, Complete Battery, Lower Primary (Grades 1 and 2), Form W, 11th Printing, 1963. Monterey, California: California Test Bureau.

2. The number of items per subtest yield grade scores from 0.0 to 4.0.

3. *Stanford Achievement Test*, Complete Battery, Intermediate II Form W, 1964. New York: Harcourt, Brace & World, Inc.

4. The number of items per subtest yield grade scores from 2.0 to 12.9.

FIGURE 6.2.   An analysis of number of items in two achievement tests

The limited number of items for each subtest in Figure 6.2 represent a sample for measuring a skill across several grade levels. For example, the 15 items used to measure reading comprehension in the *California Achievement Test* yield a reading grade score at the beginning fourth grade (4.0). Thus, the 15-item sample not only measures an important skill but also measures it across three grade levels. Clearly, item analysis does not provide information at a sufficiently specific level for instructional purposes. But an item-analysis procedure of standardized tests will provide clues for further assessment.

Validity and Reliability

Norm-referenced measures are designed to predict some future performances of students. Not only should we expect such predictions to be reasonably accurate (that is to measure what is claimed) but also to be consistent in predicting. These two expectations are commonly referred to as validity and reliability. A test is valid when it measures what it purports to measure, and it is reliable when its results are consistent. While reliability does not ensure or guarantee validity, it is a necessary condition for validity. Validity is dependent upon reliability, but a measure need not be valid in order for it to be reliable.

Validity and reliability of norm-referenced measures involve technical and complex issues. Readers are referred to texts that consider test construction. Prior to purchasing and using standardized measures, reviews concerning them should be read in volumes like those edited by Buros, which were previously cited. Only general considerations for teachers' use of normed tests are presented here.

O'Leary (1972), in an extensive discussion concerning assessing psychopathology in children, concluded that projective instruments are a waste of time because the validity coefficients, when available, are too low to warrant their use for treatment decisions. Clearly, projective measures have inherent problems of validity because they attempt to assess the inner dynamics of personality.

Aptitude and achievement norm-referenced measures tend to have better validity and reliability than do clinical tests. But when subtests from these measures are used for instructional purposes, they do not maintain the relatively high validity and reliability coefficients as do total test scores. A similar problem exists for the information processing and other diagnostic-prescriptive measures.

Coefficient of Determination

One concept that teachers should find useful when considering validity and reliability of assessment measures is offered by Guilford (1956). He suggests using the *coefficient of determination* when considering the percentage of a factor that is accounted for by the test and that percentage which has not been measured.

In order to calculate the coefficient of determination, simply square the coefficient of correlation (r) and multiply by 100. For example, test-retest reliability coefficients for the Visual Reception subtest of the *ITPA* are reported as ranging from .21 to .69 (Kirk, McCarthy, & Kirk, 1968). The coefficient of determination indicates a range of 4.41% (.21 x .21 x 100) to 47.61% (.69 x .69 x 100). This may be interpreted as indicating that performance on this subtest accounts for 4% to 48% of the aptitude. Conversely, it does not measure 96% (100% − 4%) to 52% (100% − 48%) of that same ability. Of course, we are assuming when interpreting the coefficient of determination that the test or subtest is valid in that it measures what it claims to measure.

Index of Forecasting

Teachers may use a similar approach to determine the validity of a measure. The index of forecasting efficiency (Guilford, 1956) is calculated by squaring the validity coefficient, subtracting the answer from one (1), taking the square root of the result, and subtracting the result from one (1). This amount is multiplied by 100. Using the above formula for the Visual Reception subtest of the *ITPA,* we obtain forecasting efficiency indexes of 2.2% - 27.6%. These indexes are interpreted as meaning that using that subtest prediction is between 2% and 28% better than chance. Guilford

(1956) reports validity coefficients must be about .45 in order for the index of forecasting efficiency to reach 10%. With a coefficient of .70, the index reaches 29%.

Ease of Use

Teachers should consider practical problems when selecting normed measures for assessment purposes:

> Can this test be administered without time-consuming preparation?
> Does it require individual or small group administration?
> Is it necessary to manage the remainder of the class while testing the others?
> Can the necessary conditions for administering the test be met so as not to invalidate the test?
> Does the measure yield sufficient information to warrant its use?
> How does the information yielded by the test relate to what or how the students will be taught?
> How much time will be required to score the test?
> Is there a quicker and easier means of obtaining the same information?

While ease should not be the sole or primary criterion for test selection, it is an important factor to consider. Instructional time is the most essential ingredient for teachers. If L&BD students are to be helped, time-consuming tests that provide limited results with questionable relevance for instruction should be avoided.

Nonstandardized Approaches

Information which can be obtained from nonstandardized measures is perhaps the most relevant for teaching L&BD children. Teacher-devised measures represent one of the nonstandardized approaches for assessment. Direct observations and criterion-referenced measurement constitute two other approaches.

Teacher-devised Assessment

Teachers of L&BD students need at least four types of information to teach them effectively (Stephens, 1976). Much, if not all, of this information may be obtained by teachers informally. These are:

1. *Academic skills and concepts:* Teachers should know which skills children have yet to master, have already mastered, and are in the process of mastering.
2. *Sensory channels:* Teachers should know which sensory modes are most effective for their students to receive and remember the needed instruction.
3. *Social behavior:* Teachers should have information concerning those social skills and understandings which students need to learn and demonstrate.
4. *Reinforcement system:* Teachers should know which classroom events are rewarding to their students; how frequently it is necessary to reward them to maintain desired behavior; and which reinforcement model is feasible and acceptable to the students. (Stephens, 1976, pp. 77-78)

Academic Skills and Concepts

Academic skills and concepts may be assessed using informal approaches and/or materials developed by teachers. Graded reading textbooks can be used to assess students' oral and silent reading. While a student reads a section of graded materials aloud, the teacher can record those words that are mispronounced. Following reading, the student may be asked questions as a check on reading comprehension.

Informal assessment of silent reading comprehension follows a similar procedure. With an estimate of the student's level of word comprehension, which may be obtained from a standardized reading test, the teacher should have the student begin silent reading at about two years below the student's word recognition level. Assessment continues to a point where the reading matter cannot be comprehended, as measured by the student's answers to the teacher's questions.

Other skills in reading and arithmetic may be assessed similarly using texts and other instructional materials which are readily available in the classroom. Teachers will find such assessment to be more valuable for instruction if it is conducted frequently, prior to a given segment or unit of study. Some commercial instructional materials have brief tests preceding each new unit in order to determine which skills and concepts will require special attention.

Sensory Channels[5]

The human organism has several receptive channels through which sensations are received. These receptor systems serve to provide learners with information. Intact auditory, visual, haptics, and olfactory functions are essential for learning. Children who have difficulties in discriminating and recalling stimuli through any sensory channel may find that the level of acuity is sufficient for receiving stimuli but that the discrimination and recall through any of the channels are defective, thus resulting in disturbed or hampered signals.

Knowledge of how a student learns includes knowing which receptive channels are operative for a given type of stimulus and knowing which receptors are less effective for receiving similar stimuli.

The emphasis is on assessing students' effectiveness in learning subject matter through each modality and on improving achievement in academic skill areas, rather than on testing sensory modalities or training students in an attempt to improve sensory learning.

The expressive behavior of L&BD students is important because responses suggest what students have learned. Results of students' learning are observed by their actions or responses to stimuli. These actions may take the form of moving, speaking, smelling, and touching.

A distinction should be made between assessing learning processes and assessing expression of learning. Results of assessing learning processes are viewed as aptitudes and are commonly associated with tests of intelligence that are then used to predict achievement.

Test items that purportedly measure memory span, for example, include digits or words presented aurally. Results of a student's performance on such items may be used as clues by a psychologist to suggest ways in which the student may learn effectively or poorly. Thus good performance on tests requiring memory for aural material may indicate that the student has good facility to learn aurally. We would expect a positive, but far from perfect, correlation between a score on a test that measures auditory aptitude with an achievement test score. To some degree, the two performances are related. We should expect a closer relationship, however,

---

5. Much of the content of this section has been condensed from Thomas M. Stephens, *Directive teaching of children with learning and behavioral handicaps* (2nd ed.). Columbus, Ohio: Charles E. Merrill, 1976.

between measures of aptitude in subject matter, such as arithmetic with achievement in that subject. Even with this more direct application, the correlation will not be perfect.

Assessment of expressions of learning is necessary for measuring achievement, but the purpose is not to apply the findings to an ability criterion as with results from intelligence testing. Rather, it is to determine if the student expresses academic content that presumably was assimilated through certain sensory channels.

Expression is defined here as any observable response. Expressions are rarely unitary; they often involve several modalities in consort. In assessment, however, it is helpful to isolate individual modes of expression because the purity of the response under testing conditions will suggest the extent to which that particular sensory channel can be used for learning. There is also merit in combining sensory modes when testing in an effort to assess the additive strength or weakness that results when learning activities rely heavily on two or more modalties.

Instructionally relevant information about expressions of learning should be clearly related to defective skill areas. For example, a child with a problem of reading should be assessed with reading material. It is insufficient to assume that similar processes are involved in recognizing differences among geometric designs when in fact poor achievement is noted in a failure to discriminate words.

The examples that follow describe informal ways of measuring expressions by isolation of one sense and a brief discussion about the combination of two or more senses.

Assessing visual learning. Assessment of what is learned through vision involves visual discrimination and recall. In order for effective learning to take place through sight, accurate discrimination of visual stimuli is necessary.

When problems of visual discrimination exist, careful observations of students' performances will reveal clues that can be used for teaching. L&BD students who display difficulty in differentiating visual differences among words but who discriminate words auditorily may profit from instruction that relies more heavily upon hearing than seeing. Thorough instruction in visual discrimination of words may also result in improved reading performance.

A systematic observational method for determining accuracy of visual discrimination involves selecting visual material from an academic skill area in which the student has difficulty. Set a criterion level below which discrimination will be deemed inadequate by stating in advance of testing the percentage of correct responses acceptable for passing. When establishing a criterion level, remember that the test items should be compatible with the child's age and academic achievement and that test reliability increases with additional test trials. If the test material is selected so as to represent easy and hard levels of difficulty and if each set of material is within the same subject area, successes on each succeeding trial should not greatly exceed those on earlier trials.

Assessment of visual discrimination can be summarized as follows:

1. Select visual stimuli from an academic skill area in which the student has difficulty.

2. Set a criterion level below which visual discrimination will be considered inadequate.

3. Assign exercises to the student that will test accuracy of visual discrimination. These will vary depending upon the nature of the material and its level of difficulty.

4. Ask the student to repeat those items that were incorrectly seen and, if he or she repeats the errors, tell him or her the correct responses.

5. Select instructional material to which he or she has not had prior exposure.

6. Again, test discrimination.

7. Ask him or her to repeat the items missed.

Visual discrimination may be accurate, but memory of what is seen may still be inadequate. In such instances, teaching through the vision channel may require modification of instruction or less reliance on that sensory mode. If the child's visual discrimination is accurate but his or her recall of symbols that were experienced visually is poor, the teacher may still wish to emphasize vision as a major mode for learning but will build into the instruction clues for remembering.

Memory can be categorized along a temporal dimension that includes immediate recall and delayed recall. Procedures for assessing immediate recall of visual stimuli are:

1. Select material that consists of known symbols or forms.

2. Present selected material to the child and tell him or her to look carefully at the selection because it will be removed and he or she will be asked to identify it from among other materials.

3. After a prearranged time interval remove the material and present another set of material containing similar items with the previous material embedded. Have the subject select those items that were shown to him or her on the first showing.

4. Repeated trials with equivalent materials should be conducted to ascertain that chance factors did not contribute greatly to the selections.

One of the most emphasized demands in schools is to demonstrate accuracy in recalling material, e.g., reading comprehension, spelling words, and arithmetic facts. Consequently, failure in such activities handicaps students severely in school.

Memory over time is dependent upon such factors as the effectiveness of initial learning, the meaningfulness of instruction to the learner, the effects of distractions caused by similar instruction during the interval between teaching and recalling, and reinforcement for accuracy. Irrespective of which factors influence delayed recall, knowledge of a student's performance will be helpful to his teacher.

Procedures used in assessing delayed recall of visual material follow the sequence used to assess immediate recall except that the elapsed time between steps two and three is considerably greater. Further differences occur if the child is taught material and then examined at a subsequent point.

The results of measuring recall of visual material can indicate how much reliance should be placed on memory when instruction is based on a visual approach. If the student demonstrates adequate discrimination but poor immediate and delayed recall of visual material the teacher would want to use other sensory clues to support visual instruction; overlearning could also be used to improve recall. When immediate recall is good but delayed recall is less than adequate, short periods of instruction well spaced over a long segment of time may prove effective in teaching the student to retain visual material over time.

Assessing auditory learning. Problems of auditory learning can be present even when hearing acuity is within the normal range. These difficulties include (a) auditory discrimination and (b) recall of auditorily received stimuli.

Auditory discrimination involves the extent to which sounds are distinguished from other sounds. Auditory discrimination can be assessed as follows:

1. Select material that is within the examinee's listening comprehension.
2. Set a criterion level below which performance is inadequate.
3. Pronounce the material one unit at a time; tell him or her to repeat exactly what you say.
4. Note inaccuracies in pronunciation.

Difficulties in auditory discrimination are reflected in mispronunciations of common words and the confusion of similar sounds. Teachers should use multisensory aids whenever possible in order to offset the auditory deficits.

Recall of auditory stimuli should also be assessed on a delayed and immediate memory basis. The procedure for measurement is similar to that of assessing other sensory recall. Every attempt should be made to have the student use only the sensory channel that is being evaluated. The steps for assessing immediate recall of auditorily presented material are:

1. Select material that is within the listening comprehension of the student and set a criterion level.
2. Tell the student to listen carefully because when you are finished you will ask questions about the story or you will ask him or her to repeat the rhyme.
3. Ask questions about the material.
4. Record the number of successes and failures.

Recall of auditory stimuli that were presented at any earlier time can be evaluated similarly. After 24 hours or more have elapsed, ask questions about the material.

Assessing haptic learning. The importance of the sense of touch for teaching some children with learning problems has been demonstrated by Fernald (1943). She described how memory of form is sometimes facilitated when the input is through the sense of touch in combination with other sensory avenues. Children learn through the sense of touch when they perceive objects haptically. Informal ways of assessing discrimination and recall of haptic stimuli are described below.

The effectiveness of learning haptically can be assessed by closing off the other sensory channels during the assessment process. Teachers may use a blindfold, paper bag, box with a hole in it, or a box with a drape covering one side. Students may be asked to:

— Identify environmental objects first gross then fine differences.
— Identify basic shapes in three dimension (3-D).
— Identify 3-D letters gross, then fine differences.
— Identify 3-D numerals gross, then fine differences.
— Identify 3- or 4-letter words spelled with wooden letters or sandpaper letters.
— Identify letters, numerals, or shapes traced on their hands or backs

When selecting items for identification, make certain to choose items known by the student.

1. Select instructionally relevant material that is within the demonstrated achievement level of the child.

2. With the test materials hidden, the student should be blindfolded and given one object at a time to feel. He or she should try to identify each object.

3. Each response should be recorded.

Memory can be tested with information obtained from assessing students' haptic sense. The purpose of measuring immediate recall of haptic stimuli is to determine if that sense serves as a channel for learning. Suggested procedures for assessment are:

1. Select material that has not yet been mastered by the child but is near mastery.

2. Teach the child the material through heavy reliance on haptics.

3. Test the child, upon completion of the special instruction, in order to assess the effects of practice through the haptic sense.

The effects of stimuli that are received haptically can also be measured over time. The procedure is similar to that used in assessing immediate recall, except number three occurs at a later point in time. If the student has demonstrated success on the immediate recall testing, step four below can follow in 24 hours or more to determine if the learning was maintained.

4. Retest using the same material that was taught at least 24 hours before.

Assessing olfactory learning.   Olfactory learning refers to the extent to which one distinguishes odors and associates smells with known objects. We learn to associate odors with many stimuli. Although we are aware of odors and their influence on human behavior, little has been written that is directly concerned with olfaction in learning.

Hartman (1974) studied the effects of teaching beginning readers, kindergarten students, by adding olfactory stimuli to the visual and auditory methods traditionally used. While reading performance of those in the olfactory group was superior to that of the control group, they did not exceed the performance of those children in the treatment group who did not use olfactory clues. Frew (1975) demonstrated an increase in arithmetic performance among children with measured intelligence below 80 IQ by using odor preferences as rewards contingent upon higher performance.

Recognizing odors and differentiating one fragrance from others constitutes olfactory discrimination. Steps for testing olfactory discrimination are:

1. Select at least three distinctly different odors.
2. Present the odors to the subject; restrict the use of other senses.
3. Record the number of pairs correctly matched.

The purposes for assessment of olfactory memory is to determine if the subject uses odor as a means of identifying stimuli and as a way to recall previously experienced stimuli. When assessing memory for olfactory stimuli, these steps may be followed:

1. Blindfold the child and tell him or her that you have a number of objects for him or her to smell.

2. Present an olfactory stimulus; do not permit the child to hold or to examine the objects tactually.

3. Ask him or her to smell the stimulus and to name it; record the responses.

4. Repeat the cycle using those items that were missed by the subject. Tell him or her the name of the object as he or she smells it.

5. Repeat the cycle, asking him or her to identify all the objects again. Proceed as described in steps one and two.

Social Behavior

Information concerning the social behavior of L&BD students is valuable for teachers. School-related social behavior is easily identified by teachers who are trained to be observant. Even when not observant, most teachers can describe those responses characteristic of their target students. Without prior training, however, teachers often have difficulty focusing on instructionally relevant social behavior.

Teachers may infer from what is seen without carefully observing all aspects of the behavior. A teacher who is oriented toward *describing* the behavior of a student will readily acquire information that is instructionally relevant through observation while one who makes inferences about underlying causes of what is seen will more often than not focus on irrelevancies.

Conditions under which behavior takes place in school must be known in order to effect change. It is insufficient to describe responses without being aware of events that maintain or elicit reactions. When it is not evident which stimuli elicit misbehavior, specifying conditions during the interval in which a misbehavior occurs enables teachers to determine when certain strategies should be implemented in order to modify responses.

Reactions to instruction constitute one general setting in which instructionally relevant behavior takes place. L&BD students who have difficulty in attending to instruction are engaging in behavior that interferes with learning. As a result of inattention, their responses are either inappropriate, irrelevant, or insufficient for desirable learning to occur. If children dislike the content being presented and are unwilling to participate as learners, their responses to the instruction will constitute major barriers to learning.

Reactions to others in the learning environment can result in circumstances that diminish learning because of behavior that interferes with learning or that enhances and facilitates learning. Students who respond negatively to teachers' directions or who engage in aggressive acts towards their classmates are thwarting the instructional process. In the latter instance, they may not only be hindering their own learning, but they may also be interrupting the learning of others.

Reactions to assignments by students constitute their willingness or unwillingness to engage in independent activities that have been designated as follow-ups to instruction. Assignments in workbooks, silent reading, arithmetic, and spelling practice all require cooperation from students in order for learning to occur.

Classroom observers may find these categories of in-school behavior helpful as they attempt to specify the circumstances under which behavioral responses occur.

Because teachers have many opportunities to observe children in groups, they can obtain valuable information concerning educational and social functioning of children. If purposes of observations are clearly established in advance, observers will be prepared to identify pertinent information. An observation form or inventory will aid in meeting the purposes of the observation.

Behavior ratings or checklists can be used by teachers and others to assess types of responses that are emitted by students when interacting with others. Such instruments can be devised locally or purchased from test publishers. Regardless of the source from which they are obtained, the essential features that should be incorporated into social-behavior rating devices are:

1. Formats should be relatively simple permitting ease of use.
2. Items to be checked should be observable, thus eliminating inferential or hypothetical thinking.
3. Items should specify activities and people in the environment with whom the child is interacting.

While external (predictive) validity and reliability are not essential features of instruments to be used for the purposes previously noted, validity and reliability of the observations are important. Teachers and other users of instruments should be trained in observational procedures so as to reduce the amount of observer error due to carelessness and lack of experience in school settings.

Social-behavior assessment results in an awareness of those conditions under which responses occur. When undesirable responses are emitted, baseline information can be obtained which relates to the frequencies of the behaviors and types of student responses.

Reinforcement System

A reward system consists of rewards that are preferred by a student and the necessary rate or schedule for issuing these rewards. Teachers of L&BD students need to know which rewards are effective in strengthening desirable responses. It is helpful to know how frequently responses should be rewarded in order to ensure continuation of the responses. Seldom is such information available to teachers in a systematic fashion. Nor are observation schedules or inventories readily available for use by teachers in gathering information that is concerned with reward preferences of students.

Teachers can discover through casual observations what is viewed as reinforcing to children at a given time. A teacher who wishes to be more systematic can make note of students' requests and later use these as rewards for desired performances. Such important details as the following should be noted by teachers:

Who prefers to work with whom?
Which students like which activities?
Which students enjoy attention and from whom?
Which students are strongly reinforced by peer recognition?
Which students find close physical proximity to the teacher or to others to be reinforcing?

Some assessment tactics which have been used by teachers are described below.

1. Ask students who would like to _____ (be excused from homework, have a double recess, start lunch early, get an extra drink of water). Name any *one* activity that students usually want. If there is a favorable response then indicate *how* they may obtain the reward. If there is little enthusiasm for the offer, select another possibility or drop the subject.

2. Tell the students they have 10 minutes of free time in the classroom. Observe target students and note how they spend the free time. Those activities in which they engaged that are desirable may be used later as incentives.

3. Place a list of possible events on the board. Tell students that they may write their names next to an activity they would like to do.

4. Ask: "If you had three wishes, what three things would you like to have happen in school today?" Use those that are feasible as incentives.

5. Ask students to write or tell all of the desirable (good) things that have happened in school during the past _____ (week, day, month, year).

Structured interviews can be used to assess what is reinforcing to children. Techniques discussed here include those that are designed to be used with an individual child and those that can be used within a group.

The teacher should begin with an informal discussion with the child that can serve to establish rapport and that will also provide information. During the interview, the child should be asked to identify which subject he or she believes is easiest and which subject is hardest for him or her. The teacher should pursue information by seeking answers to additional questions concerning which aspects of a subject are easy or hard.

The exchange that follows is between a teacher, serving as an interviewer, and a nine-year-old, David, and will demonstrate phase one.

Teacher: What is the easiest subject for you?
David: Arithmetic.
Teacher: What are you studying in arithmetic that you find to be easy?
David: We're learning long division and I like it.
Teacher: What subject do you have the most trouble with, David?
David: Reading and language.
Teacher: What do you find difficult about reading?
David: I have trouble figuring out new words.

The second step in the interview approach is to determine what the child views as rewarding. Potential rewards that are typically used in school with children of this age should be tried initially. The interviewer should describe and, if feasible, show potential rewards to the child, two items at a time.

Teacher: Which of these would make you feel better after you worked on new
            words in reading?
            1) a star on your paper, or
            2) hanging your paper in the room
David: Put it on the bulletin board.
Teacher: OK. Would you like that better than putting an A on your paper and
            sending it home?
David: I'd like both.
Teacher: Of the two, which is better?
David: Putting my paper on the bulletin board.

Had David responded to the question in a manner that was indicative of a lack of interest in either, the teacher would have continued offering possibilities until the most preferred reward was identified.

The student is then asked to complete an easy task based on the information provided by him. Upon the successful completion of the assigned task, he or she should be praised for his or her accomplishment. Then the child should be given a task that he or she indicated was hard for him or her. Assist the child if necessary. He or she should be rewarded for his or her attempts, using the preferred reinforcer. Note his or her reactions.

Interviews of groups can be conducted in one setting through the use of paper-pencil inventories. In an oral interview, the teacher asks a series of questions concerning feelings toward school and preferences. As each student responds, answers are recorded by the teacher.

Interviewing within a group setting sometimes is not feasible for certain age groups and with those students who have strong negative attitudes toward school. Also, teachers should be sensitive to peer pressures that can result in erroneous responses. A paper-pencil, forced-choice preference schedule can be used with students who read.

The contrived task approach (Stephens, 1970) provides an assessment of skill functioning in conjunction with an estimate of reward preference. It eliminates the necessity for obtaining separate information about a student's system of rewards and his or her academic achievement.

This approach begins by selecting a task believed to be easy for the child. As the child works on the assignment, the teacher applies a variety of potential rewards. Upon completion of the task, other reinforcers are tried. The student's performance is evaluated in terms of (1) enthusiasm for the task, (2) persistence, and (3) quality of performance. The examiner then selects the reward needed for this type of task. The cycle is repeated beginning with a more difficult assignment.

Just as tasks can be contrived and assigned to individual students for purposes of assessment, a similar approach can be used with small groups. The type of tasks may have to differ from those used with individual students because prerequisites for the tasks must be within the repertoire of each group member. Also, fewer school-related tasks lend themselves to group endeavors.

There are a number of advantages in using this approach with a group. It can serve as a natural outgrowth of group activities, and it provides valuable observations of group interactions. Group responses can serve as models for individuals who otherwise would be prone not to participate. Some of the tasks that can be contrived for use with groups are games and physical education activities, problem-solving tasks, class discussion, sensitivity training and group dynamics, and arts and crafts activities.

Procedures for assessment of behavior and rewards through the contrived task approach in groups is similar to that same approach as used with individuals.

First, an assignment is selected that is believed to be within the attainment of each pupil. While they do the task, the teacher observes and notes the enthusiasm, persistence, and quality of work displayed by each child. Second, the teacher applies social rewards (praise) as well as what could later be used as a contingent type of reward. Third, the group's attitude toward the task is evaluated by letting them discuss their product.

As a result of using this assessment technique, the teacher has a better knowledge of the group. The children's interest in this type of task, the kind of reward that appeals to them when faced with such an undertaking, and their level of accomplishment can be determined. The teacher also has an opportunity to acquire similar information about individual children.

Frequency of reinforcement is an important characteristic to assess because the pay-off for responses dictates the repetitiveness with which they will reoccur. For those responses that have not yet become internalized, rewards external to the task are essential for the continued emission of responses.

Planned reinforcement requires an established schedule that can be followed by teachers in the classroom. Two general schedules of reinforcement are commonly used: (1) continuous schedules and (2) intermittent schedules.

Reinforcement is provided after every response on a continuous schedule; reinforcement under an intermittent schedule does not occur after every response. An intermittent schedule is designed to issue rewards for correct responses without reinforcement after every response. Both of these schedules are fixed types because the rate of reinforcement does not vary.

Continuous reinforcement is used when a reward is presented every time a desired response is given. After a response is established, the schedule should be changed so that reinforcement is not presented every time the desired response takes place. When this change is made, the schedule is then termed intermittent, and it results in more stable behavior.

Direct Observations

All assessment approaches require some amount of observation. Standardized testing, for example, is best accomplished when examiners note students' reactions, attitudes, and other behaviors which may increase interpretations of the results. When the students are not required to create permanent products, such as in a paper-pencil examination, teachers can use direct observations for assessing their performances.

Observation involves systematically obtaining samples of behavior under specified conditions. Successful direct observations occur when teachers choose target behaviors, record the frequency of these behaviors, and describe the conditions under which they occur. Classroom conduct and other social behaviors are typically assessed through direct observations, although academic performances may also be analyzed in this way.

Successful observations also require the use of technology. Cooper (1974) has presented an extensive and detailed discussion for using observations in measurement and analysis. When using observations for assessing students, the necessary technology consists of selecting target behavior and recording responses.

Selecting target behavior. L&BD students characteristically display a variety of maladaptive social behaviors as well as many incorrect academic responses. While the process in observing both types of behavior is the same, factors such as conditions under which these behaviors occur and the ease or difficulty in describing and observing them encourage a separate discussion of each type.

Maladaptive social behavior. Teachers typically do not have a predetermined curriculum of social behavior against which students may be assessed. When such a curriculum does exist, maladaptive behaviors not represented in that program may be emitted by students. When such behaviors occur on a regular basis by one or more students, teachers should select these behaviors as targets to be assessed, as seen in anecdote 6.4.

ANECDOTE 6.4

Mrs. Franklin noted that several of her special class students have been referred to the building principal for misconduct on the playground. Discussion with the students, principal, and those teachers who were the playground supervisors at the times of referral indicated that:

1. three of her nine students were often cited for playground misconduct.
2. violations were most often referred by one particular teacher (Mrs. Grimes).
3. the violations were termed as "defying playground supervisors."
4. all three students (two boys and one girl) met the criteria for the social skill "fulfilling requests of teachers and those in authority" in the curriculum used by Mrs. Franklin.

Based on the above information, Mrs. Franklin decided to conduct her own observations of the three target students while they were on the playground and during those times when Ms. Grimes was playground supervisor.

Target behaviors must be highly specific in order to conduct effective direct observations. Behaviors described in general terms, such as the following, do not make adequate target observations.

— uses foul language
— fights
— has temper tantrums
— refuses to obey
— hits others
— bullies
— throws objects
— causes trouble
— lies
— cheats
— is a disruptive influence
— talks back
— sulks
— has no friends
— violates lunchroom rules
— daydreams
— engages in self-stimulation
— is sadistic

In anecdote 6.4, the teacher is faced with a problem of having too general a behavioral description. It is necessary under such circumstances to obtain more specific descriptions of the problem behavior.

ANECDOTE 6.5

Mrs. Franklin's conversations with Ms. Grimes revealed that she complained that the three students violated playground rules and, while she understood that "these types of children" often misbehaved, when she corrected them, they either ignored or ridiculed her. It was at that point that she would send them to the office. Sometimes it was necessary for her to take them to the principal.

Mrs. Franklin felt that Grimes' report was strange since these children never "ridiculed or ignored her." She considered Ms. Grimes to be somewhat overly demanding and ineffectual in managing difficult children. However, she believed that her students would often have to deal with people like Ms. Grimes and must learn to avoid conflict with them. Also, there was some reason for her to believe that these three students lacked adequate interpersonal skills.

In observing the students on the playground she noted the following disruptive behaviors:

Mike: violated playground rules by climbing and walking on the high wall on the south side of the school yard, throwing stones at smaller children, jumping from the wall onto children below.

Suzie: writing on the playground wall with colored magic markers, chasing and hitting smaller boys and girls.

Felix: spitting on other children, urinating on the playground, trying to break up games that girls were playing.

Based on this preliminary observation, Mrs. Franklin decided to obtain more observations after talking with each child about inappropriate playground behavior.

Incorrect academic responses.   Academic skills and concepts that are inadequate and/or incorrect may also be identified through direct observations. These may be revealed by examining students' written products, questioning them regarding a particular concept, and otherwise carefully observing their verbal and written emissions and responses.

Students' understandings of concepts are often difficult to assess. Some L&BD children, for example, are so verbal that their misunderstandings of concepts may be overlooked. Also, beyond the level of superficiality, concepts are not easily measured.

Skills, however, are more readily examined in a direct manner. Once teachers have identified the students and skills to be assessed, they simply need to give assignments to those students which require use of particular academic skills, as seen in anecdote 6.6.

ANECDOTE 6.6

Mr. Sickel routinely assesses students in his special class. He uses short, paper-pencil tests for checking their arithmetic performance and oral reading of selected paragraphs to assess their word attack skills and, by asking questions concerning their reading, he judges their comprehension skills.

He maintains a careful record of each student, checking them on each arithmetic and reading skill to be taught. His lesson plans are then based upon the most current assessment of the students.

Assessing students' concepts often requires small group or individual sessions in order to determine each student's precise level of understanding of a given concept. These assessment sessions may be of short duration and informally conducted as described in anecdote 6.7.

ANECDOTE 6.7

Seven-year-old Harold counts to 100 and readily names all U.S. coins through the half dollar. By checking his seatwork, however, his teacher suspects that he confuses the value of a nickel with that of a dime. She, therefore, has taken Harold aside to assess his concepts of the two coins.

Teacher:	(with a nickel and a dime on the desk in front of Harold) What do you call this coin? (pointing to the nickel)
Harold:	A nickel.
Teacher:	That's right. Another name for it is "five cents." What is another name for a nickel?
Harold:	Five cent.
Teacher:	That's *almost* right, Harold! It is five *cents*. What is another name for a nickel?
Harold:	Five cents.
Teacher:	Yes, that's correct! Now, Harold, what do you call this coin?
Harold:	Dime.
Teacher:	Good, Harold! Do you know another name for a dime?
Harold:	Five cents?
Teacher:	No, Harold, A dime is worth ten cents.

As a result of the brief assessment, Harold's teacher has identified precisely his confusion and can now proceed to teach the correct value of U.S. coins.

Recording Responses

An accurate, easy way of recording observations is useful when assessing students. Direct observations require assessors to be precise when recording responses. Cooper (1974) stresses that observational recording occurs when teachers produce records of behavior as it occurs.

Basically there are two types of conditions under which direct observations will require recording assessment information: natural conditions and contrived conditions.

Recording under natural conditions. Once teachers have identified target behaviors and target students, they can proceed to systematically assess their performances. With maladaptive social behavior, for example, teachers may find it convenient to observe and record students' responses in naturally occurring settings.

ANECDOTE 6.8

Mrs. Franklin proceeded to assess Mike's behavior on the playground after having identified his target behavior (see anecdotes 6.4 and 6.5).

She decided to observe him on the playground. Using a descriptive approach, she simply recorded his actions which were inappropriate as well as appropriate during five minute intervals for three consecutive days.

At the conclusion of the observations, Mrs. Franklin had over four sheets of paper describing Mike's playground behavior. A sizable majority of his actions were inappropriate. Among those behaviors which she found Mike to need improvement in were team games and in being more considerate of smaller children.

Naturally occurring responses to academic requirements may also be recorded for assessment purposes. Teachers may simply make notations concerning errors students make during the course of a lesson. These errors may be corrected through instruction at a future time. For example, teachers may organize small instructional groups for working with students who have demonstrated difficulty with a particular skill or concept. These temporary groups may be used for teaching a specific arithmetic process or one reading word attack or spelling skill.

Teachers will often find with L&BD students that a frequency count of a given behavior will be helpful as described in anecdote 6.9.

ANECDOTE 6.9

It appeared to Mr. Sickel that a common problem within his special class was the students' frequent shouting out instead of waiting to be recognized. He was not certain, however, that it was as frequent a problem as it seemed and decided to count the number of times any student shouted out in the classroom during an entire day.

He started the day with his right jacket pocket full of paper clips. Each time a student shouted out, he simply transferred one paper clip to his left pocket, at the close of the day, he had accumulated 68 paper clips in his left pocket.

Recording in contrived situations. Sometimes teachers may wish to assess students without waiting until the behavior occurs naturally. When assessment must be conducted at a given time, a situation can be contrived for observational purposes.

Three steps should be followed when using the contrived task approach:

1. Establish the setting. Instruct the students as to what they are to do, e.g., "during the next 10 minutes I will be busy at my desk; you may select a table game and play with whom you would like." Or, "Do these 10 arithmetic problems."
2. Record target students' responses while they are engaged in performing the tasks.
3. Evaluate students' performances in relation to their accuracy, interactions with others, and/or their persistence.

ANECDOTE 6.10

When assessing responses to academic stimuli, teachers can determine which skills the student has not yet mastered, which he or she is in the process of learning, and those that have already been learned. e.g.,

Teacher: Wilmer, each of these cards has an arithmetic problem on it. Read the problem aloud and tell me the answer. Use this pencil and sheet of paper for figuring the problems.

Wilmer's arithmetic skills are being assessed by observing his accuracy when reading problems in arithmetic computation and his understanding of various computational signs. By providing separate sheets of paper for each problem, the teacher can assess his performance and also his understanding of steps in computing.

Criterion-referenced Measures

Criterion-referenced measurement is a method of test interpretation where the measuring instrument can be a teacher-devised test, a standardized test, or any measure where an absolute level of mastery is established (Simon, 1969). By establishing an absolute standard of achievement, teachers can decide exactly what students have mastered, are in the process of learning, or have not yet begun to learn. While any test can be used, those that are specifically designed as criterion measures, tend to have more instructional value.

Characteristics

Proger and Mann (1973) identified and discussed what they termed "CRM systems," noting that most were developed for use in regular education. Noteworthy among these is the University of Pittsburgh's Individually Prescribed Instruction (IPI). Bolvin and Glaser (1968) established IPI as one of the early, if not the first, criterion-referenced programs.

While criterion-referenced measures can be used outside a given instructional system, their effectiveness and utility are increased when the measures are developed as a part of an instructional package or curriculum. Such systems generally consist of at least three components:

1. assessment or testing,
2. instruction, and
3. evaluation or reassessment.

In order for these components to be functional, it is necessary for the measures used in steps 1 and 3 to be based upon and derived from step 2. Figure 6.3 shows a criterion-referenced measure and an instructional strategy from the Directive Teaching Instructional Management System (DTIMS), which is presented more fully in chapter 9.

The criterion measure shown in Figure 6.3 contains four parts: the specific task being measured, the terminal criterion, directions which in this instance consist of what will be said to the students, and items for measuring student performance.

Assessment Task (Level I)

Given a word followed by two other words, the student will say or circle the word that has the same meaning as the first word.

Criterion: 9/10

Say the first word, then the following two and ask the student to repeat the word that means the same as the first word. E.g., say, "Listen to this word — *father.* Now listen to these two words — *dog, dad.* Which one means the same as *father?*"

1.	father	dog	dad
2.	pick	give	choose
3.	beautiful	song	pretty
4.	kind	goose	nice
5.	hurt	injure	skeleton
6.	woman	scare	lady
7.	baby	child	meat
8.	fast	tree	quick
9.	rabbit	bunny	warm
10.	painting	picture	new

Teaching Strategy

Teacher Activity:
Write the word *happy* on the chalkboard. Say, "this word is *happy.*" "Now I am going to write some words next to *happy* which have almost the same meaning."
Write *glad* on the chalkboard to the right of *happy.* Say, "this word is *glad.*"
Write *gay* on the chalkboard to the right of glad. Say, "this word is *gay* and has almost the same meaning as *happy* and *glad.*"
"One could say 'I am happy, I'm glad, I'm gay' and mean about the same thing."
Write the word *angry* on the chalkboard beginning a new line. Say, "this word is *angry.*" To the right write the words *boy* and *mad.* Say, "these words are *boy* and *mad.* One of these means the same as angry. Who can tell us which one it is?"
When *mad* is given, say, "good, *mad* and *angry* do mean the same. You can say I am *angry* or I am *mad* and have the same meaning. But you should not say, 'I am boy' when you are upset."
Then proceed to teach the first five items in the assessment task in the same way. For practice assign the last five items on a worksheet.

Evaluation:

Criterion 5/5 on worksheet, if criterion is met reassess using the assessment task. If it is not met, select the next teaching strategy.

FIGURE 6.3. A criterion-referenced measure and a related instructional strategy

Note that in DTIMS, criterion-referenced measures are embedded in the instructional strategies and that assessment and evaluation require the use of the same items. Criteria for successful performance are also stated in advance of assessment (Figure 6.3, 9/10) and instruction (Figure 6.3, 5/5), and when criteria are met following instruction mastery of the assessment task is also required.

Proger and Mann (1973) emphasized that criterion-referenced measures have meaning only when instructional goals and the contexts in which those goals are attempted are closely related. This requires specificity of items and behaviorally stated instructional objectives ("Given a word followed by two other words, the student will say or circle the word that has the same meaning as the first word").

A major feature of criterion-referenced measures is that assessment items are *task-specific,* meaning that the items to be taught are specified in the assessment component. This characteristic differs from items found in norm-referenced measures which are task-general; that is, the items are not specific to any particular skill or response.

One study has been reported (Mann, Proger, & Cross, 1973) where the *ITPA,* representing a task-general measure, was compared with a task-specific measure, the Individual Achievement Monitoring System. In seeking to identify those factors which facilitate or inhibit aptitude treatment interactions, the authors focused on sensory modality preferences as measured by the *ITPA,* the Individual Achievement Monitoring System, and teacher ratings. They concluded that the *ITPA* modality assessments are not suitable for aptitude treatment interaction research with handicapped populations where individualized instruction is necessary or important. It was suggested that this finding is due to the *ITPA's* assessment tasks which are abstract rather than school-related.

Uses

Criterion-referenced measures have been shown to be useful for assessment of entry level performances, for prescribing instruction, and for evaluating the effects of instruction. Figure 6.4 contrasts the uses of CR measures with NR measures.

Comparisons.   Normed tests compare the student's performances with other students. Criterion measures compare the individual's performance to a fixed criterion.

Instruction.   Results of normed tests are useful for curriculum development, while criterion measures are useful for immediate instruction of individuals and groups.

Counseling.   Results of normed tests are useful for counseling students on future planning. Criterion measures are useful for counseling for immediate activities.

Evaluation.   Normed tests are useful for evaluating and comparing groups of students. Criterion measures are useful for evaluating individual students.

Information.   Results of normed tests are useful for providing information to the general public concerning the schools. Criterion measures provide information to individual students, their parents, and teachers.

FIGURE 6.4.   Uses of criterion-referenced measures and
norm-referenced measures

Criterion-referenced measures are useful to teachers for individualizing instruction because the results are specific to performance, though they need not be used solely for academic instruction. Criterion-referenced measures can also be developed and used for assessing social attitudes and behaviors. Any content that has identifiable skills and concepts and that can be translated into responses is amenable to criterion-referenced measurement.

Some teachers of children with learning and behavioral problems follow a social behavior curriculum. Often such curricula are teacher devised and are used as a means of instructing students in basic social behaviors in school. When a social curriculum is followed, teachers should base their assessment on those behaviors. They may develop measures for assessing the behaviors found in the curriculum.

Sample criterion-referenced measures for two social skills found in DTIMS are shown below.

Skill: To dispose of trash in the proper container

Preliminary Assessment: The student will identify what needs to be thrown away, carry it over, and throw it into the waste receptacle.

Evaluation

1. Student exhibits the skill at an acceptable level. ____
   Mastery. No teaching necessary.
   Move to next skill.
2. Student exhibits skill occasionally at a lower than acceptable level. ____
   Instructional level. Use reinforcement strategies to increase performance.
3. Student never exhibits the skill, or no opportunity to observe performance. ____
   Use assessment task.

Assessment Task: Ask the student(s) to pick up the trash and throw it away. Observe whether student recognizes the trash and throws it away properly. Use a naturally occurring situation in which the floor is littered, e.g., after a craft project.

Evaluation

1. Student exhibits the skill at an acceptable level in assessment task. ____
   Use reinforcement strategy to maintain skill.
2. Student exhibits skill occasionally at a less than acceptable level in assessment task. ____
   Use reinforcement strategy to increase and maintain skill.
3. Student does not exhibit the skill in assessment task. ____
   Use behavior rehearsing strategy to teach the skill. Use reinforcement strategy to increase and maintain the skill.

Skill: To respond to teasing or name calling by ignoring, changing the subject, or some other constructive means.

Preliminary Assessment: The student responds to teasing or name calling by (1) ignoring, (2) changing the subject, or (3) some other constructive means.

Evaluation

1. Student exhibits the skill at an acceptable level. ____
   Mastery. No teaching necessary.
   Move to next skill.
2. Student exhibits skill occasionally at a lower than acceptable level. ____
   Instructional level. Use reinforcement strategies to increase performance.
3. Student never exhibits the skill, or no opportunity to observe performance. ____
   Use assessment task.

Assessment Task: (1) Observe student in interaction with peers. If he is teased or called derogatory names, does he ignore it, walk away, change the subject or take some other constructive action.

(2) Have the student *role play* with the teacher playing the role of name caller. (Watch severity of name calling to make sure it is not excessive for a given child.) Ask the target student to show what he would do in the name calling situation. Observe his response.

Evaluation

1. Student exhibits the skill at an acceptable level in assessment task. ____
2. Student exhibits skill occasionally at a less than acceptable level in assessment task. ____
   Use reinforcement strategy to increase and maintain skill.
3. Student does not exhibit the skill in assessment task. ____
   Use behavior rehearsing strategy to teach the skill. Use reinforcement strategy to increase and maintain the skill.

Criterion-referenced measures are useful for entry assessment at the beginning of a course or unit of study. Since students possess some prior knowledge and skills when starting instruction, those that are related to the unit of study should be assessed at entry. When criterion-referenced measures are used at entry, they serve an assessment function, permitting teachers to determine which skills and concepts have been mastered, learned, are ready to be learned, and those which are too difficult. These four levels of functioning and criteria for making a determination are shown in Figure 6.5.

Mastery. When responses are correct 100% of the time, that is, when correct behavior occurs throughout a given time interval or when responses are correct each time in a specific number of opportunities, the behavior has been mastered.

Learned. When responses are correct between 90% and 99% of the time, the task has been learned but not yet mastered.

Instructional. When responses are correct between 70% and 90% of the time, the task can be learned by students since they evidently possess the prerequisite responses. These tasks should be presented to students under teacher direction and not as independent activities.

Frustration. When responses are correct less than 70% of the time, the task is too difficult. Unless it is essential for students to learn at this time, find another task that is well within their response repertoires.

FIGURE 6.5. Criteria for mastery, learned, instructional, and frustration performances.

Criterion-referenced measures should cover all skills and concepts in the order that these are to appear in instruction. Assessment occurs prior to instruction in order to determine where teaching should begin. For modules that extend over long time periods, such as an academic year or term, content should be divided into units. Assessment should then cover content in each unit just prior to beginning instruction.

Instruction begins for individuals on tasks that have not yet been mastered or learned. As each is taught, students are evaluated as to their performances. When criteria are met, additional tasks are taught until all tasks have been mastered.

Entry measures may also be used for grouping students on a temporary basis. After assessing students and analyzing their performances, teachers may group them on the basis of tasks to be learned. As students meet criteria, regrouping of students may occur.

Criterion-referenced measures, when used for evaluating the effects of instruction, are administered following instruction as shown in Figure 6.4. Decisions are made for subsequent instruction on the basis of evaluation results. Those who meet criteria upon evaluation proceed to the next segment. When all segments in a unit are mastered, students proceed to the next unit and begin with the entry assessment.

Evaluation is best when it has immediate instructional value. Therefore, criterion measures, when used for evaluative purposes, should be used whenever possible at times when the results can be immediately helpful to students. For this reason, the most instructionally relevant time to use criterion measures for evaluation is when there is time for instruction. When instruction cannot follow evaluation, such as at the end of the school year, the results have limited instructional value. Under such circumstances, however, evaluation results may still provide a basis for guidance and counseling to students and their parents.

Procedures for Developing Criterion Measures

Steps for making criterion-referenced instructional materials follow.

Step 1: Content. Obtain the content to be taught over a given time segment. Although all the content for an entire year could be selected, it is best, initially, to focus on a limited segment of content, e.g., one unit.

Step 2: Sequence Content. Analyze the content and record the skills and/or concepts in the order that they appear in the texts or materials that are being analyzed. Record the page numbers in which each item appears.

Step 3: Easier Content. Go to another source that contains content at an easier level and proceed to do what was done in step 2. When this step is completed a sequence of items will be created for those students who may not initially possess responses of a high enough order.

Step 4: Difficult Content. Go to a source that contains content that is more difficult than that which was in the original source. At the completion of this step, a higher order of content will be developed for students who possess better responses than the typical beginning student.

Step 5: Devise Measures. Now that the skills and concepts have been listed, measures for each should be devised. Return to the list and using the pages that were recorded, select or develop from the content at least 10 items that will measure each. Place one skill or concept to be measured on a separate sheet along with the items.

Step 6: Field Test. The criterion measures are now ready for field testing. Try-outs may occur with samples from the population for which the materials were devised. Through field testing it is possible to identify tasks and items that are out of sequence, confusing, and in need of rewriting.

Instructions for using criterion-referenced measures vary depending upon the nature of the subject matter and the number of items. In all instances, however, students should be informed that the purpose is to obtain information concerning what they already know, have some knowledge of, and what they have not yet learned. It should be made clear to students that they are not expected to perform all tasks perfectly and, in fact, may not be able to respond correctly to any of the items. Make it a rule to always inform students of the purposes for assessment, stressing the immediate instructional value to them.

Step 7: Revise Material. Revise the measures based upon results of field testing. Revision of the material should become a routine matter since as the materials are used refinement will be a natural consequence.

It should be noted that while the above procedures indicate texts could be used to obtain content, teachers and others may obtain the content from many different sources.

Steps for Informal Assessment

Procedures for assessing student responses include establishing a comfortable relationship with students and obtaining relevant information regarding their functioning. Students are assessed in order to determine their instructional responses and to identify those conditions which ensure their learning. Informal assessment techniques include surveying responses, interviewing students, observing, and using simulated tasks.

Establishing Rapport

Rapport is a comfortable relationship of mutual confidence between two or more persons. It is important to establish such a relationship with children prior to assessing and teaching, although it is sometimes difficult to attain. When rapport is established, however, students tend to be cooperative and to look forward with pleasure to subsequent sessions. Steps in establishing rapport are planning for the first meeting, greeting children, selecting tasks, obtaining information during the initial session, and ending the session.

Planning.   Careful planning is a prerequisite for successful assessment sessions. Even if the assessor is also the students' teacher or is familiar with them in another capacity, assessment is a different type of activity, and students may feel uneasy while being tested. The relationship is different, particularly when students are assessed individually; they are aware of revealing their inadequate skills and concepts.

Ideally, assessment is conducted by students' teachers. Administrative arrangements can be used to facilitate assessment by teachers. Any one of or combination of these arrangements can encourage teachers to assess their students:

1. Permit teachers to begin the school year one or two weeks in advance for the purpose of assessing target children.

2. Provide teachers with a substitute teacher for a specific number of days each month in order to continue instruction while the permanent teacher assesses students.

3. On certain days have the special class come to school one hour later than usual except for those students who will be assessed.

4. Have an itinerant teacher or a consultant routinely teach the special class, on a scheduled basis, while the special class teacher is free to assess students.

When the above administrative arrangements are not available, teachers often create their own opportunities for assessing students without assistance.

Itinerant teachers or others who are assessing students should determine in advance where the session will be held. Check the room to make certain it will provide the necessary space and comfort. Make certain that desks and chairs of sufficient number of size are available for use at that time. Arrange the room prior to the session, placing the material to be used in the order which these will be needed.

Effective planning and subsequent success occur more frequently if outcomes are established in advance of each session. One plan for a first assessment session is shown in Figure 6.6.

Greeting children.   Itinerant personnel should avoid going into classrooms to get children initially because they may be embarrassed by their peers' knowledge that they are in need of help. Later, after determining otherwise, it may be appropriate to enter classrooms to get those students who do not find such attention upsetting.

If those to be assessed are not in school and are brought for assessment by parents or other adults, children and parents should be greeted together prior to working alone with the children. Sometimes young children will refuse to go with the assessor unless the parent also goes along. In such situations, try to avoid

Student _____   Date _____

Assessor _____   Session _____

Task	Outcome
1. establish rapport	child will agree to return.
2. Assess: printing skills, language skills, and motor skills	obtain sufficient information to complete first observation form.

FIGURE 6.6.   A student assessment plan

assessing children with their parents present unless, of course, it is in relation to management techniques which the parent is to conduct.

Children who hesitate to leave their parents are sometimes reassured by using one or more of the five tactics shown below. Assessors should be seated as soon as practical so as to avoid requiring students to look up.

Students should be complimented if it can be honestly done, e.g., "what a good-looking red sweater you have on." If students seem to be talkative, the assessors should begin chatting with them, but they need to be careful not to be threatening by asking too many questions. Simple small talk is needed at this time.

At this point, some children begin to discuss their difficulties in school. When this occurs, assessors should take advantage of the opportunity and encourage them to continue describing their problems. Other suggestions are:

1. Tell parents, in a loud voice so the child can hear, when you will be finished.
2. Take the child's hand.
3. Permit parents to walk with you toward the rooms.
4. Give the child a toy to take to the room.
5. When all else fails, permit parents to be in the room while you work.

Initial tasks.   An ideal introductory task is one that will be successfully performed but will still be somewhat challenging. When a task proves to be so easy that it is insulting, it should be followed immediately by one that will be more suitable.

Teacher: My, Howard, you finished that very quickly! Was it easy for you? Here is something that should be a bit harder.

By telling Howard that the next task is more difficult the teacher is getting him set for a more challenging activity and providing reassurance to him if he has difficulty with it.

The task that is evidently too difficult can be withdrawn before it results in actual failure.

Teacher: Never mind finishing this, Howard. Here is something more important I want you to try.

Teachers, in withdrawing tasks, must be careful not to reward poor work habits and lack of persistence. They should be certain that an apparent failure to respond is not due to slowness in responding. It may be necessary to focus the child's attention on one item and assist him or her in order to determine if failure in responding is due to item difficulty. When certain that the task requirements are not within the student's repertoire, an easier task should be presented. The following suggestions may be helpful when selecting beginning tasks:

1. Children between ages 5 to about 10 often feel comfortable with drawing activities.

Teacher: (With assorted pens and pencils in evidence) Howard, pick a pen or pencil that you would like to use for drawing. (Pause, giving Howard an opportunity to examine the possible selections.)

Teacher: (Placing an unlined paper before him) Draw whatever you would like.

2. Sometimes children ask for directions as to what they should draw. Encourage them to draw whatever they wish.

3. Some children respond better to copying designs. Be careful to select geometric designs that are easily drawn by the child.

Teacher: Look at this, draw one like it on your paper.

4. Try using manipulative objects for young children who are not responsive to paper/pencil tasks.

Teacher: See what I have here for you to play with! (while showing him blocks and other colored objects)

Teacher: (while placing the objects in a certain order) Do what I'm doing.

5. With older children who seem responsive to verbal stimuli, start with verbal items. Asking a series of questions distributing easy ones throughout.

Summary

Assessing students is the first step in an instructional process. L&BD children should be assessed as to their performances in academic and social areas of the curriculum, in terms of their modes of learning, and regarding their reinforcement needs.

Measures for assessing students include both formal and nonstandardized types. Standardized tests have greater value for educational planning than for instructional purposes. Nonstandardized approaches, including direct observations and criterion-referenced measures, can have instructional value. These need to be related directly to what is to be taught and should be task-specific.

Planning and Implementing Instructional Programs

7

Teachers of L&BD students try to base their instruction of students on assessment findings. This approach is common to both ability training and skill-oriented prescriptive teachers. Issues in teaching L&BD students include program scope and focus, information for teaching, and ethical considerations. Instructional tasks are selected by teachers on the bases of what to teach, when to teach it, and how to teach it. Tactics used in teaching consist of a systematic instructional plan and may include such methods as imitation, behavior rehearsing, direct reinforcement, shaping, cuing, and contingency contracting.

Introduction

Contemporary instruction of children with learning and behavioral disorders in American schools is characterized by systematic and purposeful activities. Adherents of almost all approaches to instruction of L&BD students recognize the importance of systematic instruction, providing evidence of how the prescriptive teaching movement has gained preeminence. Even summer programs have been based upon prescriptive teaching. Sabatino and Hayden (1970) described the results of a prescriptive teaching summer program for 15 elementary school children who displayed learning problems. They used a single sensory perceptual training approach where the children's strongest perceptual area for teaching was used. Their systematic approach resulted in improved conduct and language performances.

Systematic instruction is a common characteristic of all prescriptive programs regardless of the theoretical roots of the teaching practices. For example, Rice (1970) used a systematic treatment program for 10 delinquent girls judged to have learning and/or behavioral problems. For three months, these girls, ages 11 through 15 years, were institutionalized and their total time consisted of an intensive treatment program. While no rigorous evaluation of the treatment effects was made, the eclectic approach used in this study was applied systematically.

Academic skills appear to be more rapidly acquired through systematic instruction. Reading achievement among low-achieving first and second graders was higher with the use of directive teaching procedures than when taught in less systematic ways (Stephens, Hartman, & Cooper, 1973). Many other studies and authoritative opinion appear to support and encourage systematic instruction (Baker, 1973).

While current practice is moving increasingly toward systematic instruction and treatment, some authorities are predicting radical changes in the future. Rhodes (1975) believes that major changes in the future will permit more freedom, "to experience ourselves directly, without an overlay of preconditioning, is to experience others more directly, without the ritual of coded thoughts and behaviors" (p. 94). Clearly if his predictions do occur, the delivery of instruction would be radically changed.

An emphasis on self-instruction is one of the many possible forms that teaching might take. Systematic approaches might be even more necessary if individuals were to assume greater responsibilities for their own academic and social learning. It is also equally possible, of course, that systematic approaches might be less useful if there is a heavy emphasis on learning through discovery.

Currently, special education is deeply involved with managed instruction and a systems approach to education. Systems procedures require each program component to relate to the others. Such interrelatedness of program activities is believed to improve the quality of services.

Some authorities fear that systematic instruction and its attendant technology can be overemphasized in education. Broudy (1973), for example, is concerned because competency-based instruction is not rooted in any philosophy. Others agree with Shugue (1973) that it is incompatible with the academic preparation of teachers. Certainly, systematic instruction has the inherent danger of being overly mechanical as in an assembly line activity. Objectifying and routinizing instruction may obliterate those interpersonal values that are so helpful to the human experience, but such an omission need not occur. And, nonsystematic teaching does not guarantee sensitive teachers. Those who like children, enjoy helping them and interacting with them can maintain those feelings while using instructional technology purposefully.

Issues in Teaching L&BD Students

Understanding those factors which contribute to effective instruction and learning among L&BD students is limited. Many questions have yet to be asked as well as answered before teachers will be fully confident about their instruction. Similarly, program designs could be improved if some basic issues were resolved. Five such issues relate to program purposes, program scope, program focus, types of needed information, and ethical considerations. These concerns are discussed briefly here.

Purposes of Programs

By definition, school programs must have recognizable limits and objectives. Schools cannot be all things to all people. Yet it is essential that schools fulfill their basic purposes for teaching and socializing the young. Traditionally, schools provided basic instruction in the three Rs. Later, as our society became more complex, more comprehensive programs were created. And most recently, schools have begun to adjust programs in order to better meet the needs of handicapped students.

Most programs for L&BD students are directed at remediating their problems and, as a consequence, improving their academic and social performances. Some programs recognize the need for occupational preparation of L&BD students, providing work experience and on-the-job training.

What are the limits of social instruction? Should it include all aspects of living? Of emotions? Or should social behavior be limited to those school-related activities that facilitate academic learning?

Scope of Services

Should programs for L&BD students extend throughout their school lives, if necessary? Kline (1972), for example, noted that adolescents with learning problems often are overlooked and/or misdiagnosed. He views learning disabilities as problems fostered by society and those that the schools have a responsibility to correct.

Programs at high school and college levels have been started in some regions for L&BD students. Should programs for such students end upon graduation from high school? Or should colleges and postsecondary schools be encouraged to have special programs as well?

Who should be served? Should parents of L&BD students receive assistance? Should their siblings? If learning and behavioral handicaps are socially induced and/or maintained, should not the family receive instruction? And what form should the instruction take — academic centered, child management, or a type of psychotherapy?

Questions of scope can include the range of handicapping conditions as well. Should special instruction be provided in public schools for the mildly handicapped? Will instruction in public schools be available to severely handicapped children? Should extensive instruction and therapy be provided under the public school's auspices? Stuecher (1972) described a program for one autistic child which consisted of "...about 500 hours on a one-to-one basis spread out over a 5 month period" (p. 6). Can such children be taught so intensively within public school programs? Or are they beyond those programs' scope of services?

Special programs might include inservice components for all school personnel — teachers as well as noncertificated employees. Should all individuals employed by the school who interact with L&BD students be viewed as providing instruction and related services (cafeteria workers, custodians, bus drivers and clerical personnel)? Should these individuals participate in training activities which are designed to improve their understandings and attitudes toward L&BD students?

Instructional services for L&BD students may need to extend beyond the school day. Should recreation and other social activities be a part of the intervention program? Should instruction be provided after school, on weekends, and in summers for L&BD students? Where should the school's day and year begin and end for such children?

Program Focus

Special instructional programs may be focused broadly or narrowly in terms of services and curricula. Emphasis might be primarily on academic performance and school adjustment, or services could be extended to social and emotional adjustment areas that are unrelated to school activities.

Instruction could take the direction of ability training where activities for remediation are concerned with learning processes as described by Warner (1973). Or the focus could be skill training where the instructional activities relate to task-specific responses (Stephens, 1976). A broader focus might include eclectic approaches where a combination of ability and skill training is used (Hallahan & Kauffman, 1976).

In some programs, perhaps most, the instructional focus is shifted depending upon orientations of instructional personnel, types of learning problems, and/or performances of the students. Smayling (1959), for example, described six voluntarily mute children. This early study showed how an analysis of language performance and task-specific assessment were used to demonstrate how voluntary mutism was extinguished as a result of speech correction. It was one of the first published reports to show that voluntary mutism could be corrected without using psycho-therapeutic treatment.

In the end, teachers determine their own instructional focus. While program design and organizational arrangements do influence instruction, teachers bring to their classes past experiences (how they were taught), certain beliefs and attitudes concerning handicapping conditions of students (how they should teach), teaching and management competencies (how well they can teach), and a commitment to teaching (their willingness to teach).

There have been serious attempts to relate teaching behavior to personal attributes of teaching personnel (Getzels & Jackson, 1963). Scheuer (1971) considered this issue for teachers of the emotionally disturbed. He investigated the relationship between personality attributes and effectiveness of teachers. With the assumption that effective teachers of the emotionally disturbed possess the same characteristics as effective therapists, an inventory was used to measure those characteristics. Those pupils who saw their teachers as possessing a high degree of understanding, congruence, and a high level of regard showed significant gains in academic achievement. Even with the obvious failure to control significant variables in this study and accepting questionable assumptions upon which the use of the measure were based, this study does identify the importance and need for such studies.

Personal preferences and characteristics influence the instructional focus. Even within a systematically designed program, instructional decisions must be made by teachers. What they decide is based, in part, on their training, and it is through inservice and preservice experiences that teachers acquire much of their instructional focuses.

Needed Research

Among the most pressing issues in educating L&BD children is the need to establish research questions. Two major areas of concern are the effects of differential programming on these students' school success and related personnel variables.

Personnel Issues

Personnel who work in schools need to possess specific competencies and certain attitudes if they are to be effective in their work with L&BD students. Pincus (1974) described how the public school industry affects decisions of school personnel. He emphasized how incentives for innovations can be used to increase change in schools. His definition of *innovation* is that something improves educational outcomes, improves processes within school systems, and/or reduces the costs of education without impairing the quantity or quality of desired outcomes. Because of the nature of the educational enterprise, practices are often continued long after they have proven to be ineffective. Practitioners (teachers as well as teacher trainers) are often unaware of such evidence and, in some instances, refuse to accept research evidence. Teacher education practices, as well as instruction for L&BD students, often are equally as resistant to changes.

Rappaport & McNary (1970) discussed those factors which they believe influence the effectiveness of public school teachers with learning disabled students. While no research evidence was presented in support of their statements, they noted the importance of identifying which students can profit from public school instruction and under what circumstances. They believe that, in its present form, public education cannot be expected to help all children who have learning problems.

Zedler (1970) discussed the problems and issues involved in preparing teachers of children who have reading problems. In an earlier study, he had demonstrated that underachieving readers who were taught by teachers trained in "unconventional" methods made significantly higher gains in academic achievement than did the control group taught by teachers using "conventional" methods of reading instruction. Using findings from this study as a basis, Zedler described a teacher preparation program for those children who cannot learn by conventional procedures. No research evidence was presented in support of the proposed teacher preparation program, although the suggestions appear to have merit.

Bullock & Whelan (1971) reported the results of a study regarding competencies valued by teachers of emotionally and socially maladjusted students. They contrasted their findings with that of an earlier study (Mackie, Kvaraceus, & Williams, 1957). Using the same checklist items of the 1957 study, they asked 47 teachers of "emotionally disturbed and socially maladjusted children" to respond to those 88 items. Their responses were then compared with those in the Mackie study (1957). They found that teachers in their sample did not view the competencies as being as important as did the 1957 group, rated themselves as being more proficient than did the 1957 group, tended to rank the items similarly to the 1957 group on importance and on proficiency, and tended to view themselves as being proficient in the items which they viewed as important.

There are published statements of expert opinion regarding the preparation needs of teachers of L&BD students. Rabinow (1960) argued for a preparation program for teachers of the behaviorally disordered which heavily emphasizes a multidisciplinary working situation. Teachers in training, under this plan, would be steeped in psychiatry, psychology, sociology, communications, and education. Schwartz (1967), in a dissimilar approach, advocated preparing clinical teachers who would be proficient in diagnosing and remediating learning problems and behavior disorders.

Hewett (1966) indicated that seven competency areas are important for teachers of the emotionally handicapped: objectivity, flexibility, structure, resourcefulness, social reinforcement, curriculum expertise, and an intellectual model.

Adelman (1972) views the teacher education situation as ironic because teachers in training are asked to acquire effective approaches within college training programs that provide poor models. He argued for clarifying, systematically integrating, and sequencing cognitive, affective, and motivational variables into teacher preparation programs.

Clearly, there are many authoritative opinions regarding preparation of teachers for L&BD students, but little research evidence exists in support of these opinions. Those difficulties associated with obtaining relevant research findings should not be minimized. Because of the disagreements as to the characteristics of such children, confusion regarding the educational outcomes for them, and the relatively recent initiation of many teacher preparation programs, research evidence will continue to be difficult to obtain and to interpret for use across training programs (Adelman, 1971).

Effects of Instruction

Issues relating to the effectiveness of various instructional treatments upon the performances of L&BD students are complex. Not only must the treatments be clearly defined and explicated, but the performances (behaviors) and the student characteristics must be described. Within the present discussion such complexities can only be identified. No attempt is made here to deal with these issues in a comprehensive way, but perhaps readers can gain an appreciation of the difficulties to be considered regarding instructional effects in this brief discussion.

Fine (1970) considered some of the problems inherent in educating children with "cerebral dysfunction." His plea was for an experimental attitude, recognizing the tentativeness of knowledge concerning the education of such children. He cited a need to explore systematically students' behaviors and those remedial approaches which appear to be effective. He believes that there are ways to structure learning environments to match children's inner psychological states. While he cited authoritative opinions and some related research studies in support of his position, he presented no new research evidence to clarify those issues which he identified.

There are many methods and/or tactics which have been suggested as means of remediating or alleviating learning problems. For example, Rejto (1973) suggested that music instruction could serve as an aid when teaching learning disabled children with perceptual problems. The procedure consisted of visual, aural, and tactual training through the medium of piano and theory lessons over a six-month period.

Using one seven-year-old boy with speech and motor coordination problems as a subject, she supplemented his public school program and speech correction with music therapy. His subtest performances on the *WISC*, Frostig, and *ITPA* were used as guidelines for planning therapy. Posttest performances following music therapy showed gains on the three tests. However, due to her inability to control other treatment effects (schooling and speech correction) and reliability of the tests, the child's higher performance could not be attributed directly to the music therapy.

Glavin and Annesley (1971) considered the academic achievement correlates of conduct-problem and withdrawn children based upon Quay's system of grouping behaviorally disordered students. Using the Behavior Problem Checklist authored by Quay and Peterson, teachers in three elementary schools were asked to focus on those children they believed to be either extremely disruptive or overly withdrawn. The school with the largest enrollment (895) referred 5.8% of the student population, the one with the second highest enrollment (760) referred 7.5%, and the lowest enrollment school (674) referred 6% of the population. Of the group referred only boys were studied. A majority of the 130 boys who were studied were characterized by hyperactive-aggressive behavior.

Data analyzed by academic area showed that almost 82% of those classified as behavior problems were underachieving in reading and 72% in arithmetic. Among the important findings of this study was the extreme academic underachievement shown by a large percentage of behavior-problem children. These authors cited earlier studies (Glavin, Quay, & Werry, 1971; Graubard, 1964) to emphasize the importance of stressing academic achievement in order to improve social behavior (conduct). In their discussion, they refuted two popular views: (1) that conduct problems must be improved before stressing academic achievement and (2) that requiring better academic achievement from conduct-problem children resulted in an increase in behavior problems.

Another interesting finding in this study related to the lack of differences in academic achievement between those students classified as withdrawn and those considered to have conduct problems. No differences were found between the two behavioral groups on reading comprehension and reading vocabulary, and arithmetic reasoning and arithmetic fundamentals. The authors interpreted these results as indicating that the learning correlates of these two categories of emotionally disturbed children were not significantly different.

A major instructional issue concerns the effects of modality of instruction on learning (Bateman, 1968; Lilly & Kelleher, 1973; Waugh, 1973). Newcomer and Goodman (1975) categorized 167 fourth-grade students on the basis of visual or auditory modality preferences and who were taught through their preferred modalities. They found that students did not perform better when instruction was presented through their preferred modalities. The results indicated a general superiority of the visual mode for information processing regardless of individual modality preferences. They concluded that teachers of fourth-grade students need not be concerned with matching the channel of academic instruction with student modality deficits or preferences. However, Newcomer and Goodman's population consisted entirely of normal students — not L&BD students.

Issues dealing with the effects of instruction on L&BD students are varied and numerous. The relatively small amount of research evidence in response to these issues suggests that teaching practices must be approached critically with an attitude of openness toward new research findings.

Ethics

Ethical considerations are intricately related to practically all educational activities for L&BD students. Concerns include diagnosis, management with medication, management without medication, school placement, instructional approaches, and the use and maintenance of student information. Within the area of instruction, ethical issues arise as to when to use which approaches and students' participation in selecting instructional approaches.

Ethical issues are frequently discussed in relation to the use of behavior modification, though it is patently unfair to place an ethical criterion on one approach and not on others. Regardless, teachers who use behavioral approaches must face, as should others, the question of ethics.

Stolz, Wienckowski and Brown (1975) critically reviewed the major issues involved in the use of behavior modification. They identified the key question:

> ...what sort of care, caution, and control should be exercised when behavioral principles are applied precisely and systematically? (p. 1027)

While this question was discussed by the authors, no definitive answers were presented. For example, they noted that the issues and problems differ depending upon settings and populations. Noting the commonly used example of using behavioral approaches with school-aged children to teach them to be "still, quiet, and docile," they suggest that alternative goals for the children should be suggested by the "mental health professional."

Suggested procedures for behavior modification programs should take into account at least five factors: client involvement, a balance of risk and benefit, reviews by outside personnel, effectiveness of the procedures, and program accountability. It should be noted that these five items are valid ethical safeguards for all instructional and treatment approaches, and not just for classroom practices.

Client involvement. L&BD students and/or their parents (guardians) should be consulted regarding the means and goals of the special program. Consultation may occur within the framework of the special education team as described in chapter 3.

Risk and benefit. The special education team in consultation with the child's parents should consider the potential benefits for the student. They should consider the possible inconvenience and risk to the student as well. When students are competent to participate, they should be involved in decisions which affect them.

Monitoring and effectiveness of procedures. The special education team provides an administrative mechanism for reviewing students' success in programs. Ideally, a qualified, nonschool professional may serve as a consultant in student progress reviews. When students have not made reasonable progress in relation to their initial difficulties, adjustment in programs or another school placement should be made.

Program accountability. Program accountability involves reviews of individual students' progress and effectiveness of programs for those individuals. In addition to monitoring the progress of individual students, however, it includes routine and careful evaluations of each program component. The crucial question to be asked is: *How well does the program do what it is designed to do?* In addition, those school personnel who are heavily behaviorally oriented have an added ethical responsibility because of the power of behavioral tactics. Patterson (1969) has pointed out that reinforcement theory should be concerned with changing individuals' social systems rather than changing individuals. School personnel must address themselves to conditions of learning which need modifying in order to assist children. The theme *be docile, still, and quiet* should definitely not be the motto of teachers of L&BD students.

Selecting Instructional Tasks

Teachers of L&BD students, regardless of the educational provisions, face important decisions concerning what to teach, when to teach it, and how to teach it. But there are few ready answers to such questions.

Decision Points

Teachers make instructional decisions frequently. Some are routine and of limited consequence, others occur at key junctures in students' learning experiences. Important decisions are made by teachers in behalf of L&BD students at three points:

1. following assessment,
2. at mastery and/or completion of units of study or sequences, and
3. at times of unexpected need.

Decisions Following Assessment

Upon entry into an instructional setting, L&BD students should be assessed as to their performances in relation to curriculum tasks as described in chapter 6. Within a skill training approach, students are usually assessed on a segment of tasks, rather than on an entire curriculum. When skill training is implemented properly, results occur quickly. At this point, evaluation of the performance leads to additional assessment information.

In skill training, following assessment, teachers proceed to instruct the portion of skills that are: (a) within the student's instructional range and (b) at the lowest skill level. Ways to determine both the instructional range and level of skill performance are discussed under a subsequent section in this chapter, "Decision Criteria."

In clinical teaching, where tutoring is provided, the initial assessment may be more comprehensive than in a classroom setting. In anecdote 7.1, the tutor assesses Andy extensively and makes instructional decisions based upon that assessment.

ANECDOTE 7.1

Andy is seven years old and is repeating first grade. He was in Head Start for one year followed by kindergarten. In the early months of his second year in first grade, he was referred to the special education team. Following evaluation by the team, he was provided with supplemental tutoring.

Mrs. Flack, the tutor, conducted a thorough assessment of Andy's functioning in reading because it was his poorest academic area. She also assessed him in his use of sensory modalities for learning and school behavior.

Academic Assessment

Reading Readiness

Correctly matched and named eight colors cut from construction paper (red, yellow, blue, green, brown, black, purple, orange).

Drew pictures of his house and family. The major extremities were contained in the pictures of people but the bodies had no necks, ears, hands, eyebrows or other fine details. The chimney on the roof was slanted and the house had no door. His figures were large and he ran out of space and asked if he could draw himself in the air.

Does catch a ball when thrown directly to him but has very poor accuracy in trying to return it, not enthusiastic about playing "catch."

Does place box *under, over, behind, in front of, beside* table.

Does follow oral directions (sit, stand, walk, run, jump, shake my hand), does not skip.

Left and right directionality completely reversed for both hands and feet. When this was rechecked three days later he used the correct side when asked to. He always starts working from the left side of the paper.

Does not state the day, month, and year of his birth.

When asked his age stated, "Seven, eight, nine, no eight." He is seven.

Repeated two five-word sentences individually. "The cat's fur is black." "The cat has little kittens."

Did not know his address.

When asked what he liked to eat stated, "Fish hamburger, cheese hamburger." Hamburger was synonymous for sandwich.

Did not integrate five pictures into sequence of story (Charlie Brown cartoon).

When given a picture of ladies with musical instruments to create a story, his response was, "These old women made a lot of noise. The cops came and said shut-up or we'll shoot you." His sentence structure was correct. When offered other pictures to comment on he said, "Let's do something else."

Correctly identified four pictures depicting happiness, anger, sorrow, and fright.

Reading

Letter and word recognition skills.

Correctly named all letters in the alphabet except: *c* - s; *g* - h; *h* - g; and *b* - d which he then corrected.

When giving consonant sounds in isolation first gave letter name and then sound even though asked to give only sound. All correct except: *g* - u; *h* - j; *q* - gr; *z* - v; *l* - _; *w* - d; *b* - d; then corrected *y* - w; *x* - k.

Correctly named long vowel sounds when he determined that he simply had to name the letters. He had the concept of making short vowel sounds, his throat was open but he was unable to make any correctly.

When he was asked to write letters on the board from sounds given, he stalled and then asked if he could write to 100. When put under contingency contracting he wrote the letters correctly from sounds, p, b, k, r, d, and said, "Easy, easy," but the letters were very poorly formed.

The pretest of Dolch and primer words showed that he read the following words: a, an, and, up, down, said, will, who, help, not, no, I, me, you, my, this, that, red, yellow, jump, run, see, look, go, come, one, two, three, six.

Orally gave the correct beginning letter on the following words pronounced aloud to him: box, ran, see, fun, go, look, mother, no, dog, key, take; missed: what - *y* and George - *h*.

Wrote the correct ending letter from the following words pronounced aloud: *run*, *dress*, *set*, *book*, *drop*, *what*, *some*; missed big - no response.

Modality Assessment

Auditory

discrimination

  a. Twenty pairs of similar words were read aloud and Andy was to state if they were the same or different.
    Criteria: 18 (20 correct).
  b. Five pairs of words were read aloud and in each pair Andy was to identify the one containing the vowel sound pronounced just preceding the two words. His choice *italicized:*

a — cat, *cake*	a — *cat*, hop
e — *my*, see	e — bed, *dig*
i — kite, *cat*	i — go, *fish*
o — *hope*, hat	o — *pot*, me
u — *come*, cute	u — luck, *and*

  Criteria: 8 (5 correct).
immediate recall

Primer level story, well within Andy's range of comprehension, was read aloud to him: Bill said, "Look, Linda. Rags is not at home. Help me find Rags. He runs away and plays." Linda said, "I see Rags. He is at home, Bill. He is in our car."

Orally asked the following questions, Andy's answer italicized.

1. What did Bill think Rags had done? *Run away*
2. What did Bill ask Linda to do? *Help find Rags*
3. Who found Rags? *Linda*
4. Where was Rags? *In the car*

Criteria 4 (4 correct).
delayed recall

The same four questions were repeated in five days after stating, "Remember the story I read to you last week? I wonder how many of those questions you can answer."

Criteria 4 (4 correct).
Method used to assure the auditory performance would not be contaminated by visual cues: He sat facing wall with back to evaluator.

Visual

discrimination

a. Ten pairs of words were typed on a paper. Andy was to write *D* if the words were different: made, made; fat, fat; sit, sat; cat, cat; dog, bog; fog, fog; car, car; ship, boat; ball, ball.
   Criteria 9 (9 correct)

b. Test 1 — Section D of *California Achievement Test*, Lower Primary Form W. Using the first 10 pictures and identifying the correct word from 3 given through visual clues only, he attempted 9 and refused to go further when the answer choices became more than one word.
   Criteria 9 (9 correct).

c. Seven words were printed with four variations of spellings beneath each word, the same spelling was to be underlined. The following words were used; the word Andy chose is italicized: glad – *glab*; hen – *hen*; gate – *gate*; can – *can*; wnat – *want*; there – *there*; pear – *pear*.
   Criteria – 8 (7 correct).

immediate recall

a. Five plastic letters on a magnetic tray were shown. Out of his sight, one letter was removed.
   Correctly named one removed.
   Six letters on tray, one removed.
   Correctly named one removed.
   Seven letters on tray, one removed.
   Unable to name one removed.
   Six letters on tray, two removed.
   Correctly named both letters removed.
   Six letters on tray, three removed.
   Correctly named three letters removed.
   Criteria 4 (4 correct).

c. The words *help*, *sit*, *why*, and *three* were printed on a separate paper and Andy was told to study carefully the way the four words looked as he would be asked to find those same words among others of similar spelling. After studying these words for 45 seconds they were removed and he was given the following:

helg	holp	*help*	hedp
sat	*sit*	set	cet
wly	vly	wby	*why*
three	there	tree	*thee*

Criteria 4 (3 correct).
delayed recall

The words *help, sit, why* and *three* were shown directly after the Immediate Recall test and the one mistake was shown to him. He was told to study the four correct words visually again which he did. Forty-five minutes later he was given another paper with the confused words and this time his choices were: help – help; sit – sit; why – vhy; three – three.

Criteria: 4 (3 correct).

Haptic

discrimination
  a. Ten wooden uppercase letters were placed in a box with holes cut for his hands.
     He was asked to name the letters:
     The letters were: *T K W B V G C Y X E*
     The response: X K N K V H C Y H O
     Criteria 9 (4 correct).
  b. Eight lowercase letters formed with pipe-cleaners glued onto cardboard were
     placed in the box with holes for his hands.
     The letters were: *b x t r k u m a*
     The response: d t t r k n m a
     Criteria 7 (5 correct).

immediate recall

   With his hands still enclosed in the box, he was helped to trace each lowercase
letter with his finger as he was given the correct letter name and asked to repeat it.
He was then asked to identify each letter.
The letters were: *b x t r k u m a*
The response: b x t r k u n a

Criteria 7 (6 correct).

delayed recall

Forty-five minutes later the lowercase letters were again presented. He asked if he
could see the letters as he did not like putting his hands in that box. He then chose to
be blindfolded to feel the letters.
The letters were: *b x t r k u m a*
His response: d x t r k u r a
Criteria 6 (5 correct).

Olfactory

discrimination
  a. Four cotton balls were placed in numbered plastic bags and soaked in the follow-
     ing scents: (1) cider, (2) vanilla, (3) perfume, (4) ammonia. He was asked to
     identify each and he responded: 1 – *ammonia*, 2 – *chocolate*, 3 – *stuff to put on
     cuts*, and 4 – *don't know*. He knew all four were different but he did not have
     proper labels for them. He was then given four other bags with identical scents
     and told to match them which he did.
     Criteria 4 (4 correct).

immediate recall

As he matched the correct scents, he was told what each one was and he repeated
the name at that time. The numbers were then shifted out of his sight and he was asked
to tell what each of the four were. His response for each was: perfume – *orange*,
ammonia – *ammonia*, cider – *Fish and Chips stuff*, vanilla – *vanilla*.
Criteria 4 (3 correct).

delayed

Three days later the four plastic bags were again presented and he was asked to tell
what each was. His responses: perfume – *perfume*, ammonia – *ammonia*, cider –
french fry stuff, vanilla – *vanilla*.
Criteria 4 (4 correct).

A summary of Andy's performance during the modality assessment is presented in
Figure 7.1.

FIGURE 7.1. Summary of modality assessment

Sense Skill	Stimulus	Criterion Score	Performance Score	Analysis Code	0—at criterion / – – below / + –above
AUDITORY					
Discrimination	20 pairs of similar words read aloud	18/20	20	+	
Immediate Recall	Read primer story & answered 4 questions	4	4	0	
Delayed Recall	Referred to — 5 days later previous story	4	4	0	
VISUAL					
Discrimination	10 pairs of words / 10 picture words identifications	9/10 / 9/10	9 / 9	0 / 0	
Immediate Recall	5 tests of removing different letters / Study 4 words and then identify correct spelling	4/5 / 4	4 / 3	0 / —	
Delayed Recall	4 words repeated in 45 minutes	4	3	—	
HAPTIC					
Discrimination	Recognize 10 uppercase letters by touch only / Recognize 8 lowercase letters	9/10 / 7/8	4 / 5	— / —	
Immediate Recall	Identify 8 lowercase letters	7/8	6	—	
Delayed Recall	45 minutes later	7/8	5	—	
OLFACTORY					
Discrimination	Vinegar, ammonia, perfume, vanilla	4	4	0	I — Could match but did not have proper name
Immediate Recall	Same	4	3	—	
Delayed Recall	Same	4	4	0	

School Behavior

After talking with Andy's teacher concerning the behavior he evidenced in school, he was observed in class. The following is a description of a 10-minute period in the classroom towards the end of the day. The first part of the time was devoted to an arithmetic lesson and the times are correct to 30-second approximations.

Min. : Sec.

1:00	Teacher instructed class to get out arithmetic book and tear out page 32, which he did.
1:45	Watched and listened as the concept of adding was explained on board.
2:00	Andy asked teacher what number to write in and discovered he was doing wrong side of paper, stood up with knee on chair.
2:30	Answered aloud when another child was called upon.
3:00	As class was half finished with page he yelled, *I done it!*
4:00	Out of seat to get pencil sharpener from another child's desk, showed paper to neighbor behind and called, *It's easy.*
5:00	Called out answer when another child called upon, when he was told to do the rest alone he stood by his desk and said, *I done it!*
6:00	Instructed to put his head down on the desk until the rest of the class finished, he did for 15 seconds. He then got out a picture he had drawn, checked his neighbor's work and told him, *It's easy.*
7:00	Looked at another student and said, *Don't do those, you're 'posed to turn it over and put your head down.* He remained standing playing with a piece of plastic.
8:00	Waved paper in air *I'm done, it's easy.*
8:30	Called upon by teacher to add 3 + 2, replied *4* and when shown number line on board still failed to give correct answer until someone nearby said *5* at which time he called out *5.*
9:00	Turned completely around in his chair and watched the boy behind him, then shook his finger and said, *That's not right.*
10:00	When asked again what is 2 more than 3 he was unable to respond correctly.
11:00	After another child responded with 5 and was praised for knowing, Andy clapped aloud.
78:45	Total elapsed time

This is a sampling of one observation. The longest he ever remained quietly in his chair was 3 minutes 30 seconds during group singing to records with hand motions. By actual count, he was out of his seat 21 times, 2 of which were with permission. He also was excused to the bathroom once, even though he was observed having gone at the start of the period, he was there 2 minutes 30 seconds.

He checked my presence frequently. As another child brought me a paper, Andy made a face in the direction of the child.

As the classroom teacher walked near the area of the room where I was seated, Andy ran toward the teacher, slid across the floor and fell at her feet.

The other children did not seem to object to his behavior. Later the classroom teacher stated they frequently complain to her because he does not have his work completed. She also stated that Andy *loved to help other children* with their work and since there are two children in the room with lower academic achievement than he, this was sometimes possible. When he does help one of the boys he has very little patience; the teacher stated he will say to her, *You'll have to help him, he's just too dumb.*

One boy in the class the day of the observation had brought badges to give out to the members of his "army" and Andy was one of those chosen. The boy asked for the badges back, as it was time to go home, and then asked Andy if he would be in his "army" tomorrow.

A conference following the observation with the teacher, Miss N, indicated this was not an atypical day. She stated that some mornings Andy came into the room and announced, *I'm going to get my work done today* and would attend to a task, even writing which he dislikes the most, for up to 30 minutes. As the day goes on his attention becomes shorter, however.

Contingency contracting was explained to the teacher in relation to the events Andy finds rewarding. Also, social modeling tactics were suggested because he does seem to imitate other children if no attention is given to his misbehavior. During an activity song which he did not want to do, he observed his neighbor for a few seconds and then began the same activities.

Following assessment, decisions must be made based upon the results. In anecdote 7.1, the tutor, Mrs. Flack, has many items from which to select. In such a situation, the teacher will do well to select for instruction those tasks in which the child has evidenced some degree of accuracy. Note in anecdote 7.2 that Andy's tutor chose reading tasks initially which he had partially responded to correctly during academic assessment.

ANECDOTE 7.2

Mrs. Flack tutored Andy from early November until the end of that school year. During that period, he made very good progress in reading skill development. His classroom teacher reported that contingency contracting and social modeling tactics rapidly improved his in-school behavior. Following are some selected teaching strategies implemented by Mrs. Flack.

Nov. 5

Task
    To say the correct sound when shown the letters *G* and *L*.
    To say the short *a* sound.
    To sound three letter words consisting of the consonant sounds he knows and short *a* (fat, gas, map, ran, sat, lap).
Materials
    Two folded cards with the letter *G* printed on the one and *L* printed on the other.
    Felt tip marker.
    Paper with the words printed on it to be sounded out.
    Chalk and chalkboard.
Activities
    Look at chart of pictures with correct consonant sound and repeat sound aloud.
    Play game "I'm going to the store to buy a _____." (word beginning with desired sound.) Opposite player gives the shopper the correct card.
    Using felt tipped marker draw an apple and stimulate the short *a* vocal response.
    Pronounce sounds of words almost in isolation to write on chalkboard but grouped as a word. Instructor blend three sounds into word as each is completed.
    Read words from printed paper.
Approach
    Visual, auditory, haptic.
Reinforcement
    Smile and praise for each of first five correct responses then reinforce every other response. If goal achieved, he may choose from three things: Viewmaster, Logo bricks, or dictate story on wall chart.

Evaluation

Criterion: 6 short *a* words correctly read aloud.

Criterion met with 100% success. Persistence was good. Chose to dictate story to take to room and read to class.

Criterion: sounds for letters *G* and *L* given correctly aloud.

Criteria met with 100% success.

Nov. 10

Task

To write the correct letter when g, h, c are pronounced aloud.

To name aloud the letters: g, h, c when shown these printed on paper.

To determine the retention of short *a* sound and words made of known consonants: lag, fan, gap, lad, sad, rat.

Materials

Ten red construction paper letters on each: g, h, c.

Three white papers with the 10 letter outlines on each, one paper for each letter.

Red felt tip marker.

Paper with short *a* words printed on

Picture of apple he had drawn.

Activities

Using one letter at a time, say the name aloud and place it within the outline on the white paper.

If this is done correctly, instructor removes one letter at a time, saying the name aloud and allows Andy to use the flat side of the red felt tipped marker and draw in the letter as he says its name.

Discuss letter names and sounds, remind him how successful he was with sounding out words at last lesson, look at picture of apple and say short *a*.

Approach

Auditory, visual, haptic

Reinforcement

Star on each correctly done white paper.

Sticker on wall chart for reading short *a* words correctly.

Choose from: Lego bricks, cars, or crayons and paper.

Evaluation

Criteria: 3 letters written 6 short *a* words sounded out. Thirty letters to be placed were too many for one sitting. The change to the felt tipped marker in red, his favorite color, was rewarding to him. When he realized he would receive a sticker for doing the entire page, he then persisted. Criteria met with 100% success.

Dec. 1

Task

To read aloud 6 additional sight words in isolation: has, did, with, but, like, the.

To read these words aloud in sentences constructed from other known sight words.

To give the correct sound aloud for h, z, q.

Materials

Each of new sight words printed on one card in red and another card in blue plus known words treated the same.

Teacher constructed sentences containing the new words.

Words printed on Language Master Cards.

Colored chalk and balloons drawn on chalkboard.

Activities

Spend three minutes at Language Master, listen to the word once, and say the word once.

Play Concentration with the words printed on the cards, to find matching pairs to be done by student and teacher.

Silently read each sentence to self, ask for help with any unknown words, then read each sentence aloud.

Teacher print one of the letter sounds to be learned in balloon giving correct sound stimulus aloud. He may then also write the sound in another balloon with colored chalk if he gives the correct sound and a word beginning with that sound. Repeat process as many times as necessary to learn sounds.

Approach
Auditory, visual, haptic.

Reinforcement
Coupons will be given as free operants; when enough are earned, he may buy a job or game from the Job Board. The coupons will be given to reward acceptable behavior as well as correct responses to reading tasks, to be given on a variable schedule.

Evaluation
Criteria for words 5/6; criteria for sounds 3/3; criterion met 100% that day. When rewarded with coupons he asked for coupons very frequently and it was often necessary to change to contingency contracting (C-C). Coupons of 2-point value were used as an extra reward and when the points were totaled to determine what he could buy, he insisted $2 + 2$ is 22. It was necessary to count these out by ones.

January 6

Task
Easy level
Read one page silently to self from pre-primer. Answer questions about what read. Criteria answer 2 questions correctly.
Reinforcement
Smile if he looks up, praise for persistence.
Evaluation
His persistence was very good after looking over the page and commenting, *It's easy.* After answering two questions correctly, he was told, *You did that very well*, at which time he really smiled. Criteria 100%.
Task
Slightly more difficult.
Five paragraph story constructed from known words, short *a* words and two unknown words. Criteria: 90% accuracy.
Reinforcement
Free operant praise and smile at variable times. C-C to listen to a story on the tape recorder as he looks at book.
Evaluation
When he looked at the length of the story, commented, *I can't read all that.* When put under C-C to listen to a tape he said, *I'll try.* Proceeded to read story, looking up whenever he seemed to be having difficulty, a nod of the head and a smile sent him back to reading with renewed effort. When finished he looked at the story and asked, *I read all that?* Criteria: 90% accuracy met.
Task
Difficult level
Write the answers to 5 questions pertaining to the above story. Criteria 4/5.
Reinforcement
Star for correct answer and a sticker on the wall chart if all 5 are correct.
Silently read the first question and asked, *What am I supposed to write?* When told to look in the story, he asked if he really got a sticker if he got four of them correct. When assured he did he found the first answer, wrote it and a star was placed by it. The next

two he answered incorrectly and the last two he answered correctly. A star was placed by those that were correct and then he asked, *If I get those two right will I get a star then?* When told he would, he tried very hard to find the correct answers and approximations were accepted. His comment then was, *Boy those were hard; look at all the stars I got and I got 'em all right and get to put up a sticker.*

For easy tasks social reinforcers are all that are necessary. As the task becomes more difficult, the rewards must increase in frequency and value to Andy. He is most easily controlled by C-C. After the performance of a task to specified criteria he may move to another area for a reward of 4 to 6 minutes duration. He learned to set the timer himself and returned to the work table when it rang.

Feb. 12

Task

To read aloud the eight primary color words in isolation: red, blue, yellow, green, orange, purple. Plus read aloud: yellow, brown. Criteria 7/8.

To match the proper color word with the color on a chart.

To read the color words aloud correctly in the context of a story, samples after evaluation.

Correctly write answer to comprehension questions. Criteria 4/5.

Materials

Cards with color words printed in respective colors.

Cards with color words printed in black.

Teacher made matching device.

Eight primary colors felt tip markers.

Constructed story of known sight words and color words.

Comprehension question sheet about story.

Activities

Orally read color-cued cards.

Match black printed cards over color-cued cards (Associative Conditioning).

Play two games of bingo, one with instructor as caller, one with Andy as caller with black printed cards, permitted to look at color-cued card if necessary.

Lay felt tip markers on correct color words.

Draw, with proper felt tipped markers, on color-noun card. Read each color noun phrase aloud.

Match color word to color on teacher-made device.

Read constructed story aloud.

Read 5 questions silently and write correct answers.

Approach

Auditory, visual, haptic.

Reinforcement

Praise and a pat on the head when doing well and before attention lags during activities. C-C after reading constructed story aloud, a break at a game area for four minutes.

Evaluation

Criteria 100%.

It took an hour and a half to cover all the included activities but his enthusiasm was good. He remembered all eight color words over the weekend and was very pleased with himself.

The length of the constructed story bothered him each of the two times it was presented to him to read, but if given the contingency of a 4 minute break after oral reading, he very willingly complied. His persistence was good when faced with a word that troubled him, he would look up for reassurance and if given a smile he would hold the paper out and say, *I read all that!*

Instructional Decisions at Completion

Mrs. Flack, Andy's tutor, made an instructional decision following each teaching session. Because she established performance criteria, it was possible for her to determine if he had successfully learned or mastered what was taught. Note that in the 10 November session he met criteria at the 100% level. In the 1 December session, she established evaluation criteria for words (5 out of 6) which he met. Criteria for sounds were set at mastery (3 out of 3) which he met. In the 6 January session, she did not evaluate his performance on the *difficult level task*, because it was apparent to her that he had not successfully met criteria on this task. Because he failed to meet criteria on the last task, it became the major objective of subsequent instructional sessions. Thus, the performance results determined her instructional decisions.

In classroom settings, when teachers instruct small groups of children, groupings are changed as a result of evaluation. Students who have mastered a unit or segment of skills may be assigned to other instructional groups. Those who have not yet fully met criteria remain in the same group or are placed in newly formed groups for additional instruction on those skills. Because of the complexity of making instructional decisions, a tracking and record system is needed by classroom teachers. Such a system is described in chapter 9.

Instructional Decisions Based Upon Unexpected Needs

Instruction should not occur to the exclusion of other events in children's lives. Personal tragedies should be taken into consideration when teaching L&BD students. Children respond differently to similar events. A new baby is a welcome and exciting event to some children, while to others it is a threat. National emergencies and other calamities influence children's lives and performances.

Teachers need to be sensititve to such influences and recognize instructional opportunites. For example, a child in a tutoring session may feel compelled to discuss a family concern. The tutor should recognize the child's feelings of distress and discuss his or her concerns with him or her. Classroom teachers should incorporate into their instruction current events, holidays, and news items. L&BD students need, as do all children, to be aware of activities and events that influence their living.

Because instructional time is perhaps the most important variable to student performance, it is essential, however, that teachers guard against frequent distractors. They must be careful not to reinforce students for getting "off task" too often. Every event should not be treated as special. A variation on "show and tell" may provide a forum for students and yet not waste time. It may be scheduled as "group discussion time" or special announcements sometime during the school day.

Teachers should not overreact to national or personal tragedies. To do so may convey to L&BD students a sense of insecurity. As are most children, they are served best through stability and continuity in their lives.

Decision Criteria

Decisions regarding the selection of instructional tasks involve the bases for making such judgments. These include selecting tasks within the instructional range and recognizing the availability of time, competencies of teachers, and availability of instructional material.

Selecting Tasks within Instructional Range

Tasks or responses which students are *ready to learn* may be defined as those that are within their response repertoire. Thus, when a student is *able to perform,* he or she possesses the prerequisite skills and/or concepts to respond correctly in performing specific tasks. Ideally, teachers should analyze the necessary responses for a given task, but in practice it is often not feasible.

A more practical approach for determining if tasks are within students' response ranges is to select those items in which they already have demonstrated some performance. The rule, simply stated, is: *if the behavior or response occurred, the student possesses the necessary prerequisites.*

Responses may be emitted at varying levels of correctness. Students may, for example, respond correctly 1 time out of 100 chances or, 99 times out of 100 opportunities. While in either instance prerequisite responses are present, performance is closer to mastery in the second instance (99%) than in the first (1%). When teachers use the response rule, they must determine the level of accuracy which is acceptable. Performance criteria are suggested in Figure 7.2.

Level	%	Ratio
Mastery	100	100/100
Learned	90	90/100
Instructional	80	80/100
Frustration	below 80	0 to 79/100

FIGURE 7.2.   Suggested performance criteria

As indicated in Figure 7.2 when these criteria are used, those items where performance is between 80% and 90% should be taught. Those above 90% may be used for independent assignments. Those below 80% accuracy should be avoided until the performance quality is improved. It may be necessary at times to teach responses that are initially performed below the 80% level; in such instances a task analysis approach should be used.

Availability of Time

Instructional tasks should also be selected in relation to the estimated time needed to learn. This factor can be controlled by selecting those items which are close to mastery (100%) when using performance criteria.

Another way to reduce instructional time is to teach subtasks which comprise a larger task. Note how the initial specifications in anecdote 7.3 are reduced to subtasks during the instructional phase.

ANECDOTE 7.3[1]

Seven boys, all eight years old, are enrolled in a special class for learning disabled children.

Specific Objectives
1. To increase the amount of successfully completed assignments turned in daily in reading, math, and written language by the group.

---

1. Appreciation is extended to Mrs. Jane Faelchle, Springfield, Ohio Schools, for this example.

2. To assess and reduce that behavior for each student which is interfering with his learning and with his social interaction with the other members of the group and to increase the time each student is able to work independently without the continuous supportive help of the teacher.

3. To establish a classroom environment which will be quiet and conducive to effective learning for all children in the group without disruptive behavior by individual members of the group.

4. To increase student attention and participation in discussions and reduce the amount of distracting behavior in group work activities.

5. To acquire acceptable ways of moving quietly through the halls to the restroom, gym, and lunchroom without jeopardizing the safety of the crippled children in the school.

Terminal Behavior

1. Specify criteria based on assessment of the instructional level for each written worksheet in reading, arithmetic, and language and require 80%-90% proficiency to complete successfully each task.

2. Inform each student of that social behavior interfering with his effective learning and to indicate desired performance and actual functioning needed to approximate the desired performance during independent work time.

3. Require each student to listen attentively and participate in discussions in group work activities without playing with distractible objects or exhibiting interruptive behavior.

4. Require each student to move quietly in halls to restrooms, lunchrooms, gym, and the library without pushing, touching others, or making distractible noises that would distract classes in sessions or interfere with the safety of others.

Treatment and Results

A point system was used with the group to earn points for completing assignments correctly and exhibiting nondistractible or nondisruptive behavior during both the independent work time and group work activity time. The points were accompanied by praise and other social rewards. These points were exchangeable for "free time" at the end of each day for students to play games or listen to taped stories or records. A "store" was operated once a week at which time points were exchanged for toys, records, and books. Results were better grades for each student, more initially correct assignments turned in, and a higher achievement level attained by each student.

The following behaviors were rewarded.

Independent Work Time
1. stays in seat, except for permission
2. does not push, hit, or use verbally abusive language
3. works quietly

Group Work Activity
4. talks only with permission
5. pays attention
6. turns in assignments with few mistakes
7. takes care of materials
8. follows directions
9. stays in seat and works quietly when teacher is out of the room

Social Behavior, Individual
10. comes in room quietly and begins work promptly
11. works quietly without making oral noise, playing with objects or any other distractive noise
12. does not push, hit, use abusive language, tattle, argue, or make rude remarks
13. walks in halls without noise, touching walls, or members of the group

Teaching Competencies

Selection of instructional tasks is also relative to the teacher's competencies. These include knowledge of subject matter and skill development as well as instructional technology.

Teachers of L&BD students should be competent in teaching language skills (listening, speaking, reading, writing, and spelling) and arithmetic concepts and skills. Such competencies must include interpreting the results of assessment. For example, when analyzing faulty spelling of words, teachers should be able to identify errors that are due to phonetic spelling, failure to discriminate medial or vowel sounds, and other spelling errors. From an analysis, such as that in Figure 7.3, teachers can determine the spelling skills to be taught. They can arrange conditions for instruction that will minimize the skill problem. For example, phonetic spelling errors can be corrected through teaching phonetic skills and/or teaching students to use memory cues.

Staats (1963, 1968) demonstrated the use of behavioral approaches in teaching reading skills. He showed how behavioral technology may be applied for arranging events so that reading behaviors will be more likely to occur (1964, 1965). He also showed that the reading process can be structured so that the effects of reading materials can be observed (1967, 1964) and demonstrated that rewards can be used to maintain appropriate reading responses (1967). It is necessary for teachers to acquire such techniques if they are to be effective in reading instruction.

Teachers of L&BD students cannot be thoroughly competent in all skill and subject areas; however, they must be highly competent in basic skill assessment and instruction and in observational skills. And they should be capable of effectively using those teaching tactics described in the latter part of this chapter.

ERRORS	EXAMPLE: CAT
phonetic spelling	kat
hears and knows initial and final sounds but not medial or vowel sounds	cet
hears only initial sound	con
has no phonic understanding or merely guesses	go
has a reversal problem	tac
remembers last sound only	t
has an association problem	dog
poor visual memory	cAT

FIGURE 7.3. Common spelling errors (These were developed by Mr. Gene Brown, Licking County [Ohio] Public Schools.)

Instructional Material

Availability of instructional material also determines which instructional tasks will be selected. Teachers often elect to teach those tasks which are reflected in commercially available materials. A decision of this type may save time, permitting them to devote more time to instruction.

The availability of materials should not be the sole basis for selecting instructional tasks, however. When materials are not available, teachers should be capable of devising their own. A teacher-made story, for example, can often be most responsive to L&BD students' instructional needs. The tutor in anecdote 7.2 created the story shown in Figure 7.4 in response to the child's assessment performance.

A FUNNY PLAY

This is a funny play. It has something blue in it, something yellow, something green and something red.

Mother will come in with a black hat. Jane will walk up to help with an orange book. Dick will play with a purple ball. The brown dog will walk by the blue car. The three people will go away.

The dog will play with Puff with a little yellow ball. The two animals will jump and run away.

We will be here with no one. But we will have fun with the green, brown, yellow, orange, and red in the play. Who can we have work in the play?

Unknown words:

People   Animals

Review of previous lessons words:

With   But   What   Like   The

Mother's hat was *black*.
Jane had an *orange* book.
Dick had a *purple* ball.
The dog was *brown*.
The dog walked by the *blue* car.

FIGURE 7.4.   A teacher-made story

Task Analysis

Instructional tasks may be selected by analyzing outcome performance. In task analysis, teachers identify those task components that students must perform in order to demonstrate the outcome behavior (Gagné, 1965).

Task analysis serves at least four functions:

1. to determine if a student has a specific performance deficit;
2. to identify the skills, responses, and other actions necessary to perform the task;
3. to identify knowledge and behavior necessary for beginning to learn a given task;
4. to identify the most obvious instructional sequence for teaching a task.

Determining Performance Deficits

In the first function of a task analysis, an assessment activity is performed by students. The assessment may be in terms of direct observation of students under real conditions, or it may be an observation under contrived or simulated conditions. These performances are then compared with what an analysis of the task reveals the behavior should be.

ANECDOTE 7.4

Mr. Dun, a resource room teacher, analyzes beginning reading skills. He then uses the analysis for comparison with students' performances during assessment. For example, he analyzed this task:

When presented with a group of word cards, the student will distinguish categories by separating number words, color words, animal names and human names into correct piles.

He identified the following as prerequisite responses to completing this task.

1. to discriminate the words: *Number, color, animals, Names.*
2. to point to an example of each word.
3. to select words from a list that belongs in each category.

Mr. Dun then used an assessment task, requiring each student to select words on cards and place them in each of four categories. He established a criterion level of 100% for correctly categorizing the 16 words (16/16).

Those students who met criterion were assessed on other reading tasks. Those who obtained 13 to 15 correct were taught the items that they missed. Those who obtained a score below 13 were taught responses at the points in which errors occurred.

In some instances, it was necessary for him to analyze further the three prerequisite responses and to assess and teach those lower order behaviors.

In anecdote 7.4, it should be noted that task analysis permits a continuous division of tasks into smaller and smaller parts. Each task should be broken down until it meets the instructional needs as seen in Figure 7.5.

Identifying Task Responses

As seen in anecdote 7.4, task analysis also assists teachers in itemizing those responses and concepts necessary to perform the task. Each element in the task can be identified, enabling teachers to be more effective in their instruction. These tasks may be social as well as academic.

For example, teachers can identify those behaviors necessary for many social behaviors such as (1) going to the restroom, (2) using the cafeteria, (3) using the library, (4) responding to verbal assaults, (5) greeting adults.

The behavior "going to the restroom" may be analyzed by a special class teacher as follows:

   a. teacher announces that it is time for a restroom break
   b. students return to their seats
   c. students place their books and materials in their proper places
   d. when all students are seated and attending, the line leader stands and walks to the front of the room near the door.
   e. each child stands in the order that he/she is assigned and lines up behind the line leader.
   f. when all children are in line, the last student signals the line leader with a raised right hand
   g. the line leader turns room lights off and opens door
   h. after all children have gone, the last student closes the door
   i. students walk quietly and in single line to the restroom.

A similar analysis could be conducted for using the restroom and returning from the restroom.

Identifying Knowledge and Behavior

Task analysis results in identifying information about tasks as well as those skills necessary to perform the tasks. Teachers who analyze tasks will be able to discriminate subtle differences between each skill and/or step in the sequence. For

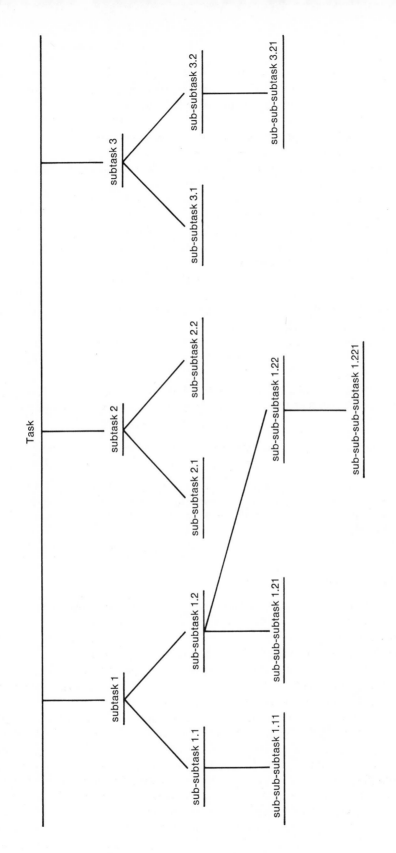

FIGURE 7.5. Task analysis

205

example, one way to improve the spelling of long words is to teach students to divide words into syllables. The following information concerning syllables is readily noted when analyzing the teaching of syllabication.

1. A syllable is a part of a word that is pronounced as a unit.
2. A syllable must have a vowel or a vowel sound in it.
3. A syllable is composed of a vowel or a vowel sound and usually one or more consonants.
4. Vowels are: *a*, *e*, *i*, *o*, *u* and sometimes *w* and *y*.
5. All other letters are consonants.
6. The letter *y* is a vowel when it has the sound of *i*, e.g., *flyer* and *easy*.
7. The letters *w* and *y* are vowels when they follow vowels in the same syllables, e.g., *lay*, *joy*, *drown*, and *follow*.
8. Sometimes two vowels together make a single sound, e.g., *boil*, *deceit*, and *laundry*.
9. If two vowels come together but are sounded separately, they form separate syllables, e.g., *usual* and *science*.
10. Double consonants are usually divided into two syllables, e.g., *dollar* and *occupy*.

After information such as the above ten items have been identified, it is possible to develop tasks for learning each item. Anecdote 7.5 shows how item 9 above can be taught.

ANECDOTE 7.5

Mr. Frank presented to his students the concept that when two vowels together are sounded separately they form separate syllables. He then demonstrated the use of this rule by writing the following words on the chalkboard, asking the students to divide each into syllables using the rule:

      rearrange   weather   theater   poison   faith

Identifying Obvious Sequences

Sometimes analyses of tasks will help teachers identify logical sequences for teaching. For example, the ten items concerning syllabication readily point to the importance of teaching items 1, 2, and 3 in that order. It also clearly identifies for the teacher that *w* and *y* as vowels must be taught as exceptions.

A task analysis may also clarify when a logical sequence is not mandatory. For example, item 4 need not be taught in that position; it may be taught preceding item 1, following it, as a part of it, or at another time.

By identifying necessary sequences for teaching a task, teachers of L&BD students will often discover gaps which students have in their learning. Because steps in a chain are often subtle, they may not have been acquired by these students. Children who do not have learning problems will, in many instances, learn skills and concepts despite careless teaching, but those with learning problems require systematic instruction. Task analysis forces teachers to examine each step, contributing to a more systematic approach to instruction.

A task analysis also helps locate points in teaching where rewards might best occur. Reinforcement can be scheduled for the end of each step, rather than at the completion of an entire task.

Reverse chaining procedures have been used to teach a chain of behavior identified through task analysis. Mechner (1967) defines chaining as "a sequence of responses where each response creates the stimulus for the next response" (p. 87). Gilbert (1962) described reverse chaining as a means of helping students acquire skills rapidly.

Reverse chaining consists of teaching the last step first and proceeding backward until the entire task has been learned. For example, when teaching long division the teacher presents the completed problem to students and then, in each succeeding presentation, presents partially completed problems until an entire problem must be completed:

$$
\text{Step 1} \quad 125\overline{\smash)11875} \quad \begin{array}{r} 95 \\ \hline 1125 \\ \hline 625 \\ 625 \\ \hline \end{array}
$$

Step 2   Complete this:

$$
125\overline{\smash)11875} \quad \begin{array}{r} 95 \\ \hline 1125 \\ \hline 625 \\ \end{array}
$$

$$
\text{Step 3} \quad 125\overline{\smash)11875} \quad \begin{array}{r} 9 \\ \hline 1125 \\ \end{array}
$$

$$
\text{Step 4} \quad 125\overline{\smash)11875} \quad \begin{array}{r} 9 \\ \end{array}
$$

$$
\text{Step 5} \quad 125\overline{\smash)11875}
$$

All tasks are not readily learned through reversed chaining. Tasks that are amenable to this procedure have at least four characteristics:

1. There is a clearly identifiable sequence of steps.
2. Each step is in a hierarchy. That is, no branching procedures are necessary.
3. The final step can be taught first.
4. The outcome (end result) is clear.

Storing and Retrieving Instructional Information[2]

School records are filled with information for serving various purposes. Because of these multiple purposes, school personnel are at times accused of maintaining irrelevant information about students. In most cases, however, the information has some educational relevance but less instructional value.

---

2. Content from this section is taken from Thomas M. Stephens, *Implementing behavioral approaches in elementary and secondary schools.* Columbus, Ohio: Charles E. Merrill, 1975, pp. 78-84.

Educational purposes include administrative needs such as family information, birthdates, previous teachers, previous school marks, standardized test results, and health information. Instructionally relevant information often consists of students' responses to academic tasks, recent performances on criterion-referenced measures, in-school conduct, social skills and attitudes, types of events that are rewarding to students in relation to task demands, and students' attitudes toward others and to school related activities.

Storing information.   Instructional information should be of recent origin, and the records should be maintained by teachers and kept in classrooms. When properly maintained, these records can be used to review previous learning, implement instructional strategies, and provide a record of performance to students and parents.

Records of students' performances on instructional tasks should be filed and later be retrieved for students' review. Since this system informs teachers as to which academic skills and concepts each student has mastered, is in the process of learning, and has not yet begun to learn, the information proves helpful in assisting students to review past learnings. Similarly, records of social behavior that has been improved may be retrieved by teachers in order to compare students' present behavior with past performances. When necessary, the instructional strategies may be repeated to improve declining social behavior.

Information acquired earlier through observations and assessments may not have been used for instruction due to limitations of time and other instructional priorities. If such information is stored, however, in an easily retrievable form, it can be useful later for devising instructional strategies.

Instructional strategies may also be filed to be used again. These can be helpful when students have difficulty learning other tasks. By incorporating successful strategies into current instruction, learning may be facilitated.

Record information on forms designed for that purpose. These may consist of individual forms for each type of information, e.g., arithmetic skills, conduct in the classroom, social skills and attitudes. From each of these forms, a composite record should be filed and retrieved when needed. In addition to filing information to be used when teaching specific students, a method should be devised for storing information by subject matter, management strategies, and reinforcement systems.

Summary records.   A summary record of assessment information can be useful. The summary is a composite of information derived from student assessment. It consists of the student's name, academic and social skills that are within his or her instructional ranges (or codes which refer to such skills), models of reinforcement which appear to be effective, and types of incentives that were used successfully. If the content to be taught has been coded, teachers need only to encircle the code for skills that students are ready to learn.

A coded form is used effectively in conjunction with criterion-referenced measures. The form may contain an entire range of skills and concepts, or it may cover a portion of the range, a unit of study, or a segment of the content. When students master all skills in a segment, assessment begins on the next portion, which is represented by another coded form.

Some content, such as social behavior, does not lend itself to coded forms, and, of course, academic content that has not been systematically analyzed and set up in criterion-referenced formats will also require less structured forms for recording information. It helps to make note of the tasks and social behavior in relation to incentives and models of reinforcement. By recording such information, it is possible to determine which behaviors are responses to incentives and to models of reinforcement.

When concerned about social behaviors, one should observe which incentives seem to be effective under normal conditions. The observer should remember that behaviors engaged in freely by students are evidently reinforcing to them and make note of such behaviors and the conditions under which these occurred.

Students who talk frequently in class evidently enjoy talking in class. Those who do their work are reinforced by it. Those who walk about the room enjoy roaming in the classroom. And those students who sleep frequently in class like to snooze in school. Such information, when recorded, can be helpful in dealing with social and school-related behaviors. Teachers can make those frequently occurring behaviors contingent upon desired performances.

Student files. Attention should be given to procedures for filing assessment information about each student. An alphabetical file should be the core of the filing system, though cross-referencing is necessary for instructing within groups since information is needed for temporary grouping of students.

The entire filing system should be cross-referenced, using important variables. One, two, or three variables are typically used depending upon the instructional responsibilities of teachers. Cross-referencing, using one variable occurs when teachers have responsibility for one subject area such as math or science.

Two variables are used when acquisition of subject matter is dependent upon related skills such as reading. In a situation of this type, student grouping may be based upon reading proficiency when the assignments require obtaining information through reading. Grouping may occur on the basis of knowledge in the subject matter if reading proficiency is not a factor. Three or more variables may be necessary in settings where teachers are responsible for instruction in several subjects such as typically occurs at lower grade levels.

Since cross-referencing is done for the purpose of grouping students on a temporary basis, the referencing system should allow for flexibility. Color codes are easily used if a small number of groups are needed.

In addition to grouping for instruction, teachers of L&BD students will also need to individualize formats for students to complete at their own rates. These are used for laboratory and seat-work assignments and are stored in each student's file. Students should be permitted to use their files for obtaining individual seatwork assignments and for evaluating their progress.

Retrieving instructional information. The basic purpose of a filing system is to have instructional information readily available. To be useful, information that is filed must be retrievable. Teachers retrieve information for at least five reasons.

1. *For temporarily grouping students.* As indicated in the previous section, regrouping is routinely accomplished as needed in order to individualize instruction. When students acquire skills, they should be given additional opportunities to learn higher order responses. This may necessitate moving individual students into other instructional groups.

2. *For evaluating teaching and student performance.* Records of learning should be readily available in order for teachers to evaluate student learning. By analyzing student progress at any point in time, teachers can make decisions con-

cerning how to assist individual students. Special instruction, regrouping of students, closer monitoring of specific students, requests for assistance from other personnel (such as school psychologists or counselors), or encouraging students to proceed as planned are possible outcomes of routine evaluations of student records.

3. *For reviewing previous learning.* By retrieving information from student files, teachers may take time from the usual routine of instruction and review with students what they have learned. Reviews facilitate maintenance of learning and also serve as a means of evaluating student performance. Reviews also tend to strengthen previous learning. Students will often gain new insights while reviewing previous learnings due to intervening experiences between the time when learning first occurred and the review sessions.

4. *For maintaining learned responses.* Some teachers retrieve material from past learnings on a set schedule in order to maintain student performance at a desirable level. Retrieval may be organized in such a manner that the material to be reviewed is accumulated across review periods. For example, if a teacher reviews spelling skills every fifth day, on the fifteenth day all of the previous skills can be practiced. But every five days, only those skills that were learned during that period of time will be reviewed.

5. *For reporting to students and parents.* Reports to parents should contain specific information concerning performance. As reports of student progress move away from the use of letter grades for school subjects and toward checklists of specific performances, retrieval of information concerning student learning becomes essential. Reports to parents may be accumulated with additional pages added as the year or term progresses. Criterion-based reports are also beneficial to students because these provide a precise overview of their learning.

Integrating Instructional Information

One way to use relevant information is to assess students prior to each instructional task, but it is inefficient to proceed in this way. Therefore, information is gathered, stored, retrieved, and used as needed. In addition, information for instruction that is interrelated will provide a much more efficient instructional application and will result in highly effective instructional strategies.

Integrating assessment information results in better teaching and learning. Skill training programs are generally composed of four components: assessing, planning, implementing, and evaluating. In such a system, recording and integrating instructional information are important.

The key in skill training is the assessment component because subsequent instruction is based upon information acquired from assessment. Each of the elements in the assessment component should be viewed in relation to each other in order to consider effective instructional plans. Thus, tasks requiring academic skills and concepts should be considered in relation to attitudes toward academic tasks and the various elements of the reinforcement system.

Relating tasks to attitudes. Most students have preferences among academic subjects. When negative attitudes are held toward any given task, students are less inclined to perform the requirements of the task. Under such circumstances, powerful incentives are more likely to be necessary. If, on the other hand, students have positive views toward specific tasks, less powerful incentives will be sufficient.

It is important to know students' attitudes toward academic tasks. When this information is known it is often possible to devise more effective instructional strategies. When teachers have knowledge of academic tasks which students prefer, these can be used as rewards following completion of less preferred tasks. For example, students who enjoy reading but dislike arithmetic may be permitted to read following completion of arithmetic.

Further integration of assessment information occurs when reinforcement is considered. First, consider the numerous types of academic tasks students are expected to attempt daily in each school subject. Then multiply these tasks by three, representing positive, negative, or neutral attitudes toward each task. Now we can obtain a notion of the varied and possible relationships tasks have to incentives.

These comparisons are further complicated when it is recognized that student attitudes and types of preferred incentives may vary from time to time without apparent reasons. The complexities of integrating various elements from assessment information should not dissuade teachers from designing and implementing instructional strategies. Because of the importance of considering these elements, storing, retrieving, and integrating instructional information should be viewed as essential activities in teaching.

Teaching Tactics

Teachers should base their instruction on the results of systematic assessment of students' performances, as discussed in chapter 6. An instructional plan, or instructional strategy, often consists of the following:

—task or items to be taught
—terminal behavior
—instructional material
—teaching tactics to be used
—reinforcement to be used
—student activities
—an evaluation of students' performances.

All of the above items are not necessarily contained in one instructional strategy; however, in most plans, these tend to be essential elements. Note in anecdote 7.6 that Eugene's tutor has thoroughly planned for the tutorial session and included the above items in the instructional plan.

ANECDOTE 7.6

Task: To discriminate the numbers 1, 2, 3, 4, and 5.

Terminal Behavior: Eugene will be shown a 2" x 3" card with the number one on it. He will be given a row of the numbers 1, 2, 3, 4, and 5 out of their proper sequence. He must draw a circle around the number one on the row of numbers. He will be given no more than fifteen seconds to do this. The numbers 2, 3, 4, and 5 will also be presented in this fashion. Eugene must circle each number in the manner described above.

Instructional Material: 2" x 3" cards with the numbers 1, 2, 3, 4, and 5 written on them; 5 sheets of paper with one row of the numbers 1, 2, 3, 4, and 5 written on each sheet (the numbers will not be in their proper sequence), rubber numbers with holes in them for pegs (rubber number has one hole for one peg; number two has two holes, etc.), sandpaper numbers, transparent plastic sheets with large numbers written on paper sheets (the paper sheet with the number one is placed under the plastic sheet, Eugene traces it on the plastic sheet), crayon, and magic marker.

Approach: Haptic, auditory, and verbal modalities will be used by Eugene.

Activities: Eugene will be presented with the sandpaper numbers. I will take his index finger and help him trace the number one. Eugene will repeat the number one after me as we trace it together.

I will then take out the rubber number one and ask Eugene if it is the same as the sandpaper number. I will ask him to place the peg in the single hole and to say "one" as he does it.

I will give Eugene the transparent plastic with the sheet of paper that contains the large number one underneath the plastic. I will ask Eugene to trace the one over the plastic with a crayon. He will say the number "one" as he traces.

We will repeat the entire process with the numbers 2, 3, 4, and 5, respectively.

I will take out a paper sheet with the numbers 1, 2, 3, 4, and 5 written on it. These numbers will be out of sequence. I will give Eugene a magic marker and say, "I am going to hold up a card with a number written on it. Put a circle around the number on your sheet that looks the same as the one I will hold up. Work quickly."

I will hold up the number one first, then the number two, then three, etc. Eugene will have no more than fifteen seconds to complete each task.

Evaluation: Eugene discriminated the numbers 1, 2, 3, 4, and 5 successfully by meeting the terminal behavior which I had set for him. I will retest him on March 1, for delayed recall.

Now that I think he can discriminate the numbers 1, 2, 3, 4, and 5, I will attempt to teach him some concept of what these numbers mean.

Eugene was fairly motivated to perform the tasks outlined above for me. I must find new ways to make learning numbers more interesting for him. He performed these tasks persistently, and he was fairly enthusiastic.

Reinforcement: I reinforced Eugene with secondary reinforcements such as "very good." Interim reinforcement was given in the form of a sticker after the entire lesson was completed. Eugene likes to sit on my lap, so I let him do this while reading a story to him.

In the future, I will reward Eugene with a one-to-one ratio at the beginning of the lesson, and then attempt variable-ratio reinforcement of the secondary type.

Teachers of L&BD students in classroom settings often need instructional strategies that are less time-consuming to develop. Note the less detailed, yet specific, instructional strategy used to teach a small group of L&BD children as shown in Figure 7.6.

FIGURE 7.6. A DTIMS teaching strategy for a small group of L&BD students. From *DTIMS Reading Strategy Book*, 1976. Reproduced with permission of the author, Thomas M. Stephens. All rights reserved.

DTIMS Strategy 194-01

1.0 The student will underline the two root words when presented compound words.

2.0 Teacher activity

    2.1 Plan R-strategy from R-menu

    2.2 Write the compound word *schoolhouse* on the board. Then point to the word and say: *This word is schoolhouse. It is called a compound word. It is a compound word because it has two words put together. I'm going to cover up the last word and see who can tell me the word remaining.* Wait for a response. *That's correct, it's school. Now I'm going to cover the first word. What word do you see now?* Wait for a response. *That's correct, it is house.*

    Now let's see if someone else can be the teacher and do what I did using this word. The teacher may repeat using other words. Teacher will present worksheet with 10 compound words. Students draw a box around root words.

3.0   Materials: Chalkboard and chalk, worksheet.

4.0   Student Response: Answer teacher questions, complete worksheet.

5.0   Evaluation: Criterion 10/10 (worksheet).

In Figure 7.6 the teaching plan specifies the task and terminal behavior (1.0), instructional materials (3.0), teaching tactics to be used (2.2), reinforcement to be used (2.1), student activities (2.2 and 4.0), and an evaluation of students' performances (5.0).

Teaching tactics consist of many different approaches. In some instances, these are selected for use on the basis of those performance characteristics of target students, the types of responses to be learned, and the teacher's preferences. There is some research evidence for basing selection of instructional tactics on different factors. For example, Lovitt and Curtiss (1969) found that higher academic response rates occurred when a pupil arranged his or her own contingency requirements as compared to when teachers specified them.

In another study, Ayllon, Layman, and Kandel (1975) showed that a behavior management program with three hyperactive children, 8, 9, and 10 years of age, could be used in lieu of medication for controlling student behavior. Under the contingency management program, and without medication, the students' behaviors improved and their math and reading performances greatly increased.

Many of the tactics which prove effective involve a combination of approaches. For example, Stephens, Hartman, and Cooper (1973) found that a systematic approach to reading instruction combined with verbal reinforcement and incentives were effective in raising the reading performances of low achieving first- and second-year students. These procedures resulted in higher gains than did standard procedures for teaching reading.

Operant conditioning appears to be an effective approach to treating selectively mute children. Nolen and Pence (1970) described the effects of using operant tactics with a 10-year-old selectively mute girl. Until age 10 she spoke only to her parents. But during an eight-month treatment program normal speaking patterns were developed. At a one-year follow-up, her speech was no different than that of her classmates.

Rosenbaum and Kellman (1973) obtained similar results with a third-grade female who did not speak in school. They used a shaping approach where each approximation was reinforced until she spoke freely in the classroom.

It appears that many teaching tactics can be selected on the bases of certain identifiable factors or conditions, but more research evidence is needed in support of many instructional tactics. In particular, many of these tactics have yet to be validated fully with L&BD students. Certainly, school personnel should be aware of the effects of different approaches on different student populations. Where evidence is not yet adequate, experimentally minded teachers can selectively determine which tactics to use and under which set of conditions.

Modeling

Modeling represents a basic way that new social behaviors and academic skills are acquired. Almost all learning can occur vicariously by observing others. Bandura (1965) has demonstrated that individuals can acquire new responses through observing behavior of others and by noting the consequences of that behavior. Modeling tactics appear to be effective for use by teachers for a diverse range of learnings. Students can, for example, acquire appropriate responses simply by observing performances of models; academic related behaviors can be assimilated rapidly; new academic skills can be emitted through "one trial" learning; and incorrect or inappropriate responses can be rectified through observational processes.

Essentially, social modeling may be defined as a form of learning through imitation. Modeling may be provided directly where students observe others, such as teachers, parents, and peers. Or it can take place vicariously through reading, viewing, and listening. Academic, as well as social, behaviors are acquired through modeling. Students may imitate behavior by observing social and academic responses. Further, when they observe that certain responses are rewarded or punished, they tend to more rapidly acquire desirable and correct responses.

Related Studies

A selected review of published studies suggests that social modeling tactics have not been used frequently in experiments with L&BD students. Minuchin, Chamberlain, and Graubard (1967) used social modeling for teaching formal elements of language to a group of delinquent children. They used role playing as a means of acting out situations with teachers and for developing skills in listening, asking relevant questions, and waiting one's turn.

In another study (Lovaas, Freitas, Nelson, & Whalen, 1967), modeling procedures were found to be effective in teaching schizophrenic students to respond. Motor tasks as well as social and academic behaviors were taught by increasing the students' attentions to cues. After they began to demonstrate finer discriminations on motor skills, they were exposed to more complex behaviors.

In an early study, Bandura, Ross, and Ross (1961) studied the effects of modeling on aggressive behavior among normal nursery school children. One group of children was exposed to an aggressive adult model and another matched group was provided with an adult model who displayed inhibited and nonaggressive behavior. The aggressive model exhibited both physical and verbal responses toward a large, inflated plastic doll. The nonaggressive model sat very quietly, ignoring both the doll and the instruments of aggression which were placed in the room. Results showed a significant increase in aggressive behavior for the group which was exposed to that kind of behavior.

In a follow-up study, Bandura, Ross, and Ross (1963) demonstrated that film-mediated models are as effective as real-life models in transmitting deviant patterns of behavior. This study as well as other studies (Kuhn, Madsen, and Becker, 1967; Lovaas, 1961) show that both inhibited behavior and aggression are modeled through films depicting humans and those showing cartoon characters.

Experimenters who use modeling as an instructional approach generally expose children to a model who is performing certain tasks. Models are sometimes shown reinforcing themselves for good performances, often verbalizing the reasons for their self-rewards, e.g., "Now that I have completed my work, I can take a break." When self-reinforcement is used, models will often also verbally reprimand themselves, explaining why they should not be rewarded, e.g., "My score was below criterion. That is not good enough work for a token."

In one such study, Bandura and Kupers (1964) found that children adopt patterns of self-reinforcement by imitating models without the use of external rewards. However, the subjects were nonhandicapped children and, as Kabler (1976) noted, there were several limitations of the study such as the type of tasks to be performed and the uniqueness of the experimental situation. Regardless of the limitations, however, the results support the effectiveness of learning self-reinforcing behavior through imitation.

Subjects consisted of 160 children, ages 7-9 years. Adult and peer models with high and low criterion for self-reinforcement conditions were used as treatment variables. Children observed models as they bowled. Models made positive verbal comments to themselves when their bowling performances met criteria and rewarded themselves with candy. When their bowling performances failed to meet criteria, they made critical comments and did not eat candy. These findings were supported in a later study conducted by Bandura and Whalen (1966).

Teachers sometimes impose standards on children but may exhibit self-reward patterns which are inconsistent with those they demand from students. There are some studies that have considered the effects of inconsistencies between an imposed standard for self-reward and a modeled standard (Mischel & Liebert, 1966; McMains & Liebert, 1968; Hildebrandt, Feldman, & Ditrichs, 1973). Findings consistently show that modeling of a standard more lenient than the one imposed on children results in their adopting self-reward criteria of a more lenient nature than that imposed. In effect, students do what they see rather than what is said.

In a study with important implications for internalizing behavior norms, Rosenhan, Frederick, and Burrowes (1968) studied the effects of four different combinations of imposed and modeled standards. Results of this study indicated that high standards for self-reward are most likely to be adopted by children when they are exposed to models who are consistent in the standards they apply to themselves and to others. They also found that self-indulgent conditions are most likely to produce students who reward themselves without regard to their performances.

Conditions for Learning through Imitation

There are some apparent conditions that facilitate learning through social modeling. One necessary condition is that of attending. Learning through observation requires that students pay attention to modeled behavior. L&BD students with limited attending skills will need to acquire these prior to profiting from modeling tactics. Instructional approaches in such situations may be similar to those used in the study conducted by Lovaas and others (1967) where a shaping procedure was used as a means of increasing the students' attentions.

Another prerequisite response for modeling instruction is that of discriminating observations. Once students are attending, they must be selective in identifying those observed responses. One way to train children to discriminate observed events is to reward responses that identify critical elements. For example, teachers may intervene with rewards when students imitate those responses which are being taught, as described in anecdote 7.7.

ANECDOTE 7.7

Among the ways Ms. Withers rewards students who accurately identify or emulate responses which they have observed are:

1. Following behavioral observation, those students who accurately demonstrate the behavior are rewarded.

2. When teaching a new arithmetic process, she asks a student to place on the chalkboard what she dictates. Those observers who can repeat the process, after watching it, are rewarded.

3. During the school day, Ms. Withers rewards those students who emit behaviors which were practiced earlier in behavior rehearsal sessions.

4. During behavior rehearsing, she praises students who display target behaviors as models.

Cuing may also be used effectively to train students to discriminate observed responses. For example, teachers may indicate that:

—when they ring a bell students should stop and carefully watch what models are doing

—those items in red on the chalkboard should be copied

—every time a student reads or says a particular word, they should pay particular attention

—they will raise or lower their voices when providing special instructions or information.

As a general rule, any novel event can serve as a cue for capturing students' attentions.

In addition to prerequisite conditions, such as attending and discriminating, four other factors tend to facilitate learning through modeling. These are characteristics of models, characteristics of the behavior, use of rewards or punishment, and directions for observing.

Characteristics of models. Imitation tends to occur more readily when models appear to possess physical characteristics similar to observers (age, sex, race) and when they are perceived as competent and powerful. As previously cited studies indicate, while students do imitate adult behavior, they generally imitate peer behavior more quickly.

Characteristics of behavior. Responses to be imitated should be clearly visible and should be demonstrated by a variety of models. The target behaviors should be repeated often in order for students to observe the responses.

Use of rewards and punishment. Behavior is learned faster through modeling when it is accompanied by rewards. Students should observe such behavior being rewarded. And, they should observe undesirable behavior being punished. When students are being trained in self-reinforcement, a consistent model is important.

Directions for observing. Students should be made aware of the target behaviors in advance of or during the observations. When a series of behaviors are to be demonstrated, students should be instructed as to which responses to note. Sometimes, it is helpful to have them record responses by counting or in some other way be engaged in recognizing target events.

Modeling Tactics

Modeling tactics include teachers serving as models, direct observations of peers, and vicarious modeling.

Teachers as models. Several studies cited earlier in this chapter used adults as models in training children in self-reinforcement (Bandura & Kupers, 1964; Rosenhan, Frederick, & Burrowes, 1968). In an extensive review of such studies, Kabler (1976) summarized his findings as follows:

...results of these studies have consistently shown that the self-reinforcement criteria and patterns of reinforcement adopted by children are influenced by the models they observe.

A number of model characteristics appear to be important factors affecting the degree of modeling of a stringent standard which takes place. These factors include: competence, power (potential rewardingness of the model), reported experience level of the model, social reinforcement received and nurturance level.

All of these factors, except nurturance level, are additively related to the extent of influence. In other words, as the level of these model characteristics increases, the model's influence on the child observer increases. Nurturance of the child by the model seems to inversely relate to his influence. Perhaps, children have learned from previous experience with adults that highly nurturing adults do not expect as much from them as do adults who are less nurturing.

Direct instruction (i.e., telling the child how to self-reinforce) was also found to be effective in transmitting self-reinforcement criteria to children. It appears that an adult can impose a standard for self-reinforcement on a child, make a discrepant lenient standard and the child will adhere more closely to the imposed than modeled standard. However, the modeling of a discrepant standard clearly weakens the effect of the imposed standard. Consistency between the imposed and modeled standard, on the other hand, is particularly effective in transmitting a stringent pattern of self-reinforcement.

As might be expected, children exposed to multiple models, adopt patterns of self-reinforcement which vary according to whether the models are consistent or discrepant. When both models exhibit a stringent criteria which has also been imposed on the child, the child adheres very closely to the stringent standard. If the models are disconcordant, the more recent model (i.e., the first model observed after the criteria are imposed) is the more powerful.

Although of less potency than live models, symbolic modeling (i.e., verbal descriptions to the child about adult behavior) likewise influences patterns of self-reinforcement. The effect of symbolic modeling was found to be in the same direction as live modeling. Some of the major implications (for classroom teachers) include:

1. Teachers who model those standards of self-reinforcement they impose on children will encourage the adoption of the imposed standards.

2. Social reinforcement of adults and children for appropriate self-reinforcement will enhance the likelihood of their students adopting the observed patterns of self-reinforcement.

3. Frequent modeling of self-reinforcement standards is important to assure that recent models are available.

4. Verbal descriptions of appropriate self-reinforcement will add to the effect of modeled and imposed standards.[3]

Readers are reminded, as Kabler (1976) quite properly noted, that generalizing these studies to other environments and populations should be done cautiously. Since these findings were derived from studies that often consisted of nonhandicapped populations, the above conclusions are tentative. They do suggest tactics, however, to be explored experimentally by school personnel who work with L&BD students.

Teachers do serve as models for their students and they can use at least four tactics to improve L&BD students' social behavior and academic performance. Each of these tactics are described in anecdote 7.8.

---

3. Reprinted from M. Kabler, *A review of research on children's self-reinforcing behaviors: A process of self-control.* Unpublished manuscript. Faculty for Exceptional Children, The Ohio State University, 1976, pp. 40-42, with permission of the author.

1. Provide good models
   Teachers can assist students in imitating their desirable behavior. They can discuss with students reasons for certain behaviors.

   After the building principal left the classroom, Mr. Crown discussed with his pupils his responses to Ms. Smith, the principal. He told them that she asked him if he would take lunchroom duty that day as the scheduled teacher was absent and the substitute teacher was unable to do the assignment (she had to return home for lunch). He reminded them that he said, "Certainly, I'll be happy to," and she responded, "Thank you, I appreciate your attitude."

2. Identify and discuss desirable behavior
   Teachers can call to students' attention desirable behavior and discuss with them reasons for the behavior and the consequences of that behavior. Desirable student behavior may serve this purpose.

   Teacher: Congratulations Jack, you completed all of your arithmetic work. You got almost all of the problems correct too!

   Or, behavior may have been observed in a TV program that many of the students saw earlier. Teachers might assign students to:

   —watch for acts of good citizenship and be prepared to discuss those behaviors.
   —watch a particular program at home and be prepared to talk about certain predetermined acts.
   —watch the evening news to identify a "good news" item.

3. Using stories as examples
   Stories may be used to exemplify desirable behavior and to demonstrate how others have overcome problems. The stories may be read to students, read by students, or told to students. Stories may be selected on the basis of certain themes that are related to specific social behavior tasks. These may include such topics as:
   How someone overcame problems
   How people make friends
   Being neighborly
   Helping others
   Being kind to animals
   Protecting the environment
   International understanding
   Good citizenship
   Biographies of eminent people
   Community workers
   Teachers should prepare students in advance of stories by discussing the story theme. In this way, students can relate previous experiences to the story and the discussion can also develop their interests in the story. In the course of the discussion, the teacher should specify those elements of the story students are to identify:
   Notice how Sylvia helps the little boy find his parents at the fair.

   Following the story, students and the teacher should have an extensive discussion concerning the target behaviors:
   What did Sylvia say to the little boy so he wouldn't be upset? Were you ever lost? How did you feel?

4. Behavior rehearsing
   Social behavior can be taught in a planned and effective way through behavior

---

4. From Thomas M. Stephens, *Directive teaching of children with learning and behavioral handicaps (2nd ed.).* Columbus, Ohio: Charles E. Merrill, 1976, pp. 222-223.

rehearsing. It can be useful with almost any specific behavior that will be displayed in a setting where teachers can evaluate and monitor the behavior. Among the social behaviors taught through rehearsal in school settings are:

—depositing litter properly
—following game rules
—cleaning up after eating
—lunchroom routines
—playground behavior
—greeting others
—telephone manners
—participating in group discussions
—caring for property
—supervising others
—using the public address system
—using A-V equipment
—using the library
—walking in the hallway
—catching a ball
—telling a joke (story)
—giving others directions
—visiting another classroom
—feeding the goldfish
—avoiding an argument (fight)
—asking questions
—asking permission from the teacher
—asking to borrow something
—expressing emotions (joy, anger, etc.)
—giving one's opinion

Behavior rehearsing should be scheduled during class periods. Some teachers give this period of time a specific title.

Schedule time during class periods in which social behavior will be taught. It is a good idea to give this period of time a specific title such as *Our Social Psychology Time.* Throughout the week problem behaviors which are noted among the students may be identified by teachers and these behaviors represent the content of subsequent social instruction. Since children with learning and behavioral problems often evidence inappropriate social behavior, instruction of this sort should be an integral part of programs for such children.

Elements for behavior rehearsals are (1) identify and discuss a specific behavior that needs improving, (2) provide information concerning the behavior, (3) rehearse that behavior, use covert and overt practice sessions and provide rewards throughout, (4) discuss the practice sessions, (5) observe students when in a real situation to determine how well they demonstrate that behavior.

Ms. Melvin noted that many of her eight special class students displayed inappropriate social behavior throughout the school day. She categorized those behaviors and began to make notes regarding those students who performed specific behaviors poorly.

Among the high priority target behaviors were:

Using the restrooms and leaving them in good condition.
Participating in a group discussion.
Expressing anger in appropriate ways.
Obtaining permission from others before taking or using their property.
Walking quietly in the hallways.

Identify and Discuss One Behavior

Ms. M. chose target behavior number five above to teach through rehearsal. She selected hallway behavior because it appeared to be well within all students' response range and because most of the students did walk quietly in the hallways. The other target behaviors would require more time to teach and she wanted to begin with a behavior that could be quickly improved, providing students and her with some satisfaction (reward).

Our psychology lesson today is on how to be considerate of others when using the hallways in school, was the way Ms. M. began the discussion. During the conversation, each student was encouraged to give reasons for behaving appropriately in the hallway. She closed the 20 minute session by helping the students summarize their reasons and citing the rules for hallway behavior (walk, don't run; be quiet; only talk in a low voice).

Providing Information

The second session started with Ms. M. having students review the rules for hallway behavior to which she added emphasis.

Rehearsal, Covert

Since time permitted, Ms. M. provided students with some covert behavior rehearsing. They were asked to close their eyes ("it's good to see that Jack and Floyd have already closed their eyes"), and, with their eyes closed, she gave them verbal instructions for leaving the room, asking them to picture, "in your mind's eyes," carrying out her instructions. She then, with their eyes opened, asked them to describe how they were to walk in the classroom.

Rehearsal, Overt

The third session started with students reviewing the previous lesson and with a quick covert rehearsal. Following this an overt rehearsal was implemented with the contingency that if all students properly followed hallway rules the class would continue outside for an extra recess following the third trial run.

Discussion

The next session consisted of a discussion of the previous practice session and the fact that, following their third trial, the class obtained an extra recess. Ms. M. reminded the students that, each time the class or one student walked in the hallways, they should remember to follow the rules.

Observation

From time to time, Ms. M. reminded the class about the hallway rules. Just prior to using the hallway she would ask students to cite the rules. She observed how well the students behaved in the hallway and occasionally she rewarded them with an extra recess.

Operant Approaches

Perhaps the most important concept for studying human behavior currently available to us is that of *operant conditioning.* It is concerned with relationships between behavior and the environment. The first rule of operant conditioning is *the frequency of occurrence of behavior is modified by consequences of that behavior.*

By demonstrating the above principle, Skinner (1953) radically changed the instruction of L&BD students. This principle has permitted us to study as well as to treat maladaptive responses. Operant tactics have been used to develop new responses, to modify existing behavior, and to remove incorrect or undesirable responses.

Students can, for example, develop new behavior through a shaping procedure whereby each approximation is reinforced until the responses form the required behavior. Existing behavior may be changed by rewarding those responses that are in the correct directions and by not rewarding or punishing those responses that are in the wrong directions. Similarly, the occurrence of nonreinforcement of a previously reinforced behavior can be used to extinguish undesirable behavior.

Related Studies[5]

Operant conditioning has been used as a treatment variable in many studies that included L&BD students as subjects. Operant tactics have been used for correcting reversal problems in handwriting (Smith & Lovitt, 1973), for improving handwriting and letter recognition (Fauke et al., 1973), for teaching emotionally disturbed children (Phillips & Haring, 1959; Haring & Phillips, 1962), for controlling hyperactive behavior (Patterson, 1965), as token reinforcement in classrooms (O'Leary & Becker, 1967; Wolf, Giles, & Hall, 1968), for reducing classroom behavior problems (Becker et al., 1967; Zimmerman & Zimmerman, 1962; Quay et al., 1966), and for establishing speech in psychotic children—to name but a few problems of learning and behavior for which operant conditioning tactics have been successful.

Considerable research evidence exists for demonstrating the effects of positive reinforcement on observable attending behaviors. Staats (1965), using a reward system for maintaining attention and work behaviors, increased the reading performance of an adolescent delinquent. Walker and Buckley (1968) developed an individual conditioning technique which increased the attending behaviors of a nine-year-old male subject from 43% during baseline to an average of 93% during treatment.

Teacher attention was used by Broden, Hall, Dunlap, and Clark (1970) to increase the attending behaviors of two boys at adjacent desks. Teacher attention and praise were made contingent upon appropriate attending behavior. These procedures resulted in mean increases in attending behavior from 31% to 33% during baseline to 71% and 74% in the final phase for subjects one and two, respectively.

O'Leary and Becker (1969) reduced a student's average classroom disruptive time from 54% to 32% simply by praising appropriate behavior and ignoring disruptive behavior. In another study, Zimmerman and Zimmerman (1962) decreased unproductive classroom behavior of two emotionally disturbed boys by removing attention and other reinforcements.

Tokens have been used as a means of implementing operant conditioning in classrooms. Meichenbaum, Bowers, and Ross (1968) instituted operant procedures with money as reinforcers in order to reduce the inappropriate and increase the appropriate classroom responses of institutionalized subjects. Ten adolescent females, with histories as major management problems, received slips of paper every ten minutes, indicating the percentage of appropriate behavior exhibited during that observation period. The slips were later exchanged for money, a maximum of two dollars daily, eight dollars weekly. A multiple baseline design was employed where treatment was introduced initially in the afternoon and later extended to the morning. Appropriate behaviors did not increase in the mornings until experimental conditions were applied, indicating that student behavior was largely under the control of the token system. The results indicated that treatment conditions significantly increased mean levels of appropriate behavior from 46% during baseline to 92% and 84.5%, respectively, during treatment.

Fifty-four emotionally disturbed students, ranging in age from 8 to 11 years, were treated using a token economy to improve specific task related behaviors (Hewett,

---

5. Dr. Gwendolyn Cartledge's (Assistant Professor, Cleveland State University) assistance in this review is appreciated.

Taylor, & Arturo, 1969). Six classes of nine students each were assigned to various combinations of experimental and control conditions.

Treatment consisted of administering checkmarks, every fifteen minutes, for starting tasks, working on tasks, and behaviors appropriate to the individual child's *developmental sequence.* Checks were exchanged on a weekly basis for back-up reinforcers such as tangible rewards. The findings indicated that the token system was effective in significantly increasing task attention behaviors of the experimentals over the controls. Students receiving experimental conditions at midyear significantly improved over the controls in task attention and arithmetic achievement. Removal of experimental conditions at mid year resulted in improved task attention for these subjects but significant gains in reading or math did not occur. These results emphasize the effectiveness of token systems in behavior control. The corresponding academic improvement, although limited to arithmetic, supports the position that certain observable behaviors are prerequisite for academic achievement.

In a similar but later study, Glavin and others (1971), in an attempt to establish an alternative to self-contained special classrooms, used similar procedures with *conduct problem* children in resource classrooms. The 27 students received tokens for task-related behaviors. Poker chips were dispensed for starting, maintaining, and completing assigned tasks.

Disruptive behavior of the experimental subjects in the resource classroom was significantly reduced and task-related behavior significantly increased when compared to the control subjects in the regular classroom. Also shown was the significantly more appropriate behavior of the experimentals in the resource room than when in the regular classroom, either prior to or during treatment. As a result of these findings, they concluded that behaviors could be changed in resource rooms but generalization does not automatically take place to regular classrooms.

Although considerable empirical evidence exists verifying the efficacy of operant procedures, efforts have been made by some researchers to examine the specific variables influencing the changes observed. O'Leary, Becker, Evans, and Sandargas (1969) in a replication of a previous study (O'Leary & Becker, 1967) examined the relative effects of classroom rules, educational structure, teacher praise, and a token reinforcement program on reducing disruptive behavior. Seven children enrolled in a second-grade class of 21 were observed for eight months. The procedures were divided into eight phases: Phase I (baseline period) — students were observed by trained observers and the teacher proceeded in the normal manner; Phase II (classroom rules) — six weeks later, rules for classroom behavior were placed on the chalkboard and reviewed at least once each morning and afternoon. This phase lasted for three weeks; Phase III (educational structure) — the class was organized into four 30-minute periods for total class participation; Phase IV — (praise and ignore) — two weeks following Phase III, praise was given by the teacher for appropriate behavior and inappropriate behavior was ignored. At the end of a two-week period, Phase V was initiated. In addition to Phases II through IV, children received tokens (ratings) four times during the two hour afternoon periods according to the degree to which they followed classroom rules. Tokens and back-up reinforcers were reinstated for two weeks during Phase VII and withdrawn again during Phase VIII. In this phase, ratings were replaced with stars and a weekly piece of candy. These procedures resulted in a marked reduction in disruptive behavior only during the token phase. Phases II through IV did not have any consistent effect on behavior, causing the investigators to conclude that rules without reinforcement are ineffective. The improved behavior of the reinforcement phases did not generalize, however, to the nontoken morning periods. This occurrence was consistent with those observed in the studies by Meichenbaum et al. (1968) and Glavin et al. (1971) where behaviors developed under treatment conditions did not generalize to similar nontreatment conditions.

Chadwick and Day (1970) used crayons and other material rewards as incentives in order to improve both social behavior and academic performances of students with severe behavior problems.

Schwitzgebel (1965) used operant techniques to shape verbal statements and promptness of 35 male delinquent adolescents. Token economy has been used to improve attending behavior in relation to an automatic timer. Packard (1970) used such a timer to control attending behavior of regular class students (kindergarten, third, fifth, and sixth grades). Students earned rewards when all students attended to their learning activities. A red light on the timer indicated that attending behavior was being recorded.

Madsen and others (1968) examined the effects of teachers' behaviors on students' behaviors. Two teachers and four target pupils in two regular primary classes were observed and rated according to specified pupil and teacher behaviors. Pupil behaviors were divided into the categories of inappropriate behaviors and appropriate behaviors. Teachers' behaviors were coded according to their responses to some pupil behavior. The experimental conditions consisted of (1) rules — teachers listed classroom rules for appropriate behavior and reviewed them several times daily; (2) rules plus ignoring — teachers were directed to ignore inappropriate behavior except in extreme cases when injury might occur; and (3) rules plus ignoring plus praise — praise was given for behaviors that facilitated learning. Significant changes in pupil behavior occurred only when praise was introduced for appropriate behavior. Rules alone were found to be ineffective.

Broden, Hall, Dunlap, and Clark (1970) examined the effects of systematic teacher attention on the study behavior of thirteen seventh- and eighth-grade special education students. Initial treatment consisted of the teachers's giving praise and attention only to students exhibiting study behavior. Later a second phase was introduced where students exhibiting study behavior when a timer rang received a check. Each check permitted the student to leave one minute earlier for lunch. In the third phase the timer was removed and a point system introduced for appropriate behaviors. Results of these procedures increased study behavior from a mean rate of 29% during baseline to 57% during social reinforcement to 74% during the timer phase to 90% in the point or token phase. Although teacher attention was effective in increasing study behavior, the greatest increase occurred during the timer and token periods. The findings from the above studies suggest that while the systematic application of teacher attention/praise may significantly change classroom behaviors, tokens and back-up reinforcers apparently are more powerful in effecting behavior change.

Osborne (1969) studied the effects of contingent and noncontingent free time on the out-of-seat behavior of six girls (11 years to 13 years) at a school for the deaf. Students were instructed to remain in their seats for 20 or 25 minute periods. At the end of this time period if they had remained in their seats, students were permitted five minutes of free time. During the noncontingent period, free time was given regardless of out-of-seat behavior. The experimental conditions significantly reduced out-of-seat behaviors. Little change was observed in out-of-seat behaviors when noncontingent conditions were introduced.

Schmidt and Ulrich (1969) attempted to reduce noise levels through a group control procedure. The authors assessed the effects of additional gym time on the reduction of the noise level and the out-of-seat behavior of a fourth-grade class during study period. The class noise level was measured by a mechanical device. For each specified period (10 minutes) that the noise level did not exceed .42 decibels, the students earned two extra minutes of gym. When the noise level exceeded .42 decibels, the experimenter blew a harmonica and reset the timer. Experimental conditions resulted in a 13.5 decibel drop in noise level.

Several studies have investigated the effects of operant procedures on social interaction behaviors. One early investigation was conducted by Allen and others (1964). Reinforcement principles were used to increase the peer interactions of a four-year-old, withdrawn, nursery school child. Maximum adult attention was made contingent on play with another child. Minimum attention was given when the subject interacted with another adult and no attention was given when she was alone. A graph of the child's behavior showed that her interactions went from 10% (peers) and 40% (adults) during baseline to 60% (peers) and 25% (adults) during the final stage of experimental conditions. The authors reported, as a result of these procedures, that the subject had become a happy, confident member of the school group.

In a related study, Hart and others examined the effects of contingent and non-contingent adult attention on the cooperative behavior of a five-year-old, nursery school child. The investigators attempted to increase the cooperative behavior of the subject, who exhibited aversive as well as uncooperative behavior of the subject, toward other peers. Initially, adult attention was given noncontingently for seven days. Contingent adult attention, for the next twelve days was given for all cooperative play behaviors emitted by the subject. For the next four- and eight-day periods, noncontingent and contingent conditions were resumed, respectively. Shaping and priming (directing other children to initiate interaction) were necessary due to the subject's low rate of cooperative play. Cooperative play behavior increased from less than 5% during baseline and noncontingent conditions to 40% during contingent conditions. Similar results were obtained in the subject's proximity to peer behavior. These findings indicated that contingent teacher attention was effective in increasing pupil peer interactive behaviors.

On a much larger scale, Phillips and others (1973) used a positive and negative token system to develop and modify social skills of six adjudicated predelinquent boys. Four different experimental conditions were established in order to increase promptness, room cleaning, money saving, and knowledge of current events. The subjects, ranging in age from 12 to 15 years, received and/or lost points for certain specified behaviors, depending on the experimental conditions. For Experiment I, the boys lost 100 points per minute when late for meals. Five hundred points could be earned for obtaining a score of 80 or more for room cleaning. A score below 80 resulted in a loss of 80 points. In the third experiment on saving, the boys earned 10 points for every penny saved. This condition was later modified so that points could be earned only on specified days. News watching for current events involved various combinations of points earned and/or lost for correct or incorrect answers to news quizzes. The points were administered daily and used to buy special privileges such as games, snacks and gifts.

In each case, the experimental conditions were effective in increasing the desired behaviors. But instructions, threats, and demands, which were used as probes in some conditions, did not have any lasting effects upon increasing appropriate behaviors.

Positive reinforcement procedures in the classroom have been implemented largely through token systems and/or social reinforcement (teacher praise and attention). Tokens, ranging from powerful reinforcers such as money to points to be exchanged for rewards of privileges, have been used extensively during the past decade and repeatedly demonstrated to be effective agents in changing undesired behaviors. Despite their proven efficacy in modifying behaviors, existing research indicates that token systems, for the most part, are situation specific. That is, behaviors developed in one setting are observed almost totally within that setting and do not generalize to other conditions without similar treatment.

Studies have shown social reinforcement to be quite effective in establishing and maintaining appropriate classroom behaviors. Teacher attention and praise appear to be more effective when paired with token reinforcement. Group management systems, utilizing principles of positive reinforcement, may serve as alternatives to the constant monitoring and cost involved in token systems and social reinforcement.

Operant Tactics

Teaching tactics derived from operant conditioning consist of direct reinforcement, shaping, cuing, and contingency contracting. These approaches may be used in teacher-directed or student-directed activities with L&BD students.

Direct reinforcement. Direct reinforcement takes place when students perform or respond correctly and the teacher rewards them. This approach to *catching students in the act and reinforcing them* requires highly observant and positively oriented teachers.

Direct operant tactics are used by teachers irrespective of their awareness since any interactions with their students can result in operant conditioning. Thomas, Becker, and Armstrong (1968) demonstrated that some teachers do unknowingly develop undesirable pupil behaviors as they interact with their pupils. This influence of teachers' behaviors on students is widespread and may occur at varying times in classrooms. Consider the events and student behaviors as a consequence of teachers' responses as depicted in Figure 7.7.

Shaping. Teachers who use operant conditioning often apply a shaping procedure. By beginning with a response that is several steps removed from the desired behavior, teachers may shape the behavior through differential reinforcement of successive approximations of the responses. A clear example of shaping is shown in the following excerpt:

A succession of tasks was devised for Scotty in order to encourage him to read orally:

1. listens to a story that is read; teacher recognition is provided in the form of verbal praise.

2. listens and holds book while story is read; verbal approval and attention from teacher are given.

3. same as 2, plus answers questions about the story; verbal approval and attention from teacher are given.

4. same as 3, plus locates answers to questions after each paragraph; verbal approval and attention from teacher are given.

5. same as 3, plus locates and reads answers to questions after each paragraph; verbal approval and attention from teachers are provided.

6. alternates with teacher in reading paragraphs of the story; attention from teacher provided when Scotty reads.

7. reads entire story aloud, assistance from the teacher is provided as needed. (Stephens, 1970, pp. 149-150)

Complex behaviors, such as reading, do require that prerequisite responses be within the student's repertoire. In the above example, Scotty had previously demonstrated a facility to read equivalent materials but refused to cooperate. Thus, the shaping procedure was used to teach him to participate willingly. Had the final step been to teach Scotty reading, the shaping procedures would have dealt more with reading skill development as contrasted with eliciting and rewarding cooperative behavior.

Event (Students)	Response (Teachers)	Student Behavior
1. Talks out without permission	Teacher calls on someone requesting permission	Raises hand for permission
2. Talks out without permission	Teacher recognizes contribution	Continues to talk out without seeking permission
3. Required to do individual assignment without possessing prerequisite skills and understanding	Teacher returns paper with low score to student	Avoids completing assignments
4. Calculates problem incorrectly	Teacher provides delayed feedback	Becomes confused as to correct calculation and must unlearn incorrect responses
5. Shows disrespect to teacher	Argues and gives student lecture on respect for adults	Continues to show disrespect
6. Does not attend to directions	Refuses to repeat directions	Is careful to attend to future directions
7. Orally misreads words	Records errors and teaches correct responses	Misreads fewer words
8. Shows disrespect to teacher	Ignores or quickly punishes student	Less disrespect is shown
9. Is courteous to teacher	Recognizes good manners	Maintains courtesy
10. Does written assignments	Consistently discards without feedback	Discontinues doing written assignments

FIGURE 7.7   Direct reinforcement of students' behaviors by teachers

Cuing.   Teachers use stimuli in order to cue students as to appropriate social and/or academic responses. Both verbal and nonverbal cues are used by teachers in classrooms. In one study, Lovitt (1972) used operant tactics with a nine-year-old learning disabled boy. His verbal answers to pictures were controlled and improved by oral instructions. Results suggested that teachers' consistent and clearly stated oral instructions can be effective in improving students' performances.

Cuing may also take the form of verbal mediation where teachers describe what processes students are to follow as cues to their responses. For example, letter formation, arithmetic computation, and other paper-pencil activities may be taught by teachers as follows:

1. Teacher at chalkboard tells student to watch and do what teacher does;
2. Teacher does and describes one step at a time;
3. As teacher performs each step, student performs it while listening to the teacher's description.

A variation of the above procedure may occur when students perform the steps as the teacher verbally instructs them. Verbal mediation, in this way, may be used in conjunction with behavior rehearsing with students responding to the verbal cues presented by the teacher.

Cuing may also be used visually. Teachers may signal students by dimming or switching lights on and off or by posting signs indicating directions for students to follow.

Hartman (1974) used odors as cues to teach beginning reading to pre-first graders. Commercially available paper, with pictures and odors embedded, were associated with common nouns. While olfactory cuing is not commonly used in schools, she demonstrated the feasibility of doing so at least in teaching beginning word recognition.

Contingency contracting.   Contingency contracting is another form of operant conditioning where rewards follow desired responses. Performances are specified along with rewards in advance. Since the contingency arrangement may extend over long periods of time, tokens, checkmarks, and other interim rewards are used to encourage students who may use these for back-up rewards. Rewards used under contingency contracting vary greatly from teacher to teacher. Some suggested exchanges in contingency contracting are shown in Figure 7.8.

Contingency contracting has been used extensively with L&BD students for improving both academic performance and social behavior. For example, McKenzie and others (1968), in an early study of contingency contracting with learning disabled children, increased the attending behavior and academic achievement of a group of eight students. Back-up reinforcers in the form of allowances were given by parents contingent upon improved performance. Children were paid at the end of each week. Eventually the length of time was extended to prepare the children for delays in a typical school situation.

In another early study, Wolf, Giles, and Hall (1968) exposed a remedial classroom to token economy in order to improve academic responses. Tokens were redeemable for objects and events. Over an academic year, report card grades and performance on a standardized achievement test indicated that students who participated in the program changed to a significantly greater extent than controls who did not receive treatment.

Extra drink (juice)
Graham crackers
Candy
Gum
Milk
Cookies
Fruit
New crayons
Balloons
Sea shells
Paper pads
Make paper airplanes
Picture postcards
Jacks
Hair ribbons
Barrettes

Puzzles
Miniature flags
Bubble gum cards
Listen to record player
Board games (Monopoly)
Use easel, chalkboard,
   feltboard
Notebook
Gum

Erasers
Use magic markers
Teacher's helper
Use Viewmaster
Messenger

Combs
Toothbrush
Membership in service clubs
Card games
Throw pillows

Dress patterns
Thread
Movie posters
Dating and personality
   conferences
Psychedelic posters
Pin cushions

Coloring books
Modeling clay
Dominoes
Chalk
Play time
Listening to radio
Pictures
Colored pencils
Pencils
Attractive rocks
Toothbrushes
Teacher's helper
Scissors
Paper scraps
Tablet backs
Story hour (teacher
   reads story)
Toy gun
Magazines
Magnets
Play chess
New tablet
Lavatory pass

Jigsaw puzzles
Maps (from service
   stations)
Rings
Industry booklets
Charms
Group leader
Magazines (*Sports
   Illustrated, Teen*)
Charms
Emery boards
Word games (Scrabble)
Cologne samples
Cookbooks or recipe
   folders
Pens or pencils
Use tape recorder

Costume jewelry

Folders

Building blocks
Design blocks
Paints
Tinker toys
Comic books
Writing on board
Grab bags
Weekly Reader
   subscriptions
Make bulletin board
   display
Seeding plants
Erasers
Colored yarn
Erasers
Plastic animals
Bubble gum prizes
Leader of group activity

Play with Barbie dolls
Listen to radio
Play checkers
Card games (Old Maid)
Free reading
Use rulers

Puzzles
New pen or pencil

Trolls
Use color pencils
Use special equipment
Comic books
Craft kits

Mirrors
Sample cosmetics
Library pass
Lotions
Records (use free ones
   from jukebox companies)
Rain hats
Sewing materials

Cookbooks or recipe

Trading stamps (Green,
   TV, etc.)

Class may save for class outing.
Free time one day a month to do whatever they wish.
Free time one period a week to do whatever they wish.

FIGURE 7.8. Suggested exchanges in contingency contracting systems (Reprinted from Thomas M. Stephens, *Implementing behavioral approaches in elementary and secondary schools.* Columbus, Ohio: Charles E. Merrill, 1975, pp. 45-46.)

Conditions. There are certain conditions which, when present, tend to facilitate the use of one operant tactic over the others. These include student variables, task demands, and instructional setting.

Contingency contracting must be learned. Students need to be aware that their behavior will result in rewards. Those who are unfamiliar with a token economy may first need to be shown the value of interim rewards and procedures for cashing in. Certainly, those too immature or otherwise unable to understand contracting will not be responsive.

Direct reinforcement is easily used with those who are unable to understand contingency contracting. It is also effective when teachers are in frequent and direct contact with students, such as in conducting a group discussion or in unplanned activities.

Shaping requires some forethought, and often a task analysis may be necessary in planning. Since each step is developed and rewarded, teachers must carefully consider those responses necessary for completing the entire behavior.

Contingency contracting can also be effectively used as a means for target students to earn rewards for their peers. In such situations, contingencies are placed upon target students, or target behaviors, for group rewards. Since a means of accounting for responses over time is often needed in contingency systems, it is necessary to use some type of token. Marks, coupons, or other interim items serve to (a) remind students that they are progressing, (b) keep a record of the amount of their progress, and (c) provide a means for cashing in tokens for back-up rewards.

Drill and Practice

Teaching tactics also involve drill and practice if those responses which have been learned are to become ingrained in students' behaviors. Drill is a routine and repeated demonstration of the learned response. Following drill, opportunities for practice should occur.

Practice activities should vary, consisting of mixed practice in different formats. If, for example, students have learned multiplication of two-place numbers by one-place numerals in a vertical format, after extensive drill they should be given practice on similar problems in a horizontal form. Subsequently, the problems should be mixed so that practice involves both horizontal and vertical problems.

Summary

Teachers use assessment information as a basis for instructing L&BD students. While by necessity their instructional decisions must be based upon many factors, they must also consider what they will teach, when it is to be taught, and how they will teach.

Teaching behavior is influenced by factors such as the instructional level of students, their own competencies and ethics, and students' academic and social needs. Recommended teaching methods for L&BD students are rooted in operant conditioning and social modeling theory. The tactics include direct reinforcement, shaping, cuing, contingency contracting, reverse chaining, drill and practice, behavior rehearsing, and learning through imitation.

8

Evaluating Instruction of Learning and Behaviorally Disordered Students

Teachers of L&BD students should carefully consider which instructional tactics to use with each individual. The most effective means of making such determinations is by evaluating the effects of their instruction.

Instruction can be evaluated by measuring behavior prior to instruction, specifying and applying the treatment, and comparing performance following instruction with pretreatment behavior. Tactics for teachers to conduct evaluations have been verified through applied research studies.

Introduction

In education evaluation may take three forms or combinations of the three. Each approach has related to it certain types of measures and, in some instances, specific methodology. These three approaches are:

1. comparing a group's performance with another group's performance,
2. comparing an individual's performance with a group's performance,
3. comparing an individual's performance against his/her previous performance.

Perhaps the most prevalent practice in general education is represented by the first approach. In this model, the concern is with comparing the relative standing of one group's performance with another group's performance. This approach almost always involves the use of standardized tests of achievement and intelligence.

The second approach is simply a variation upon the first in that an individual student's performance is considered against group standardized norms. The test instruments here, however, often consist of both group standardized measures as well as clinical tests. These latter instruments usually require trained specialists to administer.

However, when the third approach to evaluation is used, the individual's performance is compared with his/her own progress. Consequently, standardized group or clinical tests are not necessary since an individual's growth under this model need not take into account a comparison or norm group's status.

The first two models of evaluation are believed by some to be inadequate for instructional purposes, as discussed previously in chapter 6. Standardized measures are simply not capable of providing the level of precision necessary for evaluating the effects of particular instructional strategies upon individual students, and they do not yield the types of information necessary for determining which responses should be retaught or for indicating those which have been mastered.

Teachers evaluate their instruction for at least three important reasons: to help determine their students' progress, to evaluate the effectiveness of a particular instructional approach, and for making instructional decisions.

Determining Progress

Perhaps the most obvious use of instructional evaluation is for determining students' progress. When used for this purpose, it is necessary to merely obtain measures at two points in the instructional process: prior to teaching and immediately following teaching. For example, if a student correctly calculates x amount of arithmetic problems upon assessment prior to instruction and $x + 5$ of the same problems are done correctly following instruction, we have determined the amount of progress which was made (plus 5).

Various units of measurement may be used in determining students' progress. These may consist of rate of response or number of response, as in the above example for measuring arithmetic performance. Number is a tally of the correct or incorrect responses. A tally count is the simplest unit of measure used in evaluation; yet it is often valuable in determining how often a response occurs before, during, and after instruction.

In an early study, Bijou (1965) counted the number of times a preschool child emitted uncooperative behaviors and the frequency with which the child's mother responded. The mother was then instructed to ignore the child's inappropriate behavior and to respond only to his cooperative behavior. Through frequency counts it was possible to evaluate the increase of cooperative behaviors and the decrease in undesirable responses.

Rate of response is calculated by clocking the amount of time consumed from initiating a response until it is completed.[1] In the above arithmetic example, the teacher may have sought to speed up the student's work without a decrease in accuracy; clocking would have started when the student began calculating the arithmetic and stopped when the assignment was finished.

Rate may be combined with other units in measuring instructional effects. For example, first- and second-graders were subjects in a study conducted by Hopkins, Schutte, and Garton (1971). They considered rate and accuracy in printing and writing assignments. The time required to copy assigned materials and the correctness of the letter formations were both measured.

Measuring Instructional Effectiveness

Effective teachers of L&BD students frequently seek to match student assessment information with instructional strategies. Evaluating the effects of instruction is the

1. The formula is: Rate = Number of Responses/Time

best way to verify the quality of such a match. Once teachers have identified those instructional strategies which are effective with particular student performance variables, they are able to improve their knowledge and quality of instruction.

Stain, Shores, and Kerr(1976) conducted a study which demonstrates the importance of evaluating instructional tactics. Using three behaviorally handicapped, preschool boys as subjects, they gathered baseline data on two classes of behavior: motor-gestural and vocal-verbal. They also recorded two categories of teacher behavior: prompting and reinforcement. Following baseline data gathering, they implemented a treatment program. Intervention consisted of verbal and physical prompts and verbal praise contingent upon appropriate social behaviors.

Results of this study indicated that the intervention tactics increased the target students' positive social behavior and decreased inappropriate behavior. The authors also discovered an important "spillover" effect among classmates where nontarget students' behaviors also improved, even though they had different social behavior problems and different reinforcement histories than did the target students. Furthermore, these desirable "spillover" effects were greater when intervention procedures were applied to two students at once, rather than one at a time.

Although the study cited above was not conducted by the teacher, it does demonstrate the value of careful evaluation. In this instance, as a result, an important tactic was identified. It appears, based on the results, that with four-year-olds group behavior improves when two students serve as targets and are treated simultaneously.

Making Instructional Decisions

A third reason for teacher evaluation of instruction is for decision making. Teachers of L&BD students should decide:

— how well students have acquired social and academic performance tasks,
— which students need additional instruction on specific skills and concepts,
— which items should be taught next, and
— which students need practice in the use of or in applying particular social and academic skills.

Teachers often find it necessary to establish performance criteria for students in advance of the instructional activity. By doing so, they are able to make decisions quickly and on the basis of an established criteria. For example, such measures are useful for determining the effects of instruction over previously specified content. If many students fail to meet criteria, the instructional approach may need to be changed. Those students who meet criterion, upon evaluation, should proceed to the next segment of instruction.

> Evaluation is best when it has immediate instructional value. Therefore, criterion measures, when used for evaluative purposes, should be used whenever the results can be immediately helpful to students. For this reason, the most instructionally relevant time to use criterion measures for evaluation is when there is time for instruction. When instruction cannot follow evaluation, such as at the end of the school year, the results have limited instructional value, under such circumstances, evaluation results may still provide a basis for guidance and counseling to students and their parents. (Stephens, 1975, p. 60)

Types of Evaluation

Throughout the remainder of this chapter consideration is given solely to evaluation approaches for teachers of L&BD students which compare an individual's performances with his/her previous achievements. Such an approach generally consists of either criterion-referenced measures and/or systematic observations.

Criterion-referenced Measures

Criterion-referenced measures have two useful purposes in evaluation. They are used to assess students as entry measures prior to instruction and to evaluate student performance following instruction. The criterion measures in Figure 8.1 may be used for either purpose.

FIGURE 8.1.   Criterion-referenced measures

| 1. Skill: | When given the sound of *m* the student is to point to pictures that begin with the *m* sound. |

| Teacher: | Orally present the sound of *m* to the student. Then present 10 picture cards one at a time and ask the student to point to the picture card if it begins with the *m* sound. |

	1. airplane	6. dog
	2. monkey	7. horse
	3. turtle	8. mouse
	4. cat	9. pig
	5. motorcycle	10. moon

| 2. Skill: | When presented with pairs of numerals (0-9), the student will write the symbols ">" or "<" between them. |

| Teacher: | Present worksheet and say, "On this worksheet you are to put either the symbol for greater than (make symbol > on the board) or the symbol for less than (make < on the board) in the box between each set of numerals. |

PROBLEMS:

	1. 2 ☐ 7	6. 9 ☐ 2
	2. 5 ☐ 1	7. 8 ☐ 9
	3. 8 ☐ 3	8. 0 ☐ 1
	4. 4 ☐ 7	9. 5 ☐ 4
	5. 0 ☐ 6	10. 7 ☐ 6

| 3. Skill: | To identify consequences of behavior involving wrong-doing. |

Objective: The student verbally identifies possible consequences of his/her own or others' behavior involving wrong-doing.

| Assessment: | 1. Assess from previous knowledge of student OR
2. Use Assessment Task |

Assessment Task: Present student(s) with a series of situations involving the possibility of wrong-doing, for example: "You are taking a spelling test and you do not know the words. The person in front of you is sitting so you can see his paper." "You come into the classroom before school and see the teacher's purse on the desk. There is no one else in the room." "You see another student steal a bag of candy from the grocery store. He offers to give you some of it if you will not tell." Add other examples from actual situations known to the students. Have the student(s) tell different things they could do in each case and what the consequences of different actions might be. Observe target student(s) for responses reflecting understanding of possible consequences for wrong-doing.

Evaluation:

1 ____ Student exhibits the skill at an acceptable level.

Teaching procedure: Mastery. No teaching necessary. Move to the next skill.

2 ____ Student exhibits skill occasionally at a lower-than-acceptable level.

Teaching procedure: Use either social reinforcement or contingency management strategy to increase performance.

3 ____ Student does not exhibit the skill.

When criterion-referenced measures are used for evaluating students' progress, evaluation takes the form of comparing students' performances prior to instruction with those following instruction. Thus, in Figure 8.1 the same measure is used to assess a student's skill and to evaluate his/her use of the skill. For example, the first skill (matching the sound of *m* with a picture beginning with that sound) would be used as follows:

1. teacher assesses student
2. student responds correctly to 7 of the 10 pictures
3. instruction of *m* sound takes place
4. teacher evaluates student on same criterion-referenced measure
5. student responds correctly to 9 of the 10 pictures
6. teacher determines that learning has occurred (90%)
7. teacher continues to instruct on *m* sound seeking mastery (100%)

Counting the number of times students require an instructional strategy before they meet criterion has been referred to as *trials to criterion* (Cooper & Johnson, in press). With this measure the teacher simply keeps track of the number of times each student takes the criterion-referenced measure before criterion is met.

Systematic Observations

Systematic observations of students' performances provide a most useful way to evaluate instruction. This approach differs from criterion-referenced measures in several important respects. First, it allows for direct observations since students may be observed in a variety of performance situations. Second, various means of recording performances may be used. Third, criterion measures can be incorporated into systematic observations. Finally, measures of performance may be taken during instruction as well as before and after.

Baer, Wolf, and Risley (1968) described how applied behavior analysis can be effective in changing problem behavior. Crucial to such an approach are systematic observations of such behavior. They argue that an analysis of a behavior is achieved when control of that behavior is demonstrated.

They described the use of two designs for demonstrating the reliable control of a change in behavior. The *reversal design* is one, and the *multiple baseline design* is the other.

With a reversal design, sometimes referred to as an *ABAB design,* the behavior (A) is first measured over time to determine its stability. Instruction (B) then occurs. Measurement is continued to determine if the instruction is producing a change in performance. If change does occur, instruction is discontinued to determine if the performance returns to baseline conditions (A). A return to baseline conditions indicates that instruction improved performance. Instruction is then reinstated (B). Reversals of this sort may be executed several times in order to demonstrate effects of instruction.

Reversal designs have several limitations, however. In schools, for example, purposely diminishing desirable social or academic performances is not usually welcomed, and academic performances once learned may be maintained even in the absence of further instruction.

The multiple baseline approach is a better alternative for evaluation when a behavior is irreversible or when reversing the behavior is not acceptable. With this design, a number of responses are selected and measured over time for baseline purposes. The teacher may then seek to change any one of the behaviors while not treating the others. If the target behavior shows improvement while the others remain essentially stable, instruction is then assigned to another behavior. Each time it is evident that the treated behaviors improve while the others do not, the teacher is demonstrating the value of that particular instructional treatment. In subsequent sections of this chapter, the use of systematic observations for evaluating instruction are discussed more fully.

Performance Comparisons

Academic and social instruction can be readily evaluated by comparing students' performance prior to instruction with their performance following instruction. This evaluation approach can be thought of as the before-and-after method of evaluating.

Characteristics of Before-and-After Evaluations

All before-and-after treatment evaluation approaches have three common ingredients. Performance is carefully described or measured before instruction and that same behavior is described and measured after teaching. Phase one can be termed *pretreatment assessment,* while the second is considered *posttreatment assessment.* The third element in this type of evaluation is a procedure whereby a comparison is made between the two performances.

Pretreatment Assessment

Prior to instruction of a particular response or task, assessment occurs. It is equivalent to a baseline period, that is, a period of time whereby reliable observations of students' behaviors on target tasks are obtained.

Assessment may take the form of criterion-referenced measures, as shown in Figure 8.1. Reliability of measurement is not always readily established, however, with these measures for two reasons. First, the number of trials on criterion measures are limited. Thus, reliability of students' performances cannot be assured. And second, items within the measures may not be equivalent. In this situation, the items will not be measuring the same skill or response.

One way to improve the reliability of criterion measures is to increase the number of items or observations. With academic skills, 10 items in any one measure should be considered minimal, such as skills 1 and 2 in Figure 8.1. When direct observations are conducted, such as for skill 3 in Figure 8.1, it is wise to have a series of observations over several days. Even with these precautions, the issue of interobserver reliability is not considered; it is discussed, however, later in this chapter.

Criterion-referenced measures may also be used to establish a rate of proficiency in academic performance when criteria are used to evaluate rate of accuracy. Garsholt (1970) described ways to establish proficiency levels in arithmetic. She provided two students in a special class with a ditto sheet of 60 problems involving one or two movements. A product requiring one written numeral, e.g., $2 \times 3 = \_\_\_$, counted as one movement, while an answer requiring two written numerals $5 \times 7 = \_\_\_$, was considered two written movements. A posttreatment evaluation could then be conducted using a similar measure with the same maximum number of responses. When rate and accuracy are measured, the maximum amount of time consumed as well as the number of correct responses must be measured.

Once performance has been established through assessment, instruction or treatment may begin. The various approaches described in chapter 7 represent types of instructional treatment referred to here.

Posttreatment Assessment and Comparisons

Following instruction, teachers may again assess students' performances on target tasks. At this time, however, the assessment is an evaluation since it occurs following treatment. It is at this point that unreliable measures interfere with interpretation in a pre-post evaluation approach. If performance has changed, one may have no way to be reasonably certain that the change was not simply a function of unreliable measures.

In a criterion-referenced approach, the same measure should be used in posttreatment assessment as was used in pretreatment assessment. Using Figure 8.1 again as an example, student A correctly answered 7 items on skill number 2 prior to instruction and answered these same items correctly plus two others on posttreatment assessment. This comparison of student A's two performances suggests that learning has occurred. It also indicates that one item needs to be learned. At this point, the teacher may decide to teach the correct response to the one incorrect item.

Comparisons in criterion-referenced evaluation have merit in that they provide a relatively easy evaluation, but they present limitations. As already indicated, reliability of measurement can be a problem — although it can be improved. Another, more serious shortcoming is that of attributing change in performance to instruction. This is a serious problem and can be more readily controlled by using techniques commonly associated with a systematic analysis approach.

Evaluation through Systematic Observations

Cooper (1974) indicated that systematic observations in an applied behavioral approach provide teachers with techniques to answer a variety of questions. These may range from evaluating the level of effectiveness in teaching a specific computational procedure in arithmetic to the effectives of seating arrangements on academic performances. In an extension of his earlier work, Cooper and Johnson (in press) presented guidelines for teachers who wish to measure academic performances.

Guidelines for direct and continuous measurement of academic behavior, as presented by Cooper and Johnson, consisted of only those measurement techniques that classroom teachers could use without outside observers. Basic procedures included using tallies. Tallies are easily understood when communicated to parents and students since the results are in terms of number correct and/or number of errors. The measurement procedure is simple; it does not interfere with teaching; it requires little additional teacher time; and when tallies are recorded next to each item, errors may be analyzed for instructional planning.

Cooper and Johnson (in press) considered the main disadvantage to tally measurement to be that comparisons across time are unclear since the total number of opportunities for responses vary with assignments. Under such circumstances percentages may be computed by dividing the number tallied by the total number of opportunities and multiplying by 100. They caution readers not to use percentages when the total opportunities for responding are less than 20 since an increase of one response can greatly inflate percentage values. The disadvantage to the use of percentages is that they can mask gains or losses particularly when only numbers correct or errors are reported.

Rate of response and trials to criterion are other measurements described by Cooper and Johnson. Two types of measurement are needed when computing rate of response, number of responses, and time spent. Rate is calculated by dividing number of responses by time (in determining rate, time is usually reported in terms of minutes). These authors believe that trials to criterion is an appropriate measure for comparing two or more tactics or materials. Trials to criterion is defined as the number of times response opportunities are presented before the student achieves a previously determined criterion level of proficiency.

Readers are referred to Cooper's publications previously cited for detailed discussions of these guidelines. *The Journal of Applied Behavior Analysis* also contains many articles describing systematic observations for evaluating students' academic and social behavior.

Characteristics of Systematic Observations

In a review of research involving applied behavior analysis in classrooms, Hanley (1970) indicated that there are two characteristics of such analyses. First, definitions and measurements of the behaviors under investigation must be objective, Second, measurement techniques for evaluation must be reliable.

Definitions must be precise and descriptive. Among L&BD students, for example, their self-concepts are a common concern. Note how in anecdote 8.1 the resource teacher deals with this concern and meets the requirements of a precise and descriptive definition.

ANECDOTE 8.1

When Harriet was first assigned to Miss Jackson's resource room, she was described by the special education team as having moderate academic learning problems and a *poor self-concept*. Since there is no direct measure of self-concept, Miss Jackson observed Harriet and noted that her verbal behavior did suggest feelings of inadequacies.

Using a simple observation form, Miss Jackson began to count the number of negative comments Harriet emitted in the resource room concerning herself and her performances. She defined this behavior as: *any verbal statement that Harriet makes that is negative about her appearance, behavior, and/or academic work.*

Because she wanted to have some confidence that her measurements were accurate, Miss Jackson asked the special education consultant to also tally these same verbal comments during some of the same times that she did. After establishing that her definition and frequency counts were reliable, that is they agreed with the other observer at an 80% level, Miss Jackson continued to obtain baseline data concerning Harriet's "poor self-concept." Later, she implemented a treatment strategy to improve her opinion of herself.

In anecdote 8.1, the teacher descriptively defined the behavior to be measured. This description permitted an objective evaluation of the target behavior. She also conducted an interobserver reliability check on her observations. By having a second person observe simultaneously with her, she was able to determine that the measure was reliable.

Direct Measurement

Direct measurement is one characteristic of an evaluation approach through systematic observations. Four types of direct behavioral observation tactics have been identified (Hall, Hawkins, & Axelrod, 1975): event or frequency recording, duration recording, interval recording, and time sampling.

Event or frequency recording.   This is the most commonly used measurement tactic in applied behavioral analysis. It indicates the number of times a specific behavior occurs per time unit by tallying or counting the correct and/or error responses (Cooper, 1974). This type of recording requires a minimal amount of recording time and is easily applied in classroom. It does not interfere greatly with teaching, allows source of errors to be analyzed, and produces a numerical output which can be represented in the form of percentage, rate, or number of occurrences. But expressing data in number of occurrences has its disadvantages unless the number of response opportunities is held constant. Cooper (1974) warns that frequency of occurrence should only be used when opportunity for response and time are constant. Percentage of correct and/or error responses allows comparison and analysis of data across time.

To report event measures in percentages, the evaluator should divide the number of correct or error responses by the total number of opportunities for response, and then multiply by 100. Reporting data in percentages allows a large number of responses to be dealt with and makes comunication of data to others easier to understand. Presenting the data in number of occurrences also does not show proficiency. In order to show proficiency, the rate of response (correct and/or error) can be determined by dividing the number of correct and/or error responses by the unit of time taken to complete the task or the amount of time the behavior was observed. Use of rate as a basic measure of performance was originally suggested by Skinner (1953) and practiced extensively for precision teaching (Kunzelman, 1970).

Duration recording.   Duration is the measure which indicates the amount of time an individual or group is engaged in a particular behavior. Duration recording is an appropriate tactic for behaviors which occur at very frequent rates or for extended periods of time. These are usually reported as percentage of time the behavior or event continues or lasts (Cooper, 1974).

Interval recording. This consists of counting specified behaviors within fixed time intervals. The observation period is divided into intervals of equal size. Interval recording is generally inappropriate for behaviors which occur at very high or low rates. It is well suited to the measurement of discrete behavior that occurs across time and may be easily adapted to the simultaneous recording of multiple behavior categories. A symbolic representation of the behavioral category is placed in the interval that corresponds with its occurrence. Ordinarily, a behavior is recorded only once during an interval. This procedure is sensitive to both the frequency and duration of a behavior (Hall, Hawkins, & Axelrod, 1975). A major disadvantage, however, is that interval recording usually requires the undivided attention of the observer.

Time sampling. This recording procedure is convenient and practical for a teacher engaged in instruction. The observer records only the momentary state of the behavior immediately following specified time intervals.

Time intervals of minute durations are usually employed. A low-rate behavior, however, should be measured frequently. Time sampling is similar in format to interval recording, but it does not require continuous observation. Intervals are usually in minute duration, rather than seconds, and concern is placed on the behavior at the end of the specified time interval rather than during the interval.

With time sampling, the observer has to watch the subject only at particular moments. This is a particularly important advantage if the teacher is the observer.

Evaluation Designs[2]

Comparison of performances before, during, and after instruction are commonly a part of systematic behavioral observations. Three commonly used designs for purposes of evaluating classroom instruction are pre and post design, reversal design, and multiple baseline design.

Pre and Post Design

Recording student performance prior to instruction of a given task, during an observational or baseline period, represents the pre aspect of this design. Obtaining records of the students' performance following instruction is the post portion of this same design. Pre and post designs are sometimes referred to as A-B designs. Figure 8.2 shows a before-after (A-B) design.

The A portion of Figure 8.2 occurred over a five-day period where the target behavior was failure to complete math assignments. Twelve students who frequently did not complete their assignments served as the target population. The B part of Figure 8.2 shows a decline in the number of incomplete assignments among the same target group during instructional treatment. On the last day of the treatment period, only one assignment was not completed. Since the highest number was 12 incomplete assignments recorded during the baseline period, it is obvious that the instructional treatment was effective.

The major problem with a pre-post design is that it fails to prove that the treatment was the cause of behavior change. It will demonstrate if change in behavior occurs, but it does not directly attribute the change to instruction.

2. This section is adapted from Thomas M. Stephens, *Implementing behavioral approaches in elementary and secondary schools.* Columbus, Ohio: Charles E. Merrill, 1975, pp. 172-176.

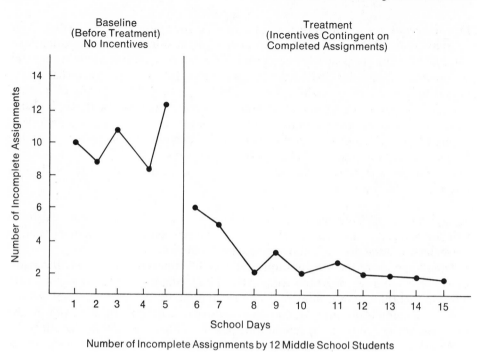

Number of Incomplete Assignments by 12 Middle School Students

FIGURE 8.2.   An example of an A-B evaluation design

Reversal Design

One type of design which will demonstrate causality is termed *reversal* (ABAB) because after change has taken place the teacher discontinues the use of that treatment which is believed to be causing the improvement. Figure 8.3 depicts our same target group when treatment was reversed or when the use of incentives was discontinued.

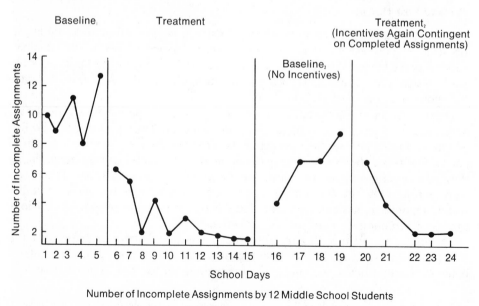

Number of Incomplete Assignments by 12 Middle School Students

FIGURE 8.3.   An example of an ABAB design

Rewarding experiences take many forms.

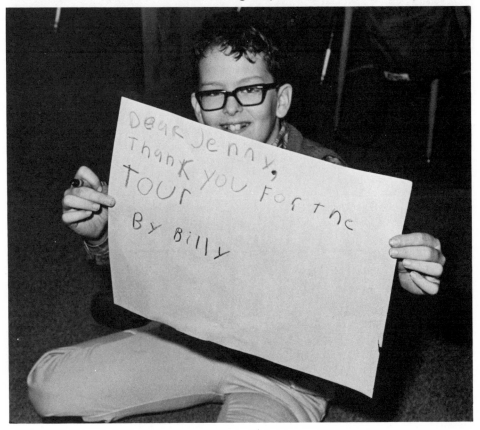

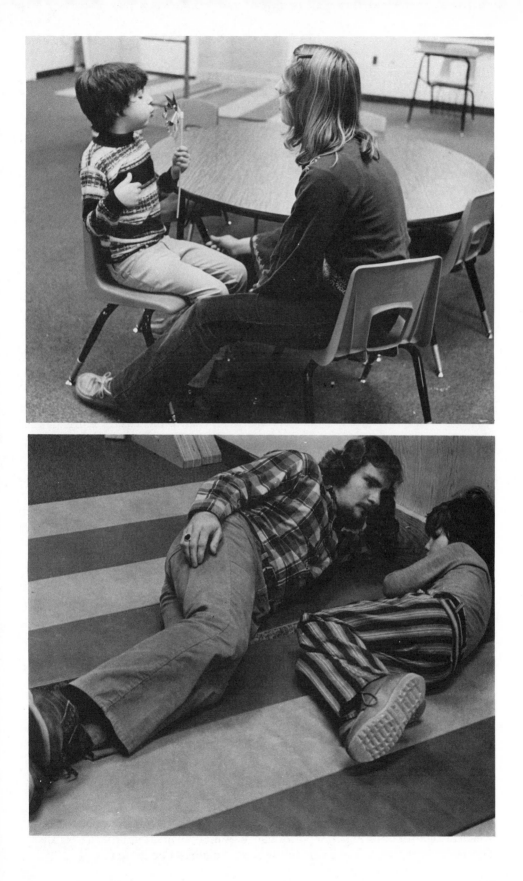

In Figure 8.3, the data clearly show that the incentives were effective in extinguishing the target behavior. Numbers of incomplete assignments decreased when incentives were used and increased when incentives were discontinued. In this instance, we can attribute the improved performance to using incentives. During the reversal phase, in which teachers were asked to return to similar conditions which were in effect during the baseline period, no incentives were used.

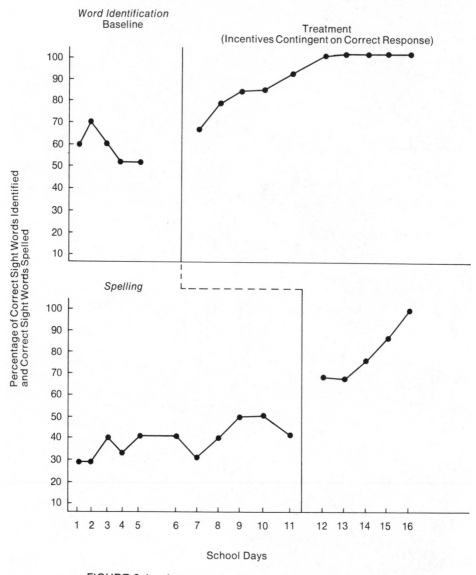

FIGURE 8.4.   An example of a multiple baseline design

Multiple Baseline Design

Teachers are naturally reluctant to use reversal designs when they are successful with a given instructional strategy because they hesitate to discontinue tactics which are contributing to better performance. A more realistic approach to evaluation under such circumstances is to use a multiple baseline design.

It is necessary when using multiple baselines to obtain observations on two or more different target students or two different behaviors among the same population of students or from the same student. If instruction improves the first behavior while the other untreated behaviors continue to remain essentially the same, improvement can be attributed to the instruction.

Figure 8.4 shows an example of a multiple baseline design. Two different behaviors were recorded among the same 12 students. Incentives were first used to reduce the number of incomplete assignments. Treatment for the second behavior (improving the percentage of correct assignments) was not begun until treatment for the first behavior showed a reduction in incomplete assignments. Since percentage of correct assignments continued to be low at that point, the treatment for the first behavior was demonstrated to be effective. Following this demonstration treatment was introduced for improving the second behavior. It resulted in an increase in the percentage of correct aassignments.

Teachers' Attitudes toward Evaluation

Ross (1976) believes that teachers of L&BD students must have objective records to determine if progress is occurring. His belief should be extended to specific behaviors that teachers of such children should use for evaluating their instruction. The following checklist can be used as a way for readers to evaluate their attitudes toward instructional evaluation.

Teacher's Checklist of Attitudes Toward Instructional Evaluation

	Always	Sometimes	Never
1. Do you keep an open mind towards new instructional techniques?	____	____	____
2. Do you use criterion measures for purposes of evaluating instructional gains?	____	____	____
3. Do you use systematic observations and behavior analysis as a means of evaluating instructional affects?	____	____	____
4. Do you use any evaluation designs for instruction such as multiple baseline, reversal, or baseline-intervention-baseline designs?	____	____	____
5. Do you specify and describe target behaviors and academic tasks?	____	____	____
6. Do you systematically apply instructional treatment, evaluating the effects of each?	____	____	____
7. Do you change your instructional approaches as a result of evaluative evidence?	____	____	____

Summary

Instructional evaluation of L&BD students is best achieved by comparing an individual's performance against his/her previous performance. In this approach, criterion-referenced measures and/or systematic observations may be used.

When criterion measures are used, teachers are applying a pre and post design. They are measuring performance before instruction and following instruction. Other designs used in behavioral analysis are reversal and multiple baseline.

Systematic observations require direct and objective measurement of classroom behaviors. These behaviors must be specified and clearly described. Their measurement may be achieved through the use of event or frequency recording, duration recording, interval recording, and time sampling.

Teachers of L&BD students are encouraged to engage in behaviors which facilitate instructional evaluation. A checklist is provided to measure the reader's attitude towards such an evaluation.

part II

Applications for Teaching Behaviors to Learning Disabled and Behaviorally Disordered Children

9

The Directive Teaching Instructional Management System

The Directive Teaching Instructional Management System (DTIMS)[1] is a skill training approach for individualizing instruction of L&BD students. It contains a curriculum for assessing and teaching arithmetic, reading, and social skills. Also inherent in the system are suggestions for classroom management and for evaluating and tracking student performances. DTIMS is used here as an example of the technology which is a part of a skill training approach to teaching and managing L&BD students. DTIMS materials and information may be obtained through the author.

Introduction

A distinction has been made previously in this text between teaching activities that are rooted in ability training theory as compared to those that are skill oriented. Because ability training has a longer history in special education, tests and teaching materials which are commonly a part of this orientation are readily available. Unlike ability training practitioners, skill trainers are less prevalent and consequently have fewer commercially available assessment and instructional materials. Yet the skill training approach is well suited for systematic instruction because it is concerned with students' observed performances.

1. Copyright 1973 and 1976 by Thomas M. Stephens. Grateful acknowledgment is made to many students, colleagues, and funding sources which supported and assisted in the development of DTIMS materials. The doctoral students were Jerry Barnett, Gwendolyn Cartledge, Thom Cooper, Denzil Edge, A. Carol Hartman, Ferris Henson, Michael Kabler, George Levin, Virginia Lucas, and Joanne Milburn. Other students were Deborah Collins, Rita Glavin, Kathy Hoff, Nancy Jelonek, Charles Klamer, Saundra Mays, George Pahl, Susan Quinn, and Emmy Spring. Technical staff members were Cheryl Elsberry, Deane Frantz, Ihsan Husseini, Edward Latessa, Joyce Lemke, Donald Lepley, Nancy Robinson, Mary Scheiderer, Douglas Smith, JoAnn VanSchaik, and Jennifer Yeagley. Colleagues were Delayne Hudspeth and Edwin Novak.

Assistance for funding was obtained through the Baltimore, Maryland Public Schools, the National Center on Educational Media and Materials for the Handicapped, the Ohio Department of Education, Division of Special Education, the Pittsburgh, Pennsylvania Public Schools, the State of South Dakota, Division of Elementary and Secondary Education, Springfield, Ohio Public Schools, and The Ohio State University. Special recognition and appreciation are extended to the two directors of the project: Dr. George Levin (1971-73) and Dr. A. Carol Hartman (1973-75).

249

The Directive Teaching Instructional Management System is one skill training approach that is designed for assisting teachers of L&BD students. In addition to providing a method for tracking student progress, DTIMS contains arithmetic and reading skills that are typically taught in kindergarten through grade three. These are, of course, also appropriate skills for any student, regardless of age and grade placement, who has not yet mastered beginning arithmetic and reading skills. The social skills curriculum may be used at any age and grade level. Although a system approach to skill training is of relatively recent origin, several other similar, but not identical, systems are available commercially. DTIMS is used here as one example of such systems. Because it is the author's, he is, of course, more familiar with it than any other existing skill system. Information concerning the use of DTIMS should be directed to the author.

Influence of Instructional Technology

Recent developments in behavioral and educational technology have made it possible to achieve three important goals for handicapped students. First, through the use of such technology, instruction can now be individualized. Second, because it is now possible to individualize instruction, many of the academic needs of handicapped students can be met within regular classrooms. Third, the educational placement of each child can be evaluated as to its success. Through regular monitoring of each student's academic progress, school personnel can meet that requirement of Public Law 94-142 (see chapter 3).

Technology of instruction refers to methods, strategies, and other practices which facilitate classroom learning. The core of an instructional technology involves a systematic approach to teaching. Individualized instruction can be achieved by carefully assessing students' responses, designing instructional strategies based upon that assessment, implementing the strategies, evaluating the effects of instruction, and modifying the instruction based upon the evaluation. Each step in this process is represented by several different techniques as shown in Figure 9.1.

FIGURE 9.1.   Directive teaching technology (Reprinted from Thomas M. Stephens, *Implementing behavioral approaches in elementary and secondary schools*. Columbus, Ohio: Charles E. Merrill, 1975, p. 78.)

1.0   Techniques for gathering descriptive information
.10 interviewing
.11 establishing rapport
.12 planning
.13 greeting students
.14 selecting initial tasks
.15 obtaining information
.16 closing the interview

.20 surveying
.21 surveying groups to identify students
.22 surveying groups to identify instructional needs

.30 simulating tasks
.31 selecting tasks
.32 assigning tasks
.33 observing student responses

.40 criterion-referenced measures
.41 determining prerequisite responses and skills
.42 identifying skills, concepts, and attitudes to be developed
.43 selecting and using sample items
.44 establishing instructional criteria

.50 observational techniques
.51 obtaining baseline information
.52 describing behavior
.53 quantifying behavior
.54 recording observations

2.0 Designing learning environments
.10 arranging physical conditions
.11 establishing reward areas
.12 establishing work areas

.20 developing psychological environments
.21 positive attitudes toward others
.22 rewarding attempts
.23 rewarding performance
.24 non-reinforcing of maladaptive performance

.30 arranging time modules
.31 establishing instructional time
.32 establishing reward time
.33 sequencing instructional time

3.0 Designing instructional strategies
.10 selecting instructional tasks
.11 determining terminal criteria
.12 selecting instructional media
.13 identifying incentives
.14 scheduling reinforcement
.15 devising delivery of reinforcement

4.0 Implementing instructional strategies
.10 providing instruction
.11 initiating instruction
.12 maintaining on-task responses
.13 rewarding performance

.20 evaluating instruction

.30 modifying instruction
.31 selecting new instructional strategies

Much of the technology shown in Figure 9.1 is built into DTIMS. Components 1.0, 3.0, and 4.0 are a part of the organized assessment and instructional strategies materials, while component 2.0 is represented by a handbook for teachers which suggests ways that they can arrange their learning environments.

DTIMS is designed to facilitate individualized instruction and to provide an organizational system for teachers of handicapped children. The general objectives of the system are:

1. to develop instructional strategies which will insure systematic instruction;

2. to provide strategies for establishing positive classroom environments for handicapped learners;

3. to provide teachers with a systematic way of selecting, delivering, and recording instructional strategies; and

4. to monitor and evaluate the effects of instruction for each student.

DTIMS follows the four basic steps in the directive teaching model: assessment, planning, instruction, and evaluation (Stephens, 1970, 1976). Content consists of imperative skills in reading, arithmetic, and social behavior. Imperative skills are those which all children are expected to master in order to be successful in school. These imperative skills were identified through a survey of basic reading and arithmetic textbooks. Skills were included in the imperative lists if they appeared in two or more materials.

Approximately 140 imperative social skills were established through a content analysis of 12 published behavior checklists, particularly those designed for use with elementary or special education populations. Those behaviors which can be observed in a school setting were identified. A consensual validation of skills was obtained by presenting the list in questionnaire form to a group of regular and special educators (Milburn, 1974).

DTIMS permits three different delivery systems: (1) manual, (2) batch, and (3) an interactive computer-managed system.

The manual system consists of materials organized to facilitate assessment, instruction, and evaluation. The skill statements, assessment tasks, instructional strategies, and references to commercial materials are presented. A reinforcement manual of directions and an assessment materials kit accompany each package.

The batch system is one of two DTIMS computer delivery options. When using the batch mode, the teacher selects skills from a sequential list and requests assessment tasks, instructional strategies, and coded materials by mail or telephone. A systems monitor inputs information and relays instructions and materials to the teacher via the mail. Time intervals between requests for and receipt of materials may vary from several hours to days. Because of delays, the batch system imposes additional planning demands on teachers, requiring assessment and instructional needs to be planned a few days in advance.

The interactive mode of delivery is a computerized system designed to meet teachers' requests almost immediately. Utilization of an interactive delivery system permits teachers to view skill lists, select skills, retrieve assessment tasks, report assessment results, select from available instructional alternatives based on student performance, retrieve teaching strategies, view coded materials, and to input information regarding length of instructional time and rate of learning or skill acquisition.

Components of DTIMS

Teachers are provided with the following products to assist them in individualizing instruction:

—specified performance objectives in reading, math, and social skills;
—criterion-referenced assessment tasks for each objective, keyed to commercial materials;
—performance criteria for each skill;
—teaching strategies keyed to commercial materials known to be available to the teachers;
—reinforcement tactics for use in conjunction with instruction.

The reading component contains over 300 imperative skill statements in levels kindergarten through the third year, a criterion-referenced assessment task with materials for each skill, a minimum of two instructional strategies per skill, and a coded reference to commercial texts for every skill.

The arithmetic component consists of imperative skill statements in kindergarten through level three, assessment tasks and materials, instructional strategies, and coded references are included for each skill.

Each social skill includes a behaviorally stated skill, an assessment task, and an instructional strategy. Included also are references to commercial texts and an index of references to problem behaviors.

Directive teaching skills are presented in small units, grouped by categories for quick reference. Arrangement is by sequence with each skill building on its prerequisite, progressing from elementary tasks to more complex ones.

Assessment Tasks

Assessment tasks provide teachers with specific information concerning skills each student has mastered and those each student has the prerequisite responses to learn. Each task includes a skill statement, 10 to 20 items for measuring the skill, a criterion score which indicates the acceptable level for meeting the task requirements, and directions to teachers for presenting the task to students. Figure 9.2 contains an example of one assessment task.

FIGURE 9.2.   Example of an assessment task

ASSESSMENT TASKS

Reading

Level 1

SO41
Student will listen to a short story and identify its appropriate topic.

Criterion: 5/5

Read story aloud to student and have him suggest main topic of story.

1)   *The Smoky House*
There were fire engines racing down the street. The house was full of smoke. The firefighters worked hard to put out the flames.

2)   *The Yellow Ball of Fur*
Peep-peep-peep-the babies were hatching from their eggs, one by one. The mother hen was very proud. There were 10 eggs, and out of each egg came a furry yellow ball.

3)   *The Ice Cream Truck*
Clang-clang-there comes the red truck. There is chocolate, vanilla, and strawberry ice cream. It is fun to hear the ice cream truck coming down the street.

4)   *The Postman*
Every day the man in the blue suit comes walking down our block. He carries a big brown bag. The bag can hold many letters. He is a very nice man and always says "Good Morning."

5)   *Too Cold to Play Outside Today*
The wind was blowing and it was snowing. Bill put on his snowsuit and went out to play. He was very cold and came back inside.

MODALITY: Auditory

MATERIALS: None

Instructional Strategies

An instructional strategy is equivalent to a teaching plan. Each strategy provides teachers with a skill statement, modalities to use in teaching, and an indication as to whether the strategy is intended for an individual or a small group.

Directions for teachers include what they are to say and/or do, a list of materials needed, and necessary responses from students. Teachers are directed to evaluate each performance following an instructional strategy. Included are guidelines for establishing a reinforcing environment, suggested teaching strategies, and a hierarchical arrangement of reinforcement, ranging from social events to objects. An instructional strategy is shown in Figure 9.3.

FIGURE 9.3.　A teaching strategy example

TEACHING STRATEGY

SO41
The student will listen to a short story and identify its appropriate topic.

MODALITY: Auditory

INDIVIDUAL OR SMALL GROUP

TEACHER ACTIVITY:
1. Plan reinforcement strategy from reinforcement menu.
2. Plan instruction.
   Teacher will say: "Listen to these two sentences. 'John went outside to play. He made a big snowman.'" "This story is about John making a snowman. What is it about?" _____ response. "Now listen to this one and see if you can guess what it is about. 'Mary ran to the swing. She began swinging very high. Soon she could not touch the ground.' What is this story about?" _____ "That's right, it is about Mary swinging." Continue with stories providing an opportunity for five correct responses. Make stories progressively longer until they involve several sentences.
   Provide reinforcement.

MATERIALS: None

STUDENT RESPONSE:
   Student will listen and respond by telling what story is about.
EVALUATION:
   Criterion: 5/5
   Criterion met? _____.
   If yes: Reassess using Assessment Task 041
   If no: Continue using same strategy or select new strategy.

Evaluating and Tracking Student Performances

Teachers are requested to evaluate performance throughout the instructional process. Results are recorded as follows:

—student performance during instruction;
—evaluation of reinforcement strategy;
—student performance on reassessment; and
—amount of time required for instruction between initial assessment and reassessment.

The above information is recorded on a pupil profile form when using the system manually. A computer-managed system may also be used for those teachers having access to a computer terminal.

The computer capacity for storage and retrieval is used to aid teachers in record keeping and planning, provide administrators with accountability and cost information, and to answer research questions regarding rate of skill acquisition, amount of time required for instruction, and sequence of skill acquisition.

Applications

DTIMS provides a systematic presentation of skills. It is used to present reading, math, and social skills to handicapped learners in small, sequenced units on an individualized basis. It is also useful as an initial program of assessment for structuring individual programs of instruction and for identifying groups of children needing the same skill instruction. It may also be used as a tutorial program. Tutors can use the material for assessing, teaching, reinforcing, and evaluating individuals or groups of children.

There are several implications for classroom instruction. Users can be expected to know and use much more specific information than is typically available to teachers. They should be able to demonstrate a student's progress on specific academic and social skills, his or her individual rate of learning, and time/cost factors.

By using a computer delivery system, teachers can readily establish flexible grouping patterns based on student performance data provided via the terminal. While the use of DTIMS will not reduce the amount of teacher time for planning, it should facilitate individualized instruction by effectively structuring the teaching/learning process and by optimizing learning for each student.

Training for Using DTIMS

The DTIMS environment has the potential to create different and perhaps more imaginative personnel roles. For example, special education consultants may serve as contact personnel for teachers. When instruction is delivered via the computer, monitoring of student performances can be done systematically. The special education consultant can identify which students and teachers are in need of immediate assistance by merely tracking the daily performances of students via computer printouts.

The type of instruction required within DTIMS has implications for training personnel in the use of the system. Teachers and other school personnel have been trained to use the system as a part of their instructional responsibilities, and special training modules have been field tested with teaching personnel. Training time for experienced teachers tends to average 60 clock hours. Regular follow-up assistance to teachers in their classroom is provided throughout the school year.

In addition to training personnel to use the system, changes in teacher attitudes are necessary if they are to be successful in using DTIMS. Teachers, principals, and other related school personnel will need to accept the basic premises of the system (Cooper, 1974). These include:

1. assessing student performance against the instructional content (as contrasted with "diagnosing" the student's problems);

2. viewing students' learning difficulties as instructional problems rather than student failure;

3. systematically using incentives to encourage student responses;

4. evaluating student learning in systematic and specific ways.

Through the use of systems such as DTIMS, L&BD students can be instructed effectively (Stephens, Cooper, & Hartman, 1973). As a result of such instruction, many of these children can be taught to acquire academic and social skills within regular education programs.

Reading, Arithmetic, and Social Skills[2]

The Directive Teaching Instructional Management System's curriculum consists of skills in reading, arithmetic, and social behavior. Criterion measures to be used for assessing students and instructional strategies are available for each skill. Teachers are trained to use these materials and to use classroom management tactics.

DTIMS Reading Skills

Reading skills currently in the DTIMS program are for students functioning at a prereading level through third grade. The major categories are Auditory Discrimination, Comprehension, Oral Reading, Phonetic Analysis, Structural Analysis, Sight Words, Visual Discrimination.

These skills are identified initially through an analysis of the seven most frequently used texts at those grade levels in Ohio.

FIGURE 9.4.   Structure of DTIMS reading curriculum

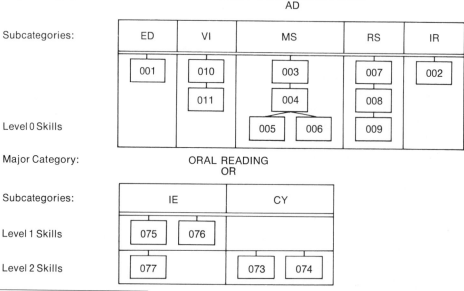

2. DTIMS reading, arithmetic, and social skills are listed in *Teaching children with basic skills*, a curriculum handbook by Stephens, Hartman, and Lucas, Columbus: Charles E. Merrill, 1978.

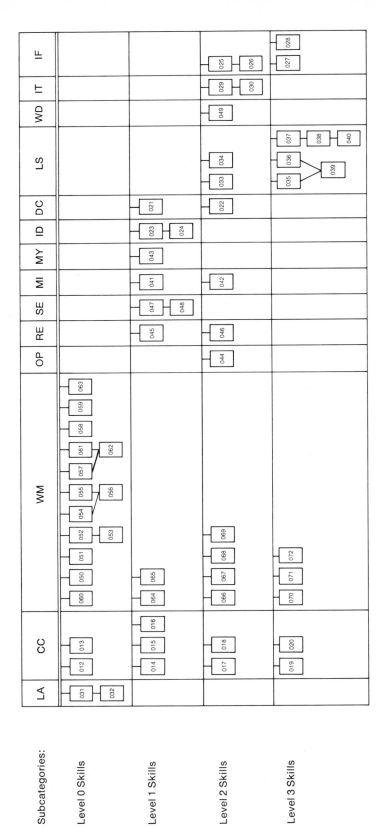

FIGURE 9.4. continued

257

PHONETIC ANALYSIS
PA

Major Category:

Subcategories:

Level 1 Skills

Level 2 Skills

Level 3 Skills

258

FIGURE 9.4. continued

STRUCTURAL ANALYSIS
SA

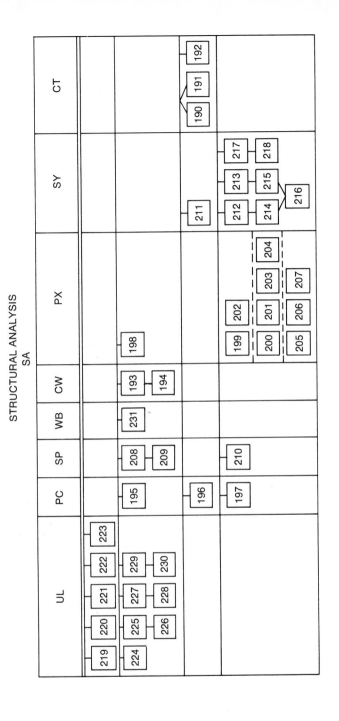

FIGURE 9.4. continued

259

FIGURE 9.4. continued

Major Category:

SIGHT WORD RECOGNITION
SW

Subcategories:	PP	PI	FI	SN	TH
Level 1 Skills	236 237 238 239 240 241	234 235	232 233		
Level 2 Skills				242 243 246 245	
Level 3 Skills					246 247 248 249

Major Category:

VISUAL DISCRIMINATION
VD

Subcategories:	LD				MT		RP			RL				RN	
Level 0 Skills	250	251	252	253	254	255	256	265	266	267	257	258	259	260	262	263

    The DTIMS skill list in reading is structured as shown in Figure 9.4. It provides a quick summary of the way the reading curriculum is organized. For example, skill 001 is found under major category Auditory Discrimination and subcategory Environmental Discrimination. This list represents reading skills for school-aged children functioning at a prereading level through the third year of school. Teachers can use these skills for (a) developing criterion-referenced assessment and evaluation measures, (b) using an observation checklist for determining which of these skills have not been mastered by selected target students, and (c) making teaching plans.

DTIMS Arithmetic Skills

Arithmetic skills currently in the DTIMS program are for students functioning at a prearithmetic level through third grade. The major categories are Measurement, Numbers, Numerals and Numeration Systems, Operations and Properties, and Sets.

    These skills were initially identified through an analysis of the seven most frequently used texts at those grade levels in Ohio. The curriculum structure is shown in Figure 9.5. This list represents arithmetic skills for school-aged children functioning at a prearithmetic level through the third year of school. Teachers may use these skills for (a) developing criterion-referenced assessment and evaluation measures, (b) using an observation checklist for determining which of these skills have not been mastered by selected target students, and (c) making teaching plans.

FIGURE 9.5. Structure of DTIMS arithmetic curriculum

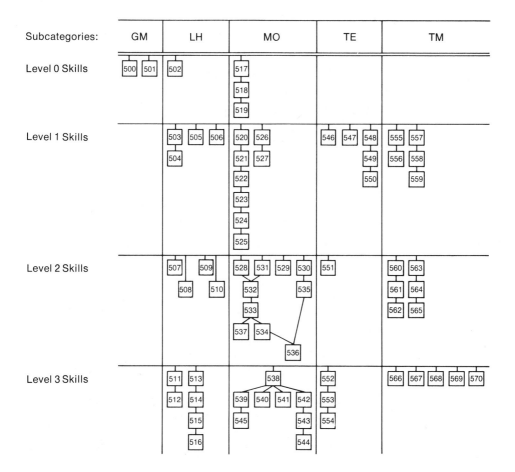

FIGURE 9.5. continued

Major Category: NUMBERS, NUMERALS & NUMERATION SYSTEMS
NN

Subcategories:	CR	NU	OE	ON	PV	RA	RM
Level 0 Skills	571 575 572 576 573 577 574 578 579	580 581 582 583 584	604 605	610 611		630	
Level 1 Skills		585 586 587 588 589 590 591 592 593	606 607 608 609		614 615 616 617 618	631 633 635 632 634 636	
Level 2 Skills		594 595 596		612	620 626 621 622 623 624 625	637 638 640 642 645 639 641 643 644	654
Level 3 Skills		597 601 598 602 599 600 603		613	627 628 629	646 647 648 652 649 650 651 653	655 656

262

FIGURE 9.5. continued

Major Category:

OPERATIONS & THEIR PROPERTIES
OT

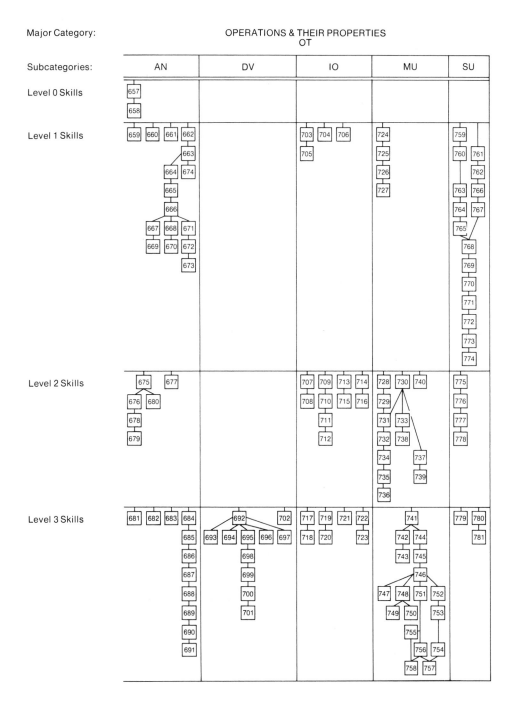

FIGURE 9.5. continued

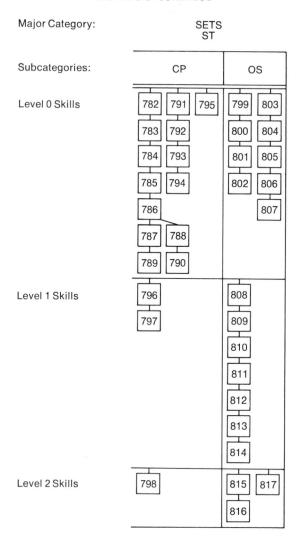

DTIMS Social Skills

Social behavior can be taught in two ways in the DTIMS program. The first is through management tactics where students are rewarded or punished for their behaviors. In this way, L&BD students learn what the effects of their desirable and/or undesirable behaviors will have upon them. Instruction in this approach may occur through classroom management tactics, which are discussed in chapter 10, and by teaching social behavior, covered more fully in chapter 11.

A second way that students are taught appropriate social behavior is through a purposefully planned instructional program. In such a program students' behaviors within the school setting are observed or assessed and those behaviors which they are not yet displaying sufficiently are taught. The DTIMS program provides a social behavior curriculum for this purpose.

Structurally, the DTIMS social skills curriculum contains four major categories and each of these is divided into subcategories as follows:

Environmental	*Interpersonal Relations*
Care for environment	Accepting authority
Dealing with emergency	Coping with conflict
Lunchroom	Gaining attention
Moving around environment	Greeting others
	Helping others
	Making conversation
	Organized play
	Positive attitude toward others
	Play informally
	Care of property
Self-related	*Task-related*
Accepting consequences	Asking and answering questions
Ethical behavior	Attending behavior
Expressing feelings	Classroom discussion
Positive attitude toward self	Completing tasks
Responsible behavior	Following directions
Self-care	Group activities
	Independent work
	On-task behavior
	Performing
	Quality of work

A list of social skills may be used by teachers to (a) identify those behaviors that are not yet prevalent among their pupils, (b) develop a checklist for use when observing target students, and (c) develop instructional plans.

Tracking and Reporting

Individualizing instruction for any group of students demands a method of tracking student progress and reporting that progress to teachers, students, and parents. DTIMS provides a means for both tracking students and reporting their progress.

Tracking Student Progress

One purpose of DTIMS is to provide teachers with specific information about those skills in the curriculum which students have already mastered, those skills which they have the necessary prerequisite responses to learn, and those skills which they are not yet ready to learn. In order to obtain the required information for planning instruction, students must first be assessed. Decisions regarding where to begin assessing skills with an individual student may be based on a number of considerations: age, school experience, previous performance data, and when known, specific skill deficits.

There are times when a teacher has little or no relevant information about a student's repertoire of skills. When this is the case it is suggested that an *entry level assessment* be used. The entry level assessments are shortened skill assessments which identify areas (major categories) of strengths and weaknesses. Results suggest where a teacher should begin assessing the student. The following is an example of the reading entry level assessment for level three.

Reading Entry Level Assessment (Level 3)

1. (A020)
   Please find these words in the dictionary by using the guidewords

                                                                YES   NO 3/3

       A. Center
       B. Mouth
       C. Umbrella

2. (A024)
   Read only the sentences which involve conversation

       One day John went for a walk. He asked his brother to
   come with him. "Bob, would you like to take a walk?"   YES   NO 3/3
   "Yes, I would like to go with you." When they got back
   from their walk their mother asked, "Where did you
   go?"

3. (A039)
   Please listen to the following questions and tell me where you would go to find this
   information
       a) Where would you look to find how many pages a   YES   NO 3/3
          particular story has?
       b) Where in your science book would you look to find a
          chapter on planets?
       c) Where would you look to find the pronunciation of
          the word *dinosaur* in your science book?

4. (A072)
   Please look at these words and tell me what they mean.
       Sale   3/3
       War
       Even
   Now tell me what these words mean.

       a) Resale   YES   NO
       b) Prewar
       c) Uneven

5. (A129)
   Please read these words
       A. Enough   YES   NO 3/3
       B. Rough
       C. Laugh

6. (A179)
   I will read the first part of the following words. Please supply the ending (*ment* or *tion*).   YES   NO 3/3
       A. Excite
       B. Act   ment or
       C. Govern   tion

7. (A197)
   Please read these sentences and put in the correct punctuation (question marks,
   periods, commas, quotation marks, exclamation points)
       A. Mother said Where did Mary go   YES   NO 3/3
       B. Help help my house is on fire
       C. I'm going swimming on Friday

8. (A202)
   Please point to and read the root word in the following words:
   A. Careless   YES   NO   3/3
   B. Undress
   C. Preview

9. (A207)
   Please add "er" and write the following words:
   A. Lazy   YES   NO   3/3
   B. Funny
   C. Bumpy

10. (A210)
    Please write the plural form of the following:
    A. shelf   YES   NO   3/3
    B. knife
    C. life

11. (A216)
    Please divide these words into syllables:
    A. Animal   YES   NO   3/3
    B. Reproduce
    C. Radio

12. (A249)
    Please read the following sentences:
    A. Do not laugh at other's mistakes   YES   NO   3/3
    B. I work for the government
    C. The system is complete

Once teachers have determined which skills are to be assessed, they locate the assessment tasks in the *DTIMS Skill Assessment Book*. The materials required to carry out the assessments are coded to the skill number. Reading skills range in number from S001 to S267. Math skills are numbered from S500 to S817; the same number is also attached to all other material related to a particular skill but the prefix letter changes.

Based on students' performances on assessment tasks, one of the following decisions is made:

1. If criterion (mastery 90-100%) is met, select new higher level assessment task and repeat assessment procedure.

2. If score is at frustration level (below 70%), select other lower level assessment task and repeat assessment procedure.

3. If score is within instructional range (70%-90%), select materials for instruction.

As assessments are completed, teachers record results on the Biweekly Update Form. The assessment number, the date, and student's performance are recorded. The teacher circles *M, I,* or *F* for Mastery, Instructional, or Frustration and *Pr* if it is a preassessment as shown in Figure 9.6.

FIGURE 9.6. DTIMS biweekly update: Assessments conducted

DTIMS BIWEEKLY UPDATE

Page _____ of _____

Date |_|_|_|_|_|_|
Month Day Year

TEACHER'S NAME _____ I.D. |_|_|_|
        Last   First   MI
SCHOOL _____ |_|_|_| |_|_|_| |_|_|_|
                                 Area Code   Telephone Number
CITY _____ STATE |_|_| ZIP |_|_|_|_|_|

STUDENT NAME _____ I.D. _____
        Last   First   MI

		Date				Circle one RANGE			Circle one	
ASSESSMENTS CONDUCTED										
Line No.	Assessment Number	Month	Day	Year	Performance	Frus-tration	Instruc-tional	Mastery	Pre	Post
1	A				/	F	I	M	PR	PO
2	A				/	F	I	M	PR	PO
3	A				/	F	I	M	PR	PO
4	A				/	F	I	M	PR	PO
5	A				/	F	I	M	PR	PO
6	A				/	F	I	M	PR	PO
7	A				/	F	I	M	PR	PO
8	A				/	F	I	M	PR	PO
9	A				/	F	I	M	PR	PO
10	A				/	F	I	M	PR	PO
11	A				/	F	I	M	PR	PO
12	A				/	F	I	M	PR	PO
13	A				/	F	I	M	PR	PO
14	A				/	F	I	M	PR	PO
15	A				/	F	I	M	PR	PO
16	A				/	F	I	M	PR	PO

Once a skill or group of skills has been identified on which a student requires instruction, teachers may select an instructional strategy from those provided in the *Strategy Book*. There are two strategy books, one for reading and one for arithmetic. Each teacher also receives a commercial reference listing. The commercial materials references cite pages in printed texts where particular skills are found. These are intended to be used as additional sources of instructional suggestions for teachers' use. Teachers record all information regarding their instruction on the back of the Biweekly Update Form. They fill in the strategy number, or Commercial Reference Code, the date and indicate if they found the material satisfactory or unsatisfactory by circling *S* or *U* as shown in Figure 9.7.

FIGURE 9.7 DTIMS biweekly update: Strategies or references used

	STRATEGIES OR COMMERCIAL REFERENCES USED									
Line No.	Circle one		Code		Commercial Reference No. Use Only With C.R.	Date			Circle one	
	Stra-tegies	Commercial References				Mo	Day	Year	Satis-Factory	Unsatis-Factory
1	ST	CR		—					S	U
2	ST	CR		—					S	U
3	ST	CR		—					S	U
4	ST	CR		—					S	U
5	ST	CR		—					S	U
6	ST	CR		—					S	U
7	ST	CR		—					S	U
8	ST	CR		—					S	U
9	ST	CR		—					S	U
10	ST	CR		—					S	U
11	ST	CR		—					S	U
12	ST	CR		—					S	U
13	ST	CR		—					S	U
14	ST	CR		—					S	U
15	ST	CR		—					S	U
16	ST	CR		—					S	U
17	ST	CR		—					S	U
18	ST	CR		—					S	U
19	ST	CR		—					S	U
20	ST	CR		—					S	U
21	ST	CR		—					S	U
22	ST	CR		—					S	U
23	ST	CR		—					S	U
24	ST	CR		—					S	U

Following implementation of instructional strategies, teachers are requested to reassess students using the same assessment tasks. Students' performances are recorded on the front of the Biweekly Update Form. They record the assessment number, date, performance, circle *M, I* or *F*, they also circle *PO* for post assessment.

If criterion is met on reassessment, teachers select new skills. If criterion is not met, teachers select a new teaching strategy and continue instruction, following the same procedures listed above.

Reporting Student Progress

The Biweekly Update Form is the only form teachers are required to complete. This profile is then used as the basis for computerized record keeping. Note that students do not interact with the computer and the computer does not tell the teacher how to teach.

DTIMS was designed to help teachers find which skills students need to learn and give them material and instructional strategies to help teach those skills. The computer is used for recordkeeping and for reporting student progress.

After teachers record assessment and strategy data, this information is fed into the computer. The information stored for each child is continually updated and teachers receive individual progress reports on each student every other week. Figure 9.8 shows a performance record for a group of students.

Teachers may request information at any time concerning a student's performance within a specific subcategory or they may request a group profile. Teachers complete a Report Request Form, filling in the student's name, identification number, the subcategory and the level. They then receive a report indicating the student's level of performance (mastery, instructional, or frustration) for each skill within that subcategory.

FIGURE 9.8.   DTIMS student progress report

DTIMS Student Performance Record

barb meyer, teacher   2/02/76

comprehension/word meaning/level 0

m s050 point to own name from set of name cards
m s051 point to correct colored object when given color name
m s052 point to left or right side of object
m s053 point to left or right side of picture
m s054 point to front of an object
n s055 point to back of an object
i   s056 point to back or front of a 2-d object
i   s057 point to top of object
f   s058 point to biggest object
f   s059 point to smallest object
n s060 point to beginning or end of words
n s061 point to the bottom of an object
n s062 point to bottom or top of a 2-d pictured object
n s063 point to common objects in room when given name

DTIMS Student Skill Status

al kohol   (s888)   2/02/76

– reading –

| id | name | last date sys. used | post-instruct. masteries | pre-instruct. masteries | |
				asmts	ela's
1000	ben zedreen	1/22/76	0	2	0
1001	sal ivate	1/13/76	516	2	3
1002	barb meyer	2/02/76	517	6	3
1003	rick o'shea	2/02/76	535	4	0
1004	lynn o'lium	2/02/76	395	3	0
1005	jerry attrix	1/09/76	14	0	0
1006	janet orr	1/27/76	1	3	1
1030	gene murdock	1/20/76	0	0	0

– mathematics –

| id | name | last date sys. used | post-instruct. masteries | pre-instruct. masteries | |
				asmts	ela's
1000	ben zedreen	1/22/76	0	0	0
1001	sal ivate	1/13/76	514	1	2
1002	barb meyer	2/02/76	533	0	0
1003	rick o'shea	2/02/76	378	0	0
1004	lynn o'lium	2/02/76	533	0	0
1005	jerry attrix	1/09/76	19	0	0
1006	janet orr	1/27/76	0	0	0
1030	gene murdock	1/20/76	1	1	1

xmit →

SKILL DATA

| | First Pretest | | | Most Recent Posttest | | | Instructional Materials Used | | |
SKILL #	Date	Criterion	MIF	Date	Criterion	MIF	ST	CR	Total
S045	09/06	08/10	I	09/20	10/10	M	045-01		1
S056	09/10	05/10	F	09/29	10/10	M	056-02	1120	2
S023	09/10	07/10	I	09/28	09/10	M	023-01	0769	2
S011	09/10	12/15	I	09/28	13/15	M		0890	1
S017	09/10	17/20	I	09/28	19/20	M	017-02	0900	2
S505	09/12	18/20	I	09/28	19/20	M		0820	1
S511	09/12	09/10	M						
S712	09/12	05/20	F						
S105	09/15	08/10	I	10/15	09/10	M	105-01	1930	2
S106	09/15	05/10	F						
S129	09/15	08/10	I						
S154	09/20	09/10	M						
S657	09/20	08/10	I	10/15	10/10	M	657-01	3320	2
S715	09/20	10/15	I	10/19	12/15	I		3890	1
S752	09/25	11/20	F						
S783	09/25	14/14	M						
S808	09/25	08/10	I						

Using the same Report Request Form, teachers may request a Group Profile by circling *G* (for group), filling in the name of the student, the student's identification number, the subcategory, and circling the level. They then receive the DTIMS Group Profile listing all the students working in that subcategory and their identification numbers. It lists the skills found in that subcategory and the level of performance of each student. Teachers can then work with groups of students who need instruction on the same skill, as seen in Figure 9.9.

FIGURE 9.9.   DTIMS group profile

AL KOHOL   10/19/75

MATHEMATICS: OPERATIONS AND THEIR PROPERTIES
                                                                         ADDITION
                                                                         LEVEL: 2

	ID	NAME
	1000	BEN ZEDREEN
	1001	SAL IVATE
	1002	BARB MEYER
	1003	RICK O'SHEA
	1004	LYNN O'LIUM
	1005	JERRY ATTRIX
	1006	JANET ORR

SKILL NUMBERS

STUDENT ID	675	676	677	678	679	680
1000	I	I	M	F	F	N
1001	I	F	M	N	N	N
1002	M	I	I	I	I	N
1003	I	I	I	F	N	N
1004	M	I	M	I	I	N
1005	I	F	F	N	N	N
1006	N	N	N	N	N	N

DTIMS is a flexible system for instructing students in small sequential steps. It is flexible because it can be used in the following way:

1. Total Program—DTIMS provides systematic presentation of skills that can be utilized as an entire program of instruction.
2. Initial Grouping for Instruction—DTIMS provides the basis for structuring individual programs through assessment.
3. Tutorial Program—DTIMS can be used in a one-to-one tutoring situation or small group.
4. Supplemental to Program for Target Students—DTIMS provides supplemental instruction that can be used with students needing remedial work on basic skills.

Summary

As skill training approaches become more prevalent, materials and entire instructional programs will be more readily available. Because skill training is based on direct observation and performance, it easily relates to instructional techniques. The Directive Teaching Instructional Management System is one program within the skill training orientation. It provides a way to individualize instruction and provides teachers with assessment and instructional plans, management suggestions, and a student reporting and tracking system.

10

Classroom Management

Competent teachers of L&BD students must be effective classroom managers. There is research evidence which relates classroom behavior to academic success.

Among the practical strategies that effective classroom teachers can use in their daily management of learning are positive reinforcement, timeout, learning centers, social rewards, interest centers, special privileges, job boards, home/school activities, tokens with backup reinforcers, and object rewards.

Introduction

In an extensive review of teaching methods for the behaviorally disordered, Swift and Spivak (1974) found that classroom instruction was differentiated for three general behavior categories: inattentiveness and short attention span, anxiety, and classroom disturbances (e.g., restlessness, blaming external forces, hyperactivity, aggression, and defiance). While some studies were found that dealt with specific tactics for each of the behavior categories, only a limited number of research studies were located. When considering the extent of maladaptive behavior in classrooms, the small number of studies on this topic is surprising.

In one such study, Becker and others (1968) demonstrated the contingent use of teacher attention and praise in reducing classroom behavior problems. They found that regular classroom teachers learned to apply behavioral tactics effectively in modifying problem students' behaviors. Their results suggested that rules alone are ineffective and that ignoring deviant responses may actually increase such behavior. But ignoring deviant behavior combined with rewarding an incompatible behavior effectively reduces maladaptive responses.

Lovitt (1973) described seven successful self-management projects. In one instance a pupil was instructed to schedule, correct, and chart his own behavior. In a second study, math and reading skills were taught by the teacher and student, alternately selecting which of the two subjects would be initially scheduled. In another situation, the pupil earned the privilege of self-scheduling. Two studies trained students to record their own maladaptive behavior. In a sixth study, effects of a pupil specifying his own contingencies were considered. And in a final study, a group of students were taught to correct, count, time, chart, and evaluate their own performances in reading.

The use of delayed timeouts has been studied as a tactic for reducing disruptive classroom behavior (Ramp, Ulrich, & Dulaney, 1971). In this study, a nine-year-old boy's disruptive behavior was eliminated by shining a light on his desk, indicating the loss of free time later in the day. The power of timeout was demonstrated by discontinuing the use of the light and timeout. When this was done, disruptive behavior returned to its previous level. The use of verbal instructions alone was ineffective in reducing the frequency of maladaptive behavior.

Soloman and Wahler (1973) demonstrated the use of peer reinforcement as a means of controlling disruptive classroom behavior. In their study five disruptive children were observed in an elementary school classroom. During the baseline period, attention from peers was found to be directed exclusively to the problem behaviors. But when peer social attention was manipulated, the maladaptive behavior of the target students diminished. One interesting feature of this study involved training the peer group in using differential reinforcement and extinction. They were also trained to identify disruptive behavior and were taught how to ignore it.

Teachers who have frequent classroom management problems often resort to punishment in attempting to reduce disruptions. While punishment does have limited effectiveness, it seldom affects behavior in permanent ways. Often it only stops behavior temporarily. When punishment is discontinued, maladaptive behavior is likely to reappear. Punishment is most effective when used immediately following maladaptive behavior. In such cases, however, it is important to reward desirable behavior also; in this way students will learn what is appropriate as well as how not to behave.

Risley (1968) demonstrated how carefully selected and used punishment tactics could be effective in a laboratory setting. After failing to eliminate disruptive and dangerous behavior of an autistic child through the use of timeout procedures and reinforcing incompatible behaviors, he used electric shock to eliminate dangerous climbing behavior. He found that this form of punishment only eliminated the dangerous behavior in the specific stimulus setting. Another aspect of this study was that no bad side effects of punishment, such as suppression of other behaviors, were found.

Classroom behavior contributes to academic performance and other school learning. Haubrich and Shores (1976) studied five upper-elementary-aged children in a residential treatment center for emotionally disturbed children. They investigated the relationship of attending behavior to academic performance. Two types of treatment were used: cubicles and contingent reinforcement. Each treatment was used for ten days.

They found that both cubicle and contingent reinforcement conditions improved attending behavior over baseline conditions. The reinforcement conditions, however, produced significantly higher rates of attending than did cubicles. Only the reinforcement condition showed a significant increase in academic performance. These findings replicated those of an earlier study (Shores & Haubrich, 1969) which showed that while cubicles increased attending behavior they did not increase academic performance.

Graubard (1971) concluded that teachers of emotionally disturbed children find about the same amount of academic retardation among their students (ages 9 to 14) as do regular classroom teachers. He found a greater amount of low academic performance among those students considered to be *conduct problems*. Because of this finding, he encouraged a greater emphasis on problems of managing and motivating disturbed students.

Noffsinger (1971) studied 45 junior high, potential dropout students, classifying them according to deviant classroom behaviors. He found no differences between classification of students and hypothesized differences and levels of aspiration. He did find, however, that setting a high level of aspiration had a significant positive effect on academic performance.

In a two-year study, Glavin, Quay, and Werry (1971) demonstrated improved academic performance and social behavior in a special class program. In the first year, they emphasized eliminating deviant behaviors and acquiring attending behaviors as precursors for academic improvement. They changed the program emphasis in the second year to stress rewarding academic performances. They concluded that their findings tended to refute the commonly held belief that maladaptive behavior of emotionally disturbed children must be changed first before stressing academic performance.

The above brief review suggests that effective classroom management of L&BD students can contribute to better social behavior as well as to improved academic achievement. Some L&BD students can be trained to collect and maintain records of their own conduct. establish a plan for improvement, modify their behavior, and evaluate the effects of their treatment. In situations where students cannot be trained to carry out such practices, behavioral technology is effective for use by trained teaching personnel.

Classroom Management[1]

This chapter is designed for teachers, tutors, aides, and other school personnel. The major emphasis is on positive approaches to classroom management. First, there is a discussion of principles of positive reinforcement. Second, components of a reinforcing environment are described. The final section contains the reinforcement menu consisting of suggestions for rewarding good behavior and performance.

Using Reinforcement

Systematic reinforcement within a classroom setting is a powerful way to improve social and academic behaviors. Classroom teachers issue many rewards to students. Reinforcers may be verbal praise and criticism, assignment of letter grades, special privileges, permission to use the restroom or get a drink of water, stars, smiling faces, and a host of other common everyday occurrences.

Teacher attention and verbal comments have been demonstrated to be powerful reinforcers, and the systematic use of praise is essential for effective classroom management. A specific statement of the behavior which is to be reinforced helps a teacher to become more systematic. For example, the teacher can say: "Morticia, when you finish this worksheet (specific task) you may write on the board for three minutes (reward)," or "Egbert, you work so quietly (specific task), when you finish, you may feed the fish (reward)."

---

1. Adapted from the *DTIMS Classroom Management Handbook* with permission of T. M. Stephens, all rights reserved. Permission to reprint should be directed to the author. Dr. A. Carol Hartman, Director, Dr. Virginia Lucas, Consultant, and the 1973-74 DTIMS Project personnel's efforts are appreciated and acknowledged.

There are many situations where rewards can increase teachers' effectiveness with children. Some typical opportunities for using reinforcement procedures are described below.

Association of Responses

When a correct response is reinforced, students associate that reinforcement with the correct response.

Ex. 1: *Teacher:* "Clementine, your work is complete and correct (correct response). You may take the lunch count to the office (reinforcement)." Clementine may think, "When I finish my work correctly, the teacher lets me do special things."

Ex. 2: *Morris:* "I want to do all my spelling words right today."
Teacher: "Morris, I like hearing you say positive things."
Morris may think, "The teacher likes me to say positive things."

Shaping Responses

Cuing. Giving clues to right answers helps students to be successful, permits teachers to reinforce, and encourages students to keep working on difficult tasks.

Ex. 1: *Teacher:* "Yesterday we talked about the words which sound alike but are spelled differently. Can someone give me an example?"
Sabbatha: "S-o and s-e-w."
Teacher: "Very good. We call sound-alike words homophones. Now Sabbatha, can you tell me the name for sound-alike words?"
Sabbatha: "Homophones."
Teacher: "Very good."

Ex. 2: *Teacher:* "This morning in music we sang a song. Some of the words ended alike. We say that words which sound alike at the end rhyme. Can someone tell we what we call words that end alike, like *bun* and *run?*"
Columbine: "Rhyming words."
Teacher: "That's right!"

Approximations. Often a teacher's expectations for pupil's behaviors are set at a level beyond the pupil's present level of functioning. When this is the case the pupil will rarely be reinforced because he or she never exhibits the behavior. For such instances, the teacher may use successive approximations. When a student attempts a difficult task, the teacher may at first reinforce responses that are approximately correct. Reinforcement of this sort encourages students to continue to try.

Ex. 1: *Teacher:* "Melba, I see that you are working very hard on your word math problems. You have selected the important numbers in the problem and you do subtract. That's excellent. Now let's see if together we can decide what to do next to solve the problem."

Ex. 2: *Teacher:* "Bob, your writing lesson looks very good to me today. Every single word is correctly spelled. I think that is worth 5 tokens. Now we need to work on spacing the words better. Perhaps tomorrow you could work on leaving a space between the words."

Strengthening Responses

When teaching pupils new responses begin by using reinforcement on a continuous basis, e.g., reinforce the correct response every time it occurs. After the behavior is well established change from a continous schedule of reinforcement to an intermittent one. When the rate of reinforcement is changed, the student will keep working and develop good work habits.

Ex. 1: At first, every time Harvey reads a sentence correctly the teacher gives him a token. After Harvey becomes regularly successful, the teacher will reinforce him at the end of each paragraph, and then each page. Harvey continues to work hard because he has associated the teacher's pleasure with his improvement, the tokens, and his own success.

Ex. 2: Zelda is often out of her seat. The teacher tells Zelda that for every three minutes she remains in her seat she earns one minute of plant watering time (a job we have observed Zelda really enjoys). This system worked well for Zelda, so after several days, the teacher begins to increase her demands on Zelda, five minutes, then ten, etc. Gradually, Zelda becomes task oriented, needing less and less reinforcement for staying in her seat.

Reinforcement Models

Two reinforcement models are direct reinforcement and contingency contracting.

Direct reinforcement.   This is a system by which a student freely responds, and the consequences of that response determines the probability of the reoccurrence of that particular response. Initially the student does not know which behaviors will be reinforced.

Ex. 1: Myrtle is correcting her spelling words. The teacher says, "Myrtle, I am happy to see you working on spelling. Here is a Happy Face for your paper."

Ex. 2: Herbert reads a story, stopping at periods. The teacher says, "Herbert, you read so nicely today, observing all the periods, you may choose a game for us."

Contingency contracting.   This system elicits desired responses by informing students in advance which behaviors will be rewarded. Teacher and pupil contract for performing specific tasks, and the teacher agrees to provide specific rewards upon the pupils' completion of the task. When the contract involves a continuing arrangement over several days or weeks, the contract should be put in writing and signed by teacher and pupil.

Ex. 1: The teacher says, "Calomine, when you finish the worksheet, you may paint for ten minutes this afternoon."

Ex. 2: The teacher says, "Lionel, when you complete four subtraction problems in five minutes, you will earn one token."

Ex. 3: The teacher says, "When you complete all seatwork assignments on time for two consecutive days, you may be 'teacher assistant' for two days." (This one should be written.)

Reinforcement Schedules

Reinforcement may either be continuous or intermittent. Continuous reinforcement is appropriate for teaching new behaviors. In such instances the teacher begins by reinforcing every time the response occurs. After the behavior has been established, the schedule of reinforcement is changed to an intermittent level. Gradually, the amount of behavior required for rewards is increased.

Continuous.   When every desired response is reinforced, the reinforcement schedule is continuous.

Ex: Agatha is told by the teacher, "Every time I see you try to do your work I will give you a token.

Intermittent.   When every desired response is not reinforced, the reinforcement schedule is intermittent.

1. *Fixed interval*

   Fixed interval is reinforcement of the first correct response that is emitted after a fixed amount of time, e.g., every five minutes. The actual interval may change from one reinforcement to the next depending upon rate of response.

Ex: The teacher gives Clarence a minute of interest center time if after a fixed interval, e.g., five minutes, he is on task.

2. *Variable interval*

   Variable interval is reinforcement given at a random interval, e.g., two, five, eight, three, ten minutes. The interval changes randomly from one reinforcement to the next.

   Ex: The teacher gives Heathcliffe a minute of interest center time if after a variable number of minutes he is on task, e.g., one, three, two, eight, three, ten minutes.

3. *Fixed ratio*

   Reinforcement is established for a fixed number of desired responses. The required number of responses is fixed and does not change between reinforcements.

   Ex: Howard receives a minute of interest center time for every five correct math problems.

4. *Variable ratio*

   Reinforcement is established for a variable number of desired responses — every four, one, three, eight, four responses.

   Ex: Jorgensen receives a minute of interest center time for varying number of correct and complete math problems, e.g., one, four, two, eight, five, ten.

Establishing a Reinforcing Environment

The vital part of a classroom environment is the application of reinforcement principles via a positive approach. That is, appropriate behavior is reinforced positively and inappropriate behavior is ignored. For example:

> An appropriate behavior is doing seatwork quietly in one's chair. We have observed that teacher attention is reinforcing to Juan. He doesn't care how he gets it, just so he gets it. A positive reinforcer for Juan would be teacher praise *when* he is working quietly in his chair. When he is out of his chair, he would be ignored and Carmen would be praised for working quietly in her chair. The eventual outcome is that Juan picks up the cue and returns to his chair and begins working quietly so that he will get the teacher's attention. Juan will quickly learn that to get the teacher's attention, he must be in his chair, working quietly.

At first Juan may not understand the *only* way to be rewarded is through appropriate behavior. In the past, the inappropriate behavior was reinforced on a random basis, e.g., teachers in the past had given him attention when he was out of his seat. When this reinforcer is removed, Juan may react by being more conspicuous, getting out of his seat more often. However, he will soon discover that in order to get teacher attention, he must be seated and work quietly.

The first step toward implementing reinforcement strategies in the classroom is to develop a positive approach. This approach ensures that appropriate behavior is being reinforced by the teacher and inappropriate behavior is not. The next step toward implementing positive reinforcement with students is assessing to determine which object, event, or activity is potentially reinforcing.

Three methods for gathering descriptive information concerning students' reward preferences are:

Observation — the teacher observes the pupil in the school environment and records the activities and/or objects that the pupil chooses when the opportunity for choice is provided.

Interview — the pupil is interviewed by the teacher in a structured manner where various potential reinforcers are presented and the pupil indicates his or her preferences.

Checklist — a list of potential rewards is presented to the pupil with instructions for him or her to check those he or she would prefer.

Observing

Teachers may observe target students' reward preferences. During free time activities within the classroom and/or on the playground, e.g., before school, recess, lunchtime, and after school, teachers can observe pupils as they make choices. They should record the activities and/or objects chosen by pupils.

More formal observations may be conducted by structuring situations in which pupils' choices are limited to activities and/or objects chosen by teachers. By allowing pupils to make a number of choices from different lists of potential reinforcers and then putting those reinforcers which were chosen on a list from which pupils again choose, it is possible to determine a hierarchy of reward preferences.

There are certain classes of behaviors which are particularly helpful to note — for example, those activities and objects for which pupils make requests are reinforcing events. Pupils who smile during an activity or after receiving an object are demonstrating that the preceding event was reinforcing to them. By noting these responses and the activities and/or objects associated with them, teachers are able to identify appropriate reinforcers for each pupil.

Interviewing

When interviewing, first identify a list of potential reinforcers that are available within the classroom and/or school. After preparing a list of potential reinforcers, interview the child. Begin with a general question and then describe, and when appropriate, show potential reinforcers to the child, two items at a time.

> Example: *Teacher:* "If given a choice after finishing an assignment, what activity that is available in the classroom, would you choose?
> *Student:* "I like listening to records."
> *Teacher:* "Now, I'm going to ask you to tell me which of two things you like better. When you finish an assignment, would you rather listen to a record at the listening center, or read *MAD* magazine?"
> *Student:* "Listen to a record."
> *Teacher:* "When you finish an assignment, would you rather listen to a record or play a game of tic-tac-toe with a friend?"
> *Student:* "Play a game of tic-tac-toe."

After identifying the most preferred reinforcer, assign the child a task and use the reward at the completion of the task. Observe the child's response.

A checklist may be used with a group of pupils. To design a checklist, identify a list of potential rewards and pupils to choose the five (or some other appropriate number) most preferred.

Sample Reinforcement Checklist

NAME _____

DATE _____

Read the list below. Ask yourself which of these things would I like most? Put the number 1 in the blank in front of your favorite. Put the number 2 in the blank next to the things you would like second. Continue until you have a number in every blank.

_____ Decorate my own desk
_____ Put up bulletin board for teacher
_____ Leave school 5 minutes early
_____ Staple papers for teacher
_____ Have my picture taken

_____ Visit the principal
_____ Be excused from homework or class assignment
_____ 5 minutes extra recess
_____ Move desk to front for day
_____ Be line leader
_____ Help teacher grade papers
_____ Go to school library

Another type of checklist consists of five potential reinforcers paired with each other where the pupil chooses his/her preferences for each pair. The teacher then tallies the number of times each item was chosen to determine the most preferred, second most preferred, and so on.

After the preferred potential reinforcer is identified, the teacher assigns the child a task, uses a reinforcement strategy with the identified reinforcer, observes the child's response, and records this information.

Issuing Rewards

A reward is any object or event which increases the probability of the occurrence of the behavior it follows. Rewards are listed here into seven categories in order of their availability in the natural classroom setting from most to least available. (Each of the categories is described in more detail and examples are provided in the reinforcement menu section.) Order of presentation also reflects a hierarchy of desirability in terms of their normal use to maintain social and academic behaviors. Social and symbolic rewards are used daily in nearly every classroom, but objects are rarely used. When selecting reinforcers to be used in the classroom, use reinforcers as high in the hierarchy as possible. In this way, you should be able to achieve quickly the goal of maintaining target behaviors with naturally occurring events.

When teachers find it necessary to use token or object reinforcers to establish an appropriate behavior, they should plan a procedure for phasing out the token or object and establishing other more naturally occurring reinforcers in order to maintain the behaviors. While teachers are encouraged to select rewards from categories nearest the top of the hierarchy, the selection must be reinforcing to the target child.

Plan reinforcement strategies for dealing with specific behavior after positive approach has been implemented in the classroom and the students have been assessed for appropriate reinforcers. Initially select an appropriate reward and then choose a reinforcement model.

Notes. One way of reinforcing students is through written notes. These notes may be:

on student's papers
to student's parents
to another teacher acquainted with the student
to the principal, custodian, secretary, cafeteria worker, anyone important to the student

The notes, of course, are positive. For example, the appropriate behavior for Josephine is finishing five subtraction problems in ten minutes.

When Josephine has completed the task, the teacher calls her over to her desk and says, "Josephine, I know you've worked very hard. And you've done a very good job. I'm going to write a note on the top of your paper so that you and your parents will know that I know how well you've done." Teacher writes on paper: "Josephine, this is very *good* work."

Before Josephine is given her paper, the teacher says, "Josephine, I know how well you can work. When you have finished this paper in ten minutes, and the timer rings, I will write a note on your paper telling you and your parents how very well you have done." When the task is completed in the allotted time, the note is written, with additional praise from the teacher.

Token economy. This is another method for rewarding in the classroom. The tokens can be in any tangible form — tickets, chips, bottle caps, popsicle sticks, points. These tokens are accumulated and may be redeemed by the student for special privileges, for "free time" or extra "free time," for time with the teacher, for time with a friend of student's choice, for jobs on the job board, for extra recess, and so forth. Examples:

1. The appropriate behavior for Jack is working on his 10 spelling words by writing one sentence for each spelling word. Jack has 20 minutes to complete his task.

Jack knows that he needs 15 chips in order to be able to buy 5 minutes of extra recess time. He does not know when he will earn these tokens. When he has completed the task, teacher calls Jack to her desk and says, "You really did a fine job on these sentences and you did it in the allotted time. Since you have done so well, I'll give you 3 chips. Nice work, Jack."

2. As teacher gives Jack his task, she says, "You will need to work very hard to do this in 20 minutes. When you have completed it in 20 minutes, you'll have earned 3 chips." If Jack completes the task, he is given the three chips. If he doesn't, then no chips are given, and *no comment is made.* Teacher may wish to give an encouraging remark, if he really worked hard, such as, "I know you worked hard. Next time I'll give you more time."

Contracts. Contracts contain a specified goal or objective for the student to meet in a given amount of time. For instance, Jeremy's written contract states that he is to complete Chapter III in his history book during the week of October 6 - 10. His contract reads: *Monday, read the chapter; Tuesday, outline it; Wednesday, answer the questions at the end of the chapter; Thursday, review chapter; Friday, take and pass the chapter test.* The contract may have been drawn up by Jeremy himself, by his teacher, or by Jeremy and the teacher together.

At the completion of each day's requirements, he will receive a check mark in the space provided on the contract. If on Friday he has 5 check marks, he may exchange them for a free period next Monday during History.

The daily evaluation of Jeremy's task may be done by Jeremy himself, by the teacher, or by both of them together. Either Jeremy or the teacher may provide the check mark on the contract at completion of each task. These alternatives should be determined before the contract is completed.

Verbal contracts may also be used. Example:

Teacher: "Jake, you may have 10 minutes of extra recess when you have completed your map of Asia."

Teacher: "You may show your paper to the principal when it is complete.

A verbal contract can also be initiated by a student, with students choosing the reward.

Peter: "Mrs. Jones, may I water the plants if I get 9 out of 10 of my math problems right?"

Susan: "If I type 70 words a minute this morning may I take the bulletin to the office?"

```
┌─────────────────────────────────────────────────────────────────────┐
│                              CONTRACT                                 │
│                                                                       │
│   Teacher  T. Jefferson                       Student  Jeremy Jones   │
│                           Date  10/5                                  │
├──────────────────────┬─────────────────────────────┬────────────────┤
│   Day                │           Task              │   Completed     │
├──────────────────────┼─────────────────────────────┼────────────────┤
│   Monday             │   Read Chapter III          │       X         │
├──────────────────────┼─────────────────────────────┼────────────────┤
│   Tuesday            │   Outline Chapter III       │       X         │
├──────────────────────┼─────────────────────────────┼────────────────┤
│   Wednesday          │   Answer Questions, pp. 93-94│      X         │
├──────────────────────┼─────────────────────────────┼────────────────┤
│   Thursday           │   Review Chapter III        │       X         │
├──────────────────────┼─────────────────────────────┼────────────────┤
│   Friday             │   Take and pass Chapter Test│       X         │
└──────────────────────┴─────────────────────────────┴────────────────┘
```

5 check marks are redeemable for 1 free period (20 minutes) on Monday.

FIGURE 10.1.   A sample written contract

Disruptive Behavior

Alternate measures to ignoring inappropriate behavior must be taken if the inappropriate behavior is such that it injures others or interrupts the learning process for others. One provision is isolation of the disruptive student. Isolation should be total, e.g., no entertainment and no students passing by. This may be accomplished by a screened-off area in the classroom. Or an empty room in the school may be used as a "timeout" area. Here is an example:

> Jeffrey hits whoever walks by him in the classroom. He has not responded to the token system set up for him. His behavior has improved but he still occasionally punches a passerby. The teacher shows Jeffrey the "timeout" room and explains: "You are better at keeping your hands to yourself, but you forget and hit someone every now and then. This cannot continue. Every time someone passes your desk and you don't hit them, I'll give you a token. Every token will buy you a minute of free time at the end of the day. Every time you do hit someone you will have a 'Timeout' for 10 minutes. You will earn no tokens when in 'Timeout.' There is nothing to do in there and no one to hit. No one will disturb you and you must sit in a chair in the empty room. Do you understand? Tokens for keeping your hands to yourself, 'Timeout' for hitting."

An approach such as the above accomplishes two purposes. First, it takes all reinforcement or attention away from the student and secondly, it removes the disturbing behavior from the classroom.

Another measure, to be used when a student is disturbing the learning process of others or injuring them bodily, is withdrawal of tokens.

For example, in Jeffrey's situation the teacher might say:

> "You are getting much better at keeping your hands to yourself, but you forget and hit someone every now and then. This cannot continue. Every time someone passes your desk and you don't hit them, I'll give you a token. Every token will buy you a minute of free time at the end of the day. Every time you hit someone, *you* will give *me* five tokens. Do you understand how that works? You earn a token for not hitting — you lose 5 of your tokens if you do."

Evaluating Reinforcement Strategies

If appropriate behavior is not developing after using the rewards, the problem may lie in one of several areas, such as these:

Type of Reinforcement: The student may not be interested in exchanging tokens for free time. He or she may prefer to exchange them for helping the custodian or painting or decorating the bulletin board. He or she may not want to earn tokens at all or may prefer a note on his or her paper. The teacher can easily find out by giving the student a choice.

Rate of Reinforcement: The student may need to be reinforced more frequently.

Difficulty of Task: The task the student is asked to complete may be too difficult for that student. If so, he or she should be reassessed and given a task at his or her instructional level.

Time Allotment for Tasks: If the task is appropriate for the student, perhaps he or she wasn't given enough time to complete it. If that is the case, he or she should be given more time to complete the task.

Source of Reinforcement: It is possible that the student is being reinforced by something other than the teacher. Perhaps the other students find him or her entertaining and that is reinforcing to him or her. If that is the case the TIMEOUT area can be used, since one student is interrupting the other's learning process. The teacher might establish a contract whereby the student will be granted "entertainment time" with friends as a reinforcer, after he or she has shown appropriate behavior. Another possibility would be to reinforce the other students for ignoring the disruptive behaviors.

Immediacy of Reinforcement: If reinforcement is being delayed, the pupil may need to be reinforced on a more immediate basis.

Summary of Procedures

To summarize the sequence of events in establishing positive reinforcement in the classroom:

1. Establish positive recognition of appropriate behavior. At the same time, lack of recognition is given for inappropriate behavior.

2. Assess individual students or the class as a whole informally.

3. Choose appropriate reinforcers and establish rate of reinforcement.

4. Choose a model for delivering systematic reinforcement to students.

Methods	*Models*
notes	direct reinforcement
tokens	contingency contracting
contracts	

5. Continue to assess reinforcers, using the guidelines given, e.g., type of reinforcer, rate of reinforcement, difficulty of task, time allotment for task, and source of reinforcement.

Learning Centers[2]

Learning centers may be used in the classroom in several ways. Teachers may choose activities which supplement, provide practice, or prepare for the academic program. A learning center is a designated space in the classroom where a variety of activities are available. These activities are related to a specific topic or skill. Also available at the learning center are rules for its use, a scoring key for students to correct their own work, and a chart for recording attendance and performance at the center.

---

2. These learning center suggestions were compiled and developed by 56 special education teachers in the Springfield, Ohio Public Schools under the direction of Dr. Virginia Lucas, Wittenberg University.

Reading Learning Center

Purpose: To increase word recognition.

Activity A

Materials: Ten cardboard bowling pins, packets of word cards — (each with *ten* words) from stories, math, reading, or science which students should be able to recognize, several copies of score sheets such as this:

Frames

Players	1	2	3	4	5	6	7	8	9	10	Total Score
John	7	9	2	7							
Fred	5	15	4	15							

Directions: Place game materials and instructions in a convenient place for playing.
1. Stand pins up and put packs of cards in a pile.
2. Each player takes a turn drawing a pack of ten cards from the pile.
3. The student tries to read each word in the pack out loud. For every correctly read word, one pin is knocked down. If you read all the words correctly, you have a strike, and get 15 points for that frame.

Activity B

Materials: Chalk, chalkboard.

Directions: Suffix train — have two trains drawn on the board with base word. Each team or participant adds a suffix to the base word receiving one point for his team by writing the suffix in a train car.

Activity C

Materials: Old newspapers, magazines, and game board.

Directions: Scavenger hunt — the children look in newspapers and magazines for sight words. They cut them out and paste on a piece of colored paper.

Activity 2. The students will use words they have selected from the newspapers and magazines and read them after spinning to take turns and moving forward or backwards on the game board. The one who finishes first will be the editor for the day.

Activity D

Directions: Label ice cream containers with the names of sports. Children write words on cards (or teacher-prepared cards) and drop the cards in the correct carton. Make a set of cards with questions about current recordings, artists, instruments, etc. Write the number of spaces to advance if the answer is correct. Put the answers on the backs of the cards and write directions on the game board which will make the game more exciting.

Activity E

Materials: Drawing of football field on posterboard. Tags with student's names. Cards with words to be learned.

Directions: Student name tags placed on 50-yard line—½ facing opposite end. The first player takes a card. If he is able to read it, he moves 10 yards toward the opposite goal. If he cannot read the card, he moves *back* 10 yards toward his own goal. When a child crosses the opposite goal line, he scores 6 points, then returns to the 50-yard line.

Learning Center Idea

Purpose: To increase reading comprehension.

Activity A

Materials: Clothes line, pins, pictures on cards with words that will build a sentence. A basket to hold the words. A piece of drawing paper, crayons.

Directions: 1. Hang the clothes on the line to make a sentence.
2. Using a piece of construction paper, draw a picture of someone wearing the "clothes sentence" you made.
3. Write the sentence at the bottom of the construction paper.

Activity B

Materials: Picture of interest to students; strips labeled to hold sentence strips, "Yes pocket," "No pocket."

Directions: 1. Take a card from the box.
2. Read the sentences on the cards.
3. Study the picture and decide if the sentence goes with it.
4. Put sentences that go with the picture in the "yes" pocket. Put sentences that do not go with the picture in the "no" pocket.
5. Check your work by turning over each card.
6. Put the sentence cards back in the box.

Evaluation: Self-check: Answers are on the back of the cards.

Activity C

Materials: Index cards, cans labeled with "F" and "O," envelopes for cards.

Directions: 1. Read the statement on each card.
2. Put a card that presents a statement of facts in the "F" can.
3. Put statements that present opinions in the "O" can.
4. Check your work by looking on the back of your card.

Evaluation: Self-check: Answers are on back of the cards.
To make the activity easier — present a statement of fact and a statement of opinion on each card, both related.

Activity D

Materials: Chart with poem Jump or Jiggle, worksheet, pencil.

Directions: 1. Read the poem.
2. Take the ditto and fill in missing words.
3. Turn in your paper.
(May use other poems.)

Worksheet

Frogs jump	Frogs jump
Caterpillars hump	Caterpillars ____
Worms wiggle	Worms wiggle
Bugs jiggle	____ jiggle
Rabbits hop	____ hop
Horses clop	Horses clop
Snakes slide	Snakes ____
Seagulls glide	Seagulls glide
Mice creep	____ creep
Deer leap	Deer leap
Puppies bounce	____ bounce
Kittens pounce	____ pounce
Lions stalk	Lions stalk
But — I walk!	But — ____ walk!

Make Bingo cards with squares — cut out pictures of these various animals from magazines or old workbooks — place the correct animal picture in the square with correct word.

Activity E

Materials: A newspaper, magic markers, scissors, construction paper, paste, tape recorder, lined paper, pencil.

Directions: 1. Pupil will find index on page one of newspaper and circle it.
2. Pupil will *underline* page on which classified ads are found.
3. Pupil will turn to that page.
4. Pupil will cut out the following headings:
   Auto sales
   Help wanted
   Rentals
   Auctions etc.

   ____

   ____

   and paste them across the top of a paper creating separate columns.
5. Pupil will read and choose three ads from each heading that he might be interested in responding to. He will paste those under their proper subject title.
6. Read one ad into the tape recorder.
7. Re-write one ad on paper.
8. Underline in red = the who? green = where? yellow = how much? blue = what they're advertising?
9. Compare with the answer key in the pocket?

Evaluation: Criterion: 4/4
Write an ad of your own for one of the following
a) to hire a person to do a chore you dislike
b) to sell something you own
c) to rent out a room in your house
Don't forget to include *who? what? where?* and *how much?* in your ad. (1 point for each.)

Ex: *Wanted,* Housekeeper to clean up my room at home every Saturday morning. Salary 25¢ an hour. Cali Harry Slobnick, 25 Apple Street, Springfield, Ohio. Call 325-0000 after school.

Activity F

Materials: Tape recorder, poem, writing paper, and pencil.

Directions: Read a poem - may be put on tape recorder as well as being placed in a very prominent place in the learning center. (Use poem of the season.)
Activity #1 - May be yes or no questions (re-assess).
Activity #2 - Specific questions about the poem (re-assess).
Activity #3 - Draw a picture of what this poem tells you.

Purpose: To reinforce spelling and recognition of sight words.

Activity A

Materials: Cassette, typewriter, magazines, magic markers, paper, pencils, scissors, glue.

Directions: 1. Type your list of words on the typewriter.
2. Pronounce and spell each word and record on the tape.
3. Illustrate your words by drawing your own pictures.
4. Illustrate your words by finding them in the magazines.
5. Using one of your words try to make it into a picture (grandfather).
6. Worksheet — supply the missing letters.
7. Write the dictated words on the tape. Using your list do the word find puzzle sheet.

Activity B
Directions: Write each of your sight words on the typewriter. Illustrate your word.

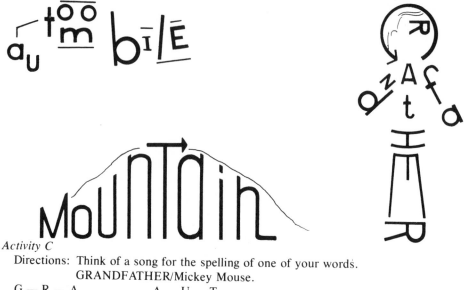

Activity C
Directions: Think of a song for the spelling of one of your words.
GRANDFATHER/Mickey Mouse.

G — R — A   A — U — T
N — D — F   O — M — O
A — T — H — E — R   B — I — L — E

Grandfather   Automobile

Purpose: To increase awareness of information obtained from a newspaper.

Activity A
Materials: Newspaper, paper, index cards.
Directions: Write on index cards problems related to repairs.
             Ex: The muffler fell off my car. Where can I buy a new muffler? How much
             would it cost? Does the cost cover installation?
             Students select a card, locate information in the newspaper and write their
             responses on paper.

Activity B
Directions: Using the employment ads —
            1. Choose the job that you are interested in for employment.
            2. Know how much education is needed.
            3. Find out what age you have to be to apply.
            4. Find out where to apply for the job.
            5. Find out about fringe benefits.
            6. Know what experience is necessary.
            7. Know what personal qualities you must have.
            8. Where do you call for an appointment? Telephone number.

Activity C
Directions: When given the daily listings index for one of the local papers, student will
            construct a collage consisting of items representative of each listed section of
            the paper.
            Task One: Cut an article from each section of the paper listed in your index
                        - i.e., sports. Ann Landers, local news, weather.
            Task Two: *Construct* a collage showing these listings with index as center.

Activity D
Materials: Newspapers containing ads of various supermarkets for the week.
Directions: Comparison grocery shopping, Activities —
1. Make a typical family grocery list. (Could be teacher supplied.)
2. List prices from various market ads.
3. Add costs for each store.
4. Determine if one market seems superior to others.

Activity E
Materials: Newspapers.
Directions: *Current Affairs*
Task One: People who work in newspaper business use certain words we say are "newspaper vocabulary." Work with others at your station and use your dictionaries to find out what these words mean:

banner headline   caption   local news story
masthead   byline   national news story
subhead   index   international news story

Task Two: Look at the chart of the front page of a newspaper. Work with others in your station and design a front page for our class newspaper. Include the following: masthead, banner headline, weather report, index (what is to be in your newspaper?). Draw the "front page" on the paper. Be careful to use a ruler to measure so the spacing between items is always the same.
Task Three: Look for stories that affect our daily lives, from local news stories, national news stories, and international news stories, such as food, fuel and wages.

Activity F
Materials: Several copies of the sports section and woman's section of the newspaper. Duplicated sheets of the five "w's"
who did it happen to?
what happened?
where did it happen?
when did it happen?
why did it happen?
Activity #2 - Front Page story - Write a news article that you would put on the front page of the newspaper - (Something exciting you saw, or happened in school.)
Activity #3 - Want Ad Section - From the index on page one find these different articles.
Task One: Pretend you have enough money to buy a boat. Find the boat you would like to have and tell us why you chose that boat.
Task Two: You have enough money to buy a motorcycle. Which motorcycle would you buy in the Want Ads and why would you buy it?
Task Three: Look through the "Help Wanted" part and choose a job you would like. Tell why you chose that job and what your salary would be (estimate if not listed).

Purpose: To increase the use of word-attack skills in decoding words.

Activity A
Materials: Cards $1'' \times 2''$ and felt marker.
Directions: 1. Write a letter on one end of card and draw an object on the other. (Domino design)
2. Child is to take a package (12) of cards and play dominoes by matching the letters and pictures according to the initial sound.

Activity B

Materials: A large piece of tagboard; pictures of objects beginning with one selected consonant and other pictures with assorted consonants; small cards with *yes* and *no* written on them.

Directions: The child looks at the pictures on the N card, one at a time. If the word begins with N, the child places a *yes* card under the picture and *no* under those that do not start with N. The student may evaluate his own work looking on the back of tagboard where the answers are located.

Activity C

Materials: Dictionary, spelling books, etc.

Directions: Students look in books and compile a list of compound words. Underline all vowels in the words.

Class divides into two teams. The teacher assigns the first parts of compound words to numbers of the other team (she can give the children cards to help them remember their words.) As the teacher calls out one of the compound words the children representing the parts hurry to write their parts on the board. Team scores for getting their part up first.

Activity D

Directions: The child will match the beginning consonant sound with the first letter of the name on a box or can of something from a grocery store with the letter on a card.

Card	Item	Card	Item
A a	apple	N n	noodles
B b	BooBerry cereal	O o	
C c	catsup	P p	pizza
D d	doughnuts	Q q	quince jelly
E e		R r	raspberries
F f	Fritos	S s	salad dressing
G g	green beans	T t	tea
H h	horseradish	U u	
I i		V v	
J j	Jello	W w	
K k		X x	xyz cereal
L l	lemon juice	Y y	yellow onions
M m	mustard		

Activity E

Materials: Letters on plain cards written large with dry marker.

Directions: Have pictures pasted on same size card. Picture with beginning sound of h and c and d. Have four extra pictures beginning with other sounds. (4 pictures with h sound; 4 pictures with c sound; 4 pictures with d sound—12 in all.) Therefore 16 pictures and 3 letter cards in a big envelope. (This has been done with teacher before put on activity table.) After finding letter card and putting in order—be sure picture cards are all face up. Then pick up one picture card— say the picture—say the beginning sounds—find correct letter and put under letter. They will know they are correct because when finished they turn picture card over and correct letter is there.

Purpose: To increase sequential memory of concepts presented visually and auditorily.

Activity A

Directions: 1. Tray containing several items.
   a. remove one object and have student tell which item is missing.
   b. continue with 2, 3, 4, 5 and 6 items.
2. Using same tray, remove entire tray and have students list as many items on it as they can.

Activity B
    Directions: Use tape recording giving a sequence of directions. After listening to tape, have students repeat directions in order.

Activity C
    Directions: Have student look at geometric pattern (quilt, block, etc.) and repeat the pattern with like pieces of fabric, paper, etc.

Activity D
    Directions: Memorizing short poem, record on tape.

Activity E
    Directions: States and capitals flash cards — match the state with the capital.

Activity F
    Materials: Cassette tape, skill sheet, pencil.
    Directions: Very simple activity that requires only a tape recording, pencil and paper. Should begin with only 1 or 2 directions and could work up to 6-7.
        Tape: 1. Take off your shoe.
              2. Scratch your head.
              3. Wiggle your nose.
              4. Write your name.
        Skill Sheet: With picture clue for those who have difficulty reading. Have the 4 directions written out of order and have them number them in the order they performed each. They can then replay tape to check themselves.

Activity G
    Materials: Story chart, writing paper.
    Directions: On a large piece of chart paper, write a story or paragraph with the sentences in the wrong order. Include one or two ideas that do not belong in the paragraph. Student writes story in correct sequence.
        Ex: At school he found that he had forgotten his lunch. The students were already going in class. The day was sunny as Tom started walking to school. The bell rang and Tom knew the teacher would be looking for him. Mother told Tom that his lunch bag was ready. Today was Friday the last day of school for this week. Tom jumped out of bed and started dressing, etc.

Activity H
    Directions: Treasure Hunt — Provide a card with several directions for locating a treasure. Students are to read the card and then follow the directions by memory.

Activity I
    Materials: *DLM* - Visual Memory Sequencing cards *or* make your own; consists of sets of graduated numbers of objects, designs, numerals, letters on main cards and individual object, design, numeral and letter cards.
    Directions: This activity requires two students, so the teacher must demonstrate why and how they must use a "buddy" system.
        Ex: Set #1: Card #1—illustrates a stop sign and milk bottle in sequential order, right to left. (2 objects.)
            Card #2—illustrates a milk bottle, spoon and stop sign. (3 objects.)
            Card #3—illustrates a fork, stop sign, spoon, milk bottle (4 objects) etc. through 10 cards.
        Each object illustrated on flash cards are also illustrated on individual cards. Spread the 10 individual object cards on table, in front of player. Mix them up. The child flashing cards, starts with number one, flashes for 5 seconds, removes. Player chooses individual picture cards and places them in order shown on flashcard. Continue through the graduated cards in order of difficulty. Flasher marks number correct for each setting. Progress to next harder level as each is mastered.

Activity J
Materials: a. Flashcards with letters, numbers, and objects; stop watch; charts.
             b. tachistoscope
Directions: 1a. Short term memory — immediate recall.
                 Given flashcards with letters, numbers, and objects, the teacher will measure the visual sequential memory of the student by showing the student 3 sets of 3 cards that have letters, numbers, and objects on them. The teacher will time the student at 10 seconds before allowing a response. The teacher will chart correct responses daily.
             1b. Given flashcards with letters, numbers, and objects, the student will correctly recall 3 sets of 3 cards (letters, numbers, and objects) using his visual contact after 10 seconds has elapsed with 100% accuracy.
             2. Use same objectives with the auditory mode, but with different sets of cards.
             3. Increase or decrease number of cards in set according to ability of student.
             4. Daily charting must be kept in order that you know what the student's ability is.

Activity K
Directions: Sequential Memory: Auditory and Visual "Going to Store" — Give list of items to be bought at store — student copies down items in sequence heard.

Activity L
Directions: Make a picture chart of father washing the car with correct sequence of pictures.

Activity M
Directions: Retell a story, movie, or TV show.

Activity N
Directions: Write a sequence for playing a game.

Activity O
Directions: Write parts of a story on cards after told on tape recorder, have student number cards to the correct sequence.

Activity P
Directions: Dictate spelling words in sentences to be written in proper sequence.

Activity Q
Directions: Make pictures of a story (own original). Student tells story on tape, have students arrange story in sequence by recording numbers on pictures in correct sequence.

Language Arts Centers

Purpose: To have student use sound to match symbol when given activities.

Activity A
Materials: Marker, tagboard or manila folder.
Directions: Mark off several squares on wrapping paper or oil cloth. Each square bears an initial consonant or blend. Students select a vowel and write as many words as they can think of for each row, using only the letters in that row.
             1. flat
             2. ram
             3. can
             4. wag
             5. pad

Activity B
Materials: Game board made by teacher, game cards — words (multisyllable).
Directions: 1. Place word cards in a pile face down.

2. The students draw a card one at a time and moves one space for each syllable found in the word. If the answer is incorrect, the student moves back two spaces.
3. The player reaching the Syllable Champ Circle first, wins.

Activity C
Materials: Envelopes, picture cards.
Directions: To reinforce phonics have a peg board with several envelopes marked with consonant sounds. Students will have pictures and then place pictures in appropriate envelope.

Activity D
Materials: Magazine picture, tape recorder.
Directions: The student will look at a picture of a cat. He will have instructions on the tape recorder to think of as many words as he can record that begin like the "c" in cat.

Activity E
Materials: Scissors and paste.
Directions: Match the small and large letters by cutting out small letters and pasting them over the letters on the alphabet worm.

Purpose: To increase listening skills.

Activity A
Materials: (a) Tape recorder. (b) paper.
Directions: Children are told to do things that involve two directions, then three, etc. These directions are taped and the child draws his response. Example: Draw a large circle and write your name in the middle.

Activity B
Materials: Tape recorder, manilla paper with pictures beginning with B drawn on it, red marker.
Directions: Child listens to tape and follows directions. With sheet in front of him, he turns on the tape and follows directions. "Look at your paper. Find the ball. When you find the ball, color it red." "Now point to the bat. Draw a circle around the bat." Go through this until all objects are identified. Directions can then be made more complex, i.e., "Draw a square inside your ball and then color the square blue." Can use compound sets of directions.

Activity C
Materials: Tape recorder.
Directions: Food recognition — On tape tell what kind of foods to put into what color dish. The student places the food in the correct dish on command. Start with 3 foods and 3 colored bowls and then increase. Example: Place the banana in the red bowl.
Five objects — Five objects placed at random on a table. On tape are directions on where to place the five objects. The child listens again to check his order or checks a card under the desk.

Activity D
Materials: Seasonal picture, community map, short story, tape recorder.
Directions: Have a picture (seasonal) with a story. Read story on tape for child to listen to — Various activities may be used.
1. Tape directions for coloring or drawing in other objects in the picture.
2. Have child answer questions (who, what, where, why) about story heard on tape—young child could make pictures to answer questions.
3. Child can put story in correct sequence.

Activity E

For older child.
Furnish map of community — Tape directions to put on map.

    1. Bus routes to c.
    2. Locate children's homes, streets — giving directions as Bob's house is on the corner of Front and Main. Color the house brown.

Activity F

On tape read a story (short) — Have child follow taped directions such as:
    1. Draw a line under who went to the store.
    2. Draw a circle around all the names of people in the story.
    3. Draw a picture to show the surprise he found at the store.

Activity G
  Materials: Tape cassette. Simple (one paragraph) stories.
  Directions: Build sparkling sentences by building from a simple sentence. Ask, what, when, where, why and how questions to make your sentence more colorful. For example:
The rain fell.
What kind of rain? "The misty rain fell."
How did it fall? "The misty rain fell softly."
Where did it fall? "The misty rain fell softly on the roof."
Record the above and then ask the student to tell (by recording) the *what, how,* and *where* about the rain.

Math Centers

Purpose: To discriminate cups, pints, quarts, gallons, ounces.

Activity A
  Materials: Milk, juice cartons, filmstrips or tapes, water, recipes.
  Directions: 1. Present containers, water, basin. List of things to discover by experimenting. *Ex:* How many cups can fit into the pint, etc?
        Evaluation — Make a record sheet of "What I Discovered." Compare with correct answer sheet.
      2. Make up — Collage, magazine pictures of containers and labels from home.

Purpose: To discriminate inches / feet.

Activity A
  Directions: Have different items at center to measure — measure a book by width and length — measure top of desk width and length — measure height of board (or similar area).

Activity B
  Directions: Measure area of specified part of room, i.e., blackboard, bulletin board in square feet, square inches.

Activity C
  Directions: Given a number problem pertaining to measuring — student draws picture, makes equation and answer and self-checks equation and answer.

Activity D
  Directions: Draw classroom according to scale, drawing in furniture in classroom.

Activity E
  Directions: Design a floor plan according to scale — placing pieces of furniture specified.

Purpose: To write and say correct answers when given multiplication facts.

Activity A
  Materials: 8″ × 8″ cardboard square, 18 snap-type clothespins, magic marker, pencil and paper.
  Directions: Divide a cardboard square into 8 diagonals. Write a multiplication fact in each space. Write answers in snap clothespins. Give cardboard and clothespin to

the student, together with a worksheet for writing problems. Student is to snap appropriate clothespin to each problem. Provide an answer key. After student checks answers, he is to write the problems.

Activity B
Materials: Game board, game card 3″ × 6″, party favor helmets.
Directions: Place cards face down in pile. Each child places a marker at opposite goal posts. Player draws a card and checks if he has the answer to any of the next three equations. Advances 10, 20, 30 yards depending on the position of match. Card is returned to bottom of pile. If not a match, no yardage gain is made. First to make touchdown wins game.

Activity C
Materials: Game board, cards with facts 3″ × 6″.
Directions: "The Road Runner" game. Place markers at start of race. Place cards face down in a pile. Player draws a card and moves his marker to the correct answer. Special citations and awards are offered during play. Winner finished game first.

Activity D
Materials: A grid, using cross number puzzles.
Directions: Fill in grid with multiplication facts, leaving blank spaces for the answer. Also have addition along with the multiplication problems. Provide answer sheets.

Activity E
Materials: 4 egg cartons, numbered 1 to 12; 2 bottle caps for each egg carton.
Directions: The child places the bottle caps inside the egg carton and closes the lid. He shakes the carton for a few seconds. Then he opens the lid. He looks at the 2 places the caps landed and these are his numbers to multiply. He then writes these two numbers on his paper and computes the fact.

   For working in pairs — one child may shake and then ask the resulting combination of another — if he answers correctly the second child then shakes for the first. When a child misses, the partner can then shake another fact for him.

Purpose: To increase and extend measurement skills.

Activity A — How do you measure?
Materials: Clock, Tape measure, yardstick, ruler, money, calendar, envelope, cards.
Directions: On index cards write a measurement question. Code each card with a number. Write the answer card and include it in the math center.
Sample questions:
   1. How long is the teacher's desk?
   2. What is the date for the 3rd Monday in March?
   3. What time does the clock show?
Place a box of measurement tools beside the envelope of task cards. Students are to write their answers on a sheet of paper and check their own responses.

Activity B
Materials: 3″ × 5″ cards, magic marker.
Directions: Write one month on each index card. Write 30 on four index cards. Write 31 on seven index cards. Write 28/29 on one index card.
   1. Give the student the month and number cards.
   2. Ask him to place month cards in correct order.
   3. Ask him to place each month card with the number card that tells the number of days in that month.
   4. Have student check his order and number of days by using a calendar.

Activity C
Materials: Ruler.
Directions: How to read a ruler (also this could deal with fractions).

Activity D

Materials: Paper, crayons, measurable objects, charts for gathering data, rulers.

Directions: Child chooses objects to measure which are about _____ feet long (length is chosen by child). *Ex:* If he chooses to measure things about 5′ long, he finds 5 things which are about this length and draws a picture of each.

Children should measure many things with their feet, their hands, a book, or toys *before* doing this work job. E.g., one child might measure a table and find it ''four spelling books long.'' Another child might measure the same table and find it ''fifteen hands-spread-out long.''

Children gradually become aware of the need for standard measurement.

Activity E

Materials: Different size containers, funnel, sponge, paper, pencil, ruler.

Directions: Liquid measurement: investigate shapes and sizes of 5 containers by filling with water and pouring the water back and forth between marked containers.

Questions: Which one is biggest?

Do they look the same?

How will you find out?

Ruler measurement: blank sheet of paper, ruler, pencil. Mark corners with A, B, C, D. Then directions will state for example:

Measure 2′′ down from A.

Make a dot, mark it E.

Draw a line from B to E, etc.

Student will be making a picture through measurement.

Activity F

Materials: Balance scale, scale measuring ounces and pounds, objects to weigh.

Directions:
1. Choose 5 things to weigh.
2. Estimate the weight of each object in ounces.
3. Weigh each object to find exact weight.
   Suggested things to weigh:
   notebook, book, crayons, stapler, pencil, tablet, purse, scissors.

1. Which object was heaviest? _____
2. Which object was lightest? _____
3. Which object was your estimate closest to? _____
4. Which object was the most difficult? _____

Activity 2: Use scale— students weigh their own weight

Use weight of all students to find:
1. average weight of group
2. draw bar graph (record)
3. percentile, etc. (find)

Activity G

Materials: Measuring cup, bucket, ruler, yardstick, thermometer, music sheets, records, scales, metric system materials, calendar, maps, maps of space and light year stuff.

Directions: Match measurement objects with correct category.
1. Liquid measurement (quarts, pints, gallons)
2. Dry measurement (bushels)
3. How tall am I (ruler, yardstick)
4. Heat measurement (thermometer)
5. Sound measurement (musical instrument cues on music — p, pp, f, ff, mp, mf, crescendo, etc.)
6. Comparisons of objects (big, small)
7. How much do I weigh? (scales, pounds, ounces)
8. Metric system
9. Calendar   (year measurement)
10. Distance (miles, etc., light years, stuff with space)
11. Time measurement (clocks)

Writing Centers

Purpose: To increase writing skills.

Activity A

Materials: Envelopes, word cards.

Directions: Write several sentences on sentence strips. Cut apart each sentence. Scramble the words in each sentence and place in the envelope. Student is to unscramble sentence by placing the words in the correct order.

Have the student write the unscrambled sentence.

Code the envelopes and provide an answer key.

Activity B

Materials: Tagboard pumpkins or other seasonal faces covered with clear contact paper, felt pens or grease pencil.

Directions: Children write corresponding manuscript and cursive (or uppercase and lowercase) letters on the pumpkin teeth.

Activity C

Directions: Listen for words that create spookiness by listening to a spooky story. List words on board. Have students use some of the words and write their own ghost story. Have students read their stories.

Activity D

Directions: 1. Each student can write favorite recipes brought from home and child chooses recipe to write and take home.

2. Copy short poems they enjoy — can collect for their own "My Favorite Poems."

3. Copy latest "pop tunes" — collect for their own — "My Favorite Songs."

Activity E

Materials: Cards containing mixed up words which become a sentence when put in alphabetical order. (Correct form on back of each card.) Box — used for card container. Paper, pencil, record sheet.

Directions: 1. Child selects card containing 5 scrambled sentences.

2. Child unscrambles each sentence by arranging words in alphabetical order.

3. Child writes correct sentence on paper—utilizing best penmanship.

4. Correct proper sequence by looking at back of card.

Ex: Crashed the tollgate car near a

Activity F

Materials: Alphabet Antics book (Zaner Bloser), paper, art paper.

Directions: Make a good f — add to it until you produce a picture of an umbrella.

There are characters for each letter in both cursive and manuscript writing.

Map Reading Center

Purpose: To acquaint students with simple maps.

Activity A

Materials: Tape recorder, map of school, strings, thumb tacks (colors—red, green, yellow).

Directions: Record directions for locating places on a map (i.e., place a yellow thumb tack on Mrs. Smith's room. Place a green thumb tack on the principal's office. Tie a string on the thumb tacks between . . . .)

Have students listen to the directions and do each thing the tape says. Provide a picture of the map with all the correct responses.

Activity B

Materials: State map, ruler, paper, pencil or pen.

Directions: The child, using a ruler, would determine which of 2 choices was further apart: (Circle correct answer.)

Dayton to Cleveland or Dayton to Columbus
Springfield to Columbus or Springfield to Akron
Athens to Toledo or Athens to Youngstown
Cincinnati to Lima or Cincinnati to Piqua

Variations:

1. Do closer together.
2. In order to learn more about state, have student find more "discreet spots" in the state, e.g., Lancaster to Kimbolton.
3. Older students might have to compute actual miles from one to another and record that on paper.

Activity C

Materials: Tagboard (24 × 36), magic marker pens.

Directions: With a simplified drawing of a 2 or 4 block area drawn on a large tagboard sheet. Identify school.

1. Write names of streets in proper places on map.
2. Identify children's homes, stores, public buildings by drawing them in and labeling each.
3. Discuss and label directions (N,S,E,W).
4. Give task cards such as (preferably *do* the activity).

John left the front door of ____ school, turned right, walked one block ____ (direction) and turned to the right and walked one block ____ (direction). What are the two street names where you would find him?

Activity D

Materials: City map, paper, pencil.

Directions: Looking at a map of the city.

1. Find your street.
2. What streets are on each side of your street?
3. What street is behind or in back of your street?
4. What street is in front of your street?

Looking at a map of the city.

1. How many railroads?
2. How many bridges?
3. Is there a water way?

Activity E

Materials: State map, paper, pencil, magic marker.

Directions: For *older* students.

Take a state map, then using a magic marker, trace the road route to a town you would like to visit. If going on an interstate, circle any rest stops along the (using the map legend) way. Use the numbers on the map to try to approximate the mileage. If student can do division, have him figure out how much gasoline would be needed and what it would cost.

For *younger* students.

Have student trace line starting at Springfield and ending at various places (Columbus, Dayton, Cleveland, etc.)

Activity F

Directions: Task cards: How many steps long is your classroom? How many string lengths long? (See below.) How many steps wide is your classroom? How many string lengths wide? (See below.)

Task cards: Cut a piece of string the same length as your step. (From the toe of the front foot to the toe of the back foot.) Using a yardstick measure the piece of string. Add the string lengths (long and wide). Multiply.

Task: How many steps to Ms. ____'s room?
How many steps to the cafeteria?
How many steps to Ms. ____'s room?
How many steps to the playground?

Culminating Task: Draw a map of the above places in our building.

Activity G
  Materials: Graph paper, larger blocks and graph paper, smaller blocks, ruler.
  Directions: Using graph paper, have each student draw the view of his bedroom at home as if he were sitting on the ceiling looking down. Have him include all furniture and label them with words.

  Next have student draw picture (map) on smaller graph paper. Instead of labeling furniture with words, have him label in a different way — either color code, initial, design, etc.

  Have him record what each symbol means at bottom of paper. (After independent work, then allow several students to exchange maps of their rooms. In a group type discussion, see if map is clear and understandable to others.)

Activity H
  Materials: City outlines, cutouts, glue.
  Directions: The student is to design his own city. He should include in his city various places such as schools, a church, stores, homes and parks. For a primary group, the child could be provided with a sheet of paper with a city outline (limits and streets). Also cutouts of the various places listed above. He could then place his building, parks, etc. where he wanted them in his city. (An older child could draw all of his own instead of using the cutouts.) After he has made and *named* his city, he could give directions to another child on how to find a certain place in his city.

Career Education Center

Purpose: To increase skills that are used in a variety of job situations.

Activity A
  Materials: Word cards, game board, envelopes, chips.
  Directions: A. Write word cards for several occupations (e.g., waitress: order, apron, menu, drink, bill) and place on the game board.
  The first player selects a card and reads the word. The player must name the occupation related to that word and move his chip to the first space labeled with the occupation.
  B. Shuffle cards and place cards into the envelopes by career categories.

Activity B
  Materials: Clock, pencil and paper, ditto of rules the employee must follow, cassette tape of oral instructions, task cards of activities, hand grooming essentials (nail file, emery board, cuticle remover, etc.), catalog of uniforms, vacuum cleaner, picture of bed — sheets, towels, etc.
  Directions: Career Education — a motel or hotel maid. The student will report to learning center and draw a task card. (Tasks might be: a schedule card for cleaning activities for the day). *Ex:*
  1. Sign in at 8:00 a.m.
  2. Report to manager at 8:10.
  3. Report to cleaning supervisor at 8:20.
  4. Clean room 106 at 8:30.
  5. Clean room 108 at 9:00, etc.
  6. ''
  7. ''
  8. ''
  9. Report to supervisor at 4:00 p.m.
  Student will use clock to set hands at various times his job responsibilities change. Draw picture of clock face for 8:00, 8:10, etc., for each change of duties.

Task card
1. Remove from catalog pictures of sheets, towels, etc., maid must take to each room.
2. Paste pictures of supplies on a sheet of construction paper.

Activity C
Materials: Child's picture book, an assortment of toys (trucks, stuffed bear, doll dishes, etc.), child's game (such as Winnie the Pooh) and a tape recorder.
Directions: 1. In this activity the student is to be working as a nursery school aide.
2. Student selects a toy, game or book.
3. Student plans how he would use his object to entertain a preschool child.
4. Student tapes his idea.
   E.g., tell the story after reading the book — explain how to play the game — make up a game (or story) using the toy.
5. Student listens to his tape.

Activity D
Materials: Pictures from magazines of waitress uniforms. A diagram of a place setting at table, an envelope with the proper objects to be set in the diagram on the table. e.g., plate, glass, knife, fork, napkin, a menu, and order pad.
Directions: The student will take the items from the envelope and place them in the proper places on the diagram of the place setting.
   Activity 2. The student will copy from the menu to the order pad the order, which he thinks a customer would order, and add the total amount.

Activity E
Materials: Newspaper ads to find different items used in a station (gas) and their prices. How to add tax to purchases (tax schedules). Credit card slips. Making change for purchase. (Tape recording of what to order if a customer.)
Directions: Students will use newspaper by cutting out items that customer can buy. Students will use paper and pencil to figure out the price and the change that is given back to customer. Students will also have customer who will use credit cards. Students should fill in item and price of purchases. Students should have pictures of mechanical devices they will be asked to repair (tire, change oil, change windshield blades, change headlights, battery, transmission fluid and radiator being filled with water). They should label the picture and give directions.

Activity F
Materials: Play money, tax chart, "Career cards," answer cards.
Directions: A series of cards could be created, each containing a situation which involves use of money.
   Ex:
      Waitress/Waiter cards: Each card would contain a check with a series of items and their prices. Also included is the amount of money paid by customer (perhaps in pictures).
      Directions: 1. Add up the cost of the customer's meal.
      2. Look on the tax chart—how much tax should you add?
      3. Total the bill.
      4. Look at the amount the customer gave you.
      5. Count out his/her change in play money.
      6. How much is his/her change?
      7. Check yourself on the answer card.

Science Education Center

Purpose: To increase an awareness of the strength of gravity.

Activity A

Materials: Magnet, string, tack, hair clip, wood, soap, nail, paper clip, etc.

Directions: Place articles on a large sheet of paper. Draw an outline of each article and label. Ask the students to identify which articles can be picked up by the magnet. Write the names of those objects on a separate paper.

B - Etch-A-Sketch, Ohio Art Co.

C - materials — stop watch, feather, marshmallow, paper wad, pencil, box with a 3-foot stand.

Students are to drop an object in the box from the 3 ft. mark and at the same time start the stop watch. Stop the watch when the object hits the box. Record object, name and time it takes to fall.

Purpose: To increase an understanding of air.

Activity B

Directions: 1. On flash cards with pictures and questions, the children will match the questions to the answers on a ditto. The pictures will deal with such as a little boy flying an airplane and the wind blowing it up. The question being: What is the wind doing to the airplane? The answer: The wind is blowing the airplane up into the air.

2. On a cardboard wheel with the top and bottom moving and in the middle a picture of clothes hanging on a line. The children will answer the questions: Look at the picture of clothes on the line. Will the clothes dry better today? Answer: No, the clothes will not dry well today. Yes, the clothes will dry well today.

Sample pictures: Winter scene
Summer scene
Windy scene
Cloudy scene

Activity C

Materials: Bike pump, balloons, water glass, tissue, shoe box, boat sails, art paper, crayons, glue, etc.

Directions: 1. The child is to show that air is everywhere by various experiments. Put freshly dug soil into water — watch the bubbles.

2. The child will pump up a bicycle tire to prove it can make the ride smoother. (Blow balloons.)

3. The child can show air occupies space — put a crushed tissue into bottom of glass tight enough that it doesn't fall out — insert glass straight down into pail of water; the air keeps the water from getting the tissue wet.

4. For art the child can draw a picture of a sailboat on water, showing air (wind) moving it along. Cut along waterline 2/3 way; paste boat on stick to move along.

Activity D

Materials: A chart with ten steps.

A pile of 25 cards with 12 numbers above 100 (101, 102, 103, 104, 105, 106, 107, 108, 109, 110, 111, 112) and 13 numbers below 100 (99, 98, 97, 96, 95, 94, 93, 92, 91, 90, 89, 88, 87).

A disc for moving the specific number of steps.

Directions: 1. Select a chart.

2. Place cards face down in a pile.

3. Select a card.

4. If the number is more than 100, move the number of spaces it is over a hundred.

5. If the number is less than 100, move the disc back the number of spaces it is less than 100.
6. The first person to get to the top is the winner.

Activity E
Materials: Magnet, pins, paper, wood, eraser, nails, coins, and other small objects. Record sheet.
Directions: 1. Spread a variety of objects on a table top, and touch the magnet to each thing.
2. Place all the objects that the magnet attracts in one pile and the remaining objects in another pile.
3. Notice that the magnet only attracts or picks up things made of iron, steel, cobalt, or nickel.
Student will record his answers on the provided sheet.

Activity F
Materials: Magnet, pennies and washers, tape, cardboard.
Directions: 1. Tape a powerful horseshoe magnet onto an 8″ × 10″ piece of cardboard. Place it about ½ of the way down and about 1 inch from a center line.
2. Turn cardboard over, prop it up against some books and slide pennies and iron washers on slugs down the center line.
3. Notice that the magnet attracts or draws the washers off to one side.
4. By using a magnet, coin vending machines can reject fake coins (slugs).

Purpose: To develop awareness of weather changes.
Activity A
Materials: Ditto clothes, boots, shoes, hats to cut out and paste on dolls (boy or girl). Using a paper doll, dress appropriately according to the card selected describing the type of weather. Alternate activity — child draws picture identifying the correct apparel to be worn for selected weather.

Activity B
Given pictures of different cloud formations, the student will make with cotton various types of clouds to be displayed at center. Write what kind of weather to expect.

Activity C
Using a coke bottle and following directions, make a barometer with a balloon and write experiment. Write observations for the following week.

Activity D
"Rains cats and dogs." "Hotter than blue blazes." Draw pictures of literal meaning and then explain what kind of weather it means.

Activity E
Materials: Pictures of seasonal scenes and activities.
Season words written on envelopes.
1. Lay out season envelopes in front of you.
spring   summer   fall   winter
2. Place pictures in correct envelopes.
3. Check your work by looking at the number on back of the envelope and each picture to see if they match.

Activity F
Materials: 2 large containers, 3′ of hose or tubing, water.
Directions: How a siphon works.
1. Fill one of the containers about 3/4 full of water and place on a stack of books to raise it above the second container.
2. Fill the tube with water, and holding both ends to keep water from running out, insert the tube ends into the container.
3. The water from the raised container runs uphill through the tube and down into the lower container.

NOTE: This is the same way water travels in pipes around a city. The weight of the water in the filled container, suction, air pressure, and gravity can cause water to follow the tube or pipes to a maximum of 34 feet (at sea level). This allows water to flow up and down small hills in a town without pumps.

Activity G
Materials: Calendar, magazines, crayons, blank paper, milk cartons, weather chart, construction paper, weather symbols, scissors.
Directions: Take four different milk cartons and cover with contact paper or construction paper. Place a symbol on the outside for each type of weather — sunny, cloudy, raining, snowing. For example, a sun for a sunny day, a cloud for cloudy, an umbrella for raining, and a snowman for snowing. Make several of these symbols and place them in each milk carton. Have the child identify the type of weather each day and place the symbol on individual calendars. Place the milk cartons next to the calendars.

Activity H
Have several magazines on hand so the children can find individual pictures of sunny, cloudy, raining, and snowing and these can be placed in a weather book made out of construction paper.

Activity I
Have crayons and blank paper for the younger children to draw picture of each type of weather.

Activity J
Place a large chart with pictures of the four types of weather (sunny, cloudy, raining, snowing) on it and additional cards with the same pictures on them on a table. Have each child match the additional pictures to the one on the larger chart.

Activity K
Put a thermometer on bulletin board in weather center. Daily weatherperson records temperatures. Daily comparison of changes (morning, noon, evening). Weekly comparisons of weather degrees. Write a weather report for the principal.

Activity L
Materials: Word strips with cloudy, sunny, snowing, foggy on them in a pocket labeled conditions. Paper thermometer that is bulged out every 10 degrees and two arrows with "HIGH" and "LOW" on them. Thermometer hanging outside window.
1. Pull out the word cards labeled "conditions." Choose the one that describes today's weather. Fasten it on the board with a thumb tack.
2. Check the thermometer outside the window in the morning when you come to school, at each recess, and at noon. Use the two arrows for "HIGH" and "LOW" and mark on the paper thermometer what the highest temperature and lowest temperature for the day is.

Activity M
Materials: Tape recorder, pencil and paper, sentence strips containing different sentences about the weather either *true* or *false,* 2 boxes — one labeled *yes* and one, *no,* 1 box that holds sentences.
The student will read each one of the sentences concerning the weather and place it in either the *yes* or *no* box. Here are some of the sentences to be used:
1. The sun shines when it is raining.
2. We wear coats and boots during the summer.
3. A thermometer tells us if it is hot or cold.
4. We see ice and snow during the summer.
5. We can go swimming during the winter.
6. When the thermometer says $0°$ it is *very* cold.
7. Ice is frozen water or rain.

Reinforcement Menu

A reinforcement menu represents those events and objects which are potential rewards for students in classrooms. Reinforcement menu categories shown in Figure 10.2 are ranked in order of desirability for classroom instruction. Teachers should use the highest ranked type of reward for students when possible. They should progress from needed rewards towards less tangible rewards as L&BD students become internally motivated to behave and perform properly.

HIGH

Social Praise
Special Privileges
Interest Centers
Job Board
Home-School Activities
Tokens
Objects

LOW

FIGURE 10.2.   Hierarchy of reinforcement menu categories

Social Reinforcement

Social reinforcers are most effective with direct reinforcement. They should be used often in order to become a natural aspect of teaching behavior.

Evaluation symbols are an interim and/or supplementary consequence. Evaluation marks on papers serve to notify students of their progress; they represent written social praise. These may be implemented with direct reinforcement or contingency contracting. They may be used on students' papers, on individual student charts, on a classroom chart, in a gradebook that students may refer to, on a school chart placed in the hall in a well-traveled area, and on the chalkboard.

Social rewards in DTIMS are categorized into five groups: positive proximity, positive physical expression, verbal comments, evaluation marks, and recognition. Suggested rewards within these groups are shown below.

Positive Proximity

> *Nearness*
> eating with children
> five minutes to discuss something with teacher
> interacting with class at recess
> pausing — while transferring objects
> principal serves as personal tutor
> sharing praise with outside person
> sitting on desk near students
> sitting within the student group
> standing alongside

> *Touching* (social, positive proximity)
> combing hair
> dancing
> gently raising chin

handshake
helping put on coats
hugging
kissing a hurt
touching
tying shoes

Positive Physical Expression

Facial Expression
Cheering
Forming kiss
Laughing (happy)
Nodding
Raising eyebrows
Rolling eyes enthusiastically
Smiling
Winking
Whistling

Bodily Expression
Bounding
Circling hand through air (encouragement to continue)
Clapping hands
High sign
Jumping up and down
Peace sign
Raising arms
Signaling OK
Thumbs up
V for victory

Verbal Comments

Spoken Comments
A good way of putting it
Absolutely right
He accepts responsibility
I admire you when you work like that
I appreciate your attention
I know you feel great
I like that — I didn't know it could be done that way
I'm glad you're here
I'm happy your desk is in order
It is a pleasure having you as a student
Keep working hard_____ (name)_____
Splendid
Student used a good example — a model
Terrific!
Thank you

That deserves my respect
That was a good choice
That was very kind of you
That's clever
That's interesting
That's right
That's sweet of you
Thinking!
You catch on very quickly
You make us happy
You're doing fine

Written Comments
Beautiful work
Bravo!
Brilliant
Congratulations
Cool
Delightful
Excellent
Exciting
Fabulous!
Fantastic!
Great
Marvelous!
Outstanding
Perfect
Positively great work!
Show this to your parents
Swell
That shows hard work
Wow!
Yeah!
You should be very proud of this
For display

Evaluation Marks

A-1
Checkmarks
Rubber stamps
Stars
Happy faces
Percentages
+
Letter grades

Recognition

Display paper on bulletin board
Student's name in school paper
Student's name on board
Student's name on honor roll

Special Privileges

Special privileges permit students to engage in some activity and to use time in extraordinary ways. Any appropriate privileges may be used as rewards in either direct reinforcement or contingency contracting. Special privileges suggested and used by teachers are listed below.

Special Privileges

Individual Classroom
Choose seat for specific time
Decorate desk
Homework in class
Early dismissal
Extra credit
Exempt a test
Exempt an assignment
Extra time for favorite subject
Free time
Gymnastics
Hot wheels
Lead discussion
Privacy
Photography
Teacher does homework
TV
Typing
Write letters

Individual In-School
Gardening
Pictures taken
Visit principal
Visit amateur class

Group Classroom
Class coke break
Competing with another class
Dancing
Extra committee meeting time
Games
Mural
Open discussion
Plan daily schedule
Present skits
Puppet theater

Group In-School
Class concert
Class party
Extend recess
Movie
Outdoor lessons
Extra curricular activities (sports, clubs)
Perform for PTA
Senior staff day

Group Out-of-School
Field trips
Time to work on community projects
Movie

Interest Centers[3]

Interest centers are areas within the classroom where students can explore and pursue their curiosities during "off task" time. Since interest centers represent reinforcing events which teachers can arrange for students, they are most readily managed through contingency contracting.

There are several advantages for using interest centers: they help to organize teachers and classrooms; they provide a variety of choices for students; they provide breaks after students have worked; and they provide opportunities for students to learn to work and play together.

Suggested Types of Interest Centers

Four suggested interest centers and rules used to manage them follow.

---

3. Adapted from Thomas M. Stephens, *Directive teaching of children with learning and behavioral handicaps* (2nd ed.). Columbus, Ohio: Charles E. Merrill Publishing Co., 1976, pp. 49-51.

TYPES	RULES
1. *Art Shop* Activities include: clay, sand, crayons and paper, paint, string, scissors, cloth, and glue. One special project activity should be introduced each week. (Macrame, sand casting, candles, mosaic, ecology boxes, tie-dyeing, photography.) Sink if available, screening is desirable.	Two children work at a time. Work quietly. Stay on newspaper. One project only. Clean-up.
2. *Reading Nook* Activities include magazines, basal readers, library books, coloring books with texts, weekly readers, phonics books, and student authorized stories. (Should be in a quiet corner, screened if possible.)	One at a time. Work quietly. Replace books. One activity only.
3. *Listening Corner* Activities include TV, radio, record player, tape cassette, puppets, and language master.	Two at a time. Listen quietly. One activity only. Replace materials.
4. *Game Field* Activities include Alphabet Twister, Moth House, Flash Cards, Phonics, race track, memory games, Spill and Spell, plus regular toys and games. A special game should be introduced each week. (Large area needed away from academics area.)	Four at a time. Play quietly. One game only. Replace games on shelf.

After the teacher has assembled interest centers, the rules for going to an interest center and staying there are specified. These conditions include behavior, time, and the amount of work necessary to earn the privilege of interest center time.

A typical arrangement is for every five correctly completed tasks, one five minute interest center pass is issued. If a center activity requires more than five minutes to complete a project, then a student must complete additional tasks to earn sufficient time.

Interest center time may be built into the structure of a classroom day as shown in the following daily schedule.

DAILY SCHEDULE

Amount of Time Needed	*Activity*
10 minutes	*Initiating the Morning — Order Period* (Each child obtains seatwork assignment — learned activity)

50 minutes	Skill Time: Language Arts
(15 minutes)	Group I - Skill Introduction
(15 minutes)	Group II - Practice Activity
(15 minutes)	Group III - Experience Table
(5 minutes)	Group IV - Total Group
10 minutes	Interest Center Time (incentive: contingent upon completion of task)
10 minutes	Recess
50 minutes	Skill Time: Mathematics
(15 minutes)	Group I - Skill Introduction
(15 minutes)	Group II - Practice Activity
(15 minutes)	Group III - Experience Table
(5 minutes)	Group IV - Total Group
10 minutes	Interest Center Time (incentive: contingent upon completion of task)
10 minutes	Summary of Morning — Readiness for Lunch
45 minutes	Lunch — Recess
50 minutes	Skill Time: Reading Comprehension
(15 minutes)	Group I - Skill Introduction
(15 minutes)	Group II - Practice Activity
(15 minutes)	Group III - Experience Table
(5 minutes)	Group IV - Total Group
10 minutes	Interest Center Time (incentive: contingent upon completion of task)
10 minutes	Recess
50 minutes	Unit Time: Social Studies, Science, Health, etc.
10 minutes	Interest Center Time (incentive: contingent upon completion of task)
15 minutes	Summary of Day — Readiness for Dismissal

It is also possible to use interest centers on an individual basis, rather than scheduling students to centers at fixed times. When scheduled on an individual basis, interest centers are used any time during the day, at different times by different students, depending upon when they complete their work.

While Frank is working on his math assignment, Julie has finished her reading task. George is just beginning his spelling assignment. Julie brings her work to the teacher for a check. It meets criterion, so she goes to the interest center of her choice. A timer is set for 10 minutes for Julie. When it rings she goes back to her desk for her next assignment. Frank and George continue with their tasks while Julie is at interest centers. When George completes his task, his work is checked. If it meets criterion, he goes to an interest center of his choice and has the timer set for 10 minutes for him. The same happens when Frank and the others in the class complete their tasks.

One advantage of the individual approach is that each student can be on-task for an appropriate amount of time and be at interest centers as time is earned. One disadvantage is that a timer is needed for every child, and it is difficult for teachers to keep track of whose timer is ringing. Each student must understand that only the teacher sets the timer since it may be tempting to reset the timer. For this reason one requirement for remaining at interest centers is that the timer be left untouched by students.

Physical Arrangements

An ideal way of providing interest centers in classrooms is to place five or six tables or stations around the room with a different interest center on each table. Interest center activities should be changed regularly, as they often lose their appeal after students have used them for a week or so. It is also wise to have a variety of activities in order to appeal to many different interests. There may be, for example, an art center (e.g., painting), a listening center (e.g., tape recorder), a building center (e.g., blocks), a learning center (e.g., felt board with letters for writing), and a game center (e.g., cards). Figure 10.3 shows a suggested floor plan for incorporating interest centers into classrooms.

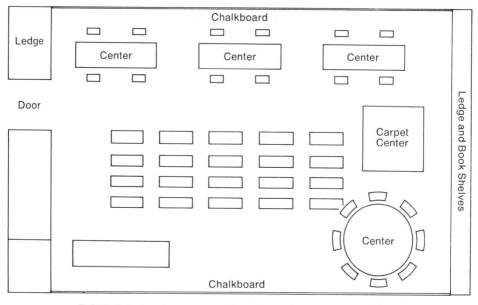

FIGURE 10.3.   A suggested floor plan for interest centers

Often a room has no space for extra tables. In this case, interest centers can be placed on ledges or shelves for checking out items to be taken to students' desks. They may invite friends to their desks to share the center.

Job Board

A job board permits the use of classroom jobs as rewards. Jobs are selected from those available in the classroom: vacuum rug, water plants, feed fish, clean sink, arrange project center neatly, operate filmstrip, answer phone, manage recess equipment, teacher assistant — to name but a few of those jobs often available in classrooms. It is best to list more jobs than students, so that every pupil can select a job. Figure 10.4 shows a sample job board.

Teachers may use jobs as rewards in either direct reinforcement or contingency contracting. Since some jobs extend over a period of time (e.g., teacher assistant) these can be assigned for varying time periods, such as half-day, one day, two days,

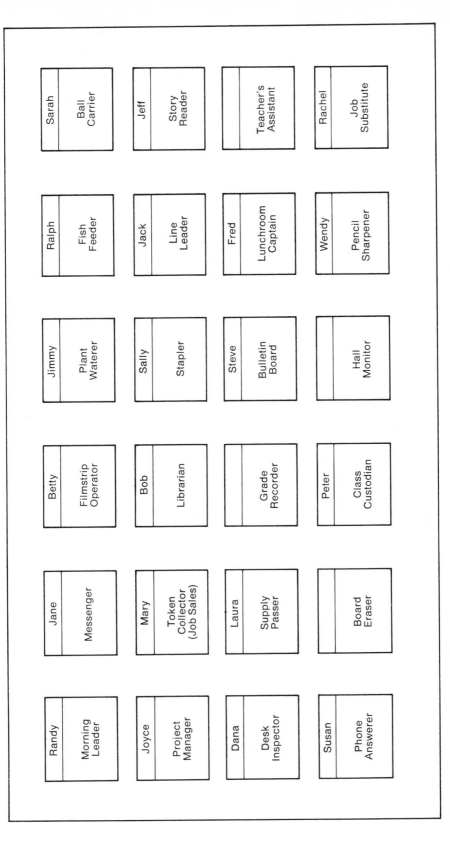

FIGURE 10.4. A sample job board

or one week. Teachers should make determinations as to what time period is most appropriate for the jobs available in their classrooms. For example:

Direct Reinforcement: Teacher says, "Sara, you did your math worksheet with 85% correct in the assigned time. That's great! You may feed the goldfish."

Contingency Contracting: The teacher says, "Sara, when you finish your math worksheet with 85% correct, you may feed the goldfish," or "Lenny, you really worked hard yesterday and finished all 5 of your seatwork assignments. Today, if you do as well, you may be teacher assistant."

Some suggested classroom jobs are listed below:

Assist teacher	Newspaper
AV monitor	Timer/Clock
-projection	Inspector
-screen	Job Board manager
-shades	In charge book corner
-lights	Project manager
Caring for pets, plants, etc.	Substitute jobs
Collect materials	Staple papers
Decorate teacher's desk	Record grades
Decorate room	Errand boy
Grade papers	Secretary's helper (phone answerer)
Help others - tutor	Janitor's helper
Janitorial tasks (erase board, floor,	Librarian
aquarium)	Patrol
Point recorders	Parking
Line leader	Ushering
Token dispenser/token collector	

Home School Activities

These activities are implemented through contingency contracting. Usually they start with a conference with one or both parents where inappropriate behavior is discussed briefly. A reinforcement tactic for shaping behavior is explained to the parents, giving the rationale and results often realized from using this approach. Then an organized program is established whereby the parent will reinforce the child at home for appropriate behavior at school. For example:

Jesse has been having difficulty completing his math papers. Nothing seems to inspire him to finish his work because he says his parents never look at it anyway. Teacher calls in Jesse's parents and explains the situation and the value of reinforcing Jesse for his good work. A program is set up whereby Jesse's parents will look over each of his math papers every day when he comes home from school. They will then sign the paper and Jesse will return it to school the next day. Every Friday Jesse should have a set of five signed math papers, a signature for each day of the week. If he does, he and his parents will do something of Jesse's choice on Friday night — go bowling, have ice cream, go out to eat, watch the ball game on TV, whatever Jesse decided he'd like to do that evening (within reason, of course — his parents may give him a choice of a few activities they know he likes to do.)

Advantages of a home/school approach such as the above are two fold. First, it helps Jesse to complete his assignments, and second, it encourages his parents to use an effective way to demonstrate their interest in his school work and to spend time with him.

Tokens

Tokens are an interim recognition of achievement. They may be used as reinforcers through direct reinforcement or contingency contracting. By issuing tokens teachers inform students that their behaviors and performances are acceptable. Tokens are distributed as a way to earn something; they are usually not effective when used without back-up reinforcers. These may include free time, special privileges, interest center time, jobs, home/school activities, or objects.

Almost anything may be used as tokens. However, it is best to use tokens that are not easily duplicated since students may try to counterfeit tokens. Token economy is a method of structuring rewards for the entire class. Appropriate behavior is explained clearly to the students, and then tokens are given when that behavior is demonstrated. At predetermined times, students exchange their tokens for back-up reinforcers from, for example, the *classroom store*.

The classroom store is the reinforcement menu teachers establish for their classes. A variety of reinforcers should be included, based on assessment of pupils' reward preferences. Back-up reinforcers may have a predetermined value; they may be sold to the highest bidder; or students with the most tokens can buy first. Back-up reinforcers may be purchased twice a day (in the morning and after lunch), once a day, or once a week depending on the needs of the students for immediate reinforcement.

Some students may decide not to spend their tokens but simply to collect tokens instead since the tokens have become reinforcing without the need to exchange them. The next step is dropping the need for tokens and being reinforced by social reinforcement alone. An example of store time follows.

Teacher or salesperson says:
"Count your tokens. It is time to buy from the classroom store. Is there anyone with more than 30 tokens?" Mary, Miguel, Jack, Joyce, and Steve raise their hands. Steve has the most with 39.

Teacher: "Steve, you may buy first."
While Steve is selecting, the teacher calls for those with 38 tokens, then 37, 36, 35, 34, etc. If two or more children have the same number of tokens, the simplest method is to stand in line. Anyone who runs or pushes should be told to return to his/her seat.

Object Reinforcement Activities

Objects may be given through direct reinforcement or through contingency contracting. There are several ways of implementing a token exchange. Objects may be purchased, giving the student ownership, or they may be leased for a given period of time. A store can be set up where items in the store would be priced according to how the students value them. A ball might be 25 tokens; a paperclip might be 1 token; and so forth. The items can be obtained in several ways; they may be purchased by the teacher, donated by the PTA, brought in by the students, or paid for through room funds.

The store may simply be a shelf somewhere in the room, or it may be somewhere else in the school. Time for exchanging tokens for objects will depend on the maturity of the students. It may be every afternoon, once a week, or once a month. As soon as possible, tokens should be exchanged for activities rather than objects.

Suggested objects for use in classroom token exchanges are shown below.

Address books	Trains	Badges
Balloons	Art supplies	Banks
Bats	Balls	Birthday hats
Blocks	Bean bags	Bookmarkers
Books	Boats	Calendars
Cartoons	Buttons	Classroom equipment
Comics	Class pictures	Comic books
Compasses	Combs	Cowboy hats
Dollhouses	Counting beads	Fans
Flashlight	Dolls	Flowers
Games	Flash cards	Jacks
Jump ropes	Grab bag gifts	Kaleidoscopes
Magazines (*Mad, Hot Rod,*	Jumping beans	Marbles
True Romance, Motor-	Make-up kits	Money
cycles)	Miniature cars	Pets
Masks	Perfume	Play dough
Musical instruments	Pictures	Ribbons
Pick-up sticks	Records	Season cards (valentines,
Puzzles	School supplies	birthday)
Rings	Stamps	Toy jewelry
Snakes	Stuffed animals	Wax lips and teeth
Stationery	Whistles	

Summary

Successful classroom management is essential to teaching L&BD students. The need for management tactics among this student population is documented in the literature, although the problem itself has not been extensively studied.

Classroom management suggestions for teachers of L&BD students emphasize positive reinforcement. Such environments include assessing students' reward preferences and issuing rewards. Learning centers can be used to supplement instruction in a positive classroom environment.

Teachers are encouraged to use a reinforcement menu for classroom management. Such a menu includes social reinforcement, special privileges, interest centers, a job board, home/school activities, use of tokens, and object rewards.

11

Teaching Social Behavior

L&BD students are often in need of instruction in social behavior. Effective instruction in this area helps to improve academic performance as well as social adjustment. Methods for teaching social behavior are derived from reinforcement theory and social modeling. Steps for developing a social skills curriculum are described. These are followed with examples from the DTIMS social skills curriculum.

Introduction

L&BD students are often found to lack certain social skills, and because of their ineptness they frequently display maladaptive behavior. Such behavior has been considered and interpreted in different ways. Those oriented toward psychodynamic explanations have interpreted maladaptive and resistant behaviors as *symptoms* of more deep-seated problems (Kubie, 1958; Fenichel, 1945; D'Evelyn, 1957; Bonney, 1960). Those who are concerned about overt manifestations of inadequate behavior view it as responses to be changed directly (Quay, 1963; Stephens, 1976; Woody, 1969). Regardless of how misbehavior is viewed, its importance in classroom learning has been firmly established (Graubard, 1971). O'Leary (1972), among others, has presented important reasons for relating social behaviors to academic performance. Improved social relations, better concentration, attention to directions, and self-control are all desirable goals for teachers to develop among their students.

There is an increasing concern with students who present conduct disorders or who otherwise behave in maladaptive ways in classrooms — a concern which extends beyond L&BD students. Most teachers want to help students who present maladaptive behavior in classrooms, but they often mistakenly believe that changing such behavior exceeds their realm of expertise, thinking that maladaptive behavior is more difficult to change than it usually is.

Basically there are two general approaches teachers can use in helping L&BD students to improve their social behavior. The first is represented by the classroom management tactics described in chapter 10. With this approach, teachers modify environmental elements in order to control students and to instruct them in the consequences of their behaviors.

Another approach involves systematically teaching L&BD students appropriate social behavior. The instruction is functional and is very much the same as effectively teaching academic skills.

Social instruction in schools is often accomplished in haphazard ways since there is rarely an articulated curriculum for teaching social behavior. Thus, students acquire social skills, attitudes, and values through a hidden curriculum which permits socialization in unsystematic and indirect ways. Saylor and Alexander (1974) point out that much important instruction in schools is unofficial and therefore not public.

Behaviors which children imitate and those which teachers reinforce in their students are those which teachers prefer where social curricula are nonexistent. Several studies have identified those student characteristics preferred by teachers (Dunn & Kowitz, 1970; Feshback, 1969; Hoy, 1967; Milburn, 1974). While the characteristics vary, teachers tend to prefer students who exhibit self-control and emotional stability.

Social Behaviors for Schooling

Milburn (1974) found that teachers rated as most important for success in their classrooms social skills concerned with order, rules, obedience, and responsibility. In addition to those behaviors viewed by teachers as important for classroom instruction, developing responsible social conduct in schools is important for other reasons as well. Through such instruction, students develop awareness of others' rights; their society and social settings are improved; desirable conditions for academic learning are created; and, as their coping skills develop, students' personal adjustments are improved.

Awareness of Others' Rights

In populated urban centers individuals are expected to be more sensitive to the presence of others. Schools present social settings in which students can learn responses which demonstrate concerns for others. Among the in-school behaviors which show consideration for others include maintaining a low noise level, using public property with care, maintaining sanitary conditions, being careful when walking in order to allow space for others, dealing with frustrations, anger, and other emotions in socially acceptable ways, and sharing time in equitable ways.

As resources for human living become more limited, it will become increasingly necessary for people to conserve energy, food, water, and other necessities of life. Therefore it becomes important to teach students at an early age how to conserve such resources so that they may be shared more widely with others.

Improves Society

Socially sensitive behavior contributes to a better society for everyone by reducing frustrations and making living conditions more pleasant, thus increasing happiness. Thousands of automobile accidents and deaths are attributable to drivers failing to heed traffic laws and to other personal acts of carelessness, rudeness or insensitivity.

A sizable amount of damage to public property is done by unthinking citizens who, without criminal intent, simply are careless in using facilities which are publically owned: highway and street signs are damaged and moved; trees and plants are carved; flowers in public parks are picked; portions of property are seized as souvenirs; parks, streets and highways are littered; radio and television volumes are increased without thought of others in nearby apartments and automobiles. School personnel must be made aware of the seriousness of these problems. They must also begin to teach systematically social behaviors and attitudes which will reduce these problems of everyday living.

Creates Desirable Conditions for Academic Learning

Schooling occurs best when students engage in behaviors which encourage learning. Students will be most responsive to those conditions which facilitate learning. An atmosphere which is both friendly and serious requires students to behave in responsible ways, thus contributing to desirable conditions for academic learning.

Students' Personal Adjustments Are Improved

Individuals who demonstrate appropriate coping skills for a given social environment are typically termed "well-adjusted."When these same skills are transferable to other settings, their personal skills are further enhanced. Students who learn to use appropriate social skills in schools are more likely to use similar responses when faced with these same conditions in other settings and in the future. (Stephens, 1975, p. 207)

L&BD students often present various maladaptive social behaviors. In many instances, their behaviors form the basis for receiving special instruction. Several studies have demonstrated the influence of students' behaviors on teachers' responses. Graubard, Rosenberg, and Miller (1971) taught seven special class children, ages 12 to 15, to influence their teachers' behavior. After being taught outside their classrooms to make eye contact, ask for extra help, make positive comments to teachers, sit up straight and nod in agreement when teachers spoke, come to class early, and ask for extra assignments, the students increased significantly positive contacts from classroom teachers.

In another study, Sherman and Cormier (1974) provided rewards to change two fifth graders' disruptive behavior without their teacher's knowledge. The percentage of positive verbal teacher responses to the students increased, and the negative verbal responses decreased.

Both studies indicate that positive social behavior of students result in improved teachers' behavior towards them. It is similarly widely recognized that inappropriate classroom behavior results in negative responses from teachers.

Methods for Teaching Social Behavior in School

There have been numerous successful attempts to develop social behaviors in schools. The methods used that have been effective have been derived primarily from operant conditioning and social modeling. There are methods which combine both of these theoretical approaches as well as variations of each.

Operant Conditioning

Contingency contracting and free operant tactics represent the operant methods commonly used to teach social behavior.

Contingency Contracting

Strategies for teaching social behavior that use contingency contracting usually involve four steps. First, the specific behaviors required of the students by the teacher are outlined. Ideally, this step is carried out in a discussion with student participation.

Second, the teacher, with student participation, identifies rewards for which they would like to work. These may be anything of value to students. The teacher may also arrange contracts in which the rewards are delivered outside the class or school, e.g., by the principal or parents. It is essential, however, that the rewards be available to students only for the desired behavior.

Third, terms of the contract are arranged, e.g., *if you do* _____, *you will receive* _____. The contract should also specify the amount and type of behavior required and the type and amount of reward.

Fourth, the teacher either watches for the behavior to occur naturally or arranges conditions so that the behavior can occur. Students are then rewarded according to the terms of the contract.

Two important factors should be considered when electing to use contingency contracting: (1) the concept may be new to some students and it will therefore be necessary to teach it, and (2) when using contingency contracting, it is assumed that the necessary behavior has been learned and must only be elicited. If either of these two conditions are not present, then a shaping approach or social modeling should be used.

Free Operant Approaches

Shaping and other operant techniques may be used without contracting with students in advance of instruction. Teachers can set the occasion for responses and then reinforce them, or they can be on the alert for desirable behavior and reinforce it when it occurs.

When teachers use free operant reinforcement, they should inform students specifically as to why they are receiving reinforcement. Teachers should provide cues to students by reinforcing other students for desirable behavior and by providing verbal, written, and other types of visual and auditory reminders. If cues and social reinforcement do not bring about an increase in desired behavior, praise should be accompanied by concrete reinforcers, such as tokens, points, and stars, to be exchanged for rewards. It is important that rewards of this sort are considered as a last resort. An effort should be made to decrease gradually the use of tangible rewards and to continue use of social rewards to maintain the behavior.

Shaping, or successive approximations as it is sometimes termed, may also be used to teach new behaviors in addition to modifying existing responses. When shaping is used to develop responses, it is necessary to identify the behavior to be taught, describe that behavior in specific and observable terms (ask what will students be doing when they have acquired this behavior?), begin to reinforce responses which may be far short of the final goal, and gradually discontinue reinforcing the lower ordered behavior and begin rewarding responses which are more closely related to the final goal. Anecdote 11.1 depicts the use of shaping.

ANECDOTE 11.1[1]

Mr. Marks' seventh grade English class met immediately prior to their lunch period. Many of the 32 students in the class evidenced little or no interest in the subject matter. Despite various attempts on Mr. M's part to make his instruction more interesting, a core of about 12 students persisted in showing little interest. This lack of interest was displayed by: (1) sleeping during class discussions, (2) careless completion of assignments, (3) non-completion of assignments, and (4) disruptive comments during class.

---

1. From Thomas M. Stephens, *Implementing behavioral approaches in elementary and secondary schools*. Columbus: Charles E. Merrill, 1975, pp. 135–136.

Mr. Marks noted that almost all of the students rushed to leave the room immediately at the close of the period to be in the cafeteria lines as soon as possible. He proceeded to use shaping as a means of improving student attitude toward the subject matter:

First, he identified the target behavior to be taught: *Constructive contributions to class discussions.*

Second, he asked: What will students be doing when they are contributing to discussions? *Students will be raising their hands seeking to contribute to class discussions. When called upon, students' comments will relate to the topic under discussion.*

Third, he began to reinforce students who merely demonstrated an interest by seeking to participate. Mr. Marks announced to the class, 15 minutes before the period was to end: "We will now have a discussion concerning the material each of you are working on." As students raised their hands and were called on and their contribution to the discussion was completed, Mr. Marks said: "_____, that was a good contribution to the discussion, you may leave now for lunch." Hearing this, more students began raising their hands hoping to be recognized. Those that were called on were excused regardless of the quality of their contributions.

The next day, Mr. Marks used the same tactic except that he rewarded those who contributed by excusing them from that night's assignment rather than dismissing them early.

Fourth, on the third day, Mr. Marks began to be more selective in issuing reinforcement. He continued this tactic for the remainder of the term. The shaping process from this point on was as follows:

1. At first when the student's contribution was clearly incorrect, he would respond by saying, "that was a good try." "You might want to check in your book to be more accurate. After you find that section, raise your hand and I'll give you another chance." Students who complied and read the correct passages were rewarded, sometimes by being dismissed early, or being excused from that day's assignment, or by receiving extra credit toward a better grade.

2. Later, students were only rewarded when their contributions were correct the first time, although Mr. Marks would recognize faulty attempts and would encourage students to correct their responses. Occasionally, he would reward a student who tried but whose response was not entirely correct, in order to shape his participation.

3. Later, more precise responses were expected and rewarded. He continued, however, to encourage students to verify their statements and permitted them to try again.

4. He phased out completely dismissing students early and excusing students from outside assignments. He continued, however, to recognize students for their attempts and to give extra credit for correct responses. When interest seemed to diminish, he would return to the earlier rewards but on more extended schedules of reinforcement.

Social Modeling

Social modeling strategies are designed to provide examples for students to follow. Vicarious modeling and overt modeling methods have been used successfully with L&BD students.

Vicarious Modeling

Role playing and bibliotherapy have been used as approaches by classroom teachers. Schubert (1975) described the role of bibliotherapy in reading instruction. It involves identifying reading material that contains characters, attitudes, values, and situations which can be used as models for students. These materials may be read to or by students. Although experimental studies are not reported showing the effects of bibliotherapy, considerable authoritative opinion and rationales have been established for its use (Emrich, 1966; Shrodes, 1955).

Role playing involves having students assume roles that are not normally their own. Or if the roles are ones that are theirs, they are enacted in settings not typical of the role. The purpose of role playing is to change behavior and attitudes in directions of those performed.

Role playing has been used widely with children in schools. Shaftel and Shaftel (1967) advocate its use in teaching social values and decision making. They consider it to be a desirable group counseling procedure for teachers' use as well as a method for teaching citizenship.

Role playing and related procedures used to aid students in changing their behavior were outgrowths of the psychodrama movement in education and psychology. Although research on behavior change through psychodramatic role playing is sparse, that movement provided several techniques which are now used systematically by behaviorally oriented professionals. Sturm (1965) described the behavioristic aspects of psychodrama. He concluded that learning theory suggests the advantages of psychodrama because it generates vivid, lifelike behavior and cues. Psychodrama requires total behavior in responding rather than merely verbal behavior.

Fictional and nonfictionalized accounts of desirable social behavior being rewarded can be used to teach social attitudes and behaviors. For young children and others who do not read, stories may be read or told to them. The purpose of using printed matter in this way is to teach appropriate social behavior vicariously.

Television and other forms of mass media shape students' attitudes and behaviors. These same means of communicating can be used by teachers to influence students. Among ways to use media for vicarious social modelings are:

1. Discuss and post news items which portray people who engaged in socially desirable behavior. Select, in particular, those accounts which describe such behavior being rewarded.

2. Show movies that display worthwhile social behavior.

3. Discuss scheduled television programs which you know depict desirable social behavior. Television magazines and news columns often describe programs in advance of their being shown. Encourage students to watch such programs and to discuss them the next day.

4. Call to students' attention books which depict behavior of a socially valuable nature.

5. Lead class discussions on topics of social importance. Encourage students to discuss ways that citizens can participate in such endeavors and what desirable consequences will occur.

6. Assign students to write short stories in which the characters perform worthwhile services for which they are rewarded.

7. Make socially acceptable behavior exciting to students. Point out how such behavior helps all people indirectly.

8. Take time to discuss, not lecture, with students socially beneficial events which occur or those scheduled to take place.

9. Use biographical accounts of noted individuals who contributed to the neighborhood's, community's, nation's or world's well-being.

10. Lead students to recognize how mankind is dependent upon each of us to behave in socially responsible ways. (Stephens, 1975, pp. 141-143)

Overt Modeling

It is important for learners to observe models being rewarded for desirable behavior since social modeling occurs when students learn new behaviors by observing others. In this way, they learn those behaviors that have positive consequences.

More complicated behaviors are also learned through modeling. Behaviors often consist of a string of responses which include both motor and verbal activities. Sometimes it is helpful to have one student verbalize responses, while others actually perform the behaviors. This technique, which Bandura (1969) has termed *verbal modeling cues,* is described by him in this way:

> However, after adequate language development is achieved, people rely extensively upon verbal modeling cues for guiding their behavior. Thus, for example, one can usually assemble relatively complicated mechanical equipment, acquire rudimentary social and vocational skills, and learn appropriate ways of behaving in almost any situation simply by matching the responses described in instructional manuals. The use of verbal forms of modeling makes it possible to transmit an almost infinite variety of values and response patterns that would be exceedingly difficult and time-consuming to portray behaviorally. (pp. 145-146)

Practicing social responses is another way to teach new behaviors. *Behavior rehearsing* is a technique where students are given instructions and sometimes models to imitate and are then assigned practice time to engage in the behavior.

Seven steps have been suggested for teachers to follow when implementing behavior rehearsing (Stephens, 1975). These are:

1. Set up a sequence of responses for students to observe. It is important to make certain that the behaviors they will observe are the desired ones.

2. Instruct students in advance as to which responses are to be noted by them.

3. Enact the behavior or have it performed by someone who will do it correctly.

4. Provide verbal descriptions for the behavior as it is occurring.

5. Reward those who are engaged in the activity as they are performing being sure that the observers see or hear the reinforcement.

6. Have students who have observed rehearse the activity, permitting students to provide verbal descriptions.

7. Repeat rehearsals as needed and have students engage in the actual behavior under authentic circumstances when possible.

How to Develop a Social Skills Curriculum

Social skills and attitudes are essential ingredients of instructional programs for L&BD students, but most school programs have not established curricula in this important area. Special teachers can, however, develop a set of skills, assessment procedures, and instructional strategies following the DTIMS format.

The social skills component of DTIMS follows the same directive teaching format as do the academic components. First, the behavior is defined and stated in behavioral terms, specifying both the observable movements which make up the behavior and the conditions under which the behavior is to occur. Next the behavior is assessed, and the student's level of performance on a particular skill is determined. Teaching strategies are prescribed to fit the student's needs as determined by the assessment. The DTIMS social skills strategies are of three types: Social Modeling, Social Reinforcement, and Contingency Contracting, with the kind of strategy to be chosen on the basis of assessment. As in other components of the system, progress is evaluated continually, and strategies are changed to fit the student's level of performance. Figure 11.1 shows the process.

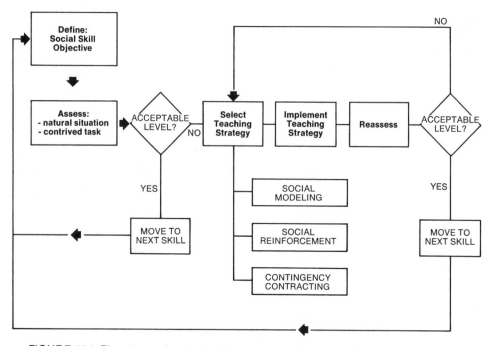

FIGURE 11.1. Flowchart of social skills assessment and teaching procedures

Step 1. Defining Behaviors to Be Taught

The social skills list.   The DTIMS social skills component presents social skills grouped into four categories, one concerned with behaviors related to the environment (ER), one with interpersonal skills (IP), one with self-related behaviors (SR), and one with task-related (TR) social skills. Within each major category are a series of subcategories and groups of sequentially ordered skills with the subcategories.

The list of skills was generated from a number of sources: classroom observations, a view of relevant literature, and a content analysis of behavior rating instruments. The list was submitted in questionnaire form to a group of special education and regular education teachers for "consensual validation." The responses of these 260 teachers indicated that they considered all of the skills to have some degree of importance for their own classes. The teachers using this component may find that skills important to them are missing, or that some of those developed here are not relevant for the structure of their class, the age group of their students, or the cultural context within which they are operating. The social skills component is developed in such a way that teachers may freely use or decide not to use a given group of skills, since except for the sequencing within subcategories, the groups of skills can be treated as independent from each other. The format of the assessment tasks and teaching strategies is easily learned, and teachers may wish to apply the techniques to the development of further social behaviors not included in this curriculum.

Coding system.   A coding system is used to facilitate access to the skills, and each skill has been assigned a code number. In the skill coded "ER/CE-0002-L1-S," for example, the first two letters ER refer to the major category "Environment Related"; the next two, CE, represent the subcategory "Care for the Environment"; and the numerals which follow (0002, 0004, 0006, etc.) represent the number of the skill within the sequence of skills in the subcategory. L1 refers to the level of difficulty of the skill, which is either Level 1 or Level 2 (L2). The final letter or letters may be *S, A, IM, IR,* or *IC* with the following meanings:

> S: Skill statement
> A: Assessment task
> IM: Instructional strategy—social modeling
> IR: Instructional strategy—social reinforcement
> IC: Instructional strategy—contingency contracting

Step 2. Assessing the Behavior

Each assessment task includes the statement of the skill as a behavioral objective and a preliminary rating scale to be completed by the teacher on the basis of his or her immediate knowledge of the child's performance on the skill. If the teacher does not have sufficient knowledge to rate the student, an assessment task is suggested which can be carried out with the student to provide an opportunity for the behavior to occur and be assessed. In rating social behavior teachers are merely asked to indicate whether the behavior is performed at an "acceptable" level.

No attempt is made to specify a criterion level. It is assumed that teachers will vary in the quantity and quality of a behavior they will accept, and that their criteria will vary at times from student to student. Using a framework adapted from Mager and Pipe (1970), teachers are asked to rate the student on the assessment sheet according to one of the following three statements:

1. Student exhibits the skill at an acceptable level.
2. Student exhibits skill occasionally at a lower-than-acceptable level.
3. Student does not exhibit the skill.

Assessment data are to be transferred to either individual or class profile sheets. The individual profile sheets can be used to record student progress, and teachers may find the class profile sheets useful for identifying several children who are deficient on a particular skill, who may then form a group for instruction.

From assessment to prescription. The rating scores, 1, 2, or 3, indicating level of performance, provide direction to the teacher for selecting a teaching strategy. The procedures are as follows:

1. A rating of *1* indicates that the student exhibits the skill at an acceptable level. The teacher need not spend time teaching this skill and may move to the next skill.

2. A rating of *2* indicates that the student exhibits the skill occasionally at a lower-than-acceptable level. The student has the behavior in his/her repertoire but conditions in the environment do not provide sufficient incentives for him/her to perform the behavior. It may be, also, that he/she is getting some "payoff" for not engaging in the desired behavior and doing something undesirable instead. A reinforcement strategy, either social reinforcement or contingency contracting, is indicated for this child. Selection of which kind of reinforcement strategy should be made on the basis of the teacher's assessment of the student's reward preferences. Does he/she respond to teacher praise and attention, or are these insufficient to

increase the amount of desired behavior? If the latter is true, the teacher may need to move to an explicit contract, specifying the behavior and the reward, using tangible rewards if necessary.

3. A rating of *3* indicates that the student does not exhibit the skill. If it appears on the basis of assessment through observation in the natural environment or on an assessment task that the student never performs the behavior, it is safe to assume that he/she may not know how. In this case the teacher begins with a social modeling strategy to teach the behavior. After the student exhibits the behavior in modeling and practice situations, the teacher needs to move to social reinforcement or contingency contracting strategies to maintain the behavior in the classroom environment. See Figure 11.2 for a schematic view of this process.

Step 3. Instructional Strategies

Social skills instructional strategies follow a prescribed format which is intended to incorporate ideas developed in the area of behavior change. Although the strategies are written in *cookbook* form with the hope that even the most inexperienced teacher may be able to follow and use the ideas, teachers are encouraged to use the strategies as a beginning point from which they can develop strategies that are most relevant for their own students. Some strategies are written for a group and some for an individual *target* child. Teachers may adapt the strategies for use with one child, with a small group, or with a large class as the need arises. A procedure for selecting teaching strategies is shown in Figure 11.2.

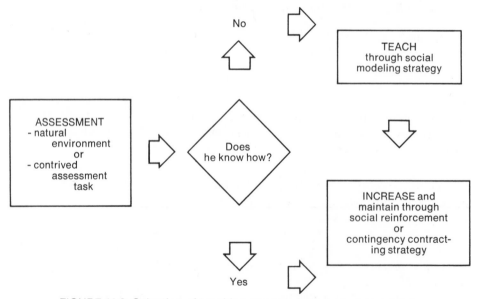

FIGURE 11.2. Selection of teaching strategy based on assessment

Social Modeling Strategies

The format for social modeling strategies is designed to provide a model for students to follow with opportunities for them to make the responses and be reinforced for their efforts. The procedures are as follows:

1. The teacher sets the stage for modeling or role playing either through a discussion, a story, a film, or some other medium which will indicate to the student

the value of learning that skill. The teacher should encourage as much student discussion around the topic as is possible and relate the behavior to events familiar to the students.

2. The teacher draws out of the discussion the specific steps which make up the behavior and makes these explicit to the students, perhaps outlining them on the chalkboard.

3. The teacher goes through the motions of performing the behavior or has a student demonstrate, asking other students to tell what was done.

4. The teacher sets up a situation in which each student has an opportunity to imitate the behavior which was demonstrated and practice it a number of times.

5. At each step the teacher watches for appropriate responses and provides either praise or corrective feedback, with an emphasis on *positive* responses for students' efforts.

When students are first learning a behavior it may not be performed in an ideal way. The teacher needs to praise for efforts in the right direction rather than for perfection, as well as look for situations in which the skill can be broken down into even smaller steps.

Social Reinforcement Strategies

Social reinforcement strategies stress using various social reinforcers which teachers have at their disposal, including looking at students, verbal praise, smiling, and touching students. In using verbal praise, teachers are encouraged to use students' names to tell students in specific terms what they are being praised for, and in most cases praise where other students can hear. Strategies also incorporate suggestions for providing cues to students through reinforcing other students or for providing verbal, written, and other types of visual or auditory reminders. If cues and social reinforcement do not bring about an increase in the desired behavior, it is suggested that praise be accompanied by concrete reinforcers such as tokens, points, stars, to be exchanged at a later point for something students value.

Contingency Contracting Strategies

Contingency contracting strategies are built around the idea of the contingency contract. Steps in the contingency contracting strategies are:

1. The teacher outlines to students the specific behaviors desired, as in Step 2 of the social modeling strategy. Ideally, this would be carried out in a discussion with the students participating.

2. The teacher, preferably together with students, identifies a reinforcer for which students would like to work. Reinforcers can be anything students value, ranging from activities to concrete objects. The teacher may also want to work out contracts in which the reward is delivered outside the class or the school. An important consideration for a reinforcer to be effective is that it must be available to students only for performing the desired behavior.

3. The teacher sets up and makes explicit the terms of the contract, i.e., "If you do _____, you will receive _____." The contract should specify both the amount of behavior required and the type and amount of reward.

4. The teacher either watches for the behavior to occur naturally or sets up a situation in which the behavior can occur, then rewards students for performing according to the terms of the contract.

Rules that have been outlined by Homme (1970) for carrying out contingency contracts are summarized below:

a) The payoff (reward) should be immediate after performance of the task.
b) The initial contracts should require small amounts of behavior.
c) Rewards should come frequently and in small amounts.
d) The contract should reward accomplishment rather than obedience.
e) Reward performance *after* it occurs.
f) The contract must be fair.
g) The terms must be clear.
h) The contract must be carried out honestly.
i) The contract must be positive.
j) Contracting must be carried out systematically and consistently.

Step 4. Evaluate

After carrying out a teaching strategy, the teacher must evaluate the effectiveness of the teaching. Is the child who previously never showed the behavior now performing the behavior at least some of the time? Is the child who exhibited the behavior only some of the time now performing at an acceptable level? If the answers to these questions are positive, the teacher can believe that the interventions are appropriate. If not, some of these changes might be made:

1) Change instructional strategy to a different kind.
2) Change reinforcer to a more powerful one, and make sure reinforcers are delivered immediately following the desired behavior.
3) Examine the task to determine whether it needs to be broken down into smaller steps.
4) Determine whether some prerequisite skills are missing and need to be taught.
5) Look at the situation to see whether there are reinforcers in the situation for inappropriate behaviors. Use extinction to eliminate competing reinforcement, or use punishment procedures to eliminate the inappropriate behaviors. Punishment and extinction procedures should only be used, however, if the appropriate behaviors are also being taught and reinforced.

Sample Assessments and Strategies[2]

The DTIMS social skills manual consists of suggestions for teaching 140 social skills using the directive teaching approach. The teacher (1) defines the skill to be taught, (2) assesses performance of the skill according to his or her criteria for acceptable performance and selects a teaching strategy based on the assessment, (3) implements a teaching strategy, either social modeling, social reinforcement, or contingency management, and (4) evaluates the effects of the instruction, changing procedures if necessary. Once a social skill is taught and performed at an acceptable level, the teacher encourages its continued performance through praise and recognition. The DTIMS social skill list is shown in chapter 9.

2. These examples are taken from The Directive Teaching Instructional Management System, Social Skills, Copyright © 1976 by Thomas M. Stephens.

Two samples from the major categories, environmental, interpersonal, self-related, and task-related, are shown below. Each sample contains an assessment task, a teaching strategy, and references to commercial materials.

Environmental

Assessment Task

CODE: S-ER-CE-0004-L1-A
SKILL: To drink properly from the water fountain.
   Objective: The student drinks properly from the water fountain by: (1) turning the fountain on, (2) bending over in front of the fountain, and (3) drinking without spilling water out of fountain.
ASSESSMENT:
   1. Assess from previous knowledge of student OR
   2. Use Assessment Task
   Assessment Task: Take the students out into the hall and ask each student to take a drink, or position yourself near water fountain after recess and watch students drink.
EVALUATION:
   1. _____Student exhibits the skill at an acceptable level. *Teaching procedure:* Mastery. No teaching necessary. Move to the next skill.
   2. _____Student exhibits skill occasionally at a lower-than-acceptable level.
      Teaching procedure: Use either social reinforcement or contingency management strategy to increase performance.
   3. _____Student does not exhibit the skill.
      Teaching procedure: Use social modeling strategy to teach the skill. Use social reinforcement or contingency management strategy to increase and maintain the skill.

Record evaluation and date on Social Skills Assessment Form and select appropriate teaching strategy.

Teaching Strategy

CODE: S-ER-CE-0004-L1-1m
SKILL: The student drinks properly from the water fountain by turning the fountain on, bending over in front of the fountain, and drinking without spilling.
Social Modeling
   1. Identify a need for the behavior through a classroom discussion of elements of the behavior, for example, discussing proper use of school equipment and public property, what happens if the water fountain is not used properly and water is spilled on the floor, and consideration for others in the use of the water fountain. Write key words on board.
   2. Identify specific behaviors to be modeled:
      a) Drinking from the water fountain at appropriate times (as defined by existing rules).
      b) Drinking by turning on the fountain.
      c) Bending over in front of the fountain, and
      d) Drinking without spilling water out of the fountain.
   3. Model drinking from the fountain for the class. Ask students to identify elements of the modeled behavior. Praise students who make good responses.
   4. Have class practice drinking from the fountain, with each student given an opportunity to drink.
   5. Praise those students who drink properly from the fountain.
   6. Maintain proper drinking through reinforcement.

Commercial Reference

MATERIALS CODE: S-ER-CE-0004-L1-M
SKILL: To drink properly from water fountain.
SCP1.111A

PUBLISHER	CONTINENTAL PRESS
TITLE	COURTESY IN THE COMMUNITY
SERIES	____
EDITION	FIRST
TYPE	TEACHER'S GUIDE
YEAR	1972
PAGE NUMBERS	003

Assessment Task

CODE: S-ER-CE-0006-L1-A
SKILL: To clean up after breaking or spilling something.
> *Objective:* The student will pick up or mop up the remains of something he has broken or spilled, leaving the area in the same condition it was in before the incident.

ASSESSMENT:
1. Assess from previous knowledge of student OR
2. Use Assessment Task
   Assessment Task: Watch for the behavior to occur or contrive a situation; for example, spread debris, such as broken pieces of pencil or crumpled papers in a small area. Ask the student to pretend that he has dropped or broken something and that these are the pieces. Observe for picking up and proper disposal of the pieces.

EVALUATION:
1. _____Student exhibits the skill at an acceptable level.
   Teaching procedure: Mastery. No teaching necessary. Move to the next skill.
2. _____Student exhibits skill occasionally at a lower-than-acceptable level.
   Teaching procedure: Use either social reinforcement or contingency management strategy to increase performance.
3. _____Student does not exhibit the skill.
   Teaching procedure: Use social modeling strategy to teach the skill. Use social reinforcement or contingency management strategy to increase and maintain the skill.

Record evaluation and date on Social Skills Assessment Form and select appropriate teaching strategy.

Teaching Strategy

CODE: S-ER-CE-0006-L1-1m
SKILL: The student will pick up or mop up the remains of something he has broken or spilled, leaving the area in the same condition it was in before the incident.
Social Modeling
1. Identify a need for the behavior through a classroom discussion. Discuss cleanliness, consideration for others, and responsibility, etc. Have students contribute ideas to the discussion. To initiate discussion, teacher may want to ask questions, such as: "What would you do if you dropped your milk carton on the floor?" "What would happen if you just left it there?" Write key words on the board.
2. Identify specific behaviors to be modeled: If you have spilled or broken something:
   a) pick up the pieces and throw them away
   b) mop up the remaining litter
   c) leave the area in the same condition it was in before the incident

3. Model the behavior for the class. Simulate having broken or spilled something. You may use bits of crumpled papers or something else as props representing the litter you need to clean up. Model cleaning up the area. Ask students to identify elements of the modeled behavior. Praise students who make good responses.
4. Have the group practice the behavior using the same props the teacher used. Give each student the opportunity to clean up the "mess." Students may be asked to evaluate how well the others have performed the task.
5. Praise those students who clean-up completely.
6. Maintain cleaning up behavior through reinforcement.

Commercial Reference

MATERIALS CODE: S-ER-CE-0006-L2-M
SKILL: To clean up after breaking or spilling something.
    SCP1.110A

PUBLISHER	CONTINENTAL PRESS
TITLE	COURTESY AT HOME
SERIES	____
EDITION	FIRST
TYPE	TEACHER'S GUIDE
YEAR	1972
PAGE NUMBERS	008

Interpersonal

Assessment Task

CODE: S-IP-AA-0004-L1-A
SKILL: To comply with request of peer in position of authority.
    Objective: The student complies with the requests of peers put in a position of authority, for example, class monitors, school crossing monitors, hall monitors.
ASSESSMENT:
1. Assess from previous knowledge of student OR
2. Use Assessment Task
    Assessment Task:
1. Observe student's behavior with student patrols in crossing streets, with hall monitors or other peers in authority.
2. Assign a student to head class. Give him instructions to request the class (or possibly just the target student) to do something which would yield a product, such as printing his name on a piece of paper or copying something from board. Judge compliance by existence of product.
EVALUATION:
1. _____Student exhibits the skill at an acceptable level.
    Teaching procedure: Mastery. No teaching necessary. Move to the next skill.
2. _____Student exhibits skill occasionally at a lower-than-acceptable level.
    Teaching procedure: Use either social reinforcement or contingency management strategy to increase performance.
3. _____Student does not exhibit the skill
    Teaching procedure: Use social modeling strategy to teach the skill. Use social reinforcement or contingency management strategy to increase and maintain the skill.

Record evaluation and date on Social Skills Assessment Form and select appropriate teaching strategy.

Teaching Strategy

CODE: S-IP-AA-0004-Ll-lm
SKILL: The student complies with the requests of peers put in a position of authority, for example, class monitors, school crossing monitors, hall monitors.

Social Modeling

1. Discuss the need to obey the requests of a peer put in a position of authority. Explain that at times a student is put in charge and that other students must obey him to keep order. Discuss with the students what might happen if they did not listen to crossing guards, hall monitors or other students who are asked to help adults. Make the point that when a student is delegated authority by an adult, he represents the adult and must be obeyed just as an adult would be obeyed. (It may be necessary also to discuss how peers put in authority should act in order not to abuse their authority.) Have students contribute ideas to the discussion of how to behave toward another who is given responsibility.
2. Identify specific behaviors to be modeled. When another student is put in charge:
   a) listen to him
   b) do what he says
   Write key words on board.
3. Model the behavior. Assign one student to be in charge of the class. Give the student a list of instructions to give to you. For example:
   "Hand in your math papers."
   "Open your reading books to page 107."
   "Margie, please close the door."
   "Would you please get me the globe from the back of the room."
   "Do the assignment on page 17 in your reading workbook."
   etc.
   Role play a student and model compliance to these orders or instructions. Ask students to describe your behavior and reward accurate responses.
4. Provide opportunity for practice. Appoint a monitor in class and give him a list of instructions to give members of the class. Reward students who comply with the monitor's instructions.
5. Maintain the behavior through reinforcement.

Commercial Reference

MATERIALS CODE: S-IP-AA-0004-Ll-M
SKILL: To comply with request of peer in position of authority
    SCP1.111A
    PUBLISHER   CONTINENTAL PRESS
    TITLE   COURTESY IN THE COMMUNITY
    SERIES   ——
    EDITION   FIRST
    TYPE   TEACHER'S GUIDE
    YEAR   1972
    PAGE NUMBERS   006

Assessment Task

CODE: S-IP-AA-0010-L2-A
SKILL: To question rules which may be unjust.
        Objective: When presented with a rule which may be unjust, the student will question the teacher about the rule in an appropriate way, for example, asking teacher politely to explain the reasons for the rule.

ASSESSMENT:
1. Assess from previous knowledge of student OR
2. Use Assessment Task

   Assessment Task: Establish a role-playing situation. Ask a student to play the part of teacher who has presented a list of rules, and ask target student to demonstrate what he would do if such a list were given to him. Observe whether he is able to raise questions about the unfair rules politely. Sample rules:
   a) No talking during reading period.
   b) No talking during recess.
   c) All coats are to be hung in the closet.
   d) All books are to be kept in desk.
   e) No pets in class.
   f) All students must pay seventy-five cents before they may go out to recess.

EVALUATION:
1. _____Student exhibits the skill at an acceptable level.
   Teaching procedure: Mastery. No teaching necessary. Move to the next skill.
2. _____Student exhibits skill occasionally at a lower-than-acceptable level.
   Teaching procedure: Use either social reinforcement or contingency management strategy to increase performance.
3. _____Student does not exhibit the skill.
   Teaching procedure: Use social modeling strategy to teach the skill. Use social reinforcement or contingency management strategy to increase and maintain the skill.

Record evaluation and date on Social Skills Assessment Form and select appropriate teaching strategy.

Teaching Strategy

CODE: S-1P-AA-0010-L2-1m
SKILL: When presented with a rule which may be unjust, the student will question the teacher about the rule in an appropriate way, for example, asking teacher politely to explain the reasons for the rule.

Social Modeling
1. Discuss the need to question and try to change unjust or unfair rules. General concepts of fairness and justice and their meaning should be explained and discussed. You may draw on historical events such as the colonists' reaction to the English taxation policies, the abolitionists' opposition to slavery, pacifists' objections to the Vietnam conflict, civil rights movements, etc. Point out that many injustices would never have been corrected if someone had not questioned the laws or rules that maintained them. Have students comment on these ideas and contribute other examples of unfair laws or rules, drawn from governmental laws, school or classroom rules. The teacher must be able to acknowledge that sometimes he or she may make a rule or decision which seems unfair and that the student is justified in raising questions about it. Students will need to be told that sometimes what seems to be fair to one person may not seem fair to another and that compromises may be necessary. Discuss with the class ways often used to change rules or laws in our society, for example, petitions, court decisions, letter to congressional representatives. You may use current or historical events to illustrate these ideas. The class may be asked to bring newspaper clippings or articles about efforts to change the laws or rules of society.
2. Identify specific behaviors to be modeled. "When a rule or decision is perceived as unjust, several steps may be taken:

a) Go to the teacher and politely ask the reasons for a rule he or she has made.

b) If the rule is a school-wide issue, ask the teacher to find out from the principal or school authority the reasons for the rule or

c) Go to see the principal by yourself or with a committee of other students to question the rule.

3. Provide a model for the behavior. Set up a role-playing situation in which the teacher (playing a student) goes to the teacher (played by a student) and models appropriate methods of questioning a classroom rule, e.g., "Mrs. Potts, the rule you made about bringing our parents on 'Open School Day' is not fair. Some of us have mothers who work, and we cannot bring them during the day. Here is a petition with the names of students whose mothers work." Ask students to describe the actions taken to question unjust rules or decisions and attempt to change them. Praise accurate responses.

4. Provide an opportunity for practice by setting up role-playing situations similar to the one above and having students take turns playing the questioning student. Have students help generate a list of situations familiar to them involving rules or decisions which they might question. Reward students who make appropriate remarks in the role-playing situation, i.e., raise reasonable objections in a polite, appropriate manner.

5. Maintain the behavior through reinforcement.

Commercial Reference

MATERIALS CODE: S-IP-AA-0010-L2-M
SKILL: To question rules which may be unjust
    RHM1.134A

PUBLISHER	HOUGHTON MIFFLIN
TITLE	FIESTA
SERIES	HOUGHTON MIFFLIN READERS
EDITION	FIRST
TYPE	TEACHER'S GUIDE
YEAR	1971
PAGE NUMBERS	039

Assessment Task

CODE: S-SR-AC-0004-L1-A
SKILL: To make apology when actions have injured or infringed on another.
    Objective: The student apologizes when his actions have injured or infringed on another.
ASSESSMENT:

1. Assess from previous knowledge of student OR
2. Use Assessment Task
Assessment Task: (1) Observe student if he has done something for which an apology would be indicated. Does he apologize to the injured party? (2) Role play: for example, the student pretends that he has just bumped into someone and knocked him down accidently. Have another student play the injured party. Does the target student apologize to the other?
EVALUATION:

1. _____Student exhibits the skill at an acceptable level.
    Teaching procedure: Mastery. No teaching necessary. Move to the next skill.
2. _____Student exhibits skill occasionally at a lower-than-acceptable level.
    Teaching procedure: Use either social reinforcement or contingency management strategy to increase performance.

3. _____Student does not exhibit the skill.
   Teaching procedure: Use social modeling strategy to teach the skill. Use social reinforcement or contingency management strategy to increase and maintain the skill.

Record evaluation and date on Social Skills Assessment Form and select appropriate teaching strategy.

Teaching Strategy

CODE: S-SR-AC-0004-L1-1M
SKILL: The student apologizes when his actions have injured or infringed on another.

Social Modeling
   1. Identify a need for the behavior through a classroom discussion. When available, use stories, films, filmstrips, or some other aid. Have students contribute ideas to the discussion. For example, "What is an apology?" "What kinds of situations require an apology?" "Why should we apologize when we accidentally injure another?" "What can we say when we want to apologize to someone else?"
   2. Identify specific behaviors to be modeled, e.g. When your actions injure or create a hardship or inconvenience for someone else, apologize for your actions by saying, "I'm sorry" or some other appropriate phrase.
   3. Model the behavior. Teacher will accidentally bump into a student and then apologize to the student.
   4. Provide opportunity for practice. Role play situations which require an apology, for example:
      a) Student bumps into another student
      b) Student has his foot in the aisle and another student trips over it
      c) Student drops something when handing it to someone else
      d) A student accidentally slams the door
      e) A student accidentally knocks another's coat on the floor
      (Develop situations appropriate to the class and age of student.) Have each student practice the behavior. Reinforce correct responses.
   5. Maintain the behavior through reinforcement.

Commercial References

MATERIALS CODE: S-SR-AC-0004-L1-M
SKILL: To make apology when actions have injured or infringed on another.

SCP1.109A
PUBLISHER   CONTINENTAL PRESS
TITLE   COURTESY AT SCHOOL
SERIES   ____
EDITION   FIRST
TYPE   TEACHER'S GUIDE
YEAR   1972
PAGE NUMBERS   006

SCP1.110A
PUBLISHER   CONTINENTAL PRESS
TITLE   COURTESY AT HOME
SERIES   ____
EDITION   FIRST
TYPE   TEACHER'S GUIDE
YEAR   1972
PAGE NUMBERS   008

RAMI.124B
PUBLISHER   AMERICAN BOOK COMPANY
TITLE   FAR AND AWAY
SERIES   THE READ SERIES
EDITION   FIRST
TYPE   STUDENT YEAR
YEAR   1968
PAGE NUMBERS   014

RAMI.129B
PUBLISHER   AMERICAN BOOK COMPANY
TITLE   GOLD AND SILVER
SERIES   THE READ SERIES
EDITION   FIRST
TYPE   STUDENT TEXT
YEAR   1968
PAGE NUMBERS   113

RAMI.134B
PUBLISHER   AMERICAN BOOK COMPANY
TITLE   HIGH AND WIDE
SERIES   THE READ SERIES
EDITION   FIRST
TYPE   STUDENT TEXT
YEAR   1968
PAGE NUMBERS   150

RAMI.139B
PUBLISHER   AMERICAN BOOK COMPANY
TITLE   IDEAS AND IMAGES
SERIES   THE READ SERIES
EDITION   FIRST
TYPE   STUDENT TEXT
YEAR   1968
PAGE NUMBERS   173

Assessment Task

CODE: S-SR-AC-0006-L2-A
SKILL: To accept deserved consequences of wrong-doing.
        Objective: When the student has done something wrong, i.e., to injure someone or
        something, the student will accept the adverse consequences of that act without
        excessive complaining.
ASSESSMENT:
   1. Assess from previous knowledge of student OR
   2. Use Assessment Task
   Assessment Task: If possible assess this behavior in the natural environment. If you
   have not had occasion to see this behavior occurring naturally, use a role playing
   situation. Have the student pretend he has just maliciously thrown a textbook out the
   window. Apply what consequences you usually would if this had actually happened.
   Does he accept the consequences without complaining?
EVALUATION:
   1. _____Student exhibits the skill at an acceptable level.
        Teaching procedure: Mastery. No teaching necessary. Move to the next skill.
   2. _____Student exhibits skill occasionally at a lower-than-acceptable level.

Teaching procedure: Use either social reinforcement or contingency management strategy to increase performance.

3. _____Student does not exhibit the skill.

Teaching procedure: Use social modeling strategy to teach the skill. Use social reinforcement or contingency management strategy to increase and maintain the skill.

Record evaluation and date on Social Skills Assessment Form and select appropriate teaching strategy.

Teaching Strategy

CODE: S-SR-AC-0006-L2-1m

SKILL: When the student has done something wrong, i.e., to injure someone or something, the student will accept the adverse consequences of that act without excessive complaining.

Social Modeling

1. Teach this skill in conjunction with SR-EB-0006, i.e., identifying consequences of behavior involving wrongdoing. In discussing possible consequences for wrongdoing, bring up also how one should act if one is punished for hurting someone or something, or doing some other wrong thing. Ask why there is such a thing as punishment, and talk about the value of punishment in helping us learn not to do things which are wrong. In the discussion recognize that no one likes punishment, (if we did, it would not be punishment) but becoming angry or complaining excessively may make the punishment worse. Have students suggest some appropriate ways to act when punished, possibly contrasted with inappropriate ways. Reinforce good responses.

2. Identify the specific behaviors to be modeled. When you have done something wrong, for example, something which injures another or destroys property of another, accept the consequences for your actions without excessive complaining.

3. Model the behavior. Select a student to role play with the teacher. Student (played by teacher) has broken a school window with a ball. Have the student role play the principal giving out a punishment. Teacher in the role of student will demonstrate desirable and undesirable ways of responding to punishment. Have students identify the behaviors.

4. Provide opportunity for practice. Have each student role play a situation where he is justly punished, demonstrating an appropriate way to respond. Sample situations:

a) Student is excluded from game for playing too roughly.

b) Student loses his turn to talk in "Show and Tell" time because he has interrupted several times.

c) Student is required to pay for breaking a mirror in the washroom.

d) Student is required to stay after school for hitting another student.

Add situations appropriate to the class involved. Reinforce good responses in the practice situations.

5. Maintain the behavior through reinforcement.

Commercial References

MATERIALS CODE: S-SR-AC-0006-L2-M

SKILL: To accept deserved consequences of wrongdoing.

RG11.125B

PUBLISHER	GINN
TITLE	THE DOG NEXT DORR
SERIES	READING 360
EDITION	FIRST
TYPE	STUDENT TEXT
YEAR	1969
PAGE NUMBERS	016

RAM1.134B
PUBLISHER   AMERICAN BOOK COMPANY
TITLE   HIGH AND WIDE
SERIES   THE READ SERIES
EDITION   FIRST
TYPE   STUDENT TEXT
YEAR   1968
PAGE NUMBERS   240

RAM1.144B
PUBLISHER   AMERICAN BOOK COMPANY
TITLE   JOYS AND JOURNEYS
SERIES   THE READ SERIES
EDITION   FIRST
TYPE   STUDENT TEXT
YEAR   1968
PAGE NUMBERS   139, 163

SAG1.110Q
PUBLISHER   AMERICAN GUIDANCE SERVICE
TITLE   DUSO MANUAL
SERIES   DUSO KIT
EDITION   FIRST
TYPE   CURRICULUM GUIDE
YEAR   1970
PAGE NUMBERS   144, 145, 146

SAG1.110Q
PUBLISHER   AMERICAN GUIDANCE SERVICE
TITLE   DUSO STORY BOOK 2
SERIES   DUSO KIT
EDITION   FIRST
TYPE   CURRICULUM GUIDE
YEAR   1970
PAGE NUMBERS   172, 173, 174, 175, 176

SAG1.110Q
PUBLISHER   AMERICAN GUIDANCE SERVICE
TITLE   DUSO RECORD 18 AND POSTER VII D
SERIES   DUSO KUT
EDITION   FIRST
TYPE   CURRICULUM GUIDE
YEAR   1970
PAGE NUMBERS   00B

Teaching Strategy

CODE: S-SR-AC-0006-L2-1r
SKILL: When the student has done something wrong, i.e., to injure someone or some-
        thing, the student will accept the adverse consequences of that act without exces-
        sive complaining.
Social Reinforcement
    Identify and praise student when he is willing to accept adverse consequences of his
behavior without excessive complaining. Call attention to his specific actions. For

example, "Tom, you accept the punishment for breaking the window without complaining. You acted very grown up;" "Don, I appreciated the way you acted when you were sent in from recess. You came in without complaining."

Provide cues for target student. Remind the student before giving the punishment that he must accept the consequences of what he did.

Note: The teacher can help lessen complaints or angry responses to deserved punishment by ignoring, being careful not to reinforce them with attention or by making complaints pay off with lessened punishment. Ideally consequences should be established in advance and should be known to the student.

Task Related

Assessment Task

CODE: S-TR-CT-0006-L2-A
SKILL: To continue working on a difficult task until it is completed.
Objective: When assigned a difficult task (below the student's mastery level), the student will persist at the task until it is done, asking for help if necessary.
ASSESSMENT:
1. Assess from previous knowledge of student OR
2. Use Assessment Task
Assessment Task: Assign the student a task below his mastery level (i.e., one with which he may have some difficulty). Does he continue to work on the task until it is completed, asking for help if necessary?
EVALUATION:
1. _____Student exhibits the skill at an acceptable level.
2. _____*Teaching procedure:* Mastery. No teaching necessary. Move to the next skill.
Student exhibits skill occasionaly at a lower-than-acceptable level.
Teaching procedure: Use either social reinforcement or contingency management strategy to increase performance.
3. _____Student does not exhibit the skill.
Teaching procedure: Use social modeling strategy to teach the skill. Use social reinforcement or contingency management strategy to increase and maintain the skill.

Record evaluation and date on Social Skills Assessment Form and select appropriate teaching strategy.

Teaching Strategy

CODE: S-TR-CT-0006-L2-1m
SKILL: When assigned a difficult task (below the student's mastery level), the student will persist at the task until it is done, asking for help if necessary.
Social Modeling
1. Identify a need for the behavior through a classroom discussion. Talk about how students feel about working on difficult assignments, that everyone has difficulties with some kinds of work, but the best thing to do is keep on working until it is finished. Elicit from students ideas about how to go on working on something which is very difficult—for example, asking the teacher or a classmate for help if necessary. If there are students in the class who are particularly persistent in the face of difficult tasks, try to have them tell what they do to make themselves keep working.
2. Identify specific behaviors to be modeled, e.g., when given a difficult task, work on it until completed, asking for help if needed.

3. Model the behavior. Take the role of a student working on difficult arithmetic paper. Ask a student to take the part of the teacher or a helping peer. Talk out loud as if to yourself as you work on the paper, describing your actions, for example, "I finished this problem, but now there is one I can't do. I'll have to get help." Raise your hand and demonstrate getting help, then resume the monologue. "Now I'll try the next problem. I think I can do it because it looks like the last one." Continue in this manner until the paper is complete. Ask students to identify your actions.
4. Provide opportunity for practice. Give each student a task which is below mastery level, i.e., one which he cannot work on completely independently. Ask students to work at the task until it is finished. Make yourself or other students available to provide assistance. Provide reinforcement to students who continue working. Praise students both for working and for completing the paper.
5. Maintain the behavior through reinforcement.

Commercial References

MATERIALS CODE: S-TR-CT-0006-L2-M

SKILL: To continue working on a difficult task until it is completed.

RSF2.115B

PUBLISHER	SCOTT FORESMAN
TITLE	MOVING AHEAD
SERIES	OPEN HIGHWAYS
EDITION	FIRST
TYPE	STUDENT TEXT
YEAR	1967
PAGE NUMBERS	106

SAG1.110Q

PUBLISHER	AMERICAN GUIDANCE SERVICE
TITLE	DUSO MANUAL
SERIES	DUSO KIT
EDITION	FIRST
TYPE	CURRICULUM GUIDE
YEAR	1970
PAGE NUMBERS	089, 090, 091

SAG1.110Q

PUBLISHER	AMERICAN GUIDANCE SERVICE
TITLE	DUSO STORY BOOK 1
SERIES	DUSO KIT
EDITION	FIRST
TYPE	CURRICULUM GUIDE
YEAR	1970
PAGE NUMBERS	088, 089, 090, 091

SAG1.110Q

PUBLISHER	AMERICAN GUIDANCE SERVICE
TITLE	DUSO RECORD 10 AND POSTER IV B
SERIES	DUSO KIT
EDITION	FIRST
TYPE	CURRICULUM GUIDE
YEAR	1970
PAGE NUMBERS	00A

RG11.110B
PUBLISHER	GINN
TITLE	A DUCK IS A DUCK
SERIES	READING 360
EDITION	FIRST
TYPE	STUDENT TEXT
YEAR	1969
PAGE NUMBERS	060

RAM1.134B
PUBLISHER	AMERICAN BOOK COMPANY
TITLE	HIGH AND WIDE
SERIES	THE READ SERIES
EDITION	FIRST
TYPE	STUDENT TEXT
YEAR	1968
PAGE NUMBERS	118

RAM1.139B
PUBLISHER	AMERICAN BOOK COMPANY
TITLE	IDEAS AND IMAGES
SERIES	THE READ SERIES
EDITION	FIRST
TYPE	STUDENT TEXT
YEAR	1968
PAGE NUMBERS	009

Assessment Task

CODE: S-TR-FD-0002-L1-A

SKILL: To follow teacher's verbal directions.
Objective: The student follows the teacher's verbal directions.

ASSESSMENT:
1. Assess from previous knowledge of student OR
2. Use Assessment Task
Assessment Task: Give student simple verbal directions. Does he follow them?

EVALUATION:
1. _____Student exhibits the skill at an acceptable level.
Teaching procedure: Mastery. No teaching necessary. Move to the next skill.
2. _____Student exhibits skill occasionally at a lower-than-acceptable level.
Teaching procedure: Use either social reinforcement or contingency management strategy to increase performance.
3. _____Student does not exhibit the skill.
Teaching procedure: Use social modeling strategy to teach the skill. Use social reinforcement or contingency management strategy to increase and maintain the skill.

Record evaluation and date on Social Skills Assessment Form and select appropriate teaching strategy.

Teaching Strategy

CODE: S-TR-FD-0002-L1-1m
SKILL: To follow teacher's verbal directions.
Social Modeling

1. Identify a need for the behavior through a classroom discussion. Discuss the importance of following verbal directions. Give examples of adults following verbal directions, for example, needing to fill out reports at teachers' meetings, driving with a friend who gives directions to the new museum. When available use stories, films, filmstrips, or other media to stimulate discussion. Have students contribute ideas to the discussion. For example, "Why should you follow the teacher's directions? What would happen if no one followed the directions? What do we have to do if we want to follow directions?"

2. Identify specific behaviors to be modeled, e.g., when the teacher gives a verbal direction, listen to what the teacher says, and do what the teacher says.

3. Model the behavior. Select a student to serve as a model. Verbalize a direction to the student which he is capable of carrying out. The student will follow through with the direction. Praise the student for following the direction. Have other students identify what the student did in following the direction and how closely it corresponded to what the teacher said.

4. Provide opportunity for practice. Teacher will give a verbal direction and call on a student to carry it out. Examples of directions: open the door; put your math paper on the teacher's desk; put your head down on your desk; shake hands with the teacher. Allow each student to have an opportunity to follow directions. Vary the complexity of the directions according to the abilities of the students. Reinforce correct responses.

5. Maintain the behavior through reinforcement.

Commercial References

MATERIALS CODE: S-TR-FD-0002-L1-M
SKILL: To follow the teacher's verbal directions.

RAM1.134B
PUBLISHER	AMERICAN BOOK COMPANY
TITLE	HIGH AND WIDE
SERIES	THE READ SERIES
EDITION	FIRST
TYPE	STUDENT TEXT
YEAR	1968
PAGE NUMBERS	071

RHM1.114A
PUBLISHER	HOUGHTON-MIFFLIN
TITLE	RAINBOWS
SERIES	HOUGHTON-MIFFLIN READERS
EDITION	FIRST
TYPE	TEACHER'S GUIDE
YEAR	1971
PAGE NUMBERS	068

Summary

Teachers are responsible for improving L&BD students' social behavior. Often their social skills and attitudes are inadequate and their school and personal adjustments can be improved through instruction.

Methods for teaching social behaviors are derived from operant conditioning and social modeling theory. These include contingency contracting, social reinforcement, role playing, and behavior rehearsal.

Procedures for developing a social skills curriculum follows the directive teaching format. First, behaviors are defined. Then they are assessed. Instructional strategies are developed and implemented. Evaluation follows instruction.

Eight examples from DTIMS are shown. Each consists of an assessment task, a teaching strategy, and commercial references.

12

Academic Instruction

Selected academic skills and how these may be taught to L&BD students are discussed. The importance of organizing and sequencing instructional content is briefly considered. Basic steps in corrective instruction begin with shaping responses, followed by demonstrating responses, getting students to imitate and produce responses, and providing practice in both simple and mixed formats.

Academic skill instruction should begin with assessment of students' performances against the skills and concepts to be taught, development of instructional plans based upon assessment results, implementation of the plans, and evaluation of the results of instruction.

Introduction

L&BD students are noted for their difficulties in acquiring academic skills and/or concepts. Consequently, their teachers should be experts in helping them to learn in school and to become independent learners. This expertise includes knowledge and competencies in organizing instruction, structuring subject matter, and charting student progress. In addition to the many other areas of ability, teachers should also be skillful in the various steps and tactics necessary for effective corrective instruction.

Importance of Structure

Academic learning is often the result of a well-organized approach to classroom instruction. In an early study Haring and Phillips (1962) demonstrated the successful application of a systematic, highly structured approach in special classes for disturbed children. Their findings broke new ground in educating such children by demonstrating the value of both structure and academic treatment.

Gallagher (1972) found that a highly structured approach, as compared with a modified structured approach, resulted in an increase in reading vocabulary. She taught 16 emotionally disturbed boys, ranging in age from 7 to 11 years, using the two approaches. In addition to increasing reading vocabulary, the highly structured approach also contributed to better attention to academic tasks.

In addition to classroom structure, as described in chapter 10, teachers should be well organized, subject matter should be structured, and instruction should be orderly and systematic.

Teacher Structure

Readers are referred to chapter 7 for a discussion of ways teachers can organize themselves for effectively instructing L&BD students. Chapter 9 also describes a system for managing instruction.

Systematic instruction generally consists of assessing students upon entry into a unit or series of concepts and skills, devising a plan based upon results of the assessment, implementing the teaching plan, and evaluating the effects of instruction. These components are typically found in instructional management systems as described in chapter 9.

Subject Matter Structure

All subject matter must be organized for effective teaching. Sometimes curriculum is organized by sequencing lower order skills as prerequisites for higher order skills, as is the case in beginning reading and arithmetic. But even when the subject matter does not require sequencing by difficulty, it must still be organized in some clearly defined way for purposes of teaching.

The structure shown in chapter 9 for DTIMS reading and arithmetic skills represents one of the common ways that such curricula are organized. Many of the lower order skills are sequenced due to prerequisite responses but the many higher order skills are sequenced on the basis of tradition, where textbook authors and curriculum developers have chosen to place them.

Charting Student Progress

Corrective instruction requires record-keeping procedures for tracking those tasks students have learned and those that they are in the process of learning. Reports of student progress permit teachers to base instruction on students' needs since they can determine exactly what students have learned. In this way, practice can be purposely assigned only for those tasks that are close to mastery. It also enables teachers to readily evaluate the success of their instruction.

By charting student progress, school personnel can provide accurate and current reports to students, parents, and other teachers. It facilitates accountability because progress reports show effects of teaching and student effort.

Steps in Corrective Instruction

There are few definitive research findings concerning instructional procedures for teaching L&BD students. Glavin and Quay (1969) identified the need for research evidence in support of effective and efficient strategies for classroom management and academic skill instruction. Sound principles which appear to have merit concerning corrective instruction do exist, however. These are rooted in the basic notion described in chapter 6.

Whenever new responses are being taught, teachers must first provide the desired response. Too frequently instruction fails because teachers instruct as if students have already acquired the new responses. Students are then forced to guess and through trial and error may acquire incorrect responses. Through assessment, teachers must distinguish between initial learning and practicing what is already learned. In example A below note that the teacher says the expected response while giving the directions. The student is then asked to repeat the response so as to ensure that what is expected is understood. During initial instruction, it is the teacher's responsibility to *teach* what is to be learned, involving telling and/or showing students the correct responses. That is, L&BD students should be assessed as to their performances, their responses to various instructional tactics, and their reinforcement systems prior to embarking on extensive instruction.

Six steps are typically effective in teaching L&BD students academic skills within the framework of assessing, planning, implementing, and evaluating. These six steps are shown in Figure 12.1.

STEP	ACTIVITY	
1	Responses are shaped toward terminal performance.	*shaping*
2	Responses are demonstrated for student.	*demon*
3	Student imitates responses.	*imitating*
4	Student produces responses.	*producing*
5	Student practices responses in simple format.	*simple*
6	Student practices responses in mixed format.	*mixed*

FIGURE 12.1.   Six steps for teaching academic skills

Step 1 is generally most appropriate when responses are not clearly within students' repertoires. The remaining five steps can be used effectively to develop skills that are composed of responses already demonstrated by students.

Shaping

Shaping tactics are useful when responses are not produced by students and when they do not respond to conventional instruction. Shaping involves the process of reinforcing those responses which resemble the desired terminal behavior. Then in successive steps reinforcement is shifted to responses which more clearly approximate the terminal performance. Once the terminal response is obtained, instruction may follow steps 2 through 6.

Demonstrating Responses

In step 2, teachers arrange conditions so that the response to be learned is presented correctly with learners attending (see chapter 10 for management tactics). Responses may be demonstrated by the teacher or students. In either case, it is important that they be demonstrated correctly each time.

EXAMPLE A

When given the sound of *m*, student points to picture with the letter *m*.

Teacher: These are the letters *Mm* (pointing to the letters on the chalkboard). Their sound is /m/ (pronouncing the sound). What sound does the letter *m* make?

Teacher: Now, I am going to give each of you a picture card. If it begins with the /m/ sound, place it on the chalk ledge when I name your picture. For example, this is a picture of a *dog*. It does not begin with the /m/ sound. So, I won't place it on the ledge.

Now, look at this picture. It shows a *mouse* and it does begin with the /m/ sound. So I will place it on the ledge.

Teacher: Now I will hold up cards with three letters on them. When I say /m/ I will point to one of you. That child will come here and point to the letter *m*.

EXAMPLE B

When presented with numeral cards 1-100, student will arrange them in natural order.

Teacher: Billy will demonstrate what we are to do. Hlere are the numeral cards (handing the pack to Billy). Billy will take cards 1 through 12 (Billy selects the 12 cards). He will then place the lowest numeral here (pointing to the ledge).

Billy: This is numeral 1 (as he places it on ledge).

Teacher: He will now place the next lowest numeral here next to the 1.

Teacher proceeds through 12 in this same way.

Imitating Responses

In step 3 teachers encourage students to imitate the responses previously demonstrated. The purpose here is to provide students with opportunities to make the responses under teacher direction. At this time if responses are incorrect, teachers can immediately intervene with corrective measures.

Responses may be imitated when teachers present models to be traced, or they may be copied when models are available for students to follow. Imitation may also occur by having students repeat what was said or done, as in example C.

EXAMPLE C

Teacher: Now that Billy has arranged his numeral cards correctly from 1 to 12, here is a set of cards for each of you. Find the same cards that Billy used and place them in the same order on your desks as they are on the ledge.

Producing Responses

In step 4 students produce responses without models present. By performing responses under teachers' directions, they can be corrected before subsequent incorrect trials occur. Example D contains descriptions of ways that teachers can arrange for students to produce responses under their supervision.

EXAMPLE D

Students will say the sound of *at*, *ake*, and *all* when shown the letter combination in a word.

Teacher provides seven cards, three cards with the letter combinations *at*, *ake*, and *all* on them, and four cards with letters *b*, *c*, *f*, and *m* on them. Holding a letter card in front of a letter combination card (example *b* and *at*), teacher says: This is the word *bat*. Say *bat* (teacher waits for a response).

The first letter *b* (holding the *b* apart) gives the word the *b* sound. The *at* (holding up the *at*) gives the word the *at* sound. Say *at* (teacher waits for a response).

At this point, the teacher has completed step 3. In the remainder of example D the students practice the response under teacher direction (step 4).

If response is correct, teacher goes through the cards using each letter, encouraging students to say the final sound again,and correctly say the entire word. If responses are not correct, teacher repeats examples. *Ake* and *all* are taught in the same way.

Practicing Responses

In step 5 students are given opportunities, assignments, and encouragement to practice responses. This activity occurs under the *general* direction of teachers. During this time, teachers should be available if needed, although they will also be involved in instructing other students. From time to time, students may need assistance during practice. This help may be provided by teachers or their assistants (students or paraprofessionals).

In example E, we return to the previous DTIMS skill.

EXAMPLE E

For practice, the teacher has prepared two large cubes (plastic, wood, or cardboard blocks). On two sides of one cube, each of the endings (*ake, at, all*) have been printed. The letters *b, c, f,* and *m* are printed on sides of the other cube.

Students take turns tossing the cubes and reading the combinations. The game continues until each child has read each of the three combinations twice correctly.

Practice opportunities may be provided by assigning individual seatwork, games, and homework.

Seatwork. Seatwork should always be geared for practicing responses that have already been learned. Seatwork activities should be individualized and most often require students to work alone.

Most commercially available texts in basic skill subjects are supplemented by workbooks containing seatwork activities. These are not often entirely suitable for L&BD students, and, in most cases, teachers will find it necessary to develop their own seatwork.

Teachers should consider several factors when developing seatwork activities. First, a teacher should decide if it is for simple practice or mixed practice. If students have not yet fully mastered the task, then the activity should be singular. That is, it should consist of the same level and type of task and require the same type of response, e.g., addition of two one-place numerals in vertical form with sums below ten, as in Figure 12.2.

Add (+) these:

1 +3	4 +1	1 +4
1 +2	2 +1	3 +1
1 +5	5 +1	1 +6
7 +1	1 +7	8 +1
1 +8	9 +1	9 +0

FIGURE 12.2.   A simple seatwork activity

After students have demonstrated the skill in practice in singular form, mixed practice activities should be assigned. Mixed seatwork assignments consist of tasks that vary somewhat from the original or from a more simple format, e.g., addition of two one-place numerals in vertical *and parallel forms*. Students who demonstrate difficulty in generalizing to new conditions should be taught the various forms of responding before such items are used in combination. As the students become more proficient, mixed practice seatwork activities may vary greatly, such as combining addition and subtraction problems in both parallel and vertical forms, as in Figure 12.3.

Do these problems.

2 +5	6 −10=	5 −4
6+12=	7 +4	9 −8
4−3=	9−8=	6 +6
9+1=	4−5=	7+3=

FIGURE 12.3. A mixed seatwork activity

Other factors to consider when making seatwork activities are clarity of instructions, length of assignments, and the relationship of the activities to the terminal behavior. Seatwork has but two purposes: to provide opportunities for students to practice skills and to serve as an evaluation of students' learning. Assignment of tasks which are solely intended to occupy students' time are always inappropriate. Teachers should always provide feedback to students on assigned work. If the activity has not already been learned and is not directly related to the terminal performance, *don't assign it.*

Games.   A game format is a good way to provide practice in academic skills because it can be more interesting and often provides students with opportunities to work in small groups. Three games (Compass, Ouch, Super Sort) coded to the DTIMS materials are shown on pp. 348–352.[1]

---

1. Taken from *Instructional activities based upon specific reading skills,* unpublished paper of the Faculty for Exceptional Children, The Ohio State University. Developed and field tested by the following graduate students: Ronald Boley, Glenn Carlton, Mary Kay Davis, Julie Kagy, James King, James Norman, and Robert Whytal.

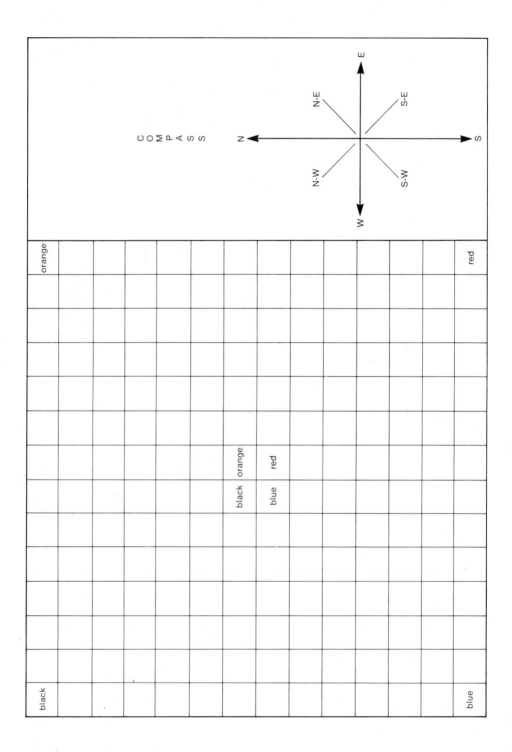

COMPASS

PURPOSE: The student will read and follow directions on a given card.
SKILL: R-CO-LS-0014
LEVEL: Three
MATERIALS: Compass game board (See p. 348.)
            Four direction cards
            Crayons (supplied by teacher or students)

MATERIALS DESCRIPTION:

Start on Red
1. Move 8 N
2. Move 9 W
3. Move 4 S
4. Move 2 E
5. Move 2 S
6. Move 1 E
7. Move 4 N
8. You are now on red.

Start on Blue
1. Move 4 N
2. Move 2 E
3. Move 1 S
4. Move 5 E
5. Move 1 N
6. Move 1 W
7. Move 2 N
8. You are now on blue.

Start on Orange
1. Move 10 W
2. Move 5 S
3. Move 6 E
4. Move 1 S
5. Move 4 N
6. Move 2 W
7. Move 4 S
8. You are now on orange.

Start on Black
1. Move 2 E
2. Move 6 S
3. Move 2 W
4. Move 3 N
5. Move 4 E
6. Move 3 S
7. Move 2 E
8. You are now on black.

DIRECTIONS:
1. To be played by two to four students.
2. Each student will take one direction card from the pile of four cards.
3. Each student will choose a corner square to start. The color of the student's card will designate the corner where she/he starts.
4. One student will read directions on card as she/he marks accordingly on the board with crayon.
5. The card will direct the student to move north, south, east or west.
6. Each student completes turns on card before next student begins.
7. The game leader checks the student's movements.
8. Each child who has moved correctly according to direction card wins the game.
MODIFICATIONS: More complicated directions can be written on direction cards (e.g., SW, NE).

OUCH

PURPOSE:	The child will read *ou* & *ow* sounds correctly from word card
SKILL NUMBER:	R-PA-DP-0002
LEVEL:	Two
MATERIALS:	Ouch game board
	five "O.K." cards
	five "OUCH" cards
	1 die
	placemarkers

OUCH

ADDITIONAL MATERIALS:

1. You will need five "O.K." cards. Each card will contain one of the following:
   a. You may sit next to your friend.
   b. Take one paper out of your folder.
   c. You can be a helper today.
   d. Move five spaces ahead.
   e. Take a drink of water.
   (Please note that you may make up your own reinforcers for the "O.K." cards)

2. You will need five "Ouch" cards. Each card will contain one of the following:
   a. Write your name ten times on paper!
   b. Move back five spaces.
   c. Do ten jumping jacks.
   d. Do ten push ups.
   e. Move back one space.
   (Please note that you may make up your directions for the "Ouch" cards)

DIRECTIONS:

1. To be played by two or three children.
2. Students begin at "start" by rolling the die and moving as many spaces as indicated by the roll. If child can say the word correctly that she/he reaches, she/he stays on the square.
3. If she/he cannot pronounce the word she/he moves back to where she/he was prior to the roll.
4. When the child lands on an O.K. or OUCH space, the child takes one card from the appropriate pile designated on the board.
5. After responding to the directions on the card, the next person takes his/her turn.
6. In order to win, one must roll the exact number to end up on the "out" square. First person to this place wins the game.

MODIFICATIONS:

1. The teacher can modify OUCH and O.K. cards to directions appropriate for the children's age and grade level.
2. When working on asking interrogative sentences, the children could be asked to use the word in an interrogative sentence.
3. Also, the game could be modified and used for verbally saying correct sentences containing the word she/he landed on.

SUPER SORT

PURPOSE: The student will say the word on the card and place the card in the appropriate box.
SKILL NUMBER: R-PA-CV-0002
LEVEL: One
MATERIALS: Super Sort game board (See p. 352.)
                28 index cards

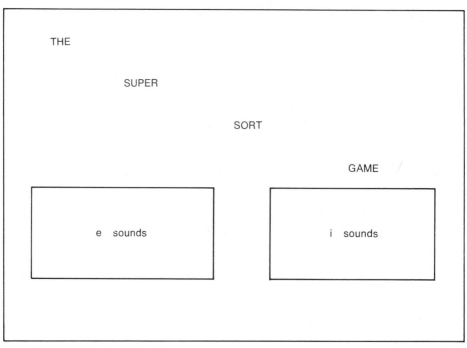

Note: Game board can be any size

MATERIALS DESCRIPTION:
1. The additional materials will include 28 index cards. Each card will contain one word, either with a long *e* or *i* final sound. The following words are used for this game:

1.	my	8.	cry	15.	pony	22.	hurry
2.	fly	9.	fly	16.	funky	23.	monkey
3.	by	10.	spy	17.	puffy	24.	happy
4.	why	11.	snowy	18.	sunny	25.	lady
5.	sty	12.	windy	19.	money	26.	baby
6.	sky	13.	rainy	20.	bunny	27.	funny
7.	try	14.	carry	21.	kitty	28.	misty

DIRECTIONS:
1. To be played by two children to two groups of two children.
2. Each child is dealt an even number of cards.
3. First child begins by saying one word on a card and placing the card in the appropriate box on the board according to the ending sound.
4. If the child responds incorrectly the game leader tells the child the correct answer.
5. The child must keep the card and the turn moves to the next player or team.
6. The first person to place all his cards on the board is the winner.
MODIFICATIONS: The words on the cards can be adjusted to fit the level of the children.

Homework.   Since practice time is one of the important factors in academic learning, it is often necessary to extend practice beyond the school day. Thus, practice assignments should be given to students to do at home. Considerations in assigning homework to L&BD students should include what to assign, where the assignment will be done, and how well students have been trained in using study time.

Assignments which have been mastered at school are appropriate for homework. Avoid assigning work that students have not yet mastered. Short homework assignments, individualized for the student, should be used.

Students may be trained through behavior rehearsing on how to study at home. With older students, charting of time and tasks completed during homework should be used as a means of helping them to evaluate their study skills.

Mixed Practicing

Step 6 is a variation of the preceding step. During this phase students are given opportunities to practice responses in a mixed format. By using mixed practice, students are helped to generalize responses to other types of activities and to relate them to other complex tasks. The discussion in the previous section concerning seatwork and game formats provides examples for mixed practice work.

Teaching Prereading and Reading Skills

Reading should be thought of as a process of communicating. It is a means of acquiring information and enriching our lives and a source of entertainment. The hierarchy of language acquisition begins with listening and speaking skills and extends to reading and writing skills. Reading requires encoding what is seen in print and decoding those symbols. While there has been much speculation as to which factors in the encoding/decoding process may be disruptive for students with language acquisition problems, teachers of L&BD students can help them by systematically assessing, planning instruction based on that assessment, following the plans when teaching, and changing their instruction on the basis of students' performances. The six steps (shaping, demonstrating, imitating, producing, simple practice, mixed practice) previously described should be followed during the instructional phase.

Teaching Prereading Skills

Teachers of L&BD students should recognize that problems in reading often are related to inadequate skills and practice with prereading tasks. Beginning readers, regardless of age, need practice in those skills that immediately precede reading.

Prereading skills can be categorized, as they are in DTIMS reading (see chapter 9), into four major categories and subcategories as follows:

    1.0. *Auditory Discrimination*
        1.1 Environmental sounds
        1.2 Following verbal instruction
        1.3 Matching sounds
        1.4 Repeating verbal sounds
        1.5 Identifying rhymes
    2.0 *Visual Discrimination*
        2.1 Likenesses and differences
        2.2 Matching symbols
        2.3 Repeating visual patterns
        2.4 Recognizing letters
        2.5 Recognizing numerals

3.0 *Comprehension*
    3.1 Labeling
    3.2 Classifying and categorizing
    3.3 Word meaning
4.0 *Structural Analysis*
    4.1 Uppercases and Lowercases

Teachers should first assess students on tasks which represent the above skills when they observe that students have serious difficulty with beginning reading. The assessment task should consist of specific responses that make up a skill such as shown in Figure 12.4.

R-AD-ES-0002
    Students will listen to a sound with their backs turned and then point to the object which made the sound.

Criterion: 8/8

Teacher will tell students to turn their backs, listen to a sound, and point to the object that made the sound.

1. hand clap
2. paper tearing
3. keys jingling
4. pencil tapping
5. book closing
6. whistling
7. feet tapping
8. finger snapping

MODALITY: auditory

MATERIALS: paper, pencil, keys, book

FIGURE 12.4.   A DTIMS prereading assessment task

Figure 12.4 shows one of the skills found in the subcategory *environmental sounds* within auditory discrimination. Note that the assessment task specifies the skill, shows what the teacher will do, and emphasizes the modality to be used, needed materials, and criterion level for mastery.

A low-level skill, such as that shown in Figure 12.4, should only be used if the student's reading performance warrants it. If the student's listening skills are adequate, teaching the skill shown in Figure 12.4 would not be necessary in order to improve reading performance.

Once assessment on relevant tasks has been completed, students should be taught those skills which they have not mastered, following the six steps described previously. A DTIMS teaching strategy for skill R-AD-ES-0002 is shown below.

SKILL: R-AD-ES-0002   Students will listen to a sound with backs turned and then point to the object which made the sound

MODALITY: Auditory, visual
TEACHER ACTIVITY:

1. Plan reinforcement strategy selected from reinforcement menu.
2. Plan instruction.

Teacher: "Everyone please close your eyes. I'm going to make a noise and you are to tell me the sound and what made the sound." (Clap hands) "Johnny, what noise did I make?" (Student response) "You're right. I clapped my hands. Now listen to this sound." (Knock on the desk) "What sound did I make?" (Student response) "Good. I did knock on the desk with my fist. Now close your eyes and we will play the game again. I'll either clap or knock on the desk and you tell me which sound you hear. Don't forget to keep your eyes closed. This time we will try it again using three different sounds." (Bell, money, paper) "When you close your eyes, I will make a noise with one of these things on my desk. When I call on you, you must come and point to what made the noise." Continue in a similar manner with several common sounds until students demonstrate mastery of this skill.

Practice: Students write names on five strips of paper with tape on back. Teacher shows them five objects (keys, ruler, chalk, light switch, door). Teacher asks students to close their eyes and when they are able to identify the sound made to raise their hands. Teacher calls on student. If correct, he/she tapes his/her name strip next to the object which made the noise. The first student to have his/her name on all five is the winner.

STUDENT RESPONSE: Student will close eyes and raise hand when he/she is able to identify the sound made.
MATERIALS: Paper, pencil, tape, bell, money, keys, ruler, chalk, light switch, door.
EVALUATION Crtierion: 5/5

In the above teaching plan, teachers can determine if students have learned the skill by comparing their performance with the established evaluation criterion (5/5). Even when they meet criterion, additional practice should be provided. Commercial textbooks contain suggestions and practice activities for specific reading skills. For example, the following text contains suggestions for teaching the skill as shown along with the pages on which the teaching suggestions are found.

Commercial Reference

Students listen to a sound with back turned and then point to the object which made the sound.

PUBLISHED	SCOTT-FORESMAN
TITLE	LEVEL 1
SERIES	READING SYSTEMS
EDITION	FIRST
TYPE	TEACHER'S GUIDE
YEAR	1971
PAGE NUMBERS 78, 114	

Within the DTIMS prereading subcategories there are 55 skills, 110 teaching strategies, and hundreds of commercial references. Space does not permit including these here. However, readers can develop assessment tasks and teaching strategies for each of the 55 skills which are shown in chapter 9.

Teaching Reading Skills

Beginning reading requires students to be skillful across many areas: reading comprehension, phonetic analysis, sight word recognition, structural analysis, and oral reading. There are numerous skills within each of these categories, and many of the beginning skills are based upon lower order, prerequisite responses, as was shown in chapter 9.

Prerequisite *experiences* are also important at all reading levels. As a general rule these should be developed by:

1. introducing new words orally and in written form prior to having students read the words,
2. introducing new words in context, not in isolation,
3. providing listening experiences to students by reading stories to them,
4. building interest in stories before assigning them to be read,
5. having a balance betwen oral and silent reading,
6. encouraging purposeful oral reading, e.g., to find information or to prove an answer.

After L&BD students have been assessed on specific reading skills, instruction should proceed as indicated in the previous section of this chapter. Selected strategies from DTIMS reading materials follow as teaching examples.[2]

Reading Comprehension (level 1)

TEACHING STRATEGY

SKILL: R-CO-WM-0024   Given a word the student will say a word that means the same as the word presented.

MODALITY: Auditory/Visual
TEACHER ACTIVITY:
1. Plan reinforcement strategy selected from reinforcement menu.
2 Plan instruction.

Teacher: "There are many words that have the same meaning—*chubby* means the same as fat. *Unhappy* means the same as sad. *Glad* means the same as _____." (Wait for response, happy, etc. — reinforce.) "Beautiful means the same as _____." (Wait for response, pretty, etc.—reinforce.) "Now we're going to play a game. I'm going to say a word. If you can think of another word that means the same, stand up. When I call your name, you tell me your word. If it does mean the same, then you may be the teacher for the next word. You'll come to the front of the room and I'll tell you what word to give to the class." Play the game until everyone has had the opportunity to respond twice. Some words you may use: gooey – sticky; skinny – thin; blinds – shades; automobile – car; rip – tear; etc. Give students a worksheet with the same words on them and have them match the words.

car	chubby
happy	shades
beautiful	automobile
angry	glad
blinds	mad
fat	pretty

If they don't know how to read a word they may ask the teacher. While the students are doing their worksheets, call each to your desk. Give him 3 words. Have him tell you a synonym.
MATERIALS: Worksheet
STUDENT RESPONSE: Student will match synonyms on worksheet and give synonym for given words.
EVALUATION: Criterion: 3/3
                  Criterion met?
                  If yes: Reassess using Assessment Task R-CO-WM-0024-LI-A.
                  If no: Continue using same strategy or select new strategy.

---

2. These strategies are taken from *The Directive Teaching Instructional Management System: Reading, arithmetic, and social skills*, Copyright © 1973 by Thomas M. Stephens.

Reading Comprehension (level 2)

TEACHING STRATEGY

SKILL: R-CO-OP-0002   The student will say the opposite of the words "up," "high," "big," "come."

MODALITY: Visual
SMALL GROUP
TEACHER ACTIVITY:

1. Plan reinforcement strategy selected from reinforcement menu.
2. Plan instruction

Teacher writes *big* and *small* on the board. Under each word the teacher places a *big* book and a *little* book, respectively. And then the teacher asks: "Are these two words the same?" (Student response) "That's right, they are very different. Who can point to the word that tells us this book is big?" (Student response) "Big and small are very different, and when words are very different, we call them opposites. Can we find other things in this room that are big, and some things that are small?" (Student response — children can either respond verbally, or physically gather items.)

Next, the teacher asks: "Who knows some other words that are *very different*, that are *opposites*?" Such words suggested by the class, (and suggested by the teacher) should be *demonstrated* (e.g., "fast" and "slow" — ask one child to walk around the room fast, and one child to walk around the room slowly). "Are they walking the same? No, they are walking very different, fast and slow are opposite."

For practice, the children, working in pairs, will demonstrate to the class the difference between opposites — including up/down, high/low, big/small, come/go, etc. The teacher will prepare cards with just one word on each (fast, high, etc.). Each group of two children will select one card and demonstrate their *word*, *and its opposite* to the class. The class must try to guess their word. Each child should get three chances to demonstrate.

List of suggested opposites to be used in game:

1. up – down	6. happy – sad	11. in – out
2. high – low	7. short – long	12. over – under
3. big – small	8. hot – cold	13. sit – stand
4. come – go	9. work – play	14. new – old
5. wide – narrow	10. far – near	15. noisey – quiet

MATERIALS: Items found in classroom, and prepared flash cards
STUDENT RESPONSE: When presented a word card child will *demonstrate* word and its opposite.
EVALUATION   Criterion: 3/3
             Criterion Met?
             If yes: Reassess using assessment task R-CO-OP-0002-L2-A.
             If no: Continue using same strategy or select new strategy.

Phonetic Analysis (level 3)

TEACHING STRATEGY

SKILL: R-PA-PW-0064   The student will read aloud in and out of context the endings *ment* and *tion* when shown the letters and a word card.

MODALITY: Visual
SMALL GROUP
TEACHER ACTIVITY:

1. Plan reinforcement strategy selected from reinforcement menu.
2. Plan instruction.

Teacher writes *basement* and *excitement* on the board. Teacher says, "Here are two words you already know. How are these two words the same?" (response) "That's right, they do end the same way. Say both words to yourself and tell me what the final syllable is in basement and excitement." (response) "That's right, it is *ment,* (write *ment* on the board) and when it occurs at the end of a word it usually sounds like /ment/. Who knows another word that ends with *ment*?" Write suggestions on the board and have pupils read the words orally. Give assistance where necessary. Next, write *action* on the board. "I know you already know this word. Say it once. How many syllables do you hear?" (response) "That's right, you do hear two syllables. Who can come to the board and underline the second syllable in *action*?" (response) "The final syllable t-i-o-n often sounds like /shun/ in a word when it's the final syllable like in this word — *fraction*." (Write *fraction* on the board.) Follow with student suggestions as outlined with the syllable *ment*.

For practice: Variation of *baseball*. Teacher marks first base, second base, third base and home plate on floor. Children are divided into two teams. The team that is "up" must be able to correctly read a word flashed to him by the other team. If he reads it correctly, he advances one base. If he doesn't read the word correctly he is out. Three outs give the other team a chance to be up. Teams score by advancing all the way around the diamond, and home. Each child should be "up" at least five times. Children may want to apply strategy — that is, presenting increasingly difficult words. Provide reinforcement.

MATERIALS: Cards with *tion* and *ment* words. Suggested words for flash cards:

moment	apartment	compartment	placement
agreement	amazement	appointment	entertainment
experiment	movement	instrument	reaction
fiction	ration	attention	affection
invitation	direction	invention	mention
protection	selection	election	question
section			

STUDENT RESPONSE: Student will read aloud words ending with *tion* and *ment* when shown flash cards.

EVALUATION: Criterion: 5/5
Criterion Met?
If yes: Reassess using Assessment Task R-PA-PW-0063-L3-A.
If no: Continue using same strategy or select new strategy.

Practice and Reading Performance

Reading performance can be improved through frequent use of reading skills. As in all academic skill areas, the more skills applied by students, the better their reading skills will be.

Teachers should encourage students to read independently. This encouragement can occur through building interest in reading, making reading materials available, and using extensive reinforcement.

Students' interests in reading can be developed by teachers in many ways. These include reading parts of stories aloud to students, having interesting displays in the classroom of books, titles, and reading topics, and story telling. Adventure stories, animal books, and biographies are popular material for students.

Teachers can make interesting reading materials available through having a book corner which can serve as a mini-library, encouraging students to visit the library, and taking them to the bookmobile when it is at the school. Teachers should take care not to impose adult or personal reading interests on the students. Teachers should identify special interests of students and build motivation for reading by locating resource books on identified topics and using these books in class. When students express desires to pursue a given topic independently, teachers can offer to help them with new words or difficult ideas. L&BD students often prefer books with many illustrations, including comics. Teachers should be supportive of such interests since practice will improve reading skills and further develop reading interests.

Extrinsic rewards for reading may consist of tokens and other forms of exchanges. A display showing the number of stories or books read can also be a powerful incentive for many reluctant readers. Permitting students to create drawings depicting a story they have completed is a common incentive.

Teachers can encourage reading by serving as models. Those who are enthusiastic about reading, who show by their behavior that they read for fun and information, will serve as a source of imitation to students. Encouragement is best shown through modeling and shaping and not by edict.

Older L&BD students have learned to compensate for their poor reading skills by acquiring information and entertainment from TV, radio, and movies. In these instances, it is difficult to encourage students to try new, often times more discouraging information and entertainment modes. Shaping practices may be most appropriate in such cases. Teachers can base reading on TV presentations, such as reading parts of a story that is to be seen on TV or reading news articles to get the details behind the newscaster's headlines. The *Teacher's Guide to Television*[3] provides program listings and teaching suggestions and resources which can be used in the classroom.

Younger children are often responsive to the language experience reading approach. Children dictate their experiences as teachers record them on chalkboard or chart paper. Teachers often find it necessary to simplify the wording and sentence structure as they record. The stories may be made into booklets which the children can illustrate and share with their classmates and parents. Since the stories are within their experiences, the contents tend to be appealing to them. This approach also serves to demonstrate to children that reading is an extension of speaking.

Teaching Handwriting and Spelling Skills

Handwriting and spelling are advanced language skills. For handwriting, students must use their fine motor skills to reproduce letters, and they must recall how to form letters. Handwriting skills are considered to be less important than they were during the "penmanship" days of education when writing was viewed as an art form, but today letter formations are important for written communications. Handwriting should be taught within the context of learning to communicate. As with all behaviors expected of students, teachers should provide initial instruction as well as opportunities to practice handwriting skills before the students are expected to function independently. L&BD students frequently demonstrate serious problems in writing. Teachers should make it a practice to encourage improvement by providing consistent and reasonable standards.

Correct spelling also improves communication skills. It requires phonetic skills, syllabication, good recall and handwriting skills. Both skill areas — handwriting and spelling — can be taught with visual imagery techniques and through the use of modeling.

---

3. One may obtain this guide by writing to the following address: P.O. Box 564, Lenox Hill Station, New York, New York 10021.

Aids to and environments for learning should be suited to the skills being taught.

Handwriting

There are two basic forms of handwriting: manuscript and cursive. Manuscript is often referred to as *printing,* while cursive is sometimes used synonymously with *handwriting.* Typically, children are taught to write in manuscript form in first and second grades and in cursive form early in third grade.

Handwriting letters are divided into uppercase and lowercase, often referred to as capital and small letters. Since formation of uppercase and lowercase letters varies in cursive and manuscript forms, some L&BD students are confused as to how to form these letters.

In addition to letter and numeral formations, other skills taught cover height of letters, spacing, and alignment. Use of punctuation marks and symbols should also be taught. These skills require forming concepts regarding the various punctuation symbols, so that students know when each should be used in writing.

Skills

Skills in handwriting are shown below, divided into readiness skills, manuscript, cursive, height, spacing, alignment, and punctuation marks.

Readiness skills
- —vertical line drawn from top to bottom
- —vertical line drawn from bottom to top
- —horizontal line drawn from left to right
- —forming circles
- —forming curves
- —slanting lines vertically
- —naming letters

Manuscript letters
- —straight line letters: *l, L, i, I, t, T*
- —circle letters: *o, c, a, e*
- —curve letters: *m, n, r, R, s, S, u, U*
- —tall letters: *d, D, f, F, h, H, b, B*
- —slant letters: *w, W, v, V, k, K, x, X, z, Z*
- —tail letters: *M, N, g, G, y, Y, p, P, j, J, q, Q*
- —straight line numerals: *1, 4, 7*
- —circle numerals: *0, 6, 8, 9*
- —curve numerals: *2, 3, 5*

Cursive letters
- —letters beginning with an undercurve:

  i, t, e, l, u, w, r, s,

  b, h, k, f, j, p
- —letters beginning with a downcurve:

  a, d, o, c, g, q
- —letters beginning with an overcurve:

  n, m, v, x, y, z
- —all uppercase cursive letters

Height of letters
- —all similar letters should be of uniform height: *t, l*
- —short letters should be about ⅓ the height of capitals: *a, u*

Spacing
  —uniform spacing between letters in a word
  —uniform spacing between words
  —spacing between lines should be uniform on unlined paper
Alignment
  —all written lines should be straight on lined and unlined paper
Punctuation
  —statements and commands (.)
  —questions (?)
  —exclamations (!)
  —dividing sentences (, : ;)
  —beginning sentences, proper names, and titles (capital letters)
  —quotations ("____")
  —abbreviations (*Pa.*)
  —contractions (*can't*)

Teachers should begin corrective writing instruction by assessing each student's handwriting skills. Assessment should incorporate prewriting and writing skills. If students are already forming letters in manuscript, vertical, horizontal, and slanted lines need not be assessed. Similarly, if students are writing in cursive, their formations of a circle, overcurve, undercurve, and downcurve need not be assessed.

When assessing, as well as teaching, letter formation and use of punctuation marks, it is important that students be able to properly name them prior to being asked to reproduce them. But they may be taught the correct names as they learn to write each by tracing or copying.

Assessment should be systematic. Students should be asked to name, copy from a model, and later to reproduce the various marks when verbally given the name and without a model present. Figure 12.5 contains a checklist which may be used by teachers in conducting a systematic assessment.

FIGURE 12.5   A checklist for assessing handwriting

Student's Name_____   Date_____

Manuscript		Copies
|	vertical line drawn from top to bottom	_____
|	vertical line drawn from bottom to top	_____
/	slanting line	_____
—	horizontal line from left to right	_____
Cursive		
O	circle	_____
⌒	overcurve	_____
‿	undercurve	_____
⟨	downcurve	_____
ℓ	loop	_____

FIGURE 12.5 continued

Letters	Names	Copies	Reproduces
A	M C	M C	M C
a	M C	M C	M C
B	M C	M C	M C
b	M C	M C	M C
C	M C	M C	M C
c	M C	M C	M C
D	M C	M C	M C
d	M C	M C	M C
E	M C	M C	M C
e	M C	M C	M C
F	M C	M C	M C
f	M C	M C	M C
G	M C	M C	M C
g	M C	M C	M C
H	M C	M C	M C
h	M C	M C	M C
I	M C	M C	M C
i	M C	M C	M C
J	M C	M C	M C
j	M C	M C	M C
K	M C	M C	M C
k	M C	M C	M C
L	M C	M C	M C
l	M C	M C	M C
M	M C	M C	M C
m	M C	M C	M C
N	M C	M C	M C
n	M C	M C	M C
O	M C	M C	M C
o	M C	M C	M C
P	M C	M C	M C
p	M C	M C	M C
Q	M C	M C	M C
q	M C	M C	M C
R	M C	M C	M C
r	M C	M C	M C
S	M C	M C	M C
s	M C	M C	M C
T	M C	M C	M C
t	M C	M C	M C
U	M C	M C	M C
u	M C	M C	M C
V	M C	M C	M C
v	M C	M C	M C
W	M C	M C	M C
w	M C	M C	M C
X	M C	M C	M C
x	M C	M C	M C
Y	M C	M C	M C
y	M C	M C	M C
Z	M C	M C	M C
z	M C	M C	M C

FIGURE 12.5 continued

Numerals	Names	Copies	Reproduces
0	_____	_____	_____
1	_____	_____	_____
2	_____	_____	_____
3	_____	_____	_____
4	_____	_____	_____
5	_____	_____	_____
6	_____	_____	_____
7	_____	_____	_____
8	_____	_____	_____
9	_____	_____	_____

Punctuations		Names	Copies	Reproduces	Concept
.	period	_____	_____	_____	_____
?	question	_____	_____	_____	_____
!	exclamation	_____	_____	_____	_____
,	comma	_____	_____	_____	_____
'	apostrophe	_____	_____	_____	_____
" "	quotation	_____	_____	_____	_____
:	colon	_____	_____	_____	_____

Directions:
1. Assess skills for *prewriting manuscript* when students are not writing in manuscript.
2. Assess skills for *prewriting* cursive when students are not writing in cursive.
3. Begin with manuscript letter assessment when students are already writing in manuscript.
4. Start with cursive letters when students are already writing in cursive.
5. Circle M and/or C under *Names* if student names the letter when shown.
6. Circle M and/or C under *Copies* when student copies correctly letter when it is present (M for manuscript, C for cursive).
7. Circle M and/or C under *Reproduces* when student correctly writes letter when asked without model present (M for manuscript, C for cursive).
8. Do not ask students to *reproduce* those letters which they cannot name.

Height	*Uniform*	*Not Uniform*
height of manuscript letters	_____	_____
height of cursive letters	_____	_____
Spacing		
between letters in words	_____	_____
between words	_____	_____
between lines	_____	_____
Alignment		
written lines on lined paper	_____	_____
written lines on unlined paper	_____	_____

In using the checklist shown in Figure 12.5, teachers should have a separate card for each item. There should be four cards for each letter: one card for each uppercase manuscript letter, one for each uppercase cursive letter, one for each lowercase manuscript letter, and one for each lowercase cursive letter. One card should also be available for each of the nine numerals.

Show students one card at a time. Ask them to name the item ("What is this called?"). When a mark is correctly named, with the model present instruct students to make one like it on a sheet of paper. During this assessment phase, check those items which students name and copy correctly on the checklist shown in Figure 12.6. Note that students are not asked to name the prewriting items.

In phase two of the assessment, ask students to reproduce, without models, each letter and punctuation mark. Simply say: "Make a capital cursive or manuscript (letter name) here." Again, check each item on the checklist as it is correctly reproduced. Students are not expected to reproduce the prewriting marks without models.

When asking them to reproduce punctuation marks without models, teachers may wish to provide clues in addition to the names, e.g., "when we want to show that someone is talking we use quotation marks; place some marks around this phrase" (pointing to a phrase on the sheet of paper).

Assessing understanding of punctuation.   Correct usage of punctuation marks requires students to have the concepts of each clearly in mind. These concepts may be assessed by asking students to point to the punctuation mark that should be used if the following were in print (teacher says):

It will be time to eat when we get home.
Help!
How old are you?
Chicago, Illinois
didn't
He said, "When we get home we will eat."
These are vegetables: cabbage, corn, peas, tomatoes, and beets.

Students who can read the above sentences, or their equivalent, should be presented with the sentences in written form minus punctuation marks. They should be asked to add punctuation marks and capital letters. The written stimuli would appear as follows:

it will be time to eat when we get home
help
how old are you
chicago illinois
didn t
he said when we get home we ll eat
these are vegetables cabbage corn peas tomatoes and beets

Special Problems

Among the special problems associated with learning handwriting, particularly among L&BD students, are relationship of writing to reading and spelling, problems of directionality, problems of handedness, problems of spacing, confusion of letters, positioning of material, and chalkboard writing.

Relationship of writing to reading and spelling.   Content used for practicing handwriting skills should be familiar to students. They should always know the correct names of the letters they are to write. *If they cannot name it, they should not be required to write it.* Similarly, they should be able to read words and phrases prior to writing them.

Spelling may be taught in conjunction with handwriting. When words are being written, students can practice both handwriting and spelling.

Problems of directionality.   Handwriting exercises should emphasize left-to-right progressions. Children with serious directionality problems should be provided with cues as to where to begin. Red marks, placed at the beginning of each line, may serve as indicators for such children. Arrows showing direction can serve the same purpose.

Problems of handedness.   Some students are confused as to which hand to use for writing. This problem is particularly serious when the young child is ambidextrous. First, determine which hand is used most often by the child in natural situations. If handedness is clearly established, that is if the same hand is almost always used, the child should be encouraged to use that hand for writing. In addition to encouragement, teachers should instruct children in properly positioning their papers and how to hold writing instruments.

If handedness is not established, it is wise to conduct a frequency count of the times writing objects are held in each hand. Situations may be contrived for this purpose. The pupil can be given paper and pencil, pen, or crayon and instructed to write or draw whatever he/she likes. This situation should be repeated over several weeks with a minimum of 20 such opportunities. The hand which is most frequently used should then be considered as the one for writing.

Problems of spacing.   Some L&BD children have difficulty in planning properly as to the use of space on paper. Assistance for this problem can be provided by drawing vertical lines on the paper leaving sufficient space for writing each letter or word. This problem can also be corrected by providing models that show correct spacing. Some teachers use a green dot on the writing paper to indicate where a letter begins and a red dot to indicate the stopping point.

Confusion of letters.   Some students have trouble in writing certain letters. They may confuse *d* with *b*, *n* with *m*, and *p*, *q*, and *j*.

Problems of this type can be reduced by teaching the writing of these letters in association with words and phonics. Rather than having the letters written in isolation, demonstrate each letter in a word. Students should say letter names as they are written and then say the word.

At first letters that are confused should be taught separately. Later students should see them together for comparison, identifying similarities and differences. As instruction continues, students can be assigned to write words beginning with the troublesome letters in the same lesson.

A multisensory approach in teaching handwriting will help to prevent problems of recall and reduce difficulties in letter formation. Encourage students to trace letters and words as they see and say them. Be certain that they are correctly naming the letters being seen.

Positioning materials.   Students who have motor problems may have trouble holding writing instruments. They can be trained through behavior rehearsal to grasp and position their writing tools properly, however. One handwriting guide describes holding the writing instruments as follows:

> The writing instrument is held between the thumb and first two fingers, about an inch above its point. The first finger rests on the top of the pencil or pen. The end of the bent thumb is placed against the writing instrument to hold it high in the hand and near the

large knuckle. The top of the instrument points in the direction of the upper arms and shoulders.[4]

Paper must also be properly positioned. It is placed straight on the desk for manuscript writing. As the student writes the paper should be moved to the left because the writing should be done directly in front of the eyes.

For cursive writing the paper is tilted. It is tilted toward the left for right-handed students and to the right for left-handed students. It is important that the paper be properly tilted for cursive writing since it is necessary to see the paper as one writes. In particular, left-handed students tend to imitate their more numerous right-handed peers and as a result will sometimes hook their hands or wrists. This tendency can be corrected by slanting the paper in the proper direction. Older left-handed students may resist this correction since they have acquired the habit of writing with a twisted wrist. Teachers should advise and encourage these students to position their papers properly but should avoid being overly demanding if the students are determined not to change, instead they should use a shaping procedure and/or contingency contracting.

Chalkboard writing. Chalkboard writing activities are commonplace in elementary schools and some training in writing properly is often necessary for L&BD students.

Writing should begin at eye level as an aid for maintaining a straight line. If much writing is done at the chalkboard by students, teachers can use a chalk marker to form lines across the board for students.

Chalk should be broken in half so that it can be held inside the hand with the end pointing toward the palm and the chalk held between the thumb and middle finger. Below grade three, oversized chalk should be used.[5]

Teaching Handwriting

Visual imagery and modeling are the methods of choice in teaching handwriting. Imagery is used at the readiness and beginning writing stages when students have not yet mastered letter names and are uncertain as to their formations.

In teaching visual imagery these steps are usually followed:

1. Teacher shows students letter or word to be written.
2. Students are told the name of the letter while it is shown.
3. Teacher asks students to study carefully the way the letter is formed.
4. Students trace the model with their fingers saying its name while tracing.
5. Students are told to close their eyes and to try to picture the letter in their *mind's eye*.
6. Students are encouraged to trace on a hard surface what they *see* with their eyes closed while saying its name.
7. Students are then told to open their eyes, look at the model, and say its name.

Visual imagery may also be used to teach the use of periods, question marks, and exclamation marks. Teachers can begin by placing each punctuation mark on the chalkboard. Students are then encouraged to discuss what each mark conveys. They are led to recognize that each mark is a means of communicating those feelings that are a part of the sentence. The teacher can then proceed to say

---

4. From *Creative growth with handwriting: Teacher guide pak™*, by W. Barbe, V. Lucas, C. Hackney, and C. McAllister. Used with permission of *Zaner-Bloser, Inc.,* © 1975.

5. See Virginia H. Lucas, *Chalkboard techniques and activities for teaching writing.* Columbus, Ohio: Zaner-Bloser, Inc., 1976.

sentences one at a time asking students to indicate which mark should be used at the end of each sentence.

Another variation of this approach was described in an earlier publication.

> Another approach can be used where students need not close their eyes; although by shutting out extraneous visual stimuli, learning may be facilitated with this approach also. Students are asked to imagine the printed symbols for what is spoken. For example, the teacher may say:
>
> "I am going to say a sentence, try to picture the punctuation marks which should be used within and at the end of the sentence. If it helps, you may close your eyes while I am speaking.
>
> The first sentence is: Stupid, he isn't!"
>
> The teacher then proceeds to ask students to write the sentence, or to select the sentence with punctuation as they heard it from a list on the chalkboard. In this same way, each of the sentences are presented:
>
> Stupid, he isn't!
> Is he stupid?
> He is stupid.
> He isn't stupid.[6]

Teaching handwriting through imitation and fading. Imitation can be used in teaching handwriting by having students trace over models. Acetate sheets can be used for this purpose. Place a sheet over the written model and have students trace over it. Students should be encouraged to say the name of the form as they are tracing it.

Fading should be used to enable students to gain writing independence. After students have traced a model, portions of it may be faded out. In the third step, the entire model is gone for tracing purposes. While it may still be displayed for students' references, they will no longer trace it.

STEP	PROCEDURE
1	Trace stimulus
2	Portions of stimulus are evident for tracing
3	Model is present for viewing while writing
4	Verbal stimulus is provided
5	Student writes without visual or verbal stimuli

Figure 12.6   A fading approach to handwriting

As seen in Figure 12.6, a visual model is not provided in step 4. Instead, the word or letter is dictated and students must reproduce it without visual clues. In the final step, students write independently without the need of visual or verbal stimuli.

Spelling

Spelling accurately is often difficult for many L&BD students. Basically, there are five reasons why some students spell poorly.

1. They do not visualize words in their minds. While the facility to "see" words is not an essential spelling skill, it is believed to be an effective one for improving spelling.

6. From Thomas M. Stephens, *Implementing behavioral approaches in elementary and secondary schools.* Columbus, Ohio: Charles E. Merrill, 1975, pp. 192-193.

2. Poor spellers often have poor phonetic skills. They have trouble assigning the proper letter symbols to sound.

3. They may try to spell all words the way they sound. For example, when words such as *laughter* and *slaughter* are spelled as they sound, they may be written as *slawter* and *laffter*. Many words are spelled exactly as they sound, e.g., hand, dog, pet, slap. Students must know which words are not spelled phonetically and which are.

4. Poor spellers often mispronounce words they incorrectly spell, such as: *probly* (probably), *hunderd* (hundred), *vegtable* (vegetable), and *preform* (perform).

5. Some words are incorrectly spelled because their meanings are unclear or unknown to students. Added to this problem are words that are confused because they sound or look alike but have different meanings, such as: *desert/dessert*, *vice/vise*, *herd/heard*, *angel/angle*, *breath/breathe*, and *chose/choose*.

Prespelling, Spelling, and Dictionary Skills

There are general skills which should be demonstrated by effective spellers. These can be grouped into prespelling skills, spelling skills, and dictionary skills.

Prespelling skills. There is a hierarchy of skills that should be mastered for *each* word L&BD students are expected to spell correctly. The sequence of prespelling skills is shown in Figure 12.7

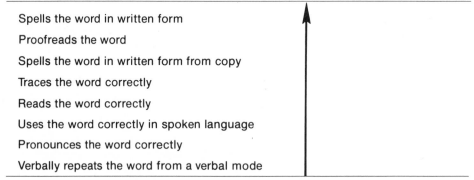

Spells the word in written form

Proofreads the word

Spells the word in written form from copy

Traces the word correctly

Reads the word correctly

Uses the word correctly in spoken language

Pronounces the word correctly

Verbally repeats the word from a verbal mode

FIGURE 12.7   A sequence of prespelling skills

Students should not be expected to spell words until they can pronounce them correctly, properly use them in speaking, read them, write them from visual models, and correct words in written forms (proofreading).

Spelling skills. There are nine spelling competencies which enable students to spell words independently. Teachers should be knowledgeable about each of these and should strive toward helping L&BD students apply them.

1. *Auditory analysis*: Students should hear words separated into their phonetic elements. Auditory analysis provides the basis for recognizing phonograms in written form. Examples:

a) Student identifies words that rhyme in jingles when spoken.

b) Student completes spoken jingles by adding ending words.

2. *Consonants:* Initial consonants should be taught prior to teaching other consonants. Teach these in relation to words within students' speaking and reading vocabulary.

Examples:

a) Students write the first letter of each word that is spoken.

b) Students are taught to spell words which begin with silent consonants, e.g., know.

Final consonants should be taught by introducing words which end with each consonant.

Examples:

c) Have students listen for the sound of *p* in stop, jump, up, help.

d) Have students write the consonant at the end of each word that is spoken.

Medial consonants can be taught by introducing words that have consonants within them.

Examples:

e) Have students listen for the sound of *p* within each word and ask them to name the consonant sound, e.g., supper, paper.

f) Have students select and write words that have medial consonants from a list of mixed words.

Consonant blends maintain the sound of each consonant blended together (*tr*, *gr*, *pr*). Consonant digraphs are two consonants representing one sound (*ch*, *sh*, *wh*, *th*). These should be taught as a part of word study and in the context of whole words.

Examples:

g) Have students underline those words in lines that begin with a particular consonant blend when given sentences or a series of words.

3. *Phonograms:* A sound unit composed of one or more vowels alone or preceded or followed by consonants represents a phonogram. Students can be taught to identify and spell initial, medial, final, and word phonograms.

Examples:

a) Have students identify and then write all words from a list which begin with the same phonogram, e.g., *ca* (as in cap).

b) Have students identify and write all words from a list which have the same phonogram in the medial position, e.g., *ar* (as in farm).

c) Have students identify and write all words from a list containing the same final phonogram, e.g., *ear* (as in clear).

d) Have students identify and write all words from a list containing the same word phonogram, e.g., *be* (as in bed, beg, before, believe, beside).

4. *Plurals:* There are five aspects of forming plurals which should be taught to pupils. These include adding *s*, adding *es*, changing *f* to *v*, medial changes, and exceptions.

Examples:

a) Have students write the plural forms of all words requiring adding *s*, e.g., boy, girl, car.

b) Tell students that singular nouns ending in *s, sh, ch, x,* or *z* form the plural by adding *es* because the plural form cannot be pronounced without an extra syllable, e.g., box, bunch, brush, quiz, gas, face.

c) Tell students that some singular nouns ending in *o* form the plural by adding *es*, e.g., mosquito, torpedo, potato.

d) Tell students that some nouns ending in *f* or *fe* change the *f* to *v* and add *s* or *es*, e.g., wolf, life, loaf.

e) Tell students that some singular nouns make a change in the middle of the word to form the plural, e.g., goose, mouse, man, woman, foot.

f) Tell students that there are many exceptions to the above examples (a through e) for forming plural words, e.g., some words ending in *o* form plurals by adding *s* (piano, solo); e.g., some words ending in *f* form plurals by adding *s* (roof, chief); e.g., some nouns form plurals by adding *en* (child, ox); e.g., some nouns have the same form for plural as for the singular (fish, deer, sheep).

5. *Syllabication:* Dividing words into syllables is one way to improve spelling. Students should learn which letters are vowels and what constitutes a syllable. Examples:

a) Have students identify vowels in known words.

b) Have students identify syllables in known words.

c) Teach students that *y* is a vowel when it has the sound of *i* as in *easy* and *play*.

d) Teach students that *w* and *y* are vowels when they follow vowels in the same syllables, e.g., how, follow, play, joy.

e) Show students that sometimes two vowels together make a single sound, e.g., boil, balloon, loud.

f) Have students divide words into syllables.

6. *Structural elements:* Prefixes, suffixes, and root words can be taught as a basis for improving spelling. Example:

a) Many words are made up of several parts (syllables). The main part of such words are called the root, e.g., *port* (portable, import), *due* (product, reduce), *prove* (approve, approval, approving).

b) Prefixes come before the roots, e.g., *ex* (except, exchange), *ad* (addition, address).

c) Suffixes come after the root, e.g., (able, less, tion, full, ize).

7. *Ending changes:* Three rules can be applied which will help in learning to spell many words. Each deals with changing word endings: final e, final y, and final consonants.

Examples:

a) Final *e* is dropped before a suffix beginning with a vowel but is kept before a suffix beginning with a consonant, e.g., vote (voting, voted). Teach students this short rule:
Before a vowel drop the e.
Before a consonant let it be.

b) Final *y* does not change if a vowel comes before y (playing, journeyed). But final *y* changes to *i* if a consonant precedes it except when adding *ing* (carrying, carries). Teach students this rule:
After a consonant y becomes i.
After a vowel y stays y.

c) For words ending in a single consonant after a single vowel in an accented syllable, double the consonant before a suffix beginning with a vowel (sto*pp*ed/sto*pp*ing, sli*pp*ed/sli*pp*ing, shi*pp*ed/shi*pp*ing/shi*p*ment). Teach students to apply this rule:
Double one consonant after one vowel if it is accented.

8. *Vowel digraphs:* A vowel digraph consists of two vowels forming one sound (e.g., ai, ea, ay, ei, ie). Among these vowel digraphs, spelling words with *ie* and *ei* are most difficult. There is a rule which can be applied, although there are several exceptions to it.

Examples:

    a) teach students this rule:

Write i before e except after c, or when sounded like "a" as in neighbor and weigh.

    b) have students spell words following the above rule, e.g., ch*ie*f, f*ie*ld, p*ie*ce (*i* before *e*).

rec*ei*ve, c*ei*ling, dec*ei*ve (*e* before *i* after *c*),

fr*ei*ght, n*ei*ghbor, w*ei*gh, (*e* before *i* when sounded like *a*).

    c) teach students to spell those words that are exceptions to the rule, e.g., (*ei*ther, h*ei*ght, n*ei*ther, th*ei*r).

    9. *Silent e:* Single syllable words ending in *e* have a long vowel and a silent *e*. Examples:

    a) Have students locate those words in a list that end in *e*.

    b) Have students pronounce those words ending in *e*.

    c) Lead them to conclude that in those one syllable words ending in *e* the *e* is silent, e.g., five, live, hive, bribe.

Dictionary skills.   Students should be trained to use dictionaries and other reference books in their word study. They should be informed that no one is expected to remember how to spell all words and their meanings. Word dividers are preferable to dictionaries for checking spelling, although either may be used for that purpose.

Words cannot be located in references if students do not know their beginning spellings. For this reason it is important to stress skills 1, 2, and 3 in the preceding spelling skills list. Once students have acquired these three competencies, they should be taught dictionary skills: alphabetizing, using pronunciation keys, and finding word meanings.

1. *Alphabetizing:* Students should be able to recite the alphabet in order. Have them list words alphabetically, first with words having different beginning letters. Later have students alphabetize words which have the same first and second letters.

As students become more proficient in alphabetizing, encourage them to use student dictionaries, showing them how to use guide words on each page. Games requiring the use of references will encourage the use of alphabetizing skills.

In order to discourage students from reciting the entire alphabet for word location, teach them to identify which letter precedes or follows other letters, e.g., which letter comes before *t*, after *s*, before *l*, after *j*? Exercises which require them to alphabetize a short range of words (such as those beginning with *l*, *m*, *n*, *o*, and *p*) will help them learn portions of the alphabet.

2. *Pronunciation marks:* Students should learn to interpret accent marks and other pronunciation keys, such as symbols and diacritical marks. Portions of dictionary listings can be used for these purposes. They should be taught one interpretation at a time. In order to avoid confusion, use the same symbols as are in students' dictionaries. Later point out to the students that each dictionary has a section in its front explaining the meaning of symbols and diacritical marks used in that dictionary. They should become familiar with dictionaries from different publishers so that they can compare the various diacritical marks and keys. In this way, students can gain the understanding that keys and marks vary depending upon the dictionary used. Students may be provided with words to be divided and for placing accent marks.

Example:
> Locate these words in your dictionary. Divide each into syllables. Show accent marks and write in brackets how it is pronounced. The first word is done for you.

expose	ex-pose′	(eks-pōz′)
address	_____	_____
raisin	_____	_____
wrench	_____	_____

It is important not to use words that are outside the students' speaking and reading vocabularies in these exercises.

3. *Word meanings:* Most words which are listed in the dictionary have several meanings. Differences in word meaning can be confusing for some children. For this reason, teachers should begin with differences in word meaning in spoken language, as in all advanced language skills. Once students have begun to note the multiple meanings for the same words and have discussed this phenomenon, dictionary exercises can be used.

Dictionary exercises should be limited at first. Have the assignments focus only on word meaning. Later, as students become proficient in differentiating word meaning usage, entire dictionary listings may be gradually included.
Example:

> Exercise 1
> Locate these words in your dictionary. *Write the first definition shown.*

medicine	1. _____
lapel	1. _____
hiccup	1. _____
agent	1. _____
scroll	1. _____
hijack	1. _____

> Exercise 7
> Locate these words in your dictionary. *Write the first two definitions shown.*

> Exercise 12
> Locate these words in your dictionary. *Write the definition that has the same meaning as used in each sentence.*

> *expose*   Jack threatened to *expose* the spy.

Dictionary skills range from simple competencies (e.g., alphabetizing) to those that are very advanced (e.g., word derivatives). With elementary-aged L&BD students only those reference skills necessary for that level work should be taught, and these should always be related to the students' daily academic needs. For older L&BD students, more advanced dictionary and reference skills should be taught in relation to their academic progress.

Word meaning is important for teaching spelling. Immediate prerequisite skills and concepts for spelling a word are (a) its meaning, (b) recognizing it in print (reading), (c) using it in meaningful spoken language, and (d) pronouncing it. Once students demonstrate these competencies, they should be taught to spell the word.

Assessing and Teaching Spelling

There is some controversy concerning the importance of teaching spelling to regular elementary students (Dunkeld & Hatch, 1975). Similarly, there is confusion as to which teaching methods result in proficient spellers (Geedy, 1975). For nonhandicapped, elementary-aged students, research evidence suggests that:

1. direct, systematic instruction increases spelling proficiency (Brothers & Hosclaw, 1969); and

2. it is more efficient to study words from word lists rather than in context and they are learned more quickly, remembered longer, and transferred more readily to new contexts (Horn, 1944, 1950, 1960).

Beyond the findings cited above, the effects of specific methods for teaching spelling are not clearly supported by research evidence. Remedial spelling techniques tend to be rooted in the Fernald approach (1943). Those remedial techniques that emphasize phonics are related to the methods advocated by Gillingham and Stillman (1966).

The study method advocated by Hillerich & Gould (1976) for *The Merrill Spelling Program* is similar to the Fernald approach (1943).

 a. LOOK at the new word.
  SAY it.
 b. CLOSE your eyes.
  THINK what the word looks like.
  SAY the word.
  SPELL the word aloud.
 c. OPEN your eyes.
  LOOK at the word again. Were you right? If you made a mistake, go back and do step 1 and step 2 again.
 d. COVER the word.
  WRITE the word. Did you spell it right? If you made a mistake, go back and do step 1 and step 2 again.
 e. COVER the word you just wrote.
  WRITE it again.

The teacher should introduce this form and go over it with the students. She should repeat this for a few days. Time should be allotted in the daily schedule for the students to work on their spelling words.[7]

The Fernald approach follows several steps: First, students are told that they will learn a word in a very successful new way. Then, the teacher writes and says the word. Third, students trace the word several times as they say it. Students then write the word on a separate sheet of paper several times while saying it. Next students write the word from memory. If incorrect, tracing and saying the word are repeated.

Teachers should have a system for students to file words when using a word study approach such as that described above. Dunkeld and Hatch (1975) recommend a practical system using three envelopes. Each student's name is written in red on one, yellow on the second, and in green on the third. *Red* is for those words which the student has yet to learn from the week's spelling list. *Yellow* represents those words the student has not yet mastered but is in the process of learning. And *green* is for those words the student has already mastered. Each student's three envelopes are stapled on a bulletin board in an accessible place.

---

7. Developed by Robert L. Hillerich and Sharon Gould for The Merrill Spelling Program, *Spelling for writing*. Columbus, Ohio: Charles E. Merrill Publishing Co., 1976.

Before selecting any one method or approach to teaching spelling to L&BD students, teachers should assess their learning approaches as described in chapter 6. A combination of the learning through imitation and phonics will probably be effective with most L&BD students.

Frequent practice in writing words is important for maintaining competency in spelling. Practice need not be dull and tedious. Games may be used to encourage students.

Example 1:

Write a number of phonograms familiar to the group (as, ape, ip, ing, all). Hold one before the group and ask one student to say sentences with a word made from this phonogram (Let's play ball. I had cereal for breakfast).

A variation of this game can be used for writing sentences and/or words on the chalkboard.

Example 2:

Have students make a spelling book from paper 6½ x 8 inches. Use white paper for the inside of the book and tinted paper for the cover. Inside these books have them paste words which they know and have cut from magazines or papers at home. They must name the words to the teacher before pasting them into their books.

Example 3:

Mount several pictures on a card. Distribute the cards, giving one to each student in the class. Ask them to write the names of the objects and to make a list of the action words. These words may be made with alphabet cards instead of written, if desired.

Example 4:

Have the students maintain spelling books. On each page have a written task for them, such as: write all flavors of ice cream that they like, the names of all the animals they know, the names of trees, the names of fruits, the names of their friends, and the names of their favorite _____ (stories, authors, TV programs, cartoon characters, athletes).

Example 5:

Prepare a set of cards 4½ x 6 inches. On each write a phonogram. Ask students to make as many words as possible from them and put them in separate lists by phonogram.

Example 6:

Write the name of a city and ask students to write as many words as they can using the letters contained in the word. Give a token for every _____ words (two, five, six, depending upon the size of the word), e.g., Minneapolis: mean, open, Minnie, lion, sin, man, pie, etc.

Assessment of spelling performance can be of two types: (1) analysis of types of errors and (2) identification of words that have been misspelled. In conducting an analysis of students' spelling errors, the teacher should use words from a prepared spelling list. Tasks may be contrived following the spelling skills shown in Figure 12.8.

The checklist in Figure 12.8 is designed to be used with task sheets related to a word list. Each task is numbered, and when it is used to assess one of the spelling skills the performance is indicated in the *results* column. For example, Task 7.04 (p. 377) was used to assess skill 7.0 for words taken from a third-grade list.

	Tasks	Results
1.0 Auditory discrimination		
.1 consonant sounds	_____	_____
.2 vowel sounds	_____	_____
.3 word pronunciation	_____	_____
2.0 Consonants		
.1 initial	_____	_____
.2 final	_____	_____
.3 medial	_____	_____
.4 blends	_____	_____
3.0 Phonograms		
.1 initial	_____	_____
.2 medial	_____	_____
.3 final	_____	_____
.4 word	_____	_____
4.0 Plurals		
.1 s	_____	_____
.2 es	_____	_____
.3 f to v	_____	_____
.4 medial changes	_____	_____
.5 exceptions	_____	_____
5.0 Syllabication		
.1 word division	_____	_____
6.0 Structural elements		
.1 roots	_____	_____
.2 prefixes	_____	_____
.3 suffixes	_____	_____
7.0 Ending changes		
.1 final e	_____	_____
.2 final y	_____	_____
.3 final consonants	_____	_____
8.0 Vowel digraphs & diphthongs		
.1 one sound (ai, ea, ay, ei, ie)	_____	_____
.2 blends (oi, ou, ow)	_____	_____
9.0 Silent e		
.1 single syllable words ending in e_____		_____

FIGURE 12.8. A spelling skills checklist

Example:

Spelling Skill Assessment Task 7.04
Directions: Present a sheet of paper to students with the following words on it. Ask them to change each word to one which you say.

7.1	7.2	7.3
1. ride_____	2. circling_____	3. size_____
4. surprise_____	5. raising_____	6. nurse_____
7. story_____	8. easy_____	9. marries_____
10. skies_____	11. fly_____	12. dirties_____
13. mud_____	14. tricked_____	15. laughing_____
16. clean_____	17. dig_____	18. war_____

Say these words to students:

1. riding	2. circle	3. sizing
4. surprising	5. raise	6. nursing
7. stories	8. easiness	9. marry
10. sky	11. flying	12. dirty
13. muddy	14. trick	15. laugh
16. cleaning	17. digging	18. warring

Criteria: 7.1 6/6; 7.2 6/6; 7.3 6/6

In the above example, the teacher would simply indicate under the *tasks* column the task number (7.04) which represents the skill number (7.0) and grade level (4). Under the *results* column, the number correct in relation to the number of items for each task would be recorded, e.g., 5/6. Following the assessment of spelling skills, teachers can proceed to use words from the spelling list for teaching the needed skills.

Criterion-referenced measures may be used for identifying words that students have not learned to spell. Procedures for designing these measures follow those outlined previously in chapter 7.

Teachers of L&BD students may have trouble determining which word list to use for developing assessment measures. It is wise to use that commercial spelling series which is used throughout the school if one has been adopted.

To develop a list of words for criterion-referenced measures, simply list those words shown in the back of each grade level book and make a measure for every 15 or 20 words. A criterion-referenced measure for 15 words from a grade 2 speller is shown below.

Criterion-referenced Measure, Grade 2[8]

Purpose: The student will write each word on the basal spelling list when auditorially presented with the word and a sentence using that word.

Criterion: 100% learned, go on to next unit; below 100% , instructional level for words missed only.

Materials: 1. List of spelling words, 1 sentence for each word
2. Pencil, paper

Directions: 1. Teacher reads word to students, reads sentence using word, reads word again.
2. Students write word.
3. List is corrected immediately by students. Teacher reads word and sentence again and writes word on chalkboard.
4. Students who have reached criterion may be tested on next basal list. Students on the instructional level should practice their spelling using the exercises shown.

Word List 2.15

see	1. Can you see him?	happy	9. I feel so happy today.
well	2. How do you feel?	took	10. He took it.
stay	3. Stay in the house.	and	11. Sam and Sue are playing ball.
an	4. Please pass me an apple.	room	12. My room is blue.
five	5. Here are five books.	fire	13. There was a fire on my block
other	6. What is in the other box?		yesterday.
my	7. My shirt is red.	girl	14. There is a new girl in my class.
that	8. I like that.	the	15. The snow is very deep.

---

8. Criterion measures, word list, and exercises were developed by Rhonda Moskowitz and Susan Quinn under the author's direction. These efforts are acknowledged and appreciated.

Following assessment, students are assigned exercises keyed to the word list where mastery was not demonstrated. Below are three practice exercises for the grade 2 word list shown above.

Practice Exercises for Word List 2.15

Purpose: When presented with a sentence with one word missing, the student will fill in the logical word from the present spelling list.
Skill: Practice for posttest — basal spelling list, grade 2
Materials: 1. Ditto sheets —

	Answers
For John's birthday there were 8 candles on his _____.	cake
One, two, three, four, _____.	five
The opposite of up is _____.	down
When she smiles she is _____.	happy
George Washington chopped down the cherry _____.	tree

2. Pencil

Criterion: 100%, learned
Directions: Teacher hands out sheets, explains what is to be done.
Purpose: When presented with a list of spelling words with mixed letters, the student will unscramble and write each word correctly.
Skill: Practice for posttest — basal spelling list, grade 2
Materials: 1. Ditto sheets —

Example	Answer
na	an
ym	my
teh	the
ees	see
yats	stay

Criterion: 100%, learned.
Below 100%, use words missed in different exercise.
Directions: Teacher hands out list and explains what is to be done.
Purpose: When presented with word auditorially and told to say word that rhymes with example and begins with _____, student will say, then write word.
Skill: Practice for posttest — basal spelling list, grade 2
Level: Grade 2
Materials: 1. paper
2. pencil
Criterion: 100%, use missed words in another exercise
Directions: 1. Teacher tells students to listen carefully, she/he is going to say a word.
2. Listen especially hard for first letter. After word is said teacher will say name of a letter.
3. Students should use new letter as first letter of word and rhyme it with original word.
4. Students write word on paper.
5. Teacher says *word*, then gives first letter of new word.

		Answers
bell	*w*	well
look	*t*	took
make	*c*	cake
deep	*k*	keep
broom	*r*	room

Teaching Arithmetic Skills

Arithmetic is the one skill subject that is consistently logical. Its structure and content facilitate systematic instruction by teachers. In many respects, arithmetic may be considered to be an advanced language since it has verbal and written symbols and serves a communication function.

In addition to teaching arithmetic skills and concepts, L&BD students should be taught and encouraged to use desk and pocket calculators, rulers, clocks, and other measurement devices. They should be taught to read tables of weights and measures and other devices which serve as tools.

Assessment and Instruction

Teachers of L&BD students can organize their instruction in arithmetic through an assessment/teaching approach. This approach is readily achieved through the use of criterion-referenced measures for assessment and instructional strategies for teaching.

The DTIMS arithmetic skills are listed in chapter 9. Below are two assessment tasks, two instructional strategies, and commercial references from each of the four major categories: (1) measurement; (2) numbers, numerals, and numeration systems; (3) operations and properties; and (4) sets. The structure of the DTIMS arithmetic skills is shown in Figure 9.5 (pp. 261-264).

DTIMS Arithmetic[9]

SETS

Assessment Task

Level 0

M-ST-CP-0001-LO-S   When presented with a collection of objects and asked to make a specified set of objects, the student will make a set of the object named.

M-ST-CP-0001-LO-A   Criterion: 10/10

Teacher: (Randomly place 3 crayons, 5 pencils, 2 popsicle sticks, 8 blocks, 1 stapler, 9 thumb tacks, 7 paper clips, 4 books, 6 rubber bands, and 5 index cards in front of the student.) "Look at the things on the table.

1. Make a set of blocks.	6. Make a set of crayons.
2. Make a set of rubber bands.	7. Make a set of pencils.
3. Make a set of books.	8. Make a set of paper clips.
4. Make a set of popsicle sticks.	9. Make a set of thumb tacks.
5. Make a set of staplers.	10. Make a set of index cards."

(Note: The student response is to be considered correct if he/she makes a set of the objects as requested. He/she *need not* use all of the objects provided. Example: When the student is asked to "Make a set of blocks," if he/she makes a set of six blocks [8 are provided] and no other object appears in that set, he/she will be correct.)

---

9. Reprinted with permission of Thomas M. Stephens from *The Directive Teaching Instructional Management System: Reading, arithmetic, and social skills.* Copyright © 1973 by Thomas M. Stephens. All rights reserved.

MATERIALS: 1 stapler, 2 popsicle sticks, 3 crayons, 4 books, 5 pencils, 5 index cards, 6 rubber bands, 7 paper clips, 8 blocks, and 9 thumb tacks.

TEACHING STRATEGY   CODE *M-ST-CP-0001-LO-I$_{01}$-VA*

SKILL: When presented with a collection of objects and asked to make a specified set of objects, the student will make a set of the object named.

INDIVIDUAL OR SMALL GROUP

TEACHER ACTIVITY:

1. Plan reinforcement strategy selected from reinforcement menu.
2. Plan instruction.

"Today we are going to learn about 'sets'. Let's have all the students who are wearing sweaters stand together here. (Point to designated place for students to stand — teacher may substitute color of clothing, ages, or any other appropriate attribute.) Now, all the students who are wearing just a shirt and not a sweater stand together over here. (Point to designated place.) Good! The students in this group (point to group with sweaters) are alike because they all are wearing sweaters. We could call this group the 'sweater set' because it is a *set* of people wearing sweaters. What kind of set is this? (Student response.) That's right, Betty."

"We could call this group (point to shirt group) the 'shirt set' since it is a set of people wearing shirts. What is this a set of? (Student response.) Very good, Eric. Now you may take your seats."

"Another name for a group of objects or a collection of objects is a set. What objects can you think of that we have or can buy as a set? (Student response.) That's very good. We can also buy a set of _____, _____." (Name sets not mentioned by students.)

Place some erasers, crayons, and pencils on a table in front of students. "Can someone pick out a set of crayons from this pile? (Student response.) Terrific, Doug." Continue procedure with erasers and pencils, giving students ample opportunity to respond.

PRACTICE ACTIVITY:

Gather the following materials: six beads, nine marbles, three cups, eight safety pins, four spools of thread, five pencils, four pieces of chalk, six spoons, seven bobby pins, ten toothpicks. Randomly place these objects in four or five baskets and hide them in different places in the room. Tell students they are going to play a "Find the Sets" game. Each student will be instructed to find a set of objects. Students must find the baskets and look in each one to find their objects. As soon as a student has found one set, he/she will show the set to the teacher and the teacher will give him/her another set to find. The student's response should be considered correct if he/she makes a set of objects as requested, even if he/she has not used all the objects available. Each student should have a chance to find at least two sets. Provide reinforcement.

MATERIALS:

six crayons, five pencils, three erasers, six beads, nine marbles, three cups, eight safety pins, four spools of thread, four pieces of chalk, six spoons, seven bobby pins, ten toothpicks, four or five baskets (or boxes.)

STUDENT RESPONSE:

The student will make a specified set of objects when presented with a collection of objects and directions from the teacher.

EVALUATION:

Criterion: 2/2

Criterion met?

If yes: reassess using assessment task M-ST-CP-0001-LO-A.

If no: continue using same strategy or select new one.

MATERIALS CODE: M-ST-CP-0001-LO-S

SKILL: When presented with a collection of objects and asked to make a specified
set of objects, the student will make a set of the object named.

3290
PUBLISHER   SADLIER
TITLE   KINDERGARTEN BOOK
SERIES   MODERN SCHOOL MATHEMATICS,
                     STRUCTURE AND USE
EDITION   REVISED
TYPE   TEACHER EDITION
YEAR   1972
PAGE NUMBERS
  053

3300
PUBLISHER   HOUGHTON-MIFFLIN
TITLE   KINDERGARTEN BOOK
SERIES   MODERN SCHOOL MATHEMATICS,
                     STRUCTURE AND USE
EDITION   REVISED
TYPE   STUDENT TEXT
YEAR   1972
PAGE NUMBERS
  006

Assessment Task

Level 0

M-ST-OS-0009-LO-S   When presented with pictured sets of objects, the student will
point to the empty set and say "zero."

M-ST-OS-0009-LO-A   Criterion: 10/10
Teacher: "Look at Group 1. Point to the empty set and say the number that goes with
it." Repeat these instructions for all ten groups.

Answers:

1. 4 apples, zero.
2. 3 triangles, zero, 4 stars.
3. 1 tree, zero, 3 balloons, 2 men.
4. zero, 1 house, 1 heart, 1 car, 1 box.
5. 1 tree, 1 cat, 1 ball, 1 sun, 1 shoe, zero.
6. 3 hearts, zero, 1 truck, 4 ice cream cones.
7. 1 bunch of grapes, 1 chair, zero, 1 diamond, 1 butterfly, 1 pencil.
8. zero, 1 airplane.
9. 2 hands, 1 apple, 1 flower, 5 triangles, zero.
10. 1 bed, 1 lamp, 1 balloon, zero, 1 star, 1 cup, 1 doll, 1 dress.

MATERIALS: Worksheet
WORKSHEET CODE: M-ST-OS-0009-LO-A

ASSESSMENT WORKSHEET
CODE: M-ST-OS-0009-LO-A

TEACHING STRATEGY

CODE: *M-ST-OS-0009-LO-I-₀₁-VA*

SKILL: M-ST-OS-0009-LO-S When presented with pictured sets of objects, the student will point to the empty set and say "zero."

INDIVIDUAL OR SMALL GROUP
TEACHER ACTIVITY:

1. Plan reinforcement strategy selected from reinforcement menu.

2. Plan instruction.

Place three containers such as small boxes on a table. In one box put one crayon and in another box put two crayons. Leave the third box empty. Point to the first box. Teacher: "This box has a set of one crayon. (Point to the second box.) This box has a set of two crayons. (Point to the third box.) This box has no crayons, it is an 'empty' set. It has a set of zero. Mary, point to the box with the 'empty' set and say 'zero.' (Student responds.) Very good! (Remove crayons and place one eraser in one box and two erasers in one box. Leave the third box empty. Point to the first box.) This is a set of one eraser. (Point to the second box.) This is a set of two erasers. (Point to the third box.) This is an 'empty' set — it has a set of zero. Tommy, point to the 'empty' set. (Response.) How much does this empty set have? (Response.) Great, Tommy. This set has zero.''

Repeat using other items in the boxes and giving each student an opportunity to respond.

Draw three circles on the chalkboard. In one circle draw two triangles, in another circle draw two squares and leave the third circle empty. Point to the first set. "Jane, what is the number of this set? (Response.) Two, that is right Jane. What is the number of this set, John (point to second set)? (Student response.) Two is correct. What is the number of this set Keith (point to empty set)? Great, Keith. This set is zero.'' Continue in this manner with several examples until students demonstrate competence in this skill.

PRACTICE ACTIVITY:

On separate sheets of paper draw large circles. Put pictured sets in some of the circles and no objects in five of the circles.

Example: Empty Set: Pictured Set:

Place sheets of pictured sets on floor making a trail. Place empty sets every second and third sheet. Each student must follow trail by stepping only on empty sets. Teacher: "Children, let's pretend we're lost in the forest. The only way out is this trail. However, we can only step on the empty sets. Each time you step on the empty set you must tell the number of the empty set. Let's begin with Oscar." (Students are to step only on the empty sets and say "zero" each time. If students forget to say "zero," remind them by saying, "What is the number of that set?"

Provide reinforcement.

MATERIALS:

Three boxes, three crayons, three erasers, and other groups of three objects; five sheets of paper denoting empty sets; ten sheets of paper showing pictured sets.

STUDENT RESPONSE:

The student will step on the empty set and say "zero" when presented on sheets of paper.

EVALUATION:

Criterion: 5/5

Criterion met?

If yes: Reassess using Assessment Task M-ST-OS-0009-LO-A.

If no: Continue using same strategy or select new one.

MATERIALS CODE: M-ST-OS-0009-LO-S

SKILL: When presented with pictured sets of objects, the student will point to the empty set and say "zero."

2740

PUBLISHER   ADDISON WESLEY

TITLE   PRIMER

SERIES   ELEMENTARY SCHOOL MATHEMATICS

EDITION   SECOND

TYPE   TEACHER EDITION

YEAR   1971

PAGE NUMBERS

074 075

2730
PUBLISHER   ADDISON WESLEY
TITLE   PRIMER
SERIES   ELEMENTARY SCHOOL MATHEMATICS
EDITION   SECOND
TYPE   STUDENT TEXT
YEAR   1971
PAGE NUMBERS
  043

3290
PUBLISHER   HOUGHTON-MIFFLIN
TITLE   KINDERGARTEN BOOK
SERIES   MODERN SCHOOL MATHEMATICS,
                   STRUCTURE AND USE
EDITION   REVISED
TYPE   TEACHER EDITION
YEAR   1972
PAGE NUMBERS
  119

3300
PUBLISHER   HOUGHTON-MIFFLIN
TITLE   KINDERGARTEN BOOK
SERIES   MODERN SCHOOL MATHEMATICS,
                   STRUCTURE AND USE
EDITION   REVISED
TYPE   STUDENT TEXT
YEAR   1972
PAGE NUMBERS
  036

NUMBERS, NUMERALS AND NUMERATION SYSTEMS

Assessment Task

Level 0

M-NN-CR-0005-LO-S When presented with pictured sets of 1-5 objects and the numerals 1-5, the student will mark the numerals as directed to match the quantities.

M-NN-CR-0005-LO-A   Criterion: 10/10
Teacher presents worksheet to student. "Draw a line to the numeral that tells how many dots you see in each circle."
Answers:
1. 3 dots   6. 5 dots
2. 1 dot   7. 2 dots
3. 5 dots   8. 1 dot
4. 3 dots   9. 2 dots
5. 4 dots   10. 4 dots
MATERIALS: Worksheet (see page 386), pencil
WORKSHEET CODE: M-NN-CR-0005-LO-A

Student Assessment Worksheet
WORKSHEET CODE: M-NN-CR-0005-LO-A

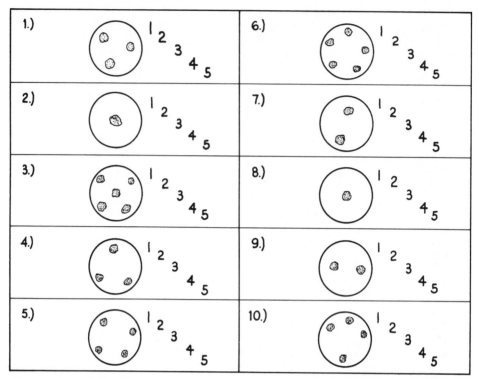

TEACHING STRATEGY
SKILL: M-NN-CR-0005-LO-S

CODE: *M-NN-CR-0005-LO-I_{01}-V*

When presented with pictured sets of 1-5 objects and the numerals 1-5, the student will mark the numerals as directed to match the quantities.

INDIVIDUAL OR SMALL GROUP
TEACHER ACTIVITY:

1. Plan reinforcement strategy selected from reinforcement menu.
2. Plan instruction.

Present each student with a set of numeral cards, 1-5. Have each student place the cards in front of himself. "Show me your 1 card. (Student response.) That's right, Mike." Repeat with 2, 3, 4, 5. Draw two circles on the chalkboard. "I have drawn two circles on the chalkboard. How many circles have I drawn? (Response.) That's right. This is the way we write two (write the numeral 2 below the circles). What does this say? (Response.) Two, that's right. When we have two objects, we can show how many we have by writing a two like this (teacher points to numeral 2)." Teacher continues with the numbers one, three, four, and five.

Draw five circles on the chalkboard. "Mary, come and count the circles. How many circles are there? (Student response.) Very good. Which card shows how many circles we have on the chalkboard? Hold it up. (Student response.) That's great, Terry. That is how we show five."

Teacher draws two circles on chalkboard. "How many circles are there in this set?" Hold up the card that tells how many. (Student response.) Good!" Continue procedure drawing sets of one to five objects and giving each student the opportunity to hold up a numeral card for a set.

PRACTICE ACTIVITY:

Present worksheet to students. "When you have a birthday, you get to make a wish and blow out the candles on your birthday cake. On this worksheet, there are many birthday cakes with different numbers of candles on them. Count the candles on each cake to see how many you would have to blow out to get your wish. Then, circle the numeral that tells how many candles there are. When you are done, you may draw your own birthday cake on another sheet of paper. Draw the number of candles that tell your age on your cake. Then write the numeral for the candles below the cake and put your name on the paper so everyone will know how old you are."

Provide reinforcement.

MATERIALS:

Numeral cards (1-5) for each student, chalkboard, worksheet, paper

STUDENT RESPONSE

The student will circle the numeral to match quantities of 1-5.

STRATEGY WORKSHEET
CODE: M-NN-CR-0005-LO-1$_{01}$

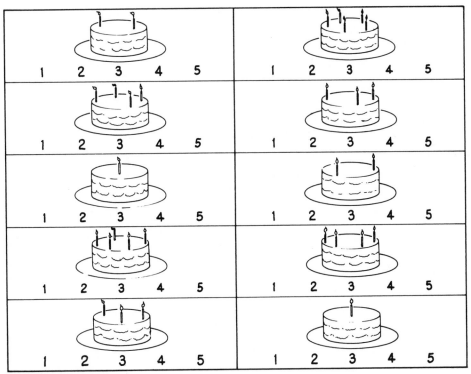

EVALUATION:

Criterion: 10/10

Criterion met?

If yes: Reassess using Assessment Task M-NN-CR-0005-LO-A.

If no: Continue using same strategy or select new one.

MATERIALS CODE: M-NN-CR-0005-LO-S

SKILL:

When presented with pictured sets of 1-5 objects and the numerals 1-5, the student will mark the numeral as directed to match the quantities.

3290	
PUBLISHER	HOUGHTON-MIFFLIN
TITLE	KINDERGARTEN BOOK
SERIES	MODERN SCHOOL MATHEMATICS, STRUCTURE AND USE

EDITION   REVISED
TYPE   TEACHER EDITION
YEAR   1972
PAGE NUMBERS
  117

3300
PUBLISHER   HOUGHTON-MIFFLIN
TITLE   MODERN SCHOOL MATHEMATICS,
                            STRUCTURE AND USE
EDITION   REVISED
TYPE   STUDENT TEXT
YEAR   1972
PAGE NUMBERS
  035   037   038
  055   056   057
  058   059   060

3860
PUBLISHER   HEATH (D.C. AND COMPANY)
TITLE   LEVEL K
SERIES   HEATH ELEMENTARY MATHEMATICS
EDITION   FIRST
TYPE   TEACHER EDITION
YEAR   1972
PAGE NUMBERS
  073

Assessment Task
Level 0

M-NN-NU-0009-LO-S   When presented with randomly arranged numeral cards (1-10), the student will put them in natural order.

M-NN-NU-0009-LO-A   Criterion: 3/3
Teacher shuffles cards and gives to student. "Put these in the right order, starting with the least number." Reshuffle cards and have student repeat task for a total of three trials.
MODALITY: Visual
MATERIALS: Numeral cards 1 through 10.

TEACHING STRATEGY   CODE: *M-NN-NU-0009-LO-$_{01}$-V*
SKILL: M-NN-NU-0009-LO-S   When presented with randomly arranged numeral cards (1-10), the student will put them in natural order.

MODALITY: Visual
INDIVIDUAL
TEACHER ACTIVITY:
1. Plan reinforcement strategy selected from reinforcement menu.
2. Plan instruction.
(Place strip of paper which has the numerals 1-3 written on it, before the student.) Teacher: "These numbers are in order. This '1' is the first number (point to 1). Point to the first number (student response). Right, that is first. It's a one. This number is next (point to 2). Two. And then this number is next (point to 3). Three. Show me the number that is first. (Student response.) Right! What comes next? (Student response.) And next?" (Student response.) Position student's hand if necessary. Repeat until student needs no assistance. The give cards 1, 2, and 3 to the student.
   "Put these cards in the same order as the numerals on this paper (point to numeral strip)." (Student response.) Cut a piece of construction paper one inch longer and

one inch wider than the numeral strip. Tape it to table on three sides, leaving the left side open. Insert numeral strip so the numeral "1" is visible. "Look at which numeral is first. Find the card that has that number on it and place it here. (Student response.) Which card comes next? (Student makes choice and puts it beside "1.") Let's see if you were right." Pull out strip so numeral "2" shows. If student has made a mistake, let him correct it. "Now put the next card here (point to space next to 2). (Student response.) Were you right? (Pull out strip to show 3.) Yes, these look like this (point to cards and numeral strip). (Push numeral strip under cover and mix order of cards.) Put these in order, then pull out the paper and see if you did it right." (Student response.)

Repeat entire procedure first with cards 1, 2, 3, 4, and 5, then with cards 1, 2, 3, 4, 5, 6, 7, and 8, and finally with cards 1, 2, 3, 4, 5, 6, 7, 8, 9, and 10.

PRACTICE ACTIVITY:

Present student with worksheet. "Cut out the numerals on this sheet (teacher demonstrates) and paste the numerals in order on the empty spaces." Teacher should demonstrate the cutting and the way numbers should be pasted.

Provide reinforcement.

MATERIALS:

Cards 1, 2, 3, 4, 5, 6, 7, 8, 9, 10; Strips (1) 1,2, 3, (2) 1, 2, 3, 4, 5, (3) 1, 2, 3, 4, 5, 6, 7, 8, (4) 1, 2, 3, 4, 5, 6, 7, 8, 9, 10

STUDENT RESPONSE:

The student will cut out numerals from worksheet and paste on strip of paper in natural order.

EVALUATION:

Criterion: 10/10

Criterion met?

If yes: Reassess using Assessment Task M-NN-NU-0009-LO-A.

If no: Continue using same strategy or select a new one.

STRATEGY WORKSHEET
CODE: M-NN-NU-0009-LO-1$_{01}$

3			4
5			7
9			8
10			6
1			2

MATERIALS CODE: M-NN-NU-0009-LO-S
SKILL:
When presented with randomly arranged numeral cards (1-10), the student will put them in natural order.

2740
PUBLISHER	ADDISON WESLEY
TITLE	PRIMER
SERIES	ELEMENTARY SCHOOL MATHEMATICS
EDITION	SECOND
TYPE	TEACHER EDITION
YEAR	1971

PAGE NUMBERS
  088   098   108

2737
PUBLISHER	ADDISON WESLEY
TITLE	PRIMER
SERIES	ELEMENTARY SCHOOL MATHEMATICS
EDITION	SECOND
TYPE	STUDENT TEXT
YEAR	1971

PAGE NUMBERS
  055   065   075

3300
PUBLISHER	HOUGHTON-MIFFLIN
TITLE	KINDERGARTEN BOOK
SERIES	MODERN SCHOOL MATHEMATICS, STRUCTURE AND USE
EDITION	REVISED
TYPE	STUDENT TEXT
YEAR	1972

PAGE NUMBERS
  076   077   078

OPERATIONS AND THEIR PROPERTIES
Assessment Task
Level II

M-OT-AN-0041-L2-S   When presented with addition problems involving three or more one-digit addends, the student will write the sums.

M-OT-AN-0041-L2-A   Criterion: 10/10

Present student with worksheet. "Find the sum for each problem."

1. 5	2. 6	3. 7	4. 7	5. 9
6	9	3	2	3
4	8	2	1	9
7	9	9	9	
			8	

6. 2	7. 3	8. 7	9. 6	10. 7
3	5	9	3	2
9	1	4	7	4
4	6		8	
			5	

MODALITY: Visual
MATERIALS: Worksheet

ASSESSMENT WORKSHEET
M-OT-AN-0041-L2-A

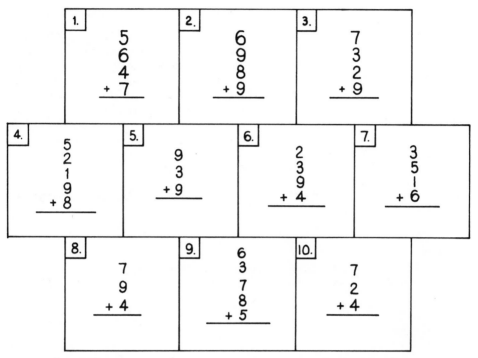

TEACHING STRATEGY
SKILL: M-OT-AN-0041-L2-S

CODE *M-OT-AN-0041-L2-I₀₂-V*

When presented with addition problems involving three or more one-digit addends, the student will write the sums.

MODALITY: Visual
INDIVIDUAL OR SMALL GROUP
TEACHER ACTIVITY:

1. Plan reinforcement strategy selected from reinforcement menu.
2. Plan instruction.

Teacher and students are seated at a table with a chalkboard nearby. Begin lesson with a review of adding two one-digit addends. Continue by saying, "Now that we know how to add problems with two addends, let's try problems with three addends." (Write 2 on the chalkboard.)

$$\begin{array}{r} 1 \\ +\ 4 \\ \hline \end{array}$$

"Look at the problem I have written on the chalkboard. We add three addend problems the same way we do two addend problems. First we start with the top two numerals (teacher points). They are two and one. How much is two and one, Arnie? (Response.) Good. Three (teacher writes 3 to the side). How much is three plus four (point)? (Response.) Great, three plus four is seven. Our answer is seven (teacher writes 7). When we have addition problems that have more than two addends, we just add two numbers at a time and keep adding until there are no numbers left to add. Let's try that again. (Write 3 on chalkboard.) What do we do

$$\begin{array}{r} 2 \\ +\ 4 \\ \hline \end{array}$$

first, Kim? (Response.) Good. We add three and two. How much is three plus two? (Response.) Good (teacher writes 5). Now what do we do, Jerry? (Response.) That's right, we add five and four. How much is five and four? (Response.) Excellent."

Write 2 on chalkboard. "Polly, will you come up and add

$$\begin{array}{r} 2 \\ + 1 \\ \hline \end{array}$$

2+2+1 for us." (Response—student repeats same procedure as demonstrated by the teacher.) Proceed in this manner until students are solving problems without teacher assistance. When students are able to successfully complete three addend problems, present four addend problems. Point out to students that regardless the number of addends, the same procedure is followed for finding the sum.

PRACTICE ACTIVITY:

Present worksheet. "Find the sums to the addition problems on this worksheet."
Provide reinforcement.

MATERIALS: Flannel board, cutouts, chalkboard, worksheet, pencil.

STUDENT RESPONSE:

The student will find the sums of addition problems with three or more addends when presented on a worksheet.

EVALUATION:

Criterion: 8/8

Criterion met?

If yes: Reassess using Assessment Task M-OT-AN-0041-L2-A.

If no: Continue using same strategy or select new one.

STRATEGY WORKSHEET
M-OT-AN-0041-L2-1

1.	2.	3.	4.
$\begin{array}{r} 4 \\ 2 \\ + 1 \\ \hline \end{array}$	$\begin{array}{r} 4 \\ 0 \\ + 2 \\ \hline \end{array}$	$\begin{array}{r} 3 \\ 3 \\ + 1 \\ \hline \end{array}$	$\begin{array}{r} 6 \\ 2 \\ + 5 \\ \hline \end{array}$
5.	6.	7.	8.
$\begin{array}{r} 3 \\ 2 \\ 1 \\ + 4 \\ \hline \end{array}$	$\begin{array}{r} 7 \\ 1 \\ 1 \\ + 2 \\ \hline \end{array}$	$\begin{array}{r} 3 \\ 4 \\ 2 \\ + 1 \\ \hline \end{array}$	$\begin{array}{r} 4 \\ 2 \\ 3 \\ + 4 \\ \hline \end{array}$

SUGGESTED PROBLEMS:

1) 4	2) 4	3) 3	4) 6	5) 3	6) 7	7) 3	8) 4
2	0	3	2	2	1	4	2
+1	+2	+1	+5	1	1	2	3
				+4	+2	+1	+4

ANSWERS: 1) 7; 2) 6; 3) 7; 4) 13; 5) 10; 6) 11; 7) 10; 8) 13

MATERIALS CODE: M-OT-AN-0041-L2-S
SKILL: When presented with addition problems involving three or more one-digit
addends, the student will write the sums.

3790
PUBLISHER   W. H. SADLIER
TITLE   PROGRESS IN MASTERING MATHEMATICS
SERIES   MASTERING MATHEMATICS
EDITION   FIRST
TYPE   STUDENT TEXT
YEAR   1969
PAGE NUMBERS
   090   015

3220
PUBLISHER   HOUGHTON-MIFFLIN
TITLE   BOOK 2
SERIES   STRUCTURAL ARITHMETIC
EDITION   FIRST
TYPE   STUDENT TEXT
YEAR   1965
PAGE NUMBERS
   114

Assessment Task

Level I

M-OT-SU-0013-L1-S   When presented with subtraction problems involving subtracting
the numbers 1-18 from the numbers 1-18, the student will write the
differences.

M-OT-SU-0013-L1-A   Criterion: 10/10
Present worksheet: Teacher: "Solve these subtraction problems. Write the difference."

17	12
−5	−7

18	13
−13	−9

11	14
−3	−7

16	15
−14	−9

18	16
−9	−7

MATERIALS: Worksheet

ASSESSMENT WORKSHEET
CODE: M-OT-SU-0013-LI-A

Name _____

```
  17              12
-  5            -  7

  18              13
- 13            -  9

  11              14
-  3            -  7

  16              15
- 14            -  9

  18              16
-  9            -  7
```

TEACHING STRATEGY   CODE: *M-OT-SU-0013-L1-I₀₁-V*
SKILL: M-OT-SU-0013-L1-S When presented with subtraction problems involving subtracting the numbers 1-18 from the numbers 1-18, the student will write the differences.

INDIVIDUAL OR SMALL GROUP
TEACHER ACTIVITY:
1. Plan reinforcement strategy selected from reinforcement menu.
2. Plan instruction.

Teacher displays number line or draws number line on chalkboard. "Today we are going to work subtraction problems using the numbers 1 to 18. Let's do this problem. (Teacher writes 17 on board.)

```
-5
```

This problem says seventeen minus five is equal to some number. Using our number line let's find what seventeen minus five is. We will start on seventeen and move back five numbers. How many should I move back? (Response.) Good, Pam. (Teacher points to 17 and counts to the left five.) When we count back five we land on twelve and twelve is our answer. So, seventeen minus five equals? (Student response.) Great!" (Teacher writes 12 below line of problem.)

Continue procedure with various subtraction problems involving the numbers 1-18. Let students come to the board to work the problems, using the number line if necessary, and write the differences. Gradually, fade out the use of the number line by instructing students to use the number line only if necessary. Encourage students to compute problems without instructional aids. Give each student an opportunity to respond.

PRACTICE ACTIVITY:
  On index cards prepare subtraction problems with sums of eighteen. Prepare enough problems so that each child can draw six. Put the cards in a box and have each student draw six. If student draws two or more cards with the same problem, he must return them and draw again. Students will write the differences to the problems on the cards they have drawn. If desired, students may present their problems to the class one at a time, reading the problem and giving the answer.
  Provide reinforcement.
MATERIALS:
  Chalkboard, number line, four index cards per student.
STUDENT RESPONSE:
  The student will write the difference to subtraction problems involving the numbers 1-18 when presented on cards.
EVALUATION:
  Criterion: 6/6
  Criterion met?
  If yes: Reassess using Assessment Task M-OT-SU-0013-L1-A.
  If no: Continue using same strategy or select new one.

MATERIALS CODE:. M-OT-SU-0013-L1-S
SKILL: When presented with subtraction problems involving subtracting the numbers 1-18 from the numbers 1-18, the student will write the differences.

2720
PUBLISHER   ADDISON WESLEY
TITLE   BOOK I
SERIES   ELEMENTARY SCHOOL MATHEMATICS
EDITION   SECOND
TYPE   TEACHER EDITION
YEAR   1971
PAGE NUMBERS
   306   307   108   109
   110   111   112   113
   115   117

2710
PUBLISHER   ADDISON WESLEY
TITLE   BOOK I
SERIES   ELEMENTARY SCHOOL MATHEMATICS
EDITION   SECOND
TYPE   STUDENT TEXT
YEAR   1971
PAGE NUMBERS
   261   262

3870
PUBLISHER   HEATH (D.C. AND COMPANY)
TITLE   LEVEL I
SERIES   HEATH ELEMENTARY MATHEMATICS
EDITION   FIRST
TYPE   TEACHER EDITION
YEAR   1972
PAGE NUMBERS
   276   282

2720
PUBLISHER   ADDISON WESLEY
TITLE   BOOK I
SERIES   ELEMENTARY SCHOOL MATHEMATICS
EDITION   SECOND
TYPE   TEACHER EDITION
YEAR   1971
PAGE NUMBERS

120	121	124	125
128	138	139	140
141	142	180	181
150	151	152	153
154	166	167	168
169	170		

2710
PUBLISHER   ADDISON WESLEY
TITLE   BOOK I
SERIES   ELEMENTARY SCHOOL MATHEMATICS
EDITION   SECOND
TYPE   STUDENT TEXT
YEAR   1971
PAGE NUMBERS

091	092	095	103	104
105	106	107	116	117
118	119	115	131	132
133	134	135	145	146

3870
PUBLISHER   HEATH (D.C. AND COMPANY)
TITLE   LEVEL I
SERIES   HEATH ELEMENTARY MATHEMATICS
EDITION   FIRST
TYPE   TEACHER EDITION
YEAR   1972
PAGE NUMBERS

118	119	122	125	144
145	149	152	164	169
171	173	225	227	228
233	236	237	246	

3190
PUBLISHER   HOUGHTON-MIFFLIN
TITLE   BOOK I
SERIES   STRUCTURAL ARITHMETIC
EDITION   FIRST
TYPE   STUDENT TEXT
YEAR   1965
PAGE NUMBERS

047	048	049	050	051	
052	054	055	056	057	
058	059	060	061	062	
063	066	068	069	070	
108	110	111	124	125	126

3310
PUBLISHER   HOUGHTON-MIFFLIN
TITLE   BOOK I
SERIES   MODERN SCHOOL MATHEMATICS, STRUCTURE
                   AND USE
EDITION   REVISED
TYPE   TEACHER EDITION
YEAR   1972
PAGE NUMBERS
   152   154   155   191   192
   193   195   222   235   342
   344   347

3770
PUBLISHER   W.H. SADLIER
TITLE   ADVENTURES IN MASTERING MATHEMATICS
SERIES   MASTERING MATHEMATICS
EDITION   FIRST
TYPE   STUDENT TEXT
YEAR   1969
PAGE NUMBERS
   024   027   045   048   051
   052   056

3320
PUBLISHER   HOUGHTON-MIFFLIN
TITLE   BOOK I
SERIES   MODERN SCHOOL MATHEMATICS,
                   STRUCTURE AND USE
EDITION   REVISED
TYPE   STUDENT TEXT
YEAR   1972
PAGE NUMBERS
   109   111   112   146   147
   148   150   175   188   285
   287   290

MEASUREMENT
Assessment Task
Level I

M-ME-MO-0007-L1-S   When presented with a penny, nickel, and dime, the student will
state its value in cents.

M-ME-MO-0007-L1-A   Criterion: 9/9

Present coins one at a time. Teacher: "How much is this coin worth in cents?

1. Penny
2. Nickel
3. Dime
4. Nickel
5. Penny
6. Dime
7. Nickel
8. Dime
9. Penny

MATERIALS: Penny, nickel, dime

TEACHING STRATEGY   CODE: *M-ME-MO-0007-L1-1$_{01}$-VA*
SKILL: M-ME-MO-0007-L1-S   When presented with a penny, nickel, and dime, the student will state its value in cents.

SMALL GROUP OR INDIVIDUAL
TEACHER ACTIVITY:

1. Plan reinforcement strategy selected from reinforcement menu.
2. Plan instruction.

Teacher shows the student(s) a penny. "This is a penny. One penny is worth one cent. (Hold up the penny.) What is this called? (Student response.) How much is it worth? (Student response.) A penny can also be called one cent because it is worth one cent. Why can a penny be called one cent?" (Student response.) Teacher holds up a nickel. "This is a nickel. It takes five pennies to make a nickel. This means a nickel is worth five cents. How much is a nickel worth? (Student response.) Very good." Teacher holds up a dime. "This is a dime. It takes ten pennies to make a dime, so a dime is worth ten cents. How much is a dime worth? (Student response.) Great."

"I am going to hold up the penny, nickel and dime, one at a time, and I want you to tell me how much it is worth in cents. For example, I will hold up this nickel and you are to say, 'five cents.'" Teacher holds up penny, nickel and dime, varying the order, and prompting students to state its worth in cents. Continue until students are responding without assistance.

PRACTICE ACTIVITY:

Prepare cards containing pictures of a penny, a nickel and a dime. Each card should have only one coin. Label classroom objects such as pencils, crayons, paper clips, tablets, etc. with prices of one cent, five cents and ten cents. Give each student a penny, nickel and dime card. The student is required to request to buy something by saying, "I would like to buy a pencil." The teacher, or a competent student, replies, "That will be five cents, please." The buying student responds, "This is five cents" and gives the teacher the nickel card. Continue until each student has "spent" his penny, nickel and dime cards. Repeat once.

Provide reinforcement.

MATERIALS:

Real pennies, nickels, and dimes; penny, nickel, and dime cards, one of each for each student.

STUDENT RESPONSE:

The student will "pay" the correct coin card and state the amount in cents when requested by the teacher.

EVALUATION:

Criterion: 6/6
Criterion met?
If yes: Reassess using Assessment Task *M-ME-MO-0007-L1-A*
If no: Continue using same strategy or select new strategy.

MATERIALS CODE: M-ME-MO-0007-*L*1-S
SKILL: When presented with a penny, nickel, and dime, the student will state its value in cents.

3870
PUBLISHER	HEATH (D.C. AND COMPANY)
TITLE	LEVEL I
SERIES	HEATH ELEMENTARY MATHEMATICS
EDITION	FIRST
TYPE	TEACHER EDITION
YEAR	1972
PAGE NUMBERS	
206 256 258	

2720
PUBLISHER   ADDISON WESLEY
TITLE   BOOK I
SERIES   ELEMENTARY SCHOOL MATHEMATICS
EDITION   SECOND
TYPE   TEACHER EDITION
YEAR   1971
PAGE NUMBERS
   216   158

2710
PUBLISHER   ADDISON WESLEY
TITLE   BOOK I
SERIES   ELEMENTARY SCHOOL MATHEMATICS
EDITION   SECOND
TYPE   STUDENT TEXT
YEAR   1971
PAGE NUMBERS
   179   123

3770
PUBLISHER   W. H. SADLIER
TITLE   ADVENTURES IN MASTERING MATHEMATICS
SERIES   MASTERING MATHEMATICS
EDITION   FIRST
TYPE   STUDENT TEXT
YEAR   1969
PAGE NUMBERS
   120

3180
PUBLISHER   HOUGHTON-MIFFLIN
TITLE   BOOK I
SERIES   STRUCTURAL ARITHMETIC
EDITION   FIRST
TYPE   TEACHER EDITION
YEAR   1965
PAGE NUMBERS
   134   135

3190
PUBLISHER   HOUGHTON-MIFFLIN
TITLE   BOOK I
SERIES   STRUCTURAL ARITHMETIC
EDITION   FIRST
TYPE   STUDENT TEXT
YEAR   1965
PAGE NUMBERS
   117   118

Assessment Task

Level II

M-ME-TM-0011-L2-S When presented with a current calendar and verbal questions about dates, the student will say the date, month, and year.

M-ME-TM-0011-L2-A   Criterion: 9/10

Teacher presents calendar. Teacher orally asks the following questions:

1. Point to the calendar and tell me what the date is today. Include the month and year.
2. What are the dates for all the Sundays in the month?
3. What are the dates for all the Wednesdays in this month?
4. What date is your birthday?
5. What date is Christmas?
6. What date is Thanksgiving?
7. What date was yesterday?
8. What date is tomorrow?
9. What is the date for last Tuesday?
10. What is the date of next Monday?"

MODALITY: Auditory/Visual
MATERIALS: Calendar (teacher provided)

TEACHING STRATEGY   CODE: *M-ME-TM-0011-L2-1$_{01}$-AV*

SKILL: M-ME-TM-0011-L2-S When presented with a current calendar and verbal questions about dates, the student will say the date, month and year.

INDIVIDUAL OR SMALL GROUP
TEACHER ACTIVITY:

1. Plan reinforcedment strategy selected from reinforcement menu.
2. Plan instruction.

Display a current calendar. Teacher: "This is the month of _____, in the year 19_____. The numerals stand for the 'date' of each day. Point to today's date and read it. This is __(month)__, __(date)__, __(year)__. What is this 'date'? (Student responds.) Good. What three things must we know to name the date? (Student response.)

Great!"

Point to numeral 25. "This date is __(month)__ twenty-fifth __(year)__. What is this date?" (Student responds.) Point to numeral 1. "What is this date, Jan? (Student responds.) Very good!"

Continue in this same manner until all students have had a chance to respond.

PRACTICE ACTIVITY:

Draw a large calendar on the floor. Have each pupil draw a card and follow its directions. The activity ends after each pupil has had five successful tries. (Note: The teacher may wish to simply present a large calendar rather than draw one on the floor. In this case, the cards should be changed to "point to."

Sample Cards:

1. Stand on and tell today's date.
2. Stand on and tell the date for the second Sunday in this month.
3. Stand on and tell the date for the first Saturday in this month.
4. Stand on and tell the date for the first Tuesday in this month.
5. Stand on and tell the date for the third Monday in this month.
6. Stand on and tell the date for the last Thursday in this month.

7. Stand on and tell the date for the second Monday in this month.
8. Stand on and tell the date for the third Wednesday in this month.
9. Stand on and tell the date for the last day in this month.
10. Stand on and tell the date for the first day in this month.
   Provide reinforcement.
MATERIALS:
   Current calendar, chalk drawn calendar on floor, direction cards (enough so each child has 10 cards).
STUDENT RESPONSE:
   Student will stand on a calendar and say the date when presented with directions written on cards.
EVALUATION:
   Criterion: 5/5
   Criterion met?
   If yes: Reassess using Assessment Task M-ME-TM-0011-L2-A.
   If no: Continue using same strategy or select new strategy.

MATERIALS CODE: M-ME-TM-0011-L2-S
SKILL: When presented with a current calendar and verbal questions about dates, the student will say the date, month, and year.

NO COMMERCIAL REFERENCES

Summary

Procedures for teaching academic skills and concepts follow the four steps in directive teaching: assess, plan, instruct, and evaluate. Fundamental to academic instruction is a well-organized, systematic approach and a structure and sequence to the content.

Instructional procedures often must start with shaping responses to acceptable performance levels. A modeling approach may then be used. It consists of demonstrating, having students imitate, encouraging them to reproduce, and providing simple and mixed practice opportunities.

Basic academic skills include reading, writing, spelling, and arithmetic. These can be taught using principles of behavior modification within a directive teaching framework.

13

Consulting with Parents and Other Personnel

Teachers of L&BD students must work cooperatively with parents, other school personnel, and with personnel from other professions. Cooperation can facilitate student learning in school and at home. Planning is necessary between parents and teachers if transfer of learning is to occur from school to home.

Effective communications with other adults in students' lives require an exchange of information on a regular basis.

Teachers can provide assistance to parents by providing information as to their children's progress and by training them to be more effective behavior managers.

Special teachers may also participate as consultants in inservice training programs. Suggested curricula for training parents and teachers in behavioral approaches are also included in this chapter.

Introduction

Teachers of L&BD students must be keenly aware of the other important adults in their pupils' lives. Foremost are parents who serve, in most instances, as childrens' first teachers. Additionally, there are school personnel, teachers, consultants, administrators, counselors, psychologists, and other educational specialists. Medical and other allied personnel may also provide vital assistance to L&BD students. But for school-aged children, teachers are the central figures in providing the necessary academic and social instruction.

Cooperation is important among and between teachers, parents, other school personnel, and allied professionals. It can result in direct benefits to the students and facilitate transfer of learning from school to other settings. Cooperation in some instances may improve teaching performance and, perhaps most importantly, should improve student learning.

Cooperation Helps Students

Kronick (1974) has shown insight and sensitivity to the social needs of the learning disabled. She noted that learning handicapped children may feel alienated from

402

their families because of their academic and social limitations. It is possible, she believes, to assist families in living with their handicapped children in ways that are mutually pleasant and effective.

Wetter (1972) found that parental attitudes toward children with learning disorders are distinctive, suggesting the need for appropriate counseling for parents of such children. His study confirmed the widely held belief that mothers of the learning disabled were overindulgent and overprotective as compared to mothers of children who did not present learning problems.

Teachers can assist L&BD students by cooperating with their parents in several different ways. Minimally, parents should be informed of their children's academic and social performances. Such information, if accumulated over time, can help parents gain perspectives concerning their children's progress.

Teachers may be asked by parents to provide information to physicians, mental health specialists, and other noneducators. They may be asked to participate in staff conferences with such personnel. While requests of this sort may be inconvenient or viewed as of dubious value, teachers should provide these services when requested by parents. They should do so with the belief that cooperation may help their students.

As L&BD students move into regular classrooms and other learning situations, cooperative activities among various school personnel become more essential. Within schools, cooperative planning may be necessary so that students can be scheduled for special instruction while their primary placement is in regular programs. Special tutoring, speech correction, adaptive physical education programs, personal counseling, and other services within the school require careful scheduling.

In addition to scheduling, provisions are necessary if the various types of instruction are to be integrated within students' performances. For example, speech correctionists and classroom teachers should be aware of students' performances and the specific tasks being taught. This awareness can result in teachers' encouraging students to practice newly acquired or developing speech skills. It can also enable speech teachers to relate their content to classroom activities and materials.

Transfer of Learning

School learnings are necessary beyond the school environment since much of what students master in classrooms is useful in everyday living. When parents and other school personnel have cooperative relationships with special teachers, occasions can be arranged so that students can transfer their learnings across conditions.

Systematic planning is necessary if teaching is to be directed toward transferring learning. Such planning is difficult to achieve, however, due to differences in theory and methods. Some instructional orientations are more compatible than others. Behavioristic approaches, for example, conflict with nondirective counseling. Ability trainers' materials and instructional emphases are at cross-purposes with skill trainers' practices (see chapter 2). An eclectic instructional approach is less likely to conflict entirely with any single treatment or instructional orientation, but, unfortunately, it is also less likely to result in as rapid performance gains as will those approaches based on reinforcement theory.

Transfer between Home and School

Fredericks et al. (1971) concluded that one of the important benefits of a parent training program was the application of behavior modification techniques to the handicapped child's siblings. His results indicate that parents can be expected to transfer their training of one child to their other children. This same type of transfer has been reported by other researchers. For example, Patterson, Shaw, and Ebner (1969) noted that parents of a deviant, hyperactive, aggressive child began applying behavioral tactics to a younger child after success with their older child.

Transfer of training from school to home and vice versa is more difficult to achieve, however. In order for transfer of learning to take place across two very different settings, the responses must be generalized from one set of conditions where the response was learned to another set of conditions where, while the response would be appropriate, it had not been learned.

Theoretically, teachers can facilitate generalizing and transferring of behavior by identifying conditions under which particular responses will be expected and by relating their instruction to those anticipated conditions. In practice, however, it is sometimes difficult to achieve transfer by anticipating home conditions. For example, Peck and Stackhouse (1973) found that families which produced reading problems were characterized by having fewer exchanges of information and more irrelevant interchanges than did nonreading problem families. Under these conditions it would be difficult to increase relevant verbalizations if these were necessary for a home-training program. Almost certainly, direct access to parents is needed if great changes in family behaviors are desirable.

Effective Communications

Consultation involves cooperation and effective communication. Communication is essential if cooperation is to develop. Communication consists of the content of messages and the delivery mode. But within these two dimensions of communication are subtleties of speech, and sometimes these subtleties result in much confusion and many misunderstandings (Farb, 1974). An information-exchange during conversation, for example, consists of verbal as well as nonverbal messages. The *ways* in which teachers refer to their students are communicated along with *what* is said.

Example 1
Teacher to Parent: Jack continues to have problems in speaking and reading, but he has made some progress since September.
Example 2
Teacher to Parent: Your son is still having trouble learning to speak correctly and to read, but with a lot of hard work I've made some progress with him since he came in my class.

Essentially, the same message is conveyed in both examples above. But the first example suggests a sensitive teacher who credits the child's success to both of their efforts. The second teacher, however, is seemingly less sensitive and less inclined to recognize the child's efforts.

In communicating, content should be free of jargon. Straightforward, descriptive terms are more likely to convey an accurate message than are technical terms. Providing concrete examples of students' performances also contributes to clear communications. Examples are particularly helpful when technical language is unavoidable. Sometimes terms that are not considered to be of a technical nature by school personnel are confusing to others. For example, when teachers refer to *individualized instruction* they mean that their teaching is differentiated on specific learning variables, but to some parents *individualized instruction* may imply that students are taught one at a time.

Modes used in communicating can affect cooperation between home and school. As a general rule, face-to-face sessions are most desirable when cooperation is the major objective. Telephone contacts also tend to be informal and probably serve as the second best way to exchange information for purposes of gaining or maintaining cooperative behavior.

Written messages are more formal than conversations. Notes are preferable to letters and memoranda for developing cooperative relationships. Of course, written messages can be made more or less informal depending upon such factors as the tone of the content and the type of salutation. Generally, the more personalized written messages are, the friendlier their tones tend to be.

Consulting with Parents

Consultation to parents of L&BD students may occur for purposes of providing and obtaining information concerning students' progress, asking the parents' assistance to encourage their children to practice those skills and behaviors at home that were learned in school, and providing assistance and training to parents.

Parental involvement in programs for handicapped children has long been considered to be important. Most efforts to involve parents, however, have not been successful. Some authorities believe that two factors appear to be associated with unsuccessful parental involvement programs: the attitudes of professional personnel toward parents and their inadequate skills in working with parents (Karnes, Zehrbach, & Taska, 1972).

Teachers should not view themselves as experts to impart knowledge; they should work cooperatively with parents in helping students. While teachers undoubtedly have information concerning students' school adjustments, parents are more knowledgeable about students' activities outside of school.

Parent Conferences

Teacher/parent conferences for purposes of sharing information should be a regular part of all special instructional programs. If possible, conferences should be scheduled at a time mutually convenient for parents and teachers, and sufficient time should be allowed (approximately 45 minutes to one hour) in order to have an unhurried exchange of information. Preferably, conferences should be held at school, although sometimes a home conference may be necessary.

Parents may feel intimidated when conferences are held at school. Others are threatened more by a home visit. Teachers should be sensitive to parents' feelings about the meeting site. But eventually, parents should visit the school and their child's room so that they can experience the physical environment where instruction occurs.

At times, other school personnel will find it necessary to conduct parent conferences. These are often for special purposes such as informing parents and seeking their permission to test and observe children, discussing students' absences from school, or discussing with the parents special health or behavior problems observed by school personnel.

Parent/Teacher Conference Procedures

Typically, parent/teacher conferences consist of four parts: establishing rapport, obtaining relevant information from the parents, providing information, and summarizing the conference.

Establishing Rapport

1. Give parents an opportunity to express their concerns first.
2. Their initial reactions to opening remarks by you should get them started: How has Jasper felt about coming to school lately?
3. Do not be defensive by explaining what you are doing with the student or by trying to "set the record straight." If they are in error, you can provide accurate information later in the session.

Obtaining Relevant Information

1. Use this time to get information that relates to your *teaching*; this can flow naturally from the earlier discussion.
2. Your questions should be phrased carefully. Avoid any hidden implications such as: Is Jasper often upset about school? What is meant by upset? The interviewer had meant to ask: Does he seem disappointed or discouraged about his school progress?
3. Get descriptive information, it is more valuable than conclusions. Descriptive: Jasper reads library books at home. Conclusion: Jasper likes to read.

Provide Information

1. Describe what is occurring in the student's instructional program. Avoid educational jargon.
2. Based on your assessment and teaching of the student, indicate what he/she knows, has yet to learn, and is ready to learn. Have documentation to support these statements available whenever possible.
3. Briefly describe the progress that the student made.
4. Indicate any instructional plans you have for the student.

Summarize

1. Briefly summarize what has been said, after making sure the parents have asked all of their questions.
2. Thank the parents for keeping the appointment.

Teachers should plan for scheduled conferences with parents. One parent conference format is shown in Figure 13.1.

FIGURE 13.1.   A parent conference form

Child_____   Date _____

Parent(s) present_____

Teacher _____

Planned Outcomes
1.
2.
3.
4.
5.

Points to Be Discussed
1.
2.
3.
4.
5.

Notes

It is usually unnecessary and cumbersome to obtain a detailed record of conferences with parents. Extensive note taking during the conference often interferes with open exchanges. In anecdote 13.1, Mrs. Flack, Andy's tutor, describes her conference with Andy's mother (see anecdotes 7.1 and 7.2, pp. 189–198, for background information).

ANECDOTE 13.1

Planned outcomes
1. Teach the parents how to construct and play word games made from designated vocabulary with Andy. "Concentration," "Bingo."
2. Show parents how to use behavioral reinforcement chart.
3. To report on the progress Andy has made.

The teacher visited the home as any other arrangement would have necessitated one of the parents taking time off from work. The mother expressed her appreciation for this, although she apologized for the appearance of the home.

We discussed my illness as Andy had mentioned at home each time I was absent. When asked how Andy felt about coming she stated he liked it and talked about working with words, sounds, letters and getting stars and stickers. She did not really understand it and then discussed at length her older son whom I had worked with last year.

We discussed the problems of working mothers and how children can help. She then went into great detail about what hard workers the boys were, how extremely eager they were to help, they never had to be asked, etc. The boys were never any trouble at home, but they had to take Andy to the Mental Health Clinic because the principal said they had to. When asked why he had done that the mother said the school psychologist's tests showed something was wrong with Andy, but the woman at the Mental Health Center could not figure out why they were there. Again she restated the boys were never any trouble at home when I happened to notice a large paddle on the television set. During all this she talked without even a pause and then she asked how Andy had done in reading.

I showed some of the papers and stories Andy had read and worked and the two teacher-made games for vocabulary. She then wanted to show games with sounds they had bought the boys and brought out two obviously new or unused games. She listened and questioned as those skills which Andy had improved were discussed.

She asked if I had children and when I said I used "Bingo" and "Concentration" with them she became very interested and asked how. When I said we had a behavior chart and gave our boys stars for the positive things they did, she asked about details but then added her boys were so good at home they did not need it but she could see how praising and rewarding good things would be a good idea.

She then told about all the places they had taken the boys and all the activities they had done with them. She then started to tell in detail about the new state museum which she had read about in a pamphlet. I mentioned the boys must have been fascinated by this and she replied, "Oh, I think they were in bed." She then showed other folders of places they had been, and I commented it was too bad every child did not have these opportunities. After further discussion about dictation stories that Andy and I had done she stated, "I'll bet it would help if I sat down with him and I let him tell in his own words what he liked and I could write it for him and he could take it to school for the other boys and girls." She said her parents were divorced when she was 11 and her husband was the youngest of seven children, and they had never gone any place as children so they went now and always took the boys with them.

During the summarization of what had been accomplished the mother commented that at times Andy was very stubborn and you could not make him do anything. When asked how she handled this she said that they just leave him alone so he won't hate it. When I commented that this type of action would handicap him at school, she said she could see that but that they tell him he has to do what the teacher says. When told about contingency contracting which had worked very well in tutoring, the mother said that might be a good idea.

Comments on Conference

The mother appears to be very interested in her children. The yard was full of every type of play equipment and they have a horse and two ponies. She was extremely defensive about discussing the boys' behavior and would only interact when discussing my boy's behavior and the management system I used.

The home was very poor even though both parents have always worked. It appears much of their money is spent on toys and outings with the boys. When Andy dictated stories in the clinic, it was with a Dick and Jane vocabulary and I never was able to identify any of the activities they had done as a family, except a synopsis of horror movies.

The father has become active in Cub Scout work to "help the boys" and last year coached a child's softball team so the boys could participate.

The mother commented at least twice that the Mental Health Clinic could not figure out why Andy was there, but she was unwilling to discuss this further. From her final comments concerning Andy's stubbornness it appears that with further conferences, progress can be made by working with the family. This will undoubtedly have to be done through the school due to the antagonism generated by the parents having been sent elsewhere.

Conducting Parental Conferences

Parental conferences are more than visits between teacher and parents. If teachers are to be effective, they should be competent in those skills that are helpful in conducting conferences with parents. These competencies are rapport building, eliciting information, recognizing parents' emotions, avoiding irrelevant areas of parental concern, and providing information and recommendations.

Building rapport. Two behaviors that teachers can use to improve rapport with parents are to engage in emotionally neutral topics of conversation and to put the parents at ease.

Teachers should remember that the intended topic of conversation is about the parents' child, one of the most important individuals in their lives. Consequently, they should not hurriedly and insensitively launch into a monologue about the student's learning and behavior problems. They should instead engage in "small talk." Comments such as the following are in order:

Teacher: Our weather certainly has been _____ (pleasant, changeable, wet, cold).

Teacher: Well, I am certainly pleased to meet you. Is this your first visit to our school?

Teacher: Hi! I hope the traffic wasn't too heavy in getting here.

Avoid discussions of topics which are likely to evoke emotional responses. Comments concerning political issues, current events, other children, and any topics where people are likely to have strong opinions are poor choices for creating small talk.

If the conference is being conducted in the school, hold it in a place where there is privacy and have full size chairs available for the parents. Offering a beverage and permitting them to smoke if they wish are ways to make parents physically comfortable.

When conferences are held in parents' homes, it is still necessary to help them to be psychologically comfortable. Being pleasant, accepting a beverage, and other behaviors which convey an acceptance of the parents' efforts to be hospitable will help put them at ease.

Obtaining information.   Teachers can obtain information from parents by stating the purpose for the conference, asking specific questions, and focusing on the student.

After the parents have been greeted, are comfortably seated, and have had a brief exchange of small talk with the teacher, reasons for the meeting should be stated.

Teacher: I wanted to discuss Harold's school progress with you.

Teacher: We haven't had a chance to meet, and I thought it was time that we talked about Sue's school work.

Teacher: As I mentioned on the phone, I wanted to have a chance to talk about Joe's progress since we last met.

Teacher: The special education team asked me to talk with you about possibly changing Ruth's placement.

Teacher: I have three reasons for needing to talk with you: to find out how you view Jerry's progress, to report to you on his daily work, and to try to answer any questions you might have concerning his school program.

Statements concerning the purposes for the conference should be followed by a question that encourages parents to give their opinions or provide information about their child. This stage in the conference is important since it sets the occasion for parents to participate early and prevents the teacher from talking at the parents and/or dominating the conference time. By obtaining current views and information from the parents before providing information, the teacher will be able to be more responsive to their concerns.

Avoid asking questions which can be answered *yes* or *no*. Instead, ask open-ended questions.

> Teacher: We have been working on students' attitudes toward reading. What types of materials is Howard reading at home for fun? (Instead of: Is Howard reading at home?)
>
> Teacher: Spelling continues to be a problem for some of our students. What do you notice about Clem's practice spelling assignments that he has been taking home? (Instead of: Is Clem practicing his spelling at home?)
>
> Teacher: We are now considering Geraldine's placement for next year. Possibly, you will be asked to agree on having her assigned to a regular fifth grade with supplemental tutoring provided. How does that plan sound to you? (Instead of: Will you agree to Geraldine being placed in fifth grade next year if supplemental tutoring is provided?)

Recognizing parents' feelings.   Parents may express anger, disagreement, and other feelings during the conference. Teachers should communicate to them that they recognize their feelings and still avoid disagreements and other irrelevant exchanges.

Angry and hostile remarks are best handled by reflecting the parents' statements:

> Parent: Jack has been in this special program for almost two years and you still haven't corrected his problem. How much longer will it take?
>
> Teacher: You feel Jack's problems have not been dealt with effectively.
>
> Parent: That's right and after two years he ought to be a lot better.
>
> Teacher: You don't feel Jack has made sufficient progress.
>
> Parent: Yes, two years wasted. When we agreed to placing him here, you told us how good it would be for him.
>
> Teacher: You don't think *any* of the program has helped Jack.
>
> Parent: Well, some progress has been made. But it seems too slow.
>
> Teacher: You see some learning taking place but wish it could be faster.
>
> Parent: Yes, that's it. When will he catch up?

In the above example, the teacher lets the parent know that his/her concerns have been identified. Yet defensive comments are not made by the teacher, such as: "Well it's hard to help Jack when I have so many students who need help." Or, "Two years really isn't a long time when you think of how serious Jack's problems are."

Teachers often find that by reflecting the parents' statements of concern first, they can gain parental cooperation more readily. But arguing with parents or ignoring their feelings tends to encourage them to be uncooperative.

Teachers, when being trained to reflect parents' feelings, sometimes are concerned about the parents' attitudes toward reflective comments. A common question is "What if parents object to my reflective statements?" as seen in this exchange:

> Parent: (following teacher's reflective statement) You didn't answer my question.
>
> Teacher: You feel that I am avoiding your question.
>
> Parent: That's right! I asked you when Jack will be able to go back into regular classes. Why can't you give me a straight answer?
>
> Teacher: You feel that is a simple question.

Parent: Well, isn't it?

Teacher: I can understand your concern and I am pleased that your wishes for Jack's return to the regular program are the same as mine. It is hard to answer your question at this time because....

As the immediately preceding exchange shows, when parents object to reflective statements, as a general rule teachers should:

1. identify parents' feeling by stating the parents' objection,
2. let the parents know that they heard the question,
3. point out the complexity of the question (if it is complex),
4. and inform the parents as to the issues as they relate to the child.

When the questions are not complex, teachers should answer them without explaining why they were making reflective statements. Explanations for tactics can be defensive in tone and serve to interfere with cooperative relationships. If parents persist, however, in questioning teachers' use of reflective statements (e.g., "Why do you keep doing that?"), they should be told that it is a conference technique for letting them know that their feelings are being considered.

Reflecting is not interpreting, and teachers should be careful not to confuse the two behaviors. Reflecting is simply restating the feeling tone expressed by the parent; interpreting goes beyond the statement and is an attempt to provide an explanation for the stated feeling, such as:

Teacher: Are you angry because Jack is not doing well in school?

The parent did not say she was angry, although she appeared to express anger. Clearly in the above example, the teacher has attempted to interpret the parent's feelings as well as provide an explanation for it ("...because Jack is not doing well in school.").

Interpreting parents' remarks is risky and unnecessary for teachers. It is risky because the interpretations may be incorrect and thus contribute to uncooperative behavior. Or if correct, it could irritate the parent since by verbally interpreting statements, the teacher has entered into a counseling relationship with the parent. Interpreting parental statements is unnecessary because counseling the parent is not, and should not be, the teacher's role. Further, since the student is central to the conference, the teacher should move toward that focus instead of away from it as interpreting parental remarks would do.

Avoiding irrelevancies.   Some parents attempt to engage teachers in their personal problems. They may seek advice concerning marital problems, try to obtain information about other children, gossip about community matters, or in other ways avoid conversation regarding their children. In such instances, teachers should bring the conversation back to the purposes of the conference.

Parent: How is Marsha Weldy doing? I understand she is now in your class.

Teacher: Yes, Marsha is in my class. I believe Ken and she have become acquainted. Ken's progress in arithmetic is something that you and I need to discuss.

Parents seeking personal assistance should not be ignored, but teachers should not provide personal counseling. Yet they can be helpful in other ways, such as suggesting a community resource.

Parent: My husband has been drinking heavily, and he refuses to go to work on Mondays because of his hangovers. Do you think that is causing Rod to be so bad?

Teacher: You might want to contact family services regarding your concerns about your husband. Rod does hit other children and is sometimes hard to manage. I have some suggestions on how we can help him.

Sometimes parents ask teachers to exceed their roles by requesting diagnostic information or by asking questions that are outside teachers' areas of expertise.

Parent: I saw a program on TV last week about dyslexia. Is that what Philip has?

Teacher: Philip does have trouble learning to read. I don't know if it is accurate to term it dyslexia since that is not an educational term.

Parent: Well, do you think he is brain damaged? You know he fell on his head when he was about three years old?

Teacher: He is making progress in reading. So, he can learn to read. I don't have any way of knowing if he is brain injured. You might want to talk to a physician about that possibility.

Providing information and recommendations. During the discussion and following some initial information from the parent, the teacher should provide specific information concerning the student's performances. Teachers should be positive. Begin with the student's gains and later discuss those areas where little progress has occurred. When feasible, dated products (papers, worksheets, and descriptive data) should be made available and shown to parents.

Anecdote 13.2 describes a parental conference conducted with Ken's mother. Ken, a 10-year-old, learning disabled child was enrolled in a special summer school program at the time this conference was held. Note that the teacher's plan served as an outline for the report.

ANECDOTE 13.2

A. Establishing Rapport

Mrs. Moore and Ken entered the conference room and were seated by a window. The ingenious method she devised to help Ken avoid losing his glasses was commented upon. She recognized the compliment and stated she was a Jack of all trades; sewing, cooking, and doing things for her children were her major interests. She said that Ken had enjoyed coming to school because of the jobs he got to do, he was recognized and paid attention to and she figured that was what he liked. She mentioned these concerns:

Ken's lack of recognition or reward in the regular school situation

Her desire that her children be obedient and well behaved in the neighborhood

Her wish that her children be approved by all the neighbors

That students be treated fairly in school

Her two retarded children at home

The lack of respect for the property of others in the school

Her lack of rapport with principal and regular teacher

Ken's difficulty with reading and writing

The regular teacher's lack of appreciation or awareness of her children's ability

B. Obtaining Relevant Information

Mother's lack of knowledge of the curriculum in his grade

Mother's lack of knowledge of helpful procedures which could be pursued at home

Ken's reaction to mother's report of her impressions of the school (behavioral expression: looked very sad, climbed into mother's lap and put his arm around her neck similar to a child much younger)

Mother's report of the lack of respect for the property of others in the school and neighborhood

Placement of both of her sons in the same classroom

Mother's dissatisfaction with lack of recognition by school authorities (in building) of her children and of herself

C. Providing Information

He is well liked by teachers and pupils in school this summer

Cooperative, worked well with teacher; complied with all requests

Came to school early each morning

Entered into playground games with much larger boys courageously

Subjects worked on, reading and handwriting, concentrated on vowel sounds, especially short *e*, as child knew letter sounds and two letter blends

Child learned best in game situations which provided repetition

Ken wrote in manuscript instead of cursive, handwriting difficult, grips pencils hard, forms letters poorly, especially letters which go above or below the line

Need to increase attention span. Can spend about five minutes on difficult task. Effort to extend time spent on difficult tasks would be helpful. Help in improving handwriting would make work easier in the fall.

Reported Ken's reaction to group situation well behaved but does not initiate or volunteer. Becomes upset if he has to take the initiative or answer a question.

Learned to recognize short *e* and to make many words containing short *e*. Volunteered (five times) in structured situation. Learned technique for improving handwriting and forming letters.

Summary

Commented on child's behavioral assets: cooperativeness, punctuality, rapport with pupils and teachers. Need to take initiative to improve reading and writing skills. Procedures mother may wish to follow in the home: contingency contracting, operant tactics, especially where instances of initiative taking were displayed. Mother expressed some interest in operant methods, reiterated child's like of this school situation but expressed doubts of any change being affected in the school situation next year. Thanked her for coming and walked to the door with mother and child.

Teachers should be careful not to overstate the gains that have been made. Provide information concerning skills which have been mastered rather than merely presenting test scores.

Products that cover similar skills over several months provide excellent materials for reporting to parents. Reports such as the one shown in Figure 9.8 (pp. 270-271) are excellent for this purpose. In that figure, dated skill statements are shown with the level of performance attained by each student. Teachers can achieve similar results by maintaining individual folders for each student. A summary chart can be used for recording the skill, level of attainment, and date. Samples of the student's performances should be filed in the folder as back-up information.

Evaluating conferences.   Teachers should try to evaluate parent conferences so that they can modify their approaches, if necessary, in subsequent conferences. Written, planned outcomes for conferences can serve evaluative purposes. They can then compare what appeared to be achieved with the previously stated outcomes. The discrepancy between what was achieved with what was planned represents areas needing improvement.

In anecdote 13.2, the teacher had the following outcomes:

1. determine Mrs. Moore's appraisal of Ken's progress in the summer program,

2. provide Mrs. Moore with information concerning Ken's progress in the summer program, and

3. provide Mrs. Moore with management tactics to improve Ken's persistence and for encouraging him to initiate more school-related activities at home.

Three outcomes are generally the maximum amount achievable in a typical parent conference. Time for rapport building and discussion reduces the chances for meeting more than three objectives in a 45-minute conference. It appears from the description in anecdote 13.2 that Ken's teacher did achieve the three stated outcomes. Note that the objectives for the conference were realistic. Since Mrs. Moore's interest in Ken's school work and her competencies were unknown, the teacher had outcomes that did not require that the parent acquire skills, e.g., to use contingency management.

Other measures of success in parent conferences include these factors:

1. *Talking.* Parents and teachers should spend an equivalent amount of time talking. If teacher or parents talk more than 60% of the conference time, it probably was not very worthwhile. This rule is based upon the belief that a conference where one of the parties dominates the time suggests a lack of cooperative activity.

2. *Child focus.* Content of the conference should consist primarily of the needs, interests, and performances of the student. While small talk is important for establishing a comfortable atmosphere, most of the discussion should deal with items of importance for the student.

3. *Clarity.* Discussion by the teacher should be clear and specific. No terms that obfuscate facts should be used. Teachers should make every attempt to explain what they mean in relation to the parent's child and in terms that parents can understand.

4. *Responsiveness.* Teachers should make concerted efforts to answer all of the parents' relevant questions. These need not be answered, however, before establishing rapport or before identifying parents' feelings, but they should be answered before terminating the conference.

Unscheduled conferences.   Sometimes parent conferences cannot be planned because they occur on an unscheduled basis. In anecdote 13.3, a tutor, Mrs. Green, describes such a conference.

ANECDOTE 13.3

Mrs. Rust describes eight-year-old Howard as very easy to get along with and as lovable and loving. While she does have to keep after him in order to be sure he gets at and finishes certain tasks, he never openly or defiantly disobeys. For example, he tries to maintain a conversation when he should be reading and he becomes preoccupied with toys or drawing a picture when supposed to be getting ready for school. Even though the parent gets quite stern with him one day he might repeat offending behavior the next day. He does keep his room clean without needing too much reminding. He does a better job at this than his brother. He and his brother usually get along fine. The parent could not describe any specific conditions under which her child becomes angry or happy. Sometimes after he has been scolded he will try to please.

Mrs. Rust has not noticed any changes of late in her child's behavior except last week when he cleaned out some dresser drawers on his own. When she asked him why, he said "just wanted to." He has talked a lot about his tutoring sessions and likes them, but she is not clear as to what he really does.

The parent feels that her child's main problem is that his reading skills are very poor. His asset is that he is so likable.

I feel this parent could be encouraged to use some planned techniques of reinforcement. She does feel a responsibility to help her child improve academically.

Parent conference conditions

Numerous times throughout the tutoring sessions, always during or following a rewarded effort, the child would make reference to his mother and how happy she would be about his efforts. Following one such comment I told him that one day I would call his mother to set a time to talk with her about what he was doing. This was a mistake due to the child's eagerness for such an interaction to occur. When I arrived for the next scheduled session on Monday, I first went to the school office to obtain the telephone number of the child's parents following clearance from the principal. I had also planned to ask the principal if she would be free to join the child's teacher and me in a conference when a convenient time could be set. The principal was not in; however, the child's mother, Mrs. Rust, and his teacher were in the office. Apparently the child had informed his mother that I wanted to see her at 9:00 A.M. The time he chose is interesting since I do not normally arrive for a session with him until 10:00. Mrs. Rust informed me she had tried to confirm the appointment by coming to the school the previous Friday at noon (she works close by the school) but that no one knew. So rather than miss a possible meeting, Mrs. Rust left work to come to the school to see me.

She asked me to clarify just why I was seeing Howard. The following is an extract of some of the more pertinent comments that I feel she made. The descriptive emotional terminology used are essentially her expressions.

Mrs. Rust had been quite concerned about Howard for the past three years, but lately, even more frustrated in that she feels "time is running out" for him (if he doesn't start doing better soon, he never will). She was briefly encouraged about his progress when he received a "C" in reading last year. Too, she has felt he has been doing better in his reading at home. But this year she has become increasingly more confused because when she talks with Mrs. Fish, the second-grade teacher, she is told that he has not improved and is doing poorly in all areas. Other times she is told that he only needs individual help with reading because he does OK with numbers.

Mrs. Rust expressed some dissatisfaction toward the school. She has talked with school personnel about what to do. Should she get a tutor in reading? What more could she do at home? She bought books and has read each night and they also listen to play-and-talk records. Some nights he does fairly well considering only a year ago she was still trying to get him to learn the alphabet. Other times he acts like his memory is bad or is just plain being smartalecky.

The school informed Mrs. Rust that they were going to have the "psychologist give him some special tests." They did not tell her the results except to say that "nothing wrong really showed up." Mrs. Fish thought she ought to take him for an eye exam even though he had been checked at school. The teacher had also asked if there was trouble in the home (tears in eyes). There had been a divorce from Howard's father a few years ago and perhaps this could have caused him to be more upset than she realized, although she did not think he acted any differently. The father repeatedly has told her that Howard's troubles are her fault. Mrs. Rust wanted to be sure I was not a psychologist and asked several times if I thought Howard did have an emotional problem.

Mrs. Rust says she tries to "crack down" on Howard about doing better. For instance, sometimes he brings a paper home with the problems worked right, but the paper is so sloppy, or he forgot to write his name on it, that he has been given a poor grade. She tries to stick with a schedule for him to study by, but when things do not work out she jumps around trying something else. She "knows" this is not good, but does not know what else to try. "Maybe she just needs to learn to be more patient."

Mrs. Fish does say that Howard is not a discipline problem which surprises her because he is all over the place at home. For instance, if a number of kids are playing, he is the one in the corner looking through a box or something.

Comments

While Mrs. Rust has demonstrated a willingness and responsiblity to work with Howard, she is uncertain and frustrated in her efforts. She seems to be asking for guidance, consistent and specific, in working with him.

She expressed some disappointment that I had spent time evaluating Howard when he had already been tested. She had hoped that I would have concentrated on his reading and while "knowing what I did was not harmful," it did not focus on his main problem area. She repeatedly asked for reassurance regarding her child's emotional status and his intellectual capabilities.

In reviewing with Mrs. Rust the proceedings of the sessions and the emphasis and results of a reinforcement system of instruction, she found it difficult to accept such an easy approach to solving his problem. However, toward the conclusion of the session she could begin to think in terms of specific behavior on Howard's part. Several approaches and ideas were discussed and written for her to think about and apply in several situations (readiness for school without constant reminders to hurry, and on the daily evening reading lessons).

This was a difficult parent conference in that it was somewhat untimely. And, unfortunately, Mrs. Rust's preconceived understanding of the purpose of the sessions with Howard was inaccurate.

Student involvement.   Student's should be included in parent/teacher conferences when they are mature enough to participate and to understand the discussion. Generally, L&BD students at the junior and senior high levels should be capable of participating in portions, if not all, the conferences. In such instances, both the parents' and students' wishes should be considered since they may prefer not to be included in the conference.

Teachers should also conduct conferences with students when they are able to profit from conferring about their performances. Procedures and activities in such conferences follow very much the same sequence as in parent/teacher conferences.

Training Parents as Training Agents

Parents' roles in the formal education and training of handicapped children have changed in recent years. Parental movements originally started school programs for the handicapped, but since these programs have become institutionalized, parents have tended to be less involved in the formal education programs. But parental involvement in training their children should be developed and maintained if transfer of learning beyond the school is to occur. In a comprehensive review and comparison of parent intervention programs for handicapped and disadvantaged children, Levitt and Cohen (1975) concluded that programs for the disadvantaged are more comprehensive and more carefully designed than those for the handicapped. They recommended the use of criterion-referenced tests for evaluating the effects of such programs. It also appeared to them that most parent-intervention programs for handicapped children are conducted with an informal, service-oriented approach without benefit of rigorous and structured activities.

However, school personnel who teach behavior modification techniques to parents tend to be well organized and are often rigorous in evaluating the effects of their training. For example, Hall et al. (1972) taught four parents to use reinforcement tactics to alleviate their children's problem behaviors. Reliability of measurement was made by people who went to the homes, and reversals of contingencies were used to demonstrate causal relationships between the procedures used as treatment and behavior change.

Wilson (1975) concluded that parental indulgence and infrequent punishment is associated with learning disorders in some children. He studied 18 children, diagnosed as having learning problems, and found that they were rated significantly lower on physical punishment and completing household tasks than were a control group of normal children.

Herbert and Baer (1972) demonstrated that parents could be trained in self-recording. Three mothers of deviant young children were taught to count their episodes of attention to appropriate and inappropriate behavior. Two of the mothers demonstrated improvement in their children's behavior and follow-up observations made over a five-month period showed durable behavior gains.

Trainers of parents of normal as well as handicapped children now have an increasing number of professional materials available, such as those sources shown below.

Becker, W. C. *Parents are teachers, a child management program.* Champaign, Illinois: Research Press Company, 1971.

Blackham, G. J., & Silberman, A. *Modification of child behavior.* Belmont, California: Wadsworth Publishing, 1971.

Bradfield, R. H. *Behavior modification the human effort.* San Rafael, California: Dimensions Publishing, 1970.

Brown, D. G. National Institute of Mental Health, Region IV, Behavior Modification in Child and School Mental Health, *An annotated bibliography on applications with parents and teachers.* National Institute of Mental Health, 5600 Fishers Lane, Rockville, Maryland 20852, DHEW Publication No. (HSM) 71-9043, 1971, for sale by the Superintendent of Documents, U.S. Government Printing Office, Washington, D.C. 20402, price 30 cents.

Dardig, J., & Heward, W. *Sign here: A contracting book for children and their parents.* Kalamazoo, Michigan: Behaviordelia, Inc., 1976.

Deibert, A. A., & Harmon, A. J. *New tools for changing behavior.* Champaign, Illinois: Research Press, 1970.

Hall, R. V. *Managing behavior parts I, II, III.* Lawrence, Kansas: H & H Enterprises, Inc. P.O. Box 3342, 66044, 1970.

Larsen, L. A., & Bricker, W. A. *A manual for parents and teachers of severely and moderately retarded children.* IMRID Papers and Reports, Volume V, No. 22, George Peabody College, Tennessee, 1968.

Patterson, G. R. *Families.* Champaign, Illinois: Research Press, 1971.

Patterson, G. R., & Gullion, M. E. *Living with children.* Champaign, Illinois: Research Press, 1971.

Smith, J., & Smith, D. *Child management: A program for parents.* Ann Arbor, Michigan: Ann Arbor Publishers, 1966.

A Parent Training Program

The following program shows a sequence of training activities that were used in training approximately 40 parents during the period 1970-1973. The project was a part of a statewide effort in Ohio entitled *Project Breakthrough.* Its major purpose was to assist special education consultants and school psychologists to be more effective as consultants to teachers and parents (Cooper, 1975).

PREPARING PARENTS AS TRAINING AGENTS[1]

Sessions

A. Assessing Parents' Management Skills
B. Introducing Management Concepts to Parents

---

1. This training program was developed by the author for use in Project Breakthrough funded by the Ohio Department of Education, Division of Special Education, 1970-1973.

C. Training Parents to Obtain Relevant Information
D. Training Parents to Establish Management Tasks
E. Training Parents to Devise Management Strategies
F. Training Parents to Evaluate Results
G. Establishing Parent-Teacher Management Systems

A. Assessing Parents' Management Skills
Purposes
1. To determine parents' styles of responding to youngsters.
2. To determine parents' styles of eliciting responses from youngsters.
3. To determine parents' methods of developing (training) responses.
4. To identify potential incentives for use by parents.
5. To obtain descriptive information regarding family life-styles.

Procedures
Step 1: Place parents at ease. Explain purposes of program in nonthreatening terms.
Step 2: Ask parents to describe everyday management barriers or "rough spots."
Step 3: Elicit information from parents regarding purposes in a systematic, nonthreatening way.
Step 4: Begin with parents' present response levels. Use successive approximations to shape and reorder their responses.

Concepts
1. All parents are training agents. This program merely aims to facilitate their training functions.
2. Descriptions of family life-styles represent baseline information.
3. Potential incentives for children at home include food, money, privileges, parental attention, eating out, shopping, TV viewing, and sibling attention.

Suggested Activities
1. Invite selected parents to a meeting to explain your parent education project. These parents may be referred by teachers, principals, or other school personnel. Parents representing one special education program may be invited as a group.
2. Serve refreshments during the meeting.
3. Involve the parents in a general discussion regarding managing children in the home. If possible, encourage them to resopnd to each other.
4. Select a few of the expressed problems as examples for use in the subsequent instructional sessions.
5. Obtain commitments from parents for at least six future meetings.
6. Ask parents to describe contacts with their children. Pay particular attention to the potential trouble times: preparing for school, meal times, bed time, and weekends.
7. Show the film *Who Did What To Whom* by Robert Mager (Research Press).
8. Complete for each parent the form: *Format for Describing Parent-Child Contacts.*

Format for Describing Parent-Child Contacts

Parent _____   Child _____

Weekdays

A.M.
Behavior Needing Improving
1.
2.
3.
P.M.
Behavior Needing Improving
1.
2.
3.

Weekends

Saturday
Behavior Needing Improving

1.
2.
3.

Sunday
Behavior Needing Improving

1.
2.
3.

B. Introducing Management Concepts to Parents
Purposes
   1. To present reinforcement in operational terms.
   2. To teach parents how they elicit appropriate and inappropriate behavior from their children.
   3. To help parents differentiate "telling" their children from training them.
   4. To help parents focus on behavior rather than speculating on causes of the behavior.
Procedures
   Step 5: Begin with a review of the previous session for the benefit of those who may not have been in attendance previously and to serve as a reminder for those who were present.*
   Step 6: Teach the concept of reinforcement.
   Step 7: Relate reinforcement to eliciting, maintaining, and developing behavior.
   Step 8: Teach parents to use functional approaches when training their children.
Concepts
   1. Reinforcement consists of events that are satisfying to the child. These events are not necessarily tangible.
   2. Immediate rewards result in learning more readily than remote rewards.
   3. Eliciting and maintaining responses require (a) prior learning and (b) cues or stimuli that are associated with desired responses.
   4. Responses that are learned or developed require instruction (experiences) in addition to reinforcement.
   5. All behavior is learned, elicited, and maintained regardless of its merit through reinforcement and experiences.
   6. Functional approaches involve (a) providing information, (b) engaging the trainee in an act (simulated or real), (c) reinforcing the desired attributer of the act, (d) discussing the trainee's performance, (e) continuing the sequence until criterion level is met.
Suggested Activities
   1. Use questions to initiate a discussion regarding reinforcement, e.g., why do people work? What are some incentives for your children to behave as you wish them?
   2. Identify some common management concerns among the parents. Use simulation and role playing to teach parents how to use free operant conditioning.
   3. Relate information obtained from *Format for Describing Parent-Child Contacts.*

C. Training Parents to Obtain Relevant Information
Purposes
   1. To train parents to be observant.
   2. To distinguish between behavior and assumptions regarding behavior.

---

*It is recommended that each session begin with a review of the last meeting.

3. To assist parents in describing their responses toward their youngsters.

4. To train parents in recording their observations.

5. To specify conditions under which the behavior occurs.

Procedures

Step 9: Teach observational skills, emphasizing descriptive information.

Step 10: Obtain descriptions of conditions in which the behavior occurs.

Concepts

1. Descriptions provide behavioral information.

2. Information concerning desirable behavior can be used for developing additional desired responses.

3. Obtaining relevant information may require careful questioning and discussions.

4. Descriptive information should be obtained before prescribing strategies.

Suggested Avtivities

1. Provide parents with a form for recording desirable and undesirable behavior. Ask them to record frequencies of occurrences.

2. Give clear examples of observances. Show how these are preferred to inferences and assumptions.

D. Training Parents to Establish Management Tasks

Purposes

1. To present behavior to be developed as tasks to be learned.

2. To break down tasks into subtasks.

3. To determine the requisite skills for performing tasks and subtasks.

4. To advise parents in selecting tasks appropriate for their children's age and development.

Procedures

Step 11: Write instructional tasks using observational information obtained from parents.

Step 12: Show how tasks may be broken down and how prerequisite skills are essential to learning the tasks.

Concepts

1. Tasks should be specific.

2. Tasks should be specified in observable terms.

3. Short-term tasks are learned more readily than long-term tasks.

4. Prerequisite skills represent responses and understandings that are essential to learning new behavior.

Suggested Activities

1. Have parents write tasks from their observations.

2. Discuss the tasks in terms of their appropriateness.

3. Use *Parent Management Form* to obtain description information from each parent. Save the information for use in the next session.

INSTRUCTIONS FOR USE OF PARENT MANAGEMENT FORM

Initiating Interview

Parents should be put at ease. It should be clearly indicated that it is their child's *behavior* that is of concern. Possible *causes* of the disorder may be of interest to the parent but are of little value for the management approach being used.

Interviewers, by their actions, can convey many feelings and attitudes to parents. Avoid asking questions that are not directly related to the behavior. Avoid imposing your values on the parent.

Ask straightforward questions with no hidden implications. Respond to parents in a friendly, helpful way.

Sometimes parents express hostility or anger. Do not become defensive or argumentative. Simply reflect the parents' expressions.

Obtaining Identifying Information

Ease into asking questions. Try to begin with the least threatening questions, e.g., the child's name, rather than his/her behavior.

"Areas of Parental Concern" are general statements that typically are obtained in the preliminary discussion, often without posing questions.

Description of Child's Behavior

Return to the areas of parental concern and assist the parent to specify behaviors that occur at home.

As you listen to the parents, note what may be potential rewards for the child. You may have to ask "What does he like to do, to eat, to wear, to hear, and so forth?"

Every child engages in some behavior that is appropriate. Help parents recognize and specify their child's "good behavior."

Parent Management Form

Parent (s) _____

Child _____ CA _____

Other Children and Ages_____

Interviewer _____ Date _____

Areas of Parental Concern
1.
2.
3.
4.
5.

Description of Child's Behavior
Code: o denotes needs improving; + appropriate behavior; − problem behavior

Behavior   *Code*
1.
2.
3.
4.
5.

Desirable Behavior (+)
1.
2.
3.
4.
5.

E. Training Parents to Devise Management Strategies

Purposes

1. To train parents in using contingency contracting, free operant conditioning, associative conditioning, and social modeling.
2. To present the use of charts in managing behavior.
3. To advise parents in selecting appropriate strategies that will achieve the desired outcomes.

Procedures

Step 13: Present each model of reinforcement as a separate technique. Provide an example for each.

Step 14: Show parents how charts and other records can be used to facilitate behavioral changes.

Step 15: Place in juxtaposition all elements that comprise management strategies. Instruct parents in implementing various strategies.

Concepts

1. Contingency management is a type of contract. It aids parents to obtain the behavior they desire while permitting their children to obtain satisfactions.

2. Free operant conditioning is used instead of, in addition to, or in conjunction with other models of reinforcement.

3. Associative conditioning provides pleasurable events in association with desired attitudes or behavior.

4. Social modeling enables individuals to learn through imitation.

5. Charts serve as reminders of progress. They also help to program parents as well as children. In addition, they provide interim reinforcement.

6. A management strategy consists of (a) Tasks, (b) Rewards, and (c) Procedures.

Suggested Activities

1. Develop a contingency management chart for parents to use. Show Behaviors, Reward, and Points Required on the chart.

2. Role play parents describing the C-M plan to their children.

3. Provide specific advice regarding when and how to confer with children regarding their progress.

4. Demonstrate the use of free operant conditioning with children.

5. Develop functional plans using the information contained on the *Parent Management Form.*

INSTRUCTIONS FOR DEVELOPING
FUNCTIONAL MANAGEMENT PLANS

Specify target behaviors based on the information obtained earlier. Target behaviors represent tasks to be learned. When more than one task is selected, make certain that the others are already being performed near an acceptable level, with mastery representing 90% accuracy or frequency. Then when three tasks are selected, one may represent a behavior needing improvement, one that is a problem, and one that is appropriate.

Indicate what the rewards or incentives will be. At this point your understanding of reinforcement principles is crucial. You may recommend a contingency management approach or an operant conditioning approach may be more appropriate. In some instances, parents may be taught to use modified forms of social modeling.

Indicate under "Notes" what you recommended. Try to give parents a written plan that they may take to assist them in initiating management strategies.

Functional Management Form

Parent(s) _____

Child _____

Consultant _____ Date_____

Functional Plan

Target Behaviors (Tasks)   Rewards

1.

2.

3.

Notes

F. Training Parents to Evaluate Results

Purposes
   1. To establish criterion levels for behavioral tasks.
   2. To compare performances against established criteria.
Procedures
   Step 16: Instruct parents in establishing criteria for each task.
   Step 17: Demonstrate how, by comparing performance with criteria, evaluation is accomplished.
Concepts
   1. Criteria should be specific and descriptive. These should relate to management tasks.
   2. Evaluation is a comparison of performance with established outcomes (tasks).
   3. When children repeatedly fail to achieve criterion levels, tasks, rewards, and procedures may need modifying.
Suggested Activities
   1. Have parents evaluate effects of their strategies.
   2. Discuss with them, problems that may arise.
   3. Assist parents to modify their management plans if necessary.

G. Establishing Parent-Teacher Management Systems

Purposes
   1. To emphasize advantages of parent-teacher cooperation.
   2. To present a way of communicating regarding management strategies between parents and teachers.
Procedures
Step 18: Involve parents in planning for generalizing behavior to other settings.
Step 19: Present a system to be used between parents and teachers to maintain reinforcement schedules for specific behaviors.
Concepts
   1. Learning is facilitated when responses are practiced under varying conditions.
   2. Transfer of learned responses occurs more readily when instruction anticipates and encourages generalizing.
Suggested Activities
   1. Present ways that conditions for learning can be changed. Give examples of subtle changes, such as requesting a learned behavior at a different time, or increasing the length of time during which desirable behavior will occur.
   2. Develop a system of cooperation between parents and teachers for improving behavior. These may include notes sent home via the child indicating how well he performed a specific behavior that he is learning, or similar C-M plans used at home and at school, or the same C-M chart which the child takes home on weekends and/or evenings.
   3. Have the parents respond to: *Evaluation of Knowledge Obtained by Parent-Participants.* Use the results as a posttest measure.

Evaluation of Knowledge Obtained by Parent-Participants

Please indicate T (True) or F (False)

1. _____ Children behave as they do because of past learning.
2. _____ Behavior can be changed.
3. _____ Talking, dressing, playing, and working are all learned behaviors.
4. _____ Whining, fighting, and temper tantrums are not learned.
5. _____ Parents respond to their children on the basis of past learning.
6. _____ Learning cannot change behavior.
7. _____ Well-meaning parents and teachers may teach children to misbehave.
8. _____ Rewards, or incentives, teach children how to behave.
9. _____ Behavior that is learned was not rewarded.
10. _____ Thanking your child after helping at home may be rewarding.
11. _____ Giving a child a quarter for shoveling snow from the sidewalks is an example of using a reward.
12. _____ Food and money are the only important rewards.
13. _____ By listening to children complain, we are rewarding complaining.
14. _____ When you stop talking when your child has interrupted you, he may be taught to continue interrupting when others are talking.
15. _____ One good example of a reward schedule is to tell a child in July that he/she will get one dollar for getting an A in arithmetic in the fall term.
16. _____ Rewards should be provided immediately following good behavior.
17. _____ By knowing what other children prefer, we will know what our children view as rewards.
18. _____ Consequences of our childrens' behavior reveal what are rewards for them.
19. _____ "John picked his clothes from the bed and hung them in the closet." This represents a descriptive behavior.
20. _____ "John failed to pick up his clothing because he has been concerned about his school work." This represents a descriptive behavior.
21, _____ It is helpful to know which desirable behaviors that a child performs.

Indicate the correct answers:

22. _____ Howard's father thanked John for helping to wash the car. This is an example of (a) contingency management, (b) free operant conditioning, (c) social modeling.
23. _____ Howard's mother told him that she would let him eat at McDonalds on Tuesday if he did three household chores on Sunday. This is an example of (a) contingency management, (b) free operant conditioning, (c) social modeling.
24. _____ Howard's father behaved like the school's bully while Howard tried to cope with him as advised by his father. This is an example of (a) contingency management, (b) free operant conditioning, (c) behavior rehearsing.
25. _____ When Howard pouts, his mother asks him what is wrong. This is an example of (a) contingency management, (b) free operant conditioning, (c) social modeling.

Answers to Evaluation of Knowledge Obtained by Parent-Participants

Questions 1 – 7 measure understanding that behaviors are learned responses.
1. T   2. T   3. T   4. F   5. T   6. F   7. T

Questions 8 – 16 measure understandings of rewards and rate of reinforcement.
8. T   9. F   10. T   11. T   12. F   13. T   14. T   15. F   16. T

Questions 17 – 21 measure knowledge of obtaining relevant information.
17. F   18. T   19. T   20. F   21. T

Question 22 (b) measures use of free operant conditioning; (c) by thanking John, his father modeled polite behavior.

Question 23 (a) measures knowledge of contingency management

Question 24 (c) measures understanding of behavior rehearsing.

Question 25 (b) measures use of free operant conditioning (inappropriate)

Helpful hints for parent trainers. Participants in the parent training component of the project were required to submit an evaluation of their training, that is, how well parents demonstrated those management tactics which were taught. Results consistently supported the advisability of training parents as child managers, although in some instances the results were less impressive than in others.

As a result of these evaluations, guidelines for conducting parent training sessions emerged.[2] Among these were the following:

1. *Use a consistent theoretical model.* Parents will be confused if training materials and consultants are inconsistent in the use of terminology and theoretical orientations.

2. *Determine in advance those skills to be mastered by the parents.* Parent trainers should have a written curriculum which specifies those skills to be taught. These should be predetermined and presented briefly in the introductory session. Remember that each skill is to be taught and demonstrated to the parent prior to his/her applying it at home. For this reason, be realistic concerning the number of skills to be taught in one session.

3. *Allow for differences in skill acquisition.* All parents will not master all skills at the same time. Individualize instruction when necessary to allow for differences in entry-level skills and rate of learning. Individual conferences, follow-up telephone contacts, and extra home-contacts may be necessary to help some parents attain skill mastery.

4. *Use a systematic and functional approach.* Assess the parents upon entry into the program. But do it through observations and informally. A pretest may discourage and frighten them. Instead, listen to them, ask questions, and watch them when they are asked to rehearse a tactic with you. Give practical assignments, activities that they can use at home.

After the introductory session, begin all subsequent sessions with a discussion of how their assignments were implemented. Encourage an exchange among the participants. And use humor, at appropriate times, when responding to their questions.

5. *Provide follow-up.* Be available for follow-up consultation after training has been completed. Follow-up may consist of telephone contacts, written feedback, or in the home consultation.

Consulting with School Personnel and Allied Professionals

Special teachers have responsibilities for working cooperatively with other school personnel in behalf of students. At times, although less often, they are expected to work cooperatively with specialists outside the school's program.

---

2. The author appreciates and recognizes the efforts of these Project Breakthrough participants (1971-72): Pat Carney, Ann Decker, Ellen Gow, Linda McCluskey, Suzanne Peters, and Jack Priser.

Consulting with School Personnel

Consulting by, with, and for school personnel has been studied on a limited basis and some reports are in the current literature. Woody (1975) identified and compared two different types of mental health consultants. Those trained in process consultation were compared with those who provided behavioral consultation. Those trained in the *process model* are client-centered in that they try to understand teachers' phenomenological worlds.

Process-oriented consultants tend to view their roles as helping teachers clarify their own thinking and determine their own goals and the ways to achieve them. Consultants working within the process model rarely direct or offer expert advice. They tend to make clarifying, supportive, or reflective responses instead of providing information, suggestions, or reinforcing responses.

Consultants working within the behavioral model view as their responsibilities identifying reinforcement contingencies, recommending behavioral techniques, and modifying target behavior. The behavioral consultant disseminates expert advice and accepts a directive and supervisory role.

Woody (1975) identified three training programs and surveyed trainees from those programs. While process consultants are more numerous, having received training in one program dating from 1955, only 26 were located and responded to the survey. Trainees from the behavioral programs who responded totaled 23.

Woody's findings showed that the assumptions about response styles and change factors of the two orientations which are described in the literature are reported as practiced by the trainees. That is, there are two distinct consultant models. The *behavioral group* attributes significantly greater importance to factors of academic information, confrontation, expert recommendations, reinforcer of actions, and specificity of expression. The *process group* stresses clarification of issues, empathic understanding, insight, and objective participation.

Stephens (1970) described a behavioral consultant's role with teachers of L&BD children. Using school psychologists as an example group, he noted that they could be involved as behavioral consultants in several ways. First, they can set up assessment procedures and develop relevant materials for assessing student behavior. Second, they can assist programmers in developing instructional strategies that relate to assessment data. Third, they can aid teachers in implementing these strategies. And fourth, they can participate in research and evaluation activities. It should be noted that special education consultants, resource rooms, and itinerant teachers could also provide these same services.

Consulting with Teachers

Special teachers and other members of the special education team should provide consultation to regular classroom teachers who are responsible for L&BD students. Coleman (1973) reported the results of consulting with a regular teacher of a fifth-grade boy who displayed disruptive behavior during class and left the classroom without teacher permission.

The consultant, a school psychologist, demonstrated a behavioral technique whereby experimentally controlled behavior was generalized and control was transferred from the consultant to the teacher and to the parent. Neither the teacher nor the parent had previous training in behavior modification tactics. The student's working behavior increased while talking-aloud and out-of-seat behavior decreased. Following baseline observations, the student was taken out of the classroom for pretraining. He was asked to pretend that he was reading at his desk.

Points contingent upon working behavior were entered on the chalkboard on a fixed interval schedule of 10 seconds. After he had accumulated 25 points, he was advised that the points could be used for purchasing items of approximately 50 cents in value. He was also told that the same procedure would be used in reading and math classes by the teacher.

Since the student was receiving a weekly allowance of $1.25 noncontingently, the parents were involved in instruction by the consultant. An accounting was sent home showing the daily record of money earned. The student's parent took him shopping each Friday evening allowing him to purchase items up to the amount earned the previous week. Money not spent could be saved but deficit spending was not permitted. Through gradual changes in point values and in recording methods, desirable behavior was extended from 15 minutes to the entire length of the class period and points were subtracted for talking aloud and for leaving his seat without permission.

Coleman's study is an excellent example of how a consultant can train regular classroom teachers and parents to use contingency contracting for helping their students and children. The procedures used by consultants using behavioral approaches are shown in Figure 13.2.

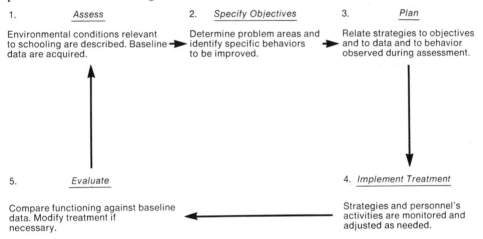

FIGURE 13.2. A schematic view of consulting procedures

Consultant training of teachers.   Project Breakthrough, referred to earlier in this chapter, had as its major objective to provide inservice training by consultants (special education personnel, building principals, and school psychologists) to regular and special class teachers. The project included a multiplier effect whereby personnel trained by this author and his colleagues (Dr. John O. Cooper and Dr. Kenneth P. Hunt were the faculty members primarily involved) trained teachers and other personnel who in turn trained students and parents.

The following training program was developed for inservice training of teachers in *Project Breakthrough.*

PROCEDURES FOR DESIGNING TRAINING
PROGRAMS FOR DIRECTIVE TEACHING[3]

These procedures are designed to be used by school practioners who have successfully completed a minimum of 100 clock hours of instruction and practicum experience

---

3. Copyright 1971 by Thomas M. Stephens and John O. Cooper.

in Directive Teaching (D-T). They are to be used for designing a program of instruction within the D-T system for:

1. Teaching Personnel
2. Parents
3. Children

A separate program should be completed for each group that you intend to instruct. Reference is made to sources for the reader to review or use. Each reference is coded and can be found under the section entitled "sources."

To be completed by the participant:

Your name _____

Your position _____

Address _____

Phone _____

This program is designed for (circle one):
1. Training teachers
2. Training parents
3. Training children

Date Program was Prepared _____

Checked and approved (do not complete)
By _____
Date _____

A. *Initial Specifications*

Step 1: Name the behavior or behaviors you want to increase or decrease.

_____

Step 2: Give your definition of the behavior. Include only definitions that generate independent observer agreements of 80% or higher.

_____

Step 3: Describe the characteristics of the population to be served; e.g., sex, age, grade, education, school success, employment, etc.

_____

Step 4: Indicate how the population will be selected; e.g., random selection, assigned by teacher, selected through assessments or criteria levels, volunteers, etc.

_____

Step 5: How many students (parents, teachers) will be selected? _____

B. *Measurable Objectives*

Step 1: Specify objectives
These objectives must be:
a) Specific
b) Measurable
c) Functional (useful to those you are treating or teaching)
Write your objectives below:
1. _____
2. _____
3. _____
4. _____
5. _____

Step 2: Indicate terminal behavior
a) Describe the conditions under which the learned responses will occur.
b) Indicate exactly what the learners will be doing so as to demonstrate their newly acquired behavior.
c) Describe how *well* the learner must perform the task; e.g., specify terminal behavior.
d) Be specific.
e) Relate the terminal behavior to each objective.

Write your terminal behavior below. Follow the same sequence as in Step 1.
1. _____
2. _____
3. _____
4. _____
5. _____

C. *Baseline Data Collection*

Step 1: Describe measurement teachnique. These descriptions should be described in enough detail so that another person could replicate your measurement tactics after reading your descriptions. You may choose to employ more than one measurement technique for your study. Choose the techniques you used from the list below and elaborate.
a) Direct measurement of permanent products (e.g., written responses)

_____

_____

b) Observational recording
Event recording (e.g., frequency of occurrence, tally, etc.)

_____

_____

Duration recording (e.g., amount of time engaged in a behavior)

_____

Interval recording (e.g.,the occurrence or nonoccurrence of a behavior within a specified interval of time) _____

_____

Time sample (e.g., the occurrence or nonoccurrence of a behavior immediately following a specified interval of time) _____

_____

Step 2: Describe materials used in data collection; e.g., stopwatch, worksheets, etc. If you use a checklist or special forms, attach them to this form.

_____

Step 3: Describe reliability measures (interobserver agreement). Attach instructions that are given to the independent observers.

_____

Step 4: Will you group your data (mean, mode, median) or make entirely separate graphs for each student (parent, teacher)? _____

_____

Step 5: Graph your data on the attached forms.

D. *Procedures*

Step 1: Indicate the procedures you will use to achieve the objectives stated under B.

   a) What independent variable (treatment) will be used to produce behavior change; e.g., reinforcement, curriculum material changes, social models and imitation, etc.? _____

   _____

   b) What are the contingency criteria for delivery of treatment; e.g., continuous, fixed time intervals, variable time intervals, fixed number (ratio) of responses, variable number (ratio) of responses. _____

   _____

   c) If you are using reinforcers or other consequences that must follow the behavior but which cannot be delivered immediately, how will you bridge this time delay? _____

   _____

   d) If others are delivering treatment (e.g., parents or teachers) how will you know that it has been delivered? _____

   _____

Describe the procedures you will follow:

   1. _____

   _____

   2. _____

   _____

   3. _____

   _____

4. _____

5. _____

6. _____

7. _____

8. _____

9. _____

10. _____

E. *Applied Behavior Analysis*

   The Reversal Design
   1. Baseline$_1$—Record of ongoing behavior prior to intervention (Step 3).
   2. Intervention procedure$_1$—Introduction of Step 4.
   3. Baseline$_2$—Withdraw intervention procedures and return to Baseline$_1$ conditions.
   4. Intervention Procedure$_2$—Reinstate the Intervention Procedures (same as Intervention Procedure$_1$)
   5. Post-checks.

   The Multiple Baseline Design
   A multiple baseline analysis can be used when two or more similar behaviors are emitted by the same subject, when the same behavior occurs in different stimulus conditions, or when the same behavior occurs in more than one subject. When these conditions exist, contingencies may be applied to one behavior then the other, in one stimulus condition then the next, or with one subject then sequentially with other subjects. Functional relationships are established if changes in each behavior correspond to experimental manipulations.

   a) Select the design you will follow in order to evaluate the effects of your instruction. Indicate the design you have chosen below:

   _____

   b) Define the criteria used for changing conditions (e.g., fixed time for each, criterion levels, "stability," etc.)

   _____

   _____

   c) Label and define, on the graph, each condition you implement. These labels and definitions should be concise, but complete enough that others would know your tactics without having to make reference to your text.

F. *Abstract*

   Population and Setting:

   Target Behavior and Interobserver Agreement:

   Treatment and Result:

   Summary Statement:

IMPLEMENTING DIRECTIVE TEACHING
WITH TEACHERS

Use this program after completing Procedures for Designing Training Programs in Directive Teaching.

Contents
A. Introducing Directive Teaching to Teachers
B. Instructing Teachers to Gather Relevant Information
C. Preparing Teachers to Specify Instructional Tasks
D. Assisting Teachers to Devise Instructional Strategies
E. Instructing Teachers to Evaluate Instruction

A. Introducing Directive Teaching to Teachers
Purposes and Terminal Behavior
1. To develop interest in using Directive Teaching approaches
   Teachers will express an interest by asking questions, or participating in discussions, or attempting to use behavioral approaches.
2. To develop positive attitudes toward behavioral approaches
   Teachers will verbalize agreement with some of the approaches that are presented.
3. To provide information concerning behavioral approaches
   Teachers will be presented with steps in Directive Teaching.

Procedures
Step 1: Meet with selected teachers to discuss your project.
Suggested activities
1. Provide refreshments in association with the meeting.
2. Visit a classroom prior to the meeting. Describe the behavioral approaches that you observed. Be supportive and positive.
3. Point out that all successful teachers use some portion of Directive Teaching but often unsystematically.
4. Ask teachers to identify a child who presents learning or behavioral problems.
Assignment: Develop a Plan for Introducing Directive Teaching to Teachers by Following Form 1-A.

Form 1-A

Your Name _____

Terminal Behavior And Criteria   *Dates* _____

Procedures

Evaluation

Do Not Complete
   Checked by _____Date _____

Step 2: Present steps in Directive Teaching
Suggested activities
1. Present one step at a time, giving examples for each step.
2. Be sure to indicate that all children need not be assessed in each area. Academic skill assessment is determined by problem areas. Expressive modalities are assessed when children display academic learning problems.
3. Discuss the steps briefly. Later, each step will be thoroughly discussed.
4. Use visual aids.
Assignment: Develop a Plan for Presenting Steps in Directive Teaching by Following Form 1-A.

B. Instructing Teachers to Gather Relevant Information
Purposes and Terminal Behavior
  1. To instruct teachers in assessing academic skills.
     Teachers will assess children's academic skill areas.
  2. To instruct teachers in assessing receptive-expressive modalities.
     Teachers will assess children's receptive-expressive modes.
  3. To instruct teachers in assessing in-school behavior.
     Teachers will assess children's in-school behavior.
  4. To instruct teachers in assessing reward system
     Teachers will assess children's reward systems.

Procedures
Step 1: Instruct teachers to assess academic skills.
  Concepts to be taught:
       1.0 Criterion level tests
       1.1 Importance of criterion level tests
       1.2 How to construct criterion level tests
       1.3 Using criterion level tests
       1.4 Establishing criterion levels
       2.0 Academic skills
       2.1 Decoding skills
       2.2 Language skills
       2.3 Arithmetic computation
       2.4 Reasoning
       2.5 Comprehension
  Suggested activities:
1. Present one assignment at a time to be implemented with a child. Follow with a meeting to discuss teachers' implementations.
2. Ask teachers to select 12 skills and concepts that are typically taught to the students assigned to them. Teach procedures for devising criterion level tests. Have teachers implement these tests with their students.
3. Have teachers chart the gains made by students who are taught skills that are within instructional range 70%-89% accuracy over a one week period. Compare these results with those obtained from students who were taught similar skills below the 70% accuracy level.
Assignment: Develop a Plan for Instructing Teachers to Assess Academic Skills by Following Form 1-A.
Step 2: Instruct teachers to assess expressive modes
  Concepts to be taught:
     1. That we have the potential to receive stimuli through five sensory channels.
     2. That some children display difficulties in receiving stimuli through any one or combination of these senses.
     3. Assuming acuity within normal ranges, problems of discriminating stimuli are present among some children.

4. Problems of acuity and difficulties in discriminating require different instruction and accommodations.
5. Recall, or memory, is an important variable to be measured.
6. Some children display problem of recall when instruction occurs through particular senses.
7. Discrimination and recall are two dimensions of sensory modes to be assessed when children present academic learning problems.
8. The integrative process, where learning occurs, is not directly measurable and must be described with hypothetical constructs. Teachers should base instruction on responses and avoid using hypothetical information.

Suggested activities:

1. Ask teachers to select a youngster who presents serious academic learning problems. Show them how to assess the child's receptive-expressive modes. Be certain to use task related materials.

2. Relate material used in this step to that used in the previous step whenever possible.

3. Show teachers how to teach decoding skills with children who present a serious receptive problem.

4. Demonstrate how to use children's strengths when they display receptive-expressive deficits.

Assignment: Develop a Plan for Instructing Teachers to Assess Expressive Modes by Following Form 1-A.

Step 3: Instruct teachers to assess students' in-school behavior

Concepts to be taught:

1. Social responses are functions of conditions under which they occur. Conditions must be described as well as the behavior. Conditions include physical setting, persons present, and activities.
2. Observations of student behavior should be obtained prior to intervening.
3. Importance of descriptive information. Consequences when using inferential, assumptive and hypothetical information.
4. Observations should be quantified for comparison later.
5. More than one observation of target behavior should occur.
6. Under-responding behavior should also be a concern of teachers.
7. The importance of acquiring samples of appropriate responses of target population.

Suggested activities:

1. Set up observation forms for teachers to use.

2. Establish beginning and terminal points for observation time.

3. Use mechanical devices for recording responses.

4. Have teachers practice observing each other for short period during the meeting.

5. Have a follow-up meeting to discuss results of observations.

Step 4: Instruct teachers to assess student reinforcement system.

Concepts to be taught:

1. Elements in reinforcement system include:
   a) type of reward, or reinforcement
   b) rate or schedule of reinforcement
   c) models of reinforcement
2. Rewards are events that satisfy individuals under given circumstances. Types of rewards include:
   a) primary rewards
   b) interim rewards
   c) secondary or social rewards
3. Begin assessing reward preference with secondary or subtle rewards. Avoid, whenever possible, using edibles and other primary rewards.

4. Reward preference is an individual matter; it varies with individuals.
5. Reward preference varies with task requirements. Difficulty of tasks, interest in performing the tasks, and other considerations require that rewards be assessed in relation to school tasks.
6. Schedule of reinforcement refers to the frequency in which rewards must be issued in order to develop or maintain responses.
7. Two schedules of reinforcement are (a) fixed schedules and (b) variable schedules.
8. Fixed schedules provide reinforcement at fixed times or intervals.
9. Within fixed schedules are included: continuous schedules, fixed-ratio, and fixed-interval.
10. Ratio refers to number of responses as compared to number of responses occurring.
11. Interval refers to clock intervals during which rewards are issued.
12. Variable schedules provide reinforcement at various times or intervals.
13. Variable schedules of reinforcement usually result in responses that continue to be maintained over longer time spans than responses that are reinforced on fixed schedules.
14. When developing new responses continuous schedules may be necessary initially.
15. Models of reinforcement include:
    a) operant conditioning
    b) contingency management
    c) associative conditioning
    d) social modeling
16. Operant conditioning is used when:
    a) a response occurs and is reinforced.
    b) a response is elicited and is reinforced.
17. Contingency management is a contract between the rewarder and the learner. It requires:
    a) announcing in advance of the activity what behavior will be rewarded
    b) and announcing what the reward will be.
18. Forms of C-M
    a) teacher operated
    b) student operated
    c) self-operated
19. Associative conditioning involves pairing a response with another event or reward. It is used to condition new responses and to develop new reward preferences.
20. Social modeling is a type of learning through imitation.
21. Procedures to use in social modeling include:
    a) give learners instruction regarding the behavior to observe.
    b) reward desired behavior.
    c) have learners discuss their observations.

Suggested activities:
1. Demonstrate each technique prior to assigning its implementation.
2. Have teachers use contrived task approach for assessing reward preference, rate of reinforcement, and operant model.
3. Base assessment of reinforcement system on prior academic and social responses.
4. Use interview approach to assess reinforcement system within a C-M model.
5. Use role training for elementary age children and role playing with older students when assessing social modeling.
6. Assign activities that will sharpen teachers' observation skills.

Assignment: Develop a Plan for Instructing Teachers to Assess Students' Reinforcement Systems by Following Form 1-A.

C. Preparing Teachers to Specify Instructional Tasks

Purposes and Terminal Behavior

1. To instruct teachers in selecting instructional tasks.

   Teachers will select academic and social instructional tasks, that are within students' repertoires.

2. To instruct teachers in writing instructional tasks.

   Teachers will specify instructional tasks in observable terms.

3. To instruct teachers in identifying prerequisite skills needed for learning academic and social tasks.

   Teachers will develop subtasks that represent prerequisite skills.

4. To instruct teachers in establishing terminal criteria and terminal behavior.

Procedures

Step 1: Instruct teachers to select relevant tasks.

Concepts to be taught:

1. Similarity of academic and social learning
2. That all behavior is learned
3. That academic responses constitute a kind of behavior
4. That social responses represent learned behavior
5. Relevance of assessment information to instruction
6. That instruction should be based on information obtained from assessment
7. That responses within instructional range should be selected for teaching.

Suggested activities:

1. Provide forms for teachers to organize assessment information.

2. Ask teachers to provide information concerning academic and social functioning of a student.

3. Select academic instructional tasks that are within students' instructional range and that are relevant to schooling.

4. Select social instructional tasks that are within students' instructional range and that are relevant to schooling.

5. Ask teachers to select at least 12 instructional tasks for each student.

Assignment: Develop a Plan for Instructing Teachers to Select Relevant Tasks by Following Form 1-A.

Step 2: Instruct teachers to write instructional tasks

Concepts to be taught:

1. Writing tasks in observable terms.
2. Descriptive terms should be used.
3. Avoid using terms requiring interpretation of behavior.
4. Tasks should be written in specific terms.

Suggested activities:

1. Provide forms on which teachers write tasks.

2. Write several social and academic tasks on a chalkboard.

3. Emphasize importance of using descriptive terms.

5. Collect the tasks written by teachers. Check what was written to determine levels of proficiency.

6. Provide appropriate reinforcement for those whose responses are in the correct direction.

Assignment: Develop a Plan for Preparing Teachers to Specify Instructional Tasks by Following Form 1-A.

Step 3: Instruct teachers to identify prerequisite skills needed for learning academic and social tasks.

Concepts to be taught:

1. Concept of prerequisite responses.
2. All responses require prerequisite skills.

   3. Prerequisite skills are not always readily identifiable.

   4. Prerequisites vary with tasks and with individuals.

   5. Prerequisite skills for a response can be identified by starting with the response to be learned and systematically recording each response that leads to the higher response.

   6. Subtasks.

   7. Prerequisite responses are represented in D-T by subtasks.

   8. Subtasks relate directly to the task under which they are subsumed.

   9. Subtasks are written in similar terms as are tasks.

Suggested activities:

1. Provide forms on which teachers write subtasks under each task.

2. Emphasize the importance of teaching subtasks.

3. Show teachers how to break down instructional tasks into subtasks.

4. Check teachers' performance.

Assignment: Develop a Plan for Instructing Teachers to Identify Prerequisite Skills by Following Form 1-A.

Step 4: Instruct teachers to establish terminal behavior and terminal criteria

Concepts to be taught:

   1. Short-term evaluation.

   2. Evaluation of instruction is facilitated by establishing terminal criteria in advance of instruction.

   3. Evaluation occurs at the close of the instructional session.

   4. Subsequent instruction can be based upon evaluation.

   5. Terminal behavior indicates what students should be doing when they have learned the tasks.

   6. Terminal criteria indicates, in descriptive terms, how well students achieve tasks.

Suggested activities:

1. Return teachers' forms that contain tasks and subtasks. Ask teachers to write terminal behavior and criteria statements after each task.

2. Present examples of how to write criterion statements. Think aloud as you write.

3. Check teachers' performance.

Assignment: Develop a Plan for Instructing Teachers to Establish Terminal Behavior and Terminal Criteria by Following Form 1-A.

D. Assisting Teachers to Devise Instructional Strategies

Purposes and Terminal Behavior

1. To assist teachers in using appropriate reinforcement systems.

Teachers will use rewards and models of reinforcement based upon assessment information.

2. To assist teachers in using receptive modes that are advantageous to students.

Teachers will use instructional approaches that facilitate receiving instruction.

3. To help teachers select instructional media appropriate for learning specified tasks.

Teachers will select instructional media based upon assessment information and instructional tasks.

4. To instruct teachers in implementing instructional strategies.

Teachers will use instructional strategies that have been written for selected children.

Procedures

Step 1: Assist teachers to use reinforcement.

Concepts to be taught:

   1. Rewards should be a part of instruction when possible.

   2. Students often indicate what is rewarding at a given time.

   3. Rewards should follow desired responses or occur simultaneously with responses.

4. Rewards should be issued not too frequently or infrequently.

5. Rewards must be rotated to prevent satiation.

6. Models of reinforcement.

7. Students sometimes must be taught to function within a particular model of reinforcement.

Suggested activities:

1. Provide teachers with a completed instructional strategy form to serve as a model.

2. Ask teachers to devise an instructional strategy for one child. After checking each, ask teachers to implement their strategy.

3. Discuss their performance. Emphasize the reinforcement aspect of the strategies.

4. Demonstrate the use of each model of reinforcement.

5. Assign teachers to try selected models of reinforcement in conjunction with their teaching.

6. Discuss their performances.

Assignment: Develop a Plan to Assist Teachers to Use Reinforcement by Following Form 1-A.

Step 2: Assist teachers to use students' receptive modes that facilitate instruction.

Concepts to be taught:

1. Use high performance modes for learning new concepts and skills.

2. Practice may occur through low performance modes.

3. Multi-mode instruction sometimes interferes with learning.

4. When to use low performance receptive modes.

5. When concepts or skills cannot be taught in any other way or after tasks have been learned, low performance receptive modes may be used.

Suggested activities:

1. Select previously stated tasks. Using the information to be delivered, change the form of the stimuli to one requiring a different receptive channel.

2. Discuss with teachers the importance of emphasizing high performance modes.

Assignment: Develop a Plan for Assisting Teachers in Using Receptive Modes by Following Form 1-A.

Step 3: Help teachers to select appropriate instructional media.

Concepts to be taught:

1. Instructional media are selected to relate directly to instructional tasks, to capitalize on students' high performance modes, and when they provide high interest to learners.

2. Instructional media should be selected on the bases of assessment information.

3. Instructional media are tools.

4. Instructional media are a part of instructional strategies not in lieu of strategies.

Suggested activities:

1. Relate assessment information to selecting appropriate instructional media.

2. Invite an instructional materials specialist to present ways to select and use instructional media.

3. Encourage teachers to measure carefully the amount of seatwork presented in one sitting.

4. Encourage teachers to experiment with new forms of instructional materials.

Assignment: Develop a Plan to Help Teachers Select Appropriate Instructional Media by Following Form 1-A.

Step 4: Instruct teachers in using instructional strategies.

Concepts to be taught:

1. Advantages of written strategies.

2. Provide a plan to follow.

3. Select time segments during each day for implementing instructional strategies.

Suggested activities:

1. Ask teachers to implement their instructional strategies.

2. Discuss problems of implementation with teachers.

3. Observe selected teachers while they implement written strategies.

Assignment: Develop a Plan for Instructing Teachers in Using Instructional Strategies by Following Form 1-A.

E. Instructing Teachers to Evaluate Instruction

Purposes and Terminal Behavior

1. To compare student performance against terminal criteria. Teachers will evaluate student performance by comparing it with established terminal criteria.

2. To base subsequent instruction on performance. Teachers will decide which tasks to teach by evaluating student performances.

Procedures

Step 1: Instruct teachers to compare student performance with terminal criteria.

Concepts to be taught:

1. When criterion is not met, determine bases for failure.

2. Bases for failure include need for more instructional time, need to change reinforcement, need for an easier task, or the need for different instructional media.

Suggested activities:

1. Following instruction, have teachers evaluate effects of their instruction.

2. Discuss problems that may arise.

Assignment: Develop a Plan for Instructing Teachers to Compare Student Performance With Terminal Criteria by Following Form 1-A.

Step 2: Instruct teachers to select instructional tasks on the bases of evaluative information.

Concepts to be taught:

1. When criterion is met.

2. Save instructional strategy to be used for review with same students.

3. Select higher order tasks from those recorded during assessment.

Suggested activities:

1. Assist teachers to select new instructional tasks

2. Present and discuss the Directive Teaching cycle: assess — treat — evaluate

3. Review major concepts in Directive Teaching

Assignment: Develop a Plan for Instructing Teachers to Select Instructional Tasks Evaluative Information by Following Form 1-A.

Consulting with Allied Professionals

Physicians are often the first professionals to recognize that preschool children may have learning and/or behavior problems. After children enter school, parents may express their concerns about their children's poor school progress to physicians and other professional personnel whom they see for their children's or their own treatment. In other instances, school personnel encourage parents to contact allied professionals in seeking assistance for their children. In such instances, it is advisable for teachers to follow advice presented in a joint organizational statement by the American Academy of Pediatrics, the American Academy of Ophthalmology and Otolaryngology, and the American Association of Ophthalmology:

The precursors of learning disabilities can often be detected by three years of age. Since remediation may be more effective during the early years, it is important for the physician to recognize the child with this problem and refer him to the appropriate service, if available, before he is of school age. Medical specialists may assist in bringing the child's potential to the best level, but the actual remedial educational procedures remain the responsibility of educators.[4]

While the above quotation is of relevance to teachers when consulting with allied professionals, other items included in this same joint statement are also important in considering expectations for certain treatments. Other relevant items in the statement are:

1. Children with learning problems have the same incidence of ocular abnormalities as children who are normal achievers and reading at grade level.
2. Eye defects do not cause reversals of letters, words, or numbers.
3. No known scientific evidence supports claims for improving the academic abilities of learning disabled or dyslexic children with treatment based solely on:
   a) visual training (muscle exercise, ocular pursuit, glasses);
   b) neurologic organizational training (laterality training, balance board, perceptual training).
4. Excluding correcting ocular defects, glasses have no value in the specific treatment of dyslexia or other learning problems. In fact, unnecessarily prescribed glasses may create a false sense of security that may delay needed treatment.
5. The teaching of learning disabled and dyslexic children is a problem of educational science. No one approach is applicable to all children. A change in any variable may result in increased motivation of the child and reduced frustration. Parents should be made aware that mental level and psychological implications are contributing factors to a child's success or failure. Ophthalmologists and other specialists should offer their knowledge. This may consist of the identification of specific defects, or simply early recognition.[5]

Limitations of the roles of noneducators which are contained in the above statement are not always recognized or accepted by allied professionals. Sometimes school personnel encourage parents to seek medical and paramedical assistance. Referrals of this sort are best managed through the school's special education team. When nonschool personnel are involved in assisting children and their parents, it should be done within a spirit of cooperation and at the parents' request, approval, or initiative. But in almost all cases, L&BD students' learning problems can only be corrected or reduced through effective teaching in school and at home.

Summary

Teachers of L&BD students are expected to serve as consultants, to cooperate with other consultants, and to communicate and work cooperatively with parents, school personnel, and allied professionals.

There are specific procedures and skills which teachers should use in conducting parent conferences. These include rapport building, obtaining information, providing information, and evaluating the conference.

Programs were presented for training parents in behavior management and for conducting inservice training programs for teachers.

Teachers should cooperate with allied professionals but should recognize that academic and social learnings are improved through effective teaching in school and at home.

---

4. "The eye and learning disabilities," Newsletter Supplement, 1 January 1972. Joint Organizational Statement, American Academy of Pediatrics.

5. Ibid.

Ackerman, P., Peters, J., & Dykman, R. Children with specific learning disabilities: WISC profiles. *Journal of Learning Disabilities*, 1971, *4*, 150-166.

Adams, R. Dyslexia: A discussion of its definition. *Journal of Learning Disabilities*, 1969, *2*, 616-633.

Adelman, H. Teacher education and youngsters with learning problems. *Journal of Learning Disabilities*, 1972, *5*, 467-480.

Adelman, H. The not so specific learning disability population. *Exceptional Children*, 1971, *38*, 528-533.

Allen, K., Hart, B., Buell, T., Harris, F., & Wolf, J. Effects of social reinforcement on isolated behavior of a nursery school child. *Child Development*, 1964, *35*, 511-518.

American Academy of Pediatrics. The eye and learning disabilities. *Newsletter Supplement*, Joint Organizational Statement, January 1, 1972.

Andronico, M., & Guerney, B. The potential application of filial therapy to the school situation. *Journal of School Psychology*, 1967, *6*, 2-7.

Atwell, A., Orpet, R., & Meyers, C. Kindergarten behavior ratings as a predictor of academic achievement. *Journal of School Psychology*, 1967, *6*, 43-46.

Ausubel, D. The use of advance organizers in the learning and retention of meaningful verbal material. *Journal of Educational Psychology*, 1960, *51*, 267-272.

Ayllon, T., Layman, D., & Kandel, H. A behavioral-educational alternative to drug control of hyperactive children. *Journal of Applied Behavior Analysis*, 1975, *8*, 137-146.

Baer, D., Wolf, M., & Risley, T. Some current dimensions of applied behavior analysis. *Journal of Applied Behavior Analysis*, 1968, *1*, 91-97.

Baker, E. The technology of instructional develoment. In R. Travers (Ed.), *Second handbook of research on teaching*. Chicago: Rand McNally & Co., 1973, 245-285.

Balow, B. The emotionally and socially handicapped. *Review of Educational Research*, 1966, *36*, 120-133.

Bandura, A. *Principles of behavior modification*. New York: Holt, Rinehart & Winston, Inc., 1969.

Bandura, A. Vicarious processes: A case of no-trial learning. In L. Berkowitz (Ed.), *Advances in experimental social psychology*. New York: Academic Press. 1965, Vol 11, 1-15.

Bandura, A., & Kupers, C. Transmission of self-reinforcement through modeling. *Journal of Abnormal and Social Psychology*, 1964, *69*, 1-9.

Bandura, A., Ross, D., & Ross, S. Imitation of film-mediated aggressive models. *Journal of Abnormal and Social Psychology*, 1963, *67*, 527-534.

Bandura, A., Ross, D., & Ross, S. Transmission of aggression through imitation of aggressive models. *Journal of Abnormal and Social Psychology*, 1961, *66*, 3-11.

Bandura, A., & Whalen, C. The influence of antecedent reinforcement and divergent modeling cues on patterns of self-reward. *Journal of Personality and Social Psychology*, 1966, *3*, 373-382.

Barone, M. *A survey of school districts to determine local policy regarding maintenance, release, and use of pupil-personnel information.* Wilkes-Barre, Pa.: Department of Education, Wilkes College, 1971.

Barr, K., & McDowell, R. Comparison of learning disabled and emotionally disturbed children on three deviant classroom behaviors. *Exceptional Children*, 1972, *39*, 60-62.

Barsch, R. A movigenic curriculum. Bulletin 25, Madison, Wis.: Department of Public Instruction, Bureau for the Handicapped, 1965.

Barsch, R. *Achieving perceptual-motor efficiency.* Seattle: Special Child, 1967.

Bateman, B. An educator's view of a diagnostic approach to learning disorders. *Learning disorders* (Vol. 1). Seattle: Special Child Publication, 1965.

Bateman, B. The efficacy of an auditory and a visual method of first grade reading instruction with auditory and visual learners. In K. Smith (Ed.), *Perception and reading.* Newark, Del.: International Reading Association, 1968.

Becker, W., Madsen, C., Arnold, C., & Thomas, D. The contingent use of teacher attention and praise in reducing classroom behavior problems. *Journal of Special Education*, 1967, *1*, 287-307.

Begley, J. Overt behavioral variables in educationally handicapped children by higher IQ and lower IQ. *Journal of Learning Disabilities*, 1970, *3*, 400-403.

Bender, L. A visual motor gestalt test and its clinical use. *Research Monograph of the American Ortho-psychiatric Assn.*, 1938, No. 3.

Benedict, P., & Irving, J. Mental illness in primitive societies. *Psychiatry*, 1954, *17*, 389.

Berkowitz, P., & Rothman, E. Educating disturbed children in New York City: An historical overview. In P. Berkowitz & E. Rothman (Eds.), *Public education for disturbed children in New York City: Application and theory.* Springfield, Ill.: Charles C. Thomas, 1960, 5-19.

Berkowitz, P., & Rothman, E. *The disturbed child.* New York: New York University Press, 1960.

Bijou, S. Behavior modification in teaching the retarded child. In C. Thoresen (Ed.), *Behavior modification in education.* The Seventy-second Yearbook of the National Society for the Study of Education. Chicago: University of Chicago Press, 1973.

Bijou, S. Experimental studies of child behavior, normal and deviant. In L. Kasner & L. Ullman (Eds.), *Research in behavior modification.* New York: Holt, Rinehart & Winston, 1965, 56-81.

Birch, H. D. (Ed.). *Brain damage in children: The biological and social aspects.* Baltimore: Williams & Wilkins, 1964.

Birch, J. Special education for exceptional children through regular school personnel and programs. In M. Reynolds & M. Davis (Eds.), *Exceptional children in regular classrooms.* Minneapolis: University of Minnesota, 1971.

Black, F. Achievement test performance of high and low perceiving learning disabled children. *Journal of Learning Disabilities*, 1974, *3*, 178-182.

Block, J. (Ed.). *Mastery learning: Theory and practice.* New York: Holt, Rinehart & Winston, 1971.

Bloom, B. Learning for mastery. *Evaluation Comment*, 1968, *1*, 1-4.

Bolvin, J., & Glaser, R. Developmental aspects of individually prescribed instruction. *Audiovisual Instruction*, 1968, *13*, 828-831.

Bonney, M. *Mental health in education.* Boston: Allyn & Bacon, 1960.

Bower, E. *Early identification of emotionally handicapped children in schools.* Springfield, Ill.: Charles C. Thomas, 1960.

Bower, E. *Early identification of emotionally handicapped children in schools* (2nd ed.). Springfield, Ill.: Charles C. Thomas, 1969.

Bower, E. The primacy of primary prevention: The metaphor of screening. *The School Psychology Digest*, 1974, *3*, 4-11.

Broden, M., Hall, R., Dunlap, A., & Clark, R. Effects of teacher attention and a token reinforcement system in a junior high school special education class. *Exceptional Children*, 1970, *36*, 341-349.

Brothers, A., & Hosclaw, C. Fusing behaviors into spelling. *Elementary English*, 1969, *46*, 25-28.

Broudy, H. *A Critique of PBTE.* Washington, D.C.: American Association for Colleges of Teacher Education, 1973.

Bryan, T. An observational analysis of classroom behaviors of children with learning disabilities. *Journal of Learning Disabilities*, 1974, *7*, 35-43.

Buktenica, N. Identification of potential learning disorders. *Journal of Learning Disabilities*, 1971, *4*, 379-383.

Bullock, L., & Brown, R. Behavioral dimensions of emotionally disturbed children. *Exceptional Children*, 1972, *39*, 740-741.

Bullock, L., & Whelan, R. Competencies needed by teachers of the emotionally disturbed and socially maladjusted: A comparison. *Exceptional Children*, 1971, *38*, 485-489.

Burgess, R., Clark, R., & Hendee, J. An experimental analysis of anti-litter procedures. *Journal of Applied Behavior Analysis*, 1971, *4*, 71-75.

Buros, O. *The seventh mental measurements yearbook*. Highland Park, N.J.: Gryphon Press, 1972.

Bush, R. The human relations factor: 1. Principles of successful teacher-pupil relationships. *Phi Delta Kappan*, 1958, *39*, 271-273.

Cantwell, D. Psychiatric illness in the families of hyperactive children. *Archives of General Psychiatry*, 1972, *27*, 414-417.

Carroll, J. Illinois test of psycholinguistic abilities (revised edition). In O. Buros (Ed.), *The seventh mental measurements yearbook*. Highland Park, N.J.: The Gryphon Press, 1972, *1*, 815-823.

Cartwright, G., & Cartwright, C. Gilding the lilly: Comments on the training based model. *Exceptional Children*, 1972, *3*, 231-234.

Cattell, R. *Personality: A systematic and factual study*. New York: McGraw-Hill, 1950.

Cattell, R. *The scientific analysis of personality*. Chicago: Aldine Publishing Co., 1966.

Chadwick, B., & Day, R. *Systematic reinforcement: Academic performance of Mexican-American and black students*. Unpublished manuscript, University of Washington, Department of Sociology, 1970.

Chalfant, J. *Factors related to special education services*. Washington, D.C.: The Council for Exceptional Children, 1972.

Chalfant, J., & Scheffelin, M. *Central processing dysfunctions in children: A review of research*. Bethesda, Md.: National Institute of Neurological Diseases and Stroke, 1969.

Cheney, C., & Morse, W. Psychodynamic interventions in emotional disturbance. In W. Rhodes & T. Tracy (Eds.), *A study of child variance, Vol. 2: Interventions*. Ann Arbor: University of Michigan Press, 1974, 253-393.

Christopolos,F., & Renz, P. A critical examination of special education programs. *Journal of Special Education*, 1969, *3*, 371-378.

Clements, S. *Minimal brain dysfunction in children*. NINDB Monograph No. 3, Public Health Service Bulletin No. 1415. Washington D.C.: U.S. Department of Health, Education and Welfare, 1966.

Clements, S., & Peters, J. Minimal brain dysfunctions in the school age child. *Archives of General Psychiatry*, 1962, *6*, 185-197.

Cloward, R. Studies in tutoring. *Journal of Experimental Education*, 1967, *36*, 14-25.

Cobb, J. *Survival skills and first-grade academic achievement*. Eugene, Oreg.: University of Oregon, Research Institute, 1970.

Coleman, R. A procedure for fading from experimental-school-based to parent-home-based control of classroom behavior. *Journal of School Psychology*, 1973, *2*, 71-79.

Connors, C. Recent drug studies with hyperkinetic children. *Journal of Learning Disabilities*, 1971, *4*, 476-484.

Cooper, J. Basic principles of directive teaching. *Theory into Practice*, 1974, *15*, 84-90.

Cooper, J. *Measurement and analysis of behavioral techniques*. Columbus, Ohio: Charles E. Merrill, 1974.

Cooper, J., & Johnson, J. *Guideline for direct and continuous measurement of academic behavior*. Unpublished, 1976.

Cooper, T. *An evaluation of a functional in-service training model for special education*. Unpublished doctoral dissertation, The Ohio State University, College of Education, 1975.

Cowgill, M., Friedland, S., & Shapiro, R. Predicting learning disabilities from kindergarten reports. *Journal of Learning Disabilities*, 1973, *6*, 577-582.

Cruickshank, W., Bentzen, F., Ratzebury, F., & Tannhauser, M. *A teaching method for brain injured hyperactive children*. Syracuse, N.Y.: Syracuse University Press, 1961.

Dauterman, J., & Amarose, R. *Assessment and placement models for social education programs*. Columbus, Ohio: Columbus Public Schools, 1974.

DeHirsch, K., Jansky, J., & Langford, W. *Predicting reading failure: A preliminary study*. New York: Harper & Row, 1966.

Delacato, C. *Neurological organization and reading*. Springfield, Ill.: Charles C. Thomas, 1966.

Deno, E. Special education as developmental capital. *Exceptional Children*, 1970, *37*, 229-237.

D'Evelyn, K. *Meeting children's emotional needs*. Englewood Cliffs, N.J.: Prentice-Hall, 1957.

Dobzhansky, T. *Mankind evolving*. New Haven, Conn.: Yale University Press, 1962.

Donahue, G., & Nichtern, S. *Teaching the troubled child*. New York: The Free Press, 1965.

Dunkeld, D., & Hatch, L. Building spelling confidence. *Elementary English*, 1975, *52*, 225-229.

Dunn, D., & Kowitz, G. Teacher perceptions of correlates of academic achievement. *School and Society*, 1970, *98*, 370-372.

Dupont, H. *Educating emotionally disturbed children readings* (2nd ed.). New York: Holt, Rinehart & Winston, Inc., 1974.

Eichorn, J. Delinquency and the educational system. In H. Quay (Ed.), *Juvenile delinquency: Research and theory*. Princeton, N.J.: D. Van Nostrand, 1965.

Elkind, D., & Deblinger, J. *Reading achievement in disadvantaged children as a consequence of non-verbal perceptual training*. ERIC ED021704, 1968.

Emrich, L. Bibliotherapy for stutterers. *Quarterly Journal of Speech*, 1966, *52*, 74-79.

Engelmann, S. *Preventing failure in the primary grades*. Chicago: Science Research Associates, 1969.

English, H., & English, A. *A comprehensive dictionary of psychological and psychoanalytical terms*. New York: Longmans, Green & Co., 1958.

Ensminger, E. A proposed model for selecting, modifying, or developing instructional materials for handicapped children. *Focus on Exceptional Children*, 1970, *1*, 1-9.

Ensminger, E., & Sullivan, M. Information processing models applied to educating handicapped children. In L. Mann & D. Sabatino (Eds.), *The second review of special education*. Philadelphia: JSE Press, 1974.

Epstein, W. The influence of syntactic structure on learning. *American Journal of Psychology*, 1961, *74*, 80-85.

Erlenmeyer-Kimling, L., & Jervek, L. Genetics and intelligence: A review. *Science*, 1963, *142*, 1477-1479.

Falik, L. The effects of special perceptual-motor training in kindergarten on second grade reading. *Journal of Learning Disabilities*, 1969, *2*, 325-329.

Farb, P. *Word play: What happens when people talk*. New York: Alfred A. Knopf, 1974.

Fauke, J., Burnett, J., Powers, M., & Sulzer-Azaroff, B. Improvement of handwriting and letter recognition skills: A behavior modification procedure. *Journal of Learning Disabilities*, 1973, *6*, 296-300.

Fenichel, O. *The psychoanalytic theory of neurosis*. New York: W. W. Norton & Co., Inc., 1945.

Ferinden, W., Van Handel, D., & Kovalinsky, T. A supplemental instructional program for children with learning disabilities. *Journal of Learning Disabilities*, 1971, *4*, 4.

Fernald, G. *Remedial techniques in basic school subjects*. New York: McGraw-Hill, 1943.

Feshback, N. Student teacher preferences for elementary school pupils varying in personality characteristics. *Journal of Educational Psychology*, 1969, *60*, 126-132.

Fieldhusen, J., Thurston, J., & Benning, J. Classroom behavior, intelligence, and achievement. *The Journal of Experimental Education*, 1967, *36*, 82-87.

Fieldhusen, J., Thurston, J., & Benning, J. Longitudinal analysis of classroom behavior and school achievement. *The Journal of Experimental Education*, 1970, *38*, 4-10.

Fine, M. Considerations in educating children with cerebral dysfunction. *Journal of Learning Disabilities*, 1970, *3*, 132-143.

Fink, A. Teacher-pupil interaction in classes for the emotionally handicapped. *Exceptional Children*, 1972, *38*, 469-474.

Fink, A., & Glass, R. Contemporary issues in the education of the behaviorally disordered. In L. Mann & D. Sabatino (Eds.), *The first review of special education* (Vol. 2). Philadelphia: Buttonwood Farms, Inc., 1973, 137-160.

Fish, B. Stimulant drug treatment of hyperactive children. In D. Cantrell (Ed.), *The hyperactive child: Diagnosis, management, current research*. New York: Spectrum Publications, Inc., 1975, 109-127.

Fleishman, E. A comparative study of aptitude patterns in unskilled and skilled psychomotor performance. *Journal of Applied Psychology*, 1957, *41*, 263-272.

Fredericks, H., Baldwin, V., McDonnell, J., Hofman, R., & Harter, J. Parents educate their trainable children. *Mental Retardation*, 1971, *9*, 24-26.

Freeman, R. Drug effect on learning in children: A selective review of the past thirty years. *Journal of Special Education*, 1966, *1*, 17-44.

Frew, T. *The utilization of odor preferences as reinforcers for academic tasks with young learning disabled children*. Unpublished dissertation, The Ohio State University, College of Education, 1975.

Frostig, M. The relationship of diagnosis to remediation in learning problems. In S. Kirk & J. McCarthy (Eds.), *Learning disabilities: Selected ACLD papers*. Boston: Houghton Mifflin Co., 1975, 119-129.

Frostig, M. *Movement education: Theory and practice*. Chicago: Follett, 1970.

Frostig, M., & Horne, D. *The Frostig program for the development of visual perception: Teacher's guide*. Chicago: Follett, 1964.

Gaasholt, M. Precision techniques in the management of teacher and child behaviors. *Exceptional Children*, 1970, *36*, 129-135.

Gagné, R. The analysis of instructional objectives for the design of instruction. In R. Glaser (Ed.), *Teaching machines and programmed learning, II: Data and directions*. Washington, D.C.: Department of Audiovisual Instruction, National Education Association, 1965, 21-65.

Gallagher, P. Structuring academic tasks for emotionally disturbed boys. *Exceptional Children*, 1972, *38*, 711-720.

Gearheart, B. *Learning disabilities: Educational strategies*. St. Louis, Mo.: The C. V. Mosby Co., 1973.

Geedy, P. What research tells us about spelling. *Elementary English*, 1975, *52*, 233-236.

Getman, G. *How to develop your child's intelligence*. Leverne, Minn.: G. N. Getman, 1962.

Getman, G. *Pathway school program*. Boston: Teaching Resources, 1969.

Getzels, J., & Jackson, P. The teacher's personality and characteristics. In N. Gage (Ed.), *Handbook of research on teaching*. New York: Rand McNally, 1963.

Gil, D. *Violence against children: Physical child abuse in the United States*. Cambridge, Mass.: Harvard University Press, 1974.

Gilbert, T. Mathematics: The technology of education. *Journal of Mathematics*, 1962, *1*, 7-73.

Gillingham, A., & Stillman, B. *Remedial training for children with specific disability in reading, spelling, and penmanship* (7th ed.). Cambridge, Mass.: Educators Publishing Service, 1966.

Glasser, W. *Reality therapy*. New York: Harper & Row, 1965.

Glasser, W. *Schools without failure*. New York: Harper & Row, 1969.

Glavin, J. Behaviorally oriented resource rooms: A follow-up. *Journal of Special Education*, 1974, *8*, 337-347.

Glavin, J. *Spontaneous improvement in emotionally disturbed children*. Unpublished doctoral dissertation, George Peabody College for Teachers, 1974.

Glavin, J., & Annesley, F. Reading and arithmetic correlates of conduct-problem and withdrawn children. *The Journal of Special Education*, 1971, *5*, 213-219.

Glavin, J., & Quay, H. Behavior disorders. *Review of Educational Research*, 1969, *39*, 83-102.

Glavin, J., Quay, H., & Werry, J. Behavioral and academic gains of conduct-problem children in different classroom settings. *Exceptional Children*, 1971, *37*, 441-446.

Glavin, J., Quay, H., Annesley, F., & Werry, J. An experimental resource room for behavior problem children. *Exceptional Children*, 1971, *38*, 131-137.

Goldfarb, A. Teachers' ratings in psychiatric case finding. *American Journal of Public Health*, 1963, *53*, 1919-1927.

Goldstein, K. *Aftereffects of brain injuries in war*. New York: Grune & Stratton, 1942.

Goldstein, K., Cary, G., Chorost, S., & Dalack, J. Family patterns and the school performance of emotionally disturbed boys. *Journal of Learning Disabilities*, 1970, *3*, 12-17.

Goslin, D., & Bordier, N. Recordkeeping in elementary and secondary schools. In S. Wheeler (Ed.), *On record: Files and dossiers in American life*. New York: Russell Sage Foundation, 1970.

Graubard, P. The extent of academic retardation in a residential treatment center. *Journal of Educational Research*, 1964, *58*, 78-80.

Graubard, P. The relationship between academic achievement and behavior dimensions. *Exceptional Children*, 1971, *37*, 755-756.

Graubard, P. Utilizing the group in teaching disturbed delinquents to learn. *Exceptional Children*, 1969, *36*, 267-272.

Graubard, P., & Rosenberg, H. *Classrooms that work*. New York: Dutton, 1974.

Graubard, P., Rosenberg, H., & Miller, M. An ecological approach to social deviancy. In B. Hopkins & E. Ramp (Eds.), *A new direction for education: Behavior analysis*. Lawrence, Kan.: Support and Development Center for Follow Through, 1971.

Guilford, J. *Fundamental statistics in psychology and education* (3rd ed.). New York: McGraw-Hill Book Co., Inc., 1956.

Hall, R., Hawkins, R., & Axelrod, S. Measuring and recording student behavior: A behavior analysis approach. In R. Weinberg & F. Wood (Eds.), *Observation of pupils and teachers in mainstream and special education settings: alternative strategies*. Minneapolis, Minn.: Leadership Training Institute/Special Education, 1975, 193-217.

Hall, R., Axelrod, S., Tyler, L., Grief, E., Jones, F., & Robertson, R. Modification of behavior problems in the home with a parent as observer and experimenter. *Journal of Applied Behavior Analysis*, 1972, *5*, 53-64.

Hallahan, D., & Kauffman, J. *Introduction to learning disabilities: A psycho-behavioral approach.* Englewood Cliffs, N.J.: Prentice-Hall, Inc. 1976.

Hammer, D. A teacher's guide to the detection of emotional disturbance in the elementary school child. *Journal of Learning Disabilities*, 1970, *3*, 517-519.

Hammill, D. Training visual perceptual processes. *Journal of Learning Disabilities*, 1972, *5*, 552-559.

Hammill, D., & Bartel, N. *Teaching children with learning and behavior problems.* Boston: Allyn & Bacon, 1975.

Hanley, E. Review of research involving applied behavior analysis in the classroom. *Review of Educational Research*, 1970, *40*, 597-625.

Haring, N., & Phillips, E. *Analysis and modification of classroom behavior.* Englewood Cliffs, N.J.: Prentice-Hall, 1972.

Haring, N., & Phillips, E. *Educating emotionally disturbed children.* New York: McGraw-Hill, 1962.

Harper, P., Fischer, L., & Rider, R. Neurological and intellectual status of prematures at three to five years of age. *Journal of Pediatrics*, 1959, *55*, 679-690.

Harris, I. *Emotional blocks to learning.* New York: The Free Press, 1961.

Hart, B., Reynolds, N., Baer, D., Brawley, E., & Harris, F. Effect of contingent and non-contingent social reinforcement on the cooperative play of a preschool child. *Journal of Applied Behavior Analysis*, 1968, *1*, 73-76.

Harth, R., & Glavin, J. Validity of teacher rating as a subtest for screening emotionally disturbed children. *Exceptional Children*, 1971, *8*, 605-606.

Hartlage, L., & Lucas, D. Group screening for reading disability in first grade children. *Journal of Learning Disabilities*, 1973, *6*, 317-321.

Hartman, A. *The effects of pairing olfactory stimuli with words on the acquisition of word recognition skills of kindergarten students.* Unpublished doctoral dissertation, The Ohio State University, College of Education, 1974.

Haubrich, P., & Shores, R. Attending behavior and academic performance of emotionally disturbed children. *Exceptional Children*, 1976, *42*, 337-338.

Hayball, H., & Dilling, H. *Study of students from special classes who have been returned to regular classes.* Ontario, Canada: Searborough Board of Education, 1969.

Herbert, E., & Baer, D. Training parents as behavior modifiers: Self-recording of contingent attention. *Journal of Applied Behavior Analysis*, 1972, *5*, 139-149.

Hewett, F. A hierarchy of competencies for teachers of emotionally handicapped children. *Exceptional Children*, 1966, *33*, 7-11.

Hewett, F., & Blake, P. Teaching the emotionally disturbed. In R. Travers (Ed.), *Second handbook of research on teaching.* Chicago: Rand McNally & Co., 1973, 657-688.

Hewett, L., & Jenkins, R. *Fundamental patterns of maladjustment, the dynamics of their origin.* Springfield, Ill.: State of Illinois, 1946.

Hewett, F., Taylor, F., & Arturo, A. The Santa Monica project: Evaluation of an engineered classroom design with emotionally disturbed children. *Exceptional Children*, 1969, *35*, 523-529.

Hildebrandt, D., Feldman, S., & Ditrichs, R. Rules, models, and self-reinforcement in children. *Journal of Personality and Social Psychology*, 1973, *25*, 1-5.

Hillerich, R., & Gould, S. *The Merrill spelling program: Spelling for writing.* Columbus, Ohio: Charles E. Merrill, 1976.

Hollingshead, A., & Redlich, F. *Social class and mental illness: A community study.* New York: John Wiley & Sons, 1958.

Homme, L., Csanyi, A., Gonzales, M., & Rechs, J. *How to use contingency contracting in the classroom.* Champaign, Ill.: Research Press, 1970.

Hopkins, B., Schutte, R., & Garton, K. The effects of access to a playroom on the rate and quality of printing and writing of first and second grade students. *Journal of Applied Behavior Analysis*, 1971, *4*, 77-87.

Hops, H., & Cobb, J. Survival behaviors in the educational setting: Their implications for research intervention. In L. Hamerlynck, L. Handy, & E. Mash (Eds.), *Behavior change methodology, concepts and practice.* Champaign, Ill.: Research Press, 1973, 193-208.

Horn, E. Research in spelling. *Elementary English Review*, 1944, *21*, 6-13.

Horn, E. Spelling. In C. Harris (Ed.), *Encyclopedia of educational research* (3rd ed.). New York: Macmillan, 1960, 1337-1354.

Horn, E. Spelling. In W. Monroe (Ed.), *Encyclopedia of educational research*. New York: Macmillan, 1950, 1247-1264.

Hoy, W. Organizational socialization: The student teacher and pupil control ideology. *Journal of Educational Research*, 1967, *61*, 153-155.

Hoyt, K. A study of the effects of teacher knowledge of pupil characteristics on pupil achievement and attitudes toward classwork. *Journal of Educational Psychology*, 1955, *46*, 302-310.

Jacobs, J. A follow-up evaluation of the Frostig visual-perceptual training program. *Journal of Program Research and Development*, 1968, *4*, 8-18.

Jacobs, J., Wirthlin, L., & Miller, C. A follow-up evaluation of the Frostig visual-perceptual training program. *Educational Leadership Research Supplement*, 1968, *4*, 169-175.

Johnson, D., & Myklebust, H. *Learning disabilities: Educational principles and practices*. New York: Grune & Stratton, 1967.

Johnson, M., & Bailey, J. Cross-age tutoring: Fifth graders as arithmetic tutors for kindergarten children. *Journal of Applied Behavior Analysis*, 1974, *7*, 223-232.

Kabler, M. *A review of the research on children's self-reinforcing behaviors: A process of self-control*. Unpublished manuscript, The Ohio State University, Faculty for Exceptional Children, 1976.

Kagan, J., & Moss, H. *Birth to maturity: A study in psychological development*. New York: John Wiley & Sons, 1962.

Kanner, L. Autistic disturbances of affective contact. *Nervous Child*, 1943, *2*, 217-250.

Karner, M., Zehrbach, R., & Teska, J. Involving families of handicapped children. *Theory into Practice*, 1972, *11*, 150-156.

Keogh, B., & Becker, L. Early detection of learning problems: Questions, cautions, and guidelines. *Exceptional Children*, 1973, *40*, 5-11.

Kephart, N. Perceptual-motor aspects of learning disabilities. *Exceptional Children*, 1964, *31*, 201-206.

Kephart, N. *The slow learner in the classroom*. Columbus, Ohio: Charles E. Merrill, 1960.

Kephart, N. *The slow learner in the classroom* (2nd ed.). Columbus, Ohio: Charles E. Merrill, 1971.

Kessler, J. *Psychopathology of childhood*. Englewood Cliffs, N.J.: Prentice-Hall, 1966.

Kirk, S. From labels to action. In S. Kirk & J. McCarthy (Eds.), *Learning disabilities: Selected ACLD papers*. Boston: Houghton-Mifflin Co., 1975, 39-45.

Kirk, S., & Kirk, W. *Psycholinguistic learning disabilities: Diagnosis and remediation*. Urbana, Ill.: University of Illinois Press, 1971.

Kirk, S., McCarthy, J., & Kirk, W. *Illinois Test of Psycholinguistic Abilities*. Urbana, Ill.: University of Illinois Press, 1968.

Kirp, D., Kuriloff, P., & Buss, W. Legal mandates and organizational change. In N. Hobbs (Ed.), *Issues in the classification of children, Volume II*. San Francisco: Jossey-Bass Publishing Co., 1975, 319-382.

Kline, C. The adolescents with learning problems: How long must they wait? *Journal of Learning Disabilities*, 1972, *5*, 262-271.

Koppitz, E. Brain damage, reading disability and the Bender gestalt test. *Journal of Learning Disabilities*, 1970, *3*, 429-433.

Kronick, D. Some thoughts on group identification: Social needs. *Journal of Learning Disabilities*, 1974, *7*, 144-147.

Kubie, L. *Neurotic distortion of the creative process*. Lawrence, Kan.: University of Kansas Press, 1958.

Kuhn, D., Madsen, C., & Becker, W. Effect of exposure to an aggressive model and frustration on children's aggressive behavior. *Child Development*, 1967, *38*, 739-745.

Kunzelman, H. *Precision teaching*. Seattle, Wash.: Special Child Publication, 1970.

Lahaderne, H. Attitudinal and intellectual correlates of attention: A study of four sixth-grade classrooms. *Journal of Educational Psychology*, 1968, *5*, 320-324.

Lambert, N. Intellectual and non-intellectual predictors of high school status. *The Journal of Special Education*, 1972, *6*, 247-258.

Lambert, N. Predicting and evaluating effectiveness of children in school. In E. Bower & W. Hollister (Eds.), *Behavioral science frontiers in education*. New York: John Wiley & Sons, 1967, 412-447.

Lambert, N., & Hartsough, C. Measurement in relation to mental health programs. *Review of Educational Research*, 1968, *38*, 478-496.

Lapouse, R., & Monk, M. An epidemiologic study of behavior characteristics in children. *American Journal of Public Health*, 1958, *48*, 1134-1144.

Lessinger, L. *Accountability in education: Every kid a winner.* Palo Alto, Calif.: Science Research Associates, 1970.

Levitt, E., & Cohen, S. An analysis of selected parent-intervention programs for handicapped and disadvantaged children. *Journal of Special Education,* 1975, *9,* 345-365.

Levin, J. *A comparison of the responses of selected educators on the effectiveness of specified procedures for reintegrating children with learning and behavioral disorders from special self-contained classes into regular elementary classes.* Unpublished doctoral dissertation, The Ohio State University, College of Education, 1974.

Lilly, S. A training based model for special education. *Exceptional Children,* 1971, *37,* 745-749.

Lilly, S., & Kelleher, J. Modality strengths and aptitude-treatment interaction. *Journal of Special Education,* 1973, *7,* 5-13.

Lippett, P., & Lohman, J. Cross age relationships: An educational resource. *Children,* 1965, *12,* 113-117.

Lovaas, I. A program for the establishment of speech in psychotic children. In H. Sloane & B. Macaulay (Eds.), *Operant procedures in remedial speech and language training.* Boston: Houghton-Mifflin, 1968.

Lovaas, O. Effect of exposure to symbolic aggression on aggressive behavior. *Child Development,* 1961, *32,* 37-44.

Lovaas, O., Freitas, L., Nelson, K., & Whalen, C. The establishment of imitation and its use for the development of complex behavior in schizophrenic children. *Behavior Research and Therapy,* 1967, *5,* 171-181.

Lovitt, T. Assessment of children with learning disabilities. *Exceptional Children,* 1967, *34,* 233-239.

Lovitt, T. Self-management projects with children with behavioral disabilities. *Journal of Learning Disabilities,* 1973, *6,* 138-147.

Lovitt, T., & Curtiss, K. Academic response rate as a function of teacher and self-imposed contingencies. *Journal of Applied Behavior Analysis,* 1969, *2,* 49-53.

Mackie, R., Kvaraceus, W., & Williams, H. *Teachers of children who are socially and emotionally handicapped.* Washington, D.C.: U.S. Government Printing Office, 1957.

MacMillan, D. Special education for the mildly retarded: Servant or savant. *Focus on Exceptional Children,* 1971, *2,* 1-11.

Madsen, C., Becker, W., & Thomas, D. Rules, praise and ignoring: Elements of elementary classroom control. *Journal of Applied Behavior Analysis,* 1968, *1,* 139-150.

Mager, R. *Goal analysis.* Belmont, Calif.: Fearon, 1972.

Mager, R. *Preparing instructional objectives.* Palo Alto, Calif.: Fearon, 1962.

Mager, R., & Pipe, P. *Analyzing performance problems.* Palo Alto, Calif.: Fearon, 1970.

Mann, L. Perceptual training revisited: The training of nothing at all. *Rehabilitation Literature,* 1971, *32,* 322-335.

Mann, L., Proger, B., & Cross, L. *Aptitude-treatment interactions with handicapped children: A focus on the measurement of the aptitude component,* 1972. ERIC ED-075-510.

Martin, D. The growing horror of child abuse and the undeniable role of the schools in putting an end to it. *American School Board Journal,* 1973, *160,* 51-55.

Martin, H., Beezley, P., Conway, E., & Kempe, C. The development of abused children. *Advances in Pediatrics,* 1974, *21,* 25-73.

McCaffrey, I., & Cummings, J. *Behavior patterns associated with persistent emotional disturbances of school children in regular classes of elementary grades.* Onondago County, N.Y.: Mental Health Research Unit, New York State Department of Mental Hygiene, 1967.

McCarthy, J., & McCarthy, J. *Learning disabilities.* Boston: Allyn & Bacon, 1969.

McFall, R., & Lillesand, D. Behavior rehearsal with modeling and coaching in assertion training. *Journal of Abnormal Psychology,* 1971, *77,* 313-323.

McKenzie, H., Clark, M., Wolf, M., Kothera, R., & Benson, C. Behavior modification of children with learning disabilities using grades as tokens and allowances as back-up reinforcers. *Exceptional Children,* 1968, *34,* 745-752.

McKinnon, A. A follow-up and analysis of the effects of placement in classes for emotionally disturbed children in elementary schools. *Dissertation Abstracts,* 1969.

McKinnon, A. Parent and pupil perceptions of special classes for emotionally disturbed children. *Exceptional Children,* 1970, *37,* 302-303.

McMains, M., & Liebert, R. Influence of discrepancies between successively modeled self-reward criteria on the adoption of a self-imposed standard. *Journal of Personality and Social Psychology,* 1968, *8,* 166-171.

McNeil, D. Developing instructional materials for emotionally disturbed children. *Focus on Exceptional Children*, 1969, *1*, 1-7.

Mecham, M., Jones, J., & Jex, J. Use of the Utah test of language development for screening language disabilities. *Journal of Learning Disabilities*, 1973, *6*, 524-527.

Mechner, F. Behavioral analysis and instructional sequencing. In P. Lang (Ed.), *Programmed instruction*, 66th Yearbook of the National Society for the Study of Education, Part II. Chicago, Ill.: University of Chicago Press, 1967, 81-103.

Meichenbaum, D., Bowers, K., & Ross, R. Modification of classroom behavior of institutionalized female adolescent offenders. *Behavior Research and Therapy*, 1968, *6*, 343-353.

Meier, J. Prevalence and characteristics of learning disabilities found in second grade children. *Journal of Learning Disabilities*, 1971, *4*, 7-20.

Merriman, P., Stephens, T., & Hartman, A. *Impact of directive teaching in 1969-1970 on children: A follow-up study*. Unpublished paper, The Ohio State University, Faculty for Exceptional Children, 1976.

Meyen, E., Vergason, G., & Whelen, R. (Eds.). *Strategies for teaching exceptional children*. Denver, Col.: Love Publishing Co., 1972.

Milburn, J. *Special education and regular class teacher attitudes regarding social behaviors of children: Steps toward the development of a social skills curriculum*. Unpublished doctoral dissertation, The Ohio State University, College of Education, 1974.

Minde, K., Lewin, D., Weiss, G., Lavigueur, H., Douglas, V., & Sykes, E. The hyperactive child in elementary school: A five-year, controlled follow-up. *Exceptional Children*, 1971, *38*, 215-221.

Minuchin, S., Chamberlain, P., & Graubard, P. A project for teaching learning skills to disturbed, delinquent children. *American Journal of Orthopsychiatry*, 1967, *3*, 558-567.

Mischel, W., & Liebert, R. Effects of discrepancies between observed and imposed reward criteria on their acquisition and transmission. *Journal of Personality and Social Psychology*, 1966, *3*, 45-53.

Moreno, J. *Psychodrama*. New York: Beacon House, 1946.

Morse, W. The education of socially maladjusted and emotionally disturbed children. In W. Cruickshank & G. Johnson (Eds.), *Education of exceptional children and youth*. Englewood Cliffs, N.J.: Prentice-Hall, 1958, 557-608.

Morse, W. The education of socially maladjusted and emotionally disturbed children. In W. Cruickshank & G. Johnson (Eds.), *Education of exceptional children and youth*. Englewood Cliffs, N.J.: Prentice-Hall, 1967, 568-627.

Morse, W., Cutler, R., & Fink, A. *Public school classes for the emotionally handicapped: A research analysis*. Washington, D.C.: Council for Exceptional Children, 1964.

Morse, W., & Dyer, C. The emotionally and socially handicapped. *Review of Educational Research*, 1963, *33*, 109-125.

Morse, W., Finger, D., & Gilmore, G. Innovations in school mental health programs. *Review of Educational Research*, 1968, *38*, 460-477.

Myers, P., & Hammill, D. *Methods for learning disorders*. New York: John Wiley & Sons, 1969.

Myklebust, H., & Johnson, D. Dyslexia in children. *Exceptional Children*, 1962, *29*, 14-25.

Nagel, T., & Richman, T. *Competency-based instruction*. Columbus, Ohio: Charles E. Merrill, 1972.

National Advisory Committee on Handicapped Children. *Basic education rights for the handicapped, 1973 annual report*. Washington, D.C.: U.S. Department of Health, Education and Welfare, 1973.

Nelson, C. Techniques for screening conduct disturbed children. *Exceptional Children*, 1971, *7*, 501-507.

Newcomer, P., & Goodman, L. Effect of modality of instruction on the learning of meaningful and nonmeaningful material by auditory and visual learners. *Journal of Special Education*, 1975, *9*, 261-268.

Noffsinger, T. The effects of reward and level of aspiration on students with deviant behavior. *Exceptional Children*, 1971, *36*, 355-363.

Nolan, J., & Pence, C. Operant conditioning principles in the treatment of a selectively mute child. *Journal of Consulting and Clinical Psychology*, 1970, *2*, 265-268.

Oakland, T. Assessing minority group children: Challenges for school psychologists. *Journal of School Psychology*, 1973, *11*, 294-303.

Oberst, B. a community approach to specific school learning disabilities: The Omaha STAAR project. *Journal of Learning Disabilities*, 1973, *6*, 421-428.

Ohio Department of Education. *Program standards for special education and legal dismissal from school attendance*. Columbus, Ohio: The Ohio Department of Education, 1973, 55-57.

O'Leary, K. Behavior modification in the classroom: A rejoinder to Winett and Winkler. *Journal of Applied Behavior Analysis*, 1972, *5*, 505-511.

O'Leary, K. The assessment of psychopathology in children. In H. Quay & J. Werry (Eds.), *Psychopathological disorders of childhood*. New York: John Wiley & Sons, 1972, 234-272.

O'Leary, K., & Becker, W. The effects of the intensity of a teacher's reprimands on children's behavior. *Journal of School Psychology*, 1968, *7*, 8-11.

O'Leary, K., & Becker, W. Behavior modification of an adjustment class: A token reinforcement program. *Exceptional Children*, 1967, *33*, 627-642.

O'Leary, K., Becker, W., Evans, M., & Sandargas, R. A token reinforcement program in a public school: A replication and systematic analysis. *Journal of Applied Behavior Analysis*, 1969, *2*, 3-13.

Onondaga County School Studies. *Persistence of emotional disturbances reported among second and fourth grade children*. Interim Report No. 1. Syracuse, N. Y.: Mental Health Research Unit, 1964.

Orton, S. Word blindness in school children. *Archives of Neurological Psychiatry*, 1925, *14*, 581.

Osborne, J. Free time as a reinforcer in the management of classroom behavior. *Journal of Applied Behavior Analysis*, 1969, *2*, 113-118.

Osgood, C. A behavioristic analysis. In J. Bruner et al. (Eds.), *Contemporary approaches to cognition*. Cambridge, Mass.: Harvard University Press, 1957.

Otto, W., McMenemy, R., & Smith, R. *Corrective and remedial teaching* (2nd ed.). Boston: Houghton-Mifflin Co., 1973.

Ozer, M., & Richardson, H. The diagnostic evaluation of children with learning problems: A process approach. *Journal of Learning Disabilities*, 1974, *7*, 88-92.

Packard, R. The control of classroom attention: A group contingency for complex behavior. *Journal of Applied Behavior Analysis*, 1970, *3*, 13-28.

Patterson, G. An application of conditioning techniques to the control of a hyperactive child. In L. Ullman & L. Krasner (Eds.), *Case studies in behavior modification*. New York: Holt, Rinehart & Winston, 1965.

Patterson, G. Behavioral techniques based upon social learning: An additional base for developing behavior modification. In C. Franks (Ed.), *Behavior therapy: Appraisal and status*. New York: McGraw-Hill, 1969.

Patterson, G., Shaw, D., & Ebner, M. Teachers, peers, and parents as agents of change in the classroom. In F. Benson (Ed.), *Modifying deviant social behaviors in various classroom settings*. Eugene, Oreg.: University of Oregon Press, 1969, 13-48.

Peck, B., & Stackhouse, T. Reading problems and family dynamics. *Journal of Learning Disabilities*, 1973, *6*, 506-511.

Perspectives on Mark Twain School. Rockville, Md.: Montgomery County Public Schools, 1975.

Peterson, G. An empirical approach to the classification of disturbed children. *Journal of Clinical Psychology*, 1964, *20*, 326-337.

Phillips, E., & Haring, N. Results from special techniques for teaching emotionally disturbed children. *Exceptional Children*, 1959, *26*, 64-67.

Phillips, E., Phillips, A., & Fizen, D. Achievement place: Modification of the behaviors of pre-delinquent boys within a token economy. In C. Franks & G. Wilson (Eds.), *Behavior therapy: Theory and practice*. New York: Brunner/Mazel, 1973.

Pincus, J. Incentives for innovation in the public schools. *Review of Educational Research*, 1974, *44*, 113-144.

Popham, W., & Baker, E. *Establishing instructional goals*. Englewood-Cliffs, N.J.: Prentice-Hall, 1970.

Proger, B., & Mann, L. Criterion-referenced measurement: The world of gray versus black and white. *Journal of Learning Disabilities*, 1973, *6*, 73-84.

Quay, H. Some basic considerations in the education of emotionally disturbed children. *Exceptional Children*, 1963, *30*, 27-33.

Quay, H. Special education: Assumptions, techniques, and evaluative criteria. *Exceptional Children*, 1973, *40*, 165-170.

Quay, H., Morse, W., & Cutler, R. Personality patterns of pupils in special classes for the emotionally disturbed. *Exceptional Children*, 1966, *32*, 297-301.

Quay, H., Werry, J., McQueen, M., & Sprague, R. Remediation of the conduct problem child in the special class setting. *Exceptional Children*, 1966, *32*, 509-515.

Rabinow, B. A training program for teachers of the emotionally disturbed and socially maladjusted. *Exceptional children*, 1960, *26*, 287-293.

Ramp, E., Ulrich, R., & Dulaney, S. Delayed timeout as a procedure for reducing disruptive classroom behavior: A case study. *Journal of Applied Behavior Analysis*, 1971, *4*, 235-239.

Rappaport, S., & McNary, S. Teacher effectiveness for children with learning disorders. *Journal of Learning Disabilities*, 1970, *3*, 75-83.

Raths, L., Harmin, M., & Simon, S. *Values and teaching*. Columbus, Ohio: Charles E. Merrill, 1966.

Redl, F. Strategy and techniques of the life space interview. *American Journal of Orthopsychiatry*, 1959, *29*, 1-18.

Rejto, A. Music as an aid in the remediation of learning disabilities. *Journal of Learning Disabilities*, 1973, *6*, 286-295.

Reynolds, M., & Balow, B. Categories and variables in special education. *Exceptional Children*, 1972, *38*, 357-366.

Rhodes, W. A community participation analysis of emotional disturbance. *Exceptional Children*, 1970, *36*, 309-316.

Rhodes, W. *A study of child variance, volume 4: The future*. Ann Arbor: The University of Michigan, Institute for the Study of Mental Retardation and Related Disabilities, 1975.

Rhodes, W. The disturbing child: A problem of ecological management. *Exceptional Children*, 1967, *33*, 449-455.

Rice, R. Educo-therapy: A new approach to delinquent behavior. *Journal of Learning Disabilities*, 1970, *3*, 16-23.

Rick, G. Single subject research designs in special education. *Behavioral Disorders*, 1976, *2* (1), 68-69.

Riegel, R., Taylor, A., & Danner, F. Teaching potentially educationally handicapped children to classify and remember. *Exceptional Children*, 1973, *40*, 208-209.

Rimland, B. *Infantile autism*. New York: Appleton-Century-Crofts, 1964.

Risley, T. The effects and side effects of punishing the autistic behaviors of a deviant child. *Journal of Applied Behavior Analysis*, 1968, *1*, 21-34.

Rist, R. Student social class and teacher expectations: The self-fulfilling prophecy in ghetto education. *Harvard Educational Review*, 1970, *40*, 411-451.

Rogan, R., & Lukans, J. Education, administration, and classroom procedures. In *Minimal brain dysfunction in children: Educational medical and health related services, phase two*. N & SDCP Monograph, Public Health Publication No. 2015. Washington, D.C.: U.S. Department of HEW, 1969, 21-30.

Rosenbaum, E., & Kellman, M. Treatment of a selectively mute third-grade child. *Journal of School Psychology*, 1973, *11*, 26-29.

Rosenhan, D., Frederick, F., & Burrowes, A. Preaching and practicing: Effects of channel discrepancy on norm internalization. *Child Development*, 1968, *39*, 291-301.

Ross, A. *Psychological aspects of learning disabilities and reading disorders*. New York: McGraw-Hill, 1976.

Roth, D. Intelligence testing as a social activity. In A. Cicourel (Ed.), *Language use and school performance*. New York: Academic Press, Inc., 1974, 143-217.

Rourke, B. Brain-behavior relationships in children with learning disabilities: A research program. *American Psychologist*, 1975, *30*, 911-920.

Rowland, P. *Beginning to read, write, and listen*. Philadelphia: J. B. Lippincott, 1971.

Rubin, R., & Balow, B. Learning and behavior disorders: A longitudinal study. *Exceptional Children*, 1971, *38*, 293-299.

Sabatino, D., & Hayden, D. Prescriptive teaching in a summer learning disabilities program. *Journal of Learning Disabilities*, 1970, *3*, 220-226.

Salvia, J., & Clark, J. Use of deficits to identify the learning disabled. *Exceptional Children*, 1973, *40*, 305-308.

Salvia, J., Schultz, E., & Chapin, N. The effect of class size on the identification of potentially disturbed children. *Exceptional Children*, 1974, *40*, 517-518.

Sandgrund, A., Gaines, R., & Green, A. Child abuse and mental retardation: A problem of cause and effect. *American Journal of Mental Deficiency*, 1974, *79*, 327-330.

Saunders, B. The effect of the emotionally disturbed child in the public school classroom. *Psychology in the Schools*, 1971, *8*, 23-26.

Saylor, J., & Alexander, W. *Planning curriculums for schools*. New York: Holt, Rinehart & Winston, Inc., 1974.

Scheuer, A. The relationship between personal attributes and effectiveness in teachers of the emotionally disturbed. *Exceptional Children*, 1971, *38*, 723-731.

Schleichkorn, J. The teacher and recognition of problems in children. *Journal of Learning Disabilities*, 1972, *5*, 501-502.

Schmidt, G., & Ulrich, R. Effects of group contingent events upon classroom noise. *Journal of Applied Behavioral Analysis*, 1969, *2*, 171-179.

Schubert, D. The role of bibliotherapy in reading instruction. *Exceptional Children*, 1975, *41*, 497-499.

Schulthesis, M. *A guidebook for bibliotherapy*. Glenview, Ill.: Psychotechnics, 1973.

Schultz, E. *The firo scales*. Palo Alto, Calif.: Consulting Psychologists Press, 1967.

Schultz, E., Manton, A., & Salvia, J. Screening emotionally disturbed children in a rural setting. *Exceptional Children*, 1972, *39*, 134-137.

Schwartz, L. Preparation of the clinical teacher for special education: 1866-1966. *Exceptional Children*, 1967, *34*, 117-124.

Schwitzgebel, R. Short-term operant conditioning of adolescent offenders on socially relevant variables. *Dissertation Abstracts*, 1965, *25*, 4819-4820.

Shaftel, F., and Shaftel, G. *Role-playing for social values: Decision-making in the social studies*. Englewood Cliffs, N.J.: Prentice-Hall, 1967.

Sherman, T., & Cormier, W. An investigation of the influence of student behavior on teacher behavior. *Journal of Applied Behavior Analysis*, 1974, *7*, 11-21.

Shores, R., & Haubrich, P. Effects of cubicles in educating emotionally disturbed children. *Exceptional Children*, 1969, *34*, 21-24.

Shrodes, C. Bibliotherapy. *The Reading Teacher*, 1955, *9*, 24-25.

Shugue, M. *Performance-based teacher education and the subject matter fields*. Washington, D.C.: American Association for Colleges of Teacher Education, 1973.

Simon, G. Comments on "implications of criterion-referenced measurement." *Journal of Educational Measurement*, 1969, *6*, 259-260.

Skinner, B. *Science and human behavior*. New York: MacMillan, 1953.

Skinner, B. *The technology of teaching*. New York: Appleton-Century-Crofts, 1968.

Smayling, L. Analysis of six cases of voluntary mutism. *Journal of Speech and Hearing Disorders*, 1959, *24*, 55-58.

Smith, D., & Lovitt, T. The educational diagnosis and remediation of written b and d reversal problems: A case study. *Journal of Learning Disabilities*, 1973, *6*, 356-363.

Smith, P., & Marx, R. Some cautions on the use of the Frostig test: A factor analytic study. *Journal of Learning Disabilities*, 1972, *5*, 357-362.

Snyder, R., & Pope, P. Auditory and visual inadequacies in maturation at the first grade level. *Journal of Learning Disabilities*, 1972, *5*, 620-625.

Soeffing, M. Abused children are exceptional children. *Exceptional Children*, 1975, *42*, 126-133.

Solomon, R., & Wahler, R. Peer reinforcement control of classroom problem behavior. *Journal of Applied Behavior Analysis*, 1973, *6*, 49-56.

Special Education for Handicapped Children: First Annual Report of the National Advisory Committee on Handicapped Children. Washington, D.C.: Office of Education, Department of HEW, 1968.

Staats, A. *Complex human behavior*. New York: Holt, Rinehart & Winston, 1963.

Staats, A. *Learning, language and cognition*. New York: Holt, Rinehart & Winston, 1968.

Staats, A., & Butterfield, W. Treatment of nonreading in a culturally deprived juvenile delinquent: An application of reinforcement principles. *Child Development*, 1965, *4*, 425-442.

Staats, A., Finley, J., Minke, K., & Wolf, M. Reinforcement variables in the control of unit reading responses. *Journal of Experimental Analysis of Behavior*, 1964, *7*, 139-149.

Staats, A., Minke, K., Goodwin, W., & Landen, J. Cognitive behavior modification: "Motivated learning" reading treatment with sub-professional therapy technicians. *Behavior Research and Therapy*, 1967, *5*, 283-299.

Staats, A., Minke, K., Finley, J., Wolf, M., & Brooks, L. A reinforcer system and experimental procedure for the laboratory study of reading acquisition. *Child Development*, 1964, *35*, 209-231.

Staats, A., Staats, C., Schutz, R., & Wolf, M. The conditioning of textual responses using extrinsic reinforcers. *Journal of the Experimental Analysis of Behavior*, 1962, *5*, 33-41.

Stain, P., Shores, R., & Kerr, M. An experimental analysis of "spillover" effects on the social interaction of behaviorally handicapped preschool children. *Journal of Applied Behavior Analysis*, 1976, *9*, 31-40.

Stennett, R. Emotional handicaps in the elementary years: Phase or disease? *American Journal of Orthopsychiatry*, 1966, *36*, 444-449.

Stephens, T. *Directive teaching of children with learning and behavioral handicaps.* Columbus, Ohio: Charles E. Merrill, 1970.

Stephens, T. *Directive teaching of children with learning and behavioral handicaps* (2nd ed.). Columbus, Ohio: Charles E. Merrill, 1976.

Stephens, T. *Implementing behavioral approaches in elementary and secondary schools.* Columbus, Ohio: Charles E. Merrill, 1975.

Stephens, T. *Organizational plans for partially seeing children in grades five and six relative to language achievement and individual differences.* Unpublished doctoral dissertation, University of Pittsburgh, 1966.

Stephens, T. Psychological consultation to teachers of learning and behaviorally handicapped children using a behavioral model. *Journal of School Psychology,* 1970, *8,* 13-18.

Stephens, T., Hartman, A., & Cooper, J. Directive teaching of reading with low achieving first-and second-year students. *The Journal of Special Education,* 1973, *7,* 187-196.

Stevens, G. *Taxonomy in special education for children with body disorders.* Pittsburgh, Pa.: University of Pittsburgh Press, 1962.

Stevens, G., & Birch, J. A proposal for clarification of terminology used to describe brain-injured children. *Exceptional Children,* 1957, *23,* 346-349.

Stolz, S., Wienckowski, L., & Brown, B. Behavior modification: A perspective on critical issues. *American Psychologist,* 1975, *30,* 1027-1048.

Stott, D. Behavioral aspects of learning disabilities: Assessment and remediation. *Experimental Publication System,* 1971, *11,* 2-45.

Stratton, J., & Terry, R. *Prevention of delinquency problems and programs.* New York: MacMillan Co., 1968.

Strauss, A., & Kephart, N. *Psychopathology and education of the brain-injured child: Volume II. Progress in theory and clinic.* New York: Grune & Stratton, 1955.

Strauss, A., & Lehtinen, L. *Psychopathology and education of the brain-injured child.* New York: Grune & Stratton, 1947.

Stuecher, U. *Tommy: A treatment study of an autistic child.* Arlington, Va.: The Council for Exceptional Children, 1972.

Sturm, I. The behavioristic aspect of psychodrama. *Group Psychotherapy,* 1965, *18,* 50-64.

Suppes, P. Modern learning theory and the elementary school curriculum. *American Educational Research Journal,* 1964, *4,* 79-131.

Swanson, M., & Jacobson, A. Evaluation of the S.I.T. for screening children with learning disabilities. *Journal of Learning Disabilities,* 1970, *3,* 318-320.

Swift, M., & Spivack, G. The assessment of achievement-related classroom behavior. *Journal of Special Education,* 1968, *2,* 137-154.

Swift, M., & Spivack, G. Therapeutic teaching: A review of teaching methods for behaviorally troubled children. *Journal of Special Education,* 1974, *8,* 259-289.

Szasz, T. The myth of mental illness. *American Psychologist,* 1960, *15,* 113-118.

Teitelbaum, V. Confidentiality of records. In C. Catterall (Ed.), *Litigation in special education: Implications for general education.* Columbus, Ohio: Faculty for Exceptional Children, The Ohio State University, 1973, 155-179.

Terkel, S. *Working.* New York: Pantheon, 1975.

Thomas, A., Chess, S., & Birch, H. *Temperament and behavior disorders in children.* New York: New York University Press, 1968.

Thomas, D., Becker, W., & Armstrong, M. Production and elimination of disruptive classroom behavior by systematically varying teacher's behavior. *Journal of Applied Behavior Analysis,* 1968, *1,* 35-45.

U.S. Department of Health, Education and Welfare. *Juvenile court statistics, 1971.* Washington, D.C.: U.S. Department of HEW, 1972.

Vaac, N. A study of emotionally disturbed children in regular and special classes. *Exceptional Children,* 1968, *35,* 197-204.

Vaac, N. Long term effects of special class intervention for emotionally disturbed children. *Exceptional Children,* 1972, *39,* 15-22.

Valett, R. *Programming learning disabilities.* Palo Alto, Calif.: Fearon Publishing Co., 1969.

Vonder Haar, T. Chaining children with chemicals. *The Progressive,* 1975, *39,* 13-17.

Wadsworth, H. A motivational approach toward the remediation of learning disabled boys. *Exceptional Children,* 1971, *37,* 33-41.

Wagonseller, B. Learning disability and emotional disturbance: Factors relating to differential diagnosis. *Exceptional Children*, 1973, *39*, 205-206.

Walker, H., & Buckley, N. The use of positive reinforcement in conditioning attending behavior. *Journal of Applied Behavior Analysis*, 1968, *1*, 245-252.

Wallace, G., & Kauffman, J. *Teaching children with learning problems.* Columbus, Ohio: Charles E. Merrill, 1973.

Wallace, G., & McLoughlin, J. *Learning disabilities.* Columbus, Ohio: Charles E. Merrill, 1975.

Wallin, J., & Ferguson, D. The development of school psychological services in school psychological services. In J. Magary (Ed.), *Theory and practice.* Englewood Cliffs, N.J.: Prentice-Hall, 1967, 8-16.

Warner, J. *Learning disabilities: Activities for remediation.* Danville, Ill.: The Interstate Printers & Publishers, Inc., 1973.

Waugh, R. Relationship between modality preference and performance. *Exceptional Children*, 1973, *39*, 465-469.

Wedell, K. Diagnosing learning difficulties: A sequential strategy. *Journal of Learning Disabilities*, 1970, *3*, 311-317.

Weissmann, H. Implications for the education of children with emotional and social disturbances. *Journal of Learning Disabilities*, 1970, *3*, 502-508.

Werry, J. Childhood psychosis. In H. Quay & J. Werry (Eds.), *Psychopathological disorders of childhood.* New York: John Wiley & Sons, Inc., 1972, 113-233.

Werry, J., & Quay, H. Observing the classroom behavior of elementary school children. *Exceptional Children*, 1969, *35*, 461-470.

Werry, J., & Quay, H. The prevalence of behavior symptoms in younger elementary school children. *American Journal of Orthopsychiatry*, 1971, *41*, 136-143.

Wetter, J. Parent attitudes toward learning disability. *Exceptional Children*, 1972, *6*, 490-491.

Whelan, R. *Semantic differential behavior of normal and emotionally disturbed school age males.* Unpublished doctoral dissertation, University of Kansas, 1966.

Wiederholt, J. Planning resource rooms for the mildly handicapped. *Focus on Exceptional Children*, 1974, *5*, 1-10.

Wiederholt, J., & Hammill, D. Use of the Frostig-Horne perception program in the urban school. *Psychology in the Schools*, 1971, *8*, 268-274.

Wilson, L. Learning disability as related to infrequent punishment and limited participation in delay of reinforcement tasks. *Journal of School Psychology*, 1975, *13*, 255-263.

Wolf, M., Giles, D., & Hall, R. Experiments with token reinforcement in a remedial classroom. *Behavior Research and Therapy*, 1968, *6*, 51-64.

Wolman, B. *Dictionary of behavioral science.* New York: Van Nostrand Reinhold Co., 1973.

Woody, R. *Behavioral problem children in the schools.* New York: Appleton-Century-Crofts, 1969.

Woody, R. *Legal aspects of mental retardation.* Springfield, Ill.: Charles C. Thomas, 1974.

Woody, R. Process and behavioral consultation. *American Journal of Community Psychology*, 1975, *3*, 277-285.

Ysseldyke, J. *Accountability of diagnostic-prescriptive teaching.* Washington, D.C.: American Psychological Association, 1974.

Ysseldyke, J., & Salvia, J. Diagnostic-prescriptive teaching: Two models. *Exceptional Children*, 1974, *41*, 181-185.

Zach, L., & Kaufman, J. How adequate is the concept of perceptual deficit for education? *Journal of Learning Disabilities*, 1972, *5*, 351-356.

Zedler, E. Better teacher training: The solution for children's reading problems. *Journal of Learning Disabilities*, 1970, *3*, 106-112.

Zifferblatt, S. Behavior systems. In C. Thoresen (Ed.), *Behavior modification in education.* The '72 yearbook of the National Society for the Study of Education, Part I. Chicago: University of Chicago Press, 1973, 317-350.

Zimmerman, E., & Zimmerman, J. The alteration of behavior in a classroom situation. *Journal of the Experimental Analysis of Behavior*, 1962, *5*, 59-60.

AUTHOR INDEX